AF521887

American Moderns on Paper

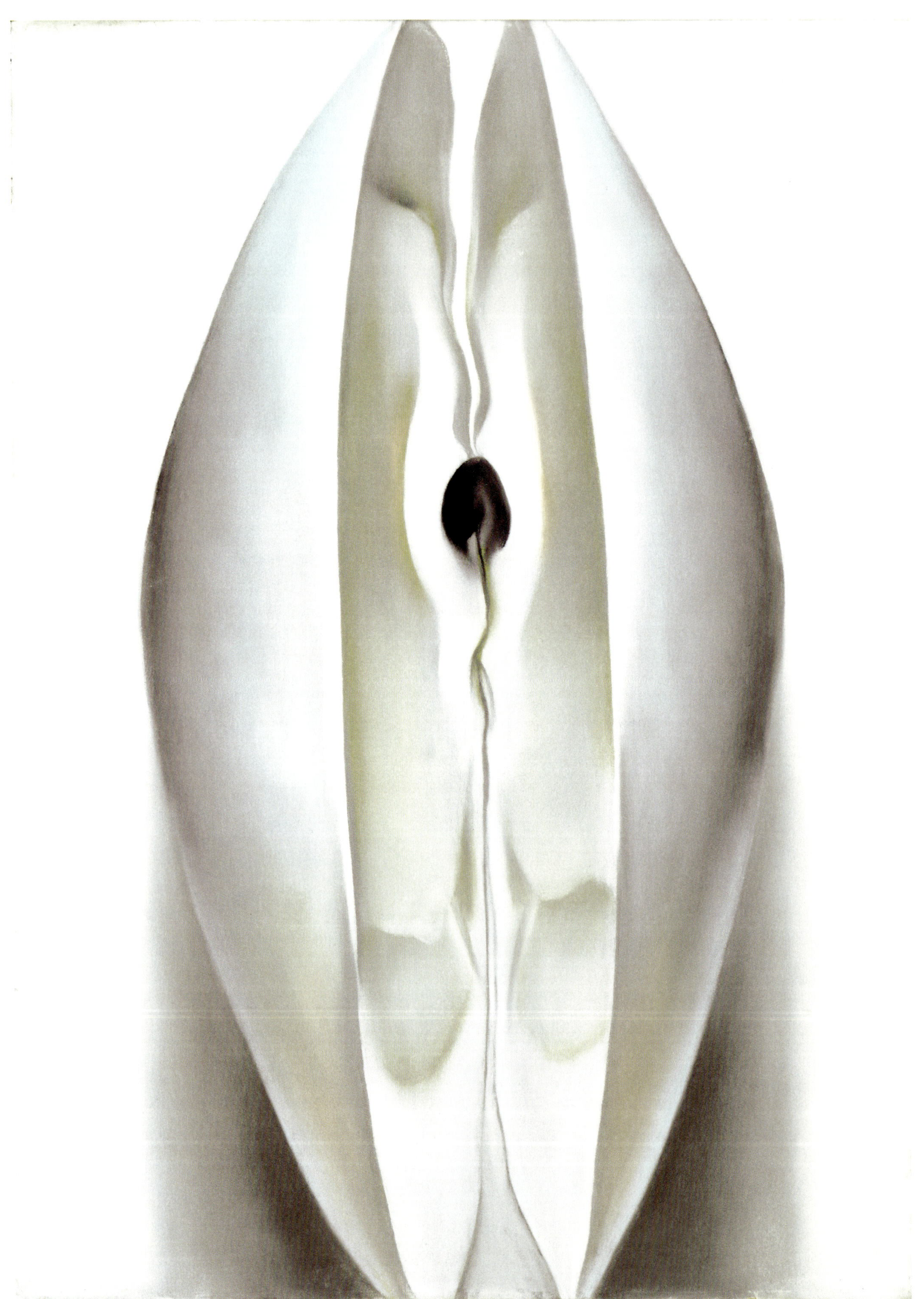

American Moderns on Paper

Masterworks from the Wadsworth Atheneum Museum of Art

Edited by Elizabeth Mankin Kornhauser

With essays and entries by
Elizabeth Mankin Kornhauser,
Erin Monroe, *and* Carol Troyen

Yale University Press, New Haven and London
in association with the
Wadsworth Atheneum Museum of Art

Published with assistance from
The National Endowment for the Arts
American Masterpieces Program
and The Henry Luce Foundation.

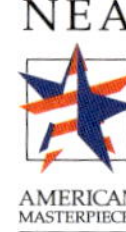

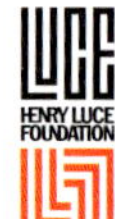

Published on the occasion of the exhibition
American Moderns on Paper:
Masterworks from the Wadsworth Atheneum Museum of Art,
organized by the Wadsworth Atheneum Museum of Art,
Hartford, Connecticut.

Amon Carter Museum, Fort Worth, Texas
February 27–May 30, 2010

Portland Museum of Art, Maine
June 22–September 12, 2010

Wadsworth Atheneum Museum of Art, Hartford, Connecticut
October 2, 2010–January 2, 2011

All reproductions of catalogue images
by Allen Phillips, Wadsworth Atheneum

Designed by Peter Good
Set in Berthold Baskerville Book
Printed in Singapore by CS Graphics

Library of Congress Cataloging-in-Publication Data

American moderns on paper : masterworks from the Wadsworth Atheneum
Museum of Art / edited by Elizabeth Mankin Kornhauser ; with essays and entries
by Elizabeth Mankin Kornhauser, Erin Monroe, and Carol Troyen.
p. cm.
Published on the occasion of an exhibition held at the Amon Carter Museum, Fort
Worth, Texas, the Portland Museum of Art, Maine, and the Wadsworth Atheneum
Museum of Art, Hartford, Connecticut.
Includes bibliographical references and index.
ISBN 978-0-300-15166-4 (hardcover : alk. paper)–ISBN 978-0-918333-25-4 (pbk. : alk. paper)
1. Modernism (Art)–United States–Exhibitions. 2. Art, American–20th century–
Exhibitions. 3. Art–Connecticut–Hartford–Exhibitions. 4. Wadsworth Atheneum
Museum of Art–Exhibitions. I. Kornhauser, Elizabeth Mankin, 1950– II. Monroe, Erin.
III. Troyen, Carol. IV. Amon Carter Museum of Western Art. V. Wadsworth Atheneum
Museum of Art. VI. Portland Museum of Art. VII. Title: Masterworks from the
Wadsworth Atheneum Museum of Art.
N6512.5.M63A643 2010
759.1309'040747463–dc22

2009026823

A catalogue record for this book is available from the British Library.

The paper in this book meets the requirements of ANSI/NISO Z39.48-1992
(Permanence of Paper).

10 9 8 7 6 5 4 3 2 1

Cover: Ellsworth Kelly, *Corn (11)*, 1959 (cat. 84)
Page ii: Georgia O'Keeffe, *Slightly Open Clam Shell*, 1926 (cat. 15)
Pages viii–1: John Marin, *Movement No. 3, Related to Downtown New York*, 1926 (detail, cat. 11)
Pages 18–19: Edward Hopper, *Marshall's House*, 1932 (detail, cat. 37)
Pages 38–39: Charles Demuth, *Still Life with Eggplant and Summer Squash*, c. 1927 (detail, cat. 19)
Pages 86–87: Charles Burchfield, *Song in the Rain*, 1947 (detail, cat. 30)
Pages 136–37: Arshile Gorky, *Untitled*, 1943 (detail, cat. 70)
Pages 182–83: Andrew Wyeth, *Granddaughter*, 1956 (detail, cat. 82)

Contents

Director's Foreword

Throughout its long and storied history, the Wadsworth Atheneum has built one of the finest American art collections held by any museum. American drawings and watercolors are an important aspect of this collection, spanning over two hundred and fifty years. However, because of their fragility and susceptibility to damage by light, many of these works have not been seen in decades. *American Moderns on Paper: Masterworks from the Wadsworth Atheneum Museum of Art* highlights our finest works from 1910 to 1960. Georgia O'Keeffe is featured among the greatest artists of this period with our most important recent acquisition, *Slightly Open Clam Shell,* 1926. This iconic pastel was purchased from a renowned private collection and adds significantly to our modernist holdings.

It is my great pleasure to introduce this landmark publication that takes its place as an invaluable reference, not only for the Atheneum's collection but also for the field of scholarly investigation and connoisseurship pertaining to original works on paper. This volume follows the 2003 publication *Hudson River School: Masterworks from the Wadsworth Atheneum Museum of Art,* which illuminates the collection of American landscapes first formed through the vision of Daniel Wadsworth who founded this museum in 1842. Wadsworth was committed to presenting works by living American artists—the modernists of his generation. In each case these volumes and their accompanying exhibitions celebrate the Atheneum's ongoing commitment to the study of American art and to the growth of the collection into the twenty-first century.

I would like to extend special thanks to Dr. Elizabeth Mankin Kornhauser, chief curator and Krieble Curator of American Paintings and Sculpture, who initiated and oversaw *American Moderns on Paper,* serving as the editor and contributor to the catalogue as well as the curator of the exhibition. Her high professional standards and curatorial vision are apparent in all aspects of this venture. She was ably assisted by curatorial assistant and administrator Erin Monroe, who began this project as a curatorial fellow.

We are proud to share these extraordinary modern works with audiences across the United States, as the collection travels to the Amon Carter Museum, Fort Worth, Texas, and the Portland Museum of Art, Portland, Maine. The exhibition will then return to Hartford for its presentation at the Atheneum.

We deeply appreciate the magnificent generosity of the National Endowment for the Arts and the Henry Luce Foundation for providing long-term support to bring this publication and exhibition to fruition. We extend special gratitude to our chairman, Susan A. Rottner, and the museum's Board of Trustees for their ongoing support.

Susan L. Talbott
Director and CEO

Preface

The Wadsworth Atheneum holds a treasury of original works on paper by artists working in America from the eighteenth century to present time. This catalogue brings to light for the first time a selection of approximately 100 of the finest watercolors, pastels, and drawings by leading modern artists in America, from 1910 to 1960, drawn from the Atheneum's renowned collection of American art.

This book and the exhibition it accompanies explore the rich roots of the Atheneum's collection, chronicling the history of the formation of the modernist works on paper collection, and placing it within a larger context that includes the national evolution of an interest in watercolor and drawings in America during the first half of the twentieth century. The people–patrons, dealers, museum directors, and curators–who were instrumental in the formation of this distinguished collection will be presented. They include the architect Philip L. Goodwin, a major patron of modern artists; the New York dealers Alfred Stieglitz, Edith Gregor Halpert, and Julien Levy; Atheneum directors A. Everett Austin Jr. and Charles C. Cunningham; and Atheneum curator Samuel Wagstaff Jr. The tension between modernist and antimodernist approaches to twentieth-century styles is explored, examining classic modern styles alongside alternate forms of modernism that were championed by A. Everett Austin Jr., including Surrealism and Neo-Romanticism. Watercolor in particular will be presented as an essentially American medium that was well suited to the restless, spontaneous, and confident American spirit. The catalogue section of the book includes artist biographies and entries, which are grouped in thematic and chronological sections as follows: section 1, "Progressive and Avant-Garde Artists"; section 2, "Regionalism, Social Realism, and American Visions"; section 3, "Surrealism and Neo-Romanticism"; and section 4, "Postwar Abstraction and the Resurgence of Realism."

The work for this book and exhibition has taken several years and benefited from the generous support of countless individuals. The Atheneum's director, Susan L. Talbott, has provided unstinting aid and encouragement along the way. We would also like to thank the Atheneum's Board of Trustees for their support. The research, writing, editing, and publication of this catalogue have taken the considerable efforts of a great many people. We are especially indebted to Carol Troyen, Kristin and Roger Servison Curator Emerita of American Paintings, Museum of Fine Arts, Boston, who helped to shape the selection and ideas for the exhibition and served as an inspired contributor to the catalogue, authoring a scholarly essay and entries. A team of interns, including Margaret Aldredge, John Beeson, Sara Kornhauser, Fionna Sherwin-Murray, Erin Webb, and Kelsea Wigmore, provided essential research for the book, in particular, for the artist biographies. The works on paper in the exhibition benefited from expert examination and treatment by Mindy Friedman Horn, private paper conservator, who provided essential information on the artists' materials and paper supports.

The staff members of numerous museums, archives, libraries, and galleries provided critical information that informed the artist biographies and entries in this catalogue. In particular, we would like to thank: Tullis Johnson, research assistant, Burchfield-Penny Art Center; Amanda T. Zehnder, assistant curator of fine arts, Carnegie Museum of Art; Heather Lemonedes, associate curator of drawings, the Cleveland Museum of Art; Karen Osburn, archivist, Geneva Historical Society, Geneva, New York; Miriam Stewart, assistant curator of drawings, Harvard University Art Museums; Eva H. Walters, archivist for Ellsworth Kelly; Amy R. Johnston, Department of Modern Prints and Drawings, National Gallery of Art, Washington, D.C.; Christine M. McCarthy, executive director, Provincetown Art Association and Museum, and Stephen Borkowski, Provincetown Art Commission; Lillian Brenwasser, Kennedy Galleries Inc.; Lisa M. Messinger, associate curator, Department of Nineteenth-Century, Modern, and Contemporary Art, Metropolitan Museum of Art; Michael Schuyler, head librarian, Munson-Williams-Proctor Arts Institute; Michael Rosenfeld and Marjorie Van Cura, Michael Rosenfeld Gallery; Carol Willis, curator and director, the Skyscraper Museum, New York; Rebecca Zurier, associate professor, History of Art, University of Michigan; Anita Duquette, Rights and Reproductions, and Carter Foster, curator of drawings, at the Whitney Museum of American Art.

We would like to express our appreciation to our Atheneum colleagues who assisted in all aspects of the catalogue and exhibition. In particular, we are grateful to Allen Phillips, director of Collection Imaging, ably assisted by Aileen Bastos, collections assistant, for creating digital images of the highest quality for this publication. In addition, thanks go to Adria Patterson, exhibitions coordinator; Stephen Kornhauser, chief conservator, Ulrich Birkmaier, painting conservator, and Zenon Gansziniec, frame conservator; and Mary Schroeder, head registrar. The manuscript benefited from careful reading by Gene Gaddis, archivist, and the editorial comments of Ann Brandwein, assistant archivist, as well as editorial support from Amy Ellis McDaniel.

At Yale University Press, thanks are due to Patricia Fidler, publisher, art and architecture; Kate Zanzucchi, senior production editor; and Mary Mayer, production manager, who very ably guided us through the publication process; as well as Miranda Ottewell, freelance manuscript editor, who provided excellent editorial assistance; and proofreader John Mordecai and indexer Cathy Dorsey. Finally we wish to thank Peter Good and the staff of the talented graphic design firm of Cummings and Good, who have provided the beautiful design for the book.

This project would never have been accomplished without the early and generous support from the National Endowment for the Arts American Masterpieces program, which provided funding for the catalogue and exhibition. We are also indebted to the Henry Luce Foundation for providing funding for the conservation of the collection.

Elizabeth Mankin Kornhauser
Erin Monroe

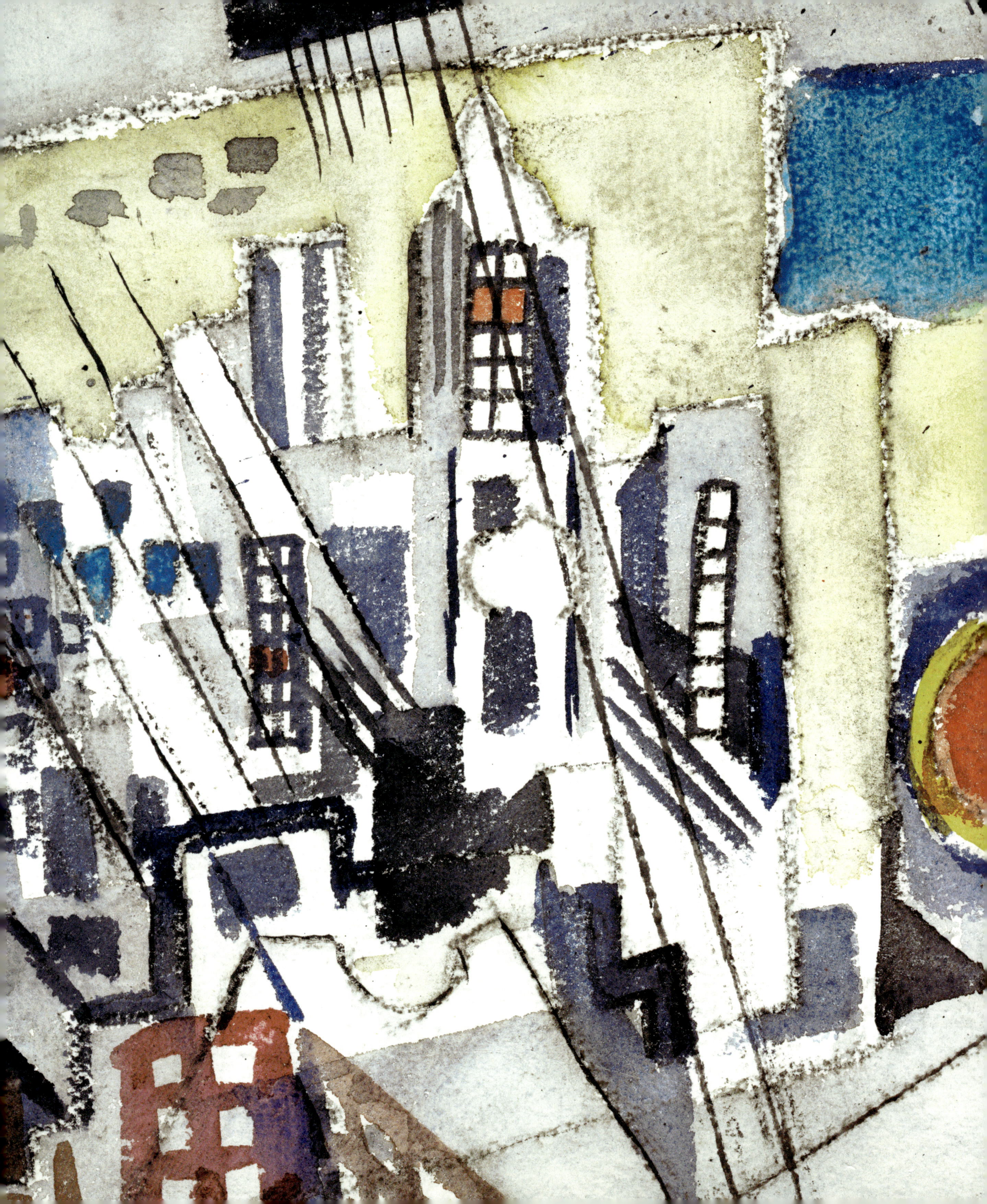

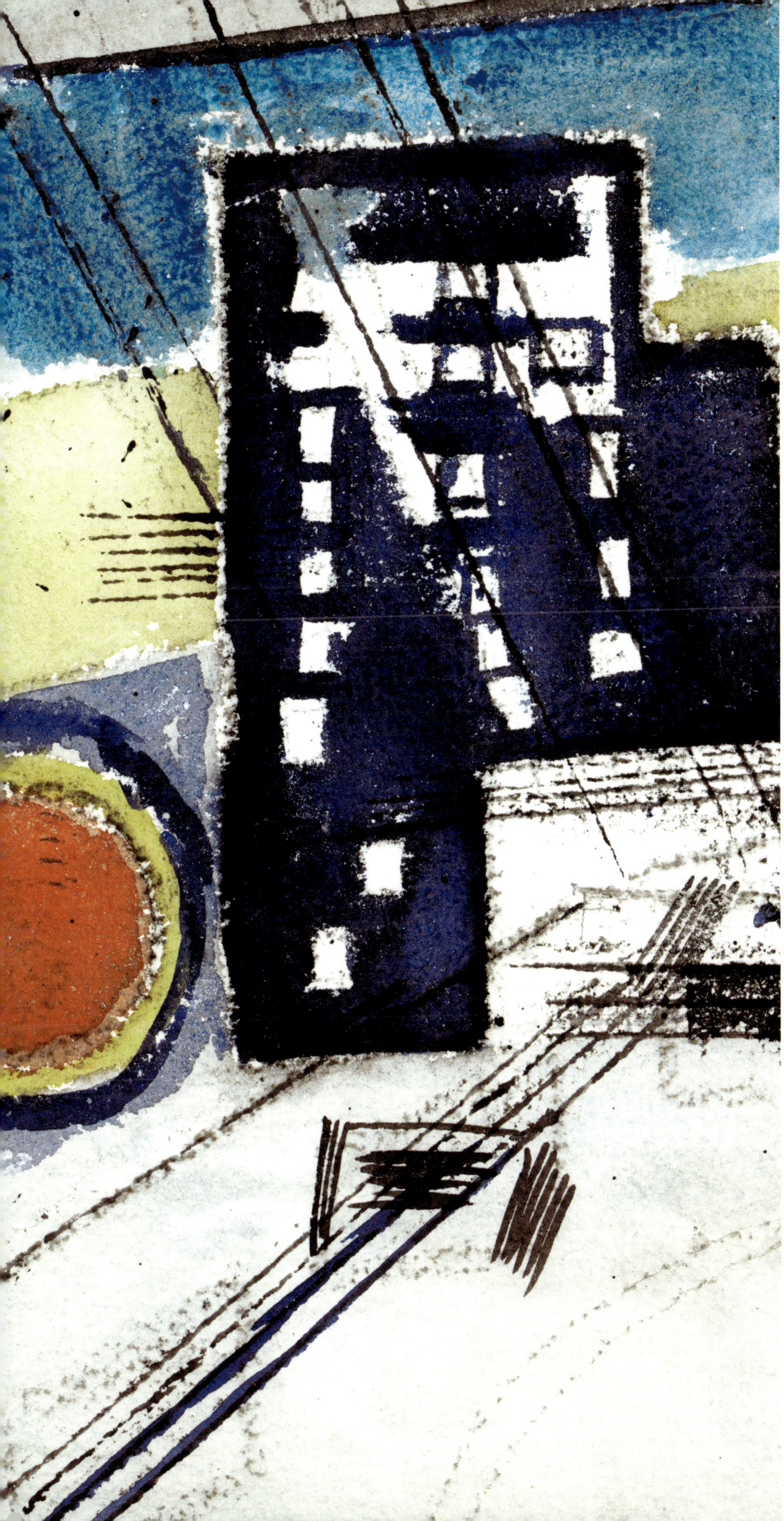

Galvanizing Hartford

The History of the American Modern Watercolors and Drawings Collection and Its Patrons

Elizabeth Mankin Kornhauser

"I think that this [John Marin watercolor] *of the typical modern American city, by a modern American painter, in a modern style, is the most interesting kind of thing, even if it shocks the old-fashioned."*

"If only the natives of Hartford could be galvanized into a little general interest in it . . ."

Philip L. Goodwin, 1923

Fig. 1. Thomas Sully, *Daniel Wadsworth*, 1807. Watercolor on paper, 6 3/8 × 5 in. (16.2 × 12.7 cm). Wadsworth Atheneum Museum of Art. Henry and Walter Keney Fund, 1987.10

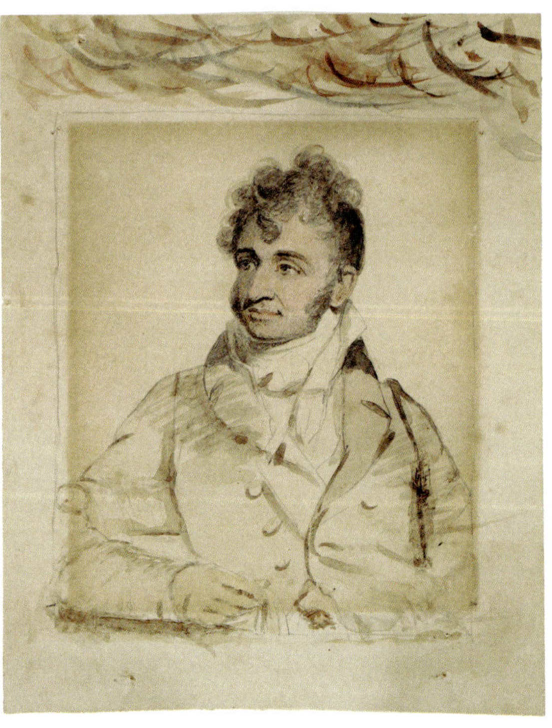

The evolution of the Wadsworth Atheneum's distinguished collection of American modern watercolors and drawings reflects the museum's long and rich history. In 1842, Daniel Wadsworth (1771–1848), a leading patron of American artists, founded the Wadsworth Atheneum, one of the earliest public art museums in America (fig. 1). It was Wadsworth himself who laid the groundwork and determined the direction of the American art collections. He commissioned major paintings from Thomas Cole, Frederic Edwin Church, and other leading members of the Hudson River School, the country's first national school of art, and these made up the core of the Atheneum's collections in the nineteenth century.[1] Wadsworth established a precedent for acquiring and exhibiting art of the moment to which the Atheneum's successive donors, museum directors, and curators would adhere.

It is therefore not surprising that the museum's strongest holdings of American watercolors, pastels, and drawings, numbering about 1,500 works, fall in the first half of the twentieth century, when museums began to value watercolors and drawings and add them to their collections. During this time American artists chose to work on paper as they pursued modern styles. In addition, America's artistic community benefited from the arrival of émigré artists who, having fled the war in Europe, enriched the artistic output of the United States. A selection of the finest examples of works on paper dating from 1910 to 1960 are the subject of this exhibition, and their makers range from members of the Ashcan school to Ellsworth Kelly.

While the collection of American paintings grew substantially following Wadsworth's bequest in 1848, only a small number of American watercolors and drawings entered the museum's holdings in the nineteenth and early twentieth centuries, and all through bequests. Among the highlights were two historically important pastel portraits inherited by Daniel Wadsworth from his father, Jeremiah. During the American Revolution, Jeremiah served as commissary general for the Continental Army and welcomed visits by George Washington to his Hartford home on many occasions. To commemorate their friendship, Jeremiah commissioned James Sharples to paint pastel portraits of George and Martha Washington in about 1795 (figs. 2, 3). The American artist John Trumbull, a close friend of the Wadsworth family, served as a mentor to young Daniel and later became related to him through marriage. Trumbull's very personal and sensitive drawing of Daniel's sister, Harriet Wadsworth, whom he was courting at the time, was left to the museum through her brother (fig. 4). In 1901 the Hartford collector Ambrose Spencer bequeathed to the Atheneum nineteenth-century American paintings as well as two accomplished watercolors of the Northeast coastline by William Trost Richards: *Marine View* (1881) and *The Old Fort, Conanicut Island* (fig. 5). Finally, the very large bequest of art and firearms Elizabeth Hart Jarvis Colt left to the Atheneum in 1905 included two watercolors by Harry Fenn of the renowned arms manufacturer's magnificent Hartford mansion, Armsmear (fig. 6).[2]

In 1912, the Hartford artist James Britton reported in the *Hartford Courant* that "water colors by celebrated American artists are gradually getting into the public galleries. Both the Boston and Worcester Museums have recently acquired works in this medium by the late Winslow Homer. Now the Boston Museum announces the purchase of a number of watercolors by John S. Sargent, the

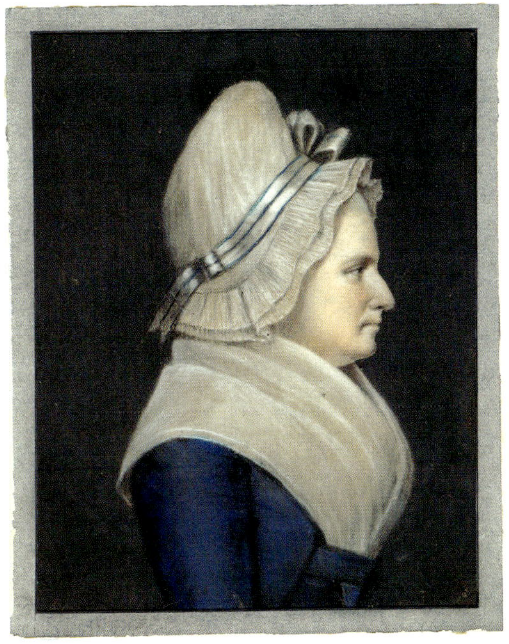

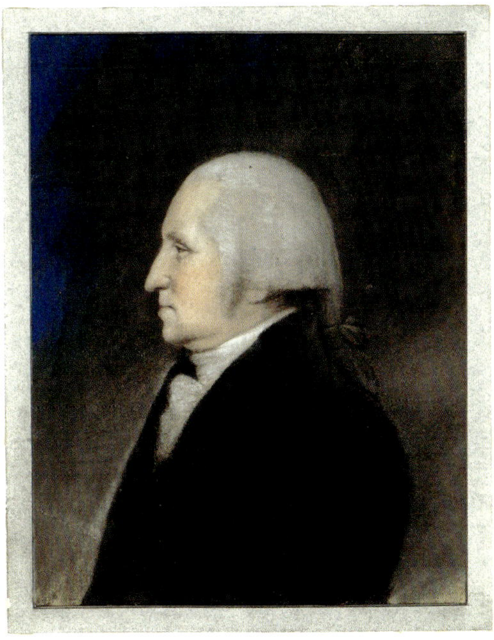

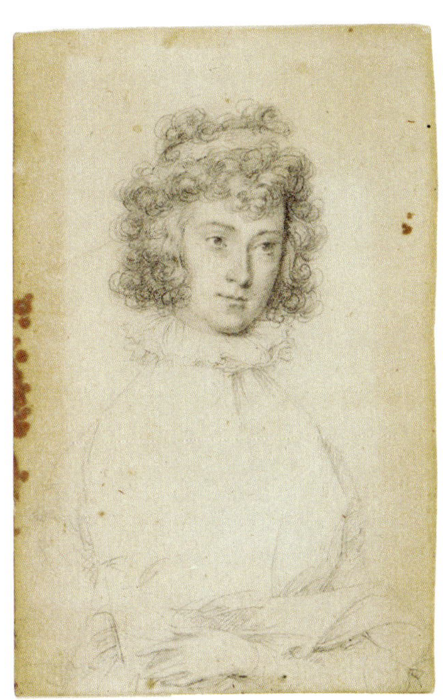

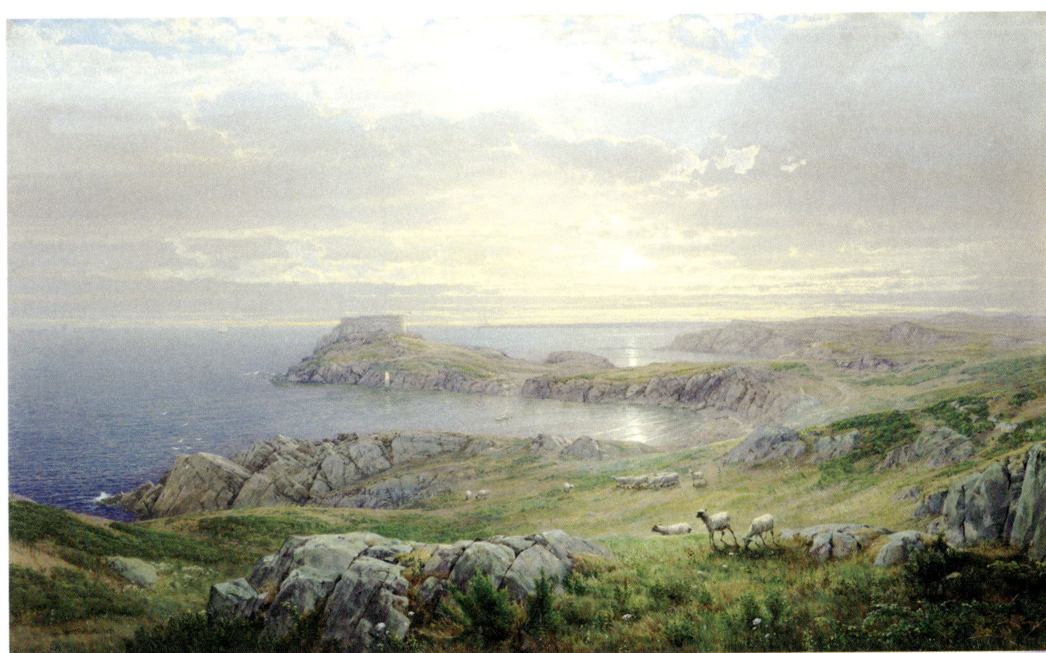

Fig. 2. (above left)
James Sharples, *Martha Washington*, c. 1795.
Pastel on paper, $9^1/_2 \times 7$ in. (34.4 × 16.7 cm).
Wadsworth Atheneum Museum of Art.
Bequest of Daniel Wadsworth, 1848.19

Fig. 3. (above center)
James Sharples, *George Washington*, c. 1795.
Pastel on paper, $9^1/_2 \times 7$ in. (34.4 × 16.7 cm).
Wadsworth Atheneum Museum of Art.
Bequest of Daniel Wadsworth, 1848.18

Fig. 4. (above right)
John Trumbull, *Harriet Wadsworth*, c. 1790–91.
Pencil on paper, $4^1/_2 \times 3^7/_8$ in. (11.5 × 9.8 cm).
Wadsworth Atheneum Museum of Art, before 1850

Fig. 5. (left)
William Trost Richards,
The Old Fort, Conanicut Island, 1877.
Graphite and transparent and opaque watercolor on paper, 24 × 38 in. (61 × 96.5 cm).
Wadsworth Atheneum Museum of Art.
Bequest of Ambrose Spencer, 1901.5

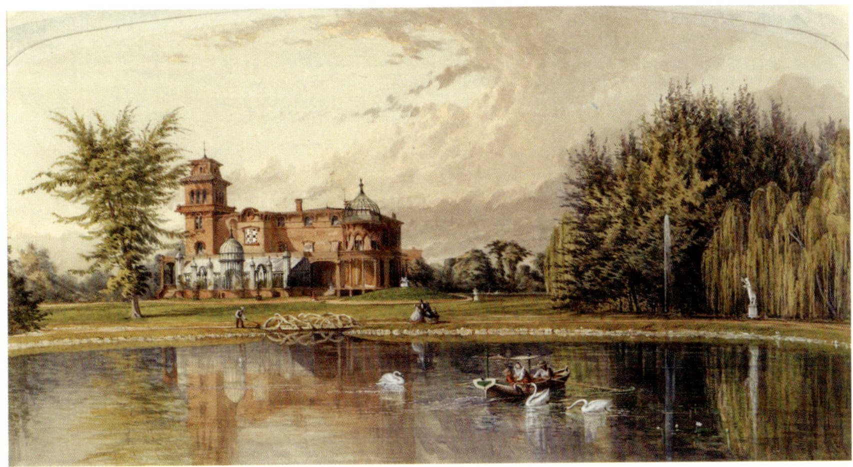

Fig. 6. Harry Fenn,
View of the Colt Residence, c. 1875.
Opaque and transparent watercolor on paper, $11^7/_8 \times 22$ in. (30.2 × 55.9 cm).
Wadsworth Atheneum Museum of Art.
Bequest of Elizabeth Hart Jarvis Colt, 1905.53

eminent portrait painter."[3] The Atheneum had not yet made a single purchase of an American work on paper by this time. However, a few years later, interest in this subject emerged in Hartford: in 1917 the Connecticut Academy of the Fine Arts, which exhibited annually in the Atheneum's Annex Gallery, held their first exhibition of watercolors and pastels, featuring works by Connecticut artists Hilda Belcher, Birge Harrison, Louis Orr, and Henry C. White.[4]

By the 1920s, the work of building a collection of American works on paper by nationally prominent American artists at the Atheneum began in earnest. The effort was led by members of the Goodwin family, a founding family of Hartford, who regularly supported the Atheneum through patronage and leadership, and by adding to the acquisition coffers. The brothers Henry and Walter Keney (Walter had married a Goodwin) established the museum's first endowment fund for art purchases in the 1890s in the amount of $50,000. That was followed in 1915 by Mrs. James J. Goodwin's gift of $50,000 for art acquisitions in memory of her husband. In 1923, at a time when her nephew Charles Goodwin served as the treasurer of the Atheneum (he would become board president in 1927), Mrs. Goodwin requested that her purchase fund be used to acquire "good American modern pictures of which there is a wide choice at the present time," decrying the lack of such works in the Atheneum's collection. She suggested focusing on such established artists as George Bellows, Mary Cassatt, Winslow Homer, and John Singer Sargent, among others.[5] In March the museum's curator, Florence Berger, reported to Mrs. Goodwin that her fund had been used to acquire Homer's watercolor *A Summer Night* from the William Macbeth Gallery, New York, for $3,000 (fig. 7), and Cassatt's pastel portrait *Child Holding a Dog* (fig. 8) from the Durand-Ruel Gallery for $2,600.[6] These were not only the first major American works on paper to be purchased for the Atheneum but the first works by these leading American artists to enter the collection as a whole. Homer died in 1910, but Cassatt was still living in Paris, and the importance of the pastel inspired the Atheneum's director, Frank B. Gay, to write directly to her regarding the work. Cassatt responded, providing information on the young model in the pastel and wishing the Atheneum "prosperity."[7]

Philip L. Goodwin (1885–1958), the son of Mrs. James J. Goodwin, played an important and sustained role in building the Atheneum's American modernist works on paper collection (fig. 9). A New York architect, he became most famous for his 1939 design, in partnership with Edward Durell Stone, for the Museum of Modern Art, where he served as a trustee. But Goodwin had deep roots in Hartford and at the Atheneum (his first cousin was Charles Goodwin), and he advocated for the exhibition and acquisition of modern American watercolors. As an early supporter and collector of these works, and those of Charles Demuth and John Marin in particular, Goodwin first encouraged the Atheneum to show works by these artists as early as 1923. He explained in a letter to Charles Goodwin, "I wanted to . . . propose . . . the interesting possibilities in holding a Spring Exhibition . . . of water colors and original drawings, by well-known modern American, French, and English artists. The reason that I suggest watercolors and drawings is . . . because they are reasonable in price, and are, therefore, within the reach of a larger number of people's purses, and . . . because such a remarkable

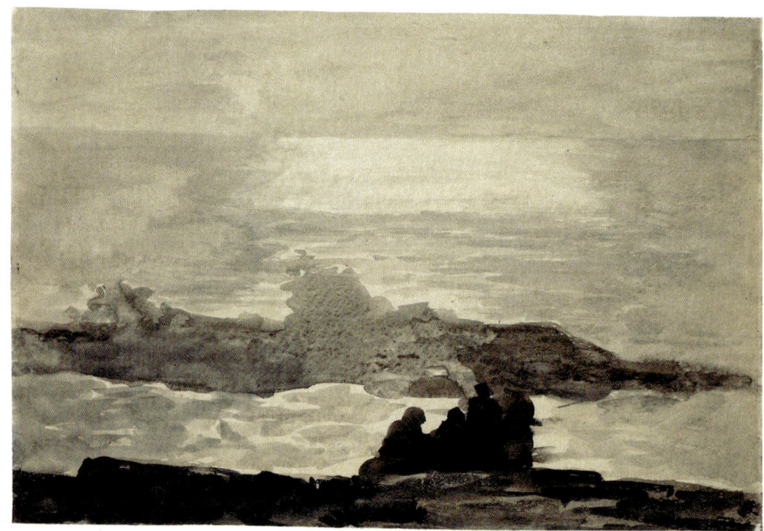

Fig. 7. Winslow Homer, *A Summer Night*, 1899.
Watercolor and wash on paper, $14^{1}/_{2} \times 21^{1}/_{2}$ in. (36.8 × 54.6 cm).
Wadsworth Atheneum Museum of Art. The James J. Goodwin Fund, 1923.82

Fig. 8. Mary Cassatt, *Child Holding a Dog*, 1908.
Pastel on paper, $21^{1}/_{2} \times 17^{1}/_{2}$ in. (54.6 × 44.5 cm).
Wadsworth Atheneum Museum of Art. The James J. Goodwin Fund, 1923.81

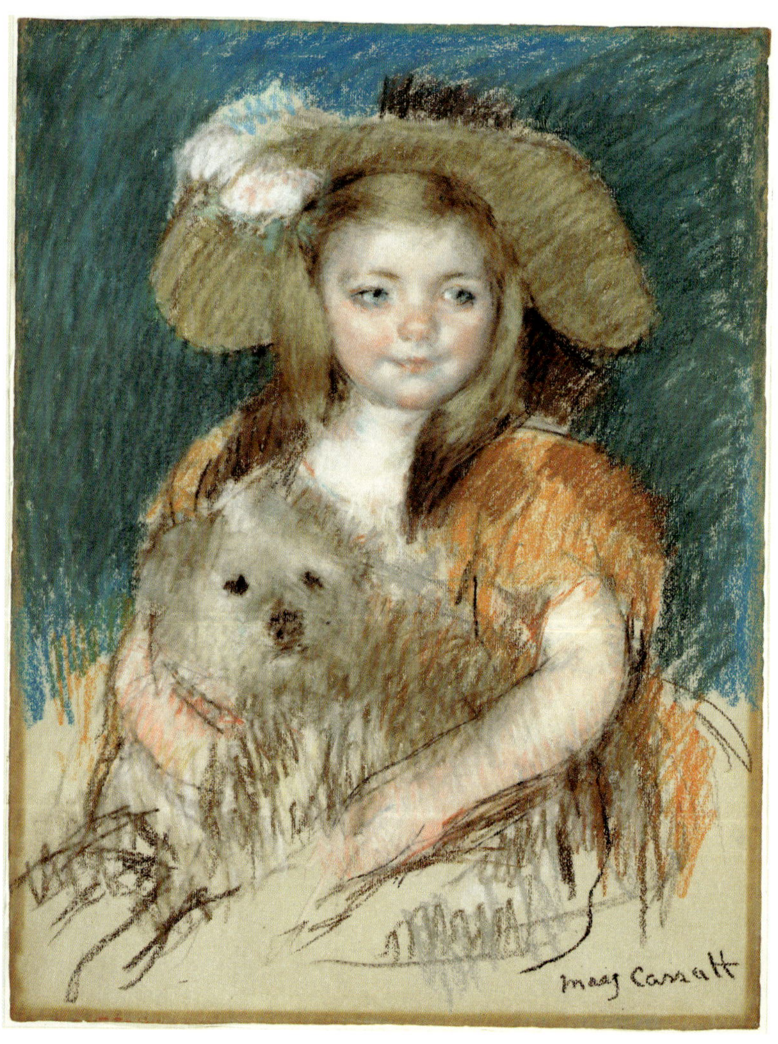

production has been made."[8] He offered to lend thirteen works from his collection and that of his mother, by such artists as Paul Cézanne, Demuth, Homer, Marin, Joseph Pennell, and Hopkinson Smith. Goodwin was aware that the works of American watercolorists, in particular, had become a subject of interest among collectors and art museums in the United States. He noted that the Metropolitan Museum had recently held an exhibition "of this sort," and indicated that the Chicago Art Institute had asked to borrow some of these works for a "similar exhibition for the following year."[9]

Just a year earlier a notable publication on the subject appeared: Albert E. Gallatin's *American Water-Colorists* (1922). Goodwin may also have been aware of the Brooklyn Museum's first biennial exhibition held in 1921, *Exhibition of Water Color Paintings by American Artists*, an impressive gathering of 365 watercolors by late nineteenth- and early twentieth-century American artists featuring a substantial number of works by Homer, John La Farge, and Sargent, and offering a smaller selection of works by such newly established modern American artists as Charles Burchfield, Demuth, and Marin.[10] This was followed by Brooklyn's 1923 *Exhibition of Water Color Paintings, Drawings and Sculpture by American and European Artists*, which had an international scope.

In addition, Goodwin was a frequent visitor to the galleries of the renowned dealer and photographer Alfred Stieglitz, who first opened his gallery 291 in 1907. (See Carol Troyen, "Modernism and Antimodernism," in this volume.) Stieglitz was partial to works on paper, and Goodwin would have seen exhibitions of watercolors and drawings by American and European modernists there.[11] By the 1920s, Goodwin began to purchase watercolors by Demuth and Marin from Stieglitz.[12] He later honored Stieglitz in a memorial tribute at the time of his death in 1946: "For twenty-five years I have known Stieglitz . . . [and] am proud to think I was a friend."[13]

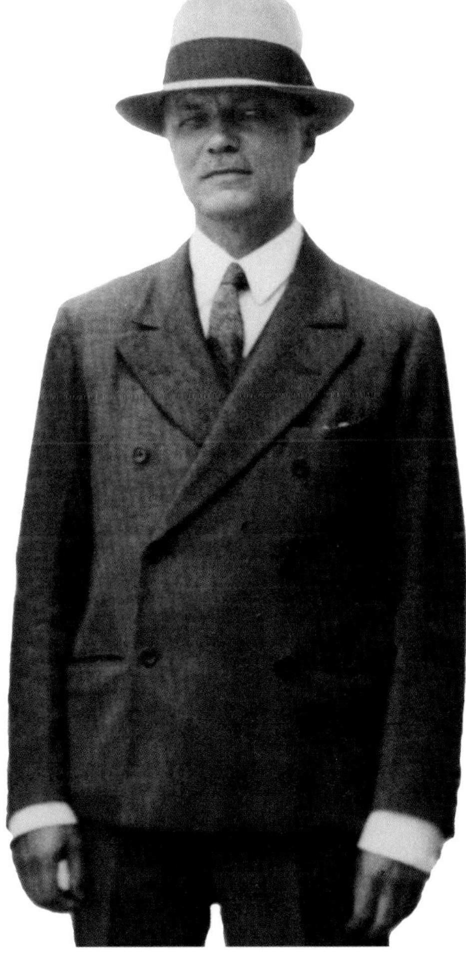

Fig. 9. Unknown photographer, *Philip L. Goodwin*, 1929. Archives, Wadsworth Atheneum Museum of Art

In October 1923 Goodwin wrote to Atheneum curator Florence Berger, expressing his pleasure that they had taken his suggestion to mount an exhibition of watercolors and drawings, so that, as he put it, "the natives of Hartford could be galvanized into a little general interest" in the subject of modern works on paper. He offered to lend seven examples from his collection, including Demuth's *Circus* and *Tree Forms*; Marin's *Tree Forms and Sea* and *Lower New York (Blue Horse)* (1920; Museum of Modern Art, New York);[14] Maurice Sterne's charcoal drawing *East Indian*; and a watercolor by English artist William Nicholson, *Mr. Ducat (from Gay's Opera, "Polly")*.[15] In a follow-up letter, Goodwin singled out the Marin watercolor of New York City, writing, "This picture of Lower New York is one of the really good modern American watercolors. . . . I think that this picture of the typical modern American city, by a modern American painter, in a modern style, is the most interesting kind of thing, even if it shocks the old-fashioned."[16]

The Atheneum's *Loan Exhibition of Watercolors, Pastels and Drawings*, held from October 16 to November 11, 1923, included 150 works borrowed from many local collectors, and, like the 1923 Brooklyn show, it included works by American and European artists. The exhibition featured established American artists such as Edwin Austin Abbey, Cecelia Beaux, George Bellows, Frank Benson, Cassatt, Irving Couse, Thomas Dewing, William Glackens, Childe Hassam, Robert Henri, Homer, La Farge, Charles Prendergast, William Trost Richards, Walter Shirlaw, and J. Alden Weir. Several works by two local favorites who had a modest national following, Hartford artists William Gedney Bunce and Dwight Tryon, were also included. Finally, the exhibition's European component ranged from Rembrandt and Leonardo da Vinci to Gustave Courbet, Claude Monet, and Camille Pissarro, among many others.[17]

The leading lenders to the show included many Goodwin family members, as well as George A. Gay (1853–1940). A Scottish immigrant who became a successful dry goods merchant in Hartford, Gay was a self-taught connoisseur and serious collector of watercolors, prints, and drawings. He was appointed curator of prints at the Atheneum in 1922 and frequently loaned his works for exhibitions. Upon his death in 1940, he left to the Atheneum his collection of 2,000 prints (launching the museum's print collection), as well as important American works on paper such as the vibrant pastel by Maurice Prendergast, *The Amusement Park* (cat. 1), a provocative drawing by Sargent, *Nude Man* (fig. 10), and Ralph Blakelock's *Landscape* (1866).

Philip L. Goodwin's loans included some of the more modern works in the exhibition, but neither of the Demuths nor the Marin, *Lower New York (Blue Horse)*, appear in the catalogue. It is possible that they were deemed to be too avant-garde for the Hartford public. Goodwin's *Tree Forms and Sea*, by Marin, appeared in the show along with a watercolor by Cézanne, *Landscape*, Augustus John's *Portrait of Mrs. John*, and Sterne's *East Indian*. In a review of the exhibition, a Hartford art critic singled out Goodwin's loans, writing, "Riots of color suggest the cubist school in 'Tree Forms and Sea,' by John

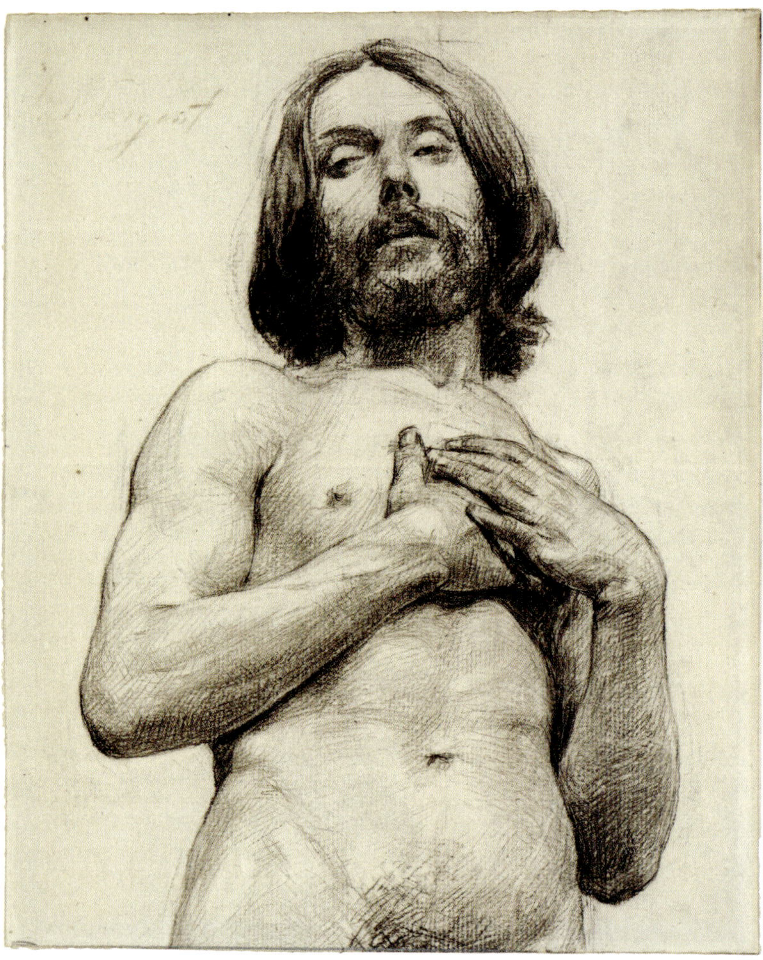

Fig. 10. John Singer Sargent, *Nude Man*, c. 1925. Graphite on paper, 9⁷/8 × 7³/4 in. (25.1 × 19.7 cm). Wadsworth Atheneum Museum of Art. Bequest of George A. Gay, 1941.447

Marin. Near at hand is a landscape by Cézanne."[18] While often frustrated in his efforts, Goodwin would continue to press the Atheneum's directors to build the collection of modern American works on paper.

The Atheneum fully embraced the modern era in 1927 with the appointment of A. Everett "Chick" Austin Jr., its first professionally trained museum director (fig. 11). Austin is celebrated for his role in promoting modern art in America by transforming Hartford, a conservative insurance capital, into a cultural mecca during his seventeen-year tenure.[19] Demonstrating a broad interest in the arts of his time, Chick sought to make the museum a center for all of the arts, presenting music, theater, dance, photography, film, and festivals. Trained in the graduate program at Harvard's Fogg Art Museum and benefiting from international study, Chick was only twenty-six when he arrived at the Atheneum in October. Hired by board president Charles A. Goodwin, Austin became a part of the Goodwin family when he married Charles's niece Helen Goodwin in 1929.

Austin was initially named acting director, and his mentor, Harvard professor Edward W. Forbes (director of the Fogg Art Museum), served as honorary director. Over the years, Chick gained fame for his individualistic approach to presenting the arts, but in his acquisition policy he adhered to the traditional hierarchy of the fine arts. His primary focus was on old master paintings, particularly the Baroque, followed by modern European works. He did not neglect contemporary American art, but showed only a modest interest and allocated fewer available funds to it.[20]

As he took the helm, Austin was dismissive of the American art that filled the museum, and he felt that there were far too many "historical" objects on display. A visitor's guide to the collections published in April 1927 provides a glimpse of what Austin encountered when he first saw the museum that June. There were only a few American works on paper on view. Upon entering Morgan Memorial, a gift of Hartford native J. Pierpont Morgan, he saw to the right of the entrance the "Pottery Room," containing the "Alfred Hastings Pitkin Collection of Early American and Bennington Pottery" as well as European and American silver and glass. To the left he entered the "Colt Collection," which featured the guns assembled by Samuel and Elizabeth Hart Jarvis Colt and, among other things, chronicled the manufacturing history of the renowned Colt's Patent Fire Arms Manufacturing Company in Hartford.[21] Downstairs was the Wallace Nutting Collection of three hundred pieces of seventeenth-century American furniture and decorative arts, which had been given the previous year as a gift of J. P. Morgan Jr. (fig. 12). The grand "Tapestry Hall" displayed tapestries and European decorative art treasures–a portion of the collection of one thousand objects given the museum through the will of J. Pierpont Morgan in 1917 (fig. 13).[22] A small gallery of American decorative arts included the Sharples pastel portraits of Washington and his wife, and a "Print Room" displayed selections from the collection of George Gay. The second floor held American Indian pottery and baskets, and an array of war medals.[23] In addition he saw natural history collections formed in the nineteenth century: minerals, butterflies, and "a bird room with eggs and skins and bird calls."[24] Paintings by Thomas Cole, Frederic Church, and other members of

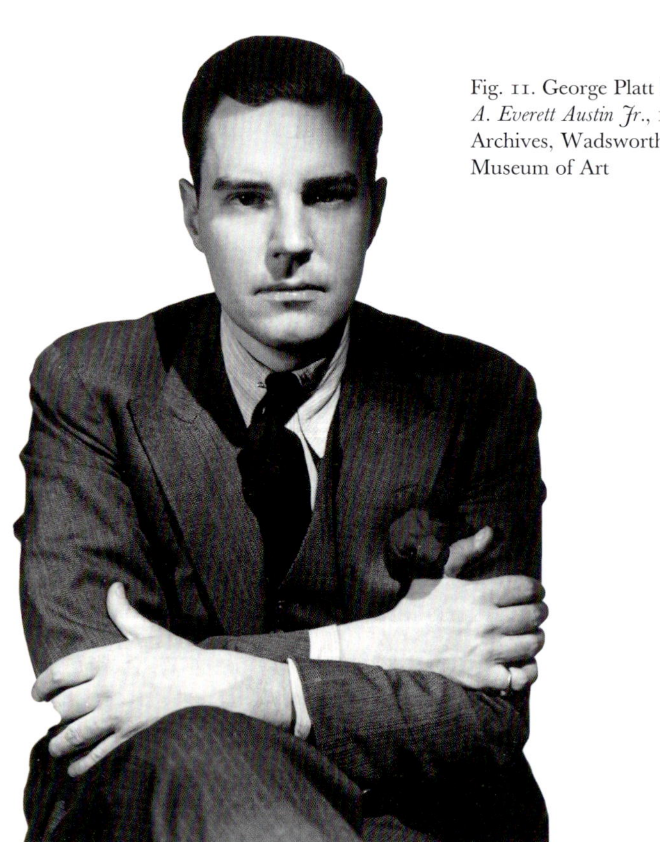

Fig. 11. George Platt Lynes, *A. Everett Austin Jr.*, 1936. Archives, Wadsworth Atheneum Museum of Art

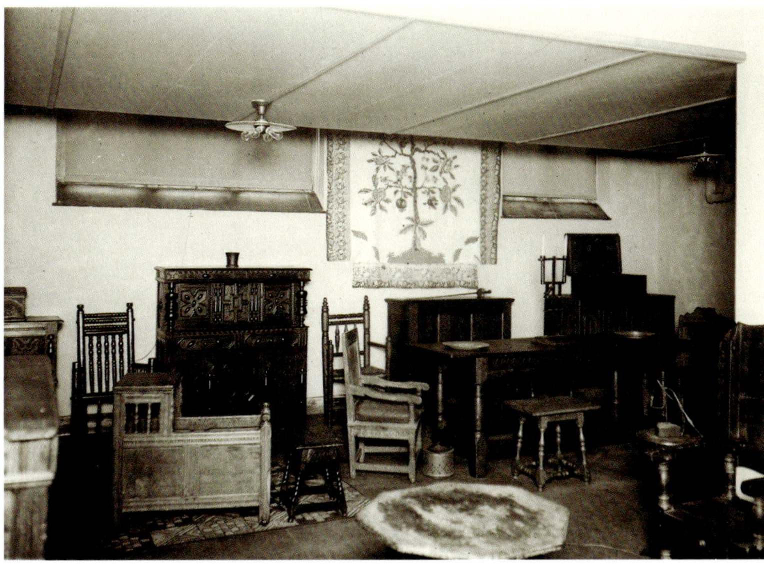

Fig. 12. *View of the Early Oak Room, Wallace Nutting Collection*, 1926. Archives, Wadsworth Atheneum Museum of Art

Fig. 13. *View of the Morgan Memorial Painting Galleries*, c. 1890. Archives, Wadsworth Atheneum Museum of Art

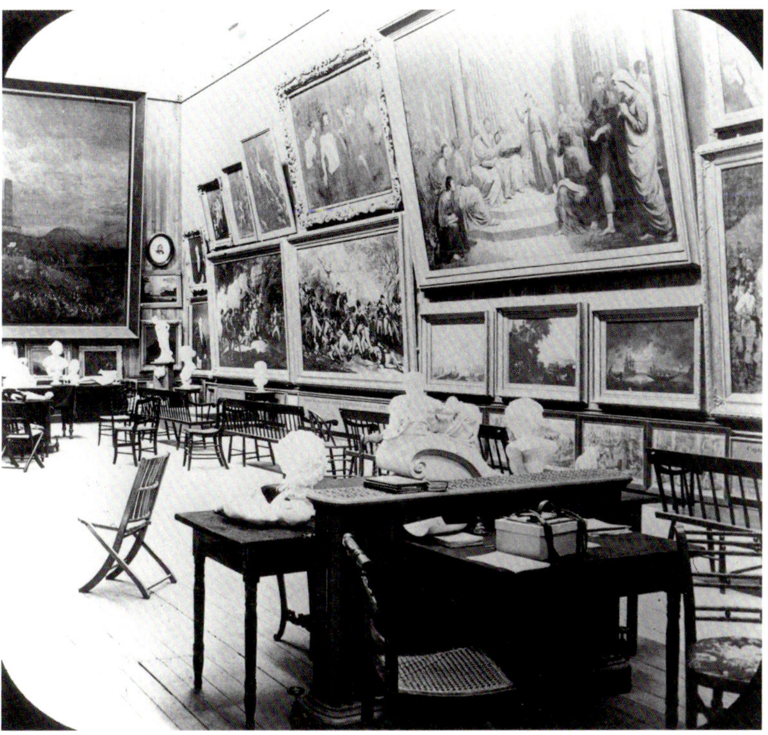

the Hudson River School were hung along with grand-scale history paintings illustrating the events of the Revolutionary War by John Trumbull, and nineteenth-century European academic works by Félix Ziem and Adolf Schreyer from Elizabeth Colt's 1905 bequest. It was an eclectic assortment of widely varying period and quality, and lacked works by the old masters and modern artists.

The buildings also housed the Connecticut Historical Society, the Hartford Public Library, and the Watkinson Reference Library, adding to the historical flavor of the institution.[25] In addition, Austin may well have attended the public lecture given by Stewart Dick in December of his first year, which the *Hartford Courant* covered with the headline "Modern Art Is Mediocre."[26] Altogether, the young director had many hurdles to overcome to achieve his ambitions.

During his first year, Austin assessed the museum's collections in a local magazine, summarizing what he saw as the important American works, singling out eighteenth-century portraits by John Singleton Copley, Ralph Earl, and Gilbert Stuart, and late nineteenth-century works by William Merritt Chase, George Inness, and James McNeill Whistler. Cassatt's pastel was the only work on paper that he felt worth mentioning.[27] He didn't take note of the remarkable collection of Hudson River School paintings, the largest and most important of its kind held by any museum, although out of favor at the time.[28]

With unconcealed disdain for his predecessors and exhibiting supreme confidence in his modern approach, he proclaimed: "The new policy of the Atheneum will be that of acquiring distinguished works of art rather than pictures of historical and decorative interest."[29] Austin knew when he accepted the position that he would be able to indulge his taste and vision in building the Atheneum's collections. In 1924, Hartford banker Frank Sumner bequeathed the Atheneum over one million dollars for an endowment fund for the purchase of "choice paintings." Conservatively invested, the fund provided Austin with approximately $60,000 to spend in his first year.[30] The money came to the museum upon the death of Sumner's wife in August 1927. Known as the Ella Gallup Sumner and Mary Catlin Sumner Collection Fund (named for Sumner's sister-in-law and his wife, an amateur watercolorist), it allowed Austin to expand the Atheneum's holdings. He moved in new directions, largely shaping the now-renowned European old master and modern and Surrealist collections.[31] The Sumner family also included approximately fifteen American drawings and watercolors by lesser-known Connecticut artists in the bequest, including works by Louis Orr, Compton Ruel Tuttle, and Mary Catlin Sumner. While the gift represented the conservative tastes of Hartford, it may also have provided Austin with the latitude to expand the definition of the Sumner Fund for "choice paintings" to include works on paper. (Nearly one-third of the works in this exhibition were acquired with money from the Sumner Fund.)

With confidence in his ability to shape the collections, Austin defined his plans for acquisitions: "It will be the policy of the Atheneum in the future, to build up a very small but very distinguished collection of works of art, buying only one important picture a year without much reference to the filling out of any given school."[32] He did not adhere to this policy of one picture a year for very long, however, as he developed a voracious appetite for new artistic agendas. He had definite ideas for augmenting the American art collection, as he explained in the interview: "At the same time, it is hoped that a collection of watercolors by modern Americans can be formed, as in this medium the American artist appears to find the ability to express himself more completely and characteristically than in the field of oils. To this end, a number of watercolors have been bought this year."[33]

Edwin Forbes likely guided Chick in his first American acquisition, made in November 1927, of a fluid and dashing watercolor by Sargent, *The Favorite Horse* (fig. 14). Chick paid $2,000 to M. Knoedler & Co., New York, using the William A. Healy Fund. Forbes had recently acquired watercolors by this artist for the Fogg Art Museum.[34] Sargent had died only two years before, and, with Homer, was considered one of the greatest American watercolorists.[35] Austin and Forbes were making up for lost time, as substantial collections of Sargent's watercolors and drawings had already been formed by the Brooklyn Museum, the Museum of Fine Arts, Boston, and the Metropolitan Museum of Art.[36]

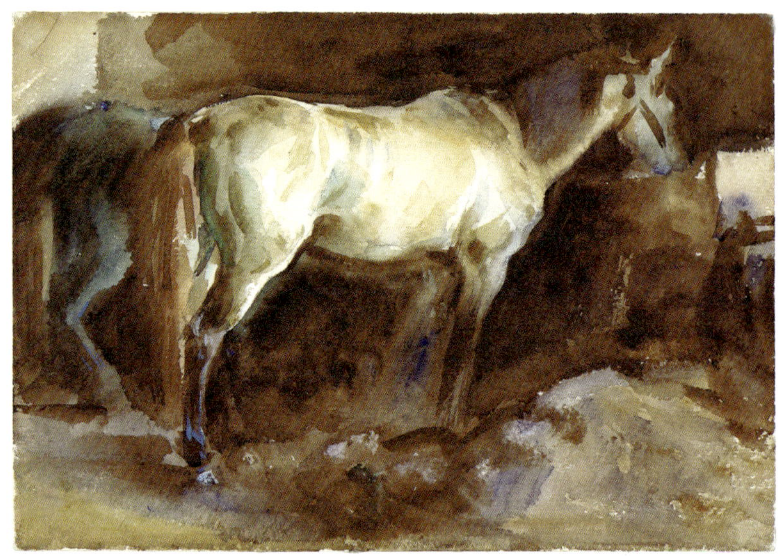

Fig. 14. John Singer Sargent, *The Favorite Horse*, c. 1910–15.
Watercolor on paper, 9 3/4 × 13 5/8 in. (24.8 × 34.6 cm).
Wadsworth Atheneum Museum of Art. The Healy Fund, 1927.613

In addition to the example set by Forbes and the growing popularity of Sargent's watercolors, the fact that watercolors were less expensive than oils made them attractive to Chick. He also had a personal interest in American watercolors through his work as an amateur artist. As early as his student days at Harvard, he had painted watercolors, which were published in the Harvard literary magazine *Hound & Horn*, founded by Lincoln Kirstein, who became Chick's friend and supporter. Austin continued to exhibit his watercolors throughout his tenure at the Atheneum. Kirstein invited him to show two watercolors in the Harvard Society for Contemporary Art's sixth exhibition, *Harvard Graduates*, and he had a solo exhibition in 1932 at the Brummer Gallery in New York (fig. 15).[37]

In 1928, his first full year as director, Austin focused on forming a collection of modern American watercolors. He began by creating a gallery for American watercolors, and with the help of Forbes borrowed works for changing displays. As he reported in the January 1928 *Wadsworth Atheneum Bulletin*, "The room of watercolors was rehung and several rare examples by Winslow Homer, Dodge Macknight, John S. Sargent, Edward Hopper, Charles Demuth, and Gifford Beal were added."[38] In January, using the Sumner Fund, he purchased Hopper's *Captain Strout's House, Portland Head* (cat. 34) from the Kraushaar Galleries for $300, and in March, Demuth's *Still Life with Eggplant and Summer Squash* (cat. 19), also from Kraushaar, for $1,200. In December, he bought Hopper's *Rockland Harbor* (cat. 32) from the Rehn Gallery for $300 and Preston Dickinson's *Power Station–Night* (cat. 21) from the Charles Daniel Gallery for $700. His interest in Hopper's watercolors was novel at this early date, as most museums were acquiring works by the American moderns promoted by Alfred Stieglitz, including Marin, Demuth, and Georgia O'Keeffe. (See Troyen, "Modernism and Antimodernism.")

To coincide with his purchases, Chick organized two modern American watercolor exhibitions that year. His first was in June, a show of sixteen works titled *Loan Exhibition of Modern American Watercolors*, which highlighted eight works by Demuth, six by Marin, and one by Preston Dickinson. He followed that with *Exhibition of Water Colors by Edward Hopper*, the artist's first solo exhibition in a museum, held at the end of November. Austin presented twelve works by Hopper, borrowing nine from the artist's dealer, Frank K. M. Rehn, and included *Captain Strout's House, Portland Head*. From

Fig. 15. A. Everett Austin Jr., *Savannah*, 1941.
Watercolor on paper, 14 5/8 × 21 1/4 in. (37.2 × 54 cm).
Wadsworth Atheneum Museum of Art.
Gift of Mr. and Mrs. Burton Tremaine, 1967.141

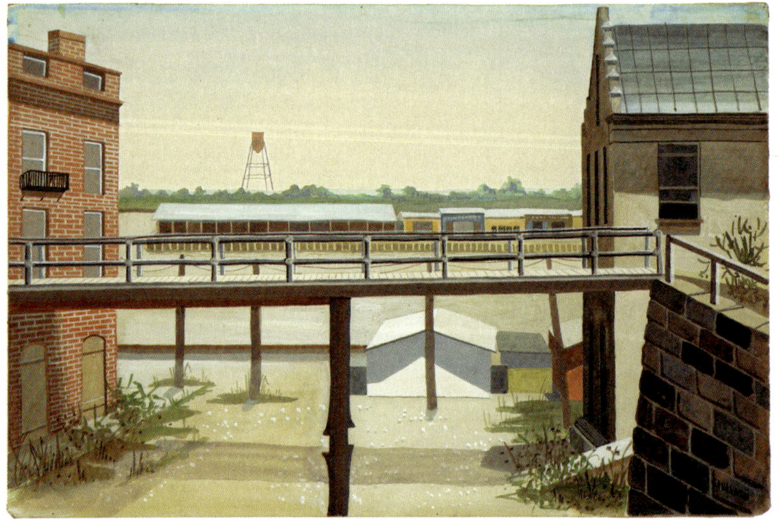

the show, he bought *Rockland Harbor*, and Atheneum trustee Robert Huntington (also an amateur watercolorist) purchased *Custom House, Portland* (cat. 33), which he later gave to the museum. Chick summarized his accomplishments in a letter to the editor of the *Hartford Times* in 1929, justifying his acquisitions with sound financial thinking:

During the past year, the Atheneum has acquired no less than six examples by prominent modern American artists—two by Hopper and one each by Sargent, Dodge MacKnight, Demuth and Dickinson. In the investment of funds in pictures, it is the wisest course always for the Museum to place its income in works of certain and recognized value rather than run the risk of buying expensive paintings by modern artists, the value of which may be considerably lowered by the criticism of the next generation. However, the policy of buying water-colors is a sound one, as in this way much smaller amounts are involved.[39]

While Chick's interest in building a collection of modern American watercolors was genuine at the time, it would prove fleeting, as he quickly moved on to new areas of interest.

After Austin's arrival, Philip L. Goodwin supported the new director's 1928 exhibition of modern watercolors by lending a number of important works. His *Lower Manhattan*, by Marin (see Troyen, "Modernism and Antimodernism," fig. 1), although missing from the Atheneum's 1923 exhibition, was included in the 1928 show and was illustrated in the *Bulletin* as a highlight.[40] Austin borrowed a second watercolor by Marin, *Green Head, Stonington, Maine* (1921; Hirshhorn Museum, Washington, D.C.), for the show from the New York Weyhe Gallery. This was a work that he wanted to purchase for the museum, but the trustees resisted because of its modern style, as well as the $650 price tag.[41] He added it to the show to convince the board otherwise; as he told Paul Vanderbilt of the Weyhe Gallery, "I am hoping in this way, I shall be able to get the picture by the Board. It looks rather difficult at the moment."[42] There were also eight works by Demuth and a pastel, *Still Life with Knife*, by Preston Dickinson (cat. 22). Goodwin generously lent the bronze portrait head *John Marin*, by Gaston Lachaise (an artist he counted as a close friend), which was placed near Marin's watercolors in the exhibition.[43] He donated it to the museum in 1943.

Austin ultimately failed to bring a watercolor by Marin into the collection that he began in 1928, even though throughout the 1930s Philip L. Goodwin strenuously lobbied for him to do just that. Goodwin frequently reminded Austin that he and his family wanted their acquisition funds to be used to buy a work by Marin. Perhaps as a way to inspire goodwill, in a letter of January 29, 1930, Goodwin offered to give the Atheneum four pictures "as good examples of the history of American watercolors": an ethereal Tonalist work by George Inness, *The Dolomites* (fig. 16); Arthur B. Davies's *Pont Neuf, Paris* (1925); the young artist Henry Schnakenberg's *Landscape with Quarry* (fig. 17); and Joseph Pennell's vigorous watercolor of the rise of skyscrapers in New York City, *Building New York* (cat. 8).[44]

In a series of letters, Goodwin continued to pressure Chick to visit Stieglitz's gallery.[45] But in 1933 Chick spent an astonishing $100,000 on a painting by Piero di Cosimo, *The Finding of Vulcan on the Island of Lemnos* (c. 1490), and months later he acquired the Serge Lifar Collection of designs for Sergey Diaghilev's Ballets Russes for $10,000, thus depleting the Sumner Fund for years to come.

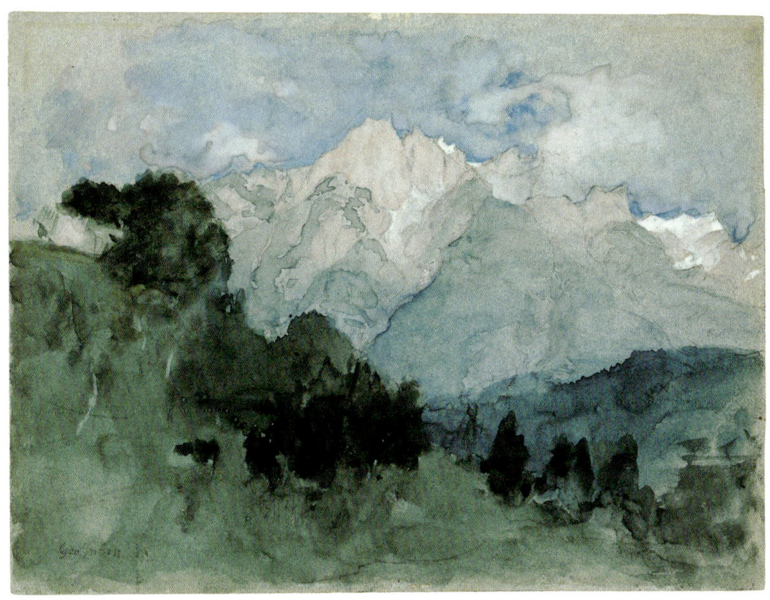

Fig. 16. George Inness, *The Dolomites*, c. 1873.
Watercolor on paper, 9 1/16 × 11 3/4 in. (23 × 29.9 cm).
Wadsworth Atheneum Museum of Art. Gift of Philip L. Goodwin, 1930.8

Fig. 17. Henry Schnakenberg, *Landscape with Quarry*, 1925.
Watercolor on paper, 11 3/8 × 17 9/16 in. (28.9 × 44.6 cm).
Wadsworth Atheneum Museum of Art. Gift of Philip L. Goodwin, 1930.10

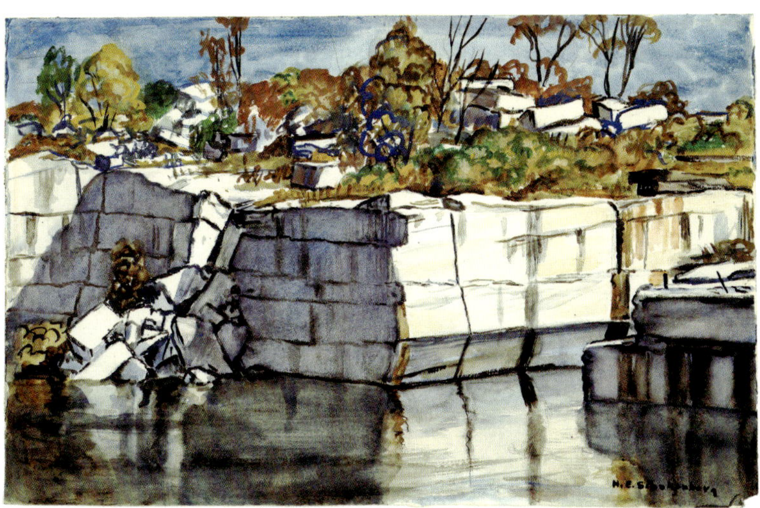

Goodwin, however, did not give up, continuing to pressure Chick to use the Goodwin funds, writing in April 1934 that he had seen several prospective Marins at Stieglitz's gallery An American Place and pleading, "You know my weakness for this painter." Chick responded that he would like Goodwin "to do the bargaining, as I find Stieglitz almost impossible to deal with."[46] It is difficult to imagine the two great egos—Stieglitz and Austin—in the small gallery space together. Austin refused to forge a relationship with the impresario of American modernism. As Stieglitz remained Marin's primary dealer until his death in 1946, a work by this artist did not enter the Atheneum's collection until the arrival of a new director.

During the 1930s, Chick moved on to artistic quests that coincided with his growing interest in performance. He maintained a frenetic pace, pushing the limits of his board's patience as he pursued new and challenging areas of European modernism, including a series of groundbreaking performances. Chick's daring response to the Depression era in America was to organize a series of exhibitions and festivals that promoted European modernism, paying scant attention to American artists.

In 1931 Austin presented an exhibition of the Neo-Romantic painters Christian Bérard, Pavel Tchelitchew, Kristians Tonny, and the brothers Leonid and Eugene Berman, who had first shown together in Paris in 1926. (See Troyen, "Modernism and Antimodernism.") Austin brought them together for the first time in a museum setting in the United States and championed their lyrical, nostalgic, and often decadent style. He proceeded to buy works from these artists, mainly on paper, as he pursued his earlier philosophy of paying "smaller amounts" for works by "modern artists." He also commissioned them to contribute their skills to stage set design and mural painting for the many performances he organized in the new Avery Theater, part of the Avery Memorial wing, which was added to the Atheneum in 1934 and included the first International style museum interior designed primarily by Austin.[47]

In the same year, 1931, Austin mounted the first exhibition of Surrealism in America, *Newer Super-Realism*, which included works by Salvador Dalí, Giorgio de Chirico, Max Ernst, André Masson, Joan Miró, Pablo Picasso, and Pierre Roy, as well as presenting three French films.[48] Other exhibitions included *The James Thrall Soby Collection*, a selection of works from the West Hartford collector of modern paintings who was discovered by Chick, becoming his friend as well as his assistant, and later a curator and a trustee of the Museum of Modern Art. This was followed by the first Picasso retrospective in America. In 1935 Chick organized an exhibition entitled *Abstract Art*, with work by César Domela, Naum Gabo, Piet Mondrian, and Antoine Pevsner. For the catalogue, he designed a single-sheet checklist with an abstract grid pattern printed on celluloid. In the same year he also showed *Paintings of Pavel Tchelitchew* and *Drawings by Eugene Berman*.

Chick was supported in these efforts by many Harvard associates, including the like-minded dealer Julien Levy. The two men shared similar tastes and approaches to contemporary art, and Levy wrote in his autobiography, "With Chick, business and friendship were outrageously, happily, and rewardingly mixed. Chick and I felt we were associates in two branches of the same business, together advancing the horizons of art."[49] Levy was quick to point out that he did not enjoy a similar relationship with the director of the Museum of Modern Art, Alfred H. Barr Jr., who did not always share Austin and Levy's tastes, in particular, their support of the Neo-Romantics. Chick acquired many groundbreaking works of art from Levy, including Joseph Cornell's *Soap Bubble Set* (1936), the artist's first box construction and his first sale to a museum, as well as many works on paper by the Neo-Romantics.

A younger Harvard alumnus, who later participated in Austin's many ventures, was Lincoln Kirstein, the man most responsible for bringing George Balanchine to America and creating the School of American Ballet. Later, he summarized his friend's achievements: "As for the intellectual background of the 'Thirties'; a lot of Chick's interest sprang from a combination of Sur-realism and a less noted movement of Neo-Romanticism, which was based on lyric observation, and neither hysteria or deformation. Both were a reaction towards the modernism that started with the Fauves, and was elegant, epicene, nostalgic and museum-oriented. It was an elite art."[50]

Chick also developed an association with the New York dealer Edith Gregor Halpert, who opened the Downtown Gallery in 1926.[51] Specializing in contemporary American artists, Halpert had in many ways assumed the mantle of Alfred Stieglitz, the pioneering dealer of American modernists. Austin began corresponding with Halpert in 1929, the year she opened the American Folk Art Gallery, at the vanguard of an interest in the works of America's folk artists. Austin maintained contact with her throughout his years as director, but bought only a few important American paintings from her, including William Harnett's *Faithful Colt* (1890), and no works on paper. Later in her life, Halpert presented a gift of works by American folk artists to the museum, included the charming drawing *Elephant* (fig. 18).[52]

Through Chick's close relationships with artists, collectors, and dealers, many gifts of American modern works on paper entered the collection. Kirstein gave two drawings by Gaston Lachaise in 1934 (cat. 65); James Thrall Soby left a large number of works to the museum in his bequest, including three drawings by

Fig. 18. Unknown artist, *Elephant*, late 19th–early 20th century. Graphite on paper, $10^1/_2 \times 15^5/_8$ in. (26.7 × 39.7 cm). Wadsworth Atheneum Museum of Art. Gift of Edith Gregor Halpert, 1958.759

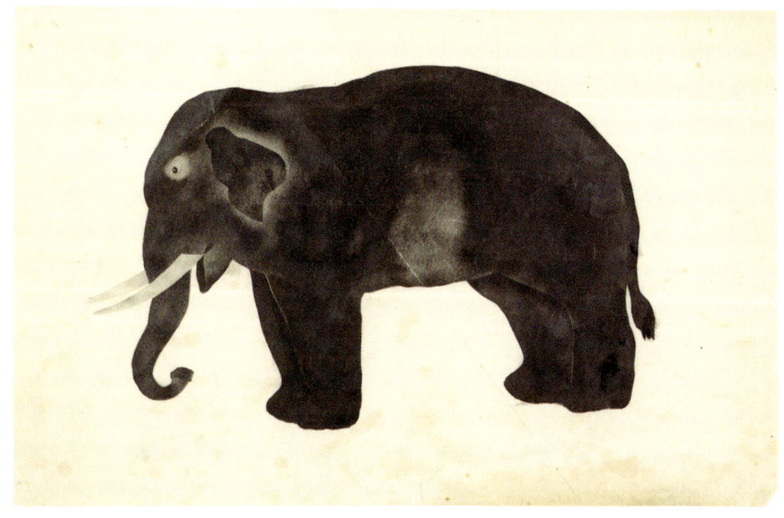

Pavel Tchelitchew (cats. 56a–c); and art historian Russell Lynes, the editor of *Harper's Magazine* and younger brother of photographer George Platt Lynes, gave a Tchelitchew drawing (cat. 52b) in 1984. In addition, many artists, some of whom settled in northwestern Connecticut, where a large circle lived and worked, donated art as a result of their friendship with Chick and their appreciation for his work at the Atheneum, even after he had resigned from the directorship. Kay Sage gave two ink drawings by her husband, Yves Tanguy, in 1963 (cat. 68). Artist Abraham Walkowitz gave one hundred of his watercolors, drawings, and pastels of the dancer Isadora Duncan in 1949, as a tribute to Austin's presentation of ballet at the Atheneum (see cats. 6a and b). Hazel Guggenheim McKinley gave a crayon drawing by Hans Hofmann in memory of Chick Austin in 1959 (cat. 77). These tributes continued into the twenty-first century, long after Austin's death. In 2001, the artist-illustrator Edward Gorey bequeathed his art collection, including several works by Charles Burchfield (see cats. 26, 31), to the Atheneum in appreciation for what Chick had done to bring the Russian ballet and George Balanchine to America. During his life, Gorey rarely missed a single Balanchine ballet.[53]

In addition to building the collections of European and American art and mounting groundbreaking exhibitions, Austin's legacy rests strongly on his talents as a showman, putting on fantastic artistic "happenings." (See Troyen, "Modernism and Antimodernism," for a discussion of the Paper Ball, which celebrated art on paper, and other art festivals orchestrated by Austin in the 1930s.) The distinguished architectural historian Henry-Russell Hitchcock, a Harvard associate who supported Austin's endeavors in Hartford, put him in perspective by defining the distinctions between the two most important museum directors of the era:

There were two people in the country who were doing new exhibitions . . . one of them was Chick Austin and the other was Alfred Barr, and they were obviously doing them from different angles. Barr's was much more the approach of the scholar, and his catalogues were monuments . . . which have been standard works ever since. . . . But certainly nothing showed to the outside world comparable to Chick's building up of that collection, providing the setting for it, and then presenting the parallel events. He had charisma. He bubbled over with ideas, and they were so stimulating that everyone was willing to work with him . . . in the art world; he knew what was going on as soon as it started.[54]

Charles C. Cunningham (1916–1979) succeeded Chick Austin in 1946 and led the museum for twenty years, making him the longest-serving director in the Atheneum's history (fig. 19). During his tenure he built the collection of modern works on paper, adding a comprehensive selection of works by Marin, as well as important examples by Burchfield, Demuth, Arthur Dove, and Hopper, and important contemporary art, including works by William Baziotes, Peter Blume, and Stuart Davis. He established professional curatorial standards in the museum, which resulted in the first efforts to research the collections. Cunningham initiated the practice of writing to all living American artists who had works in the museum. This resulted in the gathering of invaluable correspondence with American artists such as Burchfield, Hopper, and Marin, to name a few.

While not as flamboyant as his predecessor, Cunningham also had trained at Harvard and the Fogg Art Museum (and he obtained an advanced degree from the Courtauld Institute), and he adhered to the traditional hierarchy in his purchases, with European old masters as a top priority. Unlike Austin, however, Cunningham was interested in developing a comprehensive collection of American art and was willing to look back in time to remedy the many omissions he saw in that area, adding paintings and watercolors by Homer and Thomas Eakins, for example, and expanding the collection of Hudson River School paintings, as well as acquiring important American twentieth-century art.[55]

Earlier in his career, Cunningham, while serving as an assistant curator of painting at the Museum of Fine Arts, Boston, had met Edith Halpert, and purchased three watercolors by Marin from her Downtown Gallery in 1939 for $500 apiece.[56] Later as director, Cunningham was determined to add works by Marin to the Atheneum's collections, considering this artist's absence a great omission, and stating his intention to build a representative body of his works.[57] He worked to flesh out the rest of the American watercolor collection, and for both goals he turned to Halpert for help. In addition, his personal interest in the subject resulted in his own small collection of watercolors by Marin and Burchfield. He acquired Burchfield's watercolor *Snowbank and Pool* (1935) and the large watercolor *November Landscape* (cat. 29), which was later given to the Atheneum by his daughter, Priscilla Cunningham. In October 1948 Cunningham organized an exhibition to highlight watercolors by leading American artists entitled *Seven by Six: Loan Exhibition of Contemporary American Watercolors* and included seven watercolors each by Burchfield, Adolf Dehn, Lyonel Feininger, Morris Graves, Hopper, and Marin. Halpert, who by this point had a second home in nearby Newtown, Connecticut, loaned five works by Marin from the Downtown Gallery to the show, including the masterful *From the Bridge, N.Y.C.* (cat. 12), one of the artist's greatest works. Cunningham recognized its importance, writing in the exhibition brochure, "The extraordinary color harmonies in this painting and the use of the collage give form and vibrancy to this picture."[58] He

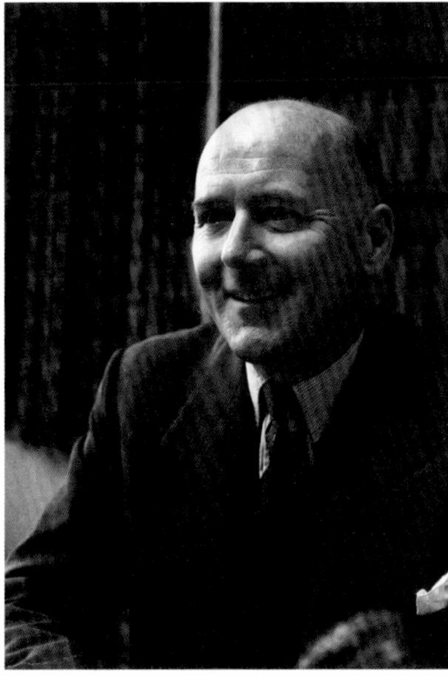

Fig. 19. Unknown photographer, *Charles C. Cunningham*, c. 1960. Archives, Wadsworth Atheneum Museum of Art

quickly convinced the Atheneum's acquisition committee to consider the work for purchase, and in December of that year he was able to get Edith Halpert to reduce the $2,000 asking price to $1,800. Halpert was thrilled to finally place a work by this artist in the Atheneum's collections, writing to Cunningham, "I feel so strongly that Marin needs that representation in New England, and I feel equally strongly about the choice you made. In my opinion this is one of Marin's truly great pictures."[59]

Not satisfied with the two major Marin watercolors he had managed to add to the collections, Cunningham continued to work with Halpert to acquire additional works by this artist. In 1949, their correspondence indicates that Cunningham purchased a Marin watercolor from Halpert for his own collection.[60] In January 1952 he wrote, "I am still looking for important Marins and would love to find several as fine as the one I bought for myself. I feel that we ought to have at least seven or eight in the museum's collection. We got left out in the cold with HOMER when the Museum of Fine Arts, the Worcester Art Museum and the Metropolitan were acquiring them and I do not want the same thing to happen to us with MARIN. Do keep us in mind when you get a really 'breathless one.'"[61] Cunningham made Marin a cause and eventually acquired enough material by this artist that the Atheneum's collection represents his entire career.[62]

Cunningham organized *Survey of American Watercolors* in August and September of 1952, featuring works from the collection and loans from collectors, dealers, and other museums. The exhibition ranged from eighteenth-century Copley watercolors to twentieth-century works by Mark Rothko.[63] He borrowed two works by Dove and two by Marin from Halpert's Downtown Gallery. He later succeeded in buying one of these from the show for the collection in 1955, adding Dove's *Sunrise* (cat. 23) and paying $127.50. At the same time, he purchased a second work by Dove, *Flour Mill II* (cat. 24) for $157.50, and bought Marin's *Small Point, Maine, Looking Up Lagoon* (fig. 20), for $500, all with the Sumner Fund.[64]

Philip L. Goodwin was undoubtedly pleased to see Cunningham's dedication in building the modern American works on paper collection. In 1957, the year before he died, Goodwin gave a 1953 pastel by William Baziotes, *Pompeii* (cat. 80a), to the museum. He had purchased it in 1954 from the Samuel Kootz Gallery in New York. Goodwin and Cunningham maintained a close dialogue about contemporary American art and informed each other about current trends at New York galleries and museums, including the growing importance of the work of Baziotes and Jackson Pollock. For example, following Goodwin's lead, Cunningham purchased Baziotes's *Figure in Foliage* (cat. 80b) from the Samuel Kootz Gallery with the Sumner Fund in 1955.[65]

Goodwin died in 1958, leaving a large portion of his collection to the Museum of Modern Art, but designated in his will a sizable number of important works in several media for the Atheneum.[66] His bequest included Marin's important New York City watercolor *Movement No. 3, Related to Downtown New York* (cat. 11), which Goodwin had acquired from Stieglitz's American Place gallery in 1945 (fig. 21). An exhibition of the Goodwin bequest to the Atheneum held that year included the Marin along with other important gifts of American watercolors and drawings: Demuth's *Eight O'Clock (Evening)* (cat. 18a); Lachaise's *Head of a Woman* (1931); and Charles Sheeler's *Stove* (cat. 38). Several modern sculptures were also part of the bequest, including Lachaise's *Statue of a Man* (1927), Elie Nadelman's *Dancer* (1918), and Isamu Noguchi's *Child of the Bell* (c. 1940s), as well as paintings by Picasso, Miró, and Pollock.[67]

Cunningham maintained a relationship with a number of artists who lived in northwestern Connecticut, including Henry Schnakenberg, who moved to Newtown, Connecticut, in 1947. Schnakenberg practiced a conservative realism in his works, which were largely landscapes painted in oil and watercolor.[68] His personal wealth allowed him to collect art from many cultures and periods. Through his friendship with Cunningham, Schnakenberg was inspired to give many important works from his collection to the Atheneum, including examples by American artists, among them original watercolors by the famous nineteenth-century naturalist artist John James Audubon. In addition, in 1950, he established the Schnakenberg Fund for the purchase of works "entirely by contemporary Americans" with an initial gift of $5,000, to which he added over the years.[69] With the Schnakenberg Fund, Cunningham purchased works on paper by Peggy Bacon (cat. 51), Paul Cadmus (cat. 74), Stuart Davis (cat. 40), William Glackens (cat. 2), Morris Graves (cat. 76), Marin (cat. 10), and John Sloan (cat. 4).[70] In 1955 Cunningham organized an exhibition of Schnakenberg's paintings and watercolors at the Atheneum and published a catalogue.[71]

Cunningham attracted a number of other Connecticut artists to give important works on paper to the museum. In 1956 Sherman, Connecticut, resident Peter Blume gave three drawings (see cat. 75) for his Surrealist-inspired painting *Italian Straw Hat* (1952), which was acquired by Cunningham in 1955. Blume was a part of the artistic circle in northwestern Connecticut that Austin cultivated in the 1930s and '40s and which included Alexander Calder, Yves Tanguy, and Kay Sage.[72]

Fig. 21. *Alfred Stieglitz Writing "Once a Year" at Desk, A.A.P.*, 1940. Gelatin silver print. Photograph by Ansel Adams. © 2009 The Ansel Adams Publishing Rights Trust

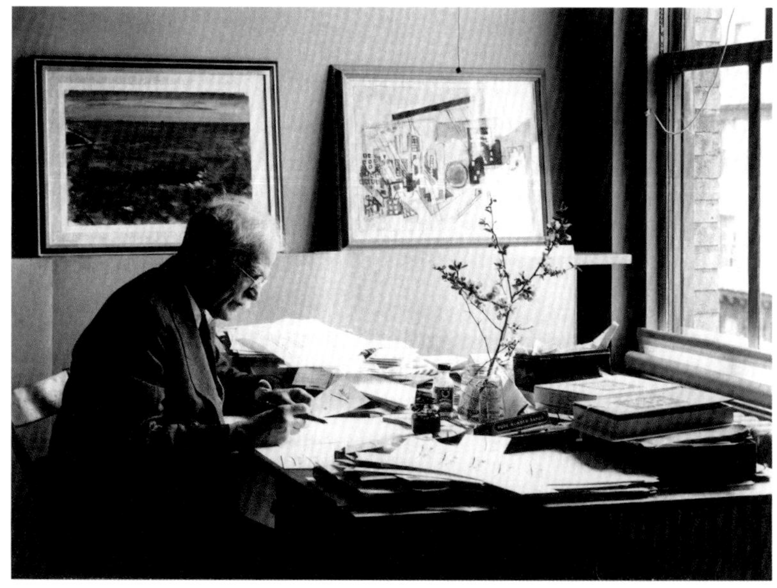

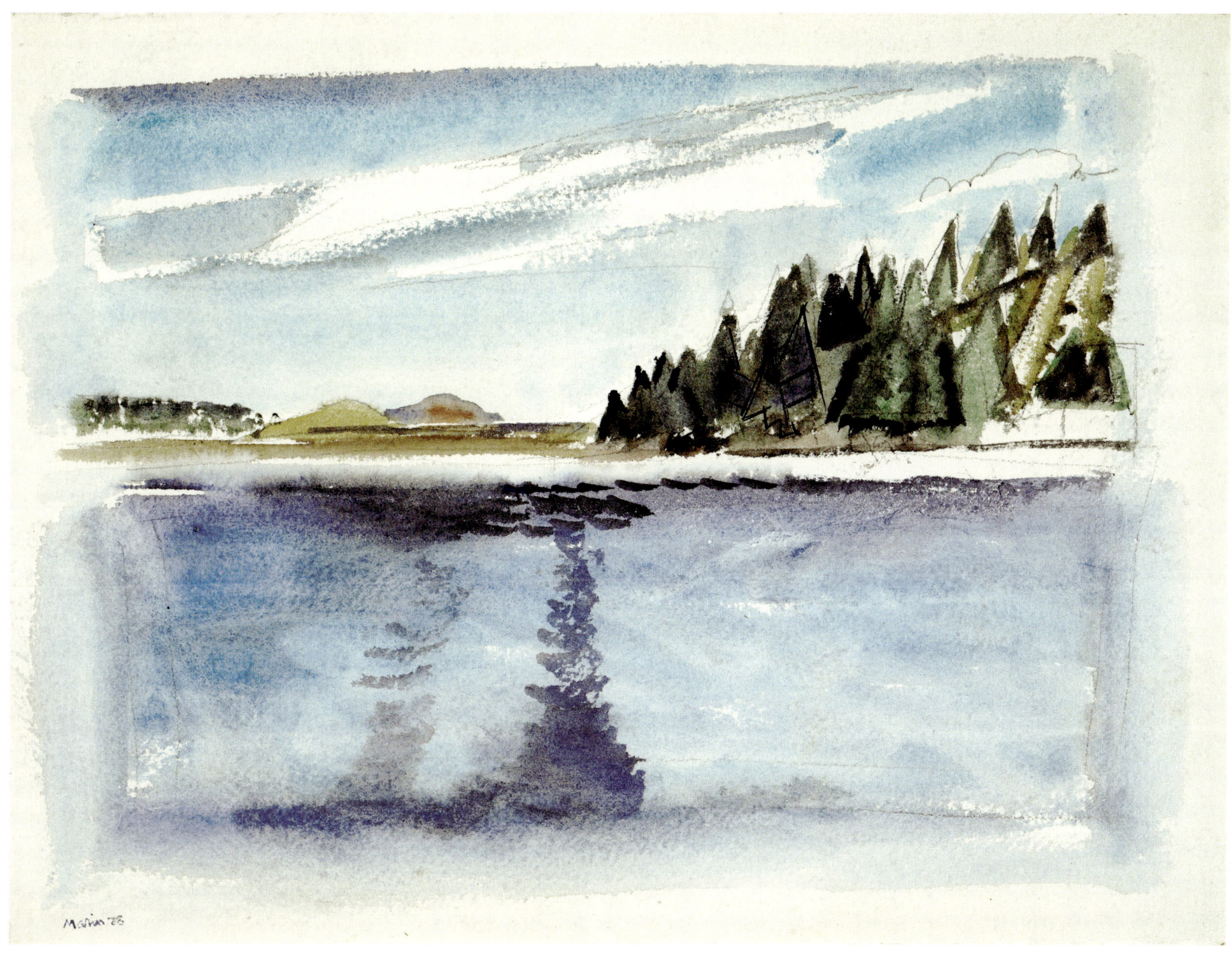

Fig. 20. John Marin,
Small Point, Maine, Looking Up Lagoon, 1928.
Opaque and transparent watercolor and graphite on paper, 14 × 18 3/8 in. (35.6 × 46.7 cm).
Wadsworth Atheneum Museum of Art.
The Ella Gallup Sumner and
Mary Catlin Sumner Collection Fund, 1955.267

In 1961, on the advice of Harvard classmate James J. Rorimer (later the director of the Metropolitan Museum of Art), Cunningham hired the young art historian Samuel J. Wagstaff Jr. as curator. They were a powerful team. Wagstaff enlivened the museum with contemporary exhibitions such as *Black, White and Gray* (1964), and made many important contemporary acquisitions. He was in close contact with artists Robert Motherwell, Ellsworth Kelly, Joseph Albers, Agnes Martin, David Smith, Lee Bontecou, Donald Judd, Nam June Paik, Richard Tuttle, Dan Flavin, Grace Hartigan, Philip Guston, and Tony Smith, among many others.[73] Wagstaff left the museum in 1968, but in 1980 he gave the Atheneum *Briar*, a drawing by Ellsworth Kelly (cat. 85) created in 1961, the year Wagstaff joined the Atheneum staff.

The scope of the present exhibition ends just as Wagstaff arrived and continued to move the Atheneum in new directions. The museum remained in pursuit of art of its own time, and indeed focused on contemporary art with the arrival of James Elliot in 1966. During his decade-long tenure as director, Elliott added superior

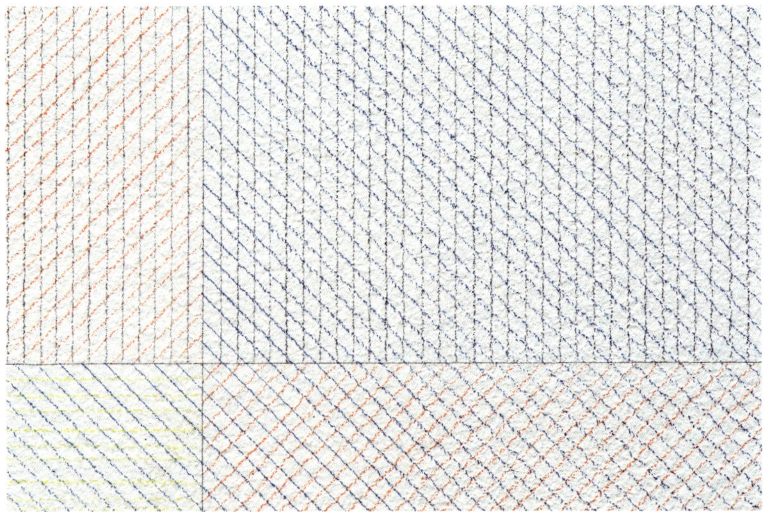

Fig. 22. Sol LeWitt, *Wall Drawing #8 A and B* (detail), 1969.
Black and colored pencil six-part drawing using all two-part combinations of lines in four directions, placed in rows of three within a rectangle.
Wadsworth Atheneum Museum of Art. Gift of the artist, 1996.10.2

works of contemporary art to the collections and, most famously, in 1974 founded the MATRIX program, which emphasized exhibitions, performances, and lectures by emerging artists. The distinguished list of over 150 MATRIX artists includes Jonathan Borofsky, Willem de Kooning, Keith Haring, Christian Jankowski, Ellsworth Kelly, Barbara Kruger, Louise Lawler, Sol LeWitt, Glenn Ligon, Sylvia Plimack Mangold, Gerhard Richter, Pipilotti Rist, Lorna Simpson, Richard Tuttle, Andy Warhol, and Carrie Mae Weems. For many artists, their MATRIX show at the Atheneum was their first one-person museum exhibition in the United States. Several MATRIX artists embraced the newer media of photography, video, and performance art, but for a large number, drawing and watercolor continued to be an essential artistic activity.

The parameters of the terms *drawing* and *watercolor* have been challenged by artists such as Warhol, Haring, and Christo. One of the most innovative and influential developments in the field of contemporary art was initiated by the Hartford native Sol LeWitt (1928–2007), whose first wall drawing was made at the Paula Cooper

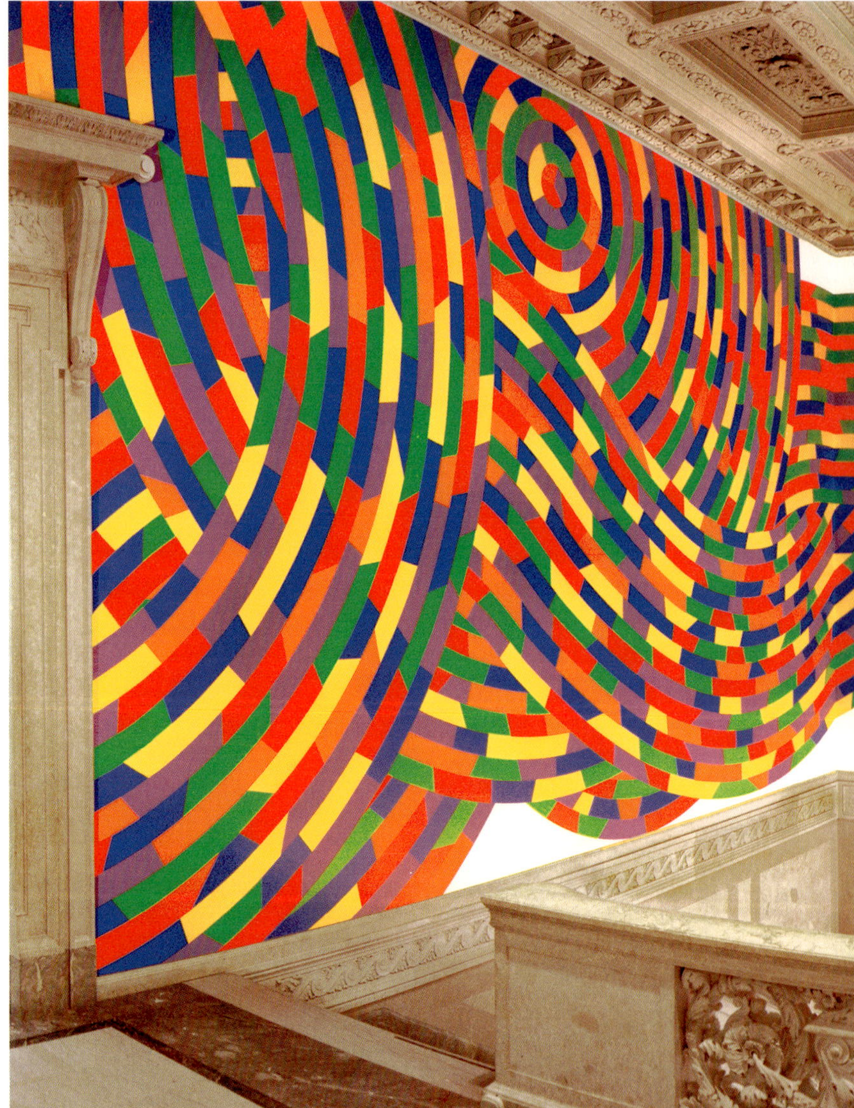

Fig. 23. Sol LeWitt,
Wall Drawing #1131 "Whirls and Twirls," 2004.
Site-specific wall drawing.
Wadsworth Atheneum Museum of Art.
The Ella Gallup Sumner and
Mary Catlin Sumner Collection Fund, 2004.12.1

Gallery in 1968. He chose to work directly on the wall and to create a work that was as flat as possible, using hard lead pencils to enhance the medium's two-dimensionality. Since then his wall drawings have changed continually, growing in scale, complexity, and impact. After his initial wall drawings, which he executed himself, LeWitt began making delicate drawings on paper, which a team of assistants would transfer to the wall. He felt that the conception of a work of art could be separated from its execution, famously stating in 1967, "The idea becomes the machine that makes the art." He intended for the wall drawings to remain in place indefinitely or to be painted over, with the possibility of re-creating them at another time. The Wadsworth Atheneum commissioned a series of six wall drawings by LeWitt, covering thirty-five years of creativity by this artist. The earliest is *Wall Drawing #8 A and B* of 1969, a black and color pencil drawing on an existing museum wall (fig. 22); the most recent, the 2004 commission *Wall Drawing #1131 "Whirls and Twirls,"* in acrylic paint on existing museum walls (fig. 23).

The approximately one hundred works on paper featured in this exhibition and catalogue entered the collections almost equally through gift and purchase, and often shortly after they were executed. The extraordinary efforts of the Atheneum's directors, curators, and benefactors led to the formation of this distinguished collection of modern American art on paper, which continues to grow in the twenty-first century. The most recent additions are three works that were added to the collection in honor of this exhibition. Two important drawings by David Smith (cats. 81a and b), the gift of a long-standing donor to the Wadsworth Atheneum, expand the collection of drawings by American sculptors, many of which are in this exhibition and catalogue. Museum acquisition funds were used to acquire the first work on paper by Georgia O'Keeffe—a masterful pastel of 1926 (cat. 15)—so that this collection and exhibition would include a work by this American modernist, who excelled on paper. Hartford's fascination with American modernist works on paper has continued into the twenty-first century, ensuring the further development of this collection for future generations.

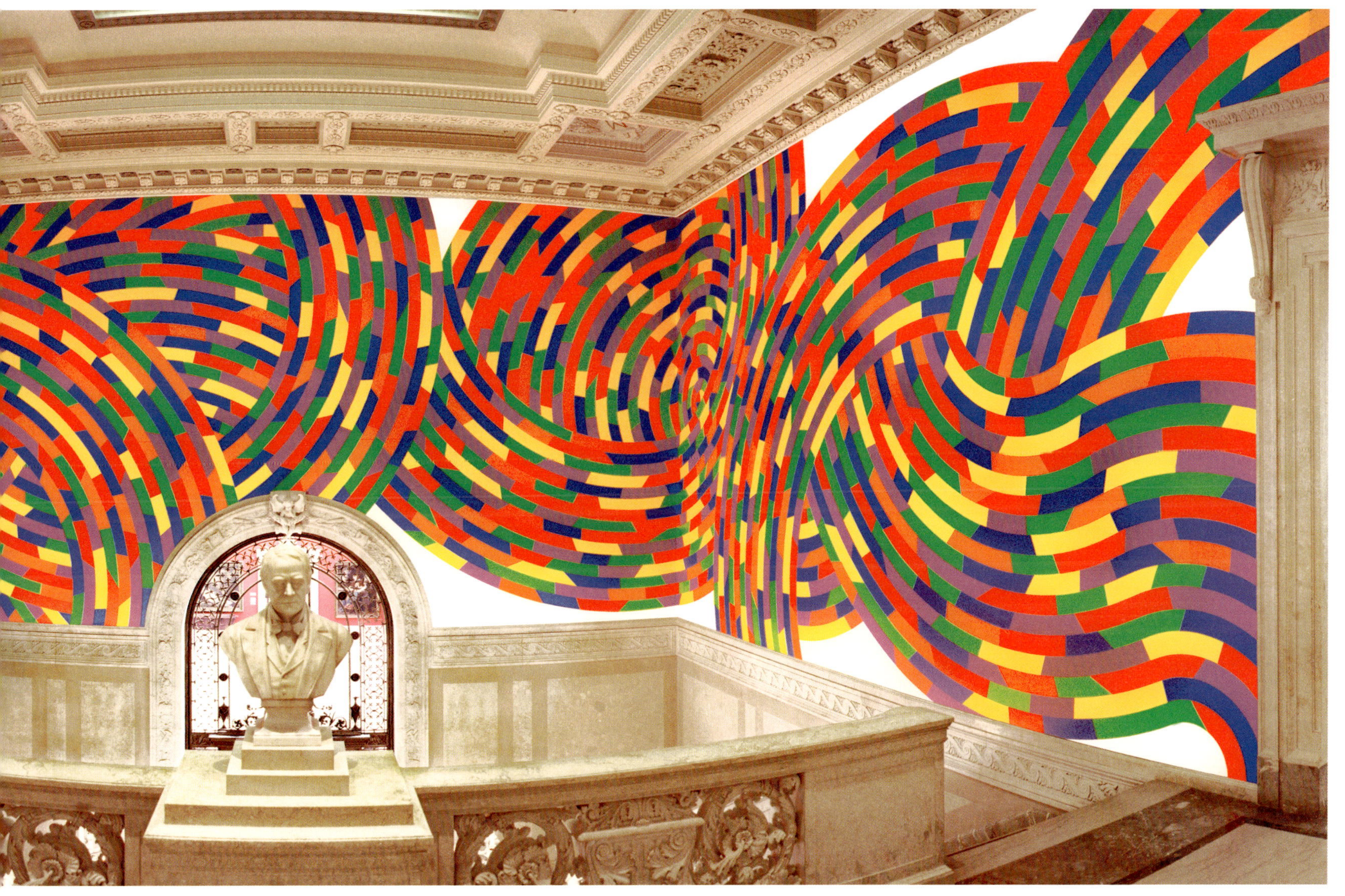

Notes

1. For a history of Daniel Wadsworth's role as a patron of American artists, see Elizabeth Mankin Kornhauser, *American Paintings before 1945 in the Wadsworth Atheneum Museum*, with contributions by Elizabeth R. McClintock and Amy Ellis, 2 vols. (New Haven, Conn.: Yale University Press in association with the Wadsworth Atheneum, 1996); and Elizabeth Mankin Kornhauser, "Daniel Wadsworth and Elizabeth Hart Jarvis Colt," in *New World: Creating an American Art,* by Kornhauser, Ortrud Westheider, and Karsten Müller (Hamburg, Germany: Bucerius Kunst Forum, 2007).

2. For a complete history of the American painting collection at the Atheneum and of these nineteenth-century patrons, see Kornhauser, *American Paintings before 1945*.

3. James Britton, "Art," *Hartford Courant*, 2 March 1912, 18.

4. "Watercolors and Pastels at Annex," *Hartford Courant*, 4 November 1917, 21.

5. Mrs. James J. Goodwin to Charles A. Goodwin, 20 February 1923, Wadsworth Atheneum Archives.

6. Frank B. Gay to Mrs. James J. Goodwin, 20 March 1923, Wadsworth Atheneum Archives.

7. Mary Cassatt to Frank Gay, 18 October 1923, curatorial files, Wadsworth Atheneum.

8. Philip L. Goodwin to Charles A. Goodwin, 20 February 1923, Wadsworth Atheneum Archives.

9. Ibid.

10. Linda S. Ferber and Barbara Dayer Gallati, *Masters of Color and Light: Homer, Sargent and the American Watercolor Movement* (Washington, D.C.: Smithsonian Institution Press in association with the Brooklyn Museum, 1998), 174–75.

11. Ibid., 153–54.

12. Philip L. Goodwin to Florence Berger, 3 October 1923, Wadsworth Atheneum Archives. This letter indicates that Goodwin purchased *Tree Forms and Sea* and *Lower Manhattan or the Blue Horse* (1920) from Stieglitz's Gallery by 1923 and owned Demuth's *Circus and Tree Forms* by 1923. He also purchased from Stieglitz *Red Cabbages, Rhubarb, and Oranges* (1929) for $1,400, and later traded it for *Green Pears* (1929). See Bruce Kellner, ed., *Letters of Charles Demuth, American Artist, 1883–1935* (Philadelphia: Temple University Press, 2000), 117. In the *New York Times* obituary for Charles Demuth, Philip L. Goodwin is listed as one of three major collectors of Demuth's works; the other two were Georgia O'Keeffe and Alfred Stieglitz. See "Charles Demuth Noted Artist Dies," *New York Times*, 25 October 1935, clipping files, Wadsworth Atheneum Archives.

13. Philip L. Goodwin, "Tribute," in *Stieglitz: Memorial Portfolio 1864–1946* (1946), n.p.

14. Sheldon Reich, *John Marin: Catalogue Raisonné* (Tucson: University of Arizona Press, 1970), 2:478.

15. Philip L. Goodwin to Mrs. Florence Berger, 20 September 1923, Wadsworth Atheneum Archives.

16. Philip L. Goodwin to Florence Berger, 3 October 1923, Wadsworth Atheneum Archives.

17. *Loan Exhibition of Watercolors, Pastels and Drawings*, Morgan Memorial, Hartford, Connecticut, 16 October–11 November 1923.

18. "Local Art Lovers View Fine Exhibition," *Hartford Courant*, 16 October 1923, 6.

19. Eugene R. Gaddis, *Magician of the Modern: Chick Austin and the Transformation of the Arts in America* (New York: Alfred A. Knopf, 2000).

20. The Wadsworth Atheneum's acquisition records for the years 1928–44 clearly demonstrate the hierarchy of spending, with European old master works receiving the largest share of funds, followed by contemporary European works. A high point was the 1932 purchase of Piero di Cosimo's *Finding of Vulcan* for $100,000. Most American paintings and works on paper averaged about $300 dollars and rarely exceeded $2,000.

21. For a history of the Colt collections given to the Wadsworth Atheneum, see Herbert G. Houze and Elizabeth Mankin Kornhauser, eds., *Samuel Colt: Arms, Art, and Invention* (New Haven, Conn.: Yale University Press in association with the Wadsworth Atheneum, 2006).

22. Linda Horvitz Roth, *J. Pierpont Morgan, Collector* (Hartford, Conn.: Wadsworth Atheneum, 1986).

23. *Short Guide to the Wadsworth Atheneum, Morgan Memorial and Colt Collection*, April 1927, Wadsworth Atheneum Archives.

24. Gaddis, *Magician of the Modern*, 73.

25. For a history of the Wadsworth Atheneum, see Eugene R. Gaddis et al., *"The Spirit of Genius": Art at the Wadsworth Atheneum* (New York: Hudson Hills Press in association with the Wadsworth Atheneum, 1992).

26. "Modern Art Is Mediocre Says Briton: Present Day Unable to Produce the Paintings and Sculpture of the Masters Dick Declares," *Hartford Courant*, 10 December 1927, clipping files, Wadsworth Atheneum Archives.

27. A. Everett Austin Jr., "Hartford's Art Museum," *Hartford Magazine*, 13 April 1928, 4. The American artist George H. Story (1835–1923) served as the curator of paintings at the Metropolitan Museum of Art from 1899 to 1906 and as the honorary curator of the Wadsworth Atheneum from 1897 until his death. Story was responsible for the addition of many of the American paintings cited by Austin as important works.

28. Kevin J. Avery, "A Historiography of the Hudson River School," in *American Paradise: The World of the Hudson River School*, ed. John K. Howat (New York: Metropolitan Museum of Art, 1987), 3–20.

29. Quoted in Gaddis, "Foremost Upon This Continent," in Gaddis, *"The Spirit of Genius,"* 19. Austin went so far as to destroy, on October 15, 1928, over thirty paintings that he felt were in poor condition or unacceptable for an art museum, many from Daniel Wadsworth's original bequest. For the most part, they were thought to be copies after old master paintings, which were acquired as part of the American Academy of the Fine Arts collections, as well as four works from the 1848 bequest of Daniel Wadsworth to the Wadsworth Atheneum; see Kornhauser, *American Paintings before 1945*, 1:10–20.

30. Gaddis, *Magician of the Modern*, 68, 74.

31. For history of the formation of these collections, see Gaddis, *Magician of the Modern*; Eric Zafran, ed., *Renaissance to Rococo: Masterpieces from the Wadsworth Atheneum Museum of Art* (New Haven, Conn.: Yale University Press in association with the Wadsworth Atheneum Museum of Art, 2004); and Eric Zafran and Paul Paret, *Surrealism and Modernism from the Collection of the Wadsworth Atheneum* (New Haven, Conn.: Yale University Press in association with the Wadsworth Atheneum Museum of Art, 2003).

32. Quoted in Gaddis, "Foremost Upon This Continent," in *"The Spirit of Genius,"* 19.

33. Austin, "Hartford's Art Museum," 4.

34. Edwin Forbes used the newly established Louise E. Bettens Fund for contemporary art to purchase works by Sargent in 1916 (including an oil of Lake O'Hara), and watercolors by Homer in 1918, Demuth in 1925, Marin in 1928, and Hopper in 1930. See Theodore E. Stebbins Jr., Kimberly Orcutt, and Virginia Anderson, eds., *American Paintings at Harvard* (Cambridge, Mass.: Harvard Art Museum in association with Yale University Press, 2008), 2:18–19.

35. See Carol Troyen, "A War Waged on Paper: Watercolor and Modern Art in America," in *Awash in Color: Homer, Sargent, and the Great American Watercolor*, by Sue Walsh Reed and Troyen (Boston: Bullfinch Press in association with the Museum of Fine Arts, Boston, 1993), xlix–li.

36. See Barbara Dayer Gallati, "Controlling the Medium: The Marketing of John Singer Sargent's Watercolors," in Ferber and Gallati, *Masters of Color and Light*, 117–43.

37. Gaddis, *Magician of the Modern*, 139, 164.

38. "Notes," *Wadsworth Atheneum Bulletin*, January 1928, 1, 8.

39. A. E. Austin, 19 February 1929, Wadsworth Atheneum Archives.

40. "Loan Exhibition of Contemporary Watercolors," *Wadsworth Atheneum Bulletin*, July 1928, 3.

41. Gaddis, *Magician of the Modern*, 94.

42. Quoted in ibid., 94.

43. *Wadsworth Atheneum Bulletin*, July 1928, 3, 20.

44. Philip L. Goodwin to A. E. Austin, 29 January 1930, Wadsworth Atheneum Archives.

45. A month later, Goodwin transmitted his mother's request to "use some of the J. J. Goodwin Fund for the purpose of purchasing a water color by John Marin." He went on to indicate that Alfred Stieglitz was willing to "make a favorable price to the museum for a really good Marin." He stressed the fact that the Atheneum had yet to acquire a work by this artist, "who is undoubtedly one of the best living American painters," concluding "I therefore beg the committee in charge to take the matter into consideration." By March Goodwin wrote to set a date for Austin to visit Stieglitz's Gallery "to show you what he has. The price varies from one to four thousand. The Fogg Museum paid the later price this year." Goodwin to Austin, 24 April 1931, Wadsworth Atheneum Archives.

46. Austin to Goodwin, 2 May 1934, Wadsworth Atheneum Archives.

47. Eugene Gaddis, *Avery Memorial: The First Modern Museum* (Hartford, Conn.: Wadsworth Atheneum, 1984), 33.

48. Deborah Zlotsky, "'Pleasant Madness' in Hartford: The First Surrealist Exhibition in America," *Arts Magazine* 60 (February 1986): 55–61.

49. Ibid., 137.

50. Lincoln Kirstein to Eugene Gaddis, 24 April 1983, Wadsworth Atheneum Archives.

51. See Marvin Sadik, *Edith Halpert and the Downtown Gallery* (Storrs: Benton Museum, University of Connecticut, 1968); Carol Troyen, "After Stieglitz: Edith Gregor Halpert and the Taste for Modern Art in America," in *The Lane Collection: 20th-Century Paintings in the American Tradition* (Boston: Museum of Fine Arts, 1983), 34–59.

52. Chick was influenced by Halpert's seminal focus on American folk art, and purchased a number of folk paintings from her gallery, including Joseph Whiting Stock's *Child with Spoon* and Thomas Chambers's *Niagara Falls*. Later in her life, Halpert gave forty folk paintings, sculptures, and works on paper to the Atheneum. See Kornhauser, *American Paintings before 1945*, 1:35–36.

53. Collector file, Wadsworth Atheneum Archives.

54. Quoted in Sybil Gordon Kantor, *Alfred H. Barr, Jr., and the Intellectual Origins of the Museum of Modern Art* (Cambridge, Mass.: MIT Press, 2002), 230.

55. Kornhauser, *American Paintings before 1945*, 1:36–37.

56. Lindsay Pollock, *The Girl with the Gallery: Edith Halpert and the Making of the Modern Art Market* (New York: Public Affairs, 2006), 220 n. 416. Cunningham acquired *Sea, Island, Tree, Maine* (1923), *Small Point, Maine* (1928), and *Mountain Form* (1918), Museum of Fine Arts, Boston, sales slip dated 18 October 1939.

57. Charles C. Cunningham to Edith Halpert, 9 January 1952, curatorial files, Wadsworth Atheneum.

58. Charles C. Cunningham, *Seven by Six: Loan Exhibition of Contemporary American Watercolors*, 27 October–28 November 1948 (Hartford, Conn.: Wadsworth Atheneum), 10.

59. Halpert to Cunningham, 15 December 1948, Wadsworth Atheneum Archives. Cunningham went on to purchase two additional watercolors from the *Seven by Six* exhibition: Adolf Dehn's *Herons at Key West* (1942) and Lyonel Feininger's *Glowering Sky* (1946).

60. Cunningham to Halpert, 8 December 1949, curatorial files, Wadsworth Atheneum Archives.

61. Cunningham to Halpert, 9 January 1952, curatorial files, Wadsworth Atheneum Archives.

62. In 1951 the Harvard art historian and Marin scholar Alan Burroughs wrote to his friend Cunningham offering to sell the Atheneum several works from his collection, including John Marin's *Big Wood Island* (cat. 10). Cunningham purchased the work for $425, thus managing to add a Maine subject by Marin.

63. Charles C. Cunningham, *Survey of American Watercolors* (Hartford, Conn.: Wadsworth Atheneum, 1952).

64. Curatorial files, Wadsworth Atheneum Archives.

65. Cunningham to Philip L. Goodwin, 21 November 1957; Goodwin to Cunningham, 25 November 1957, curatorial files, Wadsworth Atheneum. In this letter, Goodwin discusses the importance of "Pollock as an originator," and recommends the drawings by Pollock on view at Janis Gallery. He also promises to add his Pollock, *No. 8*, to his will as a gift to the Atheneum. See Cunningham to Goodwin, 4 December 1957, curatorial files, Wadsworth Atheneum.

66. His collection went to his brother James L. Goodwin and his nephew H. Sage Goodwin, who divided it, according to Philip's will, among the Museum of Modern Art, the Yale University Art Gallery, and the Wadsworth Atheneum.

67. Evan H. Turner, "Philip L. Goodwin," *Wadsworth Atheneum Bulletin*, Winter 1958, 12.

68. Lloyd Goodrich, *H. E. Schnakenberg* (New York: Whitney Museum of American Art, 1931).

69. Schnakenberg eventually dissolved the fund in 1963, as he disapproved of some of the recent purchases made by the Atheneum. Henry Schnakenberg correspondence, Wadsworth Atheneum Archives.

70. "The Schnakenberg Fund," *Wadsworth Atheneum Bulletin*, February 1951, 2; "Purchases from the Schnakenberg Fund," *Wadsworth Atheneum Bulletin*, November 1951, 1; "Some Recent Acquisitions–Schnakenberg Gifts," *Wadsworth Atheneum Bulletin*, October 1954, 1; Kornhauser, *American Paintings before 1945*, 1:71–72, 649–50.

71. Charles C. Cunningham, *The Paintings of Henry Schnakenberg; The Sculptures of Henry Kreis* (Hartford, Conn.: Wadsworth Atheneum, 1955).

72. Zafran and Paret, *Surrealism and Modernism*, 49, 55, 117.

73. James Crump, "Art of Acquisition: The Eye of Sam Wagstaff," *Archives of American Art Journal* 46, nos. 3–4 (2007): 4–13, 20.

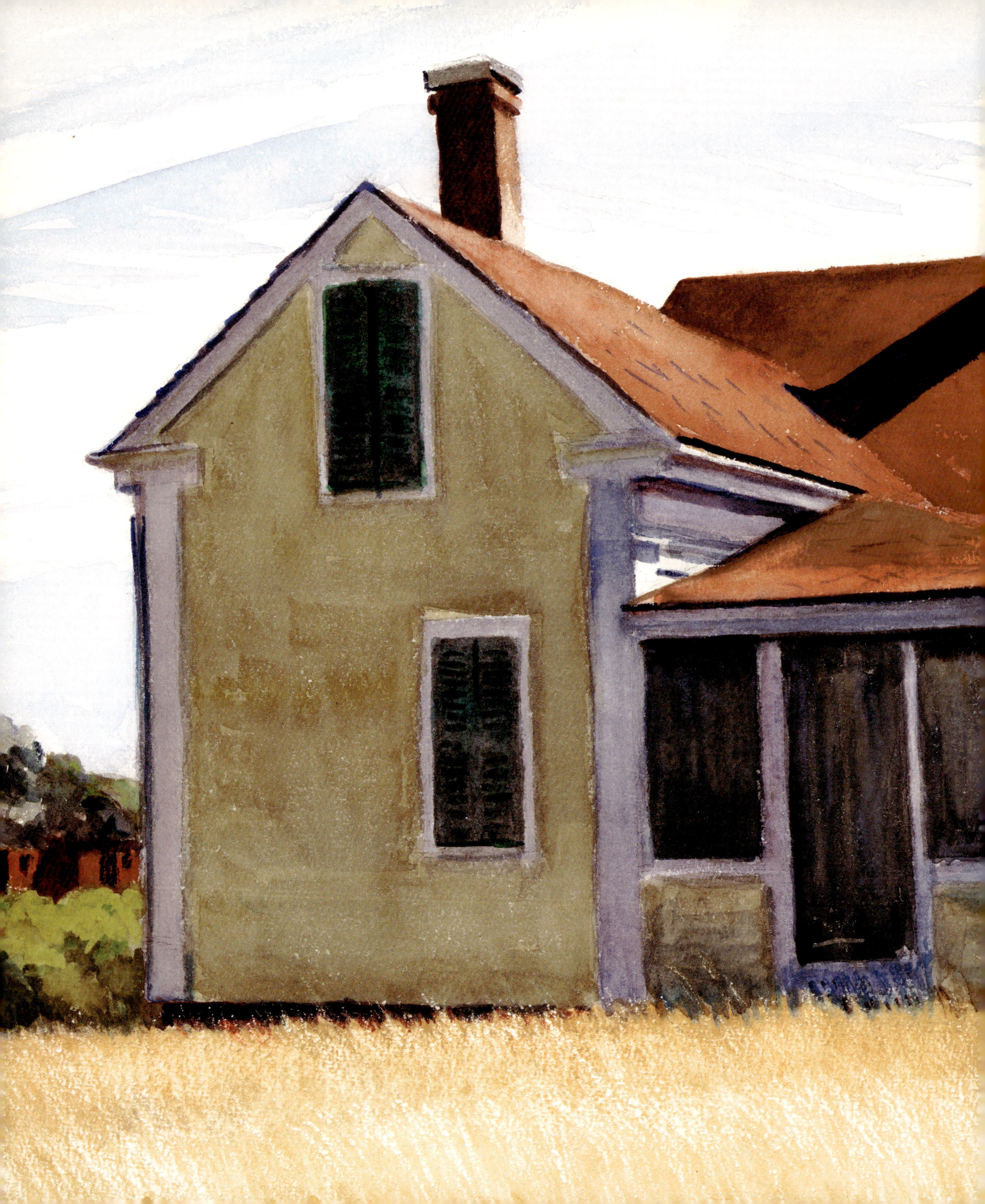

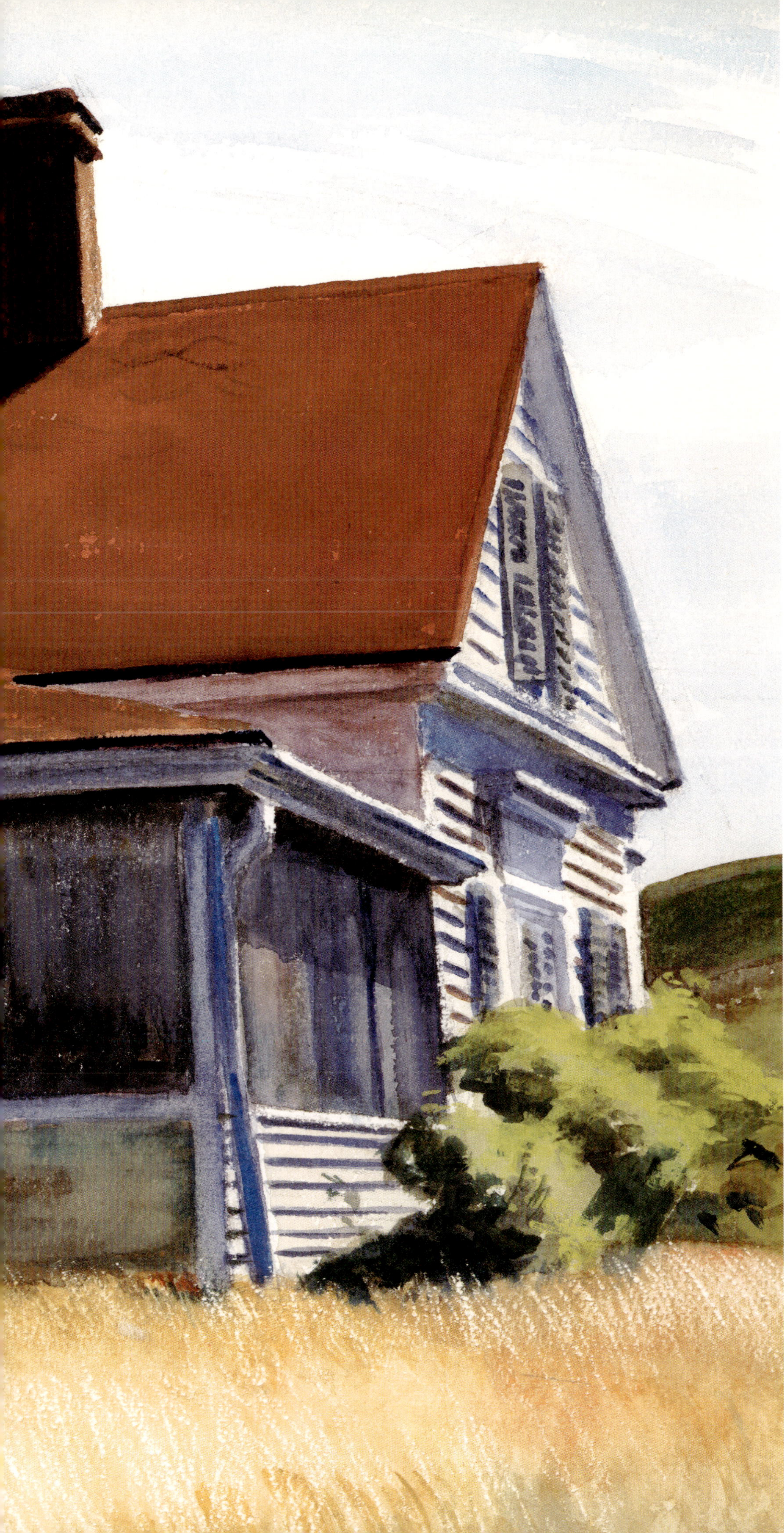

Modernism and Antimodernism

Works on Paper in the Age of Austin

Carol Troyen

Eugene Berman, the Russian-born Neo-Romantic painter and set designer, arrived in Manhattan in the spring of 1935. His American dealer, Julien Levy, showed him around the city. Levy recalled taking special pains to seek out "those elements of our landscape that might lend themselves to his technique: our vistas and courtyards, ruins and constructions, scaffolds and corridors, that expressed our own aspects of nostalgia and romanticism." At the same time, Levy thought to himself, ruefully, "But he might prefer someone show him the Statue of Liberty."[1]

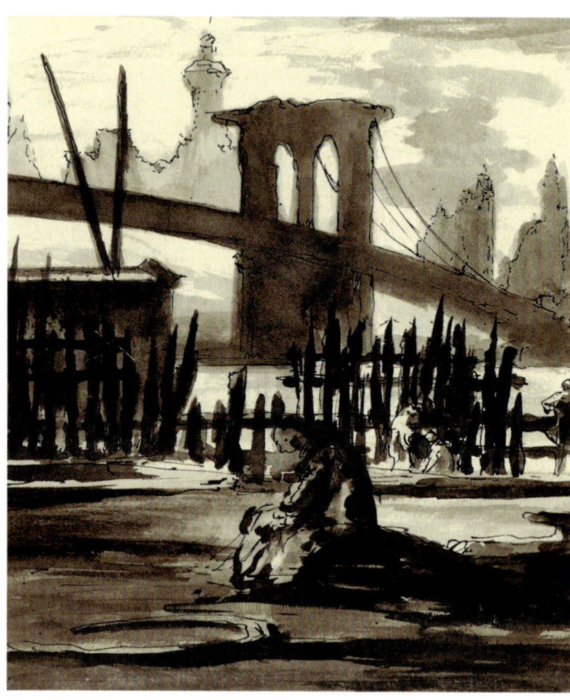

Eugene Berman, *Brooklyn Bridge*, 1935 (detail, cat. 57)

John Marin, *From the Bridge, N.Y.C.*, 1933 (detail, cat. 12)

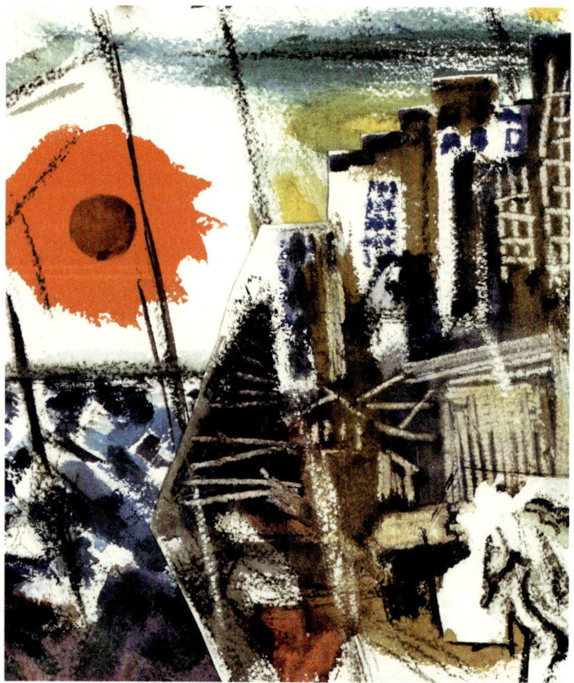

In a small wash drawing of the Brooklyn Bridge (cat. 57) made shortly after his arrival, Berman combined both aspects of Levy's quest: in his hands, a quintessentially American landmark became a setting for "nostalgia and romanticism." By 1935, the Brooklyn Bridge had long been established as an icon of American modernism. Artists such as Joseph Stella and John Marin had depicted it many times, most often from the vantage point of a pedestrian or vehicle moving across it, signaling an engagement with the bridge's vitality and promise. In *From the Bridge, N.Y.C.* (cat. 12), a watercolor made just a few years before Berman's, Marin painted the skyscrapers of Manhattan as a lively Cubist jumble. Lanky buildings crescendoing to ambitious heights are paired with zigzaggy waves and a flaming red sun, proclaiming the bridge as the ideal perspective from which to embrace America's natural and man-made wonders. Berman, on the other hand, recorded the bridge from the banks of the East River on the Brooklyn side, gazing across at a smoky gray Manhattan skyline that seems more dreamlike than real. Rather than exuberance, his view of the bridge inspires melancholy, even a sense of estrangement.

The differences between these two watercolors–one that uses a modernist icon as an observation deck from which to salute the future and one that imagines that same icon as a gateway to a lost world–dramatize the tensions in the American art community of the 1930s, with modernism and antimodernism jockeying for attention. These differences extended beyond the artists' interpretations of their subject. *From the Bridge* is big, boldly colored, and highly physical in its technique. Marin famously went at his pictures with matchsticks, his fingers, and the wrong end of the brush. Here, he used vigorous strokes of pigment and energetic scraping out; he painted broad lines of blue, brown, and green around the perimeter to create a frame for the picture. Most telling is the fragment of paper, roughly torn from another sheet and pasted here. It grafts a horse and cart (by 1933 a rarity on city streets and thus embodying the old New York) onto the bustling cityscape with its architectural and engineering wonders; Marin's collage element, like the rest of his technique, affirms the primacy of the handmade. *From the Bridge* is a modernist primer. It draws attention to its own artifice; its essential subject is the method of image-making itself. Berman's watercolor, on the other hand, is deliberately, and elegantly, anachronistic. Traditionally crafted, with delicate pen lines and soft washes in carefully modulated tones of gray, it is modest–in scale, in ambition–yet it is virtuosic. It speaks of ease of creation, of diffidence rather than muscularity. Its shadowy buildings and gloomy figure are a vision of unfulfilled desire–what modern New York would look like as the past.

Marin's form of modernism, rooted in Cubist abstraction and American dynamism, had long been championed by the brilliant photographer and impresario Alfred Stieglitz. His galleries, beginning with The Little Galleries of the Photo-Secession (known as 291, after its address on Fifth Avenue), had been the birthplace of the American avant-garde. Through the 1920s and '30s, in the spaces over which he presided (291; the Intimate Gallery, from 1925 to 1929; and beginning in late 1929, An American Place), Stieglitz continued to celebrate an indigenous modernism, and Marin was one of the standard-bearers.

Berman's form of antimodernism found an energetic advocate in A. Everett ("Chick") Austin Jr., the director of the Wadsworth Atheneum from 1927 to 1944. Austin purchased Berman's watercolor for $45 from the Julien Levy Gallery in 1935, shortly after the work was painted. In subsequent years, he would add to the Atheneum's collection dozens of works by Berman and other painters working in a similarly dreamy style. During his tenure as director, Austin gave wall space to all kinds of modern artists: Edward Hopper, Paul Klee, Joan Miró, Piet Mondrian, Pablo Picasso, even Marin (though he never bought one of his paintings[2]); he put on groundbreaking shows of Constructivist work and other forms of pure abstraction.[3] But his special enthusiasm was for art that defined itself in opposition to modernism, at least of the Cubist sort. Austin was a pioneering supporter of Neo-Romanticism and Surrealism, and he particularly admired figurative art. He was attracted to the Baroque, admiring its naturalism and its theatricality, and much of the contemporary art he favored shared these traits with the old masters he was buying for the museum. He was well known for his hospitality to émigrés, folding the art they made in the United States into the story of contemporary American art he presented at the Atheneum. Austin's enthusiasm for modern art extended to—and in the case of the Neo-Romantics, focused especially on—works on paper. His taste, both eccentric and farsighted, gives the Wadsworth Atheneum's collection, including its works on paper, its unique and fascinating character.

Early in his tenure as director, laying out his acquisition program for the Atheneum, Austin observed, "It is hoped that a collection of watercolors by modern Americans can be formed, as in this medium the American artist appears to find the ability to express himself more completely and characteristically than in the field of oils."[4] Austin remained true to his word, buying contemporary American works on paper rather than oils; in fact, among his first purchases of any sort were watercolors by Edward Hopper, Preston Dickinson, and Charles Demuth, which he added to the collection within months of arriving in Hartford.

Austin's opinion that American artists had a special affinity for watercolor represented a subtle inflection of Stieglitz's celebrated defense of works on paper. In both words and actions, Stieglitz rejected the traditional hierarchy of the media as established by the academy: "[I do] not see why photography, water colors, oils, sculptures, drawings, prints . . . are not of equal potential value. I cannot see why one should differentiate between so-called 'major' and 'minor' media. I have refused so to differentiate in all the exhibitions that I have ever held."[5] Admittedly, these views were somewhat self-serving. Stieglitz was, after all, a photographer himself; works on paper, being generally smaller than paintings or sculpture, were cheaper and easier to transport; and their size made them better suited to the intimate spaces of 291 and his subsequent galleries. Nonetheless, the sketchpad and watercolor block—cheap, portable, and ready to receive spontaneous inspiration—freed the artist from the studio, the academy, and establishment theories and standards. Stieglitz was one of the first to embrace the so-called minor media as an act of modernist rebellion.

Stieglitz had made his reputation with pioneering shows of watercolors and drawings by Auguste Rodin (1908, 1910), Henri Matisse (1908, 1910, 1912), Paul Cézanne (1911), and Picasso (1911). But in the years following World War I, his pride in his internationalism, as manifested in exhibition brochures introducing "Picabia of Paris" (1914) or "Severini of Italy" (1917) was replaced by a sometimes vituperative isolationist posture ("No one respects France less than I do").[6] Stieglitz substituted for his polyglot program an all-American one, and one that frequently focused on works on paper. Among the artists he promoted most heavily were those, like Marin, who worked almost exclusively in watercolor or those who created their breakthrough works on paper, such as Arthur Dove and Georgia O'Keeffe.

Watercolor in particular could be put forward as an essentially American medium—one that no other national school had claimed, and one that was well suited to the restless, spontaneous, and confident American spirit. Closing at least one eye to the facts, Stieglitz celebrated these artists as truly native, that is, as being of sound Yankee stock and free of foreign influence in their art. And (O'Keeffe aside) watercolor could be promoted as a manly art. This, too, was a somewhat rebellious posture, contradicting the traditional association of the medium with schoolgirl and amateur artists. Again and again, Stieglitz and his associates praised Dove's "virile and profound talent" or Marin's "rude, strong, primal" work.[7]

But by the time Austin assumed the leadership of the Wadsworth Atheneum, Stieglitz's gallery, once cutting-edge, had become museumlike. The pace of exhibitions had slowed, and Stieglitz (who was sixty-five years old in 1929 when he opened An American Place) dedicated most of his efforts to promoting O'Keeffe, Marin, and Dove, whom he considered the aristocracy of American modernism. The gallery, always serious, had become, according to photographer and Stieglitz devotee Ansel Adams, "a deep pool of clear water in a desert," a self-consciously calm, solemn sanctuary for an enduring national modern art.[8]

Austin, on the other hand, was eager to pursue the new. A few years after his appointment, he reminded his Hartford public that an essential part of his job as director was to introduce artists who had "an original and distinctive contribution to make to your artistic experience." Such artists might "possibly form the style of a new movement," but on the other hand, their work "is not being offered to you with the assurance that it will eventually be great."[9] For Austin, part of the attraction of building practically from scratch a collection of contemporary art for the Wadsworth Atheneum was the element of risk. This explains, in part, his lack of interest in Stieglitz's artists. Those artists had been cutting-edge in the 1910s and early 1920s, but by the time Austin arrived in Hartford they defined the modernist establishment. More exciting to him were the art and artists just beginning to be known in the United States: the Neo-Romantics and the Surrealists, either émigrés or those Americans, like Alexander Calder, who worked in their orbit. For Austin, Stieglitz's mission of nurturing and enshrining a definably national modern art held little appeal. The watercolor he purchased in 1928 by Demuth was the only Stieglitz-circle picture he ever bought.[10]

And in fact, the Demuth watercolor was acquired not from Stieglitz but from the Kraushaar Galleries just a few months before Austin mounted his first show of contemporary American art, *Modern American Water Colors*.[11] Demuth, with eight works, was one of two artists featured in that sixteen-object show. Marin, with six watercolors, was the other (fig. 1); Preston Dickinson and (anomalously) Paul Cézanne were represented by one watercolor each. All but one of the pictures in the exhibition were borrowed either from the Fogg Art Museum at Harvard (where Austin was trained) or from Philip L. Goodwin (a supporter of contemporary American art who later married one of Austin's cousins; see Elizabeth Mankin Kornhauser, "Galvanizing Hartford," in this volume). The show's contents may reflect Austin's still somewhat limited list of contacts as much as his taste, but Demuth, at least, fit with his preference for the cosmopolitan, the delicate, and the well crafted.

Although Demuth was included in shows at the Intimate Gallery and An American Place, Stieglitz never promoted him with the same enthusiasm as he did the other artists. Demuth had only three solo shows with Stieglitz, the first in 1926, in contrast to Marin and O'Keeffe, who beginning in the 1910s were shown almost every year, Marin sometimes twice. Demuth had been described, regretfully, by photographer and Stieglitz follower Paul Strand as "a very sensitive rather than a robust talent" and bearing the mark of "contemporary French influences and of a certain too delicate niceness."[12] But the very worldliness that made Demuth an uncomfortable fit for Stieglitz's rugged, all-American group recommended him to Austin. Demuth's watercolors are elegant, sophisticated, even decorative. They are technically accomplished, in a restrained, classical manner. They are tinged with homoeroticism (see, for example, *Eight O'Clock*, cat. 18b, included in the Atheneum's 1928 exhibition). And Demuth's technique, in which eloquent use is made of blotting and otherwise lifting up and removing color (see cat. 19) and of pencil lines that fade and disappear as they move outward from the center of the composition, makes his works seem mysterious and ephemeral.

A few months after *Modern American Water Colors*, Austin organized *Exhibition of the Water Colors of Edward Hopper*, which opened at the Atheneum in November 1928. Hopper was just then becoming known, and this was his first solo museum exhibition. He had come to public attention five years earlier, in the second biennial exhibition of watercolors presented by the Brooklyn Museum. Brooklyn's initial show, in 1921, had been a survey of American achievements. A milestone in establishing watercolor as a medium of the first rank, it featured such "old masters" of watercolor as Winslow Homer, John Singer Sargent, and John La Farge, as well as Impressionists such as Childe Hassam and Dodge Macknight. It also highlighted a few fresh faces, among them Charles Burchfield, who had had his inaugural New York solo exhibition at Kevorkian Gallery the year before (see cat. 27).[13] In contrast, the 1923 biennial had fewer "old masters" and was more daring in its presentation of unfamiliar talents. Hopper was the best of these; six of the watercolors he made the previous summer in Gloucester, Massachusetts, were selected for the show, and one of them, *The Mansard Roof* (fig. 2), won the museum's $100 purchase prize. Hopper's success in the biennial led to a series of attention-getting exhibitions (in 1924, 1927, and 1929), of watercolors for the most part, with Frank K. M. Rehn, the leading dealer of contemporary American realism in New York.

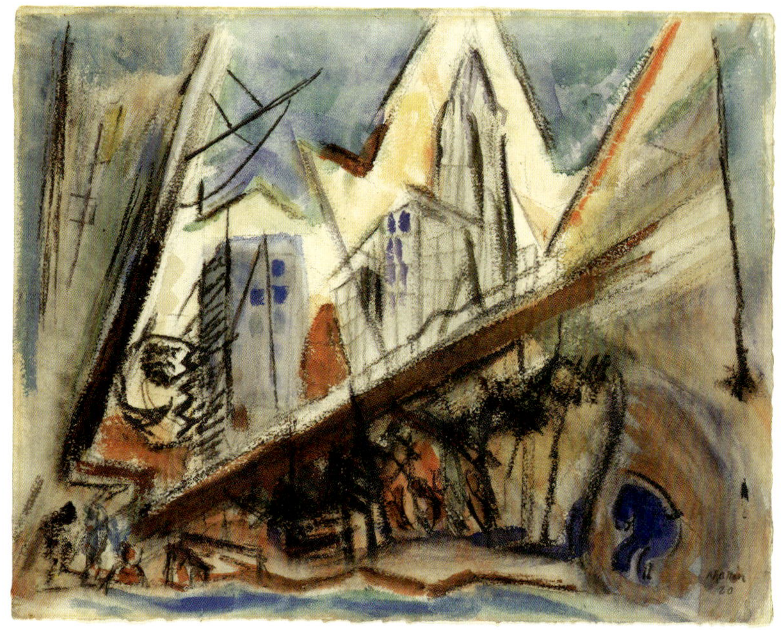

Fig. 1. John Marin, *Lower Manhattan*, 1920.
Watercolor and charcoal on paper, 21 7/8 × 26 3/4 in. (55.6 × 68 cm).
Museum of Modern Art, New York.
The Philip L. Goodwin Collection, 104.1958

Fig. 2. Edward Hopper, *The Mansard Roof*, 1923.
Watercolor over graphite on paper, 13 7/8 × 20 in. (35.2 × 50.8 cm).
Brooklyn Museum. Museum Collection Fund, 23.100

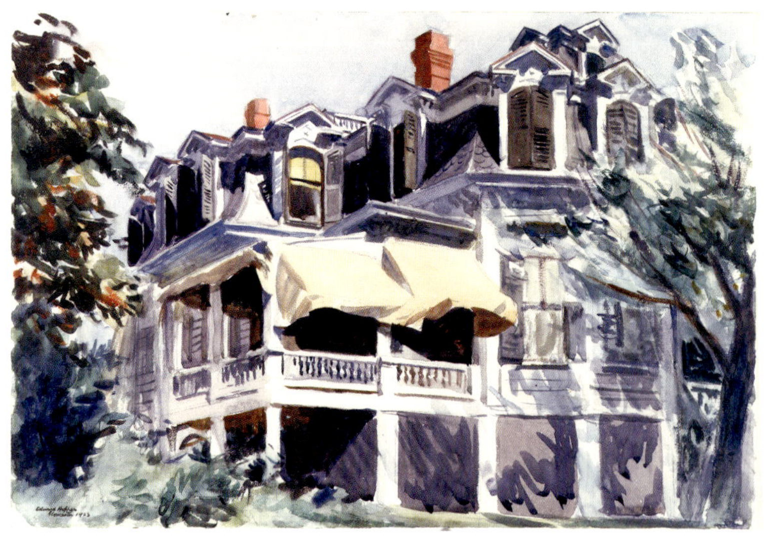

Hopper's newness on the scene, his formal discipline, and the matter-of-fact yet edgy nature of his vision may explain why Austin chose to show his watercolors at the Atheneum. Like *Modern American Water Colors*, the Hopper show was small, consisting of only twelve works, three of which (cats. 32–34) were already or would become part of the Atheneum's collection.[14] Austin's discussion of *Captain Strout's House*, the first Hopper he bought, revealed what would be a lifelong dedication to the kind of representational art that went beyond the merely descriptive: "[Hopper] appears to be a realist," he explained, "but . . . has gone much further than realism. . . . His own idea . . . is to create a great amount of starkness in his form, with no loss of emotional quality."[15]

Over the next several years, Austin put on a number of loan exhibitions that reflected his increasingly adventurous taste and his ever-widening circle of supporters. Austin's artistic family—a group of scholars, dealers, collectors, critics, and patrons—would share in his artistic endeavors for the next several decades. Many of these he knew from classes at Harvard's Fogg Art Museum led by Edward Forbes and Paul Sachs—the architectural historian Henry-Russell Hitchcock, Museum of Modern Art director Alfred H. Barr Jr., and dealer-collectors Kirk Askew and Julien Levy. The slightly younger Lincoln Kirstein was part of an extraordinary trio of undergraduates who created the Harvard Society for Contemporary Art, from which the Atheneum borrowed several exhibitions.[16] Some of Austin's cohorts were artists, and a very few—most significantly James Thrall Soby, the scholar-collector from West Hartford—were local.[17]

Many of these friends provided enthusiastic support for Austin's first antimodernist project. Opening in April 1931, the exhibition *Five Young French Painters* presented the work of five artists known as Neo-Romantics (Eugene Berman and his brother Leonid, Christian Bérard, Pavel Tchelitchew, and Kristians Tonny), all of whom were young but only one of whom was French.[18] They were certainly romantic. Composer (and Austin associate) Virgil Thomson, who befriended them during his years in Paris, described Tonny as "blond, muscular, and Dutch, with the sea at the back of his eyes."[19] These painters were virtually unknown in the United States; in fact, the Atheneum show was their first museum exhibition anywhere.[20] The Neo-Romantics had made their European debut at the Galerie Druet in Paris in 1926, and were introduced in New York at the Marie Harriman and Balzac galleries—the latter's show heralded as presenting "what the younger men in Paris are up to . . . a right-about face from the Matisse-Braque-Picasso formulae."[21] Thomson echoed this view: "[Their work was] in full reaction against cubism and striving steadfastly to express, as Picasso had loved to do two decades earlier, tenderness, mystery, and compassion."[22] Hitchcock, who was the first of Austin's circle to discover their works, in Paris in 1928, described them as "new painters of sentiment and mystery."[23] And Soby, who lent several works to Austin's show, explained that they "deliberately renounced the value of all abstract art." He described their work as "fine painting in the traditional sense" and "hauntingly elegant," noting that "the emotional restraint of Cubism . . . is replaced by a search for poetic intensity."[24]

Austin's enthusiasm for the Neo-Romantics stemmed from the fantasy and theatricality in these artists' works,[25] and also from their virtuosity—their refined draftsmanship and careful composition. He was furthermore committed to the belief that museums should

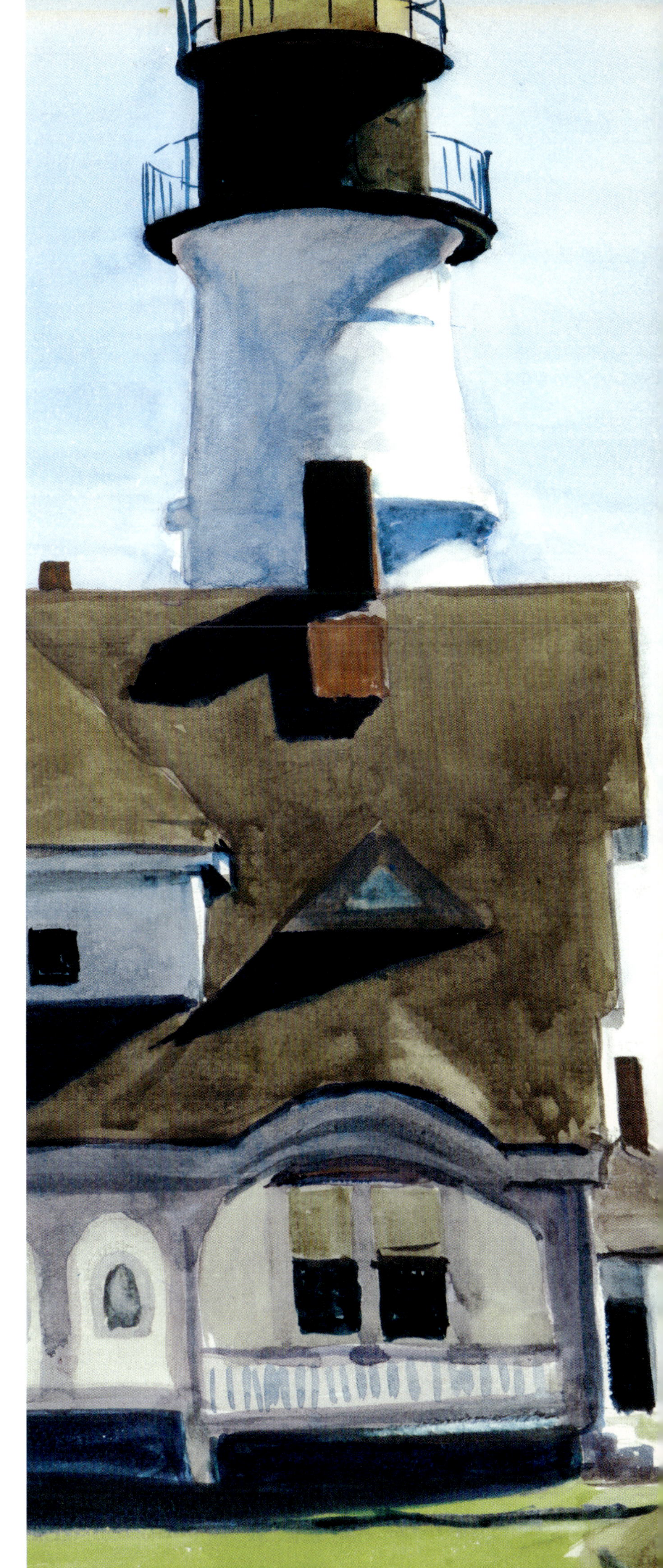

Edward Hopper, *Captain Strout's House, Portland Head*, 1927 (detail, cat. 34)

emphasize both "living things" and "fine examples of the past."[26] The Neo-Romantics, with their melancholic reflections on the modern condition and their homage to classical and Renaissance art, gratifyingly did both at once. As Julien Levy said of the first pictures Berman painted in New York, "he began to conceive of pictures not as dark New York phantoms but as rainbowed Baroque egrets. Berman's New World style . . . became a theatrical old world memory."[27]

Following *Five Young French Painters*, the Neo-Romantics were shown in solo and group exhibitions that were often shared between the Wadsworth Atheneum and Julien Levy's gallery, which opened on Madison Avenue in New York in November 1931. The Julien Levy Gallery quickly became a leading outpost for antimodernist, yet modern, styles.[28] Berman's 1932 exhibition of drawings and a few paintings at Levy's gallery, which the reviewer for *Art News* gratifyingly described as exotic, romantic, classical, and modern,[29] was subsequently seen in Hartford. Tchelitchew's drawings were shown at Levy's gallery in 1933 and again in 1934; the latter exhibition then traveled to the Wadsworth Atheneum, where it was incongruously paired with a show, borrowed from MoMA, that reintroduced the forgotten nineteenth-century Missouri painter George Caleb Bingham—Austin was attracted to exciting new discoveries whatever the century.[30]

The critical reaction to Neo-Romanticism was decidedly mixed, as is indicated by the responses to the overlapping displays of Berman's work in Hartford and New York in the spring of 1935. *World-Telegram* critic Emily Genauer called him a "superlatively fine draftsman." T. H. Parker, reviewing the Atheneum's show of seventy-five drawings for the *Hartford Courant*, saluted Berman's "technical finesse and sensitivity to his medium." He noted the "classical temper" and traditional manner of his drawing—the "observance of . . . conventions of those earlier periods." But he found the mood and subject of the works "based more on artifice than art" and suffering from "a paucity of ideas." E. A. Jewell, the *New York Times'* earnest reviewer, agreed, complaining of the pictures at Levy's, "The new work is less impressive than the old," and dismissing it as "decorative in tone."[31] "Decorative," which for Austin, Levy, and their sophisticated, Europe-oriented circle, conveyed an overarching beauty, was something of a pejorative for Americans, who associated the term with the frivolous, superficial, even feminine. It was a special problem in the Depression-weary 1930s, when much art doubled as social commentary (see, for example, fig. 3), and thus the simply elegant and well made were viewed with suspicion. Still, the consensus was that the Neo-Romantics were at their best on paper, where their tendency to lightness and fantasy was complimented by the delicacy of the medium. *New Yorker* critic Lewis Mumford, who called the Neo-Romantics the "greatest flop" of the 1934–35 season in New York, nonetheless wrote poetically about Berman's next show at Levy's, in the spring of 1936:

Eugene Berman's drawings . . . bear the same relation to his paintings that the sweet disorder of the dressing-table does to the properly gowned and painted woman who emerges from the boudoir. These drawings are not . . . the aesthetic equal of the paintings; they represent, rather, a more inchoate state of thought and feeling. Perhaps the most interesting examples in the present show are the water-color drawings for stage designs; these often have a fine architectural sense, and they are far less subdued than the oils.[32]

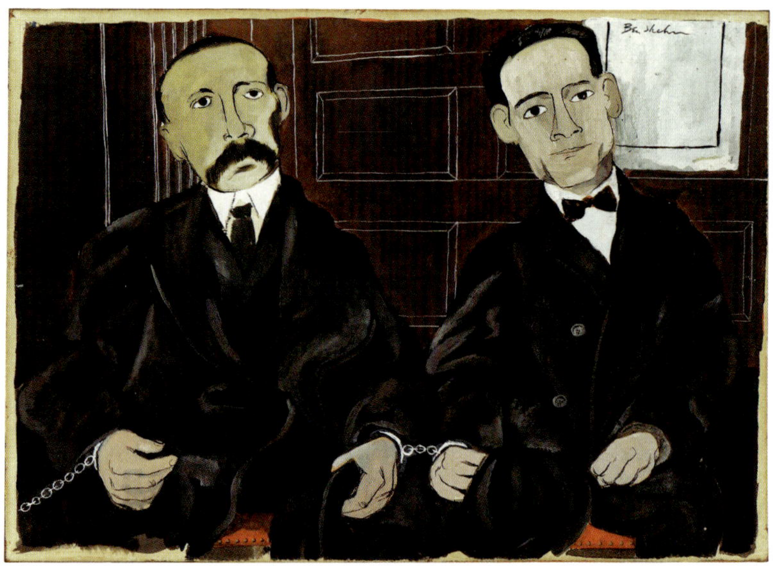

Fig. 3. Ben Shahn, *Bartolomeo Vanzetti and Nicola Sacco*, from the series The Passion of Sacco and Vanzetti, 1931–32. Gouache on paper mounted on board, 10 7/8 × 14 5/8 in. (26.7 × 36.8 cm). Museum of Modern Art, New York. Gift of Abby Aldrich Rockefeller, 144.1935

Regardless of the critical response, Austin remained loyal to the Neo-Romantics. He showed their work consistently through the 1930s and '40s, and urged his friends to support them. As a result of his and Levy's continuing enthusiasm, Kirk and Constance Askew amassed an important collection of Tchelitchew's work, and James Thrall Soby became one of the Neo-Romantics' most eloquent defenders.[33] Austin, too, continued to buy their works for the Atheneum, maintaining a special interest in their drawings and watercolors throughout his directorship.[34] But his most visible way of supporting Berman, Tchelitchew, and Tonny was the decorative work he commissioned from them for the various theatrical projects he put on at the Atheneum.

As Hartford's most influential tastemaker and cheerleader for the new, Austin declined to limit himself, or his museum, to the visual arts,[35] and beginning in 1928, he organized a succession of dazzling events at the Wadsworth Atheneum. These were always collective efforts, involving an international group of composers, choreographers, painters, and performers, as well as enthusiastic amateurs from the community. Among the entertainments staged at the Atheneum were the debut of a Virgil Thomson quartet with decorations by Tchelitchew (1934); the first performances of the ballet *Yankee Clipper* performed by Lincoln Kirstein's Ballet Caravan with music by Paul Bowles (1938); and the world premiere of the Thomson–Gertrude Stein opera *Four Saints in Three Acts*, with sets by Florine Stettheimer (1934). One of the most ambitious of these projects was the Hartford Festival (February 9–16, 1936), a week-long celebration of the arts that included concerts, dance, film, vocal recitals, and displays of paintings and drawings. The festival was an extraordinary collaborative performing arts enterprise, often bringing together the classic and the contemporary—recitals of recent music were given not on a bare stage, for example, but before backdrops featuring Renaissance-style architecture designed by Berman (see cats. 58a and b); ballets to music by Mozart had costumes and sets by Tchelitchew and Calder. The culminating event of that week was the Paper Ball, an elaborate costume party held at the Atheneum on Saturday, February 15. It was attended by both Hartford's elite and the artistic community befriended by Austin.[36]

Inspired by the "ragpickers' balls" that originated in Europe among the urban underclass and replicated by the aristocracy, the Paper Ball was a celebration of the *style pauvre* admired by the Neo-Romantics (see cats. 52a and b). All costumes and decor were to be made from paper—a material that was both inexpensive and ephemeral, and that called for a great deal of artistic ingenuity. Austin invited Eugene Berman to provide some of the decor, and Berman and Calder created a number of the costumes. But the principal designer was Tchelitchew (see cats. 52a and b, 53, 54a–c). In about six weeks' time, he produced costumes, designed the invitation and program cover, and, using little more than discarded newsprint, converted the austere International style Avery Court, an addition to the Atheneum completed only two years before, into "an enchantment, fragile, snowy, elegant, direct from the Winter Palace of Leningrad" (fig. 4), in the words of delighted Paper Ball attendee Henry McBride. McBride rhapsodized, "The cumulative effect of so much careless beauty was almost unbearable."[37]

The Paper Ball was an exquisite entertainment that brought to life the qualities—refinement, imaginative richness, and above all, virtuosity—that Austin consistently sought in works on paper. Reflecting on the event a month later, he praised Tchelitchew's transformation of Avery Court into "a sort of newspaper heaven of incredible delicacy, shimmering with extraordinary color." His admiration for craftsmanship found its ultimate expression in Tchelitchew's ability to make art out of nothing. The "careless beauty" that McBride found so affecting was to Austin not just the backdrop for a party but "one of the most beautiful exhibitions that the museum has ever held."[38] By the next morning, of course, all was in tatters, and then quickly gone. Tchelitchew's magical art was deliberately designed to have only a momentary lifespan. The arrogance of such a creative enterprise didn't seem to concern its sponsors, nor did its paradox: the production of art intended to disappear in the midst of a building designed for art's preservation. Revelers at the Paper Ball thrilled to the grandeur of imminent decay; the Neo-Romantics' mysterious, Renaissance-inflected, spectral designs created an atmosphere all the more magical for being so transitory. Furthermore, the ball was the ultimate expression of Austin's delight in the theatrical, the ephemeral, and the fantastic, and in subverting art's sense of permanence, seriousness, and authority. As Lincoln Kirstein perceptively noted,

Tchelitchew shared Austin's rather recklessly aristocratic disdain for survival. After all, art was also an amusement. . . . In fact, the excitement of excess, of wastefulness, of the whims of spoilage and the very luxury of impermanence in a museum building devoted to . . . salvage . . . was half the fun. Fantasy, craftsmanship, hard work—all aimed at a service of some three hours; there is such a potential of excellence in talent that it can be thrown away, like old newspapers.[39]

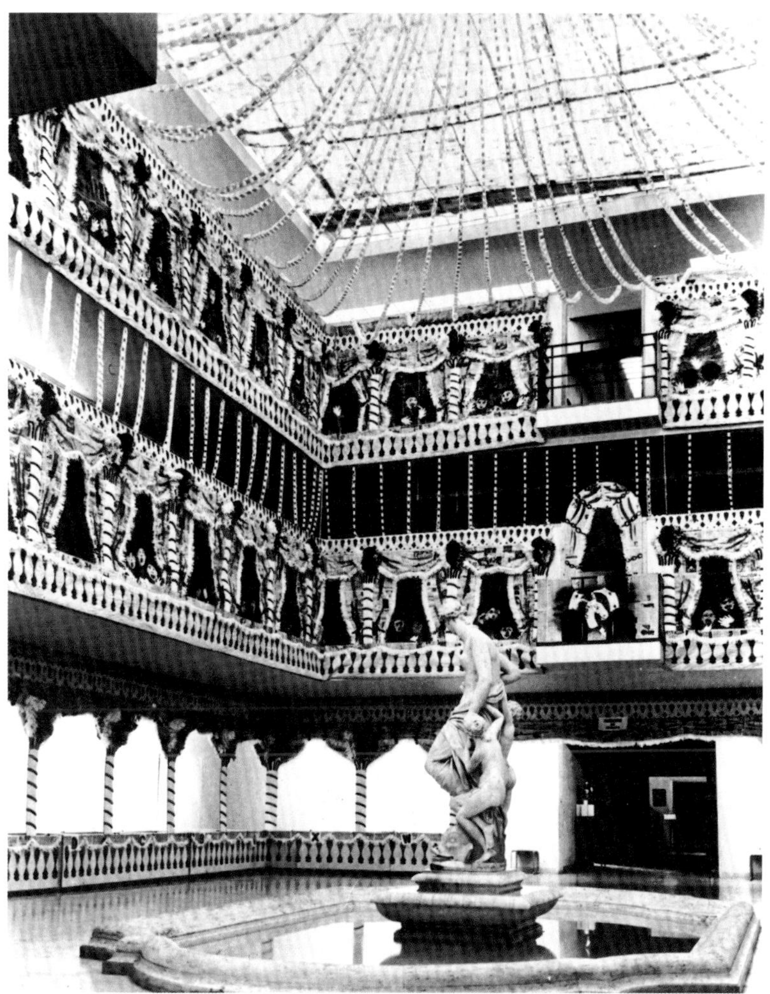

Fig. 4. *Avery Court Decorated by Pavel Tchelitchew for the Paper Ball of February 15, 1936.*
Archives, Wadsworth Atheneum Museum of Art

What remains of the Paper Ball are some photographs, one of the costumes (fig. 5), and several groups of drawings and watercolors made by Berman and Tchelitchew for the ball and other Hartford Festival activities. Austin bought these sketches as a way of compensating the artists for their work on the ball.[40] They are often small and on poor-quality supports. Compared to some of the other American works on paper Austin acquired around that time—eloquent architectural compositions by Hopper, Burchfield's monumental watercolors, or even Reginald Marsh's quiet view of the Manhattan Bridge (cat. 47)—these sketches are not entirely satisfying as works of art. They were clearly not made for display or made to last. But as souvenirs of "one of the most beautiful exhibitions that the museum has ever held," they have a particular, and somewhat poignant, value.

The above-mentioned acquisitions of works on paper by Hopper, Burchfield, and Marsh reflected Austin's preference for representational art. They were also as close as he would come to mainstream taste for contemporary American painting. That taste was epitomized by the collection of Abby Aldrich Rockefeller,

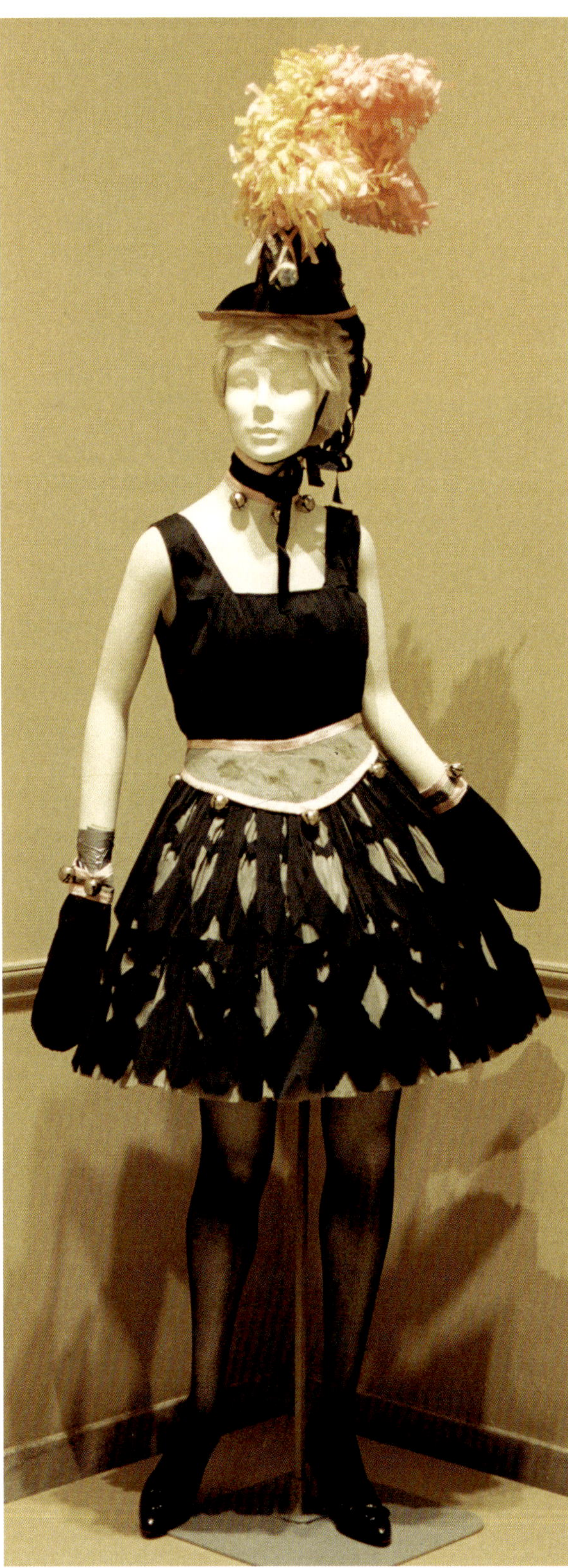

Fig. 5. *Dress and Hat for the 1936 Paper Ball, designed by Pavel Tchelitchew.*
Wadsworth Atheneum Museum of Art.
Gift of Mrs. Robert Hyde Smith, 1983.759A,B

assembled over ten years and donated to the Museum of Modern Art in 1935. The entire collection—more than one hundred drawings and watercolors and thirty-five oils by living American artists—was shown at MoMA in January and February of 1936, coinciding with the Hartford Festival and Paper Ball. Rockefeller's taste, forged by the dealer Edith Halpert,[41] was part Stieglitz-circle modernism and part conventional realism. The gift, with its preponderance of works on paper, underscored the growing conviction that watercolor was a medium in which Americans surpassed the achievements of any other national school.[42] Furthermore, it added a group of American modernists to the museum's increasingly influential roster. Demuth, Marin, Charles Sheeler, Ben Shahn, and Pop Hart (see cats. 18–20, 9–13, 38, 44, 45) were now enshrined at MoMA alongside Cézanne, Matisse, and Picasso. Yet few of the American artists would be represented in the Atheneum's collection until after Austin's directorship. He did buy, from Levy in 1941, a major watercolor by Shahn, the eerie *Vacant Lot* (cat. 44). Predictably, Austin was drawn not to Shahn's social realist side (as represented, for example, by the celebrated images he made in response to the Sacco and Vanzetti case, one of which Rockefeller had given to MoMA; fig. 3), but to his surreal side. Equally predictably, Austin was not at all interested in another major trend of American art of the early to mid-1930s: American Scene painting. The Atheneum did not pursue works by John Steuart Curry or Grant Wood, either on paper or on canvas; its only Thomas Hart Benton (cat. 49) came much later.

During this period Benton, and the mural movement he spearheaded, was hard to avoid. His 1925 *Self Portrait* appeared on the cover of *Time* magazine in December 1934 to introduce a story on "The U.S. Scene." He had gained wide recognition for the murals he painted for the New School for Social Research in New York (1931) and the Whitney Museum (1932). Benton's *America Today* and *The Arts of Life in America* were among the works that inaugurated a decade-long investment in mural painting in this country, especially as the Works Progress Administration (WPA) and later the Public Works of Art Program (PWAP) commissioned murals for public buildings in order to sustain otherwise out-of-work, impoverished artists during the Depression. At the same time, the Mexican muralists were active in the United States—José Clemente Orozco painted his murals for the New School in 1930 and for Dartmouth College in 1932–34; Diego Rivera's ill-fated *Man at the Crossroads* for Rockefeller Center was begun in 1933. In 1932 Lincoln Kirstein organized the exhibition *Murals by American Painters and Photographers* for MoMA. Artists were invited to submit designs on the theme "The Post-War World": Kirstein (and Julien Levy, who also wrote about photomurals for the catalogue) then selected about fifty of these for the show. Their goal was to interest "architects and others responsible for the selection of mural designers" in the works, "with special reference to the possibilities of beautifying future American buildings."[43] But in 1937 when Austin sought a painter to decorate the walls of the Avery Theater, he did not turn to Benton or the muralists of the Mexican Renaissance or any of the progressive artists featured in MoMA's exhibition.[44] Instead, he hired Kristians Tonny, one of the Neo-Romantics, who was greatly admired for his draftsmanship and dedication to art of the past and for creating images both dreamy and decadent. That Tonny had no experience as a mural painter undoubtedly appealed to Austin's propensity for taking risks.

Austin was gratified that Tonny's images flew in the face of prevailing assumptions about what a modern mural should be. The four panels created for the side walls of the theater are not strong, boldly colored graphic designs that can be read at a distance but rather elegant white line drawings—chalklike markings on slate-gray walls (see cats. 62a and b). Instead of the robust mannerism of Benton's murals or Rivera's forceful, politically inflammatory realism, Tonny's decorations have the delicacy and lightness of the Rococo (he referred to them as "capriccios" and "rhythmical arabesques").[45] And their subject matter differed from the solemnly political, historic, or boosterish quality of most murals of the era. The best T. H. Parker, the *Hartford Courant's* art critic, could do to explain the meaning of the flying horses with their nude riders, wild cattle, mountains, and fairy-tale buildings scattered across the theater's walls was to invoke the wall drawings at Lascaux: "The general theme of the murals [is] an uncertain, primitive coursing in a fantasie realm." But at least for Parker, the perplexing novelty of these murals was a virtue:

So accustomed are we to a muralese of muscle-bound Labor, blindfolded Justice, Education in mortar-boards and Red Men saying "Ugh!" to the City Founders that Mr. Tonny's painting, turning its back on puling symbolisms and allegory, may require a readjustment of mural reflexes, especially on the part of all to whom painting must be "about" something. As a matter of fact, Mr. Tonny's murals are not about anything. They are purely decorative paintings and "mean exactly what meets the eye."[46]

This, of course, was just what Austin intended. "We have gone through a period of literature and political subject matter in mural painting," he said. "We are sick of Mexican communist preachments and of ladies representing civic virtues and the pastoral vices. Here we have no story, no propaganda, merely a dreamy space peopled with rushing figures."[47] Austin reveled in the dramatic, the antididactic, the decorative and the virtuosic. Murals that are not about anything appealed to his sense of art as a fugitive pleasure. And images that are a strange combination of the dreamy and the violent resonated with the other art movement Austin embraced in the 1930s, Surrealism.

If the Neo-Romantics were antimodernist in their Baroque theatricality and [homo]erotic longing, the Surrealists offered a cooler alternate modern art, one that rejected the extremes of previous avant-gardes (such as Cubism's fragmentation of reality, or Futurism's celebration of the machine and of war) and offered instead a new, if disturbing, kind of order. The Neo-Romantics and the Surrealists (particularly the imagistic Surrealists like Salvador Dalí and René Magritte) nonetheless had much in common. Their works were meticulously crafted. They shared a debt to Giorgio de Chirico, translating into their own idiom his penchant for mysterious scenes set in incomprehensible spaces. They gravitated toward theatrical effects and narrative subjects. And both groups embraced the authority of dreams. But while the Neo-Romantics' pictorial fantasies evoke a lyrical, melancholy past, the Surrealists derived their themes from the subconscious. Their work could seem futuristic, presenting a morbidly fascinating vision of the disintegration of contemporary culture. Their molten watches, decimated landscapes, and bleached bones were called up from the unconscious to populate pictures with such ominous titles as *Paranoiac–Astral Images* and *Europe after the Rain*. These—both paintings and drawings—were rendered in an exquisite, hyperrealist style and arranged in spaces governed by subtly subverted traditional perspective systems. The Surrealists' images were offered as revelations of a higher reality, but a reality that was irrational, bizarre, and sometimes brutal.

While the Surrealists were serious and cerebral, a number of them also demonstrated a flamboyant, provocative personal style that appealed to Austin's sense of theater. In an era of somewhat dreary isolationism and earnestly political art, they were foreign, exotic, stylish, and non-doctrinaire. And they were young and, to American audiences, as yet unknown. Although there had been a few solo shows of Surrealist artists in New York galleries in the late 1920s,[48] the Atheneum's *Newer Super-Realism* exhibition, presented in November and December of 1931, and Levy's *Surrealisme*, mounted at his Madison Avenue gallery a month later, were the first American surveys of the new movement. Other shows would follow, culminating in the mammoth, multimedia *Fantastic Art, Dada, Surrealism*, organized by Alfred H. Barr Jr. at the Museum of Modern Art in 1936.[49]

The differences in the organizers' explanations of the cryptic art their shows introduced are telling. Barr insisted that "Surrealism as an art movement is a serious affair and that for many it is more than an art movement: it is a philosophy, a way of life, a cause to which some of the most brilliant painters and poets of our age are giving themselves with consuming devotion."[50] In defending the Atheneum's show, Austin took his cue from the Harvard Society for Contemporary Art, whose avowed mission was to present art whose merits were "still frankly debatable"[51]:

Fashion in art is very much like fashion in dress. Most of our clothes are bought with the idea of ultimately discarding them and few indeed with the idea that they will ultimately be acquired by museums, yet we do not hesitate to dress in fashion because we fear that next year the mode will alter. . . . These pictures which you are going to see are chic. They are entertaining. They are of the moment. We do not have to take them seriously to enjoy them. . . . Many of them are humorous and we can laugh at them. Some of them are sinister and terrifying but so are the tabloids. It is much more satisfying aesthetically to be amused, to be frightened even, than to be bored by a pompous and empty art which has become enfeebled through the constant reiteration of outmoded formulae.[52]

Levy, who didn't have a board of trustees to cajole, initially presented the Surrealists as amusing, but later gave them more credit: "In the history of art surrealism is a revolution, first against the bondage of realism, secondly against the snob monopoly of *abstract painting*."[53]

But the figurative artists of the Surrealist movement were not entirely revolutionary, at least not in their attitude toward drawing. Dalí, for example, worked in a highly finished, academic manner in the mid-1930s. Several drawings in this style (see cat. 64) were acquired by Austin and Soby at the time of the artist's 1934 solo show at Levy's gallery (the show then traveled to the Atheneum). A decade earlier, Dalí had experimented with a more intensely linear, edgier version of this style in a portrait of his father and sister (*Don Salvador and Ana Mariá Dalí*, 1925; Juan Abelló Collection, Madrid).[54] Commenting on that work, Dalí invoked Jean-Auguste-Dominique Ingres, particularly the French artist's celebrated maxim, "Drawing is the probity of art."[55] The revival of interest in Ingres was part of the "return to order" of the 1920s; Dalí's veneration of academic drawing, however, bordered on the spiritual: "It is also the weapon of objective lucidity against the nihilism of esthetic subjectivism. Drawing remains the most insoluble mystery in the 'sensory representation of knowledge.'" Another antecedent for Dalí's detailed illusionism was the "classical realist" work of Picasso (himself an admirer of Ingres).[56] But Dalí explained his use of an academic drawing style by conjuring up an even more exalted touchstone: "In the domain of my drawing, my whole ambition is to rediscover the tradition of the old masters."[57]

Dalí was just one of a number of artists of the era who drew in a classical drawing style and saluted the art of the past. In the 1930s, Tchelitchew (who was associated with both the Neo-Romantics and the Surrealists) drew portraits in this austere manner in hard pencil or pen and ink (see cat. 55), as well as in the highly demanding Renaissance medium of silverpoint. For Joseph Stella, whose work was shown at the Atheneum in the 1940 exhibition *Some Newer Forms of Beauty, 1909–1936*,[58] the act of drawing was talismanic ("Not one day without a line," he vowed[59]). During the 1920s he produced similarly hyperreal silverpoint portraits (fig. 6). Stella had worked in a futurist style and then rejected it in favor of an idiosyncratic realism. He exhibited at the Valentine Gallery, another Surrealist outpost, during the early 1930s, when Dalí and Tchelitchew were showing at the Levy Gallery. He often presented his subjects in the severe profile format of ancient and Renaissance reliefs. Using silverpoint not only linked him to the old masters, but also enabled him—as he claimed—to distill a more incisive moment from the disorder of the everyday.[60] The same use of purified line also characterizes Stella's still lifes in silverpoint and crayon, in which botanical definitiveness and sensuality are fused (see cat. 14). For Peter Blume, who showed with Julien Levy, Netherlandish art of the fifteenth century was the standard. Through the 1930s and '40s he used a highly detailed, academic drawing style to produce hallucinogenic vignettes he later incorporated into his oils (for example, fig. 7). The intensity of his observations produced images of startling power.

All these artists remained dedicated to representation, to using a heightened realism—a decidedly antimodernist language—to reflect on the modern condition. Yves Tanguy, who immigrated to the United States in 1939 and had his first American museum show at the Wadsworth Atheneum in January 1940,[61] created imagery that formed a bridge between figurative and abstract Surrealism. Like Dalí and others, he worked in a patient, self-effacing, precise technique. But he used it to bestow a vivid legibility on shapes that had no counterpart in nature. His fantastic yet utterly believable bone-shaped forms (see cat. 67) appear to be made of marble, with an elegance of silhouette that evokes classical sculpture. Even in the tiniest of gouaches, they occupy a space rich in atmosphere that extends to infinity. Inspired by the haunting scenes of De Chirico (whom Tanguy greatly admired), Tanguy's dreamscapes seem governed by Renaissance perspective gone awry, transformed by the irrational, the subconscious, the hallucinatory.

The alternate modernism of the Surrealists was greeted with amusement, serious interest, and some trepidation by both critics and the public. James Thrall Soby, a devotee of Surrealism, acknowledged

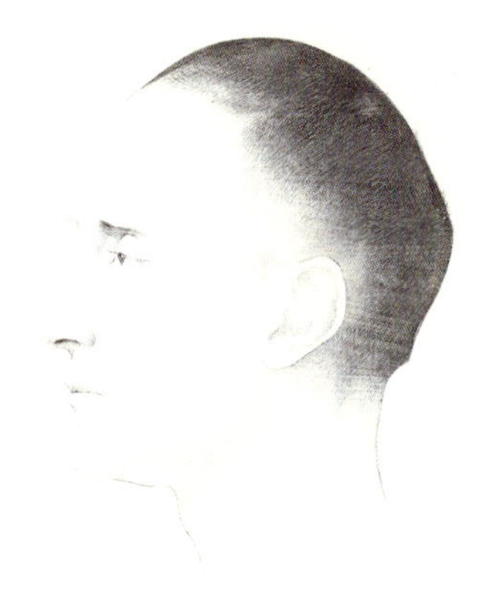

Fig. 6. Joseph Stella, *Marcel Duchamp*, c. 1920.
Silverpoint on paper, 24 1/4 × 18 3/4 in. (61.6 × 47.6 cm).
Museum of Modern Art, New York.
Katherine S. Dreier Bequest, 210.1953

Fig. 7. Peter Blume, *Rock and Stump #44*, 1942.
Black chalk and graphite,
with stumping and incising on cream wove paper,
18 13/16 × 22 7/8 in. (47.8 × 58.1 cm).
Princeton University Art Museum.
Gift from the collection of Millard Meiss, Class of 1926,
and Margaret L. Meiss, X1994-90

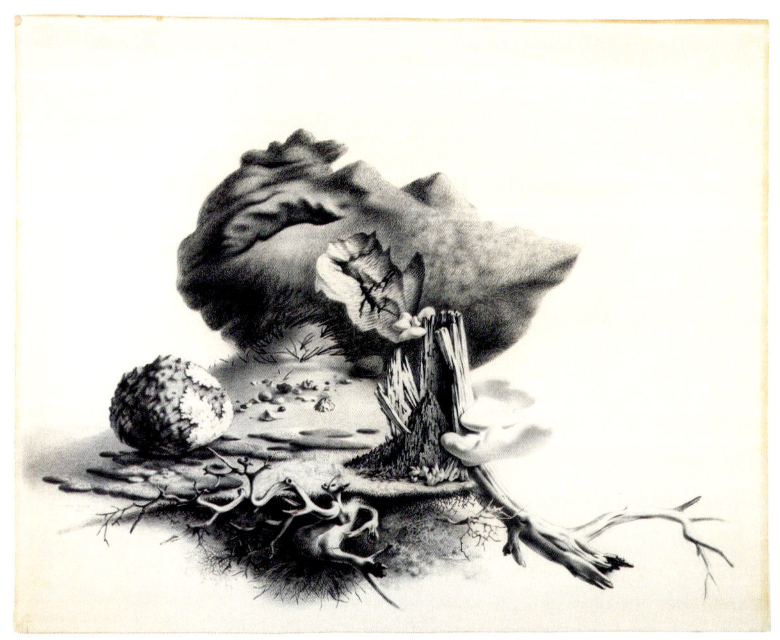

its surprisingly broad appeal: "Whereas Cubism is extremely beautiful to an initiated few, Surrealism does seem able to communicate at least a part of its message to people without special knowledge of art. While few people have penetrated the professional secrecy of Cubism, many are at least strangely excited by Dalí's limp watches."[62] E. A. Jewell found the 1936 MoMA show overwhelming and perhaps a bit suspect, describing it as "an opulent circus" (it did contain nearly seven hundred objects), "more artistry than art," and just possibly already out of date.[63] Lewis Mumford presciently admired Surrealism less for what it was ("a good part of it is rubbish") but for what it might lead to. Perhaps responding to those who suspected some of the artists of fakery or decadence, he also saw Surrealism as providing a moral lesson for the times:

It would be absurd to dismiss Surrealism as crazy. Maybe it is our civilization that is crazy. . . . Surrealism makes us conscious [that] . . . before we can become sane again, we must remove the greatest of hallucinations—the belief that we are sane now. Here surrealism, with its encouraging infantile gestures, its deliberately humiliating antics, helps break down our insulating and self-defeating pride. Even in perverse or sinister or silly forms, the surrealists are restoring the autonomy of the imagination.[64]

During the mid-1930s, the debate between the advocates of a purely nativist art and those espousing a more global view continued. While Austin and his coterie remained steadfastly international, MoMA straddled the fence, generally championing abstract movements from Europe (for example, *Cubism and Abstract Art* of 1936, a comprehensive exhibition that nonetheless included only two American artists) while promoting realist currents in American art. Austin agreed that realism was "the true American métier," but dismissed much American art as provincial.[65] Countering this sort of snobbery was a certain amount of isolationist swagger. A number of critics held up works on paper, watercolors in particular, as an area of national supremacy.[66] They embraced the medium as an embodiment of essential aspects of national character. Watercolor, they said, is decisive (that is, unfettered by convoluted European theories), manly, and morally sound.[67] *Christian Science Monitor* critic Dorothy Adlow had already thrown down the nativist gauntlet in her tribute to Edward Hopper's *Marshall's House* (cat. 37), which the Wadsworth Atheneum had purchased in 1933 and loaned to MoMA's Hopper retrospective in November of that year. She praised Hopper's watercolor as "purely native in what [it] sets out to express," a "hearty, wholesome transcript" of the American scene, and thus superior to the "frenzy and agitation, the enigmatic and distorted devices" of the Surrealists.[68] Of John Marin's 1936 retrospective at MoMA, which immediately preceded the Surrealism show there, Lewis Mumford wrote, "In its freedom from sentimentality, Marin's attitude toward nature is as healthy as that of a trapper, a hunter, or a fisherman. . . . [His] paintings are as American as an old coverlet."[69]

By this time, museums were regularly mounting exhibitions celebrating American watercolors (for example, the Museum of Fine Arts, Boston's *Ten American Watercolor Painters*, 1939) or using an international context to highlight American accomplishments (e.g., the Art Institute of Chicago's *18th Annual International Watercolor Exhibition*, which included retrospectives of the watercolors of Hopper and John Whorf, also 1939). In 1942 the Whitney Museum presented *A History of American Watercolor Painting*. That show, a survey of the medium from the late eighteenth century, placed special emphasis on the watercolors of Winslow Homer, "whose work inspires clarity and probity of method, directness of vision and aesthetic courage." The by this date rather unadventurous "modern" component of that show included works by many of the same artists featured in the Rockefeller collection (see cats. 19 and 35). Catalogue author Alan Burroughs paid special tribute to those moderns—Hopper, Marsh, and Burchfield—who had "escaped French influence" and who instead had "owe[d] much of their individual power to what they have observed in Homer's work."[70] This patriotic equation of watercolor with national accomplishment, and with Homer dominating a robust and native cast of characters, reached its apogee in the 1945 exhibition *American Watercolor and Winslow Homer*. That show, organized for the Walker Art Center in Minneapolis by Lloyd Goodrich, then research curator at the Whitney Museum, nominated artists as stylistically and temperamentally diverse as Hopper, Marin, and Marsh as heirs to the "intransigently masculine" and "entirely original" Winslow Homer (see fig. 8).[71] This posture, part wartime boosterism and part deserved pride in American achievement, may also have been a strategy to camouflage a deep-seated artistic inferiority complex.

Ironically, these shows, celebrating "intransigently masculine," earnestly nativist art, took place in the late 1930s and early 1940s, just at the moment when significant numbers of European artists were coming to the United States to avoid the war. The artists were welcomed, especially by the more cosmopolitan side of the American cultural community. A number of them already had representation in New York: Julien Levy showed Dalí, Max Ernst, and Matta; Pierre Matisse showed André Masson and Tanguy; and Austin's friend Kirk Askew of Durlacher Brothers took over some of Levy's artists, notably Tchelitchew, when Levy entered the army. And when the artists arrived, they quickly entered the social circles of their advocates, who dominated the New York–Hartford cultural axis. Many followed the pattern described by Eugene Berman of his own sojourn, earlier in the decade: "No sooner had I landed in New York than I was whisked away . . . to see the Hartford museum and to meet the almost legendary man behind it: Chick Austin."[72] By the late 1930s much of the international modern art community had been transplanted to the United States, and Austin was its godfather.

The most significant demonstration that the new center of the Western art world was no longer Paris but New York was Pierre Matisse's exhibition *Artists in Exile*. Opening in early March 1942 (just as the Whitney's resolutely American watercolor survey closed its doors), the exhibition presented fourteen "world-famous artists who have come to America to live and work."[73] Among the artists were Berman, Marc Chagall, Ernst, Fernand Léger, Matta, Mondrian, and Tanguy, most of them already represented in the Atheneum's collection. By and large, the exhibition and the artists were well received. But while critics did not question the importance or quality of their paintings, some were concerned about whether they might overshadow native production. Patriotism vied with the desire to step onto the international stage. "Perhaps," wrote Margaret Breuning of the *Journal-American*, "some of our provincialism will wear off from such contacts, but we shall never become imitators of a cosmopolitan accent."[74]

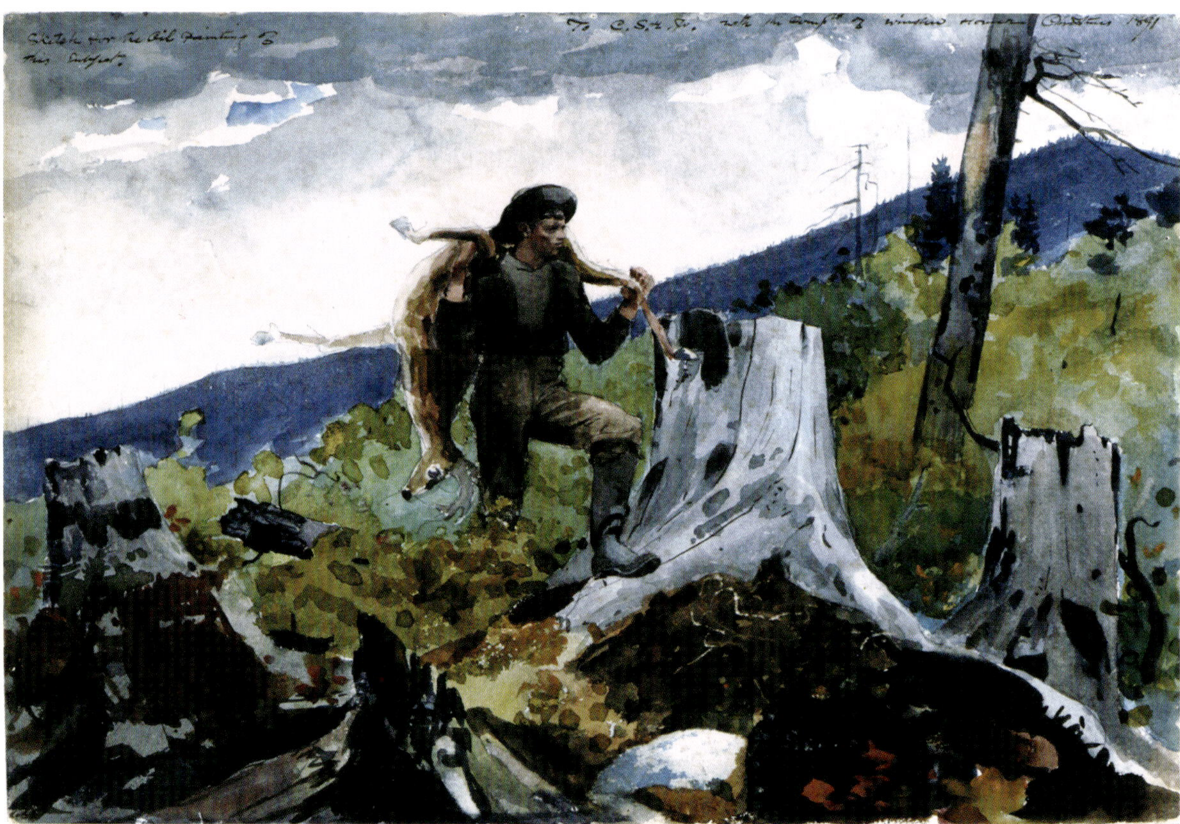

Fig. 8. Winslow Homer, *Guide Carrying a Deer*, 1891.
Watercolor and ivory on wove paper, 14 × 20 1/8 in. (35.6 × 51.1 cm).
Portland Museum of Art, Maine.
Bequest of Charles Shipman Payson, 1988.55.10

Artists in Exile was a paintings show, but its artists would exhibit works on paper as well as oils in a number of subsequent exhibitions. The Wadsworth Atheneum's response to *Artists in Exile*, held in May 1942 and titled *Painters in Attendance* (Austin hoped that the émigrés represented would come to Hartford for the opening; disappointingly, only Tanguy showed up), included works on paper by Ernst, Matta, and Tanguy, among others.[75] Two years later, MoMA put the drawings of these émigrés in a broader international context in its exhibition *Modern Drawings*. That show, beginning with a Edgar Degas from 1885 and ending with a Paul Cadmus from 1943, included about 120 artists from fifteen countries and contained a significant number of both Neo-Romantic and Surrealist drawings. American artists were well represented, from the late nineteenth-century expatriates Mary Cassatt and Sargent through Ashcan school draftsmen and the artists of the Stieglitz group. There were some younger practitioners as well—Peggy Bacon, Blume, Calder, and Marsh. Despite the numbers of works included, the show's organizers were candid in their assessment of the quality of American achievements, noting that "Americans have not, by and large, excelled in audacious and imaginative drawings." But precisely because large numbers of European artists were adopting the United States as their new home, America no longer had to suffer from a sense of cultural inferiority. These artists could now be counted as Americans, thereby bolstering the national artistic image, and enabling the United States to become the most promising location for the creation of a new and exciting art:

Although American patriotism about art has been proud in spirit, its narrowness of intellectual outlook has sometimes been discouraging in effect. This appears especially in the way Americanism is estimated—far more strictly and exclusively than the French output has been in this country. The School of Paris was only half French. If Picasso, Brancusi, Modigliani, Pascin, Soutine, Chirico, Chagall, Lipchitz, Miró and Dali were Frenchmen in those days, then Léger, Masson, Tanguy, Mondrian, Lipchitz, Ozenfant, Tchelitchew, Berman, Dali and Matta are Americans at the moment; and some of them will not leave us when peace is declared. The New York School of tomorrow may not be very idiosyncratically American but this is an international era, for better or worse; and for art it should be better.[76]

The Wadsworth Atheneum was a generous lender to MoMA's drawings exhibition. Among its contributions were drawings by Bérard, Klee, Amedeo Modigliani, Dalí, and a large colored pencil drawing by Chilean émigré Matta (cat. 69), a recent acquisition. Although by the time of MoMA's drawings exhibition Matta was only thirty-three years old and had been in the United States less than five years, he had already become a pivotal figure in the development of abstract Surrealism in America. He was the youngest of the "Artists in Exile" and, as Julien Levy recalled, made a vivid first impression: "He appeared in my gallery, confident, exuberant, and mercurial and produced a portfolio of explosive crayon drawings."[77] Matta was admired for his craftsmanship as much as for his personality.

Praising a show of his works at Pierre Matisse (from which the Wadsworth bought its drawing), Henry McBride enthused, "[Matta's] 'oil-pencil' drawings . . . are spirited, and electrically colored and with contrasts of texture that the artist seems to manage just as easily in this difficult medium as he does regular oil paint."[78]

In the winter of 1942, Matta organized workshops in his New York studio to spread the gospel of automatism. He had been a protégé of André Breton, who in 1924 had codified automatism as a key Surrealist technique. Matta's gatherings were a challenge to the imagistic, or figurative, Surrealists, who worked in a precise, academic manner using traditional illusionistic techniques to generate bizarre, disorienting, dream-world imagery. Under Matta's tutelage, a group of young Americans—including William Baziotes (see cats. 80a and b), Robert Motherwell, and Jackson Pollock—learned to use automatism and other chance procedures to evolve a new mythology, one that provided visual equivalents for various states of consciousness.[79]

Automatism, a drawing technique based on chance and the stimulation of the unconscious, was both anarchic and intellectually ambitious. It was prompted by the Surrealists' underlying doubts about the rationality of civilization, and it sought to express—through random lines and ambiguous forms—their psychic and emotional responses to that irrationality. The technique enabled these artists to make visible those things—dream images, memories—that could not be seen. Neither improvisational nor decorative, automatism was pursued with intensity and seriousness. Even works seemingly as playful as Calder's constructions and collages (cat. 66) were at their core about bringing together seemingly unrelated images (a green rose, a bowler-hatted vaudevillian) whose juxtaposition revealed a deeper truth.

Although Matta's group met only a few times, the artist remained a significant link between the Surrealists and the artists who came to be known as the New York School. Their interaction was a critical factor in the internationalization of American art during the war years. Matta and the other émigrés were catalysts, exposing a younger generation of American painters to an unorthodox, energetic way of making art; encouraging them to believe in the contents of their own imaginations and the imagery it spawned; and introducing techniques, such as automatism, collage, and montage, that seemed to break down decisively the hierarchy of the media and the tyranny of the easel painting. Surrealism enabled Adolph Gottlieb, Pollock, Mark Rothko, and others (a number of whom were émigrés themselves) to liberate themselves from prevailing models—the provincial styles of the Regionalists and urban realists on the one hand and the dogma of pure abstraction (as espoused by the American Abstract Artists organization) on the other. They could put to rest for good the legacy of Cubism—not just as represented by the hallowed artists of the Stieglitz circle but also by the jazzy, vibrant latter-day Cubism of artists such as Stuart Davis (see cats. 40, 41). The Surrealists gave the New York School the license as well as the means to forge a monumental American art, a new modernist style.

In the realm of drawing, Matta's radical ways of thinking about the medium proved particularly influential. In many drawings he erased or smudged lines to evoke layers of consciousness. These erasures bore witness to the evolving content of the drawing, documenting both ideas accepted and those abandoned. Matta also used sharp, precise lines, a legacy of his training as an architectural draftsman. Those lines described a world of weird, colliding forms that were variously biomorphic and sensuous or mechanistic and sinister, creating brittle skeins and mazes that seem to float just beneath the surface of his drawings. Such linear markings, pale and elegant, paved the way for the allover calligraphies of artists as diverse as Pollock and Mark Tobey (cat. 79).[80]

Of the radical artists working in New York in the early 1940s, it was Arshile Gorky on whom Matta had the greatest influence. Matta and Gorky met about 1940, and whereas both artists profited from their interaction, Gorky's work seems to have become more fluid after exposure to Matta's graceful line.[81] Matta apparently counseled Gorky on matters of technique, urging him to thin down his pigment so it would spread and flow. By allowing his oil to mimic the effects of transparency and bleeding characteristic of watercolor, Gorky arrived at images that were more lyrical and spontaneous. Matta also encouraged Gorky to make the most of the accidents inherent in using such thinned-down media, turning unplanned drips and splotches into active compositional elements. Although Gorky would later renounce Surrealism as "academic art under disguise,"[82] the automatism he learned about from Matta loosened his style. He also shared with Matta the use of erasures, smudges, and razor-sharp lines; Gorky was known to have sharpened his pencils to an inch-long point and used them, as he said, "like a surgeon's tool."[83] And paralleling Matta's abstract, conflated images—part organic, part mechanistic—were Gorky's own "hybrids," shapes derived from observation, invention, and memory (see cat. 70).[84]

In August 1944, the increasingly influential critic Clement Greenberg published an essay in the *Nation* deriding Surrealist painting. It was for the most part an attack on the figurative Surrealists, whom Greenberg accused of causing "a certain vulgarization of modern art." Their narrative subjects and academic techniques were to blame: "for the sake of hallucinatory vividness the Surrealists have copied the effects of the calendar reproduction, postal card chromeotype and magazine illustration." And under this heading of betrayers of the avant-garde he lumped the Neo-Romantics and magic realists as well.[85]

Greenberg was slightly more sympathetic to the abstract Surrealists (although he would later call Matta "that prince of comic-strippers"[86]), acknowledging that they had some influence on the formalist New York School painters he had begun to promote in those years. Yet the Abstract Expressionists and the magic realists were not polar opposites, as he suggested, and had more than their debt to Surrealism in common. Both were struggling to find a language to express wartime and postwar anxieties, and to identify and convey meaning in a seemingly irrational, repressive, and violent modern culture.

The magic realists were given a major show at MoMA in 1943. In the catalogue, Lincoln Kirstein explained the movement: "Magic Realists try to convince us that extraordinary things are possible simply by painting them as if they existed,"[87] that is, by using a painstaking drawing style and minimizing paint texture and gestural handling to achieve heightened illusionistic effects. The exhibition was later described by Alfred H. Barr Jr. as one of a series organized by MoMA "designed to present the movements, trends or divisions of modern art"—two other shows in the series having been *Cubism and*

Abstract Art and *Fantastic Art, Dada, Surrealism*.[88] As was frequently the case when MoMA introduced new trends, many of the participating artists in *American Realists and Magic Realists* had first been brought to attention in solo or group shows at Julien Levy's. Peter Blume was shown at Levy's gallery in 1937, Jared French in 1939, Ben Shahn in 1940. And as was also the case, the Wadsworth Atheneum was one of the first museums to buy their new work, and lent generously to MoMA's exhibitions, sending to *Magic Realists* Shahn's *Vacant Lot* and a gouache by John Atherton (fig. 9), among other pictures.

However, Levy was not omniscient. And Austin was restricted by his own essentially modern-but-not-modernist taste, and by an increasingly restive board of trustees, who eventually forced him out of the directorship. An assessment of Levy's limitations by his gallery assistant Eleanor Perényi might also be applied to Austin:

Julien did rather miss the boat on Abstract Expressionism. He showed Matta, who was a forerunner, but he ignored Pollock and Rothko and the other Americans who were being promoted by Peggy Guggenheim, for one. Gorky apart [Levy gave Gorky his first solo show in 1945 and remained his dealer until the artist's death], he bet on the Surrealists and the Neo-Romantics, and he seems to have bet wrong.[89]

The up-and-coming Abstract Expressionists played no part in the collection Austin assembled for the Wadsworth Atheneum. He left the directorship at the end of 1944, perhaps before he was fully aware of the early efforts of artists such as Willem de Kooning, Motherwell, or Pollock–but their work, with its basis in formalism, gesture, and a defiance of academic tradition, is unlikely to have appealed to his antimodernist taste. Whereas in oils these omissions have mostly been filled by subsequent curators and directors at the Atheneum, the same cannot be said for works on paper. The Atheneum acquired an eloquent Gorky drawing (cat. 70) in 1955, but for the most part the gestural tradition of the New York School is represented by drawings made by sculptors, among them Seymour Lipton, Theodore Roszak, and David Smith (cats. 73, 72, and 81a and b).

Austin left other gaps–notably artists of the Stieglitz circle, American Cubism, and 1930s regionalist art–in the collection of American works on paper he built for the Wadsworth Atheneum. The museum's strong Stuart Davises, its Sheeler, its Doves, all came later. Nonetheless, the Austin legacy is striking for its prescience, and for the quality of the objects he championed. The twentieth-century works on paper he brought to the Atheneum present an extraordinary illustration of a side of modern art that, while not modernist, is poetically descriptive, exquisitely crafted, and provocative. Long before the belief in modernism as an ongoing linear development began to unravel, Austin promoted alternate forms of modern art. He formed a collection that expanded the understanding of the American tradition into an international sphere.

Fig. 9. John Atherton, *Invasion: The Acrobats*, 1941.
Gouache on drawing board, 12 × 18 in. (30.5 × 45.7 cm).
Wadsworth Atheneum Museum of Art.
The Ella Gallup Sumner and Mary Catlin Sumner Collection Fund, 1942.379

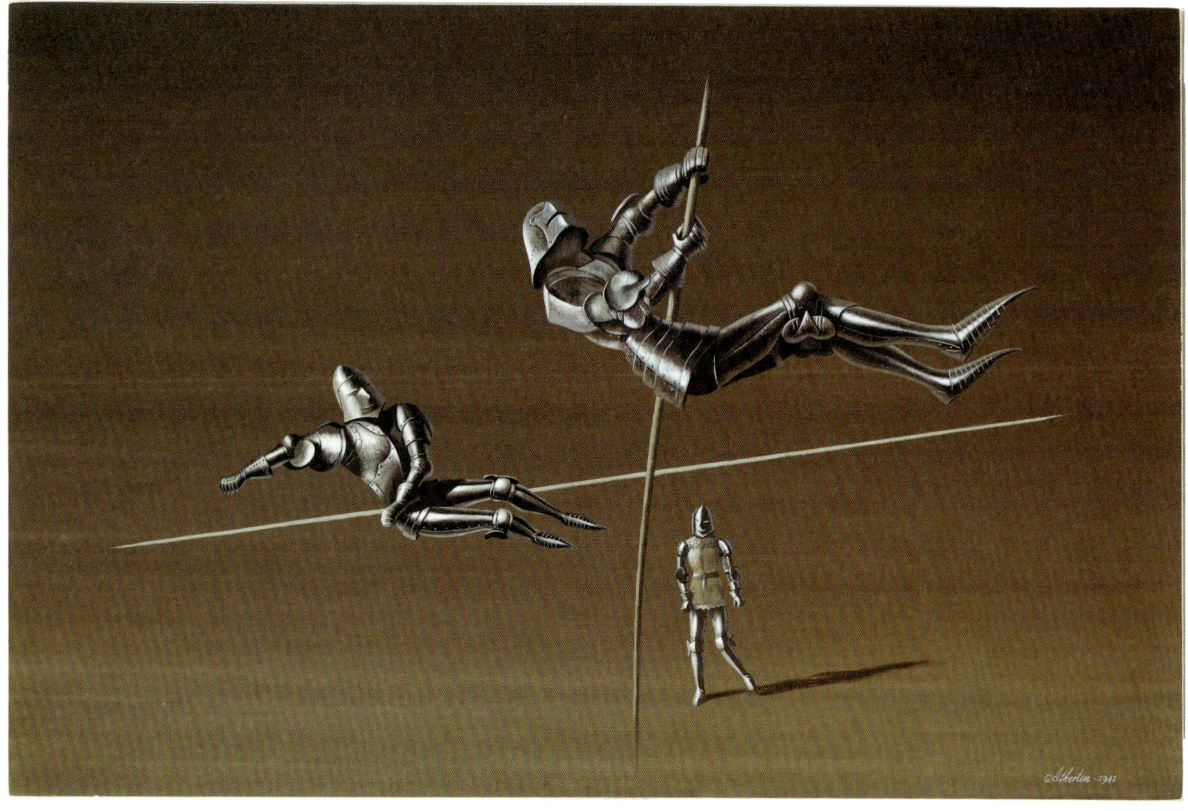

Notes

I am grateful to Betsy Kornhauser for the opportunity to participate in this project, for Erin Monroe's cheerful research help, and for Ann Brandwein's insightful editorial comments that inspired improvements found throughout this essay.

1. Julien Levy, *Memoir of an Art Gallery* (1977; repr., Boston: MFA, 2003), 181.

2. In 1928, Austin had Marin's 1921 watercolor *Green Head, Deer Isle, Maine* (Hirshhorn Museum and Sculpture Garden, Washington, D.C.) sent to the museum from the Weyhe Gallery in New York as a potential acquisition. Perhaps because of its radical style (but equally likely because of its $650 price), Austin decided against presenting it to his conservative board of trustees. See Eugene R. Gaddis, *Magician of the Modern: Chick Austin and the Transformation of the Arts in America* (New York: Alfred A. Knopf, 2000), 94.

3. For example, he organized *Abstract Art* in 1935 (the year before the Museum of Modern Art showed *Cubism and Abstract Art*). Austin's show featured work by the Russian Constructivists Antoine Pevsner and Naum Gabo and the Dutch Neo-Plasticists Mondrian and César Domela, as well as two pieces by Alexander Calder.

4. Austin, "Hartford's Art Museum," *Hartford* 13 (April 1928): 4.

5. Dorothy Norman, ed., "Writings and Conversations of Alfred Stieglitz," *Twice a Year* 14–15 (1947), quoted in Barbara Rose, *Readings in American Art since 1900: A Documentary Study* (New York: F. A. Praeger, 1968), 45.

6. Stieglitz, 1923, quoted in Debra Bricker Balken, *Debating American Modernism: Stieglitz, Duchamp, and the New York Avant-Garde* (New York: American Federation of Arts/Distributed Art Publishers, 2003), 32. This view was echoed by Stieglitz's acolytes. For example, Paul Rosenfeld wrote in 1923, "The fight against provincialism in America is the crucial one. We do all sorts of stupid things principally because we have no sense of ourselves as Americans. I am sick of foreign reputations and France-worship." Rosenfeld to Stieglitz, 1 September 1923, Alfred Stieglitz Papers, Beinecke Rare Book and Manuscript Library, Yale University, New Haven, Conn.

7. For the importance placed on being of "Yankee" stock, see Paul Rosenfeld on Marin: "The nervousness of Marin's pictures is deeply American, deeply Yankee." Rosenfeld, "The Water-Colours of John Marin," *Vanity Fair* 18 (April 1922): 54. On Dove, see again Rosenfeld, "American Painting," *Dial* 71 (December 1921): 665. For Marin, see Henry McBride, "Modern Art," *Dial* 70 (May 1921), quoted in "Some Critics on John Marin," in *Exhibition of Water Colors Oil Paintings and Etchings by John Marin* (New York: Montross Galleries, 1922), n.p. The issue of watercolor creating a modern, American cultural identity is discussed in Carol Troyen, "A War Waged on Paper: Watercolor and Modern Art in America," in *Awash in Color: Homer, Sargent, and the Great American Watercolor*, by Sue Welsh Reed and Troyen (Boston: Museum of Fine Arts in association with Bulfinch Press, Little, Brown, 1993), xxxiv–lxxiv; and Barbara Dayer Gallati, "Language, Watercolor, and the American Way," in *Masters of Color and Light: Homer, Sargent, and the American Watercolor Movement*, by Linda S. Ferber and Gallati (Washington, D.C.: Smithsonian Institution Press in association with the Brooklyn Museum of Art, 1998), 143–69.

8. Ansel Adams to Alfred Stieglitz, 29 November 1936, Yale Collection of American Literature, Beinecke Rare Book and Manuscript Library, Yale University.

9. Austin, *Hartford Courant*, 4 April 1931, quoted in Gaddis, *Magician of the Modern*, 152.

10. See n. 2, above. After *Modern American Water Colors* (discussed below), Austin did not exhibit Stieglitz-circle artists in any quantity until 1935, when he included a number of Marins, Doves, Demuths, and O'Keeffes in the exhibition *American Painting and Sculpture of the 18th, 19th & 20th Centuries*.

11. Kraushaar was one of a number of dealers specializing in the new American art. Among the others were the Charles Daniel Gallery, the Carroll Gallery, and, beginning in 1926, the highly successful Downtown Gallery. Austin seems to have visited most of these with some regularity; on the other hand, he seems not to have worked with Stieglitz, perhaps in part because both men had larger-than-life personalities but very different styles. See Kornhauser, "Galvanizing Hartford."

12. Paul Strand, "American Water Colors at the Brooklyn Museum," *Arts* 2 (December 1921): 151–52.

13. Henry McBride called Burchfield's New York debut at Kevorkian "the most interesting 'first appearances' of the winter." "Charles Burchfield," *Dial* 69 (August 1920), reprinted in *The Flow of Art: Essays and Criticisms of Henry McBride*, ed. Daniel Catton Rich (New York: Atheneum, 1975), 159.

14. Austin bought *Captain Strout's House* shortly before the Hopper show and *Rockland Harbor* immediately after. *Custom House, Portland* was purchased in 1929 by Robert Huntington, a local collector, who gave it to the Atheneum in 1946.

15. "Edward Hopper," *Wadsworth Atheneum Bulletin* 6 (April 1928): 13–14.

16. For example, in 1930, four of the Atheneum's shows came from the Harvard Society for Contemporary Art: *Dymaxion House*, *Modern Mexican Art*, *Modern German Art*, and *Photography 1930*.

17. For Austin's lifelong friendship with Soby, who later became a highly influential curator and trustee at MoMA, see Gaddis, *Magician of the Modern*, 142–43 ff.

18. As explained by Gertrude Stein, who first adopted them and then grew tired of them: "The group then consisted of the russian, a frenchman, a very young dutchman, and two russian brothers. All of them except the dutchman about twenty-six years old." Gertrude Stein, *The Autobiography of Alice B. Toklas* (1933; repr., New York: Vintage, 1990), 226. Stein's remarks about Bérard's work, made in 1933, sum up her final judgment on the group: "They are almost something and then they are just not." Stein, *Autobiography*, 228.

19. Thomson's attraction to these artists was clearly romantic as well as aesthetic. They were all part of a creative, mostly homosexual, community in Paris in the 1920s; Thomson referred to them repeatedly as "my own painters." Virgil Thomson, *Virgil Thomson* (1966; repr., New York: E. P. Dutton, 1985), 109, 110.

20. There was some interest in the Neo-Romantics among other museums at this time, but it was quirky. According to Julien Levy, the Museum of Fine Arts, Boston's 1932 purchase of Eugene Berman's *Young Man Asleep* occurred "almost by accident" (that is, it was a provisional acquisition, bought for the "reserve" collection); see Levy, *Memoir of an Art Gallery*, 110. And between 1931 and 1933, when Austin made his first purchases of Neo-Romantic works, the omnivorous Duncan Phillips bought five works by Eugene Berman and two by his brother Leonid, but then seems to have lost interest in the group.

21. "Exhibitions in New York: Tchelitchew, Berman, Leonide, Bérard," *Art News* 29 (28 March 1931): 13.

22. Thomson, *Virgil Thomson*, 92.

23. Hitchcock, "New Painters of Sentiment and Mystery," typescript [1931], Austin Papers, Wadsworth Atheneum Archives, cited in Gaddis, *Magician of the Modern*, 445 n. 4.

24. James Thrall Soby, *After Picasso* (Hartford, Conn.: Edwin Valentine Mitchell; New York: Dodd, Mead, 1935), 5–7.

25. A number of them would have distinguished careers as set designers.

26. "I have tried to make of the Avery Memorial in Hartford a museum of living things–paintings, sculpture, architecture, decorative arts, even movies and music–as well as fine examples from the past." Austin, fragment of a typescript, Austin Papers, quoted in Gaddis, *Magician of the Modern*, 309.

27. Levy, *Memoir of an Art Gallery*, 181.

28. As James Thrall Soby remembered, "[Julien Levy] was for a long time the only New York dealer who handled the work of the Surrealists and Neo-Romantics. . . . Nor did he neglect some of the best younger American painters, sculptors, and . . . photographers. It was at his various galleries in the 57th street area that I first saw the paintings of Ben Shahn, the photographs of Atget and Walker Evans and of many other artists whose names now seem secure in art's ever-changing constellation. . . . The two New York galleries that both Chick Austin and I frequented most were those of Julien Levy and of Durlacher Brothers." James Thrall Soby Papers, Museum of Modern Art Archives, quoted in Ingrid Schaffner and Lisa Jacobs, *Julien Levy: Portrait of an Art Gallery* (Cambridge, Mass.: MIT Press, 1998), 20 and 54 n. 1.

29. "Eugene Berman," *Art News* 30 (19 March 1932): 9.

30. The Bingham exhibition originated at the Saint Louis Art Museum (then the City Art Museum of Saint Louis).

31. Genauer, quoted in *Art Digest* 9 (15 April 1935): 19; T. H. Parker, "Drawings by Berman on Exhibition," *Hartford Courant*, 22 March 1935; Edwin Alden Jewell, "Among Current Shows," *New York Times*, 7 April 1935.

32. In addition to the Berman show at Levy's, the Neo-Romantics were represented in exhibitions dedicated to Tchelitchew and Leonid [Berman] and in a group show. Mumford, "In Capitulation," *New Yorker* 11 (1 June 1935), and "Drawings and Illustrations–Pictures for the Public," *New Yorker* 12 (16 May 1936), reprinted in *Mumford on Modern Art in the 1930s*, ed. Robert Wojtowicz (Berkeley and Los Angeles: University of California Press, 2007), 165, 198.

33. Soby's *After Picasso* (see n. 24, above), written in 1935, was the pioneering study of these artists as well as the Surrealists.

34. Austin bought Tchelitchew's *Derby Hill* sketches and Berman's elegant watercolor, *Natural Bridge*, in the 1940s.

35. See n. 26, above.

36. The Paper Ball was not the first event of its kind staged for these overlapping social circles. In the spring of 1928, Austin staged a "Venetian Fete" to raise funds for the Atheneum; it was a costume ball that transformed the museum into a Venetian palazzo. The event was glamorous, its aura of mild dissipation titillating, and because it was scheduled to coincide with the opening of a show of modern French painting, it defanged the potential threat of that art to Hartford's conservative museum patrons. A year before the Paper Ball, Joella Levy (Julien's wife) and socialite Caresse Crosby organized a "Bal onirique" in honor of Gala and Salvador Dalí, for which guests were asked to come dressed as their favorite dream. Among the attendees were the Barrs and the Askews. Austin bought the Atheneum's first Dalí drawing (cat. 64) the day before the bal onirique.

37. Henry McBride, "All Arts United in Hartford," *New York Sun*, 22 February 1936. McBride was enraptured: "No words will give you the richness of the decoration achieved by this Russian artist with a few hundred tons of abandoned newspapers." The courtyard was surrounded by "boxes filled with painted guests from the witty brush of Mr. Tchelitchew, and above them ropes of paper chains stretched to the ceiling., and the ceiling itself was entirely covered with a flat surface of newspapers which . . . had the fairy-like texture of silken fabric."

38. Typescript of radio broadcast by Austin, delivered 5 March 1936, quoted in Gaddis, *Magician of the Modern*, 303.

39. Lincoln Kirstein, "The Ballet in Hartford," in *A. Everett Austin Jr.: A Director's Taste and Achievement* (Hartford, Conn.: Wadsworth Atheneum, 1958), 71.

40. See Gaddis, *Magician of the Modern*, 307–08.

41. The core artists of Rockefeller's collection would be introduced by Halpert at her Downtown Gallery in the exhibition *Seven Masters of Watercolor*. It featured works on paper by Demuth, Preston Dickinson, Hart, Marin, Sheeler, Abraham Walkowitz, and William Zorach, and was held in the spring of 1931, just before Austin presented *Five Young French Painters*.

42. Rockefeller's collection is described in Dorothy C. Miller, "Contemporary American Paintings in the Collection of Mrs. John D. Rockefeller, Jr.," *Art News* 36 (annual supplement; 26 March 1938): 104–16.

43. Lincoln Kirstein and Nelson Rockefeller, foreword to *Murals by American Painters and Photographers* (New York: Museum of Modern Art, 1932), 5.

44. Austin was quite familiar with these muralists. He had borrowed the Harvard Society for Contemporary Art's *Modern Mexican Art* show in 1930 and, having spent a summer in Mexico working on Mayan wall paintings as a college student, returned to the country in 1939 and bought a dozen modern works for the Atheneum. See Gaddis, *Magician of the Modern*, 60–61, 332–35. Austin had organized a small Benton show at the Atheneum in 1932. It included mural sketches borrowed from Benton, who lectured at the museum on his mural techniques during the course of the show. I am grateful to Ann Brandwein for this information.

45. Tonny, quoted in Marian Murray, "Avery Ready to Unveil Kristians Tonny Murals," *Hartford Times*, 6 January 1938, Scrapbooks, vol. 28 (1937): 94, Wadsworth Atheneum Archives.

46. T. H. Parker, "Veil Drawn on Tonny's Work Here," *Hartford Courant*, 7 January 1938, Scrapbooks, 28:95, Wadsworth Atheneum Archives.

47. Austin, quoted in Murray, "Avery Ready to Unveil Kristians Tonny Murals."

48. Between 1927 and 1930, various New York galleries–among them Valentine Gallery, Brummer Gallery, and Balzac Gallery–devoted exhibitions to De Chirico, Miró, Klee, and others. See Deborah Zlotsky, "'Pleasant Madness' in Hartford: The First Surrealist Exhibition in America," *Arts Magazine* 60 (February 1986): 57.

49. Among the other shows was the Harvard Society for Contemporary Art's *Surrealisme*, held February–March 1933, which explained that the movement "has been on the ascent both in literature and painting for the last nine years. It is a revolt against intellectualization, and a return to literary and psychological content." Harvard Society for Contemporary Art, *Fourth Annual Report*, 1932–33, n.p.

50. Alfred H. Barr Jr., preface to *Fantastic Art, Dada, Surrealism* (New York: Museum of Modern Art, 1936), 8.

51. Statement of Purpose and Membership Form, The Harvard Society for Contemporary Art, Inc., reproduced in Nicholas Fox Weber, *Patron Saints* (New York: Alfred A. Knopf, 1992), 6.

52. Austin, "Museum Plans Major Exhibits," *Hartford Times*, 7 November 1931, quoted in Gaddis, *Magician of the Modern*, 160.

53. Levy, *Surrealism* (1936; repr., New York: Da Capo Press, 1995), 9.

54. Dalí would continue to use this style for portraits through the 1930s. Perhaps the best known of these is his graphite and ink portrait of Harpo Marx (1937; Philadelphia Museum of Art).

55. Dalí cited Ingres's celebrated pronouncement–"Drawing is the probity of art"–and two other statements by the French painter in the exhibition catalogue for his first solo show, *Exposició S. Dalí*, Galeries Dalmar, Barcelona, November 14–27, 1925, cited in Dawn Ades and Michael R. Taylor, *Dalí* (New York: Rizzoli in association with the Philadelphia Museum of Art, 2004), 66.

56. Picasso's drawings in this manner are characterized by a stringent linearity coupled with intense shading of certain areas of the figure, most often the head. See Ades and Taylor, *Dalí*, 66.

57. Salvador Dalí, "Dalí to the Reader," in *Dalí* (New York: M. Knoedler, 1943), n.p.

58. The exhibition presented about seventy works from the Société Anonyme, a wide-ranging collection of modern art assembled by Connecticut patron of the arts Katherine Dreier with the advice of Marcel Duchamp. *Some Newer Forms of Beauty* included a number of Austin favorites, among them De Chirico, Klee, and Miró, as well as works by artists unfamiliar to Hartford audiences, Arshile Gorky, John Graham, and Stella among them. See Eric Zafran, "Springtime in the Museum: Modern Art Comes to Hartford," in *Surrealism and Modernism from the Collection of the Wadsworth Atheneum Museum of Art* (Hartford, Conn.: Wadsworth Atheneum Museum of Art in association with Yale University Press, 2003), 121–22.

59. Stella attributed this motto to Giotto; see Joann Moser, *Visual Poetry: The Drawings of Joseph Stella* (Washington, D.C.: Smithsonian Institution Press, 1990), 19.

60. "For drawing I found the unbending inexorable silverpoint the efficacious tool to seize . . . out of reality integral caustic evidences of life." Stella, quoted in Irma Jaffe, *Joseph Stella* (Cambridge, Mass.: Harvard University Press, 1970), 91.

61. The exhibition premiered at the Pierre Matisse Gallery and then was seen at the Atheneum and the Arts Club of Chicago. Austin, Barr, and Soby were among the lenders.

62. Soby, *After Picasso*, 7.

63. Edwin Alden Jewell, "Fantasy in Perspective," *New York Times*, 13 December 1936.

64. Lewis Mumford, "Surrealism and Civilization," *New Yorker* 12 (19 December 1936), reprinted in *Mumford on Modern Art*, 230–31.

65. Austin attributed the American penchant for realism to a deficiency among its artists ("the Anglo-Saxon mind is pictorially . . . unimaginative") and also to a simplemindedness in American taste (realism is "what the greater part of our public is most capable of enjoying"). Austin, foreword to *American Painting and Sculpture of the 18th, 19th & 20th Centuries* (Hartford, Conn.: Wadsworth Atheneum, 1935), 3–4, as quoted in Gaddis, *Magician of the Modern*, 273.

66. E.g., Holger Cahill: "The best American watercolorists have no superiors in the world today." Cahill, *Modern American Water Colors* (Newark, N.J.: Newark Museum, 1930), 8.

67. In her review of the 1934 American Watercolor Society annual, *Brooklyn Daily Eagle* art critic Helen Appleton Read noted "the instinctive predilection and flare which the American artist evinces for the water color medium. . . . [It] lends itself to native traits of spontaneity and haste and impatience with theorizing." "Water Colors are 'Waving a Gay Banner,'" *Art Digest* 9 (15 November 1934): 6.

68. Dorothy Adlow, "The Home Forum," *Christian Science Monitor*, undated clipping, curatorial files, Museum of Fine Arts, Boston.

69. Mumford, "John Marin," *New Yorker* 12 (31 October 1936), reprinted in *Mumford on Modern Art*, 215.

70. Alan Burroughs, introduction to *A History of American Watercolor Painting* (New York: Whitney Museum of American Art, 1942), 14. Burroughs also acknowledged the conservatism of their practice ("Present techniques are on the whole only a little more varied than those of the last century").

71. James W. Lane, "Aquarellia Americana," *Art News* 41 (15–28 February 1942): 12. (Lane begins his essay, "In the family of American artistic mediums, watercolor is king. The American painter takes to watercolor like a duck to water. He has found it the ideal medium for expressing the adaptability of the national temper. . . . The oil medium is too static to express American restlessness." Lane, 11.) Goodrich picks up this theme, and reminds the reader that Homer was "of old Yankee stock." Lloyd Goodrich, *American Watercolor and Winslow Homer* (Minneapolis: Walker Art Center, 1945), 23–24.

72. Eugene Berman, "Legendary Chick," in *A. Everett Austin, Jr., A Director's Taste and Achievement* (Hartford, Conn.: Wadsworth Atheneum, 1958), 48.

73. Genauer, *New York World Telegram*, 7 March 1942, quoted in William M. Griswold, *Pierre Matisse and His Artists* (New York: Pierpont Morgan Library, 2002), 189–90.

74. Breuning, quoted in "Artists in Exile Hold Stimulating Show," *Art Digest* 16 (15 March 1942): 9. A similar show had been held at the Addison Gallery of American Art in Andover, Massachusetts, the previous October. A somewhat different group of artists was represented, but they were identified as "progressive moderns." The show, titled *European Artists Teaching in America*, reassured the public that no single style or school would be imposed on American students, but on the contrary, these émigrés would "help break up America's natural tendency toward standardization." "Addison Asks: 'What Effect Will Europe's Upheaval Have on U. S. Art?'" *Art Digest* 16 (1 October 1941): 5, 17.

75. Other shows featuring works on paper by the "artists in exile" included a Matta drawings show at Pierre Matisse, March 1942; *Aspects of Modern Drawing* (with works by Chagall, Ernst, Masson, and Tanguy, among others) at Buchholz Gallery, May 1942; and drawings by Ernst at Levy, May 1943.

76. Monroe Wheeler and John Rewald, *Modern Drawings* (New York: Museum of Modern Art, 1944), 14.

77. Levy, *Memoir of an Art Gallery*, 247. Levy had mixed feelings about Matta, calling him "the most fertile and untrustworthy of the younger Surrealists."

78. Henry McBride, "Matta and the Henry Cliffords," *New York Sun*, 3 April 1942, in *The Flow of Art: Essays and Criticisms of Henry McBride*, ed. Daniel Catton Rich (New York: Atheneum, 1975), 390.

79. Elizabeth A. T. Smith and Colette Dartnall, *Matta in America: Paintings and Drawings of the 1940s* (Chicago: Museum of Contemporary Art, 2001), 20.

80. For the different uses made of automatism and other techniques by the Surrealists and the New York School, see Robert Hobbs, "Surrealism and Abstract Expressionism: From Psychic and Plastic Automatism," in *Surrealism U.S.A.*, by Isabelle Dervaux (New York: National Academy Museum, 2005), 56–65. The interrelationships between the two movements are thoroughly chronicled in Martica Sawin's *Surrealism in Exile and the Beginning of the New York School* (Cambridge, Mass.: MIT Press, 1995). See also Sidney Janis's pioneering *Abstract and Surrealist Art in America* (New York: Reynal & Hitchcock, 1944).

81. According to Julien Levy, "For Gorky, automatism was a redemption. And it was also this new visceral freedom which brought him close to the Surrealists who were now in America–Ernst, Tanguy, Masson, and in particular Matta and Andre Breton." Levy, foreword to *Arshile Gorky Paintings Drawings Studies*, by William C. Seitz (New York: Museum of Modern Art, 1962), 8.

82. Gorky, letter to his sister Vartoosh, quoted in Diane Waldman, *Arshile Gorky, 1904–1948: A Retrospective* (New York: Solomon R. Guggenheim Museum, 1981), 60.

83. Willem de Kooning, "Remembrances of Gorky," *Ararat* (Fall 1971): 50, quoted in Lisa Mintz Messinger, *Abstract Expressionism: Works on Paper; Selections from the Metropolitan Museum of Art* (New York: Metropolitan Museum of Art, 1992), 34. See also Seitz, who suggests this kind of line, which became especially apparent in the drawings produced during his two summers in Virginia, had historic roots as well: Gorky worked with "his pencil sharpened to a long, tapering point, applying a technique schooled by his study of Ingres and Picasso." Seitz, *Arshile Gorky*, 29.

84. Unlike Matta, however, Gorky's forms were increasingly rooted in nature, and in his need to give shape to sensuous experience. As André Breton wrote in his statement for the brochure accompanying Gorky's first solo show at Julien Levy's gallery in 1945, "[Gorky created] hybrid forms in which all human emotion is precipitated. . . . Gorky is, of all the surrealist artists, the only one who maintains direct contact with nature–sits down to paint *before* her." Breton, "Arshile Gorky: The Eye-Spring," in *Arshile Gorky*, trans. Julien Levy (New York: Julien Levy Gallery, 1945).

85. Clement Greenberg, "Surrealist Painting," *Nation*, 12 and 19 August 1944, reprinted in John O'Brian, ed., *Clement Greenberg: The Collected Essays and Criticism* (Chicago: University of Chicago Press, 1986), 1:225, 229, 230.

86. Greenberg, "Art," *Nation*, 24 March 1945, in O'Brian, *Clement Greenberg*, 2:13.

87. Kirstein, introduction to *American Realists and Magic Realists*, ed. Dorothy C. Miller and Alfred H. Barr Jr. (New York: Museum of Modern Art, 1943), 7.

88. Alfred H. Barr Jr., preface to *Romantic Painting in America*, by James Thrall Soby and Dorothy C. Miller (New York: Museum of Modern Art, 1944), 5.

89. Eleanor Perényi, quoted in Schaffner and Jacobs, *Julien Levy*, 168.

Notes to the Reader

Entries are arranged in historical sections that are chronological. Works by a given artist are arranged chronologically, with those of the same date arranged alphabetically. A biography of the artist, followed by a select bibliography, precedes each group of entries. Each work is reproduced; secondary illustrations are included where appropriate.

Contributing Authors

The artist biographies were written by a team of interns and by the three coauthors. The initials of the author of the entry or entries for each artist follow each entry for that artist. The three coauthors are Elizabeth Mankin Kornhauser (EMK), Erin Colley Monroe (ECM), and Carol Troyen (CT).

Conservation

Most of the objects in the exhibition were not previously treated, and many still have their original mats and frames. Whenever possible, the drawings received minimal conservation treatments in order to preserve as much of the artist's intentions and working methods as possible. Original mats and frames were used in the exhibition, when possible.

Cross-references

When an artist listed in the catalogue is mentioned in the biography or an entry for another artist, the name is followed by "(q.v.)." When a biography or entry refers to a specific work listed elsewhere in the catalogue, the mention is followed by "(cat. 00)."

Measurements

Every individual support was remeasured in preparation for this catalogue. Dimensions are given in inches, followed by centimeters in parentheses. Height precedes width.

Medium and Support

In preparation for this catalogue, Mindy Friedman Horn, private conservator of works on paper, examined every drawing, pastel, and watercolor. These works are executed on paper or paperboard in a wide variety of media. In the catalogue entries, the predominant medium is recorded first. The color and composition of the paper and the composition of the mount, if any, to which the paper is affixed are given wherever they could be determined.

Signatures, Dates, Inscriptions, and Watermarks

The artist's signature and any inscriptions as well as their location are given in the catalogue entries. A firm date, or an approximate date based on documentary and stylistic evidence and listed as "circa," is supplied whenever the artist did not date a work. Any watermarks and supplier's marks and labels are also described. Marks known to have been made by the museum, including accession numbers and stamps, are not recorded.

Catalogue

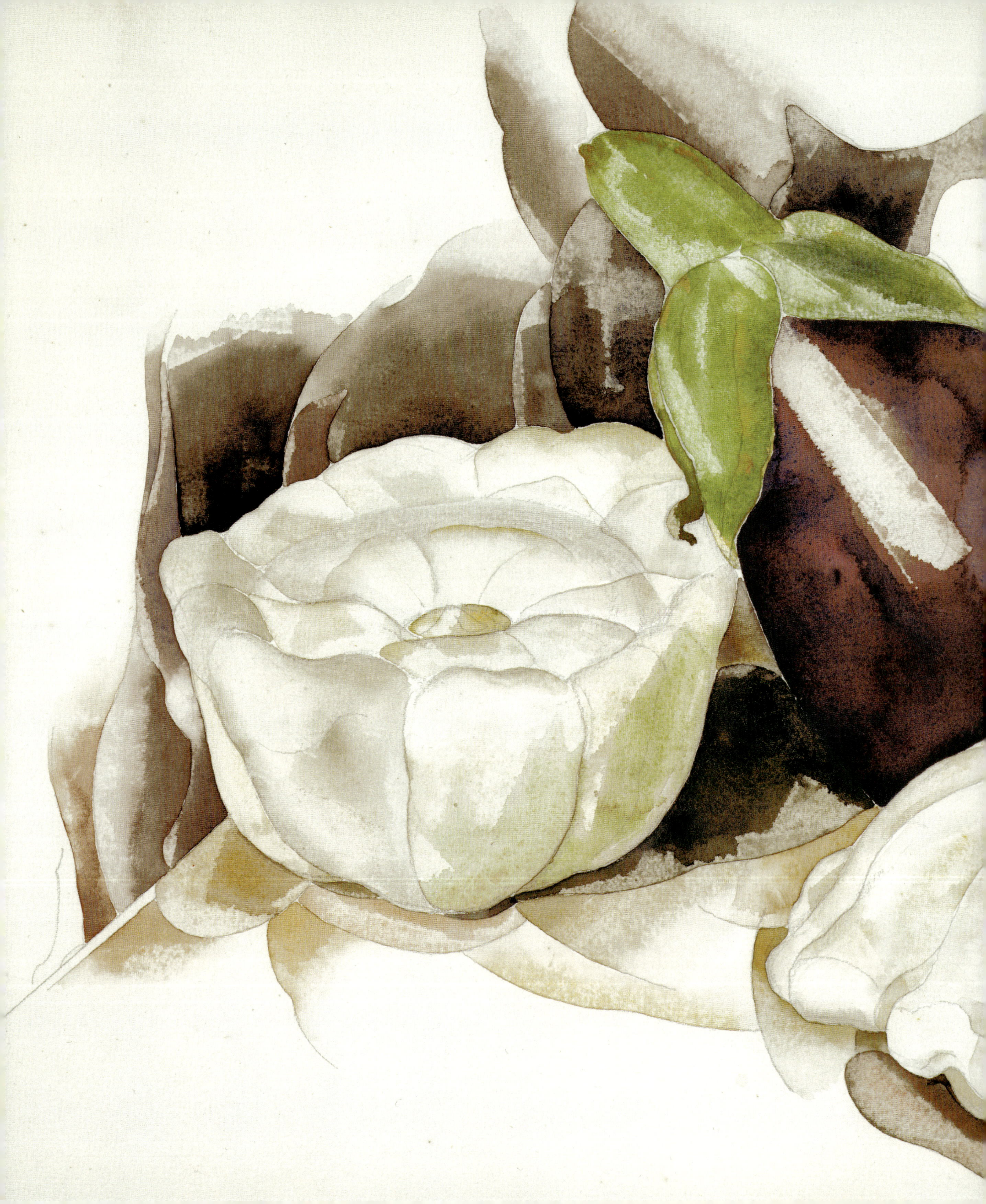

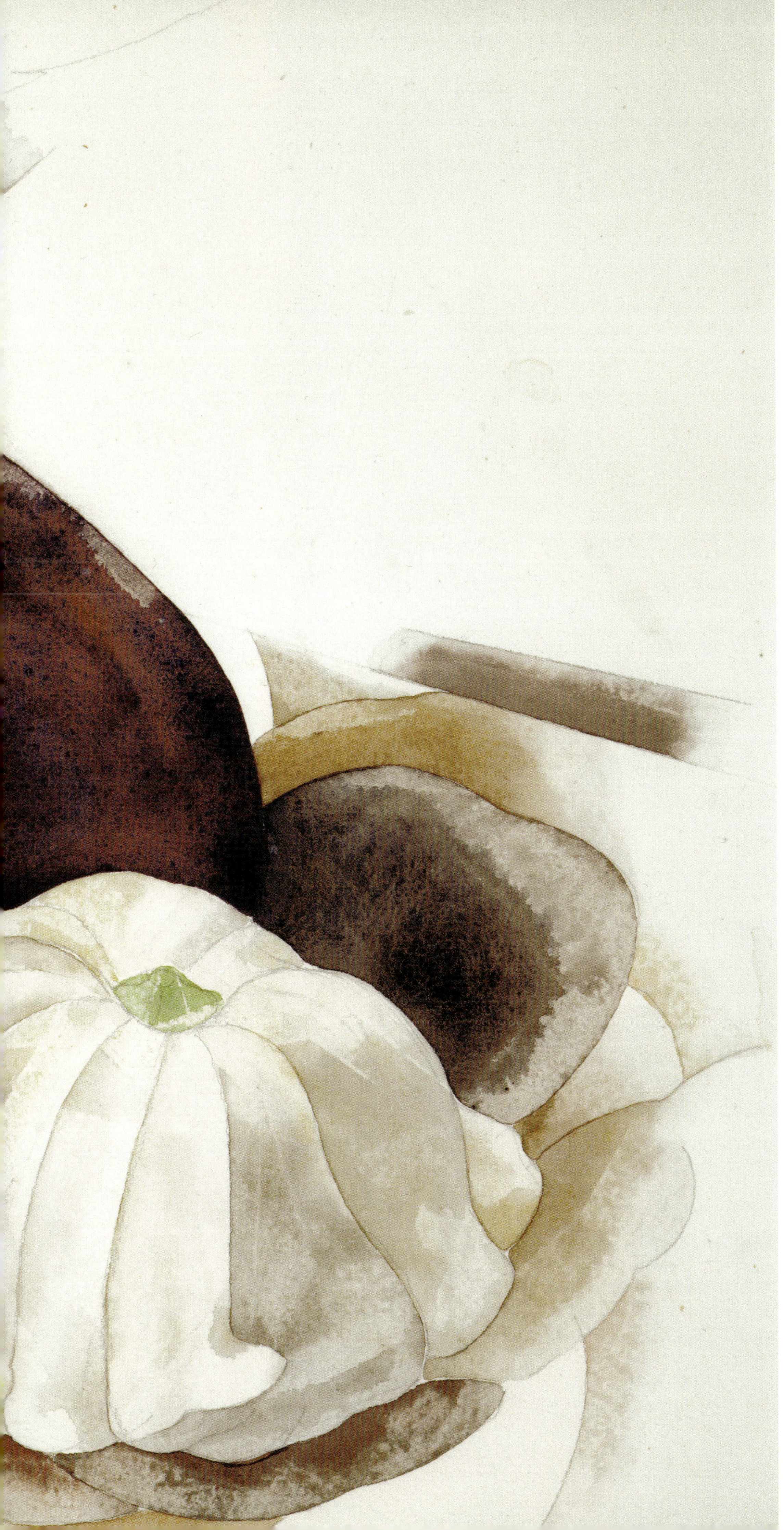

1.

Progressive and Avant-Garde Artists

Maurice B. Prendergast

Born in St. John's, Newfoundland, 1858; died in New York, 1924

Maurice Prendergast moved from Newfoundland to Boston with his family in 1868. He never married, and was supported throughout his career by his brother Charles Prendergast (1863–1948), who was a gifted artist and framemaker. His formal artistic training included study at the Académie Julian and at the Colarossi studio in Paris. He traveled frequently to Europe and was exposed to modern art movements, including Postimpressionism, which he began to incorporate into his own work. He was inspired by the art of the Nabis, by James McNeill Whistler, and by the watercolors of Paul Cézanne, all of whom influenced his focus on surface patterning and expressive color.

While in Boston from 1894 to 1898, he worked mainly in watercolor and monotype; he began exhibiting in 1895, when he showed two watercolors at the Boston Art Club. He painted in oil at the turn of the century and associated with other progressive artists, including Arthur B. Davies, William Glackens (q.v.), and Walt Kuhn.

After a trip to Paris in 1907, Prendergast returned to New York, and in 1908 he participated in the show of The Eight at the Macbeth Gallery, New York, and in 1910 at the *Exhibition of Independent Artists*. He helped organize the Armory Show in 1913 and showed his own work there as well. In 1914 he and Charles moved to New York, where he remained, although he summered on the North Shore of Massachusetts. Excelling in watercolor as well as oil, Prendergast drew on modern European styles, including Fauvism, to depict scenes of modern life. He focused his attention on bustling urban crowds, visitors to city parks, and holiday beachgoers, transforming them into dazzling scenes of movement and color. He was supported by leading collectors, including Duncan Phillips, Lillie P. Bliss, Albert C. Barnes, and John Quinn.

Select Bibliography

Van Wyck Brooks. "Anecdotes of Maurice Prendergast." In *The Prendergasts: Retrospective Exhibition of the Work of Maurice and Charles Prendergast*. Andover, Mass.: Addison Gallery of American Art, Phillips Academy, 1939.

Carol Clark, Nancy Mowll Mathews, and Gwendolyn Owens. *Maurice Brazil Prendergast and Charles Prendergast: A Catalogue Raisonné*. Williamstown, Mass.: Williams College Museum of Art, 1990.

Nancy Mowll Mathews. *Maurice Prendergast*. New York: Whitney Museum of American Art, 1990.

1

Maurice Prendergast
The Amusement Park (also possibly *Ferris Wheel*), c. 1902, reworked c. 1915–17
Pastel over opaque and transparent watercolor and graphite on wove paper, laid down on mat board
18 3/4 × 16 1/2 in. (47.6 × 41.9 cm)
Signed lower left in pencil: Prendergast / Prendergast
Ex coll.: with the artist; to his brother Charles Prendergast, by 1924; with the Kraushaar Galleries, New York; purchased by George A. Gay, Hartford, Connecticut, in 1927
Bequest of George A. Gay, 1941.172

Maurice Prendergast was exposed to the contemporary art scene in Paris in the 1890s, where he painted scenes of Parisian parks and boulevards in a profusion of bright colors and patterns. Upon his return to Boston and later, working in New York, Prendergast took delight in portraying contemporary American life, particularly showing a broad range of people enjoying recreational spaces including parks and the seashore. *The Amusement Park* is characteristic of his American subjects. A lively procession of women and girls wearing brightly colored dresses and yellow hats, one holding a parasol, stroll in the foreground. They are joined by a large orange-striped cat in the center foreground, and at the far right is a seated black cat. In the middle distance a ring of figures approaches the entertainment area, which includes an exotic onion-domed building topped with an American flag; looming above the park is a Ferris wheel.

Prendergast explored his favorite subject in this work, but the variety of media used is unusual: a combination of brilliant pastel strokes broadly applied over more delicate translucent watercolor. The foreground figures have been heavily outlined in black, and the pastel colors of bright blue, orange, green, pink, and red are roughly worked. The figures in the middle ground, however, are faintly brushed in more muted, shimmering watercolor tones. Many unfinished watercolors by Prendergast survive, and he is known to have frequently reworked them. Prendergast scholars have suggested that the distinct discrepancy in style and media found in this work suggests that the artist reworked an earlier watercolor from about 1902, applying pastel and heavy outlines to the foreground figures and to the trees in about 1915, at a period when he was using pastel.[1]

A related watercolor by Prendergast titled *Amusement Park*, from about 1900 to 1905, shows a similar subject, including a large Ferris wheel, and the location is identified by an inscription on the sheet: "New York City; 86th Street and East River." This was the site of a popular public park that is now known as the Carl Schurz Park.[2] It is possible that the Atheneum's pastel and watercolor is of the same subject. The Atheneum's work was included in an exhibition at the St. Botolph Club, in Boston, with the title *Ferris Wheel*, but entered the Atheneum's collection with the title *The Amusement Park*. This work retains its original carved polychrome and gilt frame by the artist's brother, Charles Prendergast (fig. 1).
EMK

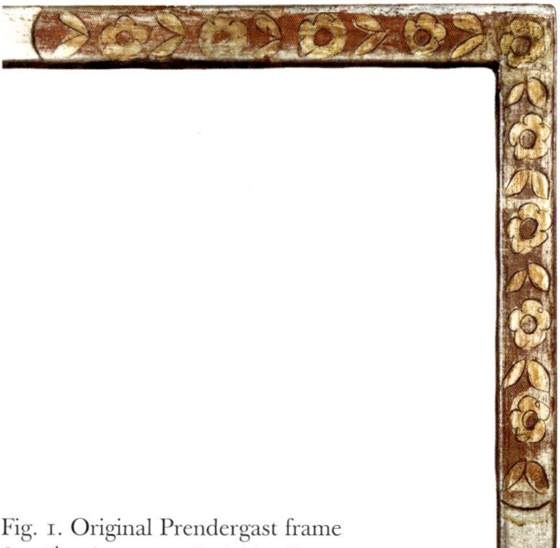

Fig. 1. Original Prendergast frame for *The Amusement Park* (detail)

1. Carol Clark, Nancy Mowll Mathews, and Gwendolyn Owens, *Maurice Brazil Prendergast and Charles Prendergast: A Catalogue Raisonné* (Williamstown, Mass.: Williams College Museum of Art, 1990), 420–21; and Hedley Howell Rhys, "Maurice Prendergast: The Sources and Development of His Style" (Ph.D. diss., Harvard University, 1952), 189.
2. Rhys, "Maurice Prendergast"; and William H. Whyte, *The WPA Guide to New York City* (1929; repr., New York: New Press, 1995), 250.

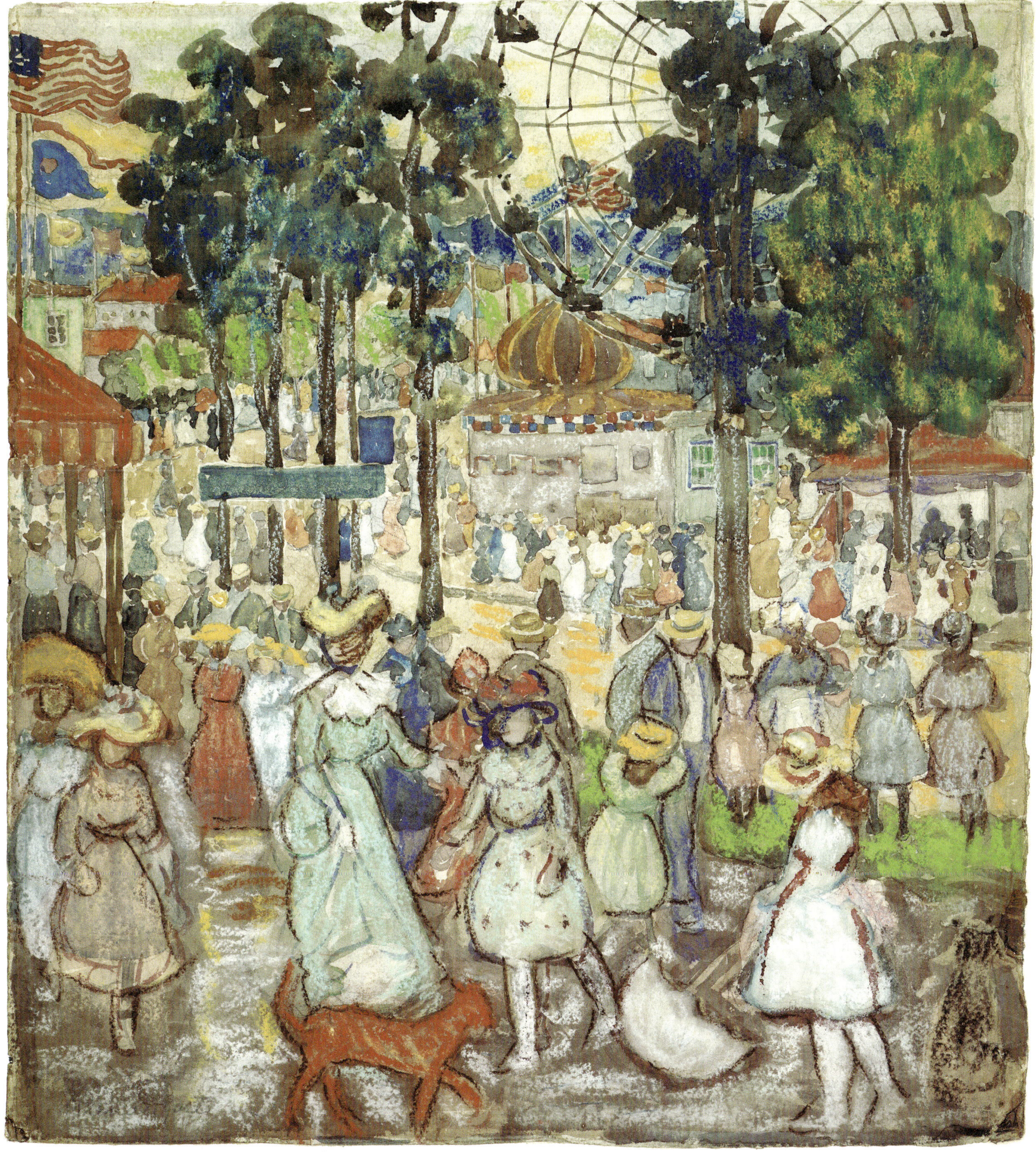

Cat. 1

William Glackens

Born in Philadelphia, 1870;
died in Westport, Connecticut, 1938

William Glackens attended Central High School in Philadelphia, with John Sloan (q.v.) and the collector Albert C. Barnes, graduating in 1889. He began his career as an illustrator for the *Philadelphia Record*, and later for the *Philadelphia Press*. There he worked with artists Sloan, Everett Shinn, and George Luks, all of whom would join him in the 1908 exhibition that established the group called The Eight, dubbed the Ashcan school by its detractors. Glackens attended night classes at the Pennsylvania Academy of the Fine Arts, and with encouragement from his mentor, Robert Henri, he traveled to France in 1895.

Upon his return to the United States in 1896, Glackens moved to New York, where he worked as an artist-reporter and magazine illustrator and began painting. In 1898 he accompanied the U.S. Army to Cuba to record the Spanish-American War for *McClure's Magazine*, executing such sketches for illustrations as the Atheneum's *Night after San Juan, Attending the Wounded* (1898). After his return to New York he met Edith Dimock, an art student from a prominent Hartford, Connecticut, family, whom he married in 1904. Glackens turned more exclusively to painting at this time and successfully exhibited his work in Philadelphia and New York. He became an associate of the National Academy of Design in 1906, and exhibited with The Eight at Macbeth Gallery, New York, in 1908. His paintings at this time reflect the dark realist style of Henri and his fellow artists, who rejected academic conventions by supporting progressive styles and choosing everyday street life as their subject. His earlier experience as a sketch-reporter for the newspapers, with its requisite quick-sketch technique, lent itself well to his later sketches and paintings of New York City urban life.

In 1913, Glackens served as chairman for the selection committee of American art for the Armory Show, and participated in the exhibition. He became the first president of the Society of Independent Artists in 1917. He divided his time between France and the United States from 1925 to 1932, and his later paintings reflect his admiration for the works of such French artists as Édouard Manet, Pierre-Auguste Renoir, and Claude Monet.

Select Bibliography

Ira Glackens. *William Glackens and the Ashcan Group: The Emergence of Realism in American Art.* New York: Crown, 1983.

Rebecca Zurier, Robert W. Snyder, and Virginia M. Mecklenburg. *Metropolitan Lives: The Ashcan Artists and Their New York.* New York: W. W. Norton, in association with the National Museum of American Art, 1995.

Rebecca Zurier. *Picturing the City: Urban Vision and the Ashcan School.* Berkeley and Los Angeles: University of California Press, 2006.

2

William Glackens
Far from the Fresh Air Farm (East Side), 1910–11
Charcoal heightened with pale blue and red chalk on wove paper
$24^{1}/_{4} \times 16^{1}/_{2}$ in. (62.2 × 41.9 cm)
Inscribed at lower left: W. G. / [?] 9.9
Ex coll.: with Kraushaar Galleries, New York; Henry Schnakenberg, Newtown, Connecticut, until 1954
Gift of Henry Schnakenberg, 1954.121

While working as a sketch reporter for New York newspapers and illustrated magazines, Glackens walked the city streets and rapidly executed on-the-spot sketches. Later, he drew from these sketches for the fully realized and intricately detailed large-scale drawings executed in his studio, including *Far from the Fresh Air Farm (East Side)*. John Sloan (q.v.) recalled the strength and vivacity of these works, noting that Glackens's "drawings of New York streets, tenements, fire escapes, pushcarts, people were full of incidents and more alive than life could ever be. He would make a drawing over and over again until he got what he really wanted. He was never satisfied."[1] Glackens's painstaking working method and acute observations of urban life can be seen in the preliminary studies in his sketchbook and the large preparatory drawings he created for one of his most celebrated illustrations, *Far from the Fresh Air Farm . . .*, which was published on the cover of *Collier's* magazine on July 18, 1911.

The Atheneum's charcoal and crayon drawing was preceded by numerous sketches in the artist's notebook, including those of individual figures and vignettes of the street itself.[2] Employing his knowledge of Lower East Side tenement life, Glackens chose a wide-angle view for his large-scale drawing of this crowded street scene, thought to be Tompkins Street.[3] Glackens conveys the frenetic activity and throngs of this dense street scene in rapidly scribbled lines that are reworked to take distinctive architectural and human form. In the drawing, Glackens has captured innumerable architectural details, among them cast iron balconies and fire escapes, in the buildings that frame the street. The crowded street is filled with individualized figures spanning generations and the rich mix of cultures of the East Side neighborhood—in the right foreground, for example, clothing peddlers, workers in the garment industry, have distinctive Jewish faces. Street signs and overflowing pushcarts filled with fruit and clothing suggest the lively outdoor marketplace. Finally, Glackens added soft touches of color—pale blue for a figure of a woman at the lower left and red on a building at the upper left.

The Atheneum's drawing was followed by a more finished gouache and crayon drawing measuring $24^{1}/_{2}$ by $16^{1}/_{2}$ inches, *Far from the Fresh Air Farm . . .* (fig. 1). As Rebecca Zurier has noted, "using heavy outlines, stylized poses, and exaggerated energy, this drawing employs a cartoonist's way of seeing."[4]

Fig. 1. William Glackens,
Far from the Fresh Air Farm . . ., 1911.
Gouache and crayon on paper,
$24^{1}/_{2} \times 16^{1}/_{2}$ in. (62.2 × 41.9 cm).
Museum of Art, Fort Lauderdale, Nova Southeastern University. Bequest of Ira Glackens, 91.40.152

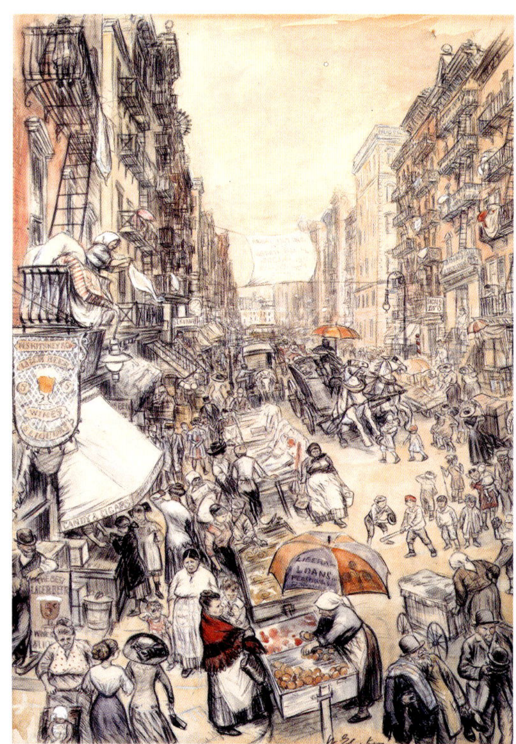

The published illustration was accompanied by a caption: "The crowded city street, with its dangers and temptations, is a pitiful makeshift playground for children." This moral is conveyed in the Atheneum drawing through a series of vignettes, including the center scene of a horse and carriage careening down the busy street as the horses rear up to avoid hitting a young girl carrying a baby and followed by a toddler. Just beyond, boys are playing baseball, and at lower left, children can be seen buying candy from a vendor. Although Glackens's message is that this is not a proper place to raise children, he conveys this message with humor.
EMK

1. Quoted in Rebecca Zurier, *Picturing the City: Urban Vision and the Ashcan School* (Berkeley and Los Angeles: University of California Press, 2006), 181.
2. Illustrated in ibid., 210.
3. Ira Glackens, *William Glackens and the Ashcan Group: The Emergence of Realism in American Art* (New York: Crown, 1983), 115.
4. Zurier, *Picturing the City*, 183.

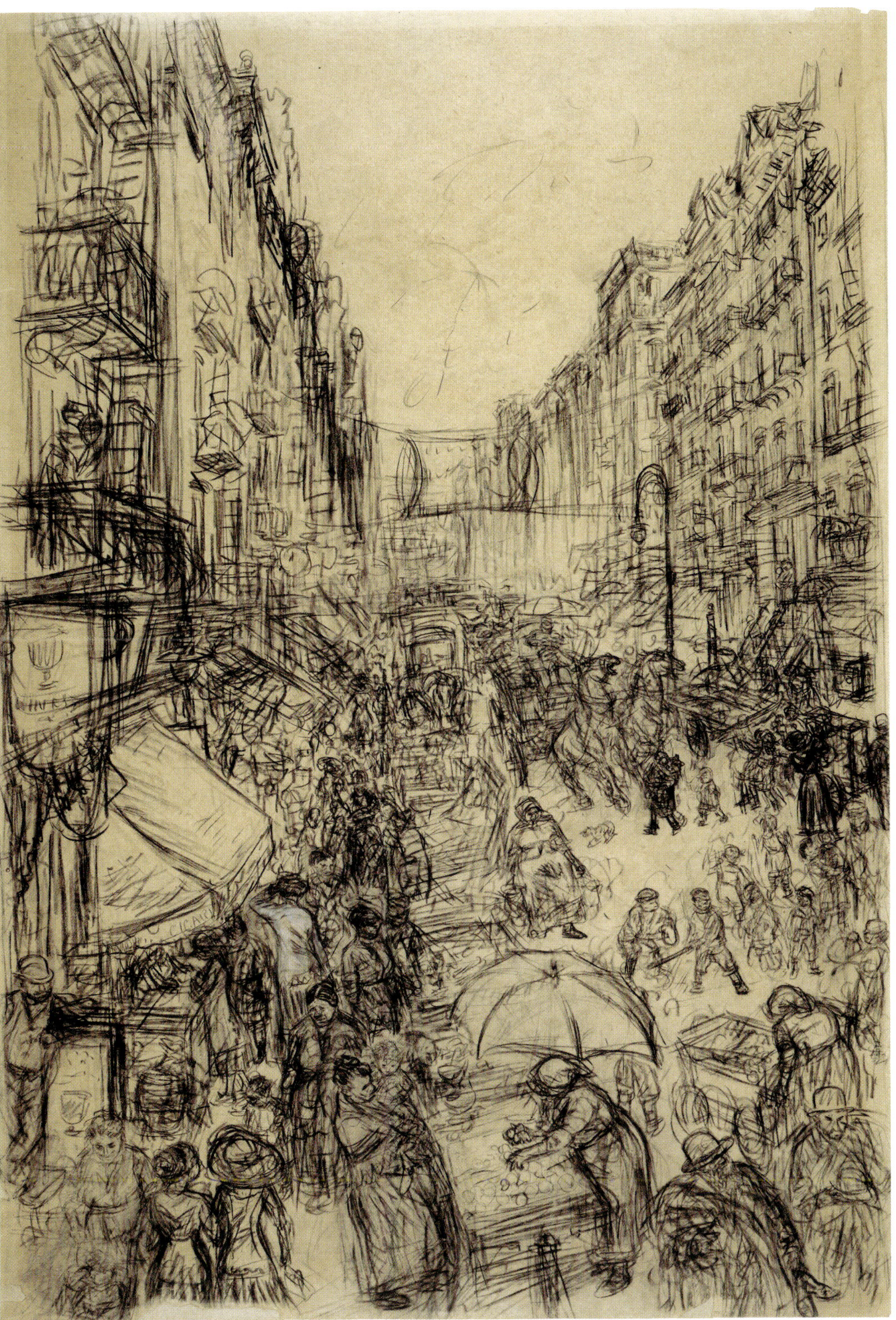

Cat. 2

John Sloan

Born in Lock Haven, Pennsylvania, 1871; died in Hanover, New Hampshire, 1951

John Sloan enrolled in 1892 at the Pennsylvania Academy of the Fine Arts, where he studied under Thomas Anshutz. Sloan and his classmate Robert Henri founded the Charcoal Club in 1893, which included fellow illustrators William Glackens (q.v.), Everett Shinn, and George Luks. This group formed the nucleus of the maverick circle of New York realist painters who exhibited as The Eight in 1908, challenging the more genteel imagery of the National Academy. Later, they were derisively called the Ashcan school. Sloan worked as a newspaper illustrator for the *Philadelphia Inquirer* from 1892 to 1895, and for the *Philadelphia Press* from 1895 to 1904.

In 1904, encouraged by Henri, Sloan and his first wife, Dolly, moved to New York City, where he illustrated for *Collier's* and *Century Magazine*. His series of etchings from 1905 to 1906 depicting Fifth Avenue and the Tenderloin district, titled New York City Life, demonstrate a direct realism that is also visible in his paintings from this time. As a leader of the independent movement, Sloan helped to organize and participated in *The Eight* at the Macbeth Gallery, New York, in 1908, and the *Exhibition of Independent Artists* in New York in 1910.

Sloan held liberal political views and joined the Socialist Party in 1910; he became the art director for the socialist magazine *The Masses* in 1912, contributing illustrations to it until 1916. He began teaching at the Art Students League, and in 1914 he submitted two paintings and five etchings to the Armory Show. Having honed his skills of observation and reportage through his work as an illustrator, he developed a direct and vigorous painting style to capture the urban scene.

By the mid-1910s, Sloan adopted a brighter palette and turned his attention to nude studies. While summering in Gloucester, Massachusetts, from 1914 to 1919, he produced plein-air landscapes. Sloan traveled to Santa Fe, New Mexico, in 1919, which became a second home for the artist and which led to a new series of paintings inspired by the desert landscape and the rituals of the southwestern Indians. In 1939 Sloan published his *Gist of Art*, based on his lectures at the Art Students League. Sloan is best remembered for his application of the realist style to urban subjects.

Select Bibliography

John Sloan. *Gist of Art: Principles and Practice Expounded in the Classroom and Studio.* With Helen Farr. New York: American Artists Group, 1939.

Van Wyck Brooks. *John Sloan: A Painter's Life.* New York: Dutton, 1955.

John Sloan. *New York Scene: From the Diaries, Notes, and Correspondence, 1906–1913.* Edited by Bruce St. John. New York: Harper and Row, 1965.

David W. Scott and E. John Bullard. *John Sloan, 1871–1951.* Washington, D.C.: National Gallery of Art, 1971.

Rowland Elzea. *John Sloan's Oil Paintings: A Catalogue Raisonné.* 2 vols. Newark: University of Delaware Press, 1991.

Rebecca Zurier. *Picturing the City: Urban Vision and the Ashcan School.* Berkeley and Los Angeles: University of California Press, 2006.

3

John Sloan
Study for Hairdresser's Window, 1907
Conté crayon on thin wove paper
(watermark: Indenture Bond)
6 3/4 × 5 1/8 in. (17.2 × 13 cm)
Signed lower right: John Sloan
Ex coll.: with Kraushaar Galleries, New York, by 1947; with Bernard Danenberg Galleries, New York, by 1973; with Beacon Hill Fine Art, New York, by 1998
The Dorothy Clark Archibald and Thomas L. Archibald Fund, 1998.7.1

Following his arrival in New York City in 1904, Sloan focused his attention on city street life, walking several miles a day memorizing and only occasionally capturing fleeting scenes of interest in rapidly executed drawings. His drawing *Study for Hairdresser's Window* records a scene, perhaps from memory, that he later incorporated into one of his most celebrated paintings of city life, *Hairdresser's Window* (fig. 1).[1]

Sloan later recalled the inspiration for the drawing and finished painting in his diary entry for 5 June 1907: "Walked up to Henri's studio. On the way saw a humorous sight of interest. A window, low, second story, bleached blond hairdresser bleaching the hair of a client. A small interested crowd about." On June 6, he continued, "Walked out to take another look at the Hair Restorer's Window. Came back and started to paint it."[2]

Urban women were a favorite subject of Sloan's, and here he treats them with novelty and humor.[3] In the drawing, Sloan portrays the hairdresser—who herself has bleached blond hair—possibly "Madame Malcomb," as indicated by the sign at left in the painting. She wears gloves to protect her hands from the harsh chemicals and is engaged in brushing bleach into the hair of her seated client. At the left, a young woman leans into the scene to assist the hairdresser by holding the cup of bleach. In quickly rendered, abbreviated lines, Sloan captures the novel process of bleaching hair that he saw through the window as he walked along Sixth Avenue. In the finished oil, a crowd of passersby gather on the street below and look up, enjoying the scene above them. Sloan faithfully followed the outlines of the drawing in his finished painting, but made the figure of the assistant less prominent.

When the Wadsworth Atheneum purchased the painting *Hairdresser's Window* in 1947, Sloan wrote to the museum, "It is a great satisfaction when one of my old 'New York City' works is safely installed in an institution such as the Athenaeum.'"[4] This drawing was purchased to compliment the painting and gives a sense of the artist's working method. An architectural sketch is executed in pen and ink on the verso.

EMK

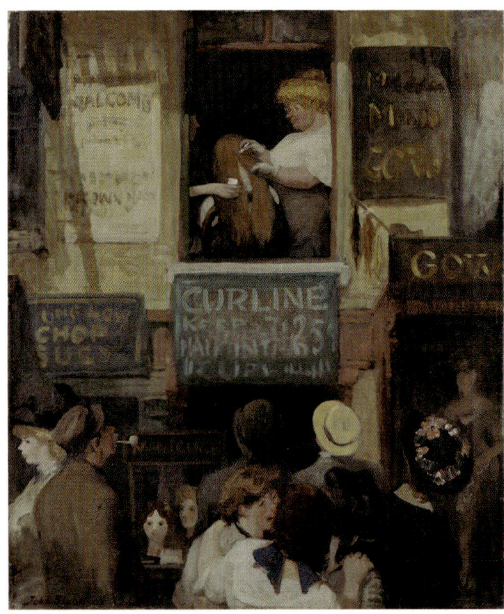

Fig. 1. John Sloan, *Hairdresser's Window*, 1907. Oil on canvas, 32 × 26 in. (81.3 × 66 cm). Wadsworth Atheneum Museum of Art. The Ella Gallup Sumner and Mary Catlin Sumner Collection Fund, 1947.240

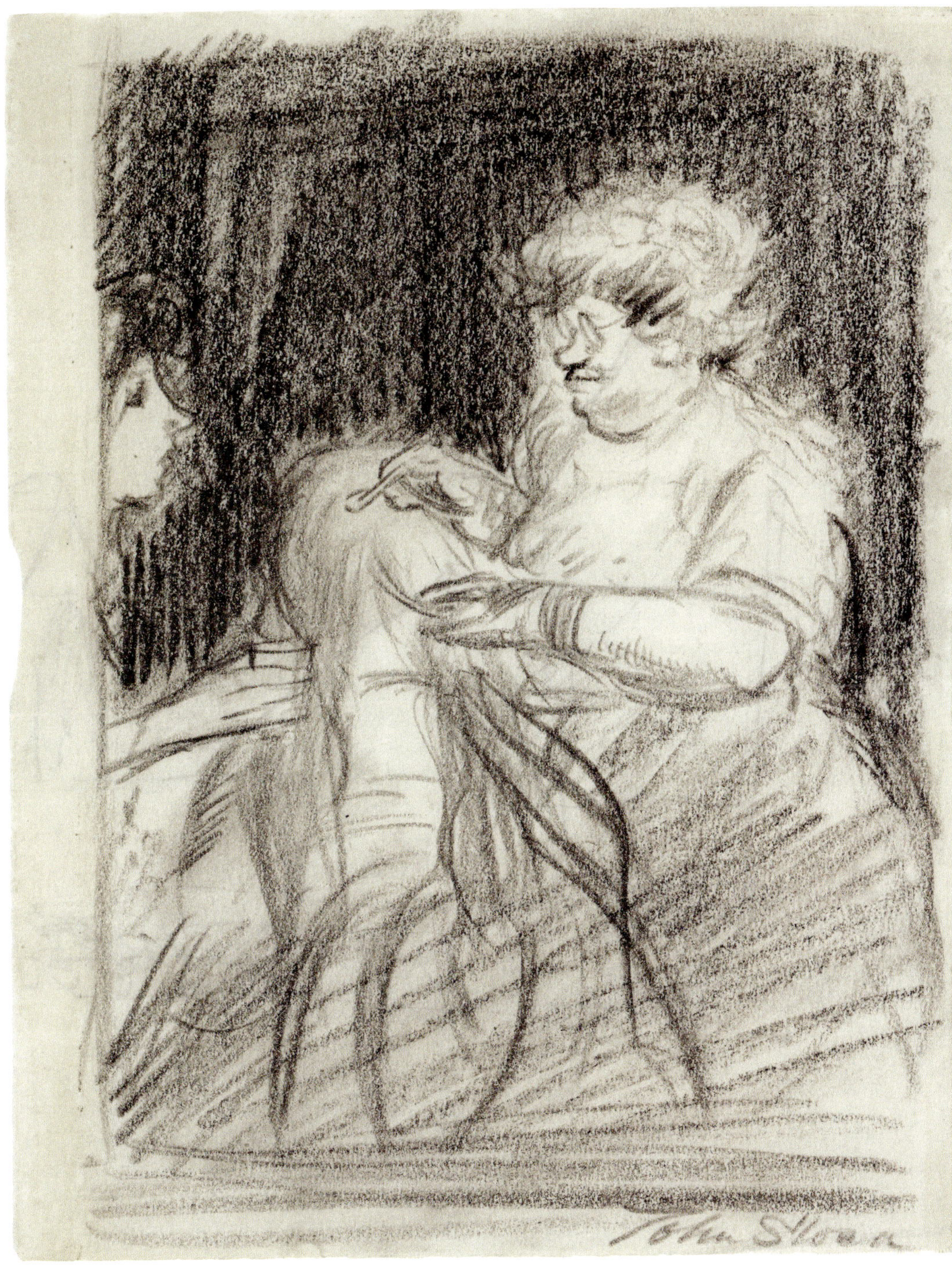

Cat. 3

4

John Sloan
Picture Hat, c. 1914–15
Black crayon on thin wove paper
13 × 9 in. (33 × 22.9 cm)
Signed at lower right: John Sloan
Ex coll.: Henry E. Schnakenberg, Newtown, Connecticut, until 1952
Gift of Henry E. Schnakenberg, 1952.72

"A beautiful day and the breezes about the Flatiron Building show the beautiful forms of the women in their summer gowns. There are so many lovely women in New York and they dress so very charmingly, I'd like to spend hours watching them," wrote John Sloan in his diary.[1] As a leading member of the Ashcan school of painters, Sloan was the primary chronicler of the youthful urban women who were seen on the streets of New York City. Sloan was in the habit of walking the streets, observing women from all walks of life.[2] *Picture Hat* is a rapid sketch of an attractive young middle-class woman—perhaps a shop-girl—who is fashionably attired. As the title of the work indicates, she wears a large veiled hat, the height of fashion at the time this sketch was taken.[3] With her head tilted slightly to the left, she looks downward with a dreamy gaze. Her hands are clasped together in front of her, and the bottom of her skirt blows up to reveal attractive legs beneath. Sloan sets the figure against a series of squiggly lines at the bottom of the drawing—all the artist conveys as a backdrop—providing a sense of the energy of New York City.

While Sloan revealed his socialist political views in his cartoons and illustrations, he did not do so in his paintings. As Sloan insisted, "I was never interested in putting propaganda into my paintings. . . . I saw the everyday life of the people, and on the whole I picked out bits of joy in human life for my subject matter."[4] This drawing is an example of the artist's depictions of "everyday life" in its straightforward portrayal of a young urban woman.

EMK

1. Elizabeth Mankin Kornhauser, *American Paintings before 1945 in the Wadsworth Atheneum*, with contributions by Elizabeth R. McClintock and Amy Ellis (New Haven, Conn.: Yale University Press, 1996), 2:660–63.
2. John Sloan, *New York Scene: From the Diaries, Notes, and Correspondence, 1906–1913*, ed. Bruce St. John (New York: Harper and Row, 1965), 133.
3. For a discussion of Sloan's penchant for the subject of urban women in his art, see Rebecca Zurier, *Picturing the City: Urban Vision and the Ashcan School* (Berkeley and Los Angeles: University of California Press, 2006), 264–67.
4. John Sloan to Charles C. Cunningham, 26 July 1947, curatorial files, Wadsworth Atheneum.

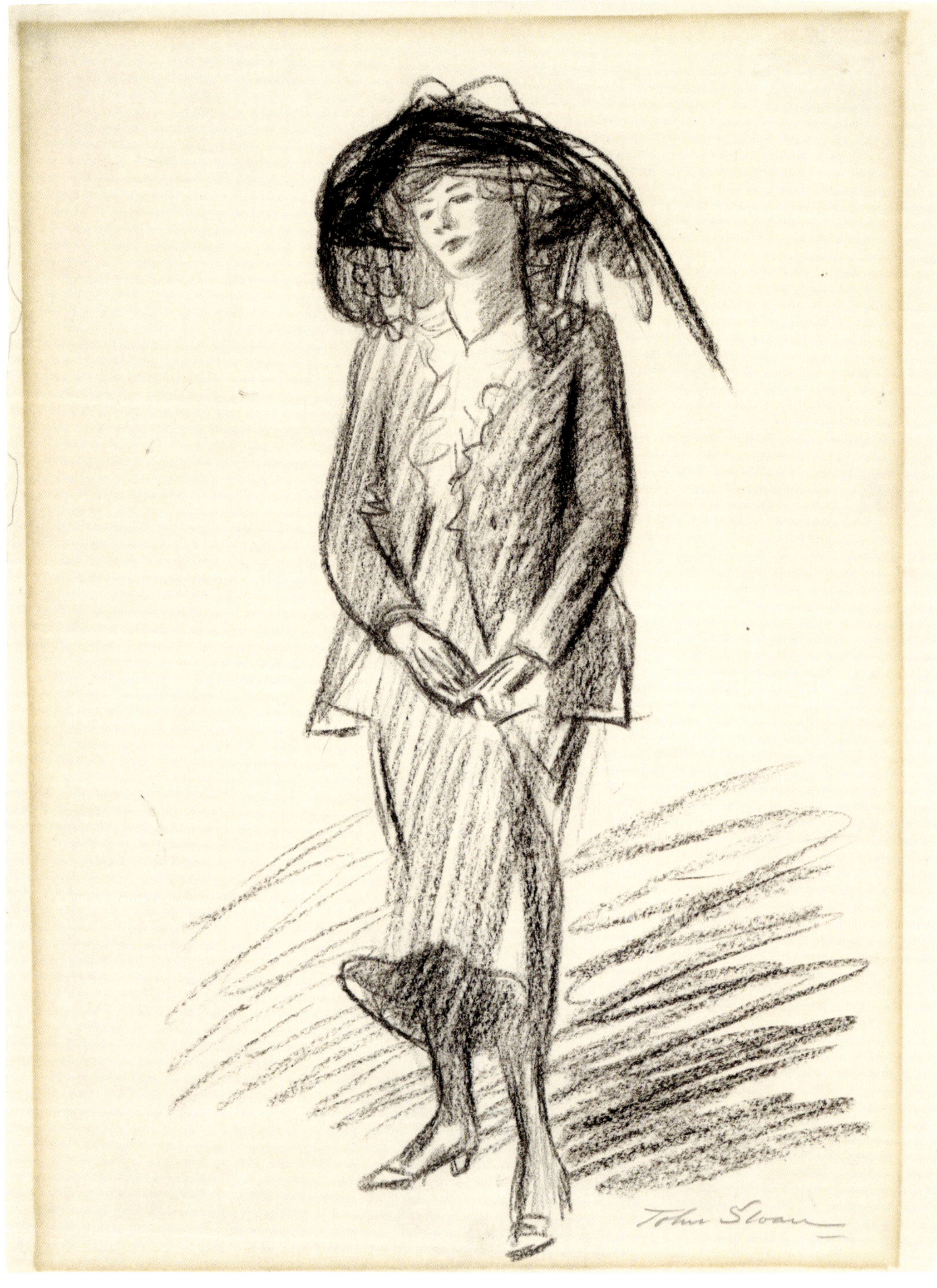

Cat. 4

1. John Sloan, diary, 15 July 1908; quoted in Karen Sherry, "Form and Meaning in John Sloan's Representations of the Female Body," in *The Gist of Drawing: Works on Paper by John Sloan* (Newark: University of Delaware, 1997).
2. Many scholars have written of Sloan's penchant for portraying women; see Rebecca Zurier, *Picturing the City: Urban Vision and the Ashcan School* (Berkeley and Los Angeles: University of California Press, 2006), 266; and Ellen Wiley Todd, *The "New Woman" Revised: Painting and Gender Politics on Fourteenth Street* (Berkeley and Los Angeles: University of California Press, 1993), 19–27.
3. My thanks to Lynne Z. Bassett, costume and textile historian and consultant to the Wadsworth Atheneum, for her expert insights on the subject's attire and the date of the sketch.
4. John Sloan, "Early Days," in *American Art Nouveau: The Poster Period of John Sloan*, ed. Helen Farr Sloan (Lock Haven, Pa.: Hammermill Paper Co., 1967), n.p.; quoted in Patricia Hills, "John Sloan's Images of Working-Class Women: A Case Study of the Roles and Interrelationships of Politics, Personality, and Patrons in the Development of Sloan's Art, 1905–1916," in *Reading American Art*, by Marianna Doezema and Elizabeth Milroy (New Haven, Conn.: Yale University Press, 1998), 311.

Abraham Walkowitz

Born in Tyumen, Siberia, 1878;
died in Brooklyn, 1965

One of the pioneers of the modern movement in America, Abraham Walkowitz was primarily a graphic artist, working most successfully in watercolor and charcoal. He immigrated to the United States in 1889, where he settled with his family in New York City, on the Lower East Side. He studied art at the Cooper Union and, in about 1898, at the National Academy of Design, where he mastered figure drawing and studied etching with Walter Shirlaw. He began exhibiting his work at the Educational Alliance in New York, where he taught from 1900 to 1906.

Walkowitz moved to Paris, where he lived until 1907, studying at the Académie Julian and engaged with the avant-garde, including Max Weber (q.v.) and Walter Pach; he encountered Gertrude and Leo Stein, saw the Paul Cézanne watercolor exhibition of June 1907, and was influenced by Henri Matisse and Pablo Picasso. It was also at this time that he first saw the performances of the American dancer and choreographer Isadora Duncan, whose style of free movement in dance influenced Walkowitz's approach to portraying the figure.

Returning to New York in the summer of 1907, Walkowitz had his first solo exhibition at the Haas Gallery. Through Marsden Hartley, he was introduced to Alfred Stieglitz, who supported him with four exhibitions at his gallery 291 between 1912 and 1917. As a member of the progressive art movement in New York, he exhibited at the Armory Show of 1913 and at the Forum Exhibition of Modern American Painters in 1916. He became the director of the Society of Independent Artists in 1918, and two years later, he joined the Société Anonyme, composed of European and American modernists, including André Derain, Man Ray, Wassily Kandinsky, Hartley, and Joseph Stella (q.v.). He is best remembered for his vibrant watercolors and drawings of New York City, and the thousands of drawings he made of his muse, the dancer Isadora Duncan.

Select Bibliography
Abram Lerner and Bartlett Cowdrey. "Oral History Interview with Abraham Walkowitz." December 8 and 22, 1958. Smithsonian Archives of American Art, Washington, D.C.

Martica Sawin. "Abraham Walkowitz, Artist." *Arts Magazine* 33 (March 1964): 42–45.

Sheldon Cheney. *The Art of Dance: Isadora Duncan.* New York: Theatre Art Books, 1969.

Sheldon Reich. "Abraham Walkowitz, Pioneer of American Modernism." *American Art Journal* 3 (Spring 1971): 72–88.

5

Abraham Walkowitz
Future New York, 1912
Graphite on thin wove paper
10 3/8 × 6 in. (26.4 × 15.2 cm)
Signed at lower right, in ink: A. WALKOWITZ
Signed at bottom, in graphite:
A. WALKOWITZ / 1912
Ex coll.: the artist
Gift of Abraham Walkowitz, 1949.246

For Walkowitz's publication *Improvisations of New York: A Symphony in Lines*, writer and photographer Carl Van Vechten provided the following tribute:

Having glorified the American dancer, Isadora Duncan, in over 5,000 drawings, that indomitable artist, Walkowitz, has now determined, apparently, to perform a like aesthetic service for the city of New York. In his sketches for this tortured, terrifyingly aspiring and ambitious metropolis, the artist has borrowed an idea from Gertrude Stein and employs repetition for emphasis. None of these pictures is exactly like its predecessor, but each one of them carries the intention one step further. Towers shoot upward in endless carefully arranged projections, now as flames, now as rhomboids, now as stalagmites, now as phallic obelisks, growing out of the sewers below and overshadowing the groveling populace.[1]

The book, which appeared the year before Walkowitz gave *Future New York* to the Atheneum, reproduces hundreds of drawings and watercolors of New York, sometimes singly, sometimes twenty-five to a page. It surveys Walkowitz's many different renderings of the city. A number of them are completely nonobjective. In some, buildings are reduced to flat outline shapes. In others, there is a pileup of tall, blocky forms, with regularly spaced wash or watercolor splotches designating windows; in several of those, thirty or more

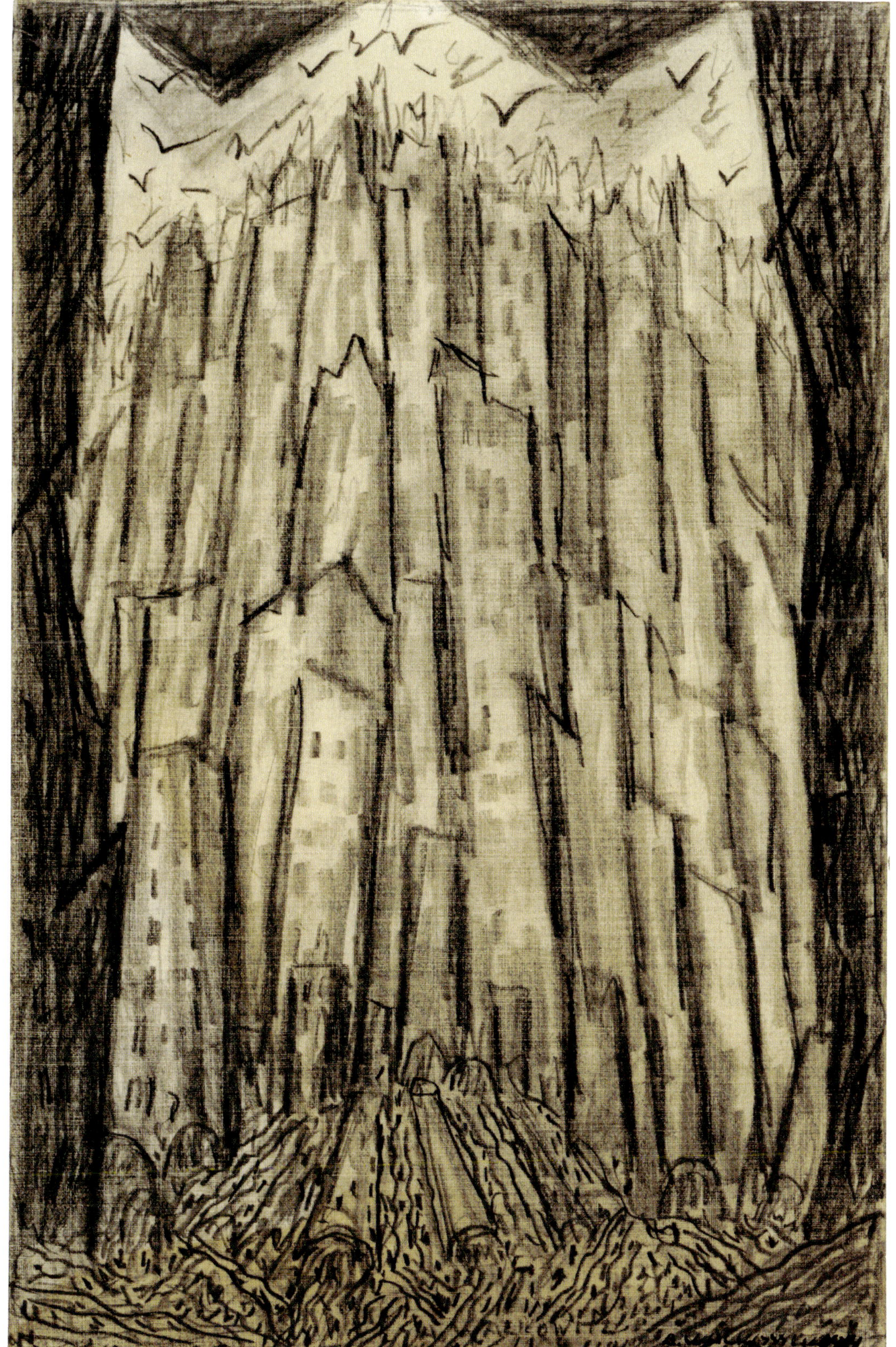

Cat. 5

skyscrapers seem to fan out across the sheet. And in still others, a large, heroic building is silhouetted against a nighttime sky or surrounded by an aureole of light. But unlike his contemporaries' responses to New York—for example, Marin's exuberant watercolors of the Woolworth Building or Stieglitz's photographs of the view from his window in the Shelton Hotel—none of Walkowitz's drawings refers to an actual building or even a neighborhood. In fact, his images (which he started to produce shortly after his return from Europe in 1907) all celebrate a "future New York"—striving, cacophonous, dense, exhilarating, alarming.

In the Atheneum's version, Walkowitz puts his skyscrapers onstage. The buildings are arrayed behind a jagged, proscenium-like frame and seem to jostle and shove one another for more prominence in the space. At the same time, a host of thick, irregular lines, tubular forms (are they meant to be horns? Van Vechten's sewer pipes?), and staccato pencil marks spill forward across the apron of the stage, suggesting a stream of pedestrians, or vehicles, or the remains of a ticker-tape parade. The drawing was undoubtedly made quickly: the lines are rough, even crude; the contrasts in tone are perfunctory. Yet Walkowitz's elemental, gestural style is powerfully evocative, especially as he used it for drawing after drawing: repetition makes his futurist vision seem inevitable. As Van Vechten noted, "The emotion in these drawings, indeed, is inherent in the city itself."[2]
CT

1. Carl Van Vechten, "Comment," in *Improvisations of New York: A Symphony in Lines*, by Abraham Walkowitz (New York: E. Haldeman-Julius, 1948), n.p.
2. Ibid.

6a and b

Abraham Walkowitz
Isadora Duncan, 1917
Pastel on colored laid paper
(partial watermark: Montgolfier, France)
19 × 12 1/2 in. (48.3 × 31.8 cm)
Signed at lower left, in ink: A WALKOWITZ / 1917
Signed at lower right, in graphite:
A. WALKOWITZ
Ex coll.: the artist
Gift of Abraham Walkowitz, 1949.232

Isadora Duncan, 1917
Pastel on colored laid paper
(partial watermark: Montgolfier, France)
19 × 12 1/2 in. (48.3 × 31.8 cm)
Signed at lower left, in ink: A WALKOWITZ / 1917
Signed at bottom, in graphite: A. WALKOWITZ
Ex coll.: the artist
Gift of Abraham Walkowitz, 1949.233

Abraham Walkowitz was nearly thirty years old and still seeking his own modernist voice when he first saw Isadora Duncan, the captivating pioneer of modern dance, perform at a private salon in Paris in 1907. He attended numerous performances over the next decade and, responding to her celebration of improvisation, emotion, and the body, produced thousands of sketches of her, in charcoal, pen and ink, watercolor, and pastel. He called her his muse (although it is not certain that they ever met[1]), and from about 1917 on, when New York's Daniel Gallery mounted a solo exhibition of his images of Isadora Duncan,[2] these would be the works for which he was best known.

Walkowitz claimed to have given away countless Duncan drawings—they were "like my visiting card," he said[3]—and in 1949 he donated a group of one hundred of them to the Atheneum. These range in date from 1908 to 1931; among the most elegant are four pastels on colored paper produced in 1917. Two of the four are included in this exhibition.

Walkowitz placed Duncan at the top of his pantheon of creative Americans ("Her body was music. It was a body electric, like Walt Whitman"[4]). His images of her are not portraits—like Auguste Rodin, whose drawings these resemble,[5] he seldom suggested facial features—rather, they are an attempt to convey the fluid, intuitive, and wholly natural quality of her performance. Here he shows her dressed in a filmy, vaguely Grecian costume, its transparency indicated by a few soft strokes of pale yellow chalk. The gown parts to reveal her muscular thighs. In one pastel, her hair is neatly arranged in a bun. In the other, her head is thrown back so wild strands of hair stream behind her, and her bright red scarf—a signature prop—billows out like a sail in the wind. Walkowitz uses blunt contour lines and rather patchy modeling in black and white chalk to detach Isadora's body from the colored paper that defines both background and figure. This method of suggesting three-dimensionality is a modernist revision of traditional life-drawing techniques, although Isadora never posed for Walkowitz—his images of her were made from memory.[6] In one pastel, her arms stretch behind her and her leg is raised high and twisted forward in a pose that seems both archaic in its contortions and jazzy in its rhythms. In the other pastel, her body and scarf form an expressive unit that is centered on the sheet yet pushes beyond its boundaries. Her figure is balanced like a work of Hellenistic sculpture yet threatens to move out of sight like a character in a film. With these combinations of the classical and the modern, the measured and the ecstatic, Walkowitz evokes "the body electric," expressing both Isadora's vitality and the ephemeral nature of her dance.
CT

1. As suggested by Virginia Zabriskie, Walkowitz's dealer at the end of his career, Walkowitz's was "a one-sided romance from his seat in the theater." Zabriskie, quoted in Eric Zafran, *Ballets Russes to Balanchine: Dance at the Wadsworth Atheneum* (Hartford, Conn.: Wadsworth Atheneum, 2004), 42.
2. *Interpretation of the Dances of Isadora Duncan*, Charles Daniel Gallery, New York, 12 April–12 May 1917.
3. A tape-recorded interview with Abraham Walkowitz conducted by Abram Lerner and Bartlett Cowdrey in New York, 8 and 22 December 1958, published in the *Journal of the Archives of American Art* 9 (January 1969): 15.
4. Ibid.
5. Walkowitz knew Rodin in Paris. The inspiration of the French master's drawings was undoubtedly reinforced by the exhibitions of his works on paper at Alfred Stieglitz's gallery 291 in 1908 and 1910.
6. Martica Sawin, "Abraham Walkowitz, Artist," *Arts Magazine* 33 (March 1964): 44. Sawin quotes Walkowitz: "I never worked from posed models. I learned that when I visited Rodin's studio. Rodin always had his models walk around. That's the first principle of life: you must be free to see."

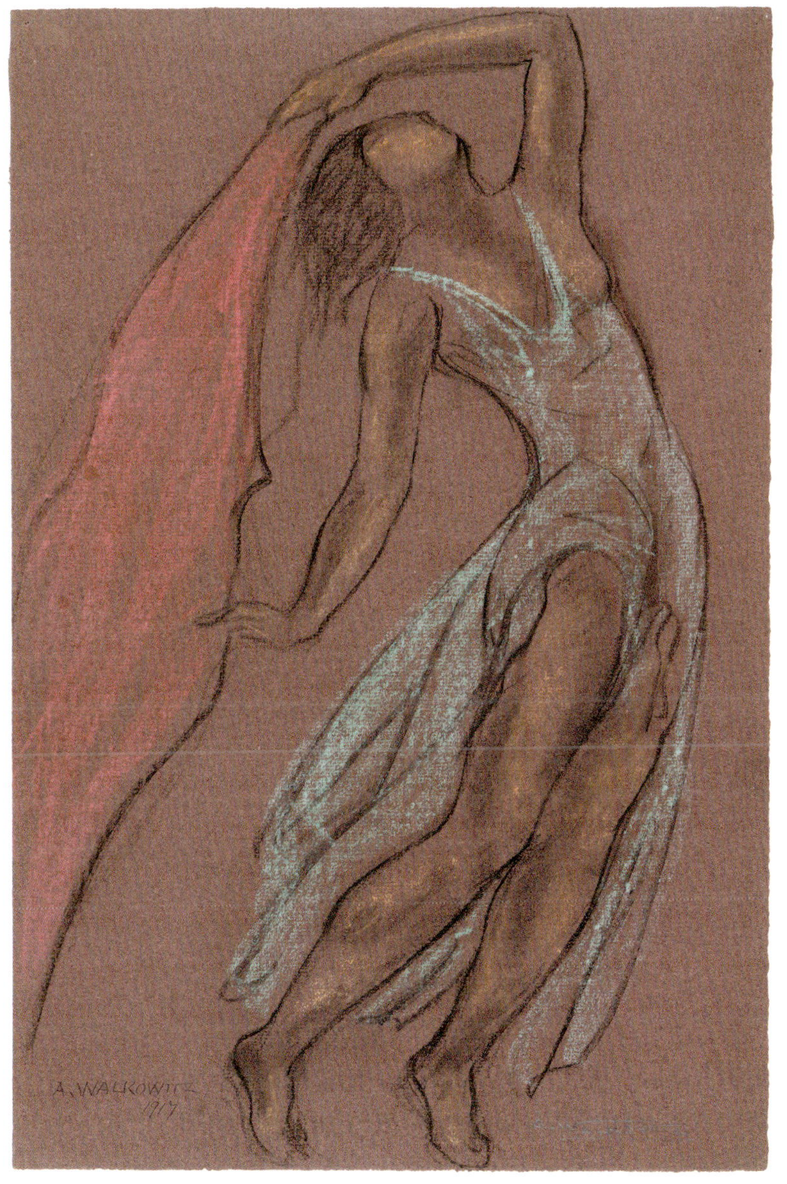

Cat. 6a

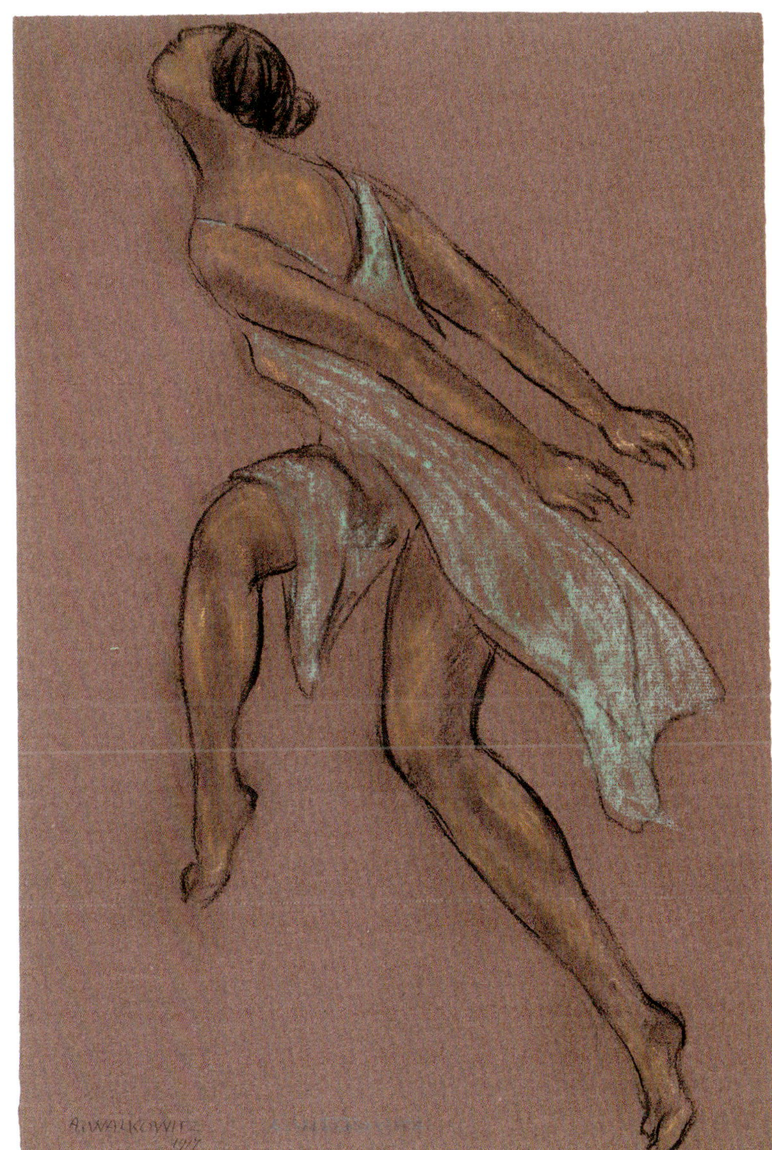

Cat. 6b

Max Weber

Born in Belostok, Russia
(now Białystok, Poland), 1881;
died in Great Neck, New York, 1961

Max Weber and his family immigrated to the United States from Russia in 1891 and settled in Brooklyn. He struggled through poverty to receive an education in art, studying at the Pratt Institute, on a scholarship, where he was mentored by Arthur Wesley Dow. Dow, who had studied with Paul Gauguin, was an influential teacher who championed the use of flat masses of color and a vibrant line. Soon after graduating, Weber moved to Virginia to teach art in public schools and then became head of the drawing and manual training program at the State Normal School in Duluth, Minnesota.

Weber traveled to Paris late in 1905; there he came into contact with the beginnings of the modern movement. He developed a friendship with Henri Rousseau and helped organize a class with Henri Matisse as the instructor. While in Europe, he encountered firsthand the development of the Fauve and Cubist styles and was greatly influenced by Matisse's use of color, Paul Cézanne's use of space, and Pablo Picasso's Cubist theories.

In 1909, Weber returned to New York, where he was championed by Alfred Stieglitz (although the two had a falling-out several years later) and, in an effort to introduce Cubism to American art, began writing essays on art. Weber was instrumental in organizing several key exhibitions at Stieglitz's gallery 291, including shows of his own work. One of these was an important early exhibition of American modernism with his own work and that of Arthur Dove (q.v.), Marsden Hartley, and John Marin (q.v.). During this period, Weber's style fully embraced the Cubist theories of space, color, and form. His early work incorporated the blocky planar forms into his painted figures: the primitive, angular facial features of his figures recall Picasso's *Demoiselles d'Avignon*, completed in 1907. Weber also worked as a sculptor and printmaker, but his preferred medium was oil painting.

In the 1920s and '30s, Weber returned to figuration and began to introduce Jewish themes into his work. Although he was the first artist to be given a retrospective at the Museum of Modern Art (1930), his late work was overshadowed by new developments in American art, including the predominant Abstract Expressionism. Still, he is credited with transforming European modernism, particularly Cubism, into a distinctive American art form. Weber remained an active member in New York art circles and exhibited regularly until his death in 1961.

Select Bibliography

Lloyd Goodrich. *Fifty Years of Painting by Max Weber*. New York: Bernard Danenberg Galleries, 1969.

Alfred Werner. *Max Weber*. New York: Abrams, 1975.

Percy North. *Max Weber: American Modern*. New York: Jewish Museum, 1982.

7 a and b

Max Weber
Three Figures, 1910
Opaque and transparent watercolor on laid paper, laid down to thick paper board
20 × 25 3/4 in. (50.8 × 65.4 cm)
Signed and dated at lower right:
Max Weber '10
Ex coll.: The Downtown Gallery, New York
The Ella Gallup Sumner and Mary Catlin Sumner Collection Fund, 1963.457

Meditation, 1917
Pastel on laid paper
(partial watermark: faint crest visible top right)
24 1/2 × 15 1/4 in. (62.2 × 38.7 cm)
Signed and dated at lower right:
Max Weber '17
Ex coll.: The Downtown Gallery, New York
Ella Gallup Sumner and Mary Catlin Sumner Collection Fund, 1963.456

Three Figures was completed in 1910, the year after Weber returned to New York from Paris. Clearly, the avant-garde paintings of Pablo Picasso and Georges Braque remained fresh in his mind. The compressed grouping of figures with masklike faces reveals Weber's engagement with the early phase of Cubism and primitivism. One of the Cubists' major innovations was breaking down the distinctions between the figure and its surrounding space. Here, Weber compressed three figures into a shallow picture plane; their heads and torsos overlap with one another, almost to the point of confusion. Their angular features are reminiscent of African sculpture, which Weber is known to have acquired for his personal collection.[1]

Many of Weber's compositions from 1910 to roughly 1912 were large-scale works that included compact groups of female nudes, often in groups of three, with stylized features and contorted figures. The boldness of the figures and their close arrangement recall Picasso's influential painting *Les Demoiselles d'Avignon* (1907; Museum of Modern Art, New York).[2] Of note, however, is that Weber retained the integrity of forms in space so that his images appear less perverse and grotesque than Picasso's.[3] In *Three Figures*, for example, the landscape setting is still legible and the women's facial features are less distorted.

By 1917, when he completed *Meditation*, Weber was more daring in his own style, although his work is still reminiscent of that of the Cubists. With its pattern of geometric shapes dissolving into one another, *Meditation* is more visually complex than Weber's earlier work. The nude body is depicted from multiple viewpoints simultaneously, formal qualities that were hallmarks of Analytic Cubism. Weber's vertical, fractured form may have been inspired by two works he had the opportunity to see in New York: Picasso's charcoal *Standing Female Nude* (1910; Metropolitan Museum of Art, New York), which was exhibited at Stieglitz's gallery 291 in 1911, and Marcel Duchamp's *Nude Descending a Staircase, No. 2* (1912; Philadelphia Museum of Art) which debuted at the Armory Show in 1913. Weber's use of pastel to shade the area around the figure is evocative of Picasso's charcoal drawing, and though less directly related, the deconstruction of the female form brings to mind Duchamp's famous nude. These two works demonstrate how Weber responded to different variations of Cubism but discovered his own distinct artistic voice in the process.
ECM

1. Alfred Werner, *Max Weber: Early Works on Paper* (New York: Bernard Danenberg Galleries, 1971), 2. Also at this time Weber continued to visit the ethnographic section of the American Museum of Natural History in New York. Michael FitzGerald notes that Weber owned a Congolese statue that he bought during his stay in France. Michael FitzGerald, *Picasso and American Art* (New Haven, Conn.: Yale University Press, 2006), 23.
2. Weber met Picasso in 1908 at Gertrude Stein's studio and may have seen the original painting while in Paris at that time. He may also have seen a reproduction in New York in Gelett Burgess's article "The Wild Men of Paris," *Architectural Record* 27 (May 1910): 400–414.
3. Percy North, *Max Weber: American Modern* (New York: Jewish Museum, 1982), 37.

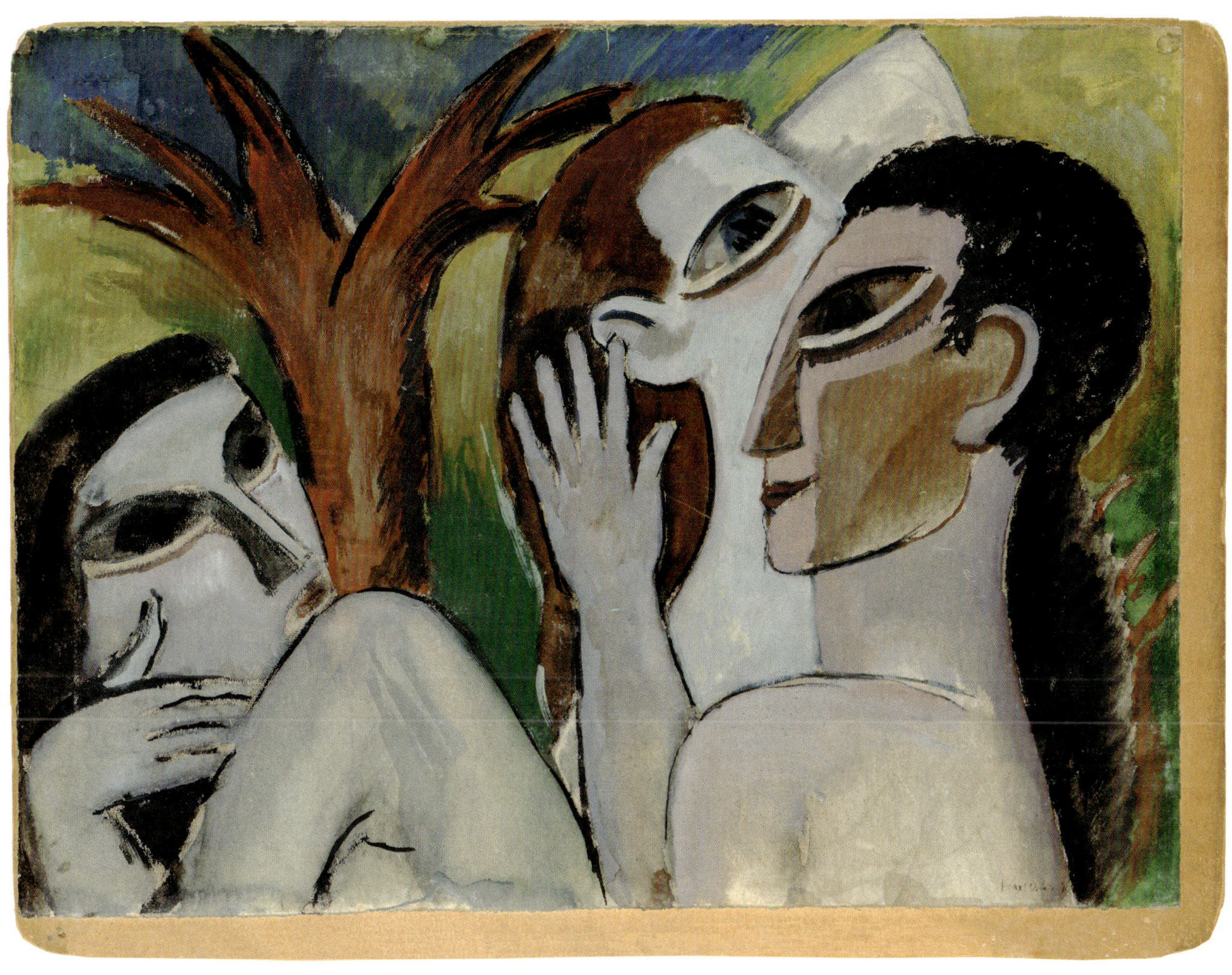

Cat. 7a

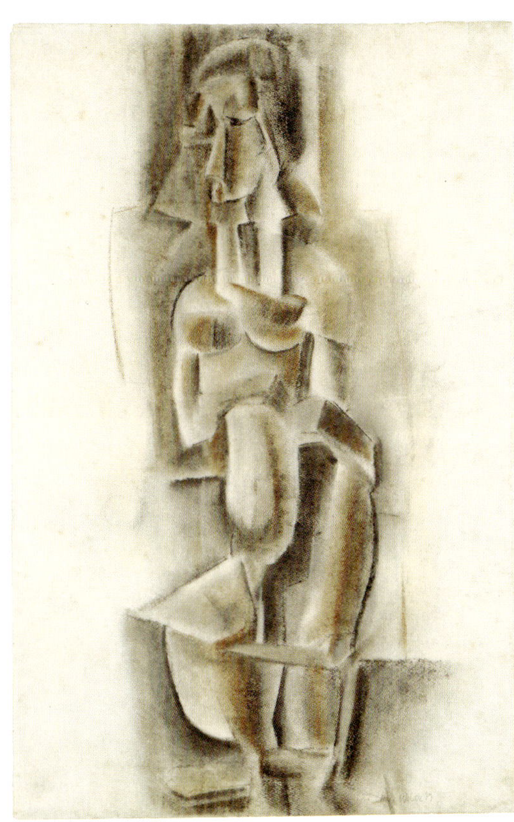

Cat. 7b

Joseph Pennell

Born in Philadelphia, 1857;
died in New York, 1926

Joseph Pennell was born into a Philadelphia Quaker family; his parents wished him to pursue a career in business, but he chose to be an artist, attending evening classes at the Philadelphia Industrial Art School and at the Pennsylvania Academy of the Fine Arts, where he took Thomas Eakins's life class. In 1880 he worked as a magazine illustrator, and by 1883 he left for Europe, making London a home base until 1917, when he returned to the United States.

Pennell was influenced by the work of James McNeill Whistler, with whom he became a close friend. With his wife Elizabeth Robins (whom he married in 1884), Pennell wrote a biography of Whistler (published in 1908) and collected his prints, books, and letters, which he donated to the Library of Congress. He wrote a number of additional publications, including *Pen Drawing and Pen Illustration* (1899), and *Modern Illustration* (1895). Pennell became a leading sketch artist and printmaker during the course of his career, specializing in architectural subjects. As a result, he became a successful illustrator for travel literature. He also executed pen-and-ink drawings, watercolors, and pastels. His works won numerous medals at international exhibitions, including the Paris Exposition of 1900 and the St. Louis Exposition of 1904.

In 1917 Pennell settled in New York, where he used his substantial talents as a printmaker and illustrator to depict the architecture of New York, including the rise of skyscrapers, as well as nearby industrial subjects such as the Pittsburgh steel mills, wartime munitions plants, and shipyards.

Select Bibliography

Frederick Keppel. *Joseph Pennell: The Print Collector's Bulletin*. 3d ed. New York: Frederick Keppel, 1909.

Elizabeth Robins Pennell. *The Life and Letters of Joseph Pennell*. 2 vols. Boston: Little, Brown, 1925.

Joseph Pennell. *The Adventures of an Illustrator*. Boston: Little, Brown, 1925.

8

Joseph Pennell
Building New York, c. 1920
Transparent and opaque watercolor with chalk on laid paper (with Ingres watermark; sketchbook page with perforations along top)
11 3/4 × 8 3/4 in. (29.9 × 22.1 cm)
Inscribed on verso in ink: Building New York
Ex coll.: Philip L. Goodwin, New York, by 1923
Gift of Philip L. Goodwin, 1930.7

Joseph Pennell devoted his artistic career to etching and illustration, with a specialization in representations of architecture. He was particularly successful in illustrating popular travel literature, which led to extensive travel abroad and extended residency in foreign cities—for example, he lived in London from 1884 to 1917. But Pennell was frequently inspired by New York. He lived there off and on with his wife, Elizabeth Robins Pennell, over the course of his career; after the war, he settled there from about 1920 until the end of his life. The artist was especially interested in New York's skyscrapers, to which he devoted numerous print series. Pennell wrote of the city, "New York rises a vision, a mirage of the lower bay. . . . The color by day more shimmering than Venice, by night more magical than London. In the morning the mountains of buildings hide themselves to reveal themselves in the rosy steam clouds that chase each other across their heights . . . with the city . . . finer than any in any world that ever existed."[1]

In the past, Pennell has been written off as lacking in true talent as a draftsman, but this work demonstrates his mastery of the watercolor medium and ranks as one of his most loosely executed and painterly works.[2] Around this time, Pennell indicated in his autobiography that the "drawings of New York, I did for myself . . . with no authors to bother me, and they were issued without text in The Century [magazine]."[3] The artist used loosely applied watercolor, in shades of blue, green, and purple, to produce the forms of rising skyscrapers in the distance. The view is from Liberty Street in lower Manhattan, looking west past Nassau Street to Broadway. *Building New York*, which depicts the Federal Reserve Bank under construction, was likely painted in 1920, the year that the building was completed.[4] The lively street activity in the foreground shows crowds of pedestrians indicated with thickly applied black strokes; an automobile; and heavy equipment, including tall cranes used to construct the steel frame of the building. The center of the composition focuses on a cloud of white steam, executed in thickly applied opaque watercolor. The steam emerges from a black pipe, drawing the viewer's eye to the lower portion of the building site. Rapidly scribbled black charcoal lines in the foreground emphasize the vitality and pace of a large city. The skyscrapers directly behind the Federal Reserve Building chronicle the recent building program of lower Manhattan: at the far left is the Singer Building (completed in 1908—and demolished in 1968); in the center is the Liberty Tower (completed in 1911); and to the right is the Woolworth Building (completed in 1913).[5]

Building New York was acquired by Philip L. Goodwin, a New York architect most famous for the Museum of Modern Art, which he designed with Edward Durrell Stone in 1939 (see Elizabeth Mankin Kornhauser, "Galvanizing Hartford," in this volume). Given Goodwin's profession, and the fact that he was also an admirer of American works on paper, it is not surprising that the subject of this work interested him. He offered to lend a work by Pennell (likely this one) to the Atheneum in 1923 for a show that he proposed of watercolors and drawings, and later made a gift of it to the museum in 1930.[6]
EMK

1. Reproduced in Frederick Keppel, *Joseph Pennell: The Print Collector's Bulletin*, 3d ed., Dec. 28, 1909 (New York: Frederick Keppel, 1909), 35–36.
2. In Sadakichi Hartmann's survey *A History of American Art* (Boston: L. C. Page, 1902), 2:139, Pennell is described as "skillful, but without much individuality," and the artist was dismissed as "never a highly gifted or original artist" in Theodore E. Stebbins Jr., *American Master Drawings and Watercolors* (New York: Harper and Row, 1976), 258.
3. Joseph Pennell, *The Adventures of an Illustrator* (Boston: Little, Brown, 1925), 316.
4. Carol Willis, Skyscraper Museum, New York, to Erin Monroe, 1 August 2008, curatorial files, Wadsworth Atheneum.
5. I am indebted to Carol Willis, Skyscraper Museum, New York, for lending her expertise in identifying the buildings.
6. Philip L. Goodwin to Charles A. Goodwin, 20 February 1923, Wadsworth Atheneum Archives.

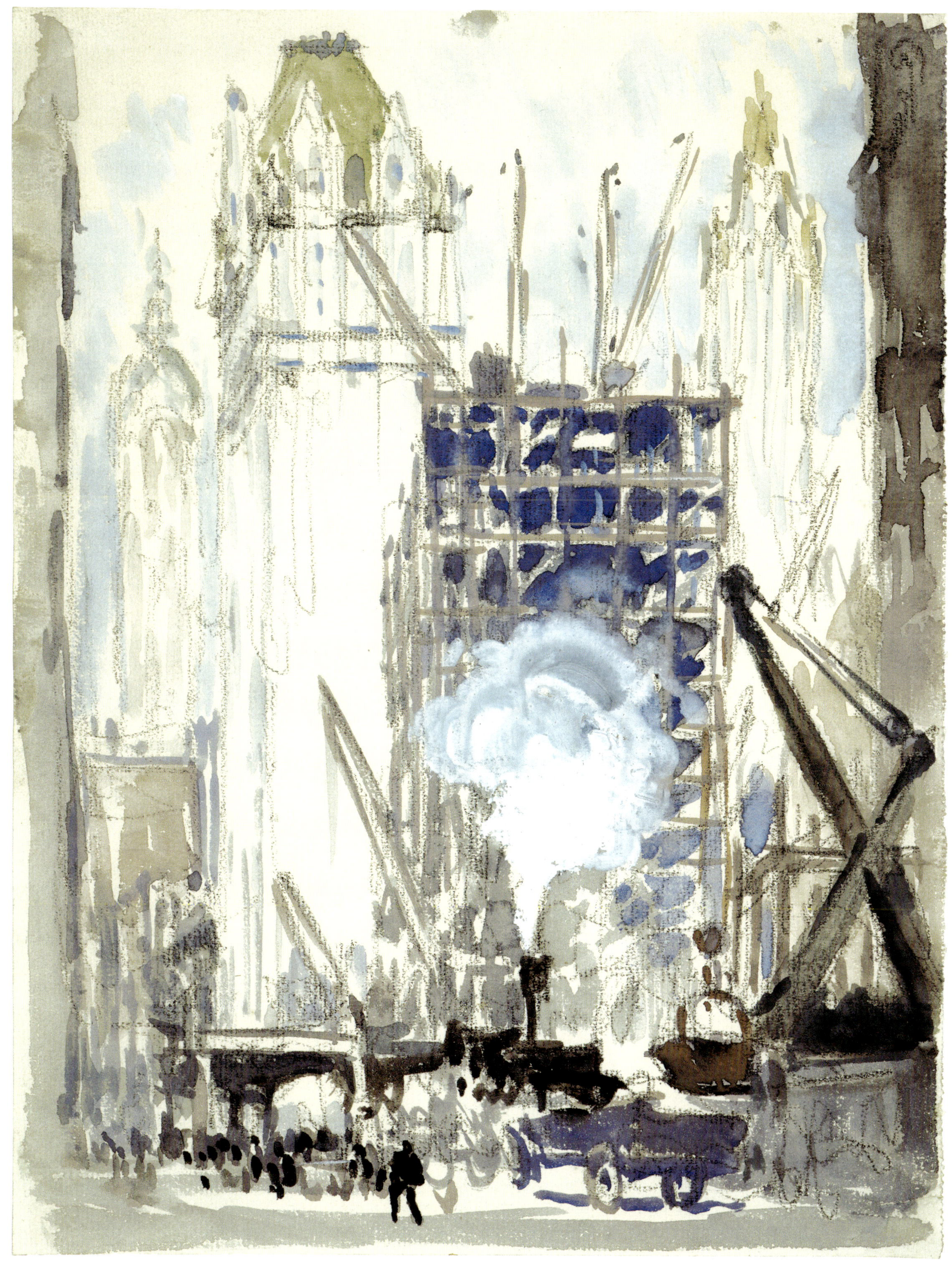

Cat. 8

John Marin

Born in Rutherford, New Jersey, 1870;
died in Cape Split, Maine, 1953

In a career spanning half a century, John Marin became one of the most acclaimed modern artists in America. He worked briefly as an architect before studying at the Pennsylvania Academy of the Fine Arts from 1899 to 1901, under Thomas P. Anshutz, William Merritt Chase, and Hugh Breckenridge. He also studied at the Art Students League in New York before departing for a lengthy European sojourn, from 1905 to 1910, where he was exposed to modern European art and formed important associations with the avant-garde. He exhibited his works—reminiscent of the work of James McNeill Whistler—in the Paris Salons. In 1909 he met Edward Steichen, who introduced him to Alfred Stieglitz. When Marin returned to the United States with a pronounced talent as a watercolorist, Stieglitz, as his dealer and friend, promoted him and presented an exhibition of his watercolors nearly every year.

Although he painted in oil, Marin is celebrated primarily for his watercolors and etchings. Like Stieglitz and other artists in the dealer's circle, Marin found inspiration in both urban and rural landscapes, and he divided his time between New York and rural locations, the coast of Maine in particular. His earlier work as an architectural draftsman may have contributed to his fascination with the buildings of New York; he explored such monuments as the Woolworth Building in dynamic semi-abstract drawings, watercolors, and prints.

During the 1920s Marin's style became expressive and abstract as he continued to depict both urban and rural subjects. He revealed a sensitivity toward and a love of nature, traveling mainly in the summers to the Hudson River Valley and the Adirondacks, New York; to Taos, New Mexico; and to various places in New England, where he focused on landscape as his primary interest. In the tradition of Winslow Homer and Marsden Hartley, Marin's name became associated with the state of Maine, where, beginning in 1914, he spent part of every year until his death. He painted landscapes as well as seascapes, which became an increasingly important motif for his art. During the 1930s, Marin was interested in the circus as a subject, and he executed images of ringmasters, trapeze artists, lions, and elephants in his drawings and watercolors.

Marin received great acclaim during his sixty-six years as a working artist, participating in the most important art exhibitions of the time, including the Armory Show of 1913; the Forum Exhibition of Modern American Painters of 1916; the Brooklyn Museum's survey of contemporary American watercolors in 1921; and, finally, a major retrospective of his work at the Museum of Modern Art in 1936. He was remarkably prolific, executing over three thousand drawings, watercolors, etchings, and oils. He enjoyed the sustained patronage of such major collectors of contemporary American art as Philip L. Goodwin, Ferdinand Howald, Duncan Phillips, and Alfred Stieglitz (see Elizabeth Mankin Kornhauser, "Galvanizing Hartford," in this volume). Toward the end of his career, he was named America's number-one artist by a poll conducted in 1948 by *Look* magazine. In 1950, he was featured at the twenty-fifth Venice Biennale.

Select Bibliography

John Marin Watercolors, Oil Paintings, Etchings. New York: Museum of Modern Art, 1936.

Dorothy Norman. *The Selected Writings of John Marin.* New York: Pelligrini and Cudahy, 1949.

Sheldon Reich. *John Marin Drawings, 1886–1951.* Salt Lake City: University of Utah Press for the University of Utah, Museums of Fine Arts, 1969.

Carl Zigrosser. *The Complete Etchings of John Marin.* Philadelphia: Philadelphia Museum of Art, 1969.

Sheldon Reich. *John Marin: A Stylistic Analysis and Catalogue Raisonné.* 2 vols. Tucson: University of Arizona Press, 1970.

Ruth E. Fine. *John Marin.* New York: Abbeville Press in association with the National Gallery of Art, 1990.

9

John Marin
Downtown New York, c. 1913
Graphite on wove paper
(watermark: Berkshire Bond)
10 × 8 1/4 in. (25.4 × 21 cm)
Signed at lower left: Marin
Ex coll.: with Edith Halpert,
the Downtown Gallery, New York, by 1960
Purchased through the gift of the Henry and Walter Keney Fund, 1960.226

While primarily celebrated for his watercolors, John Marin was a talented draftsman who created drawings throughout his career. Although he did not execute these works for exhibition, he did sign his drawings consistently, and he often used them as studies for his watercolors and prints.[1] Marin began making drawings of New York City as early as 1910, and beginning in 1912, he focused his attention on the city as his prime subject in series that explored the rapid building of modern New York. As he observed at the time, "The city was passing through a corporate convulsion, a frightening and bewildering kind of high-tensioned life. It was like watching the first days of creation."[2]

By 1913, the year that *Downtown New York* was probably executed, Marin had begun his series of drawings, watercolors, and etchings of the Woolworth Building (under construction from 1910 to 1913) and the Brooklyn Bridge. Both of these series are celebrated for their energy and dynamic execution, including slashes and calligraphic squiggles that show a large degree of abstraction.[3] The Atheneum's drawing, executed on thin paper, is more precisely rendered with a finer line than that seen in the majority of his New York drawings from this period. Marin combined thin and thick straight lines with subtle areas of shading.

Here the artist has taken great care in delineating architectural details. In 1913, he and his wife lived on the corner of Twenty-eighth Street and Fourth Avenue, in the upper two floors of a house, where Marin worked in a makeshift studio.[4] While it is difficult to identify the specific buildings in the drawing, it is possible that the view is from out the artist's second-story studio window. In this view, Marin contrasts old and new New York. Recently constructed skyscrapers flank either side of the composition, rising above the picture plane. These are contrasted with older, more human-scale low-rise buildings that recede in the distance. A clothesline draped with laundry, running across the foreground, further emphasizes the juxtaposition of old and new. A large sun is seen in the distant sky—the sun would appear in successive drawings and watercolors of New York (see cats. 11, 12).

This drawing relates to the photographs of Marin's friend and dealer, Alfred Stieglitz. For example *From the Back Window—"291" (I)* (1915; Museum of Fine Arts, Boston) also shows a city in rapid transition and contrasts new and old buildings, even including a clothesline with laundry hanging.[5] In a catalogue for one of his many shows at Stieglitz's gallery 291, Marin observed, "I saw great forces at work; great movements; the large buildings and the small; influences of one mass on another greater or smaller mass."[6]

In *Downtown New York*, Marin squared off the image with graphite lines and signed the drawing at lower left, below the line (not a

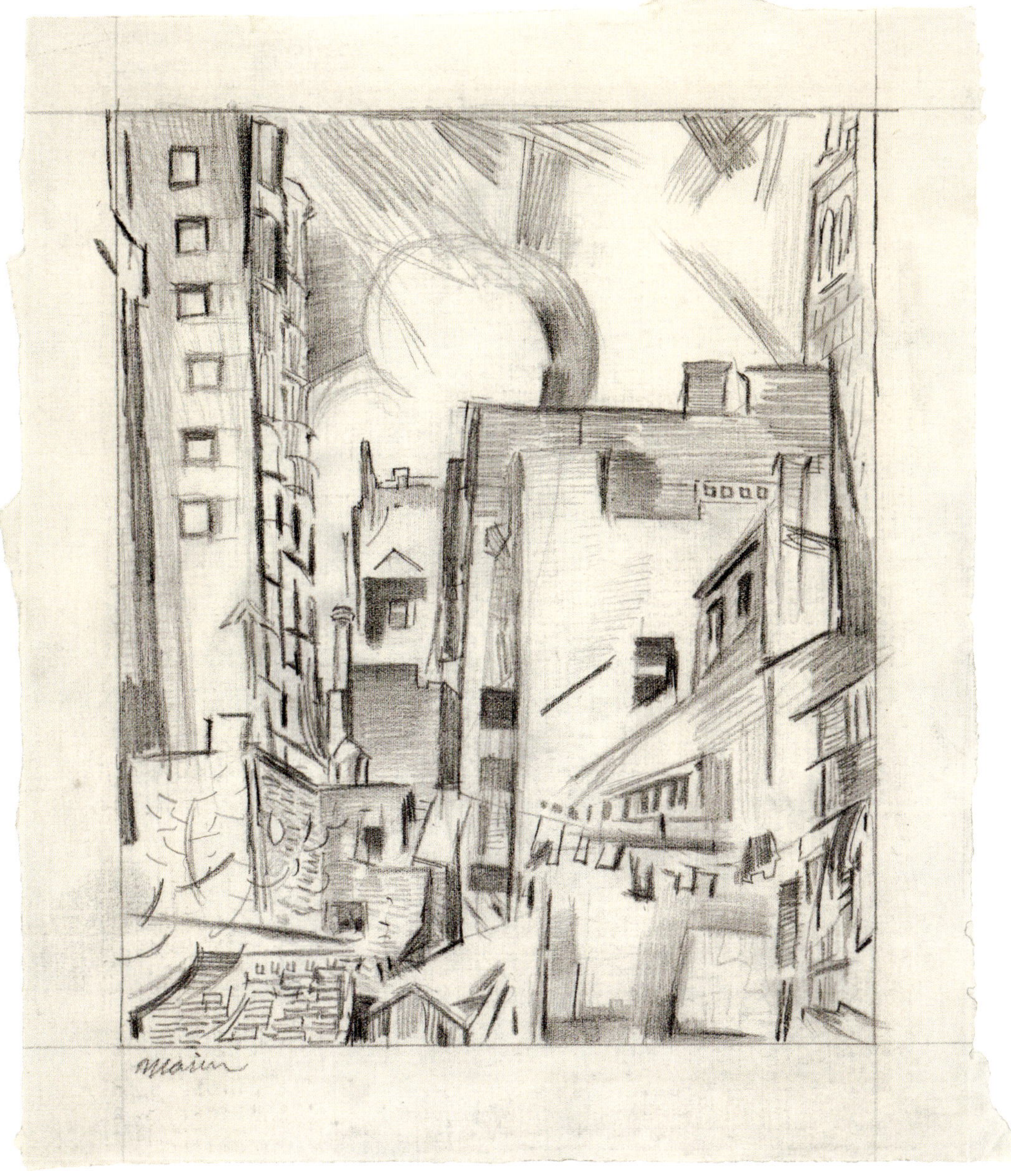

Cat. 9

common practice for the artist's drawings, but seen in many of his etchings). However, this work has not been identified as a source for one of his watercolors or etchings. It was acquired from the Downtown Gallery, New York, in 1960 for $270 by Atheneum director Charles C. Cunningham, who sought to build a comprehensive collection of Marin's works for the American collections (see Elizabeth Mankin Kornhauser, "Galvanizing Hartford," in this volume).
EMK

1. Ruth E. Fine, *John Marin* (New York: Abbeville Press in association with the National Gallery of Art, 1990), 119–20.
2. E. M. Benson, *John Marin: The Man and His Work* (New York: J. J. Little and Ives, 1935), 35.
3. Ibid., 119–65. This drawing does not appear in Sheldon Reich's catalogue raisonné.
4. The date of 1913 for this work was first established by Edith Halpert, who offered it for sale at the Downtown Gallery, New York. The back of the mount on the drawing carries a label, "The Downtown Gallery / John Marin / Downtown New York / 1913 / No. D13 / 1."
5. See Elizabeth Mankin Kornhauser, Amy Ellis, and Maura Lyons, *Stieglitz, O'Keeffe and American Modernism* (Hartford, Conn.: Wadsworth Atheneum, 1999), 36–37.
6. Dorothy Norman, *The Selected Writings of John Marin* (New York: Pelligrini and Cudahy, 1949).

10

John Marin
Big Wood Island, 1914
Opaque and transparent watercolor over graphite, on thick wove watercolor paper laid down on mat board with heat set tissue
14 1/4 × 16 3/8 in. (36.2 × 39.1 cm)
Signed and dated at lower left: Marin / 14
Verso: watercolor diluted with water
Ex coll.: with Alfred Stieglitz, 291, New York, by 1915; acquired by Philip L. Goodwin, New York; to Alan Burroughs, Little Compton, Rhode Island, until 1951
The Henry Schnakenberg Fund, 1951.275

This watercolor of the Casco Bay region was executed during John Marin's first visit to the coast of Maine in August and September 1914. At age forty-four, Marin first stayed at Small Point, a promontory at the eastern edge of Casco Bay; he returned to Maine for nearly every summer after that until the end of his life. According to the artist, he painted this work from "Carrying Place Head at Small Point, Maine," looking toward Big Wood Island.[1] Shortly after his arrival, Marin wrote to Alfred Stieglitz, describing the site as "fierce, relentless, cruel, beautiful, fascinating, hellish, and all the other ish's place. . . . At high tide . . . our little shack is 15 feet from the water on a ledge of rock running down into the water." A letter from Stieglitz, attached to the back of another watercolor, *Small Point, Maine* (1914; private collection), reveals that Marin's first summer in Maine was a very happy and productive time in the artist's career—his wife was pregnant with their first and only child, and the artist's "output was full of unusual buoyancy and happiness."[2]

In this exuberant watercolor of a beautiful, hot summer day on the coast of Maine, Marin uses bright colors of blue, green, and pink in a vigorously executed view of the rock ledges at Carrying Point, looking toward Big Wood Island. Two trees anchor the composition, one at the far left and one just off center. Marin's brushstrokes combine the use of a dry brush technique for the trees, revealing the paper beneath, and wet-on-wet watercolor to capture the luminous blue and greenish-blue ocean. The ledges are defined by lightly brushed pink tones, and the distant island, which links the sea and the sky, includes dark strokes of blue to define the fir trees. In the foreground, Marin added touches of green seaweed and deep blue tidal pools on the ledges. There is a lyrical quality to this work that is characteristic of his early Maine watercolors.[3]

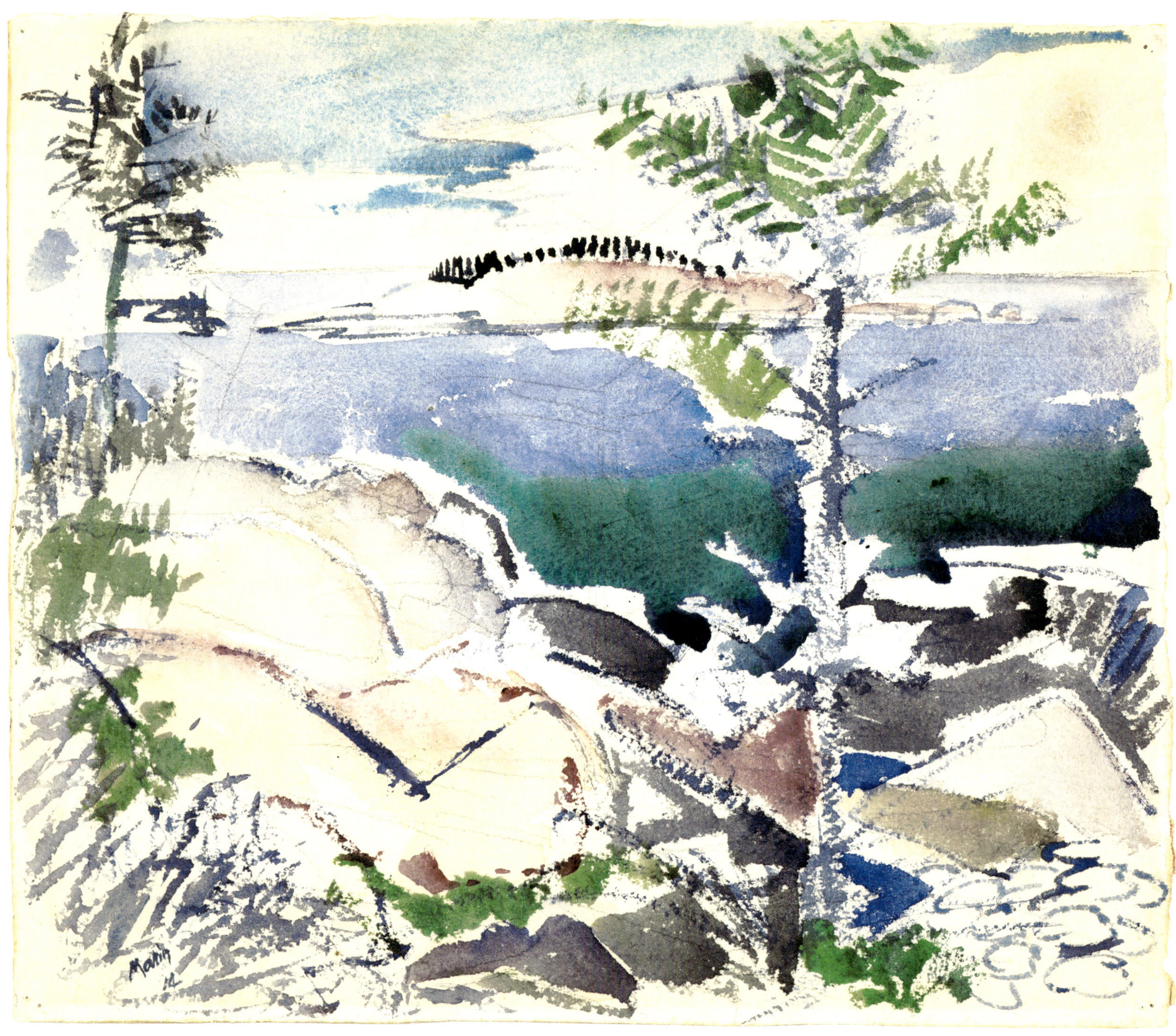

Cat. 10

This watercolor was acquired by Atheneum director Charles C. Cunningham from Alan Burroughs, a scholar of American modernism and the works of Marin in particular. (Burroughs curated a survey of the history of American watercolor for the Whitney Museum of American Art in 1942.) It was a favorite work in Burroughs's collection, as he commented in a letter to Cunningham; "It is a good picture and in a small way an historic one because of its lyric mood. Who would think that the fierce and austere Master had moments of lazing in the sun? And in 1914 at that. I really regret parting with it."[4] Marin used the back of the paper for a watercolor sketch that appears to have been diluted with water, and executed in a vertical format depicting a seascape with rocky ledges in the foreground and a sailboat on the water. This work retains its original wood frame with a simple reverse concave molding, painted white. EMK

1. Edith Halpert to Charles C. Cunningham, 23 February 1952, Wadsworth Atheneum Archives.
2. Sheldon Reich, *John Marin: A Stylistic Analysis and Catalogue Raisonné* (Tucson: University of Arizona Press, 1970), 2:398.
3. Ruth E. Fine, *John Marin* (New York: Abbeville Press in association with the National Gallery of Art, 1990), 168.
4. Alan Burroughs to Charles C. Cunningham, 26 December 1951, Wadsworth Atheneum Archives.

11

John Marin

Movement No. 3, Related to Downtown New York, 1926

Opaque and transparent watercolor over charcoal on thick wove paper, laid down on mat board with heat set tissue

$17\frac{1}{2} \times 22\frac{3}{8}$ in. (44.5 × 56.8 cm)

Signed and dated at lower right: Marin 26

Ex coll.: with An American Place, New York, to 1945; Philip L. Goodwin, New York, 1945–58

Gift of James L. Goodwin and Henry Sage Goodwin from the Estate of Philip L. Goodwin, 1958.229

In his laudatory review of Marin's exhibition at the Museum of Modern Art in 1936, *New Yorker* columnist Lewis Mumford expressed special enthusiasm for the artist's dynamic vision of New York:

> *No other contemporary has better caught the beat and tempo of the great city: its crazy exultation and its restless surge, the disordered march of slow beats and fast beats, the dead spots that seem an eternity spent on a stalled subway train, and the live spots, so packed with unmanageable vitality that the juice overloads the circuit and causes a blowout.*

The "Movements Related to Downtown New York" and the "Lower Manhattans" he said, "are splendid."[1]

Three watercolors from 1926 bear the title, "Movement Related to Downtown New York." All were shown at Stieglitz's Intimate Gallery in 1927 and again in Marin's retrospective at MoMA. But while associated by title, the watercolors depict different vistas. *Movement No. 1* (Metropolitan Museum of Art, New York) and possibly *Movement No. 2* (fig. 1) are views of Lower Manhattan from the Hudson River, with the newly completed Telephone Building dominating the skyline.[2] *Movement No. 3*, while sharing certain compositional features with *Movement No. 2*, nonetheless depicts the other side of Manhattan, that is, the skyscrapers visible from the East River. Marin frequently returned to successful compositions at various points in his career. When in 1932 he reprised *Movement No. 3*, the most graphic and jazzy work of the 1926 group, he called the new watercolor *Region of Brooklyn Bridge Fantasy* (fig. 2). The title not only identifies the location of Marin's scene but also clarifies the meaning of the parallel

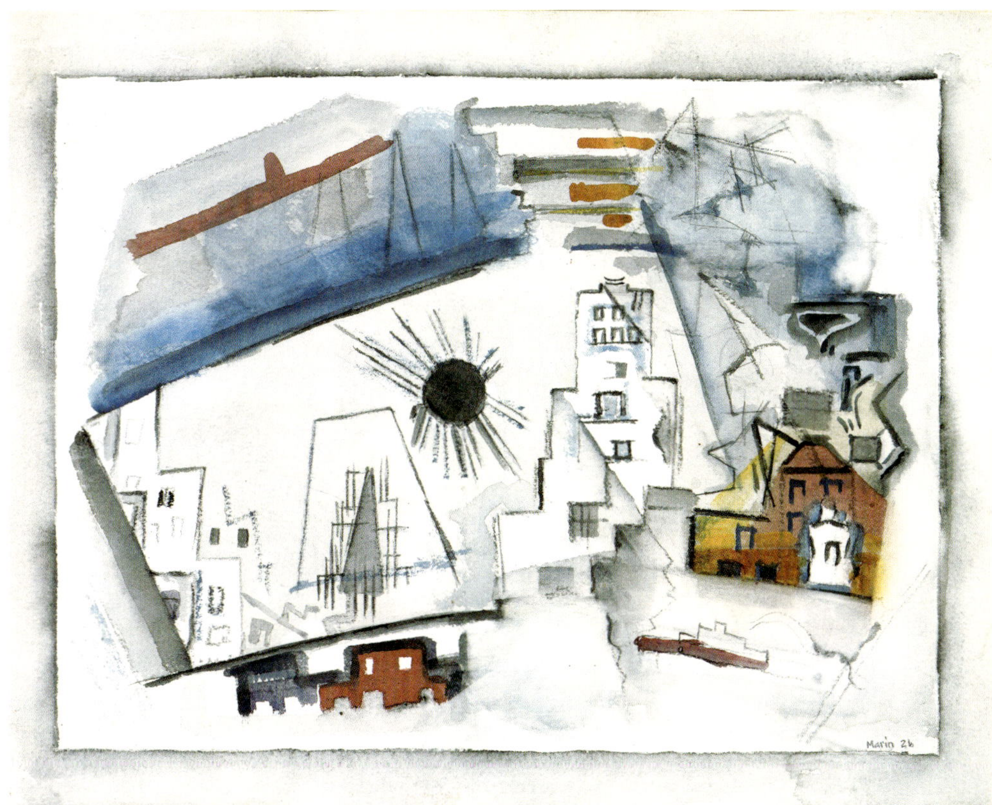

Fig. 1. John Marin, *Related to Downtown New York, Movement Number 2, The Black Sun*, 1926. Watercolor and charcoal on wove paper, $22 \times 27\frac{3}{4}$ in. (55.9 × 70.5 cm). The Metropolitan Museum of Art, New York. Alfred Stieglitz Collection, 1949, 49.70.135

Fig. 2. John Marin, *Region of Brooklyn Bridge Fantasy*, 1932. Watercolor on paper, $22 \times 28\frac{3}{16}$ in. (55.9 × 71.6 cm). Whitney Museum of American Art, New York. Purchase, 49.8

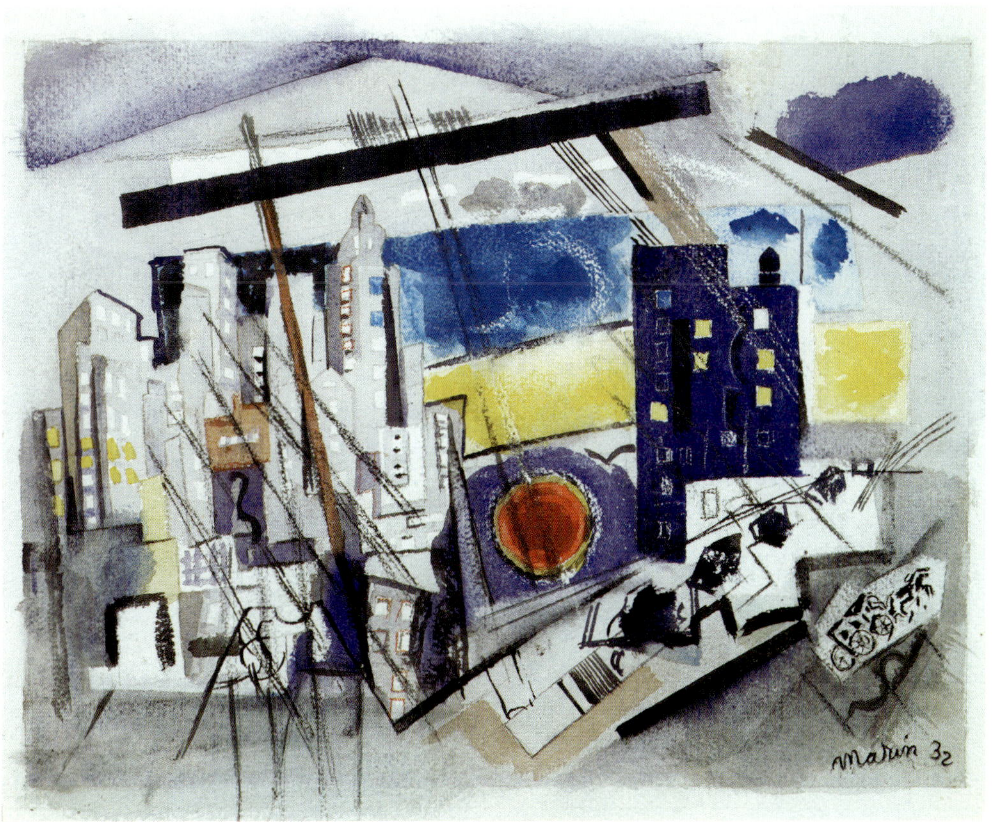

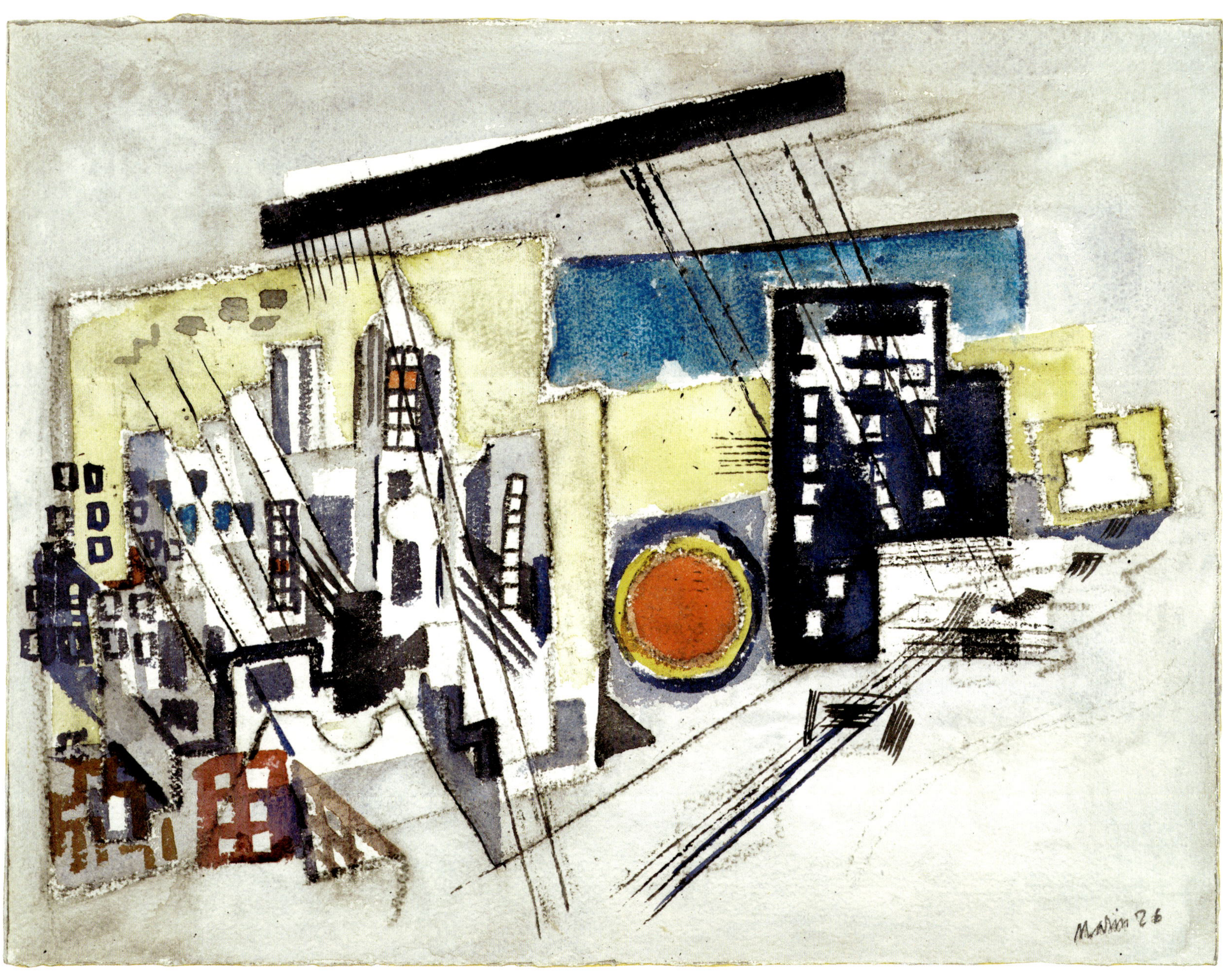

Cat. 11

lines slanting down from a heavy black bar in the Atheneum's watercolor: they represent the cables of the Brooklyn Bridge, and were one of Marin's favorite ways of framing a view (see also cat. 12).

There are otherwise no obvious landmarks in *Movement No. 3*; the watercolor is a brilliant exercise in geometric rhythms. The building at right appears as a generalized, flat, boxy shape colored a deep blue. Balancing it on the left side of the picture is a "disordered march" of buildings that evoke the graduated pipes of a calliope more than a progression of skyscrapers. At far left, windows float free of buildings and dance on the picture surface. The image is concentrated, taut: there is little sense of ground, sky, or atmosphere. Even the sun–which in *Movement No. 2* appears as a strange black orb whose rays nonetheless seem to illuminate the landscape–is here colored like a target and placed quite low in the picture space. Returning to the design in 1932, Marin retained all the outlines of the earlier composition but nonetheless evoked a much more naturalistic cityscape, one darker, heavier, and governed by gravity.

The prismatic, angular style of *Movement No. 3* is markedly different from the more organic views of New York Marin produced in the 1910s and equally distinct from his lush, expressive views of Maine. The richness and variety of his work (what Mumford, in the same review, called his "endless invention" and "range of resources"[3]) won him the admiration of many critics. The value Marin's contemporaries placed on his creative diversity is illustrated in a photograph by Ansel Adams of Alfred Stieglitz at An American Place (see Elizabeth Mankin Kornhauser, "Galvanizing Hartford," in this volume, fig. 21). Stieglitz was Marin's great champion, showing his work every year; both artists were mentors to the much younger Adams.[4] In the photograph, Adams shows the elderly Stieglitz working at his desk. On the wall next to the desk, in the place of honor, are two eloquent and stylistically disparate watercolors. Representing Marin's organic side is the dark, brooding *Sea, Green and Brown, Maine* (1937; Art Institute of Chicago). Representing Marin the abstract artist is the intense and graphic *Movement No. 3, Related to Downtown New York*.
CT

1. Lewis Mumford, "John Marin," *New Yorker*, 31 October 1936, reprinted in *Mumford on Modern Art in the 1930s*, ed. Robert Wojtowicz (Berkeley and Los Angeles: University of California Press, 2007), 214.
2. In 1936 Marin returned to the general outlines of *Movement No. 1* in the watercolor *Motive, Telephone Building, New York* (Metropolitan Museum of Art, New York). The location depicted in *Movement No. 2* is less certain. While the white skyscraper's square, set-back profile is reminiscent of the Telephone Building (see commentary by Stephen Rubin in John K. Howat, Rubin, and Victor Koshkin-Youritzin, *American Watercolors from the Metropolitan Museum of Art* [New York: American Federation of Arts in association with Harry N. Abrams, 1991], 178), the diagonals framing the view of the skyline recall the cables of the Brooklyn Bridge.
3. Mumford in *Mumford on Modern Art*, 215.
4. For the relationship between Adams, Stieglitz, and Marin, see Anne Hammond, *Ansel Adams: Divine Performance* (New Haven, Conn.: Yale University Press, 2002), 90–92.

12

John Marin
From the Bridge, N.Y.C., 1933
Opaque and transparent watercolor with charcoal and collage on thick wove paper
21 7/8 × 26 3/4 in. (55.6 × 68 cm)
Signed and dated at lower right: Marin 33
Ex coll.: the artist; with the Downtown Gallery, New York, 1948
The Ella Gallup Sumner and Mary Catlin Sumner Collection Fund, 1948.479

Marin recorded the view of Lower Manhattan through the cables of the Brooklyn Bridge nearly a dozen times and in several media between the mid-1910s and the mid-1940s. Among the oils, watercolors, drawings, and prints in this group are at least four watercolors in which the scene is presided over by a vivid red sun, and in which the composition is divided between a lively cluster of skyscrapers and the equally lively waters of the East River.[1]

In these works a horse, entering the composition from lower right and silhouetted against tall buildings, is used as an emblem of the city's past. The juxtaposition of the horse and cart with New York's ambitious skyline recapitulates a theme beloved of modernists, and one that Marin addressed many times: the coming together of past and present New York.[2] In the watercolors with the red sun, the cables of the Brooklyn Bridge (itself a modernist icon) form a transparent screen between the two worlds. *From the Bridge, N.Y.C.* is the latest and largest of these, and the most complex and technically inventive.

In the Atheneum's watercolor, Marin makes expressive use of scraping out to create an energetic pattern of windows ascending the skyscrapers. He leaves unpainted the area around the sun, which appears all the more fiery in contrast to the white paper. He renders the cables with slashing diagonals that begin as black strokes of paint near the top of the sheet and turn into white, scraped-out lines as they descend. He interweaves charcoal lines with areas of opaque watercolor and with thinned-down washes that he allows to pool and spread. The spots and drips of red pigment at lower left are a further demonstration of the authenticity, the spontaneous passion, of Marin's execution.

What particularly distinguishes this watercolor from the others in the group is Marin's use of collage. The skyscrapers were painted on a second sheet and cut out and pasted here; then an irregular shape, roughly torn from another piece of paper, was attached on top, and the horse and cart painted over that fragment. Marin's means of creating these elements were deliberately chosen: he produced his view of the modern metropolis with a scissors, creating sharp, mechanical edges, while the second element was crafted entirely and obviously by hand, so that the horse and cart appear soft, even ephemeral.

Marin frequently created his own frames, both external and painted on the object, and they complement—and sometimes comment on—the images they contain. Here, he painted long strokes of blue, reddish brown, and celadon around his image to create an internal frame. These successive border lines in alternately deep and soft colors set up a sly allusion to a French mat, whose old-masterish delicacy and pretension are amusingly at odds with the robustness of Marin's execution and the modernity of his theme.

From the Bridge, N.Y.C. was first exhibited in 1948, in a survey of Marin's New York pictures organized by the Downtown Gallery in celebration of the city's Golden Jubilee. Marin's foreword for the show's catalogue describes the dynamic relationship between old and new captured in the watercolor: "I see . . . great movements; the large buildings and the small buildings; the warring of great and small; I can hear the sound of their strife and there is great music being played."[3]
CT

1. The watercolors are *The Red Sun, Brooklyn Bridge* (1922; Art Institute of Chicago); *Lower Manhattan* (c. 1925; formerly collection of E. M. Benson, Philadelphia [current location unknown]); and *From the Bridge* (1931; private collection). Marin also painted two very abstract watercolors in about 1925 (*From Brooklyn Bridge* and *From the Bridge*, both in private collections) that are small and schematic versions of this composition. See Sheldon Reich, *John Marin: A Stylistic Analysis and Catalogue Raisonné* (Tucson: University of Arizona Press, 1970), vol. 2, nos. 22.109, 25.34, 25.35, 25.47, 31.7, and 33.13.
2. The photographer Alfred Stieglitz was one of the first to explore this theme, notably in his 1910 photograph *Old and New New York*.
3. Marin, foreword to *Paintings and Drawings by John Marin: New York—1910–1944* (New York: Downtown Gallery, 1948), quoted in Sam Hunter, "Among the New York Shows," *New York Times*, 15 August 1948.

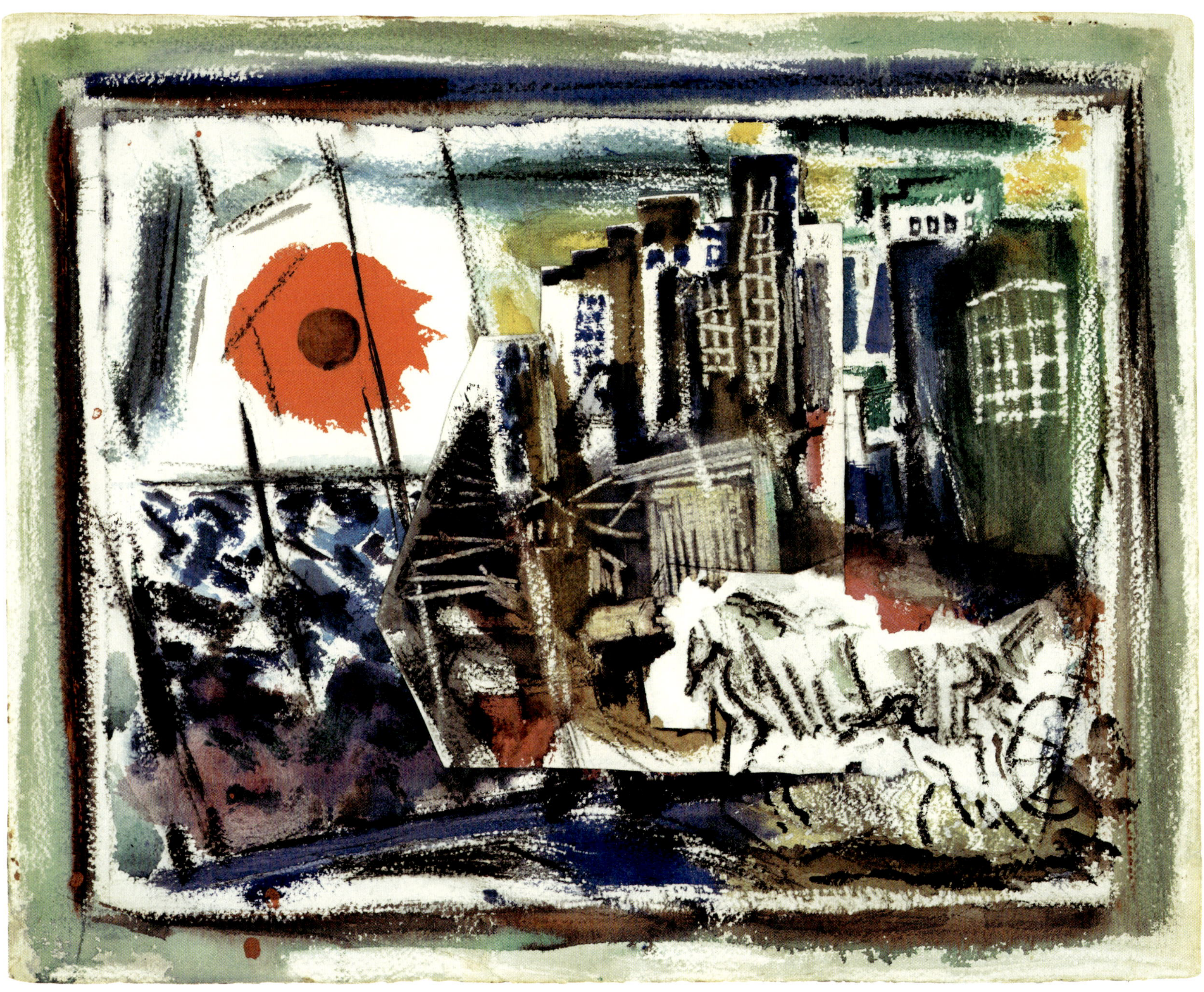

Cat. 12

13

John Marin
Green Sea, Cape Split, Maine, 1941
Opaque and transparent watercolor over graphite on wove paper laid down on illustration board with heat set tissue (board ink stamp: Royal Watercolor Society / All Pure Linen / Handmade paper / Grumbacher)
15 1/2 × 22 1/2 in. (39.4 × 57.2 cm)
Signed and dated at lower right: Marin 41
Ex coll.: with Alfred Stieglitz, An American Place Gallery, New York; collection of Philip L. Goodwin, New York; collection of Arthur P. Day, Connecticut
Bequest of Arthur P. Day, 1952.405

In 1933, Marin, then sixty-three, spent his first summer at Cape Split, Maine. The location was farther down the coast than the Casco Bay area, where he had spent the last twenty years. Despite the greater distance, he was attracted to this new locale and bought a cottage there the following year. He and his family spent their summers there for the rest of his life. Often painting directly from his porch, which was set near the rocks, with the sea beyond, he observed, "Here the Sea is so damned insistent that houses and land things won't appear much in my pictures."[1]

This late watercolor, *Green Sea, Cape Split, Maine*, takes the sea as its primary subject, as is the case with many of Marin's Cape Split works. It is an expressive painting that demonstrates the interaction of Marin's watercolors and oils at this time. Marin began to execute oil paintings in the 1930s, continuing until the end of his career, and most were depictions of the sea. This watercolor bears a strong visual relationship to Marin's oil paintings of the same time. For the Atheneum's watercolor, Marin used heavily applied brushstrokes to capture the vigorous movement of the sea over the rock ledges. Three-quarters of the composition is devoted to the richly colored green waves, with touches of blue and red that swirl around the dark black rocks. The strip of sky above consists of the exposed white paper with streaks of pink and yellow, and pools of black pigment.

This watercolor was included in an exhibition at Stieglitz's gallery An American Place in New York in 1948. The exhibition was devoted to Marin's Maine subjects from this period, and included eight oils and fifteen watercolors. One of the oil paintings in the show was a work titled *My Hell Raising Sea* (1941; collection of Mr. Barney A. Ebsworth), a similar composition of the sea "with its dappled, densely layered paint," including a rich palette and vigorously applied brush strokes capturing the sea, rock ledges, and sky.[2] In both works Marin employs expressive rapid brushstrokes loaded with pigment (whether oil or watercolor), and pares down his forms to near abstraction.
EMK

1. Quoted in Ruth E. Fine, *John Marin* (New York: Abbeville Press in association with the National Gallery of Art, 1990), 229.
2. Ruth Fine, "John Marin: An Art Fully Resolved," in *Modern Art and America: Alfred Stieglitz and His New York Galleries*, ed. Sarah Greenough (Washington, D.C.: National Gallery of Art, 2001), 350–51.

Cat. 13

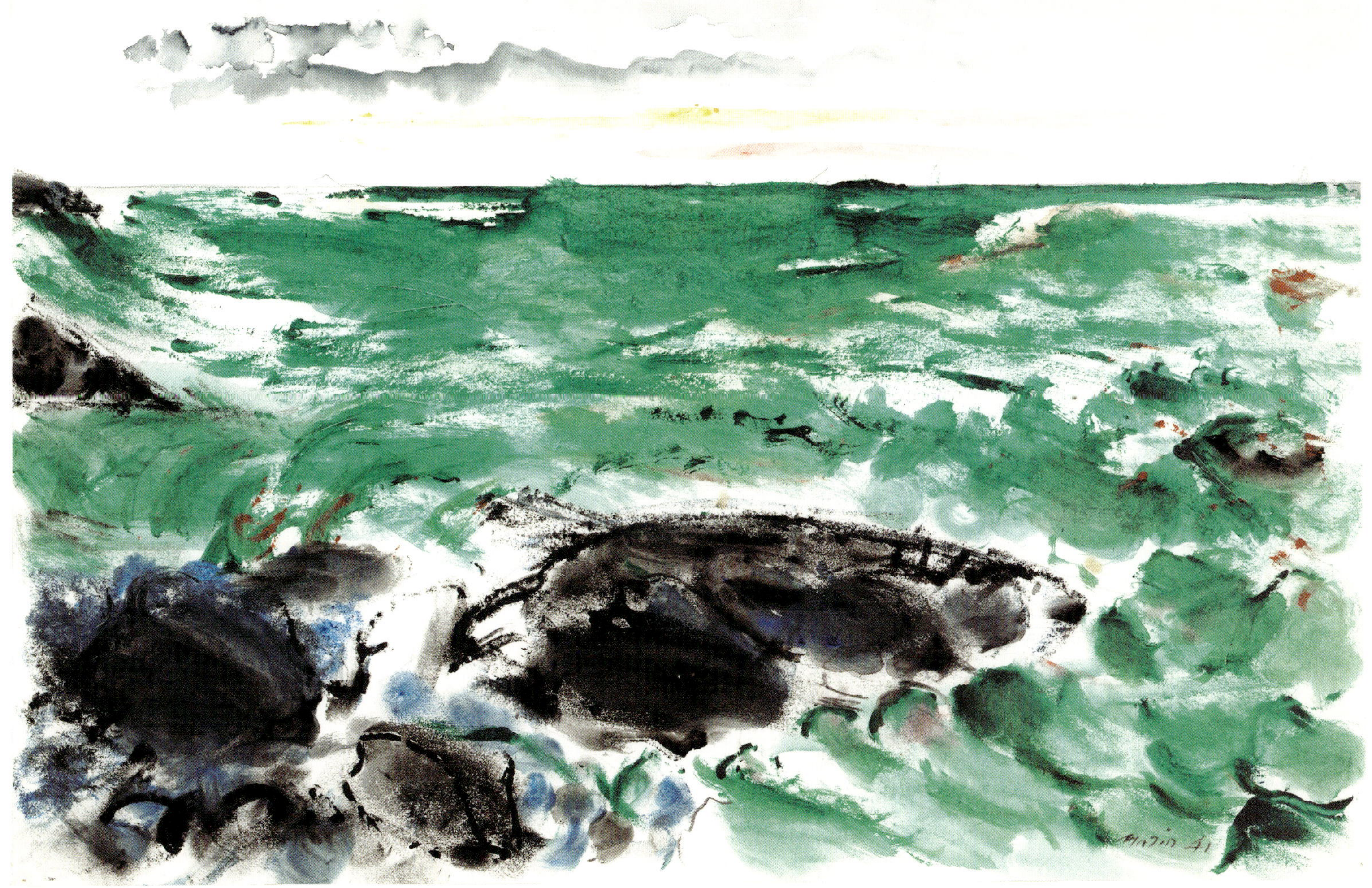

Joseph Stella

Born in Muro Lucano, Italy, 1877;
died in New York, 1946

Italian-born Joseph Stella was a painter, draftsman, and collagist who immigrated to New York at the age of eighteen. He studied at the Art Students League and then with William Merritt Chase at the New York School of Art. His early work is similar to that of his contemporaries of the Ashcan school and focuses on industrial and urban America. His first important commission was to depict the industrial workers in Pittsburgh for the *Survey*, a social reform journal.

A trip to Paris in 1911 exposed him to avant-garde painting and drawing, particularly that of the Futurist artists such as Gino Severini (1883–1966), whose work had the greatest impact on Stella. Beginning in 1913, Stella produced a group of major Futurist-inspired paintings such as *Battle of Lights, Coney Island* and *Mardi Gras* (1913–14; both Yale University Art Gallery, New Haven) that helped established him as one of the leading modern painters in America. He exhibited two paintings in the landmark Armory Show the same year. Stella defied classification, creating almost simultaneously complex, large-scale canvases, small-scale botanical drawings, and experiments in collage. Over the next two decades he returned to Naples several times and visited North Africa and Barbados. The influence of these trips is seen in his painted tropical fantasies of the 1930s and '40s; they are among his most passionate and original works.

Stella exhibited under the auspices of the Société Anonyme, the modern art organization founded by Marcel Duchamp, Man Ray, and Katherine Dreier, in 1920. Dreier became one of Stella's most loyal patrons; their association lasted until his death in 1946. Stella was celebrated in several important posthumous exhibitions, including a solo exhibition of his drawings at the Museum of Modern Art in 1960, and retrospectives at the Whitney Museum of American Art in 1963 and 1994.

Select Bibliography

Irma B. Jaffe. *Joseph Stella*. Cambridge, Mass.: Harvard University Press, 1970.

John I. H. Baur. *Joseph Stella*. New York: Praeger, 1971.

Joann Moser. *Visual Poetry: The Drawings of Joseph Stella*. Washington, D.C.: Smithsonian Institution Press, 1990.

Barbara Haskell. *Joseph Stella*. New York: Harry N. Abrams, 1994.

14

Joseph Stella
Frangipani, c. 1920
Silverpoint and colored crayon over off-white ground on gray card stock
9 5/8 × 7 3/4 in. (24.5 × 19.7 cm)
Signed at lower right: Joseph Stella
Ex coll.: with the Rabin and Krueger Gallery, Newark; with the Felix Landau Gallery, Los Angeles, as of 1969
The Ella Gallup Sumner and Mary Catlin Sumner Collection Fund, 1969.127

Around 1919, Joseph Stella shifted his focus from painting the American industrial scene to drawing botanical subjects. He refined his technique to meet the needs of a more delicate subject matter. As exemplified by *Frangipani*, Stella started working in silverpoint, a method of drawing with pointed rods of silver, and wax crayon. This medium was demanding and impossible to erase or cover up. Nevertheless, Stella went to great lengths to use silverpoint, including making his own specially treated paper.[1] The results are exquisitely detailed drawings of flowers, plants, and birds, in which every blossom, leaf, and feather is carefully observed by the artist.[2]

The fragrant frangipani, also called plumeria, is native to tropical climates. Stella may have selected it as a reminder of his childhood in Italy or from his travels abroad in the early 1920s, which included time in southern Italy, his birthplace. The availability of plants blooming year-round enabled him to draw and paint them throughout the year.[3] Upon his return to New York, Stella frequented the greenhouses of the New York Botanical Garden in the winters for source material.

With little formal training in drawing, Stella brought a fresh, modern approach to the traditional subject matter of still life. His cool, spare style emphasized the pure, simple beauty of the natural world. The delicate cluster of flowers is disconnected from its original setting and thus appears timeless, everlasting. As one scholar observed, "Stella was motivated by an attempt to invent the material world with spiritual significance and to create a symbolic language of form with which to express his personal fantasies, dreams, and visions."[4]

At this point in his career, Stella had developed competing themes in his art. He was equally intrigued by the modern industrial landscape and the natural world, often addressing these different concerns simultaneously. Stella admitted he swung "like a pendulum" from one subject to the other, but found himself continually inspired by botanical subjects. As he explained, "[I was] spurred by inciting expectation of finding thrilling surprises, especially going through the luxuriant gardens of the Bronx, I was seized with a sensual thrill in cutting with the sharpness of my silverpoint the terse purity of the lotus leaves or the matchless stem of a strange tropical plant."[5]
ECM

1. Barbara Haskell, *Joseph Stella* (New York: Harry N. Abrams, 1994), 123. It was the precision that Stella enjoyed. As Haskell points out, it enabled Stella to attain lines of incredible thinness and purity that shimmered when they caught and refracted light. Dissatisfied with commercially prepared papers, Stella prepared his own surface by thinning zinc white gouache to the consistency of light cream and applying it evenly onto paper with a swipe of a brush.
2. John I. H. Baur, *Joseph Stella* (New York: Praeger, 1971), 41.
3. Kate Davis Satz and Richard T. York, *Passion and Reverence: Joseph Stella and the Natural World* (New York: Richard York Galleries, 1998), 7.
4. Joann Moser, *Visual Poetry: The Drawings of Joseph Stella* (Washington, D.C.: Smithsonian Institute Press, 1990), 61.
5. Joseph Stella, "Autobiographical Notes," Joseph Stella Papers, Archives of American Art, New York, roll 346, frames 1260–76; also in Joseph Stella, "Discovery of America: Autobiographical Notes," *Art News* 59 (November 1960): 13.

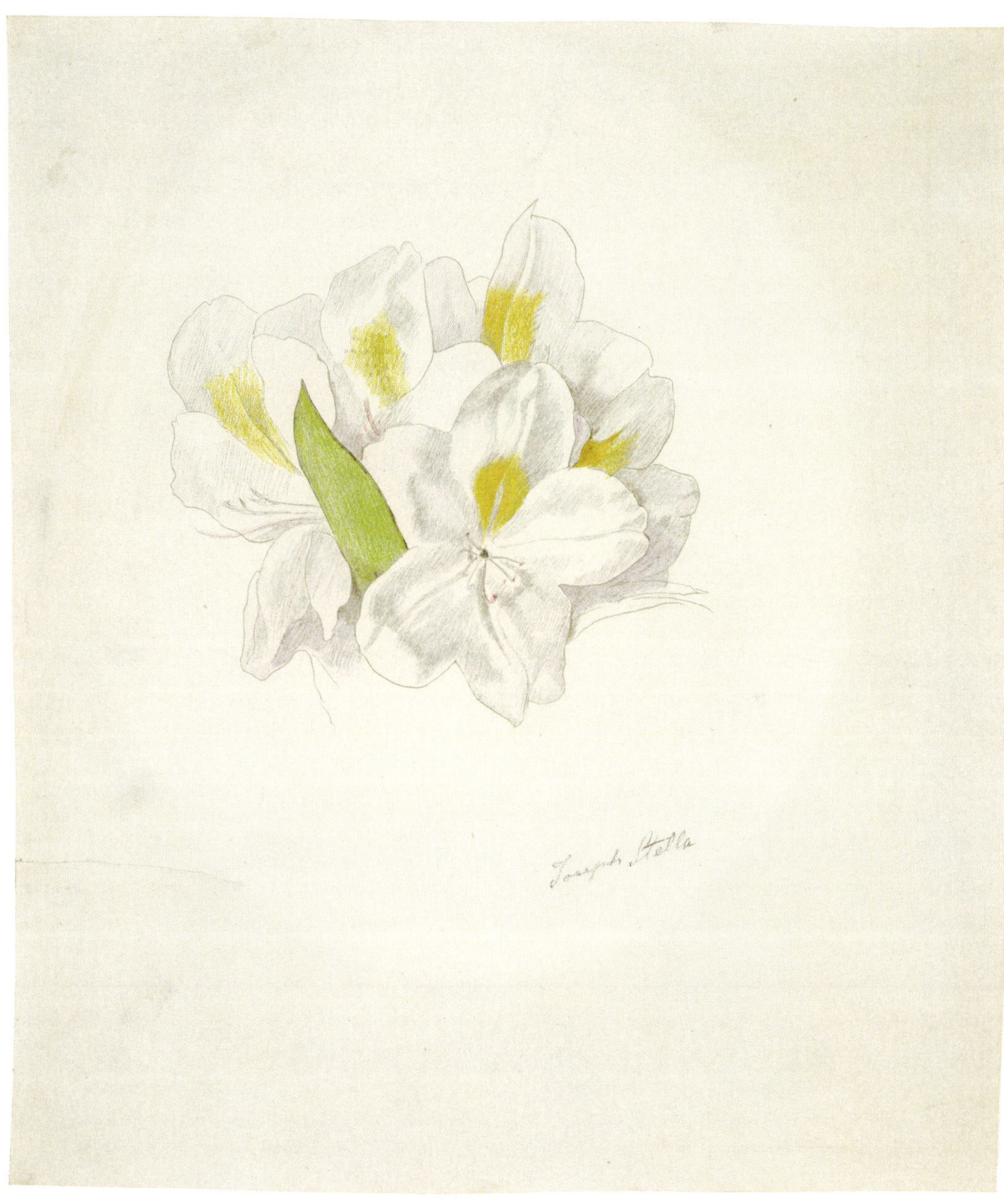

Cat. 14

Georgia O'Keeffe

Born in Sun Prairie, Wisconsin, 1887;
died in Santa Fe, New Mexico, 1986

Georgia O'Keeffe was a leading proponent of modernism in America. Her early charcoal drawings, her watercolors executed between 1915 and 1918, and her later pastels and oil paintings—works executed during a career that lasted for nearly a century—contributed significantly to the advancement of progressive art in the United States. She was a prominent member of the group of modern artists promoted by photographer and gallery owner Alfred Stieglitz, in New York.

O'Keeffe enrolled in the School of the Art Institute of Chicago in 1905 and, two years later, went to New York, where she attended classes at the Art Students League under William Merritt Chase. Between 1908 and 1914 she worked as a commercial illustrator and taught art in the public schools in Amarillo, Texas. O'Keeffe returned to New York in 1914 to study at Teachers College, Columbia University, with Arthur Wesley Dow. Two years later, she accepted a teaching post as head of the art department of West Texas State Normal School, Canyon, Texas. She remained there until 1918, when at Stieglitz's invitation, she returned to New York City to pursue her artistic career full-time.

In 1916, Stieglitz exhibited a group of charcoal drawings by O'Keeffe at his gallery 291, purportedly without the artist's permission. He also mounted her first solo show the following year and, beginning in 1923, exhibited O'Keeffe's works annually at his successive avant-garde galleries until his death in 1946. The couple married in 1924, and Stieglitz championed her work, remaining intimately involved in her career, at times to the dismay of O'Keeffe. Beginning in 1918, O'Keeffe spent summers at the Stieglitz family estate at Lake George in upstate New York, where she developed an interest in nature abstractions, evident in her close-ups of plants and flowers, and evocations of the landscape. While spending winters in New York City, she painted masterly abstract renderings of Manhattan skyscrapers.

In 1929, at the invitation of Mabel Dodge Luhan, O'Keeffe made the first of her nearly annual summer pilgrimages to New Mexico. There, the sun-bleached imagery of the desert transformed her life and art. Captivated by the landscape of the region, she found a measure of artistic independence. She moved to Abiquiu, New Mexico, in 1949, three years after the death of Stieglitz, and stayed there for the rest of her life.

O'Keeffe's art has been the subject of numerous retrospectives, beginning in 1927, at the Brooklyn Museum, and an astonishing number of thematic exhibitions, many organized by the Georgia O'Keeffe Museum Research Center, Santa Fe, New Mexico. Among the many honors conferred on O'Keeffe during her lifetime were memberships in the American Academy of Arts and Letters and the American Academy of Arts and Sciences; she was also awarded the Medal of Freedom in 1977, the nation's highest civilian award. In her later years, O'Keeffe continued to paint and took up pottery, creating pieces that suggest the desert.

Select Bibliography

Lloyd Goodrich and Doris Bry. *Georgia O'Keeffe.* New York: Whitney Museum of American Art, 1970.

Jack Cowart and Juan Hamilton. *Georgia O'Keeffe: Art and Letters.* With Sarah Greenough. Washington, D.C.: National Gallery of Art, 1987.

Barbara Buhler Lynes. *O'Keeffe, Stieglitz, and the Critics, 1916–1929.* Chicago: University of Chicago Press, 1989.

Barbara Buhler Lynes. *Georgia O'Keeffe: Catalogue Raisonné.* 2 vols. New Haven, Conn.: Yale University Press in association with the National Gallery of Art, 1999.

Elizabeth Hutton Turner. *Georgia O'Keeffe: The Poetry of Things.* New Haven, Conn.: Yale University Press in association with the Phillips Collection, Washington, D.C., 1999.

Ruth E. Fine, Elizabeth Glassman, Barbara Buhler Lynes, and Judith C. Walsh. *O'Keeffe on Paper.* Washington, D.C.: National Gallery of Art, 2000.

15

Georgia O'Keeffe
Slightly Open Clam Shell, 1926
Pastel on white ground on pressed artist's board
18 1/2 × 13 in. (47 × 33 cm)
Inscribed with title, date, and artist's star device on the backing: "Slightly Open Clam Shell—26 OK"
Ex coll.: the artist until 1957; with the Downtown Gallery, New York; private collection, New York, 1958; descended in family; [Christie's, New York, sale no. 8790, lot no. 87, 4 December 1997]; Curtis Galleries, Inc., Minneapolis, until 2009
The Douglas Tracy Smith and Dorothy Potter Smith Fund, 2009.1.1

Edith Halpert, proprietor of the Downtown Gallery, recommended that O'Keeffe come up with a "theme" for the artist's first solo show at the gallery, scheduled for February 1952. O'Keeffe suggested a survey of her career through the medium in which she had worked consistently—and brilliantly—since about 1914: "What would you think of a pastel show—It could cover all the years as it is something I have always returned to."[1] From among her pictures of the 1920s, when she produced many of her most exquisite pastels, O'Keeffe chose for the show the deeply personal *Slightly Open Clam Shell*, a work not seen in public since its debut at the Intimate Gallery in 1927.

On both occasions, critics responded to the elegance of her use of materials. Margaret Breuning, reviewing the 1952 exhibition for *Art Digest*, commented: "Pastel, always a gracious medium, seems to acquire special qualities of richness and depth at the hands of O'Keeffe." Twenty-five years earlier, critic Henry McBride had observed, "The tones melt smoothly into each other as though satin . . . were the base."[2] O'Keeffe had used pastel to refine her aesthetic; techniques perfected there would become part of her practice in oils. By preparing the cardboard support for *Slightly Open Clam Shell* with a white ground and a gray priming layer, O'Keeffe arrived at the satiny quality McBride admired—a method and a result similar to her oils. And her barely textured surfaces were marked by soft blending of color—McBride's melting tones. The resulting balance between refinement of surface and strength of color and design carried over to her oils.[3]

In the case of *Slightly Open Clam Shell*, the connection between pastel and oil is direct and specific. *Slightly Open Clam Shell* forms a group with two oils of shells, one closed and the other slightly open, as here (each 20 × 9 inches; private collection). All three works show the clam on its end in a vertical slice of space, its form barely contained by the narrow proportions of the picture—a device that makes the shells seem monumental while creating a sense of intimacy and communion.

O'Keeffe was drawn to seashells at York Beach, Maine, where she had gone, alone, late in the summer of 1926. The trip may have resulted from a need to distance herself from Alfred Stieglitz and his smothering attempts to direct her career and her persona. It may also have been prompted by a desire to avoid the scrutiny of those critics who, while applauding her work, insisted on seeing her images as a direct revelation of her psyche and her sexuality.

During the month at York Beach, O'Keeffe took long walks along the shore to gather shells. She delighted in their handsome shapes and in their self-sufficiency: "Each shell was a beautiful work in itself," she wrote later.[4] The images of shells—the trio of vertical clam shells in particular—became metaphors for her need to simultaneously reveal and conceal aspects of herself. This sense of connection offered and withheld was not only part of O'Keeffe's personality but also a universal human trait, and was seen as one of the attractions—and enigmas—of her art: "Picture after picture," one critic wrote, "beckons the eye with promises, only to shut up like a clam when the gaze becomes too inquisitive."[5]

Slightly Open Clam Shell may also express O'Keeffe's simple need for privacy in the face of the many pronouncements about the meaning (usually seen as sexual) of her work that were published in the 1920s. The erotic quality of this pastel is obvious. It may be that, in producing an image of a shell slightly parted to reveal a glimpse of a soft, tender interior, and then displaying that image prominently at the Intimate Gallery in 1927, O'Keeffe was motivated in some measure by a spirit of defiance. Critics and friends took the bait, responding rapturously to the show, and to O'Keeffe as a goddess of passionate femininity. She was proclaimed "priestess of Eternal Woman . . . imaginative biologist of all creation," one who played "grand, maternal music, which . . . reveal[ed] woman as an elementary being, closer to the earth than man."[6]

However, a few critics arrived at a more sensitive reading of her work, recognizing that in works like *Slightly Open Clam Shell*, O'Keeffe was providing a glimpse into the world of a living creature, one both armored and vulnerable. In a review for the *Brooklyn Daily Eagle*, Helen Appleton Read defended O'Keeffe's work against those who

read into it things which have nothing to do with painting. . . . Because of her interest in clean, perfect shapes it was inevitable that she should have painted the clean perfect shapes of sea-shells. . . . There are few conceivable subjects which so put to test her ability to paint cleanly and clearly a simple unrelated object, and yet relate it to all of life.[7]

CT

1. O'Keeffe to Halpert, Abiquiu, 10[?] September 1951, in *Georgia O'Keeffe: Art and Letters*, by Jack Cowart and Juan Hamilton, with Sarah Greenough (Washington, D.C.: National Gallery of Art, 1987), no. 109, 261.
2. Margaret Breuning, "Fifty-seventh Street in Review," *Art Digest* 26 (1 March 1952): 18; Henry McBride, "Georgia O'Keefe's [*sic*] Work Shown: Fellow Painters of Little Group Become Fairly Lyrical Over It," *New York Sun*, 15 January 1927.
3. "Throughout the 1920s, O'Keeffe's oil paintings increasingly came to look like her pastels." Judith C. Walsh, "The Language of O'Keeffe's Materials: Charcoal, Watercolor, Pastel," in *O'Keeffe on Paper*, by Ruth E. Fine et al. (Washington, D.C.: National Gallery of Art, 2000), 71, 58, and 79 n. 38.
4. Georgia O'Keeffe, *Georgia O'Keeffe* (New York: Viking Press, 1976), n.p., text accompanying entry 79.
5. "Exhibitions in New York: Georgia O'Keeffe, Intimate Gallery," *Art News* 24 (13 February 1926): 7–8.
6. Oscar Bluemner, "A Painter's Comment," in *Georgia O'Keeffe: Paintings 1926* (New York: Intimate Gallery, 1926), n.p.; Louis Kalonyme, "Musicians Afield–Local Art Notes. In New York Galleries: Georgia O'Keeffe's Arresting Pictures," *New York Times*, 16 January 1927.
7. Read went on to argue, "The writers, who insist upon interpreting her work in terms of biology and psychology, not only miss its real beauty as painting, but have done her actual harm in the eyes of the art-loving public." Helen Appleton Read, "Georgia O'Keefe [*sic*]," *Brooklyn Daily Eagle*, 6 January 1927.

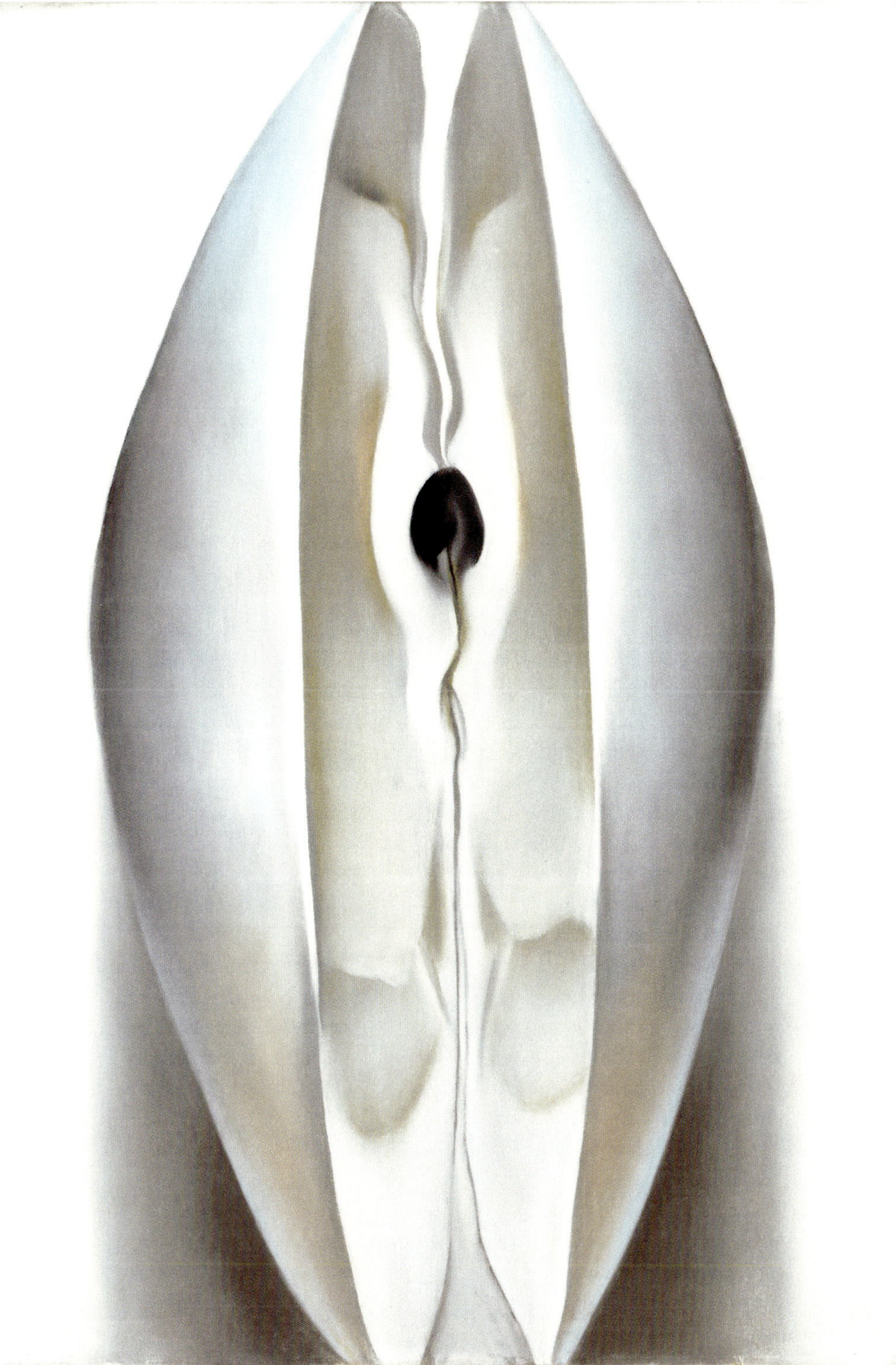

Cat. 15

Yasuo Kuniyoshi

Born in Okayama, Japan, 1893;
died in Woodstock, New York, 1953

A native of Japan, Yasuo Kuniyoshi moved to the United States in 1906 and took odd jobs to pay for school. He studied at the Los Angeles School of Art and Design for three years before moving to New York in 1910, where he first studied with Robert Henri and then with Kenneth Hayes Miller, both at the Art Students League, from 1916 to 1920. There he met Alexander Brook, Reginald Marsh (q.v.), Peggy Bacon (q.v.), and Katherine Schmidt (whom he later married); he and Brook became close friends, and through Brook, Kuniyoshi came in contact with the collector Hamilton Easter Field. Field invited the artist to spend a summer in Ogunquit, Maine, where he ran a summer school. Kuniyoshi summered in Ogunquit from 1920 to 1926. His early paintings from this period often combined landscapes, figures, and flowers in dreamlike compositions, partly inspired by American folk art.

Kuniyoshi had his first solo exhibition in 1922 at the Daniel Gallery, New York, and later exhibited regularly at Edith Halpert's Downtown Gallery, New York. He traveled Europe and eventually settled in Paris in 1928, where he studied lithography. While in Europe, he was greatly impressed by the work of Chaim Soutine, Pablo Picasso, and Jules Pascin. Like Pascin, Kuniyoshi focused on painting women and still lifes in the late 1920s. He often set his subjects in the center of a white page, where they appear ungrounded and seem to float in space. By the 1940s, his compositions grew more complex and his palette more colorful.

Although the Japanese-born artist was prohibited from becoming an American citizen, Kuniyoshi was an active member of the American art community. He was one of the founding members of the American Artists' Congress, and he served as the president of the Artists Equity from 1947 to 1951. He was the first living artist to be given a one-person show at the Whitney Museum of American Art in 1948. He also had a successful teaching career at the Art Students League from 1933 to 1953 and the New School for Social Research in 1936.

Select Bibliography

Lloyd Goodrich. *Yasuo Kuniyoshi: A Retrospective Exhibition.* New York: Whitney Museum of American Art, 1948.

Richard A. Davis. *Yasuo Kuniyoshi: The Complete Graphic Work.* San Francisco: Alan Wofsy Fine Arts, 1991.

Jane Myers and Tom Wolf. *The Shores of a Dream: Yasuo Kuniyoshi's Early Work in America.* Fort Worth, Texas: Amon Carter Museum, 1996.

16 a and b

Yasuo Kuniyoshi
Wild Flowers, 1922
Pen and black ink and ink wash on wove paper
17 5/8 × 12 in. (44.8 × 30.5 cm)
Signed at bottom, along leaf:
YASUO KUNIYOSHI 1922
Ex coll.: William E. Hill, Redding Center, Connecticut, to 1959
Gift of William E. Hill, 1959.17

Grapes in White Bowl, 1923
Black ink and watercolor applied using pen and brush, heightened with graphite and clear glaze on wove paper (partial watermark: Whatman 1921 [?] England B [?])
22 1/8 × 15 1/4 in. (56.2 × 38.7 cm)
Signed at bottom: YASUO KUNIYOSHI '23
Ex coll.: William E. Hill, Redding Center, Connecticut, to 1959
Gift of William E. Hill, 1959.16

Between 1921 and 1925, Kuniyoshi produced more than sixty elegantly crafted pen and ink drawings. Many of these were shown, to great acclaim, at the Charles Daniel Gallery in New York City. These drawings are for the most part still lifes representing ordinary objects. At first glance they seem straightforward and realistic; on further study, they appear idiosyncratic, strange, and somewhat amusing. The drawings' complicated tone was discerned by the critic for the *New York Times*, who described the drawings in Kuniyoshi's 1924 show at the Daniel Gallery as having "a puzzling quality of distance and mystery, though the method is most concrete." Of *Grapes in White Bowl* and the closely related still life *Dish with Banana* (1923; Art Institute of Chicago), the reviewer noted, "Each side of [the bowl] . . . is independently designed, one side balancing the other, and in the white bowl lies [the fruit], trying unsuccessfully to look innocent."[1]

Kuniyoshi attributed a personal meaning to his pictures of grapes, for he had harvested grapes as a child in California, and described eating them as a voluptuous and somewhat clandestine experience:

I used to go to the field very early, before sunrise, the air is cool then and vines and grapes are wet with dew. The big black bunches hang down so heavily, one on top of another. First thing I did was grab a soft slippery bunch and stuff as many into my mouth as it would hold. They were so juicy and cold.[2]

The grapes in this picture have a prickly, slightly menacing quality, sitting erect in the bowl. With their faint tints of color, a device Kuniyoshi introduced into his black-and-white drawings that year,[3] they read as three-dimensional forms against the bowl, which seems largely two-dimensional, despite the ring of graphite shading at the rim. The compote itself seems to float in space, its odd shape a product both of the modernist tension between illusionism and flatness and of Kuniyoshi's enthusiasm for American folk art.[4] With its deckled foot, the compote resembles nineteenth-century bisqueware and other utilitarian ceramics; its jauntily distorted contour and its oddly soft, velvety surface pay homage to traditional theorem painting (fig. 1).

Wild Flowers, on the other hand, has as its touchstone still lifes of extreme sophistication: the lush and colorful floral watercolors of Charles Demuth (q.v.), Kuniyoshi's friend and fellow exhibitor at the Daniel Gallery, and Japanese ink drawings. The extreme verticality of Kuniyoshi's composition, as well as his delight in rich, sooty blacks, seems to evoke *sumi-e* ink drawings. However, Kuniyoshi's emphasis on detail—the saw-toothed profile of

Fig. 1. Unidentified artist, *Blue Compote Filled with Fruit*, c. 1840. Watercolor and pencil on wove paper, 13 7/16 × 15 1/4 in. (34.1 × 38.7 cm). Abby Aldrich Rockefeller Folk Art Center, Colonial Williamsburg Foundation. From the Collection of Abby Aldrich Rockefeller, Gift of the Museum of Modern Art, 1933.304.4

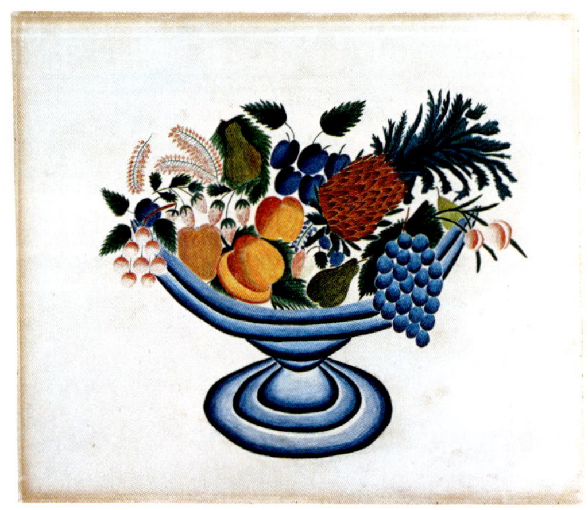

the leaves at left, for example—and the precision of his line differ from traditional Japanese practice.[5] Similarly, while he depicted ordinary flowers, as Demuth did, and showed them in an organic arrangement, Kuniyoshi's compositions remain austere, disconcerting yet appealing in their sinuous vitality. As modernist critic Henry McBride perceptively noted,

Kuniyoshi disturbs conventional art lovers . . . by a reversal of the usual color values. Kuniyoshi is quite capable of indicating the color of a flower by a rich black . . . in a way that is quite inimitable. . . . He manages to make it stand out from the background and to have an unmistakable feeling of air in the picture. Stodgy people who are fixed in their notions take one look at a Kuniyoshi flower and fly the room, outraged to their souls; but if they could only outstay their first consternation they would soon see that Kuniyoshi is not taking away anything from art but adding to it, and that all his work is full of vivacity and life.[6]

CT

1. "Exhibitions of the Week: Yasuo Kuniyoshi," *New York Times*, 6 January 1924.
2. Kuniyoshi, "Universality in Art," *League Quarterly* 20 (Spring 1949): 7, quoted in Jane Myers, "Independent Creations: Kuniyoshi's Ink Drawings of 1921–25," in *The Shores of a Dream: Yasuo Kuniyoshi's Early Work in America*, by Myers and Tom Wolf (Fort Worth, Texas: Amon Carter Museum, 1996), 64.
3. Alexander Brook, "Yasuo Kuniyoshi," *Arts* 5 (January 1924): 27. Noting that Kuniyoshi's introduction of color into ink drawings in 1924 was a departure from the pure black-and-white work of the previous year, Brook noted that Kuniyoshi handled color "with originality and reserve, merely a tint here and there most tastefully selected. The actual workmanship of [the drawings] . . . is marvelous to behold. So neat and immaculate are they that a wayward atom of otherwise innocuous dust falling upon them would immediately be noticed as a disturbing excrescence. Particularly I am thinking of the Grapes in a White Bowl."
4. Kuniyoshi was one of a number of artists who worked for several summers at publisher Hamilton Easter Field's artists' colony in Ogunquit, Maine. The artists' cottages were furnished with local folk art, and as a result Kuniyoshi and many of his colleagues began collecting such works and finding in them inspiration for their own creations. See Doreen Bolger [Burke], "Hamilton Easter Field and His Contribution to American Modernism," *American Art Journal* 20, no. 2 (1988): 79–107.
5. Myers, "Independent Creations," 57, 62.
6. McBride, "A Kuniyoshi Retrospective," *New York Sun*, 11 February 1928, reprinted in *The Flow of Art: Essays and Criticisms of Henry McBride*, ed. Daniel Catton Rich (New York: Atheneum, 1975), 240.

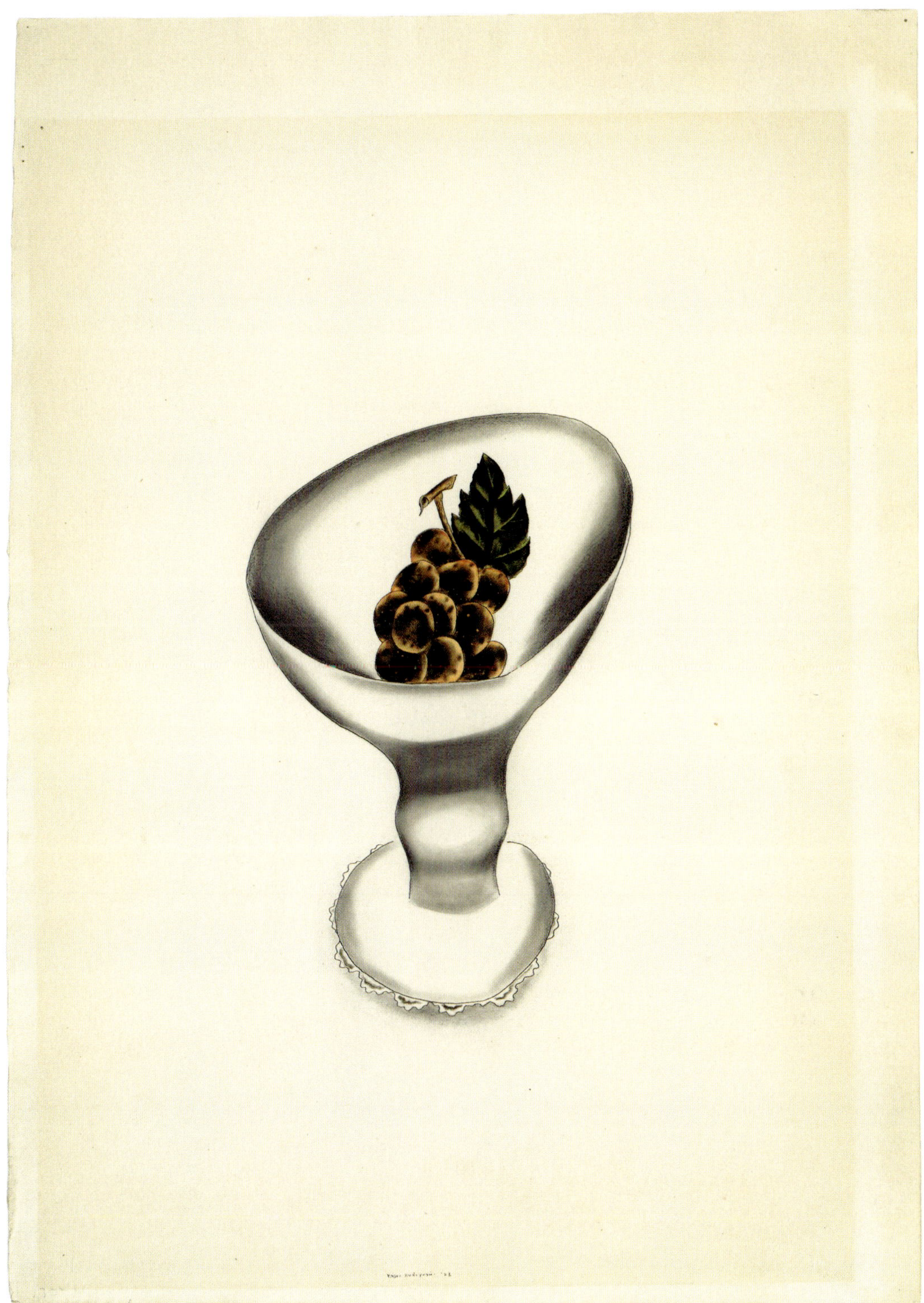

Cat. 16b

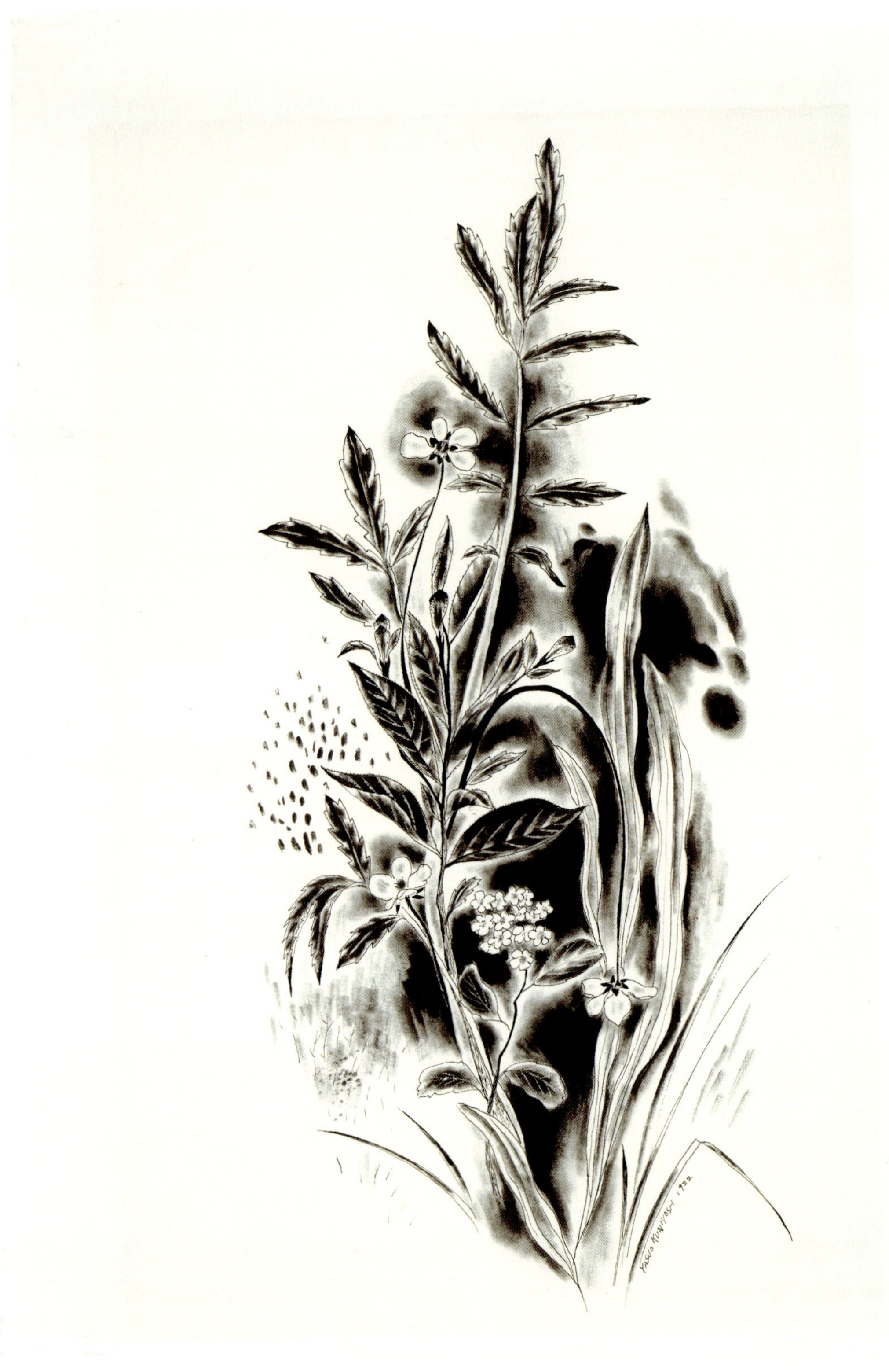

Cat. 16a

Isamu Noguchi

Born in Los Angeles, 1904;
died in New York, 1988

Isamu Noguchi was an American sculptor and designer. The son of writers—his American mother was a writer and his Japanese father was a poet—Noguchi was inspired by an Asian aesthetic that believed in a common link among all the arts. He was brought up in Japan (1906–18) before he was sent to the United States to attend high school in Indiana. In 1922, he moved to Connecticut where he was an apprentice to the sculptor Gutzon Borglum (1867–1941), the sculptor of Mount Rushmore. Noguchi moved to New York to study medicine and attended night classes at the Leonardo da Vinci Art School.

In 1927 and 1928 Noguchi lived in Paris and worked as Constantin Brancusi's studio assistant. Working alongside other American artists such as Alexander Calder (q.v.) and Stuart Davis (q.v.) and foreign artists in the independent academies of Paris, Noguchi quickly became attuned to modernism and, specifically, modernist sculpture. From Brancusi he picked up an awareness of the power of the simple shape and organic forms. Upon his return to New York during the Depression, he came in contact with socially aware artists such as Arshile Gorky (q.v.), John Graham, and Moses and Raphael Soyer. In the late 1930s and '40s, Noguchi addressed his social concerns in several large public commissions. By the 1950s, his interest in the relationship between sculpture and architecture had intensified. His later projects included two sites in Connecticut that exemplify this: the garden terrace for the Connecticut General Insurance Company, Bloomfield (1956–57), and the Sunken Garden for the Beinecke Rare Book and Manuscript Library, Yale University, New Haven (1960–64).

Noguchi was also a successful set designer and worked with influential performers such as Martha Graham, George Balanchine, and Merce Cunningham. From the late 1920s to the late 1960s, Noguchi's intensive involvement with theater led to his awareness of movement and a feeling for a relationship of an object in its environment, and subsequently influenced his work as a sculptor. In 1968 and 1978 Noguchi was given landmark retrospective exhibitions at the Whitney Museum of American Art and the Walker Art Center, respectively. He represented the United States in the 1986 Venice Biennale. At the end of his career, he turned to furniture and lighting design.

Select Bibliography

Dore Ashton. *Noguchi: East and West.* New York: Knopf, 1992.

Bonnie Rychlak, ed. *Isamu Noguchi: A Sculptor's World.* New York: Harper and Row, 1968; Göttingen, Germany: Steidl, 2004.

Masayo Duus. *The Life of Isamu Noguchi: Journey without Borders.* Translated by Peter Duus. Princeton, N.J.: Princeton University Press, 2006.

17

Isamu Noguchi
Nude, c. 1920
Black chalk on thin wove paper laid down on gray cardboard with heat set tissue
17 1/8 × 11 in. (43.5 × 27.9 cm)
Ex coll.: with the Weyhe Gallery, New York, as of 1959
Purchased through the gift of Henry and Walter Keney, 1959.85

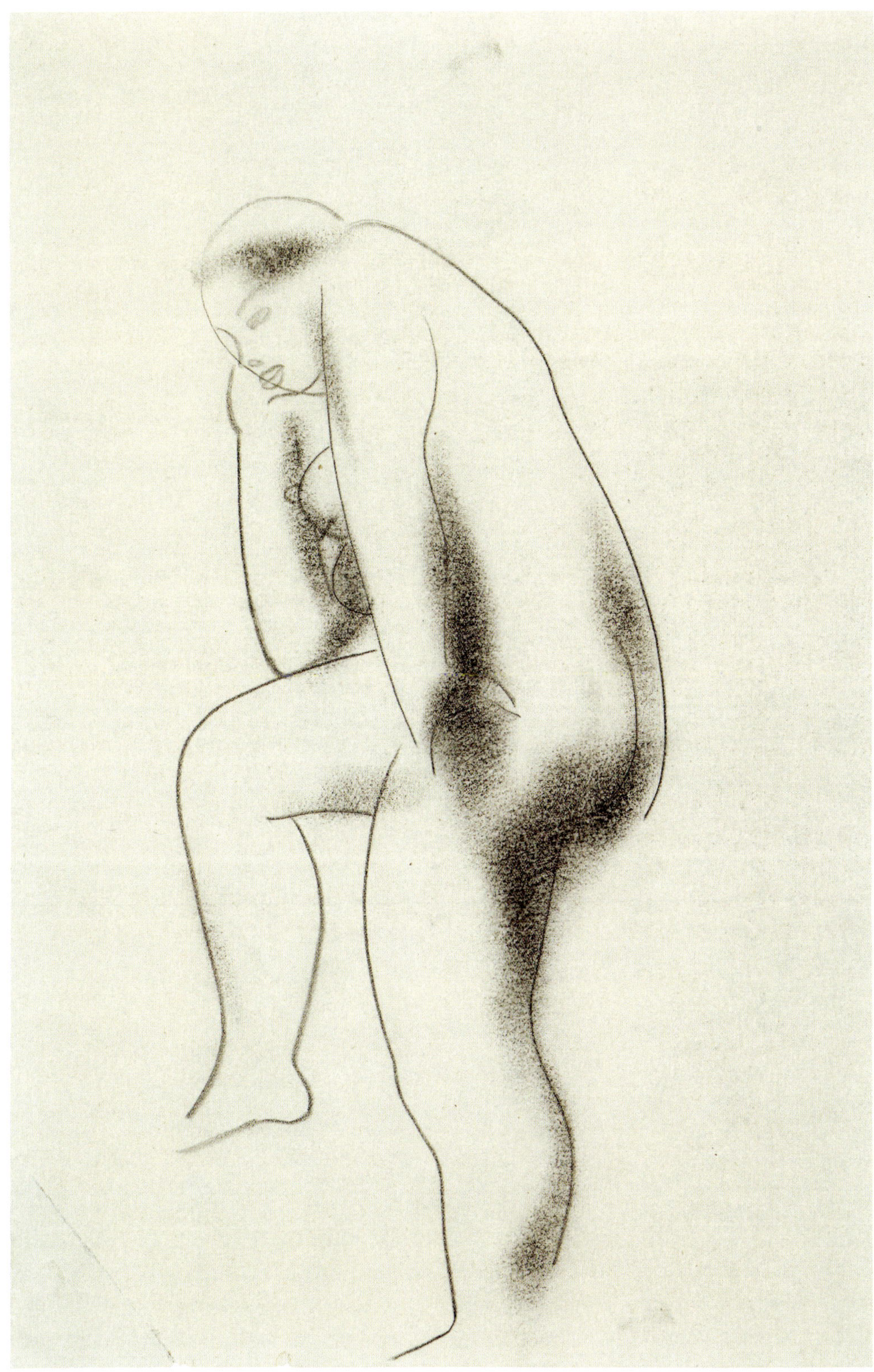

Cat. 17

Celebrated primarily for his sculpture, Isamu Noguchi was a multifaceted artist whose work included a wide range of creative production, including garden and stage design and the fabrication of useful objects for the home.[1] Noguchi was also a talented draftsman, and for him, drawing functioned as a way of thinking about actual pieces as well as an activity independent of his sculpture. Noguchi created four cohesive bodies of drawings during different phases in his career: crayon drawings of live models, geometric and biomorphic abstractions in black-and-white gouaches, large ink-brush drawings, and constructions made with paper that showed the elements of his interlocking sculptures.[2] *Nude* belongs to the first group, completed in the late 1920s in Paris, just as Noguchi was developing his first abstract sculptures inspired by Constantin Brancusi.

As a young sculptor, Noguchi worked in an academic style, until 1926, when he saw an exhibition of Brancusi's modernist works in New York and was influenced by his abstract style. In the late 1920s, Noguchi completed a series of drawings ranging from rough sketches to highly finished sculptural forms.[3] *Nude* occupies a middle ground in this series: more complete than a sketch but with certain rough and haphazard characteristics, such as the facial features. The body is outlined, and selected areas are shaded to create volume and dimension. Compared to another drawing from this series, *Female Nude* (1928–29; Columbus Museum of Art, Georgia), *Nude* appears cursory, less finished. In the Atheneum drawing, the figure's pose is more strained than the upright, fully exposed pose of the Columbus version.

Exhibiting a gamut of emotion and mood, these figurative drawings display Noguchi's appreciation for rounded, silhouetted forms. While it was not specifically based on these drawings, his sculpture from the period addressed similar aesthetic concerns. In *Globular* (1928; Isamu Noguchi Museum, Long Island, New York), the smooth contours and verticality of his nude drawings are translated into a three-dimensional tour de force in polished brass.
ECM

1. Charles T. Butler, ed., *Lines of Discovery, 225 Years of American Drawings* (Columbus, Ga.: Columbus Museum, 2006), 114, cat. no. 42.
2. Ibid., 114.
3. Ibid.

Charles Demuth

Born in Lancaster, Pennsylvania, 1883; died in Lancaster, Pennsylvania, 1935

Charles Demuth was born to an affluent family that ran a well-established tobacco shop in Lancaster, Pennsylvania. Although he spent substantial periods of time in such cities as Philadelphia, New York, Paris, and Provincetown, his hometown provided much of the subject matter found in both his early and late work. He enrolled at the Drexel Institute of Art, Science, and Industry in 1903, and later transferred to the Pennsylvania Academy of the Fine Arts where his teachers included Thomas Anshutz and William Merritt Chase.

Demuth was one of the first American artists to be receptive to modernism, which he discovered and explored during three extensive trips to Europe between 1907 and 1921. While abroad, he became familiar with such European art movements as Cubism and Futurism. Demuth learned of avant-garde ideas on frequent trips from Lancaster to New York, where he became acquainted with Alfred Stieglitz, Georgia O'Keeffe (q.v.), Marsden Hartley, and Marcel Duchamp. Charles Daniel, of the Daniel Gallery in New York, was among the first to exhibit early American modernists; he mounted a solo exhibition of Demuth's work in 1914. Later, Demuth exhibited at Alfred Stieglitz's gallery, An American Place.

Demuth is best known for his meticulous oil and tempera paintings of abstract architectural structures. These works caused him to be described as a Precisionist. He also used that taut style for some of his exquisite still lifes in watercolor, which depict flowers, fruit, and vegetables from the family garden in Lancaster. At the same time, Demuth painted a series of watercolors inspired by vaudeville themes—equally by the New York clubs and the local theater in Lancaster, an important stop for performers at the time. He painted these figurative subjects in a looser, more flowing and transparent style, demonstrating an extraordinary command of the expressive range of the watercolor medium. From the mid- to late 1920s, Demuth produced a series of symbolic "poster portraits" of several friends, including John Marin (q.v.), O'Keeffe, and Arthur Dove (q.v.), among others.

Select Bibliography

Emily Farnham. *Charles Demuth: Behind a Laughing Mask*. Norman: University of Oklahoma Press, 1971.

Betsy Fahlman. *Pennsylvania Modern: Charles Demuth of Lancaster*. Philadelphia: Philadelphia Museum of Art, 1983.

Barbara Haskell. *Charles Demuth*. New York: Whitney Museum of American Art, 1987.

Jonathan Weinberg. *Speaking for Vice: Homosexuality in the Art of Charles Demuth, Marsden Hartley, and the First American Avant-Garde*. New Haven, Conn.: Yale University Press, 1993.

Betsy Fahlman. *Chimneys and Towers: Charles Demuth's Late Paintings of Lancaster*. Fort Worth, Texas: Amon Carter Museum, 2007.

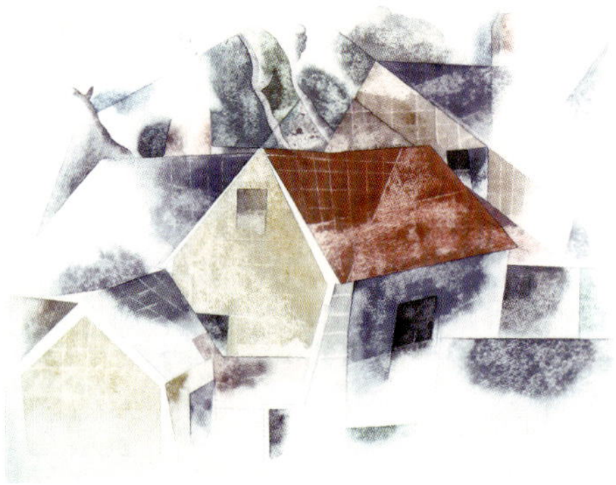

Fig. 1. Charles Demuth, *Red-Roofed Houses*, 1917. Watercolor and graphite on paper, 9 15/16 × 14 in. (25.2 × 35.6 cm). Philadelphia Museum of Art. From the Samuel S. White and Vera White Collection, 1967-30-25

18 a and b

Charles Demuth
Eight O'Clock (Evening), 1917
Transparent watercolor over graphite, on thin wove paper (watermark: Genuine Irish Linen)
8 × 10 3/8 in. (20.3 × 26.4 cm)
Signed and dated bottom center:
8 o'clock-/C. Demuth. 1917-
Ex coll.: George J. Dyer, Norfolk, Connecticut, before 1950
Gift of George J. Dyer, 1951.261

Eight O'Clock (Morning) #2, 1917
Transparent watercolor over graphite, on thin wove paper (watermark: Genuine Irish Linen)
7 7/8 × 10 13/16 in. (20 × 27.5 cm)
Signed and dated lower left:
C Demuth./1917-/8 o'clock.
Ex coll.: with Kraushaar Galleries, New York; Philip L. Goodwin, New York, in 1928 until 1958
Gift of James L. Goodwin and Henry Sage Goodwin from the Estate of Philip L. Goodwin, 1958.228

By 1917, Charles Demuth had launched his successful painting career in New York with annual shows at the progressive Charles Daniel Gallery that were applauded by adventurous and mainstream critics alike. He was also part of the city's bohemian community, frequenting nightclubs and tearooms, and attending vaudeville and circus performances with poets, political activists, and fellow artists—Marsden Hartley, Carl Van Vechten, and Eugene O'Neill were among his compatriots. Demuth documented their haunts in an ongoing series of figurative watercolors that he displayed at the Daniel Gallery alongside architectural studies done in Provincetown and Bermuda (fig. 1). The latter show clear Cubist influence, with sharp planes and crisp lines. The figurative watercolors, on the other hand, are more fluid, mannered, technically idiosyncratic, and emotionally intense.[1]

The Eight O'Clock group is among the most ambiguous of these. Demuth painted one scene titled *Evening* (cat. 18a) and two titled *Morning* (cat. 18b and fig. 2). While the evening and morning scenes are clearly connected by the repetition of characters and props (most tellingly the white silk scarf and top hat placed prominently in each picture), the narrative is by no means clear. In *Evening*, a formally dressed butler serves tea to two men while a third dresses—or perhaps undresses—before the fire. In the first version of *Morning*, one figure, in his underwear, extends a hand to a second, pajama-clad, figure who sits, distraught, on a daybed; a third man washes himself in the bathroom. In the second version, one man dresses while a second is in the tub and a third is at far right, watching from the bed.

Fig. 2. Charles Demuth, *Eight O'Clock—Morning #1*, 1917. Watercolor and graphite pencil on paper, 8 1/16 × 10 5/16 in. (20.5 × 26.2 cm). Whitney Museum of American Art, New York. Gift of Carl D. Lobell, 93.108

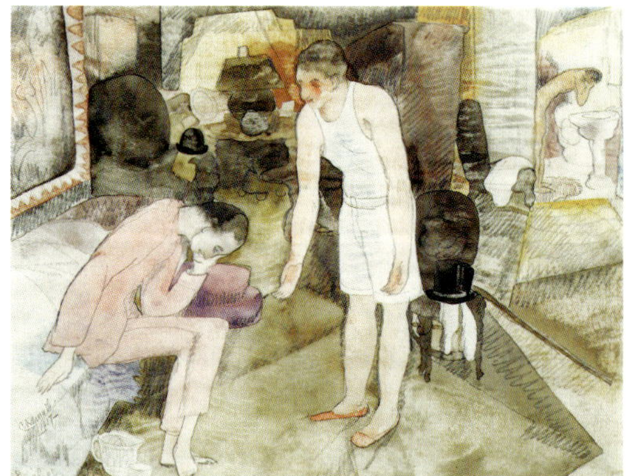

These watercolors have been explained, blandly, as "views of bachelor quarters" and as "depictions of three young men on an evening in town." More recently, the pictures have been described in terms of their gay subtext, as representing settings in which "homoerotic activity [is] about to happen or [has] already occurred."[2] But as scholar Jonathan Weinberg astutely points out, in 1917 such images of men about town would likely be read as innocuous masculine camaraderie. Demuth cleverly loaded the pictures with curious details and ambiguous gestures. The tea-drinking man in *Evening* appears naked beneath his open dressing gown; the figure extending a hand in *Morning #1* could be a friend offering consolation to a fellow reveler suffering from a tremendous hangover but is equally likely a male prostitute demanding payment. Demuth could expect that his watercolors would be interpreted simply as scenes of male companionship; only the initiated would see beyond the camouflage.[3] Weinberg notes, "The seeming innocence of the series was confirmed when *Eight O'Clock (Morning #1)* was purchased by such a respectable collector as Mrs. John D. Rockefeller."[4]

Just as Demuth's image subtly undermines expectations of conventional propriety (at least to those in the know), so his technique deliberately undermines expectations of the well-constructed, elegantly crafted watercolor, and establishes the emotional contrasts between the scenes. Loose, if controlled, pencil line in *Evening* gives way to rather more messy, even clumsy, drawing in *Morning #2*: the hatching lines are little more than scribbles, and the arms of the blond man are strangely proportioned. Reserved paper—for the white scarf and the underwear—creates a bright note of expectation in *Evening*, but in *Morning* those areas have been toned back with gray wash, contributing to the downbeat mood of the "morning after." Demuth used small sheets of smooth, thin watercolor paper, which caused pigmented areas to buckle slightly in places and to pool in others. In *Evening*, the rippled effect, enhanced by blotting up of color, gives a watery, miragelike texture to the scene. But in *Morning*, the same technique (on the back of the maroon chair, for example) makes the furniture seem worn. The pooling of pigment creates tide lines. These are especially noticeable in the yellow curtains, where they look like stains on the fabric, and underscore the seedy, dispiriting quality of the surroundings.
CT

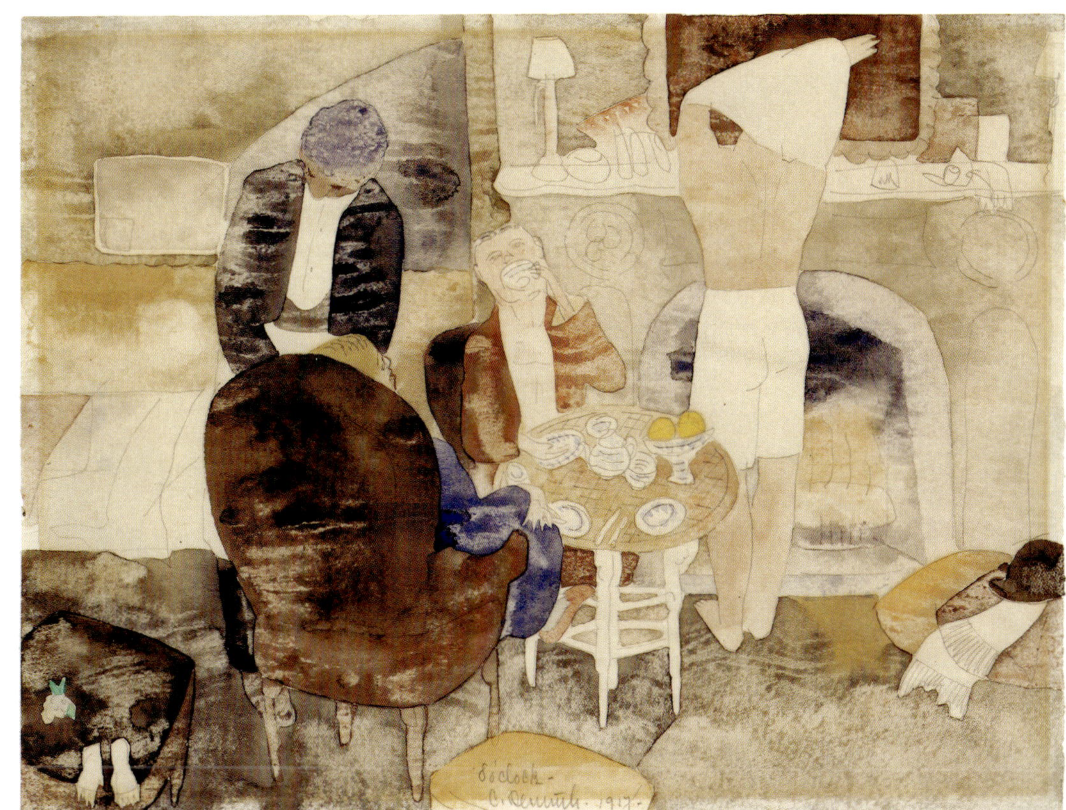

Cat. 18a

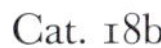

Cat. 18b

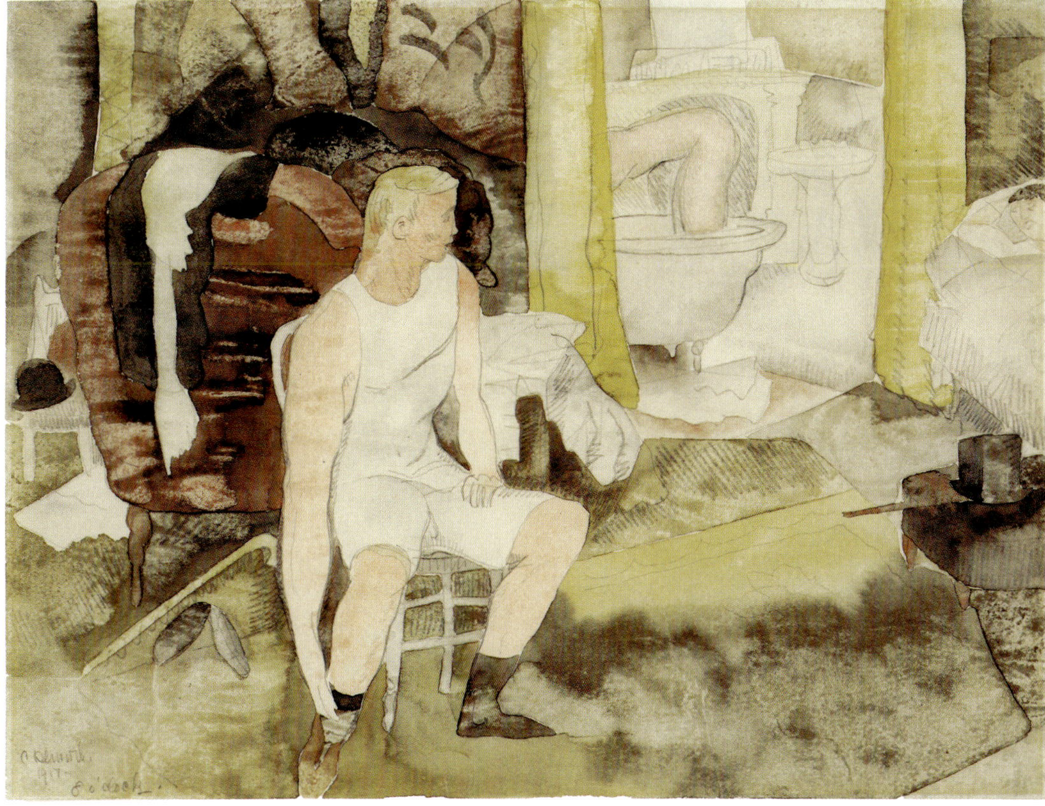

1. Demuth's contemporary watercolor illustrations for such books as Henry James's *Turn of the Screw* and Emile Zola's *Nana* are painted in the same style.
2. Emily Farnham, *Charles Demuth: Behind a Laughing Mask* (Norman: University of Oklahoma Press, 1971), 98; Alvord L. Eiseman, *Charles Demuth* (New York: Watson Guptill, 1982), 14; Barbara Haskell, *Charles Demuth* (New York: Whitney Museum of American Art, 1987), 62.
3. For Jonathan Weinberg's excellent discussion of these watercolors, see Weinberg, *Speaking for Vice: Homosexuality in the Art of Charles Demuth, Marsden Hartley, and the First American Avant-Garde* (New Haven, Conn.: Yale University Press, 1993), 24–29. Weinberg suggests that Demuth anticipated most viewers would be unaware of the pictures' homoerotic content, but it presumably would be understood by those in his social circle–not just gays but also "those who shared some of the same spaces with the various homosexual subcultures–the motley group of intellectuals, artists, eccentric patrons, and hangers-on that made up the community of avant-garde life in such places as New York, Provincetown, and expatriate Paris." Ibid., 29.
4. Ibid., 28. *Eight O'Clock (Morning #2)* was bought by New York architect Philip L. Goodwin, who loaned it to the Wadsworth Atheneum's 1928 exhibition *Modern American Water Colors*. One of eight Demuths in the show (the others were all still lifes or landscapes), *Eight O'Clock* elicited no comment from the press.

19

Charles Demuth
Still Life with Eggplant and Summer Squash, c. 1927
Opaque and transparent watercolor over graphite on wove paper (partial watermark: 1942 Unbleached Arnold)
$13^{1}/_{2} \times 19^{3}/_{4}$ in. (34.3 × 50.2 cm)
Ex coll.: with Kraushaar Galleries, New York, 1928
The Ella Gallup Sumner and Mary Catlin Sumner Collection Fund, 1928.40

In the mid-1920s, critics had begun to embrace the American vernacular and to applaud certain American artists for their ability to reveal the beauty in the everyday.[1] Since the beginning of the decade, Demuth had depicted the industrial architecture of his birthplace, Lancaster, Pennsylvania; these pictures were admired for their aesthetic redemption of dreary aspects of contemporary culture and also for their whimsy.[2] During this time, Demuth also became known for his elegant watercolor still lifes representing ordinary fruits and vegetables from the garden plot in his mother's backyard.

Plump eggplants (always the common variety rather than Japanese, striped, or other less familiar types) appear often in these watercolors, generally in combination with other fruits and vegetables. Some of the compositions, in which the produce is spread on tablecloths or arranged in bowls, allude to the market basket or the supper table (for example, *From the Kitchen Garden*, 1925; McNay Art Museum, San Antonio). Others, such as *Eggplant and Pears* (1925; Museum of Fine Arts, Boston) and *Still Life with Eggplant and Summer Squash*, are more abstract, and have only a minimal suggestion of setting.

That these still lifes were perceived as richly evocative despite the plainness of their subjects is apparent from the widely differing ways in which they were perceived. Modernist critic Henry McBride, one of Demuth's most dedicated supporters, praised their sensuous quality, writing rapturously of "the glittering polish of the aubergine."[3] Albert Gallatin, no less admiring, found Demuth's images austere: "His fruits and vegetables are very cool. . . . This is not voluptuous fruit . . . it comes from a country whose *vin du pays* is iced water."[4] When *Eggplant and Squash* was purchased by the Wadsworth Atheneum shortly after it was painted, it was presented as the cornerstone of "a collection of water colors by American painters" that the institution intended to build. The watercolor was credited with "a strange beauty" that came from its technical and formal properties ("He applies the water color washes with luxurious variations and nuances of the surface. . . . Demuth . . . is interested in the intellectual perception of forms"[5]) rather than its descriptive qualities. Yet even as reductive and abstract a composition as *Eggplant and Squash* can be seen as somehow animate: the eggplant appears to cuddle up affectionately to the upturned pattypan squash, while the other squash, resembling a sea creature as much as a vegetable, seems ready to scuttle across the table. License for such an anthropomorphic interpretation was provided by Demuth himself, who wrote to Alfred Stieglitz about an earlier still life, *Eggplant and Peppers* (1922; Fisk University, Nashville), "I'm so glad you want the eggplant. I kept it here, it turned into a heart–maybe mine."[6]
CT

1. For example Edward Hopper, who was called "forcefully eloquent upon the hitherto concealed beauty of some supposedly hideous buildings built during the Garfield administration." See Henry McBride, "Edward Hopper's Water Colors Prove Interesting–Also Sell," *New York Sun*, 25 October 1924. Charles Sheeler was similarly credited with demonstrating the grace in ordinary objects; this ability continued to be seen as a virtue throughout his career. See "Sheeler Finds Beauty in the Commonplace," *Life*, 8 August 1938, 42–45.
2. "These unlovely things, belonging so distinctly of our era of commercialism and mass production, have been made lovely by Demuth's rare art. . . . Not only beautiful, on account of their harmony and unity, these paintings of modern industrial America would at times almost to seem to strike a note of gaiety. The titles, too, are witty." A. E. Gallatin, *Charles Demuth* (New York: William Edwin Rudge, 1927), 7–8.
3. Henry McBride, "Water-Colours by Charles Demuth," *Creative Art* 5 (September 1929): 635.
4. Gallatin, *Charles Demuth*, 9.
5. "Charles Demuth," *Bulletin of the Wadsworth Atheneum* 6 (April 1928): 12.
6. Demuth to Stieglitz, 29 January 1929, Stieglitz Papers, Collection of American Literature, Beinecke Rare Book and Manuscript Library, Yale University, New Haven, Conn.

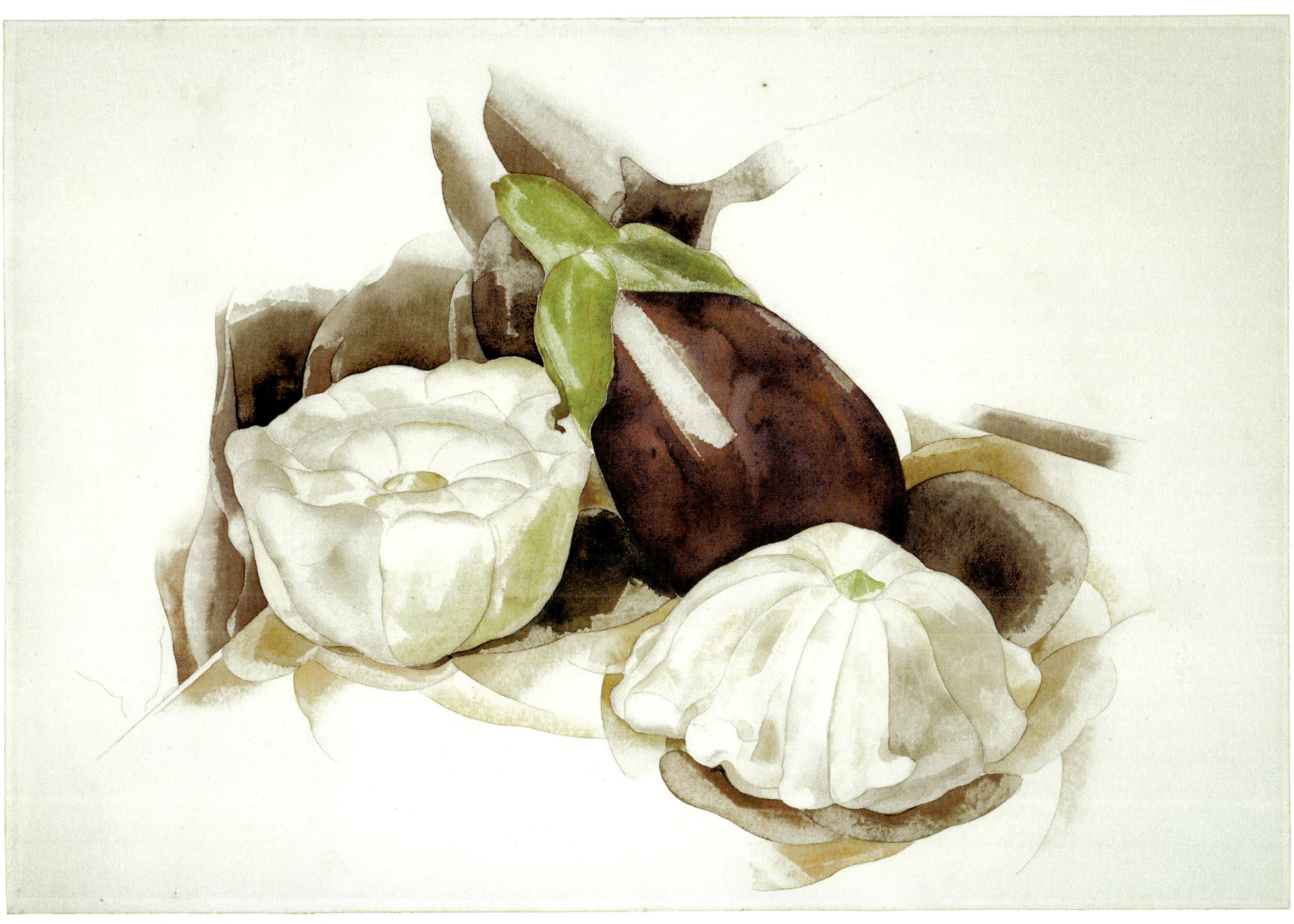

Cat. 19

20

Charles Demuth
Jonquils, 1928
Opaque and transparent watercolor over graphite on wove paper (partial watermark: Whatman 1919 England)
17 5/8 × 11 3/4 in. (44.8 × 29.9 cm)
Signed and dated at bottom: C. Demuth- / 1928- / Lancaster- / Pa.
Ex coll.: George J. Dyer, Norfolk, Connecticut, until 1958
Gift of George J. Dyer, 1958.179

In 1928 Demuth was living in his mother's house in Lancaster, Pennsylvania, struggling with his deteriorating health. He wrote to Stieglitz, who had shown his paintings since 1925, that he felt isolated and was dissatisfied with his work.[1] Nonetheless, that year he produced his greatest painting, *I Saw the Figure Five in Gold* (1928; Metropolitan Museum of Art, New York), his homage to his friend the poet William Carlos Williams, and another of his "poster portraits," *Longhi on Broadway* (1928; Museum of Fine Arts, Boston), as well as nearly a dozen watercolors.

The Lancaster watercolors depict plants Demuth found in his mother's garden or at the local farmers' market. He had little interest in hothouse flowers or exotic species, preferring zinnias, gladioli, hyacinths, and jonquils, as here. His choice of subject resulted, in part, from his poor health. He told friend and critic Henry McBride that he lacked the energy for figure painting, implying that it was all he could do to paint what was readily at hand.[2] But he loved flowers, especially simple ones, and from these unpretentious subjects he was able to craft watercolors of great sophistication.

In *Jonquils*, Demuth's technical virtuosity served both his keen powers of observation and his quest for formal purity. His skillful layering of pale green over yellow washes at the necks of the jonquils evoke the papery skin from which the blossoms emerge; the blotting along the slender leaves suggests the powdery decay and drying out along the tips that mark the season's end. The hyacinths are intertwined with the jonquils as though still growing in an unplanned clump in the yard. Yet behind Demuth's persuasive naturalism is a carefully ordered design. Some of the hyacinth blossoms are left unpainted, creating negative spaces that flatten the composition even as the flowers seem to bend and turn in space. The entire bouquet is pushed to the right side of the sheet, except for one jonquil, shown in profile, which arches into the empty space. There is no vase or lawn to locate Demuth's eloquently asymmetrical gathering. The flowers are only given a context by abstract arcs of grayed purple and brown wash that Demuth has blotted to make them more atmospheric and ephemeral; these washes then fade away to empty outlines. The image is entirely natural yet elegantly crafted, possessing great purity of design while conveying the charming ungainliness of spring blossoms.
CT

1. "It's almost time for you to be going [to Lake George]. . . . I wish that I could too, go to the sea, some place on the Mad Cape. . . . I'll stay here and work—I don't see anything else—I like a few places and a few people, but I see them seldom. Perhaps I wouldn't work at all if I did. Still, I don't like most of my work—and maybe that's what keeps me working." Demuth to Alfred Stieglitz, 4 June 1928, quoted in Bruce Kellner, ed., *Letters of Charles Demuth, American Artist, 1883–1935* (Philadelphia: Temple University Press, 2000), 106.
2. Henry McBride, "Charles Demuth, Artist," in *Charles Demuth Memorial Exhibition* (New York: Whitney Museum of American Art, 1937), n.p. Demuth produced a similar image of spring flowers (*Field Flowers: Daffodils and Bluebells*, 1922; current location unknown) after gathering some from the grounds of the Physiatric Institute in Morristown, New Jersey, where he was being treated for diabetes. Emily Farnham, "Charles Demuth: His Life, Psychology and Works" (Ph.D. diss., Ohio State University, 1959), 2:578, no. 423.

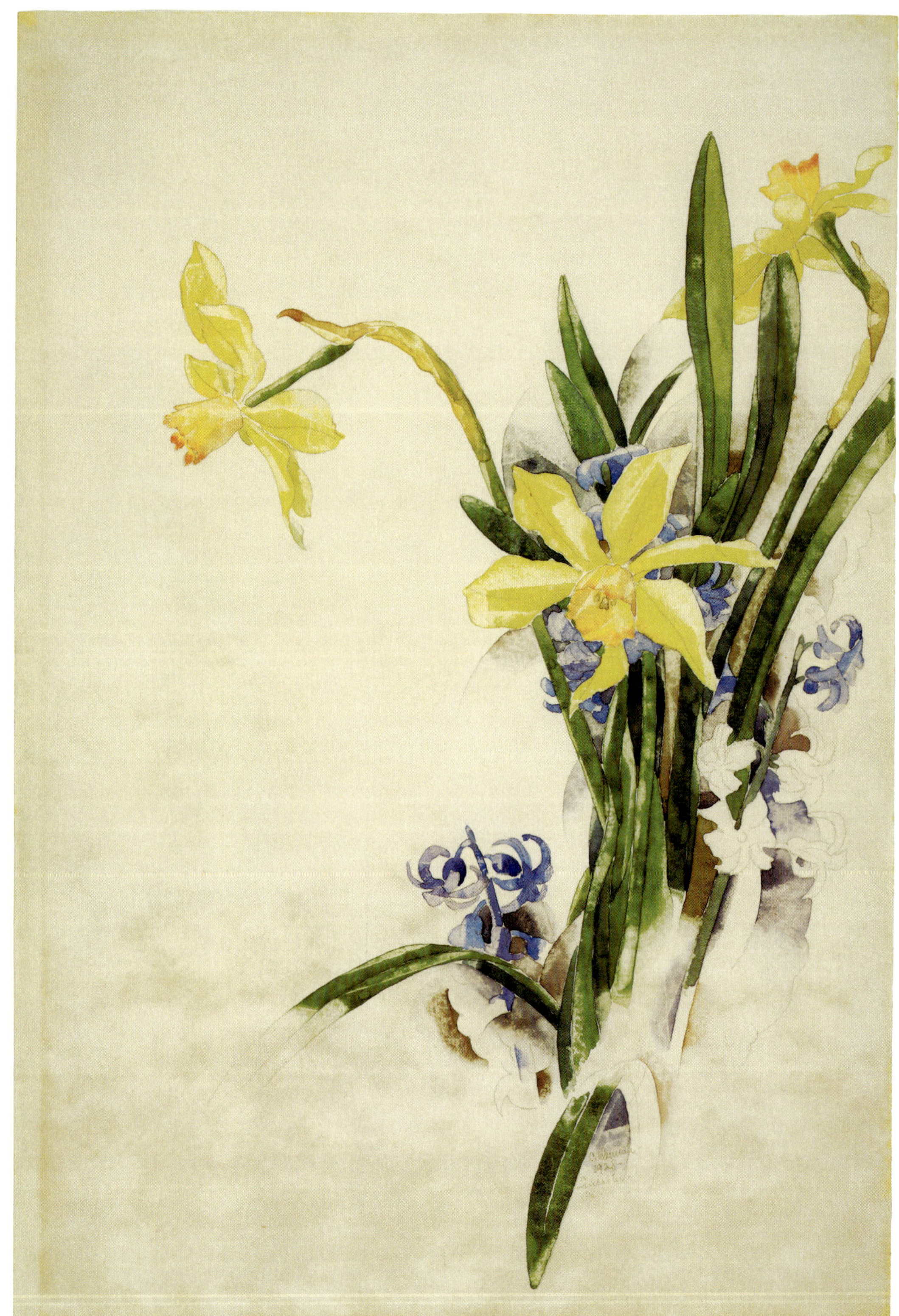

Cat. 20

Preston Dickinson

Born in New York, 1889;
died in Irun, Spain, 1930

Preston Dickinson was born into a working-class family in New York City. After his father's death in 1900, Dickinson was forced to quit high school to help support his mother and his sister. Aided by the financial assistance of his employer, Dickinson attended the Art Students League from 1906 to 1910, where he studied with William Merritt Chase and Ernest Lawson. From 1910 to 1914, he studied in Paris at the École des Beaux-Arts and then at the Académie Julian. During this time he gained exposure to art forms that influenced his mature style, most notably Japanese prints, Cubism, and Futurism. The discovery of contemporary European artists such as Juan Gris, Georges Braque, Pablo Picasso, and most importantly Paul Cézanne propelled Dickinson's art into a more formal direction. From Cézanne Dickinson assessed the organization, design, and use of color in his work. Dickinson excelled in pastel, his favorite medium, but his best-known work after 1920 was done in oil. In Paris, in 1912, he participated in his first two exhibitions, at the Salon des Indépendants and the Salon des Artistes Français.

With the outbreak of World War I, Dickinson returned to New York City in 1914. He became closely aligned with other artists working in the modernist idiom, many of whom were represented by Charles Daniel, owner of the Daniel Gallery. Daniel was among the most active supporters of the Precisionist painters in the 1920s, including Dickinson, Charles Demuth (q.v.), Elsie Driggs, and Charles Sheeler (q.v.). The architecture of New York inspired Dickinson and his fellow Precisionists; bridges and buildings were seen as symbols of industrial achievements in America. Dickinson's first one-man show at the Daniel Gallery was in 1923, followed by solo exhibitions in 1924 and 1927.

Dickinson continued to exhibit throughout the 1920s, but despite artistic successes he was plagued by economic and personal problems. His career failed to provide him with an adequate living, in large part due to his drinking habits. Increased problems with his health and well-being led to his decision to return to Europe, in search of an inexpensive place to live and paint. In 1930 he and his companion Oronzo Gasparo, also an artist, settled in northwest Spain. Dickinson died later that year of double pneumonia at age forty-one.

Select Bibliography

Ruth Cloudman. *Preston Dickinson, 1889–1930*. Lincoln: Nebraska Art Association, 1979.

Karen Tsujimoto. *Images of America: Precisionist Painting and Modern Photography*. Seattle: University of Washington Press, 1982.

Thomas S. Holman. "Preston Dickinson, 1889–1930: Paintings and Drawings." Zabriskie Gallery, http://www.zabriskiegallery.com/exhibition.php?ex=50&page=140.

21

Preston Dickinson
Power Station–Night, 1924
Pastel and graphite, heightened with opaque watercolor, on laid paper laid down on paper board
25 1/4 × 18 3/4 in. (64.1 × 47.6 cm)
Signed at lower left: Preston Dickinson 24
Ex coll.: with Charles Daniel, Daniel Gallery, New York
The Ella Gallup Sumner and Mary Catlin Sumner Collection Fund, 1928.323

In the decade after World War I, the economic growth and progress in the United States attracted the interest of an emerging group of modern American artists. This fascination with industrial and mechanical forms can be seen in the work of Preston Dickinson, whose images of factories, bridges, and smokestacks reflected this changing American landscape.

After returning from Paris in 1914, Dickinson settled in the Bronx. Over the next decade, he painted the structures along the Harlem River in northern Manhattan, such as the Washington Bridge and High Tower. Dickinson worked in oil and pastel, but the latter was his medium of choice for its delicate texture and soft lushness. In 1924 he accepted an invitation from a patron to visit Omaha, Nebraska. That summer he completed a series of pastels inspired by the grain elevators and buildings that towered over the flat, desolate Nebraska plains.[1] The foreshortened vantage point, the emphasis on verticality, and the flatness of form and color all contribute to the beautiful complexity of these 1924 works. *Power Station–Night* was likely part of this Nebraska series.

This industrial scene is composed of an array of geometric shapes and forms set against the dark night sky. The frenetic activity within the power station is symbolized by the billowing smokestacks. An intense spotlight from the right suggests an approaching transient barge or boat on the Missouri River, a vital source of Omaha's economic development at that time. The thrusting diagonals of light are reminiscent of the dynamic movement in Futurist paintings.[2] In addition to their shared interest in modern machines, American modernists such as Dickinson and his friend Charles Demuth (q.v.) were inspired by the diagrammatic designs of Italian Futurist paintings, as exemplified by Gino Severini's *Armored Train* (1921; Museum of Modern Art, New York). Strong lines were meant to symbolize the energetic potential within an object. Dickinson and Demuth both employed similar tactics in their work. Demuth's *Modern Conveniences*, for example, contains transparent beams superimposed across the composition that bisect a tall, vertical structure (fig. 1).[3] Dickinson and Demuth, both represented by the Daniel Gallery, often exhibited side by side. Though Dickinson's brushwork and colors were more expressive than Demuth's, there were strong visual connections between their paintings. A reviewer of a 1924 exhibition in the *New York Times* proclaimed, "Dickinson and Demuth are robust standard bearers of modernist art in this country; the more gallant that their modernism is under such adequate control and their individuality unconquerable by formula or theory."[4]
ECM

Fig. 1. Charles Demuth, *Modern Conveniences*, 1921. Oil on canvas, 25 3/4 × 21 3/8 in. (65.4 × 54.3 cm). Columbus Museum of Art, Ohio. Gift of Ferdinand Howland, 1931.137

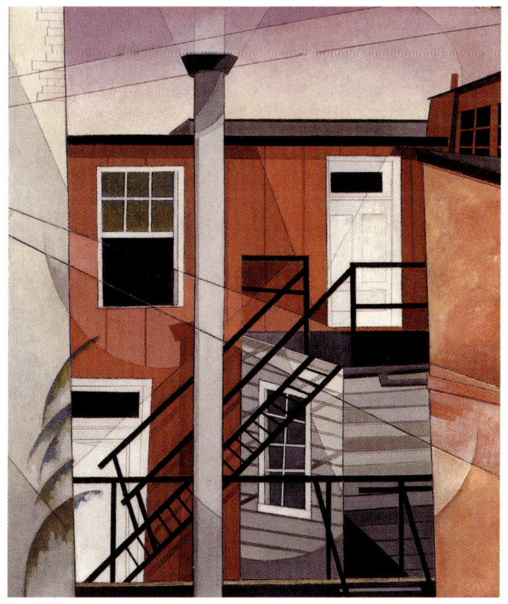

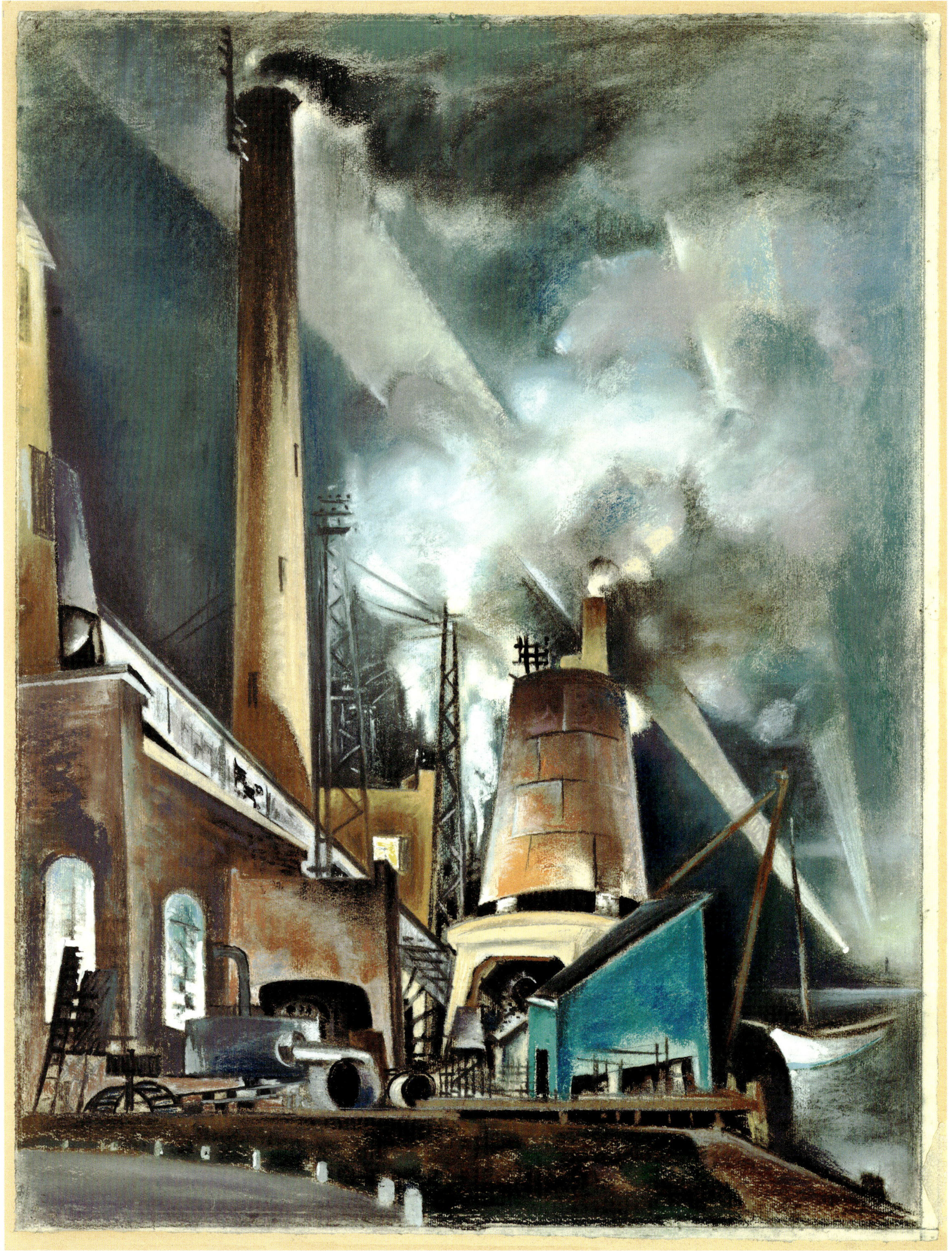

Cat. 21

1. Thomas S. Holman, "Preston Dickinson, 1889–1930: Paintings and Drawings," Zabriskie Gallery, http://www.zabriskiegallery.com/exhibition.php?ex=50&page=140.
2. Karen Tsujimoto, *Images of America: Precisionist Painting and Modern Photography* (Seattle: University of Washington Press, 1982), 27. Dickinson, with fellow Precisionist painters Charles Demuth and Joseph Stella, was in Paris in 1912 when the Futurists held their first major exhibition.
3. Tsujimoto, *Images of America*, 27.
4. "The World of Art: Art in the House and in the Galleries," *New York Times*, 20 July 1924.

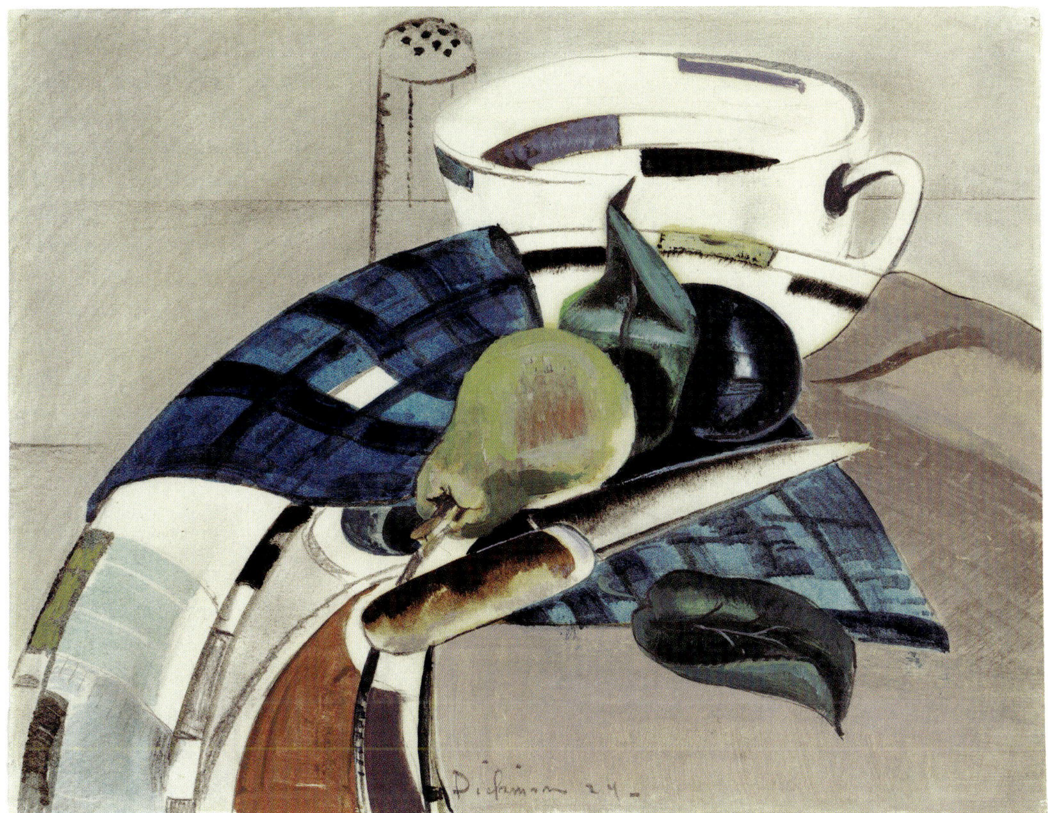

Cat. 22

22

Preston Dickinson
Still Life with Knife, 1924
Oil paint and transparent watercolor over graphite on thin wove paper (watermark: Capitol Bond)
$8^1/_2$ × 11 in. (20.3 × 27.9 cm)
Signed at lower center: Dickinson 24-
Ex coll.: the artist; Stanley Weiser, Sioux Falls, South Dakota; Mrs. Maurice Sickel, Sioux Falls, South Dakota; Hackley Art Gallery, Muskegon, Michigan, 1935; Maynard Walker Gallery, New York, 1959
The Ella Catlin Sumner and Mary Catlin Sumner Collection Fund, 1959.288

Preston Dickinson painted both the industrial landscape (cat. 21) and intimate impressions of modern life, including the domestic interior and still life. In 1924, he began a series of still lifes employing a repertoire of familiar objects that often included fruit, a paring knife, and a wine bottle. Dickinson arranged these objects upon different containers, including patterned plates and bowls, which provided ample opportunity to experiment with texture, color, and volume.

In *Still Life with Knife*, a pear, a plum, and a paring knife are placed on a blue napkin, which has been draped across a white plate. Behind the plate are a white teacup and a salt shaker. Though the composition is inherently "still" in its subject matter, Dickinson creates movement within it by emphasizing the flat geometric patterns of the napkin and plate on which the fruit and knife are arranged. The plate is unusually large in comparison to this cluster, and its round edge sweeps across the composition. This circular motion is echoed in the teacup with matching decorative trim.

Dickinson's new work, possibly including this still life, was exhibited at the Daniel Gallery in April 1924. The reviewer for the *New York Times* praised the artist as "a master of still life . . . [whose compositions] are luxuriously rich in form and magnificent in color."[1] Dickinson's eye for color and richly textured surfaces crystallizes in his still lifes. His varied brushstrokes emphasize the texture and pattern of each object, breathing new life into a classical mode, updating it for the twentieth century.

ECM

1. "Art: Exhibitions of the Week, Old Masterpieces," *New York Times*, 4 May 1924. The exhibition at the Daniel Gallery opened on April 24. There is no checklist for the exhibition, but it is possible *Still Life with Knife* was on view. The exhibition likely remained on view through the summer as suggested by a later review, "The World of Art: Art in the House and in the Galleries," *New York Times*, 20 July 1924.

Arthur Dove

Born in Canandaigua, New York, 1880;
died in Centerport, New York, 1946

Arthur Garfield Dove was raised in Geneva, New York, and attended Hobart College, and Cornell University, where he graduated in 1903. He supported himself as a commercial illustrator for *Harper's* and the *Saturday Evening Post*, in New York, but, against his family's wishes, he decided to become a painter. He enrolled in art classes in New York and made professional contacts with John Sloan (q.v.) and William Glackens (q.v.). During an eighteen-month trip to Europe from 1907 to 1909, Dove joined a community of expatriate American artists in Paris that included Alfred Maurer and Max Weber (q.v.), and through them became conversant with modernism, and experimented with the heightened palette of Postimpressionist and Fauvist painting.

In 1909 Dove returned to New York, where he met Alfred Stieglitz the following year. Stieglitz became his dealer, friend, and lifelong advocate. After settling in Westport, Connecticut, Dove exhibited at Stieglitz's gallery 291 along with Maurer, John Marin (q.v.), Marsden Hartley, and Max Weber (q.v.). Stieglitz gave Dove his first solo exhibition in 1912; this show, which included a series of abstract pastels later labeled The Ten Commandments, established Dove's reputation as a leading member of the American avant-garde. During the 1920s, Dove's work also attracted the attention of the prominent collector Duncan Phillips, who became the artist's most loyal patron. In 1921, Dove left his first wife and moved with his companion Helen "Reds" Torr, also an artist, to a houseboat on the Harlem River. From 1924 to 1933, they lived, for the most part, on a sailboat on Huntington Harbor, off of Long Island. They were married in 1932.

Between 1924 and 1930, Dove experimented with various mediums, creating assemblages and witty collages containing verbal and visual puns, influenced, in part, by Cubist and Dadaist art. While living on the boat on the coast of Long Island, Dove painted scenes inspired by the coastal waters. In the 1930s, Dove took up watercolor and continued to paint watercolors throughout his career. Many inform his oil paintings.

Financially strapped throughout most of his adult life, Dove returned to his hometown of Geneva, New York, in 1933, following the death of his mother, to settle the estate of his parents and to protect his inheritance. Despite feeling culturally isolated—Dove could afford to make only one trip to New York City during the five years he spent in Geneva—he found inspiration in the landscape surrounding the Finger Lakes. The emotional stress and harsh conditions of his five years in Geneva living on the family farm led Dove to produce some of his most powerful work. Dove and his wife returned to Long Island, where they purchased a house in Centerport.

In his final years, in the late 1930s and early '40s, Dove suffered from a heart condition and Bright's disease, an inflammation of the kidney. Despite his ill health, he produced an important group of abstract paintings and experimental color studies on paper. Like many artists in the Stieglitz circle, Dove was interested in creating an "American" form of modernism; from the outset, the reverence for nature evident even in his most abstract work led observers to view his paintings as a continuation of the nineteenth-century landscape tradition.

Select Bibliography

Barbara Haskell. *Arthur Dove.* San Francisco: San Francisco Museum of Modern Art, 1974.

Ann Lee Morgan. *Arthur Dove: Life and Work, with a Catalogue Raisonné.* Newark: University of Delaware Press, 1984.

Ann Lee Morgan, ed. *Dear Stieglitz, Dear Dove.* Newark: University of Delaware Press, 1988.

Ann Cohen DePietro, ed. *Arthur Dove and Helen Torr: The Huntington Years.* Huntington, N.Y.: Heckscher Museum, 1989.

Charles C. Eldredge. *Reflections on Nature: Small Paintings by Arthur Dove, 1942–1943.* New York: American Federation of the Arts, 1997.

Debra Bricker Balken. *Arthur Dove: A Retrospective.* With contributions by William C. Agee and Elizabeth Hutton Turner. Cambridge, Mass.: MIT Press in association with the Addison Gallery of American Art and the Phillips Collection, 1998.

Debra Bricker Balken. *Arthur Dove Watercolors.* New York: Alexander Gallery, 2006.

23

Arthur Dove
Sunrise, 1936–37
Opaque and transparent watercolor and pen and black ink on thick wove watercolor paper
Signed at lower center in black ink: Dove
5 × 7 in. (12.7 × 17.8 cm)
Ex coll.: The Downtown Gallery, New York
The Ella Gallup Sumner and Mary Catlin Sumner Collection Fund, 1955.265

While living in his family's farmhouse in Geneva, New York, Dove noted in his diary on 29 August 1936 that he had begun to execute a series of large paintings of the sunrise. He was required to get up early to observe his subject, as he wrote to Stieglitz: "Weather shouldn't be so important to a modern painter—maybe we're still 'too human.' . . . Must get up to work. Have been trying to since 5 a.m."[1] His close observation of nature led to abstract images of the sun, presented in concentric circles of color. He continued to work on the Sunrise series intermittently for a six-month period, until the end of January 1937. He numbered the series I through IV in the order of their completion.[2]

Dove's Sunrise series is a metaphor for conception, which unfolds as a story of creation. In *Sunrise I*, a phallic form enters the center of the sun to fuse with the cell. In *Sunrise II*, the surrounding rings of the sun have been penetrated by two cellular forms. The Atheneum's watercolor is a study for *Sunrise III* (fig. 1).[3] Melanie Kirschner has noted that in Dove's watercolors from this period, he eliminates the drawn line, "relying instead on unrestrained color to create a softness."[4] For the Atheneum's watercolor *Sunrise*, Dove simplified forms and used color as the essence of his imagery. He

Fig. 1. Arthur Dove, *Sunrise III*, 1936. Oil and wax emulsion on canvas, 25 × 35 1/16 in. (63.5 × 89.1 cm). Yale University Art Gallery. Gift of Katherine S. Drier to the Collection of the Société Anonyme

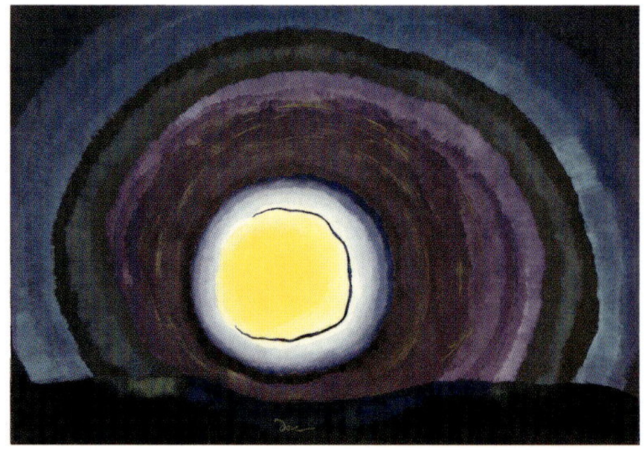

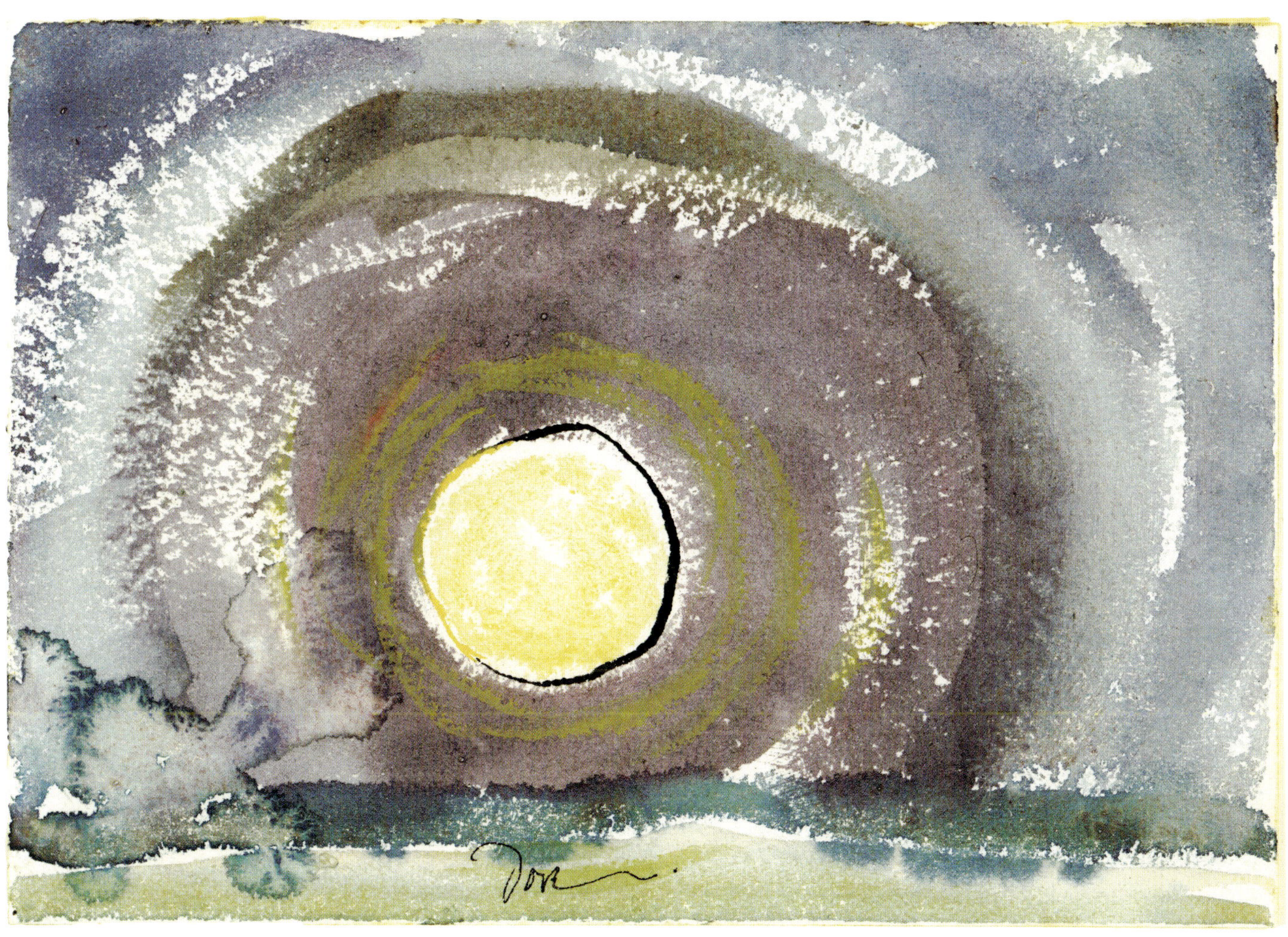

Cat. 23

applied concentric circles of layered translucent colors to capture a radiant light. He has scumbled the brushstrokes to reveal flecks of white paper that surround the pale yellow core of the sun, defined by a partial black line. Splashes of blue watercolor in the lower left enliven the image. Dove followed the outlines and forms of the watercolor closely for his large wax emulsion and oil painting, *Sunrise III*. He used darker colors for the oil and placed the sun just off center in both images.

Atheneum director Charles C. Cunningham borrowed *Sunrise* from Edith Halpert's Downtown Gallery in 1952 for an exhibition he organized titled *Survey of American Watercolors*, and he later purchased the watercolor for the Atheneum's collection. (See Elizabeth Mankin Kornhauser, "Galvanizing Hartford," in this volume.)
EMK

1. Arthur Dove to Alfred Stieglitz, 24 October 1936, quoted in Ann Lee Morgan, ed., *Dear Stieglitz, Dear Dove* (Newark: University of Delaware Press, 1988), 363.
2. The oil paintings are in the following collections: *Sunrise I* (1936), Museum of Fine Arts, Boston; *Sunrise II* (1936), private collection; *Sunrise III* (1936), Yale University Art Gallery, New Haven, Conn.; *Sunrise IV* (1937), Hirshhorn Museum, Smithsonian Institution, Washington, D.C.
3. Robert L. Herbert, Eleanor S. Apter, and Elise K. Kenney, eds., *The Société Anonyme and the Dreier Bequest at Yale College: A Catalogue Raisonné* (New Haven, Conn.: Yale University Press, 1984), 204–5.
4. Melanie Kirschner, *Arthur Dove: Watercolors and Pastels* (New York: George Braziller, 1998), 53.

24

Arthur Dove
Flour Mill II, 1938
Pen and black ink and transparent watercolor on thick wove paper
9 × 7 in. (22.9 × 17.8 cm)
Signed at lower center, in black ink: Dove
Ex coll.: The Downtown Gallery, New York, in 1955
The Ella Gallup Sumner and Mary Catlin Sumner Collection Fund, 1955.264

In 1937, his last year in Geneva, New York, Dove and his wife Helen "Reds" Torr moved from the Dove family farmhouse, where they had lived for five years, into town. They took up residence on the third floor of a large building in the center of Geneva that had been owned by Dove's father, and which he had cast on the facade: Dove Block. The artist suddenly had new views to contemplate from this building overlooking the town. He could also see Lake Seneca, whose banks were lined with commercial properties. His summer and fall were productive; his work reflects the urban and industrial subjects he encountered in his new surroundings. Dove's method at this time was to sketch ideas in watercolor on the spot, later deciding which ones he would expand into paintings, calling them his "models to build from."[1]

Flour Mill II is a watercolor study of the new Agway grain elevator (built in 1937 and demolished in the 1980s or early 1990s) on Lake Seneca (fig. 1).[2] Dove positions the viewer at the base of the giant industrial structure, which juts upward in a strong, vertical thrust; he compressed the composition on the sheet. The round cylinder shapes of the elevator and the shaft that soars above into space are simply defined by slender black lines, and thinly brushed translucent watercolor strokes of pale gray and yellow reinforce its upward direction. Lightly applied strokes of blue define the sky beyond. He used a dry brush technique (loading the brush with a minimum of color and dragging it across the sheet) that allows the paper to show through, emphasizing the simple forms of the composition. (Small brush marks of discolored rubber cement are found at the lower right and the center of the image.)[3] Here he has reduced elements to their simplest form, relying on color and space, while deemphasizing descriptive details.

Flour Mill II, which was shown at Stieglitz's gallery, An American Place, in 1938, served as a study for the larger oil *Flour Mill II*

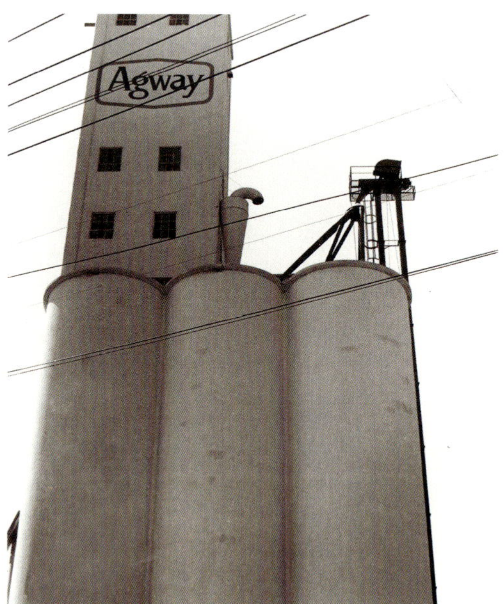

Fig. 1. Robert E. Doran, M.D., *Agway Grain Silo*, c. 1965. Photograph. Geneva Historical Society, Geneva, New York

Fig. 2. Arthur Dove, *Flour Mill II*, 1938. Oil and wax emulsion on canvas, 26 1/8 × 16 1/8 in. (66.4 × 41 cm). The Phillips Collection, Washington, D.C. Acquired 1938

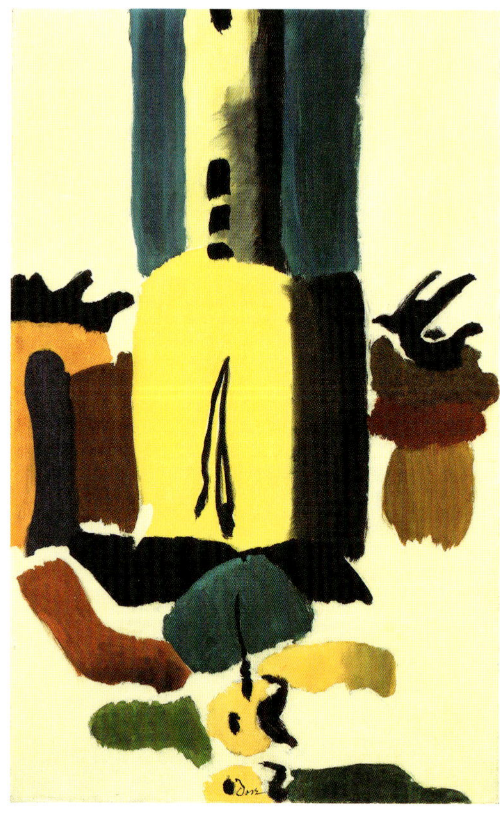

(fig. 2).[4] The finished oil departs from the watercolor in a number of ways. While the watercolor is tightly cropped at the bottom, in the oil, Dove paired down his brushstrokes of strong bright colors, using abstract strokes in the foreground leading to the base of the structure and cropping the top shaft to create a nondescriptive space. The form of the flour mill is even more abstracted in the final oil. He has placed his abstract forms against an off-white background.

This watercolor was acquired by Charles C. Cunningham for the Atheneum from the Downtown Gallery (see Elizabeth Mankin Kornhauser, "Galvanizing Hartford," in this volume) following its exhibition in *Dove and Demuth Watercolors*, Downtown Gallery, New York, April 1954.[5]

EMK

1. Arthur Dove to Alfred Stieglitz, 19 July 1930, quoted in Debra Bricker Balken, *Arthur Dove: A Retrospective* (Cambridge, Mass.: MIT Press in association with the Addison Gallery of American Art and the Phillips Collection, 1998), 102.
2. Our thanks to Karen Osburn, archivist, Geneva Historical Society, Geneva, New York, for providing this information as well as archival photographs of the grain elevators.
3. Mindy Horn, paper conservator, was able to diminish these areas, which were applied unintentionally by the artist, who had coated the back of the paper with rubber cement. Conservation report, 1 December 2008, curatorial files, Wadsworth Atheneum.
4. Suzanne Mullet Smith Papers, Archives of American Art, microfilm reel 1043, frame 964, cited in Melanie Kirschner, *Arthur Dove: Watercolors and Pastels* (New York: George Braziller, 1998), 53.
5. John Marin Jr., Downtown Gallery, to Charles C. Cunningham, 29 October 1955, curatorial files, Wadsworth Atheneum.

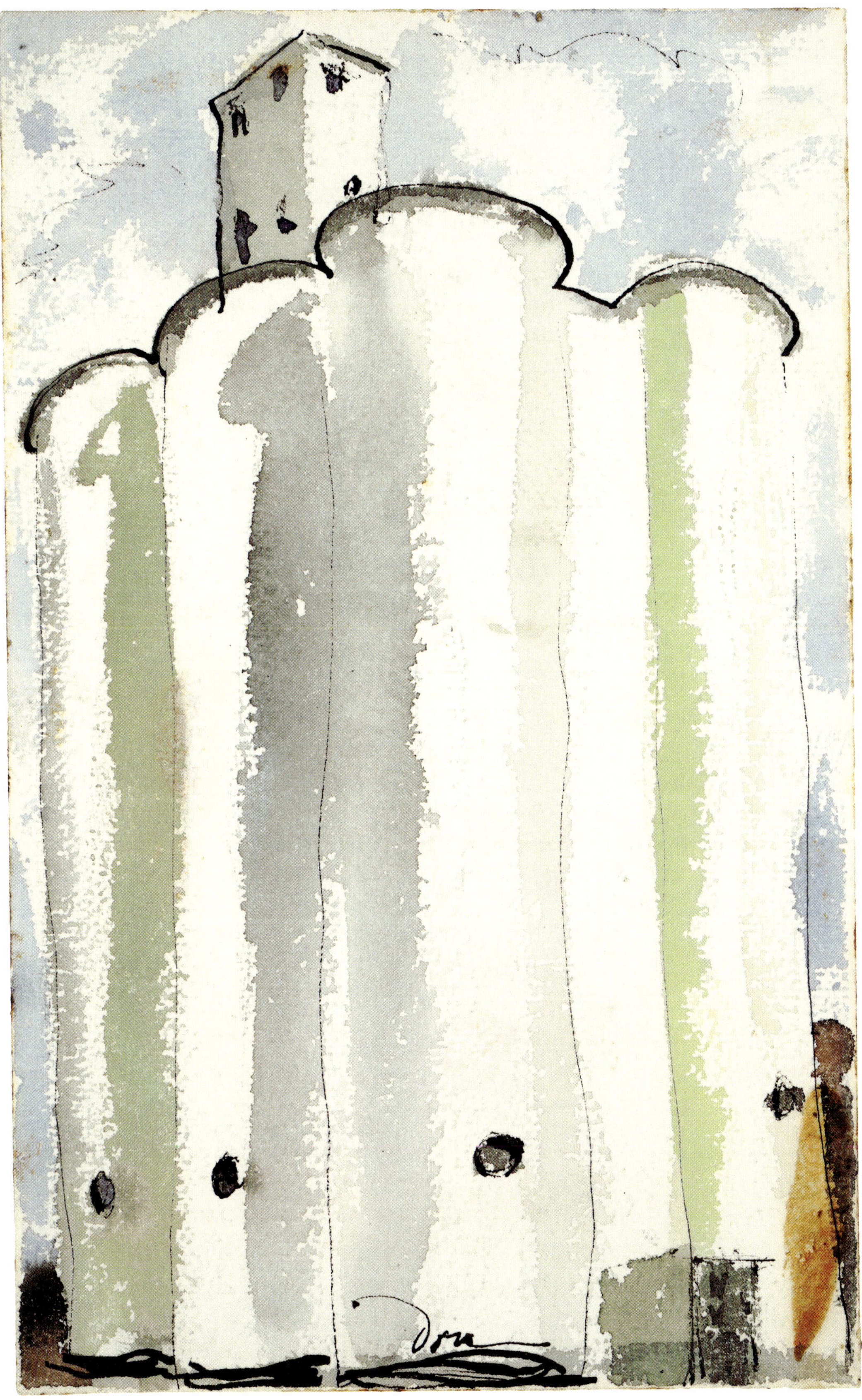

Cat. 24

25 a–f

Arthur Dove
Untitled
(#1 in a portfolio of 24 sketches), 1942
Wax-based paint, possibly modified with watercolor, oil paint, gums, and resin, on wove paper (sketchbook page perforated along left edge)
7 × 5 in. (17.8 × 12.7 cm) (sheet)
Inscribed at lower left: 180
Dated at lower center: 8.27.42
Inscribed at lower right: P+B Aurora Y. / Mars
Ex coll.: with the artist until 1946; to the artist's son, William C. Dove, until 1989
Gift of William C. Dove, 1989.61.1

Untitled
(#4 in a portfolio of 24 sketches), 1942
Wax-based paint, possibly modified using watercolor, oil paint, gums, and resin, with pen and black ink on wove paper (sketchbook page perforated along left edge)
7 × 5 in. (17.8 × 12.7 cm) (sheet)
Inscribed at lower left: 120
Dated at lower center: 7.30.42
Ex coll.: with the artist, until 1946; to the artist's son, William C. Dove, until 1989
Gift of William C. Dove, 1989.61.4

Untitled
(#8 in a portfolio of 24 sketches), 1942
Wax-based paint, possibly modified using watercolor, oil paint, gums, and resin, on wove paper
7 × 5 in. (17.8 × 12.7 cm) (sheet)
Inscribed at lower left: 247 [??]
4.VI.blk.cob+w.b.s.
Dated at lower right: 6.27.42
Ex coll.: with the artist until 1946; to the artist's son, William C. Dove, until 1989
Gift of William C. Dove, 1989.61.8

Untitled
(#15 in a portfolio of 24 sketches), 1942
Wax-based paint, possibly modified using watercolor, oil paint, gums, and resin, with pen and black ink on wove paper (sketchbook page perforated along left edge)
7 × 5 in. (17.8 × 12.7 cm) (sheet)
Inscribed at lower left: 244
Dated at lower center: 6.25.42
Inscribed at lower right: wx egg / oil
Ex coll.: with the artist, until 1946; to the artist's son, William C. Dove, until 1989
Gift of William C. Dove, 1989.61.15

Untitled
(#22 in a portfolio of 24 sketches), 1942
Wax-based paint, possibly modified using watercolor, oil paint, gums, and resin on thick wove paper (from watercolor paper block)
7 × 5 in. (17.8 × 12.7 cm) (sheet)
Inscribed at lower left: 110
Dated at lower center: 9.3.42
Inscribed on the back: M.H.
Ex coll.: with the artist, until 1946; to the artist's son, William C. Dove, until 1989
Gift of William C. Dove, 1989.61.22

Untitled
(#24 in a portfolio of 24 sketches), c. 1942
Wax-based paint, possibly modified using watercolor, oil paint, gums, and resin on wove paper
3 × 4 in. (7.6 × 10.2 cm)
Ex coll.: with the artist, until 1946; to the artist's son, William C. Dove, until 1989
Gift of William C. Dove, 1989.61.24

The final years of Dove's life were spent in Centerport, Long Island, where he had moved with his wife "Reds" in 1938. The couple lived on a millpond in an abandoned post office, which they converted into a studio and living space. Despite Dove's declining health, these were productive years for the artist. He reported to Stieglitz that his recent works "are very clear, clean-cut, and there is something new that I think worth fighting for."[1]

In a brochure for an exhibition of his late works held at An American Place, Dove commented, "I would like to make something that is real in itself, that does not remind anyone of any other thing, and that does not have to be explained."[2] At this time, in the years 1942 and 1943, Dove painted several hundred small-scale mixed-media and watercolor "Sketches," as he called them, of an intimate size and vision (the images measure three by four inches, and they are executed on sheets measuring five by seven inches).[3] This miniature format not only allowed the artist to be exceedingly productive despite his failing health but also resulted in compact works of bold creativity. His son, William C. Dove, who inherited these sketches, explained his father's reasoning for adhering to a uniform scale and format for these pieces. In his earlier career, the artist had been known to use a pantograph to enlarge his sketches for transfer to large oil paintings. But due to his frailty in the early 1940s, he instead chose to use a magic lantern for enlargement; his sketches were proportioned to fit the lantern.[4] Several of these sketches were in fact transferred to large canvases, while many others served as independent works in and of themselves.

Six of these sketches are presented here and represent the variety of imagery and technique that Dove experimented with in these works. Their small size challenged him to distill his lifelong study of the nature of abstraction into a dense, concentrated form. The sketches served as a visual diary. Dove recorded his experiments with different media, including watercolor, oil paint, wax emulsion, gum and resin, and egg yolk. Earlier, during his years in Geneva, New York, Dove read and was impressed by Max Doerner's *Materials of the Artist and Their Use in Painting, with Notes on the Techniques of the Old Masters* (1934), and he was inspired to work with a variety of mediums.[5] According to his diary entries, he began using wax emulsion in 1935, and also tried his hand at egg, oil, and wax emulsion combined with gasoline.[6] His experimentation intensified in these later sketches, as indicated by the pencil notations along the bottom of the sheets; for example *Untitled #15* is inscribed "wx egg oil" indicating a mixture of wax, egg, and oil for his composition. Several of the sketches were first outlined in pencil, including numbers 1 and 22.

Dove also used a wide variety of intense color combinations. In many of the sketches, including the examples presented here, he inscribed the sheets with the date of execution as well as abbreviated references to the colors used. For example, in *Untitled #1*, Dove inscribed "Y. Mars.," which may indicate his use of the pigment Mars Yellow.

Dove's watercolor sketches are remarkably varied in design and function. Of the six works presented here, only one, *Untitled #1*, dated 27 August 1942, is known to have been used as the basis for a large oil painting, *Flight* (fig. 1). The rich colors of the sketch, including Mars Yellow, are used in the finished oil, but Dove substituted brown and mauve in portions of the oil. The two compositions mirror each other faithfully.

While many of the studies are abstract compositions, a few suggest representational forms. For example, *Untitled #24* appears to be a landscape with a rooftop in the foreground and a bright yellow sun in the sky. Dove's late sketches are considered by scholars to be among his finest works and a high point in the history of watercolor in American art.

William Dove, who inherited these sketches from his father, generously gave groups of them to a selection of American museums, including a gift of twenty-four to the Atheneum, in 1989.[7]
EMK

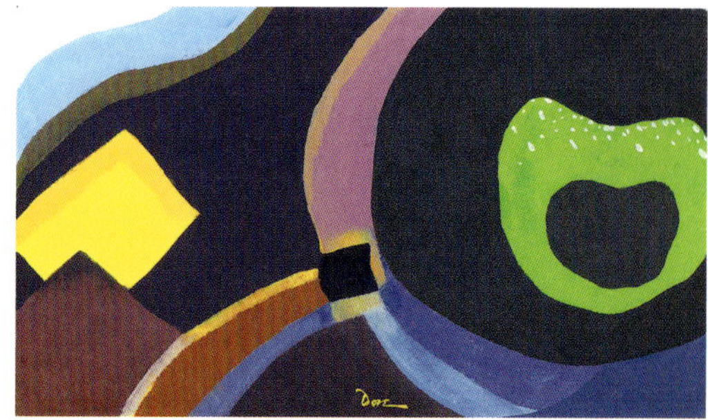

Fig. 1. Arthur Dove, *Flight*, 1943.
Wax emulsion on canvas, 12 × 20 in. (30.5 × 50.8 cm).
The Phillips Collection, Washington, D.C.
Bequest of Elmira Bier, 1976

1. Arthur Dove to Alfred Stieglitz, c. December 1940, quoted in Ann Lee Morgan, ed., *Dear Stieglitz, Dear Dove* (Newark: University of Delaware Press, 1988), 451.
2. *Arthur G. Dove Paintings, 1942–43*, An American Place, New York, 11 February–17 March 1943.
3. Debra Bricker Balken, *Arthur Dove: A Retrospective*, with contributions by William C. Agee and Elizabeth Hutton Turner (Cambridge, Mass.: MIT Press in association with the Addison Gallery of American Art and the Phillips Collection, 1998), 142, 152 n. 32.
4. Anne Cohen DePietro, "A Form Finding a Form: An Interview with William C. Dove," in *Arthur Dove and Helen Torr: The Huntington Years* (Huntington, N.Y.: Heckscher Museum, 1989), 79.
5. Balken, *Arthur Dove*, 152 n. 32; Justine S. Wimsatt, "Wax Emulsion, Tempera or Oil? Arthur Dove's Materials, Techniques and Surface Effects," unpublished paper, 1982, curatorial file, Wadsworth Atheneum; and Margaret Holben Ellis, Chairman, Conservation Center, New York University, to Elizabeth R. McClintock, 7 November 1991, curatorial files, Wadsworth Atheneum.
6. DePietro, *Arthur Dove and Helen Torr*, 43.
7. Among the museums that received gifts of Dove's late sketches are the Amon Carter Museum, the Metropolitan Museum of Art, the Pennsylvania Academy of the Fine Arts, the Philadelphia Museum of Art, the Museum of Fine Arts, Boston, and the Wichita Art Museum.

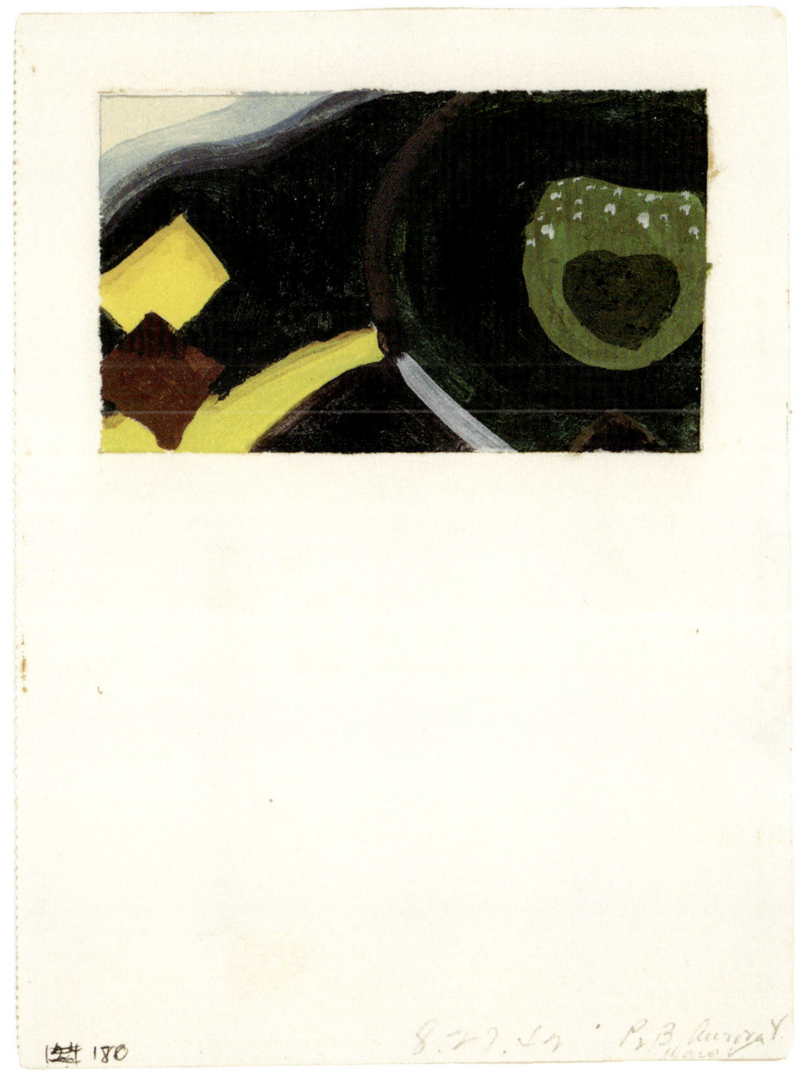
Cat. 25a

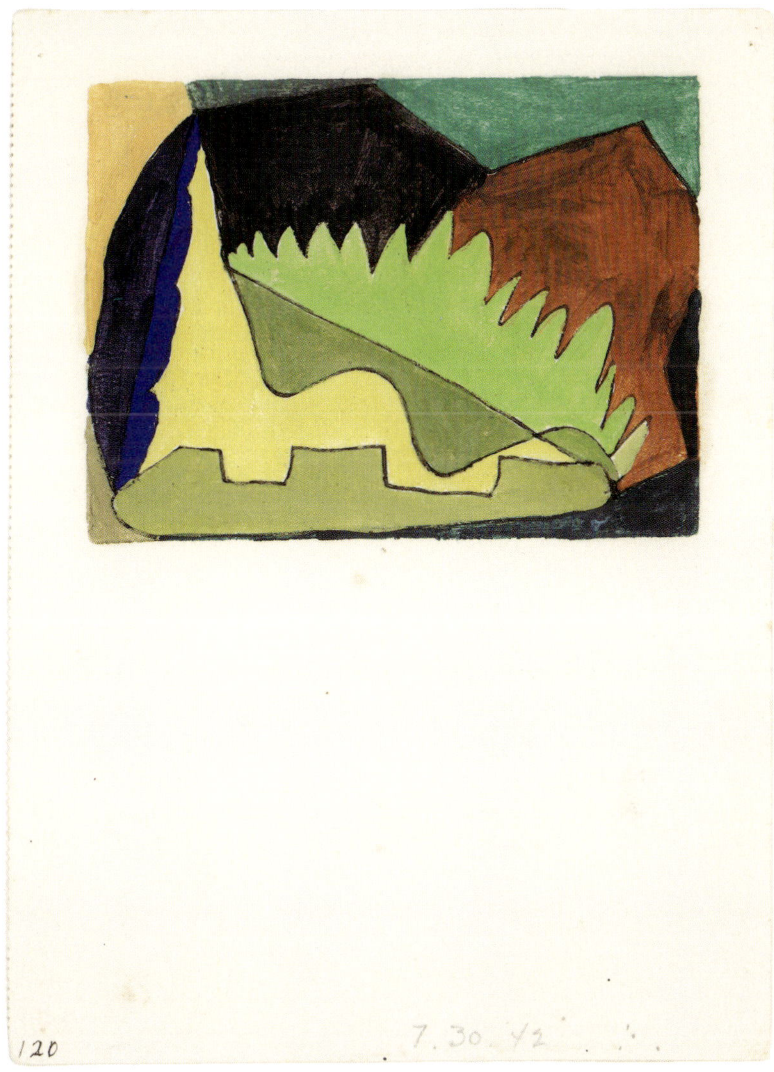
Cat. 25b

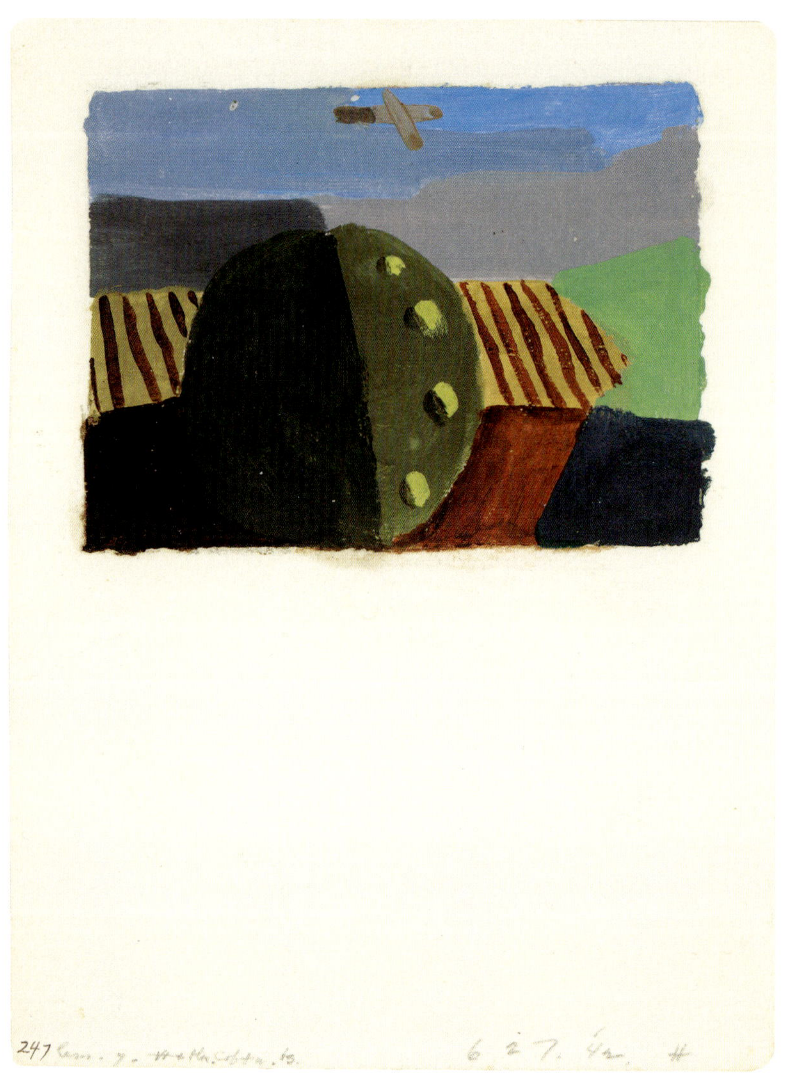

Cat. 25c

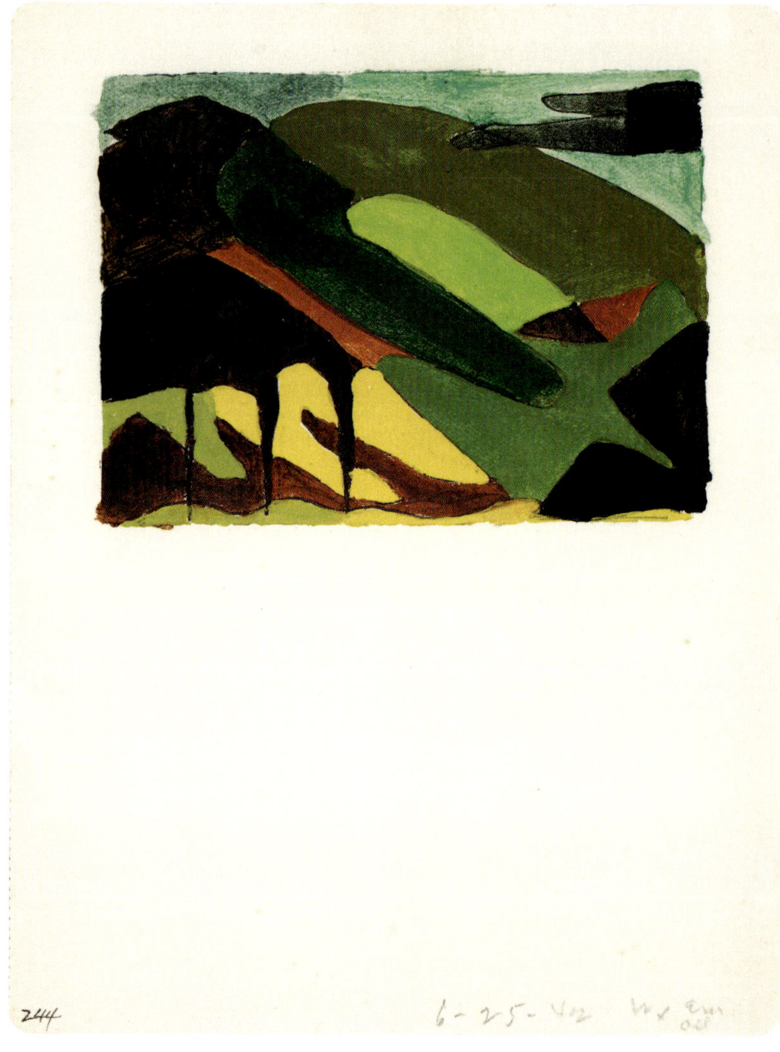

Cat. 25d

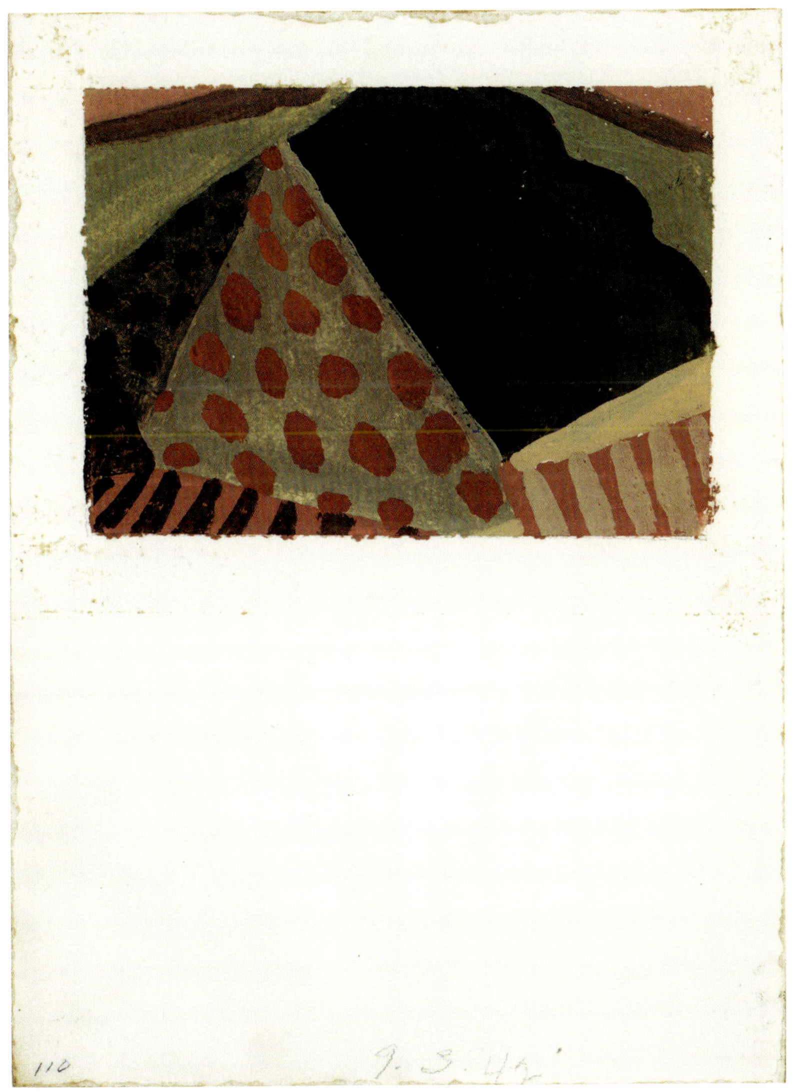
Cat. 25e

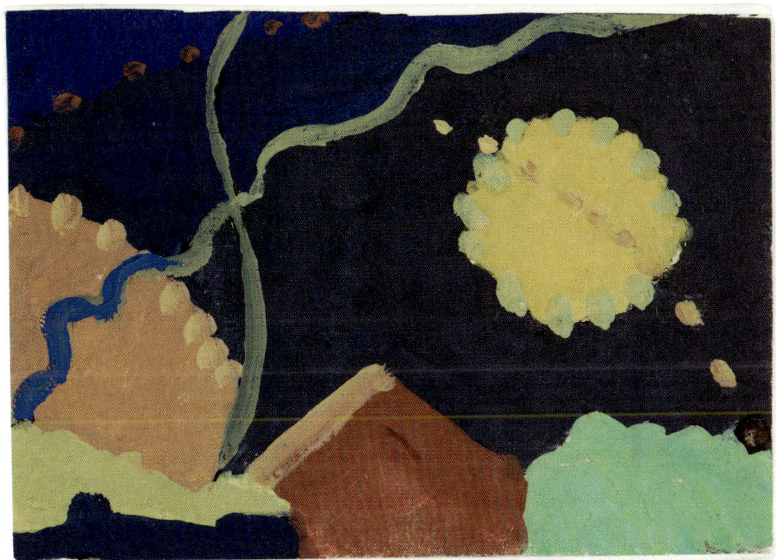
Cat. 25f

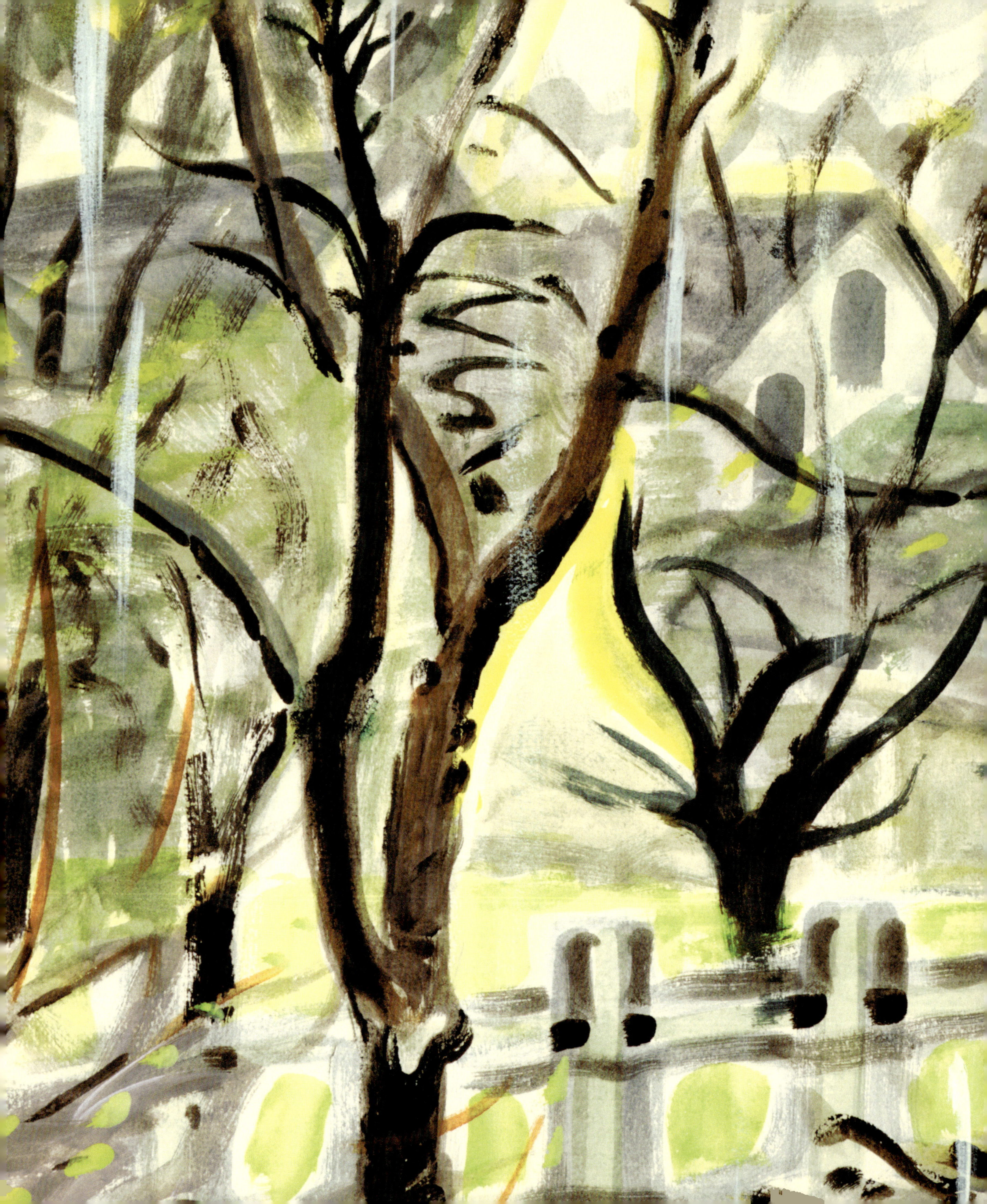

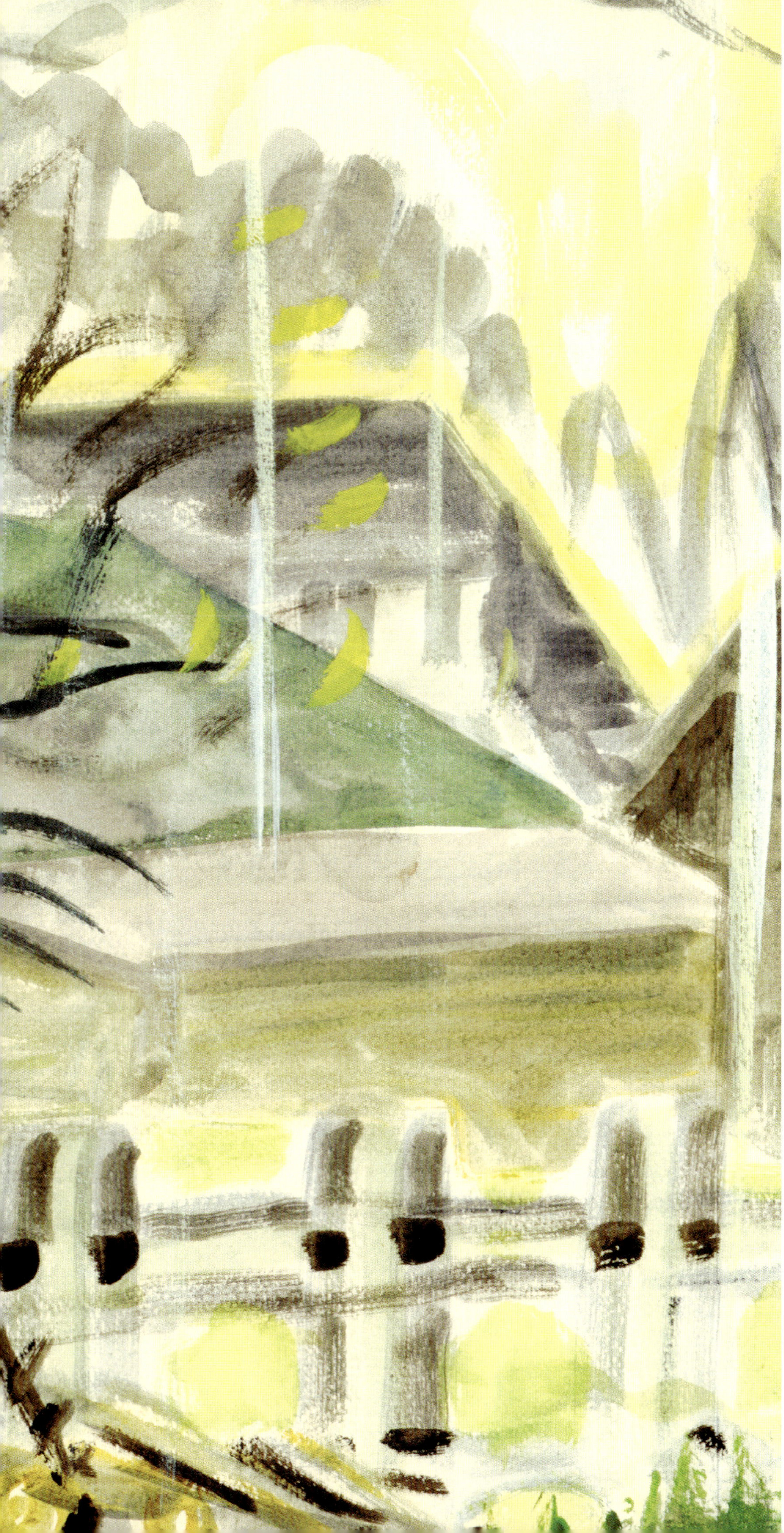

2.

Regionalism, Social Realism, and American Visions

Charles Ephraim Burchfield

Born in Ashtabula Harbor, Ohio, 1893; died in Buffalo, New York, 1967

Charles Burchfield is best known for his individualistic watercolors inspired by nature. Burchfield was raised in Salem, Ohio, and his earliest imagery of flowers and trees can be traced back to his teenage years. Recognized for his proficiency as a young artist, Burchfield attended the Cleveland School (now Institute) of Art on scholarship from 1912 to 1916. After graduation, Burchfield returned home to Salem, where he worked full-time at a local manufacturer. Although his painting was limited to weekends, lunch hours, and vacations, these years were crucial to his artistic development and discovery of a distinctive, expressionistic style in watercolor.

In 1921 Burchfield moved to Buffalo, New York, to work as a designer for the M. H. Birge & Sons Company, one of the nation's most prominent wallpaper companies. He married Bertha Kenreich the following year and later relocated to the suburb of Gardenville, where he raised a family and remained until his death. By the end of the 1920s, the Frank K. M. Rehn Gallery in New York was representing Burchfield, enabling the artist to resign from his day job to paint full-time. In the 1930s, Burchfield began to focus on the urban landscape and his paintings had somber overtones and a muted palette.

Gradually, Burchfield returned to the ideas and style of the early phase of his career. By the 1940s, he was literally drawing inspiration from earlier watercolors; he reworked compositions from 1917–18, pasting them onto larger pieces of paper and expanding them into more exuberant designs. These larger works display with greater intensity the artist's mystical view of nature—its fantastic and transcendent sights and sounds. His late works are almost double the size of his earlier paintings, and they present a bolder combination of expressive lines and distortions in form and color.

Burchfield had several important solo exhibitions at the Museum of Modern Art (1930), the Albright Art Gallery in Buffalo (1944), and the Whitney Museum of American Art (1956). Between 1949 and 1953, Burchfield taught at Ohio University, the University of Minnesota, the Art Institute of Buffalo, and the Buffalo Fine Arts Academy.

In 1966, one year before Burchfield's death, the Charles Burchfield Center at Buffalo State College was created in honor of his artistic achievement. Today, the Burchfield Penney Art Center (renamed in honor of a significant gift from Charles Rand Penney), a museum dedicated to the art and vision of Charles E. Burchfield, possesses the world's largest and most comprehensive collection of his art, as well as archival materials, studio objects, and memorabilia related to the artist's life.

Select Bibliography

Charles Burchfield: His Golden Year. Tucson: University of Arizona Art Gallery, 1965.

John I. H. Bauer. *The Inlander: Life and Work of Charles Burchfield, 1893–1967*. Newark: University of Delaware Press, 1982.

J. Benjamin Townsend. *Charles Burchfield's Journals: The Poetry of Place*. Albany: State University of New York Press, 1993.

Charles E. Burchfield: Romantic Lands. New York: Kennedy Galleries, 1999.

26

Charles Burchfield
Nature's Mystic Spiral, 1916
Opaque and transparent watercolor, heightened with graphite, on wove paper
12 × 9 in. (30.5 × 22.9 cm)
Signed at lower right: Chas Burchfield / 1916
Inscription on verso: Nature's Mystic Spiral / April 1916
Ex coll.: Edward Gorey, Yarmouthport, Massachusetts
Bequest of Edward Gorey, 2001.13.32

In 1915–16, Burchfield was developing his technique and establishing a series of motifs that would recur throughout his art. This is apparent in *Nature's Mystic Spiral* and a drawing from the year prior, *Sunburst and Clouds*, that contain similar vertical arrangements of semiabstract forms (fig. 1). Both scenes are divided into three sections (sun, clouds, earth) and topped by a similar "spiral"—a radiant light source surrounded by concentric circles. Both compositions depict the sun as an orb with linear and circular rays, partially covered by clusters of clouds and other strange shapes. These sharp, pointy forms possess a more sinister feel than fluffy, rounded clouds. As suggested by the title of the Atheneum's watercolor, Burchfield may have invented these forms to convey the magical or "mystic" qualities of Mother Nature.

At this time, Charles Burchfield had just graduated from the Cleveland School of Art and received a scholarship to the National Academy of Design in New York. His move to New York was truncated by homesickness and financial struggles, and after one month he returned to his hometown of Salem, Ohio, seeking respite from the city in the rural countryside. Despite these interruptions, however, Burchfield's productivity remained strong, and by year's end he had completed over two hundred watercolors.

This initial phase of Burchfield's artistic career was detailed in his journal entries. From 1915 to 1918, he wrote of personal struggles with depression and a desire to escape from reality. He described having physical/sensory reactions to trees, birds, and clouds that sometimes bordered on hallucination.[1] This combination of factors—an obsessive interest in the natural world and feelings of alienation—shaped Burchfield's early forays as an artist. *Nature's Mystic Spiral* can thus be interpreted as a visual record of Burchfield's emotional state.

Fig. 1. Archival photograph of *Sunburst and Clouds*, 1915. Burchfield Penney Art Center, Buffalo, New York. Frank Rehn Archive

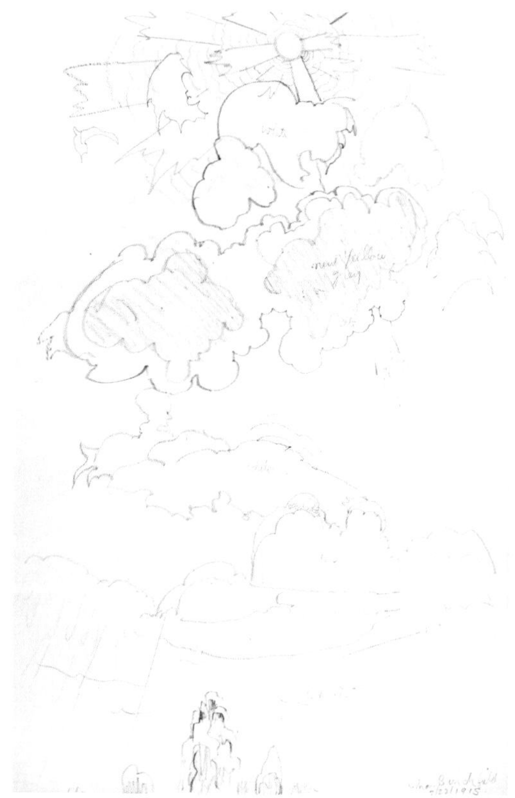

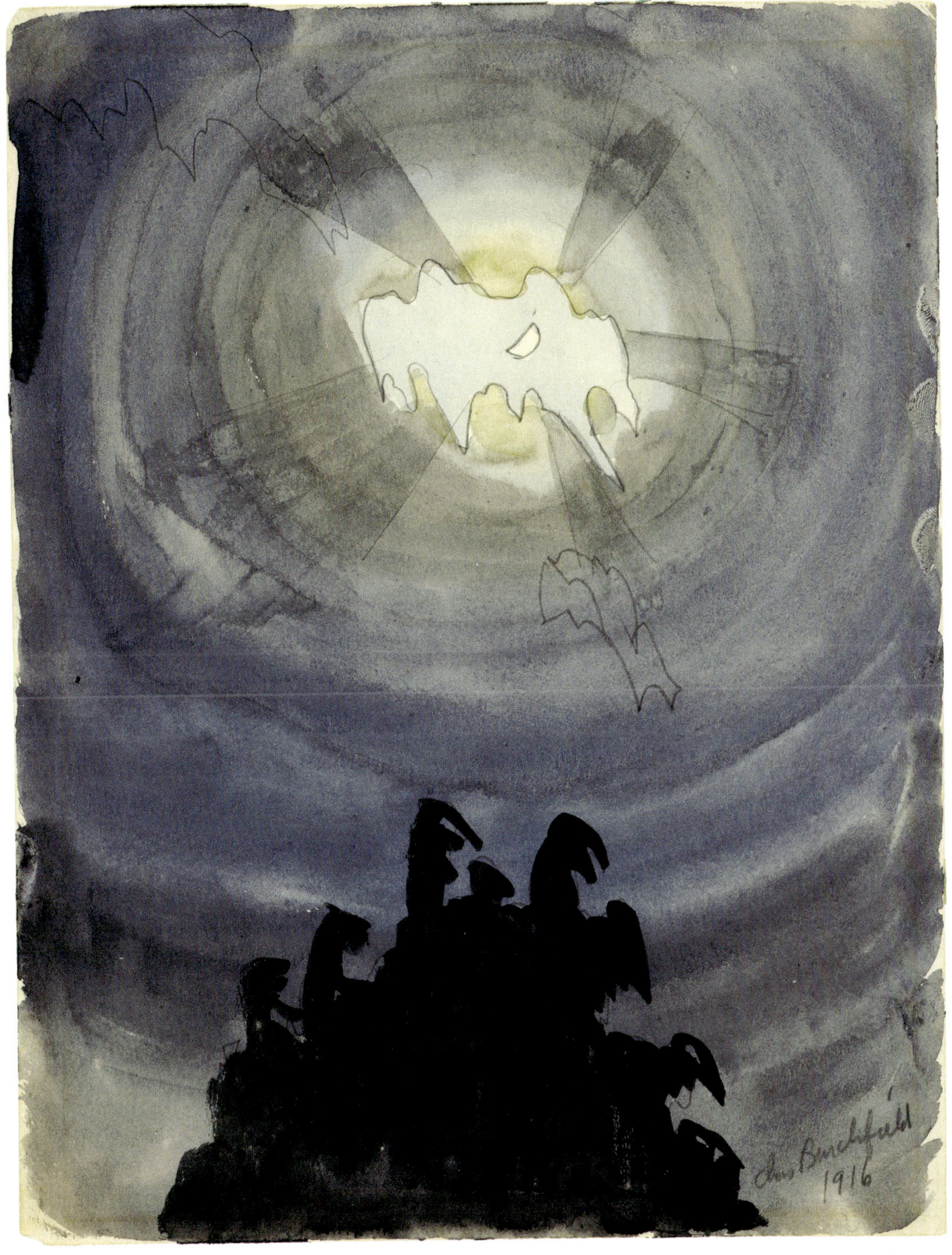

Cat. 26

The radiating sun and its hazy, hypnotic rings are the artist's sensory responses to nature. The scene is painted with a thin, semitransparent layer of watercolor with varying degrees of opacity, which enhances the atmospheric feeling. The composition appears moody, tentative; the absence of detail makes it difficult to identify the time or place.
ECM

1. J. Benjamin Townsend, *Charles Burchfield's Journals: The Poetry of Place* (Albany: State University of New York Press, 1993), 332.

27

Charles Burchfield
Spring Evening (Salem), 1917
Opaque and transparent watercolor, over graphite, on wove paper laid onto cardboard
20 × 13 7/8 in. (50.8 × 35.2 cm)
Inscription at lower left: Chas Burchfield / 1917
Inscription on verso, in artist's hand: Spring Evening / April, 1917 / An impression of a spring evening emphasizing the delicate transparency of budding trees.
Ex coll.: Frank K. M. Rehn Gallery, New York
The Ella Gallup Sumner and Mary Catlin Sumner Collection Fund, 1940.27

Charles Burchfield labeled 1917 as "the golden year" of his career, from the standpoint of production and innovation.[1] This was all the more impressive since he was working full-time at the W. H. Mullins Company, a manufacturer, and time for painting was limited to the evenings, lunch hours, and vacations. Not surprisingly, many works from this year, such as *Spring Evening*, depicted views in and around his home.

The body of work completed in 1917 reflected a burst of creativity and foretold the direction of Burchfield's mature work, namely the discovery of his expressionistic style patented by a loose, relaxed brushstroke.[2] This watercolor was painted from an upstairs window in his house in Salem; the view is of a budding tree and the nearby row of houses.[3] The houses are roughly sketched; it is the natural elements that are the focus of this scene. The emphasis on the sensory experience of nature in *Spring Evening* was fundamental to the distinctive style that emerged in Burchfield's early works. He often used cartoonlike outlines to translate the sounds and vibrations of nature into pictorial images.[4] For instance, the foliage of the central tree is framed by light purple lines that vary in opacity and thickness. This halo effect became more prominent and more intense in later years, as seen in the Atheneum's *Song in the Rain* (cat. 30).

Spring Evening was included in two important exhibitions in Burchfield's career. *Drawings in Watercolor by Charles Burchfield*, at the Kevorkian Gallery, New York, February 1920, was among one of his first solo shows; twenty years later, *Early Watercolors 1917–1918, November 1939*, organized by Burchfield's dealer, Frank K. M. Rehn, functioned as a mini-retrospective. In his review of the 1939

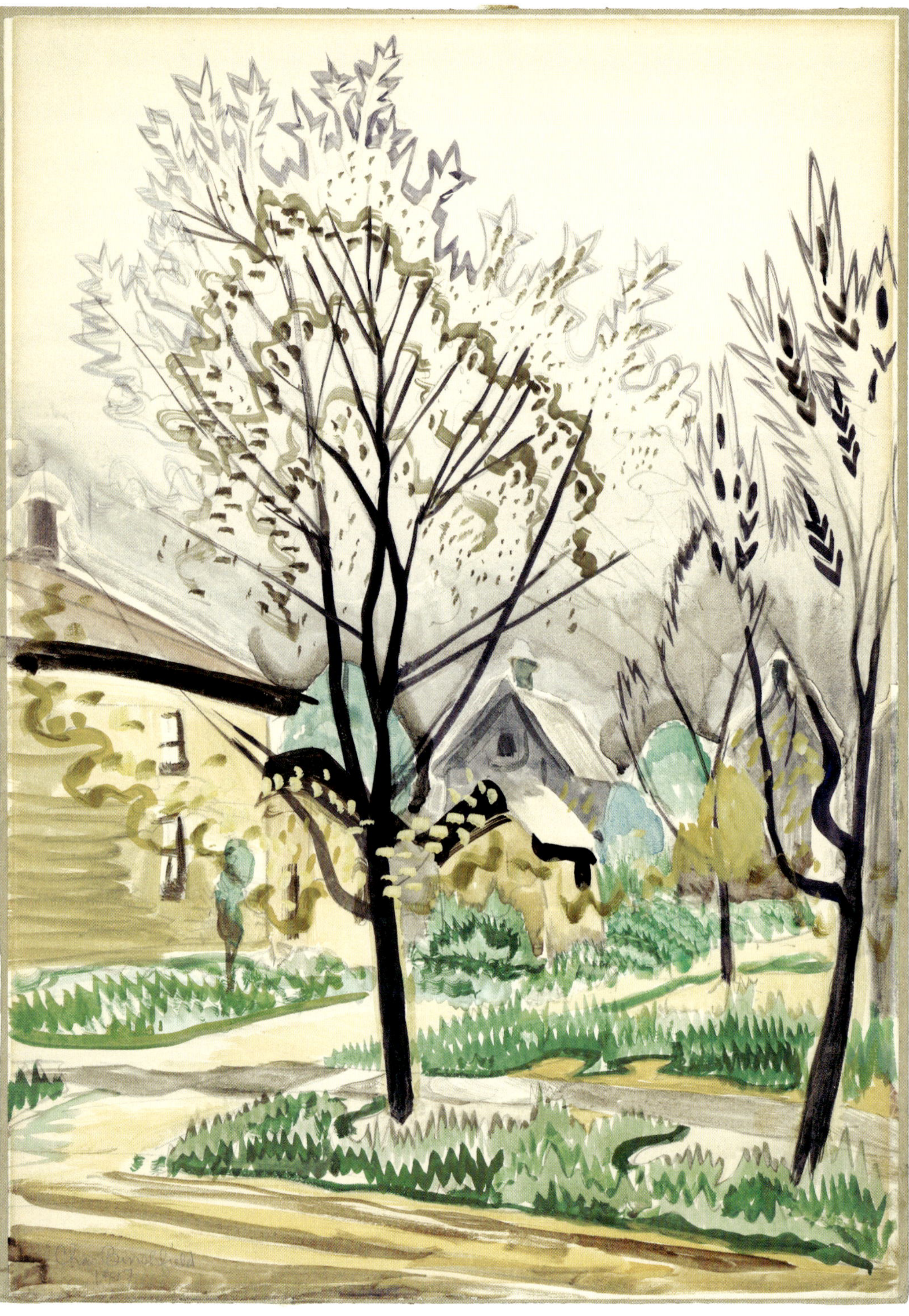

Cat. 27

exhibition, Edward Alden Jewell described the watercolors from Burchfield's "youth" as "romantic and [possessing] an imaginative power that reaches out and up."[5]
ECM

1. *Charles Burchfield: His Golden Year* (Tucson: University of Arizona Art Gallery, 1965), 20. See also J. Benjamin Townsend, *Charles Burchfield's Journals: The Poetry of Place* (Albany: State University of New York Press, 1993), 436.
2. Bridget Moore, "Charles Burchfield: Art and Nature," in *Charles Burchfield Paintings, 1915–1964* (New York: D. C. Moore Gallery, 2005), 11.
3. Charles Burchfield to Charles C. Cunningham, 11 February 1951, Wadsworth Atheneum Archives. The artist explained, "The scene is opposite my home [in Salem] done from an upstairs window."
4. Townsend, *Charles Burchfield's Journals*, 436.
5. Edward Alden Jewell, "Burchfield Shows Water-Color Art," *New York Times*, 21 November 1939.

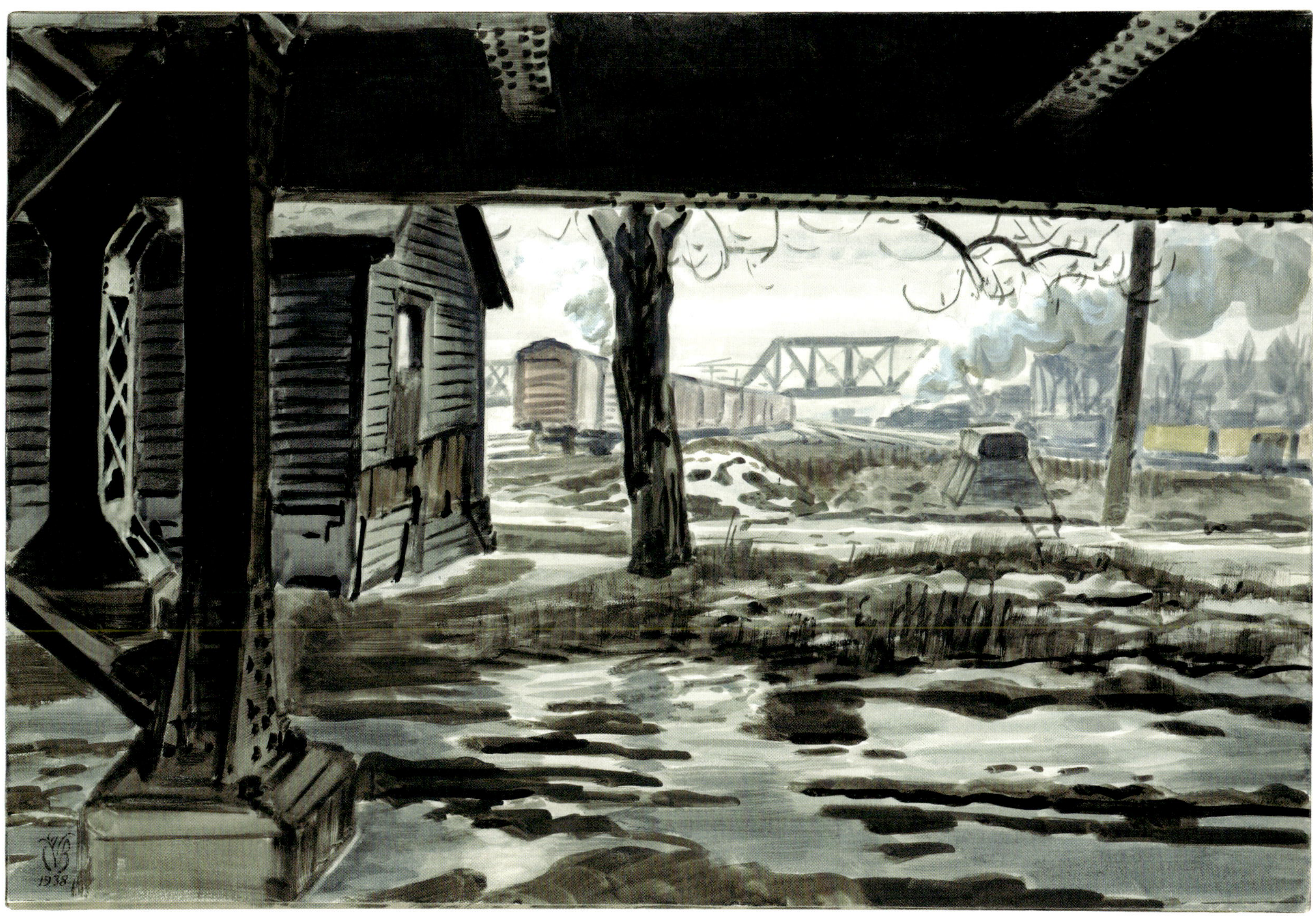

Cat. 28

28
Charles Burchfield
Looking Through a Bridge, 1938
Opaque and transparent watercolor, over graphite, on wove paper, laid onto cardboard
22 5/8 × 33 in. (57.5 × 83.8 cm)
Signed and dated at lower left: CEB (monogram) / 1938
Ex coll.: with the Frank K. M. Rehn Gallery, New York
The Ella Gallup Sumner and Mary Catlin Sumner Collection Fund, 1939.208

Looking Through a Bridge was painted during the middle phase of Burchfield's career, which was characterized by a marked change in subject matter. After a period of adjustment to the move from his native Salem, Ohio, to Buffalo, New York, and then the suburb of Gardenville, Burchfield found inspiration in his new surroundings. As seen in *Looking Through a Bridge*, Burchfield was stimulated by the grit and decay of the railroad yards, the harbor, and other places that conveyed the industrial city. Watercolors from this middle period are characterized by a somber palette of black, brown, and dark green. As John I. H. Baur observed, "[These paintings] had a new austerity, a greater degree of realism, than any of his earlier work. They also had a largeness of structure and design that was almost classical in form though plainly romantic in feeling."[1]

By the late 1930s, Burchfield had secured the prominent Frank K. M. Rehn as his dealer in New York and thus resigned from his position at M. H. Birge & Sons to devote more time to painting. Free to paint all day, Burchfield embarked on daily expeditions to surrounding areas, often returning to Buffalo, since it provided ample subject matter: rows of working-class houses, railroad, docks, bridges, and bleak weather. *Looking Through a Bridge* was painted during one such visit to Buffalo and is based on an area adjacent to the harbor known as the Industrial Flats.[2] As the artist recalled, "I painted it in late January, outdoors on the spot. It was one of those relatively mild days in winter when it was possible to paint in water-color." The artist described the scene as having a murky atmosphere that he attempted to convey using touches of opaque watercolor.[3] More than most of Burchfield's vivid and ecstatic depictions of nature, this work expresses a Depression-era mood. The setting is akin to the gritty urban scenes more commonly depicted by American artists such as Raphael Soyer and William Glackens (q.v.). In 1939, Atheneum director A. Everett Austin purchased two urban-themed watercolors from Frank Rehn, *Looking Through a Bridge* and Reginald Marsh's *New York* (cat. 47). ECM

1. John I. H. Baur, *The Inlander: Life and Work of Charles Burchfield, 1893–1967* (Newark: University of Delaware Press, 1982), 152.
2. Charles Burchfield to Charles C. Cunningham, 7 October 1946, Wadsworth Atheneum Archives.
3. Burchfield to Cunningham, 11 February 1951, Wadsworth Atheneum Archives.

29

Charles Burchfield
November Landscape (formerly *November*), 1946
Opaque and transparent watercolor, over traces of charcoal, on two sheets of conjoined wove paper, laid onto cardboard
33 7/8 × 26 in. (86 × 66 cm)
Signed and dated at lower right: CEB (monogram) / 1946
Inscribed on old label removed from verso: November Landscape / 34 × 26 / 1946 / Burchfield
Ex coll.: Mr. and Mrs. Charles C. Cunningham, Chicago, as of 1947; Ms. Priscilla Cunningham (his daughter), New York
Gift of Priscilla Cunningham, 1991.42

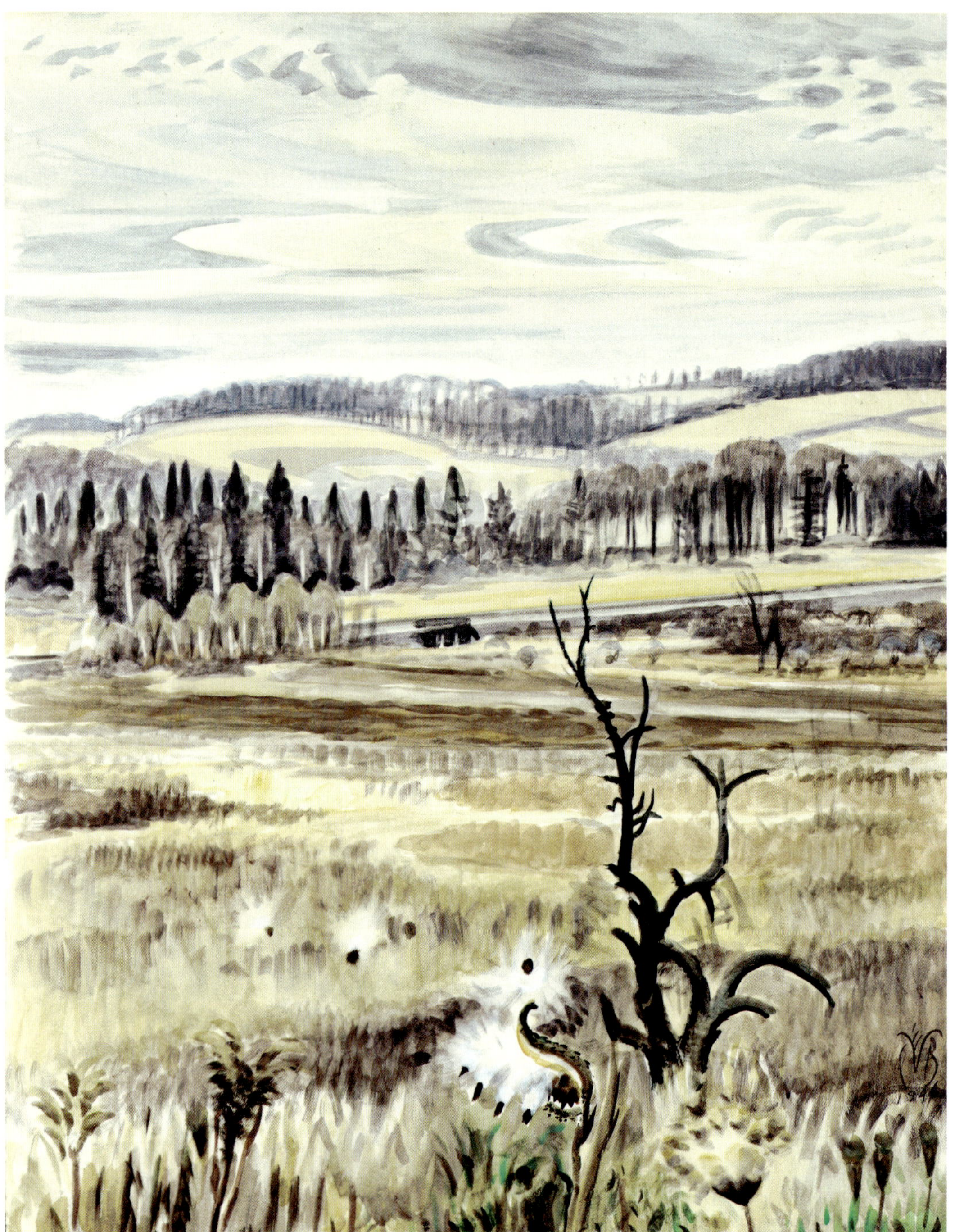

Cat. 29

Burchfield's principal concern in the 1930s was industry in an urban setting, but in the following decade he returned to nature and the country, as seen in *November Landscape*. Burchfield's transition from the "realism" of Buffalo's urban decay to the more expressionistic style of his early watercolors was gradual, however. Seeking the boldness and bravura of his early, imaginative watercolors, he began rereading his early journals and reexamining his paintings from 1917 and 1918. He found inspiration in the freshness and spontaneity of this work and began to rework and expand many of his earlier compositions. Many of his paintings from this decade were larger in scale.[1] Reconnecting to earlier work manifested a major breakthrough, and many of Burchfield's best-known paintings, such as *The Sphinx and the Milky Way* (Munson-Williams-Proctor Arts Institute, Utica), were completed in 1946, a watershed year.[2]

As John I. H. Baur has observed, in the 1940s Burchfield also moved toward "a clearer evocation of mood, of the powers that shake nature, and, by implication, of the inner powers that shake humankind."[3] In *November Landscape*, Burchfield captures the poetic feeling of seasonal change. The muted autumnal colors and the stark, barren fields exemplify the month of November. In the foreground, a milkweed plant scatters its pods before the winter hibernation. Beneath the stem of the milkweed, blades of bright green grass dot the bottom of the composition. These and the silky white filaments of the milkweed are reminders of the death and rebirth that will take place in months to follow.

The quality of brushwork in *November Landscape* also is evidence of the technical strength of Burchfield's later watercolors, in which he combined a variety of brushstrokes: the texture of the grasses and fields is illustrated by short, abbreviated strokes, whereas the sky and rolling hills are painted with layers of light wash. In addition, *November Landscape* was painted on two conjoined pieces of paper and is almost twice the size of his earlier works. ECM

1. Nanette V. Maciejunes, "A Biographical Sketch," in *Charles E. Burchfield: Romantic Lands* (New York: Kennedy Galleries, 1999). Burchfield began pasting blank strips of paper to existing watercolors and reworking the compositions into what he called "reconstructions."
2. J. Benjamin Townsend, *Charles Burchfield's Journals: The Poetry of Place* (Albany: State University of New York Press, 1993), 503.
3. John I. H. Baur, introduction to *Charles E. Burchfield: The Middle Years, 1929–1950* (New York: Kennedy Galleries, 1978).

30

Charles Burchfield
Song in the Rain, 1947
Opaque and transparent watercolor on wove paper, with a conjoined strip at the left, laid onto cardboard
40 3/8 × 28 1/4 in. (103.8 × 71.8 cm)
Signed and dated at lower left: CEB (monogram) / 1947
Ex coll.: with the Frank K. M. Rehn Gallery, New York
The Ella Gallup Sumner and Mary Catlin Sumner Collection Fund, 1957.16

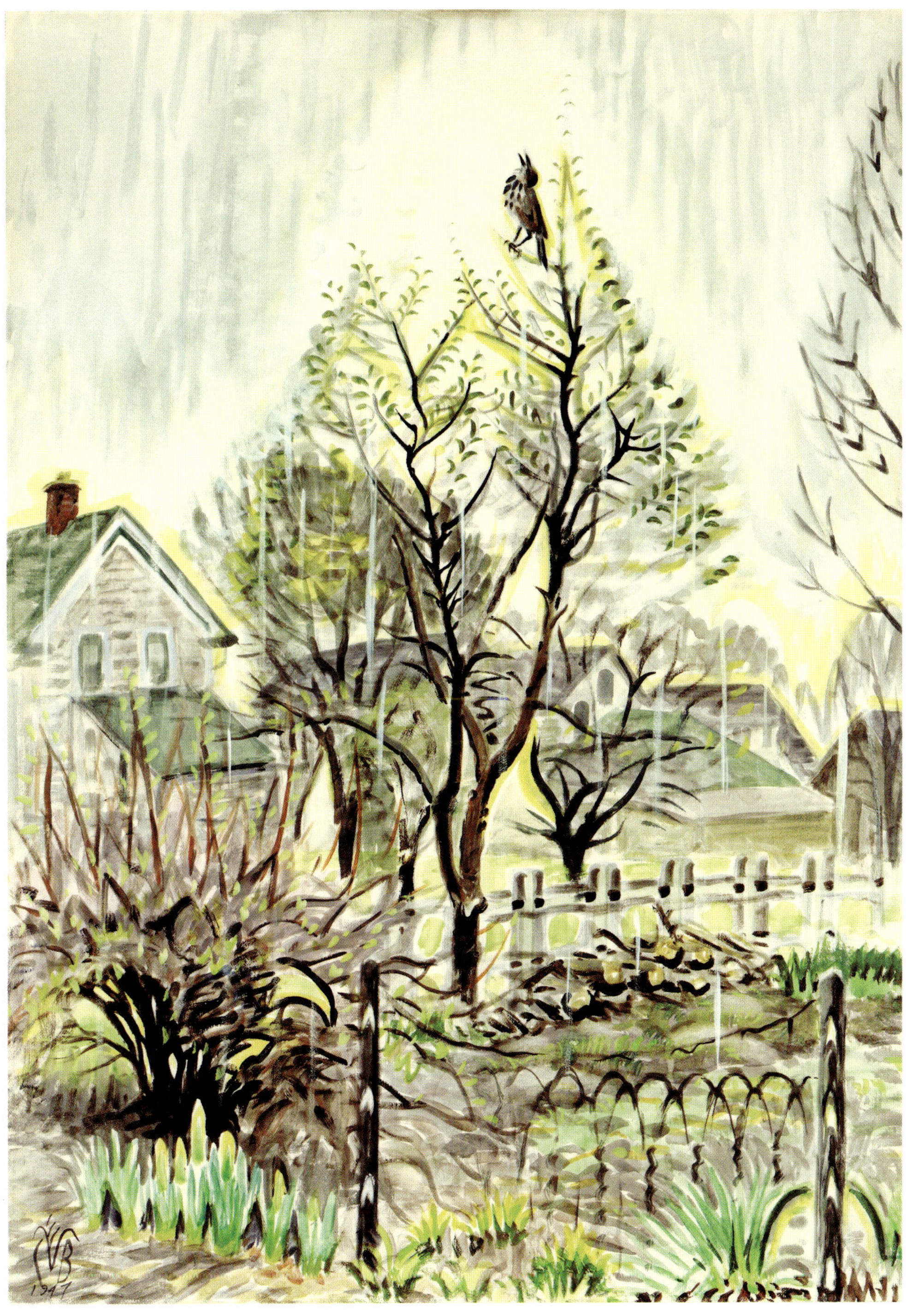

Cat. 30

Song in the Rain, like Burchfield's watercolor *November Landscape* (cat. 29), dates to the middle phase of his career. In the watercolors from this period, Burchfield moves away from the realism of the previous decade toward an expressionistic depiction of nature, indicated by emphasis on the weather, the changing seasons, insects, and birds. In contrast to the somber mood of *November Landscape*, *Song in the Rain* celebrates the vibrant and energetic spring season with patches of concentrated color. Burchfield worked almost exclusively in watercolor—he rarely painted oils—and pushed the medium to bold, new levels. As seen here, he increased the scale of his compositions by using multiple sheets of paper for one composition.

The composition, set near the artist's home in Gardenville, New York, is of a sparrow perched atop a cherry tree in a neighbor's backyard. Burchfield's recollection of this demonstrates his intimate association between nature and emotion:

Each year a pair of song sparrows build their nest in some underbrush not far from the studio—from early March to late May, the male delights me with his lovely song. On this particular day when the painting was made, it was raining; the bird seemed to enjoy the rain, for again and again he would perch in the top of the wild-cherry tree, and lifting his head, literally seemed to burst into song. And so, under my beach umbrella, the painting came into being.[1]

In his detailed memory, Burchfield reveals how a single bird created a transcendent experience. *Song in the Rain* evokes this moment by suggesting the fresh colors of spring growth, the soothing pattern of raindrops, and above all, an exuberant bird in song.

With a renewed boldness of color, Burchfield juxtaposed bright greens and yellows with dense blacks and browns. The major forms in the composition—the trees, bushes, and row of nearby houses—are highlighted by electric yellow contours. Around the top of the central tree, where the bird is perched, the artist has made use of negative space—Burchfield uses an area of light wash to create an almost white invisible cloud, an aura that is meant to be the visual equivalent of the bird's melodic song. Painted over the elaborately designed landscape is a veil of raindrops suggested by long, pale strokes. This layering of pattern and colors is communicative of the awe and rapture Burchfield experienced. The artist Peter Blume (q.v.) described him as having "a romance with nature itself . . . to which he could never get close enough. He would have liked to learn the song of the grasshoppers, in order to follow the dance of the flowers."[2]
ECM

1. Charles Burchfield to Charles C. Cunningham, 21 February 1957, Wadsworth Atheneum Archives.
2. Peter Blume, "A Tribute to Charles Burchfield," in *Charles Burchfield, Memorial Exhibition: Paintings and Drawings* (New York: American Academy of Arts and Letters, 1968).

31

Charles Burchfield
Study of Bats in Flight, c. 1954–63
Conté crayon on wove paper laid onto paperboard
13 5/6 × 19 1/2 in. (35.1 × 49.5 cm)
Stamp at lower right:
C. E. Burchfield Foundation / B-307
Ex coll.: with Charles E. Burchfield Foundation; Kennedy Galleries, Inc., New York; Edward Gorey, Yarmouthport, Massachusetts, as of 1978
Bequest of Edward Gorey, 2001.13.34

Study of Bats in Flight has been identified as relating to three compositions with bat motifs: the Conté crayon *Abandoned House at Twilight* (1956; Burchfield Penney Art Center, Buffalo), the watercolor *Haunted Twilight* (1954–62; Burchfield Penney Art Center, Buffalo), and the unfinished watercolor *Twilight Phantom* (fig. 1).[1] The motif of flying creatures—predominantly insects and birds—appears regularly in Burchfield's repertoire of images. Bats, however, were less common. Burchfield's drawings were compositional studies for paintings and the Atheneum's study of bats may be a preparatory work for one of the more finished compositions.[2]

The bats are scattered across the page and are depicted from a variety of angles. The degree of finish of the drawings varies, ranging from childlike doodles to meticulous detail. The two bats at the center of the page are distinct; they are larger, viewed from above rather than in profile, and are more finished in their appearance. Burchfield has made greater effort in these two sketches to accurately render the animal. He has clearly defined the animals' thumbs (the first finger at the top of the wing), legs, and feet, and has carefully rendered their fur and skin. Their slightly open mouths give the bats an oddly human expression, though this does not lessen the creatures' spooky quality.

Another noteworthy feature about this drawing is its connection between the artist and its former owner, Edward Gorey.[3] Gorey, an acclaimed writer, artist, and illustrator, also completed theatrical set designs. He purchased this drawing just as he finished scenery and costume designs for the Broadway production of Bram Stoker's *Dracula*.[4] Burchfield's drawing likely appealed to Gorey's taste for the macabre and reminded him of his own bat-embellished set designs. In "Grand Curtain," for example, bats populate the scene, both obvious and concealed; the profusion of dark bodies and pointy ears create feelings of apprehension and mystery (fig. 2). Similarly, they decorate the sky in a manner that recalls Burchfield's study and *Bats at Twilight*. The stylized and mysterious literary and theatrical world of Edward Gorey was not unlike the fantastic quality of Burchfield's paintings. Although Gorey created imaginary characters and invented animals, his passion for the real thing was quite sincere. Among the numerous animal welfare groups he supported was the Bat Conservation International Foundation in Austin, Texas.[5]

ECM

1. My thanks to Tullis E. Johnson, research assistant, Burchfield Penney Art Center, Buffalo, New York, for help dating this drawing and additional research assistance.
2. Leona E. Prasse, *The Drawings of Charles E. Burchfield* (Cleveland: Cleveland Museum of Art, 1953).
3. Jean Martin, "The Mind's Eye: Writers Who Draw," *Drawing*, July–August 1980, reprinted in *Ascending Peculiarity: Edward Gorey on Edward Gorey*, ed. Karen Wilkin (New York: Harcourt, 2001), 90. Burchfield was one of the painters Gorey admired, and he owned several watercolors and drawings by the artist, including *Nature's Mystic Spiral* (cat. 26).
4. My thanks to Martha J. Fleischman of Kennedy Galleries, Inc., New York, for providing this information.
5. Susan Lumenello, "Vita: Edward Gorey; Brief Life of an Artful Author, 1925–2000," *Harvard Magazine*, March–April 2007, 3.

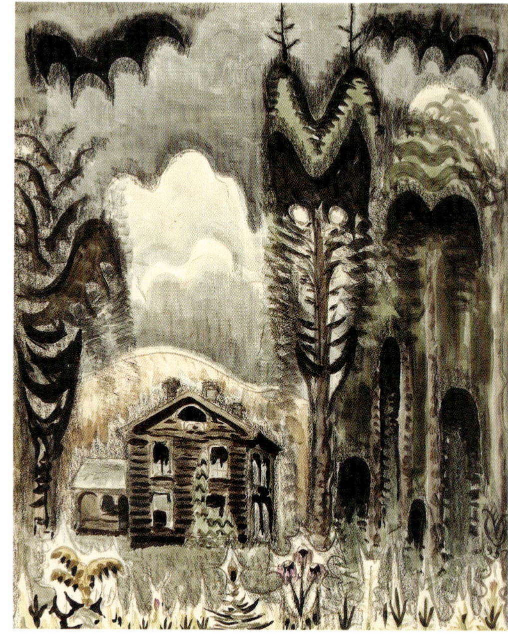

Fig. 1. Charles Burchfield, *Twilight Phantom*, 1957. Watercolor on paper, 21 1/2 × 16 1/2 in. (54.6 × 41.9 cm). Private collection

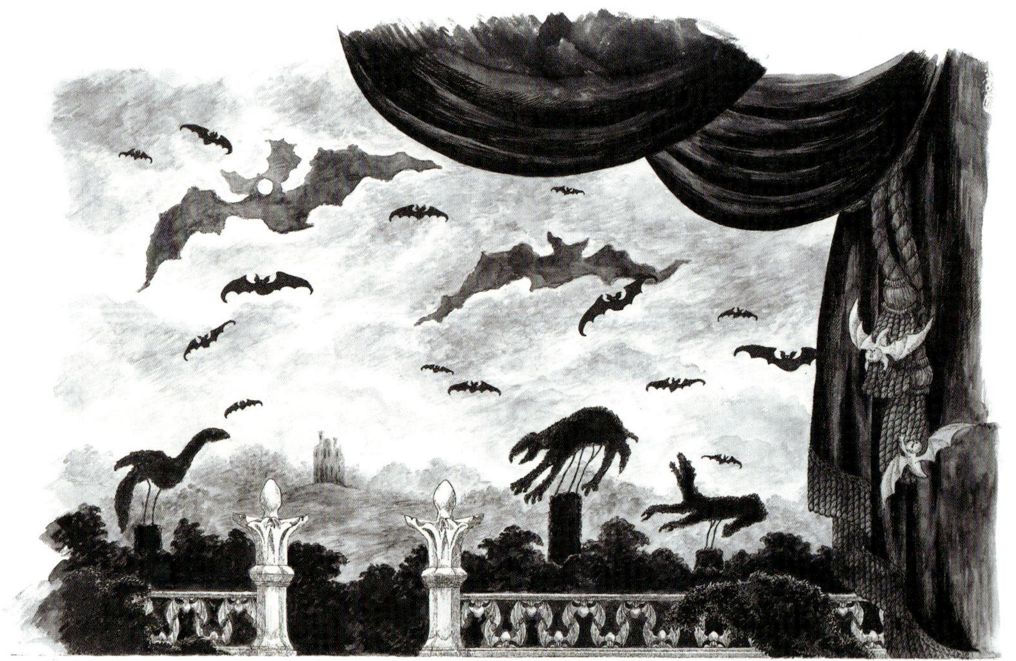

Fig. 2. Edward Gorey, "Grand Curtain" for *Dracula*, 1977. Pen, ink, and watercolor, 20 1/2 × 27 in. (52.1 × 68.6 cm). Collection of Frances Massey Dulaney

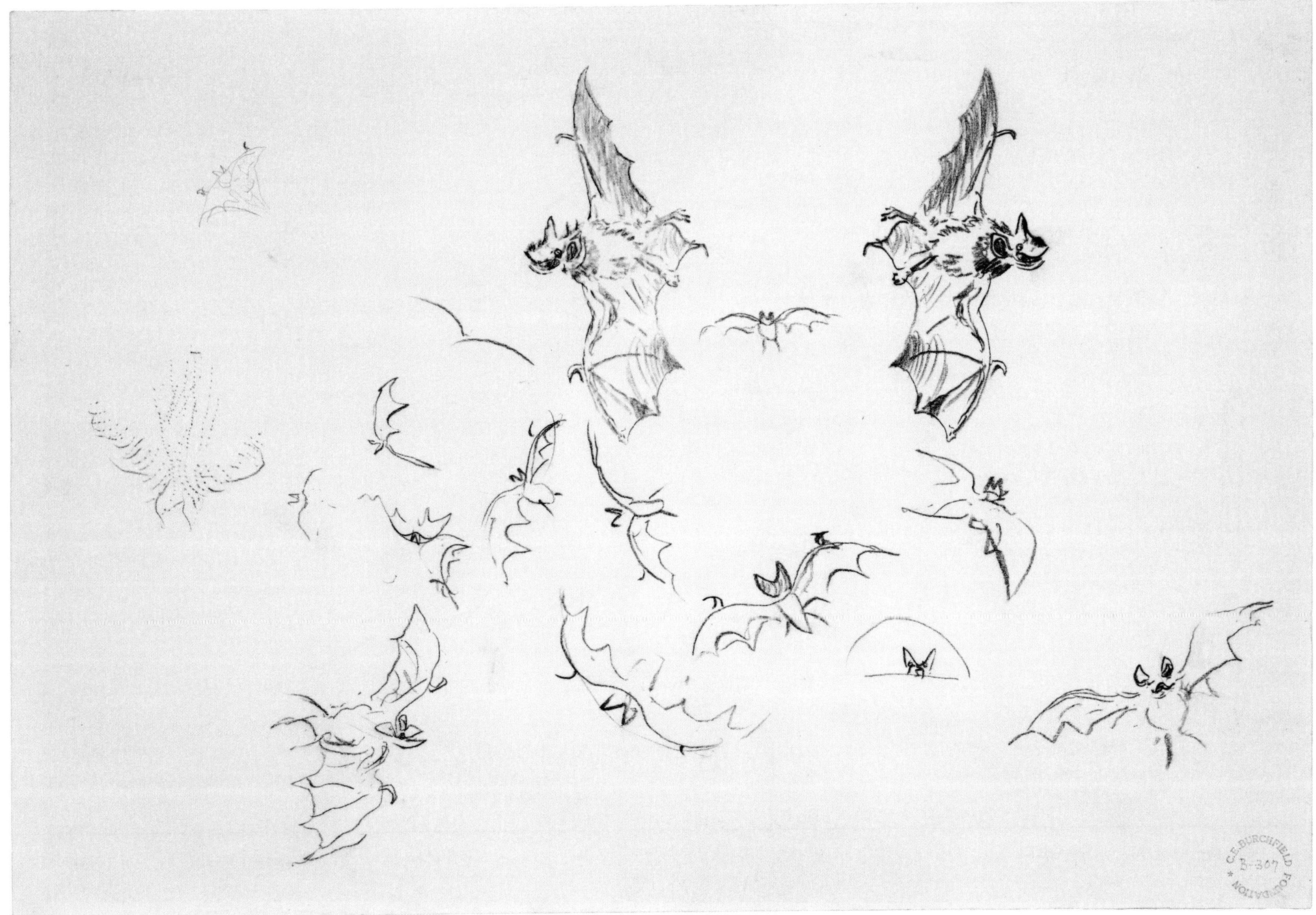

Cat. 31

Edward Hopper

Born in Nyack, New York, 1882;
died in New York, 1964

Hopper's formal art training began in 1899 at the New York School of Illustrating. After one year, however, Hopper left the program to pursue a broader education in fine arts at the New York School of Art, where he remained until 1906. There, he studied with William Merritt Chase, Kenneth Hayes Miller, and Robert Henri. In Henri's class, Hopper studied alongside artists such as Stuart Davis (q.v.), George Bellows, and Patrick Henry Bruce, but remained independent from any particular school or movement.

Hopper traveled to Europe three times between 1906 and 1910, spending most of his time abroad in Paris. His Parisian oils were rendered with a looser brushstroke and lighter palette reminiscent of Impressionist painting, which he would have seen while in Europe. A few years after his return to New York, he moved into an apartment at 3 Washington Square North in Greenwich Village, which would be his home and studio for the rest of his life. Until he was about forty years old, his career was marked by disappointment; he only sold one painting, and was rarely able to get into gallery shows. He supported himself through commercial illustration, which he disliked, and printmaking, which won him critical recognition.

Hopper's breakthrough came in 1923 when the Brooklyn Museum bought his watercolor *The Mansard Roof*. The following year he married fellow painter Josephine Nivison and began showing his work with prominent New York art dealer Frank Rehn. Solo shows made Hopper's reputation, and among his earliest was a 1928 exhibition of watercolors at the Wadsworth Atheneum Museum of Art.

In 1933 Alfred H. Barr Jr., founding director of the Museum of Modern Art, recognized Hopper as one of America's leading modern artists and held a retrospective of his work at the newly opened museum. Hopper was only the third living artist to receive this honor. The exhibition included many of his signature subjects: Victorian houses, New York restaurants and theaters, as well as views into quiet middle-class apartments. He painted during his summer travels to Gloucester, Maine, and, after 1930, to Truro, Cape Cod, Massachusetts. In 1934 he and his wife, Jo, built a house in Truro where they spent almost every summer.

Although Hopper continued to travel, his best-known works came from his solitary wanderings in New York. These include *Early Sunday Morning* (1930; Whitney Museum of American Art, New York), which shows Greenwich Village shop fronts before people were in the streets, and *Nighthawks* (1942; Art Institute of Chicago), an image of a diner late at night. During his long career, Hopper saw the rise of many different avant-garde moments, including Surrealism, Abstract Expressionism, and Pop Art. Despite the popularity of these styles, so different from his, he remained esteemed by critics and the public alike. In 1950, the Whitney Museum gave him a major retrospective, and he was featured on the cover of *Time* magazine in 1956. In 1967, the year of his death, he represented the United States in the prestigious São Paolo Biennal.

Select Bibliography

Gail Levin. *Edward Hopper: A Catalogue Raisonné*. 4 vols. New York: Whitney Museum of American Art in association with W. W. Norton, 1995.

Gail Levin. *Edward Hopper: An Intimate Biography*. New York: Alfred A. Knopf, 1995.

Virginia M. Mecklenburg. *Edward Hopper: The Watercolors*. Washington, D.C.: National Museum of American Art, Smithsonian Institution, 1999.

Carol Troyen et al. *Edward Hopper*. Boston: Museum of Fine Arts, 2007.

32

Edward Hopper
Rockland Harbor, 1926
Opaque and transparent watercolor over graphite on wove paper
13 7/8 × 20 in. (35.2 × 50.8 cm)
Signed at lower right:
Edward Hopper / Rockland Me
Ex coll.: with Frank K. M. Rehn Gallery, New York, 1926; Dr. T. L. Bennett, 1927; with Parke-Bernet, New York, fall 1927; with Frank K. M. Rehn Gallery, New York, 1927
The Ella Gallup Sumner and Mary Catlin Sumner Collection Fund, 1928.324

Arriving in Rockland, Maine, in early July 1926, Hopper wrote to his dealer, Frank Rehn, "[Rockland is] a very fine old place with lots of good-looking houses but not much shipping. . . . I've made two sketches here within two days, which is not so bad."[1] Hopper was traveling through Maine that summer in search of paintable subjects. He was eager to replicate the stimulating experience of recent visits to Gloucester, Massachusetts, where in the summer of 1923 he rediscovered the medium of watercolor and where, more importantly, at the age of forty-one he at last had found his mature voice and an audience for his work.[2] Rockland was very much like Gloucester. It was an active fishing community and busy port (Hopper was wrong about the shipping), accessible by boat and train, and its housing stock was dominated by the Victorian architecture that had become one of his signature subjects.[3] Hopper stayed in Rockland for seven weeks and painted more than twenty watercolors there.

Rockland Harbor is one of the most complex watercolors Hopper produced that summer. It is deliberately antipicturesque: the artist took pains to emphasize the harbor's hardworking character by showing a dark, heavy pier jutting into the water, a pile of bricks in the lower right corner, and across the way a succession of blocky, no-nonsense buildings that cast deep shadows. The strong colors—white, rust red, and smoky black—and the blistering sunlight evoke work, not recreation: the boats that enter this harbor, Hopper implies, are not the romantic sailing ships of New England legend but the runty, efficient beam trawlers he painted again and again in Rockland.

Hopper sent *Rockland Harbor* to Frank Rehn at the end of the summer. It was first exhibited in 1928, which proved to be a banner year for the artist. His sales totaled more than $8,000;[4] and he was represented in twenty-three different exhibitions, including two solo shows of his watercolors, in March, at the Utica Art Society, and in November, at the Wadsworth Atheneum. The *Hartford Courant*'s critic, Albert Coote, wrote enthusiastically about the Wadsworth show, and singled out *Rockland Harbor* for its "sculpted solidity and color value."[5] He noted that the watercolor had already been purchased by the museum, making it the second Hopper (after *Captain Strout's House*, cat. 34) to enter the permanent collection that year.
CT

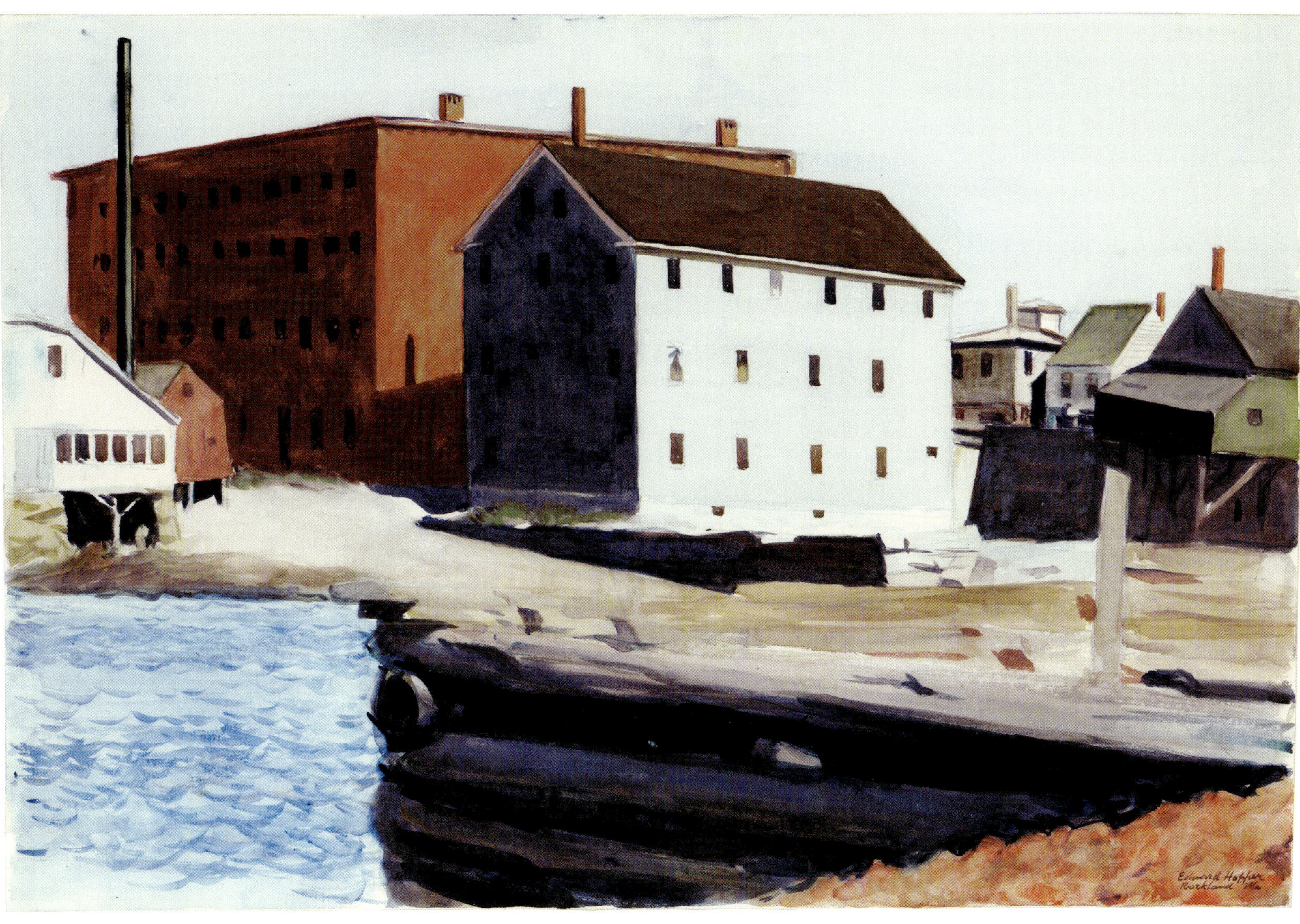

Cat. 32

1. Hopper to Rehn, 6 July 1926, in *Edward Hopper: An Intimate Biography*, by Gail Levin (New York: Alfred A. Knopf, 1995), 198.
2. In 1923, after years of painting landscapes and city views in a quasi-Impressionist manner and going largely unnoticed by the critics, Hopper submitted several watercolors depicting Gloucester's nineteenth-century houses and its fishing boats–both new subjects for him–to the Brooklyn Museum's annual watercolor show. Six were accepted and one, *The Mansard Roof*, was purchased by the museum for $100–Hopper's first sale of a painting in ten years. He was subsequently offered a solo show of his Gloucester watercolors at the Frank K. M. Rehn Gallery, the most prestigious venue for contemporary realist paintings in New York, to which both critics and collectors responded with enthusiasm.
3. For Rockland, see Janet L. Comey, "Painting Sunlight on the Coast of Maine," in *Edward Hopper*, by Carol Troyen et al. (Boston: Museum of Fine Arts, 2007), 89–91.
4. By this time his oils were commanding as much as $1,500 and his watercolors $300.
5. Albert W. Coote, "Fine Examples Of Water Colors Are On Display: 12 Paintings by Edward Hopper Exhibited At Morgan Memorial," *Hartford Courant*, 1 December 1928.

33

Edward Hopper
Custom House, Portland, 1927
Opaque and transparent watercolor over graphite on wove paper (partial watermark: Whatman 1925 England)
14 × 20 in. (35.6 × 50.8 cm)
Signed lower right:
Edward Hopper / Portland, Me.
Ex coll.: with Frank K. M. Rehn Gallery, New York, 1927; Robert W. Huntington, Hartford, 1929
Gift of Robert W. Huntington, 1946.232

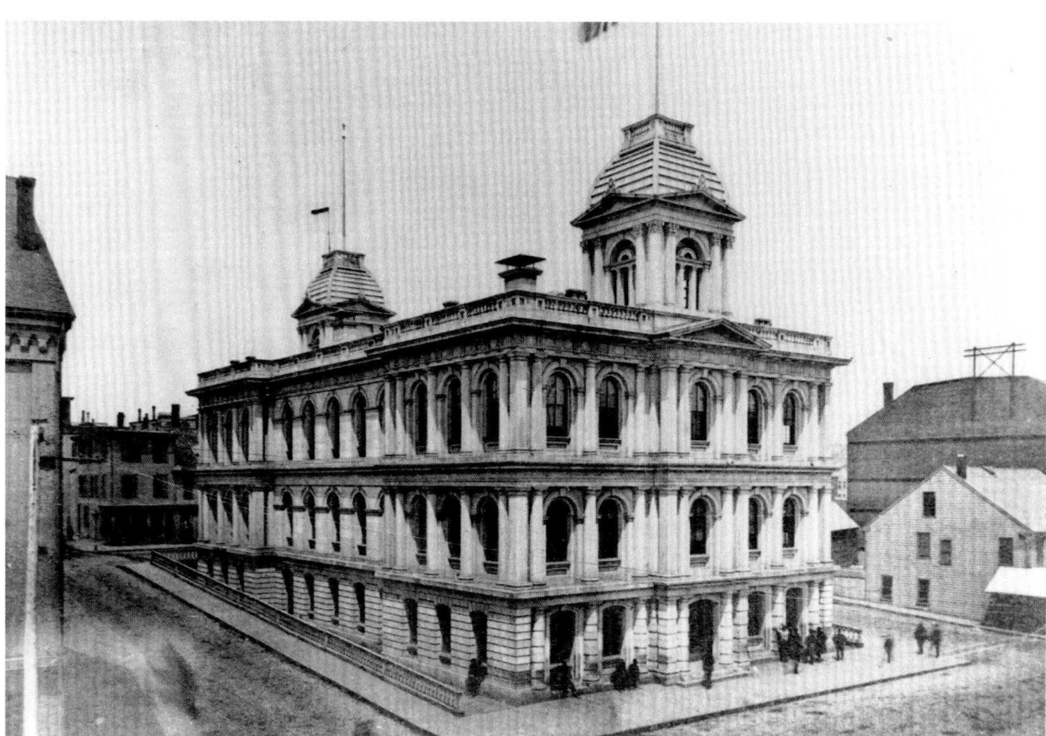

Fig. 1. Custom House, Portland, c. 1880. Collections of Maine Historical Society

The U.S. Customs House in Portland, Maine, is one of the city's finest post–Civil War buildings. Designed by Alfred B. Mullett (supervising architect for the U.S. Treasury between 1886 and 1874) in the French Second Empire style and completed in 1872, the majestic three-story granite building dominates the block between Fore and Commercial streets on the city's waterfront (fig. 1). It is one of the few architecturally significant buildings Hopper (a dedicated painter of vernacular architecture) ever chose to depict.

Late in life, Hopper described Portland as "our finest New England city,"[1] but even so, when he painted this landmark, he showed it from the side, rather than presenting it frontally and in the center of the space, as its symmetrical design would seem to demand. He minimized its architecturally significant features: he undermined the elegance of the entrance with its handsome circular stairway by rendering it in profile, he cut off the building's imposing elevation at the first story, and–an even greater indignity–he interrupted the view of the corner with a sagging utility pole. Beyond the Customs House at left Hopper showed an undistinguished commercial building whose function is not identified, although the partially legible lettering on the façade suggests a relation to the boat-building industry.

Hopper's Portland pictures are sometimes connected with the watercolors of Charles Burchfield (q.v.), whom he admired.[2] Although Hopper vehemently denied any influence, the drab, somber palette, the anthropomorphized windows, and the slightly eerie, empty quality of *Custom House*[3] can be seen as paralleling Burchfield's renderings of Victorian streets that satirize small-town life. *Custom House* has also been seen as an indication of Hopper's sensitivity to architectural pretension. By pushing the Custom House to the side of the composition and pairing it with an ordinary building, Hopper seems to be suggesting that a French-influenced classical-style building was "entirely incongruous on the streets of Portland, Maine."[4] But Hopper was less a social critic than a dedicated observer of the urban experience. In *Custom House*, he shows Portland from the vantage point of a pedestrian, for whom the utility poles mark intervals along the street as he passes, and who absorbs the juxtaposition of buildings of many different styles and eras, taking in as a matter of course the succession of the architecturally distinguished and the mundane, each with its own degree of interest.

1. Hopper to Donald Adams, 7 August 1955, in *Edward Hopper: An Intimate Biography*, by Gail Levin (New York: Alfred A. Knopf, 1995), 208.
2. Hopper's relationship with Burchfield is summarized in Janet L. Comey, "Painting Sunlight on the Coast of Maine," in *Edward Hopper*, by Carol Troyen et al. (Boston: Museum of Fine Arts, 2007), 93–95.
3. The drabness and emptiness have their basis in direct observation, since apparently Hopper painted this watercolor on a rainy day, from the seat of his parked car.
4. Virginia M. Mecklenburg, *Edward Hopper: The Watercolors* (New York: W. W. Norton in association with the National Museum of American Art, Smithsonian Institution, 1999), 73.

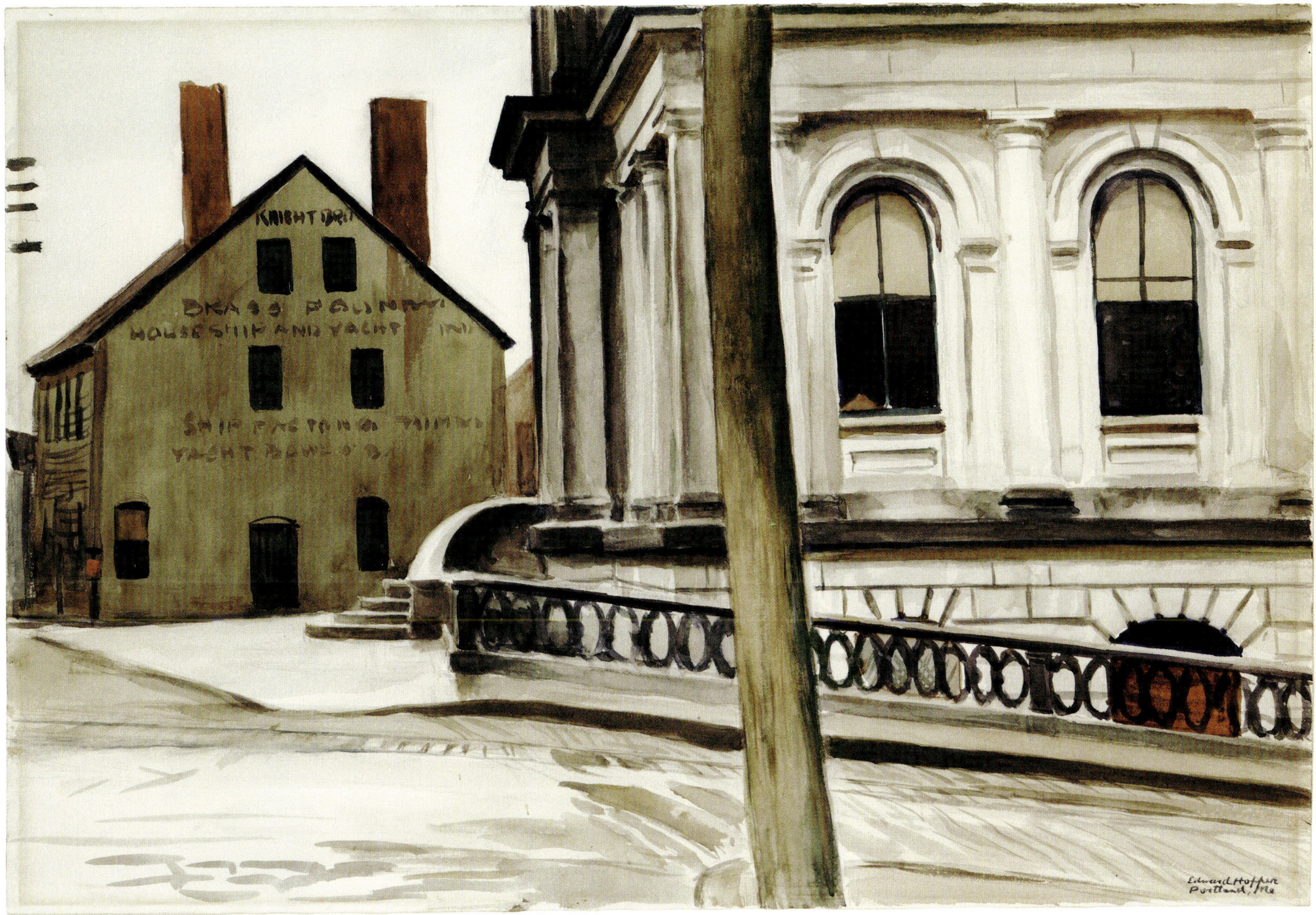

Cat. 33

34

Edward Hopper
Captain Strout's House, Portland Head, 1927
Opaque and transparent watercolor over graphite on wove paper (partial watermark: Whatman 1925)
14 × 20 in. (35.6 × 50.8 cm)
Signed at lower left:
Edward Hopper / Portland Head
Ex coll.: with Frank K. M. Rehn Gallery, New York, 1927
The Ella Gallup Sumner and Mary Catlin Sumner Collection Fund, 1928.3

Located on Cape Elizabeth, southeast of Portland, Maine, Portland Head Light, with the adjacent keeper's house, is now a tourist destination visited by painters, photographers, and busloads of sightseers every year. There was little interest in it in Hopper's day, however, despite its breathtaking setting and historic significance—the lighthouse overlooks Casco Bay and is the oldest in Maine, commissioned by George Washington and completed in 1791. A few painters sought it out earlier—George Luks was there in 1919—but it was Hopper who drew attention to the complex with his group of watercolors of the scene.[1]

Having made several working trips to Maine (one just the summer before), Hopper returned in 1927 in more comfortable circumstances. He had recently sold a painting (*Two on the Aisle*, 1927; Toledo Museum of Art) for the substantial sum of $1,500 and bought his first car, which made travel easier and provided him with a mobile studio. He drove around scenic Cape Elizabeth, painting views of the village, Coast Guard station, and twin lighthouses at Two Lights; a church at the inland community of Spurwink; and four watercolors at Portland Head Light.

Captain Strout's House and the closely related *Lighthouse and Buildings, Portland Head, Cape Elizabeth, Maine* (fig. 1) are the most picturesque of Hopper's Cape Elizabeth watercolors. In them, Hopper used his characteristic yellow-green, blue, and brown palette and his customary simple technique, in which layers of pale wash are applied over the most schematic of pencil outlines. Both watercolors are animated by the dazzling light of a summer's day, which Hopper achieved through use of a deep clear blue for water and sky and the brilliant white of the paper to represent the direct light of the sun. In *Lighthouse and Buildings, Portland Head*, Hopper stretched out the buildings along a diagonal (the keeper's house is at right); the lighthouse juts above the horizon like a skyscraper, dominant and heroic. In *Captain Strout's House*, Hopper showed the keeper's house from the front, with the lighthouse in partial shadow behind. He named the watercolor after the house's occupant—Captain Joshua Strout had been keeper since 1904, having taken over from this father[2]—ensuring both house and owner a kind of immortality.

Hopper had made his reputation painting Victorian houses, first in Gloucester and then in Maine. He gave Captain Strout's house (built in 1891) an unusually anthropomorphic character. With its dormers, porches, and jagged roofline casting the intriguing shadows, it has a fairy-tale quality that is especially appealing. Its charm was not appreciated at the time, however (Victorian architecture was very much out of fashion in the 1920s); in fact, Hopper's architectural watercolors were frequently described as being attractive despite their unfortunate subject matter. When the Wadsworth Atheneum bought the watercolor in 1928, the announcement of the acquisition paid special tribute to Hopper's ability to reveal the evocative power and beauty in the uninspiring: "He chooses for the subjects of his pictures buildings which ordinarily seem to be of the ugliest varieties—lighthouses, Victorian residences, tenement blocks, railroad signal stations, roofs and bridges—but to the painting of these structures, he adds the peculiar beauty of his art. One is made to feel that these objects exist with such intensity that the stimulation results in a definitely aesthetic yield."[3]
CT

1. The lighthouse, now automated and operated by the Coast Guard, is in the center of Fort Williams Park. The keeper's house is now a museum.
2. Virginia M. Mecklenburg, *Edward Hopper: The Watercolors* (New York: W. W. Norton in association with the National Museum of American Art, Smithsonian Institution, 1999), 71.
3. "Edward Hopper," *Bulletin of the Wadsworth Atheneum* 6 (April 1928): 14.

Fig. 1. Edward Hopper, *Lighthouse and Buildings, Portland Head, Cape Elizabeth, Maine*, 1927. Watercolor over graphite pencil on paper, 13 1/2 × 19 1/2 in. (34.3 × 49.5 cm). Museum of Fine Arts, Boston. Bequest of John T. Spaulding, 48.723

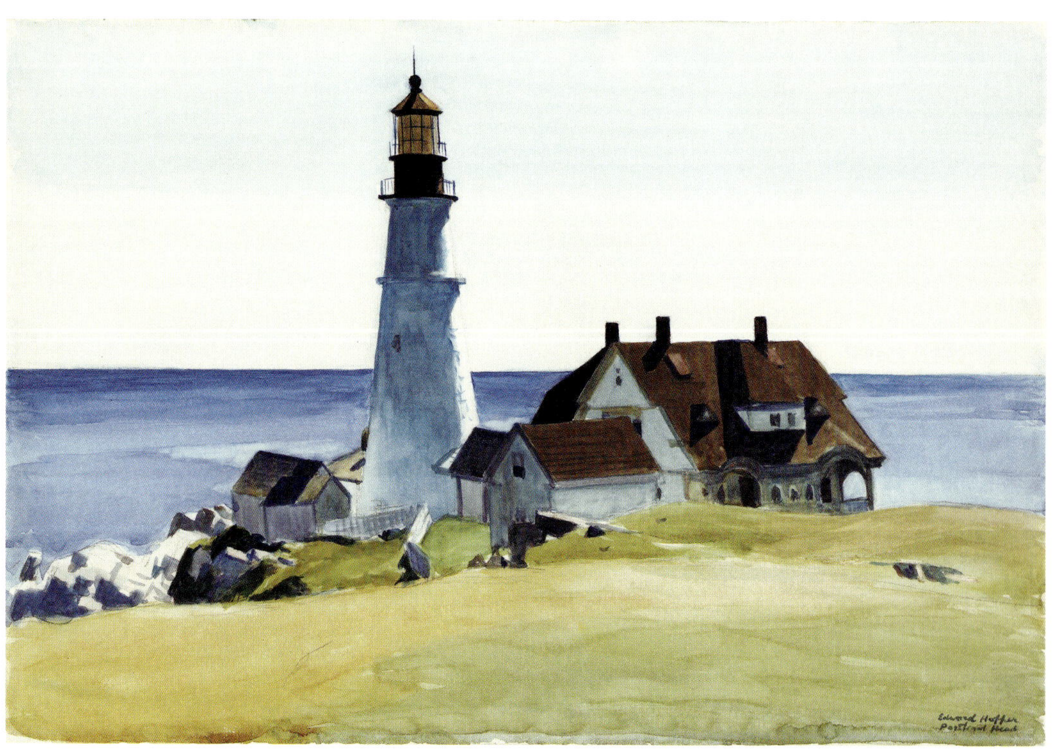

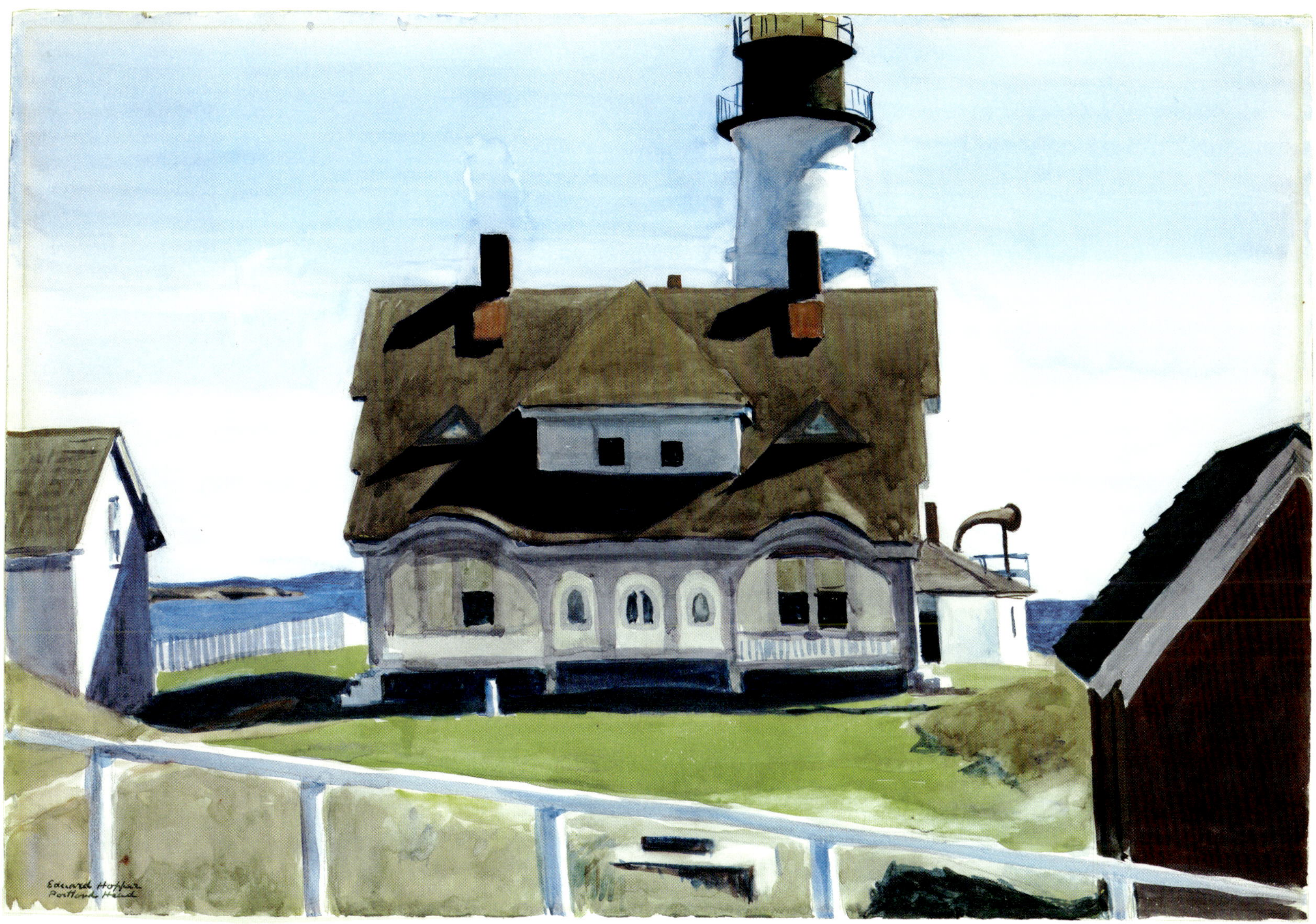

Cat. 34

35

Edward Hopper
Methodist Church Tower, 1930
Opaque and transparent watercolor over graphite on thick wove paper
25 × 19¾ in. (63.5 × 50.2 cm)
Signed at lower left:
Edward Hopper / Provincetown
Ex coll.: with Frank K. M. Rehn Gallery, New York, 1930; Lesley G. Sheafer, New York, 1931 to at least 1950; with Frank K. M. Rehn Gallery, New York
The Ella Gallup Sumner and Mary Catlin Sumner Collection Fund, 1951.19

During his first summer on Cape Cod, Hopper experimented with larger (approximately 20 × 25 inches, as opposed to 14 × 20 inches) and more heavily textured sheets of watercolor paper. Within a few years he was using these more substantial papers frequently to better enable him to render the outer Cape's vast open spaces. The larger format also underscored the function of his watercolors as major exhibition pieces, increasingly compositionally complex and imposing. The vertical format of *Methodist Church Tower*, almost unique in his oeuvre, makes it even more impressive. And indeed, Hopper was satisfied with this picture. Shortly after it was purchased, Jo (who generally spoke, and corresponded, for her husband) wrote to Charles C. Cunningham, director of the Atheneum, that the watercolor was a "great favorite." She then described the circumstances under which Hopper made it: "Painted in back seat of car parked on Main St., a little to side of the church where shops pile up making fine composition of angles for foreground."[1]

The church itself, built in the mid-nineteenth century, is located on Commercial and Center streets (not Main Street, as Jo had it) in Provincetown, and was for nearly a century the home of the Center Methodist Episcopal Church.[2] For Hopper, who generally preferred to paint idiosyncratic Victorian buildings or humbler Cape Cod cottages, the church inspired a rare foray into depicting the Georgian style. It was also an unusual excursion into working in Provincetown altogether—it is one of only three Provincetown subjects he painted in more than thirty summers on the Cape.

Hopper chose an unusual vantage point for this composition. He depicted the church from street level, looking up, so that its tower and the roofs and gables of the neighboring houses are compressed into a lively pattern of overlapping geometric shapes. He had used this viewing angle once or twice before (notably in his 1926 watercolor of Gloucester's Universalist Church—also a Georgian-style building); *Methodist Church Tower* also echoes the composition of Charles Demuth's 1920 watercolor of the same church (fig. 1), which Hopper may well have seen when it was exhibited at the Montross Gallery in New York in 1924.[3]

Methodist Church Tower is one of thirty-seven watercolors Hopper included in his 1933 exhibition at the Museum of Modern Art—his first museum retrospective, and only the third solo show organized by the museum to honor the work of a living American artist. The exhibition was generally well received. In paintings like *Methodist Church Tower*, Hopper was applauded for his ability to reveal the nobility of American artifacts ("the spare angularity of New England architecture"[4]) and for his brilliance as an abstract designer. For Alfred H. Barr Jr., founding director of the Museum of Modern Art, New York, champion of the international avant-garde, and organizer of Hopper's exhibition, works like *Methodist Church Tower* defined both Hopper's place in art history and his contribution to modernism: "Hopper has like Corot and Cézanne and certain Italian primitives an alert eye for the interplay of blocks and angles in buildings, as is proven by . . . *Methodist Church*. . . . In fact a few compositions . . . approach remarkably in appearance, though not in method, certain phases of Cubism."[5]
CT

1. Jo Hopper to Charles C. Cunningham, 31 March 1951, Wadsworth Atheneum Archives.
2. It now houses the Provincetown Library, and is a National Historic Landmark property.
3. *Original Paintings, Drawings, and Engravings Being Exhibited with The Dial Folio/The Living Art*, Montross Gallery, New York, 26 January–14 February 1924, no. 8. Demuth's watercolor may also have been included in the artist's 1920 solo show at the Daniel Gallery, New York (*Arrangements of the American Landscape Forms by Charles Demuth*, December 1920). I am grateful to Lisa Messinger of the Metropolitan Museum of Art for this information.
4. Helen Appleton Read, "Edward Hopper," *Parnassus* 5 (November 1933): 10.
5. Alfred H. Barr Jr., "Edward Hopper," in *Edward Hopper Retrospective Exhibition* (New York: Museum of Modern Art, 1933), 13.

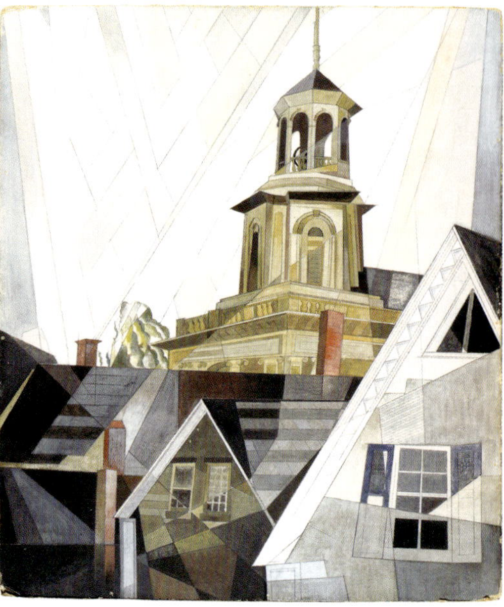

Fig. 1. Charles Demuth, *After Sir Christopher Wren*, 1920. Watercolor, gouache, and pencil on cardboard, 24 × 20 in. (61 × 50.8 cm). The Metropolitan Museum of Art, New York. Bequest of Scofield Thayer, 1982, 1984.433.156

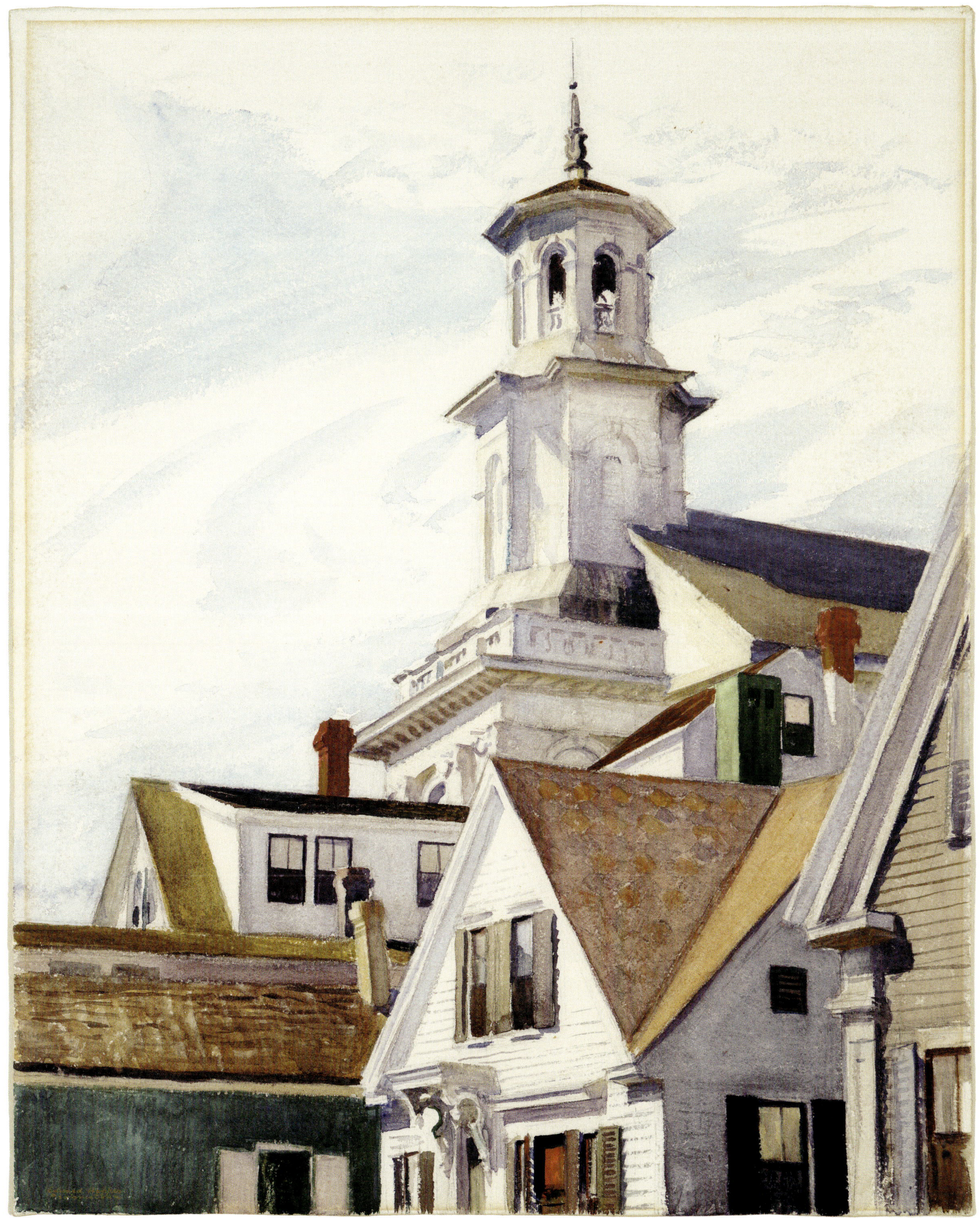

Cat. 35

36

Edward Hopper
Truro Station Coal Box, 1930
Opaque and transparent watercolor over graphite on thick wove paper
[from watercolor block]
(partial watermark: 1925 Unbleached Arnold)
14 × 20 in. (35.6 × 50.8 cm)
Signed at lower right: Edward Hopper / Truro
Ex coll.: with Frank K. M. Rehn Gallery, New York, 1930
The Ella Gallup Sumner and Mary Catlin Sumner Collection Fund, 1934.9

In July 1930, the Hoppers made their first visit to the tiny community of Truro, Massachusetts, between Wellfleet and Provincetown on Cape Cod. Although Jo, Hopper's wife, was drawn to the dynamism of Provincetown, then as now a lively artists' colony, the reticent Edward preferred the quieter atmosphere of Truro. He described it as "a desert on a small scale with fine dune formations, a very open almost treeless country,"[1] and it became a rich source of subject matter. The Hoppers returned to Truro almost every summer and fall for the rest of their lives.

In *Truro Station Coal Box*, Hopper created a luminous view of the "open almost treeless country." His watercolor shows a stretch of sand in the foreground, loosely painted with layers of tan wash, and a broad view of the grassy dunes beyond. To the right of center is the small, house-shaped coal box, its "eaves" nearly synonymous with the low horizon line. The station building occupies a sliver of the picture space on the far right side; the rest of the composition is given over to the softly modulated sky. It is one of the most restrained and minimal images Hopper ever produced; in the record books he and Jo kept of his work, he tersely described it as "rather spare."[2]

Despite the startling emptiness of *Truro Station Coal Box*, Hopper clearly regarded it as a finished work. He signed the watercolor and delivered it to his dealer in October 1930 along with more than a dozen others he painted in Truro that summer. In 1934, director Chick Austin chose it for the Wadsworth Atheneum. Many years later, Jo Hopper wrote to Charles C. Cunningham, who had succeeded Austin as director, that the "subject occasioned much question in the community + amazement that it ever should be bought,"[3] referring both to the unlikelihood of the small, drab coal box as a suitable focus for a picture and to the sparseness of the composition. Yet presumably it was the picture's radically pared-down quality that had especially appealed to Austin. When he bought it in 1934, he had just overseen the construction of the Atheneum's International style Avery Memorial wing, a building of abstract spaces, elegant unadorned surfaces, and dazzling luminosity. Austin was clearly drawn to analogous qualities in the watercolor: its subtle balance of geometrical shapes and voids, its shimmering light, and its austerity. He referred to it as his favorite among the Hopper watercolors he had bought.[4]
CT

1. Hopper to C. K. Chatterton, 23 July 1930, in *Edward Hopper: An Intimate Biography*, by Gail Levin (New York: Alfred A. Knopf, 1995), 230.
2. Hopper Record Book 1:73, Whitney Museum of American Art. See Gail Levin, *Edward Hopper: A Catalogue Raisonné* (New York: Whitney Museum of American Art in association with W. W. Norton, 1995), 2:W-246, 215.
3. Jo Hopper to Charles C. Cunningham, 31 March 1951, curatorial files, Wadsworth Atheneum.
4. Eugene R. Gaddis, *Magician of the Modern: Chick Austin and the Transformation of the Arts in America* (New York: Alfred A. Knopf, 2000), 269.

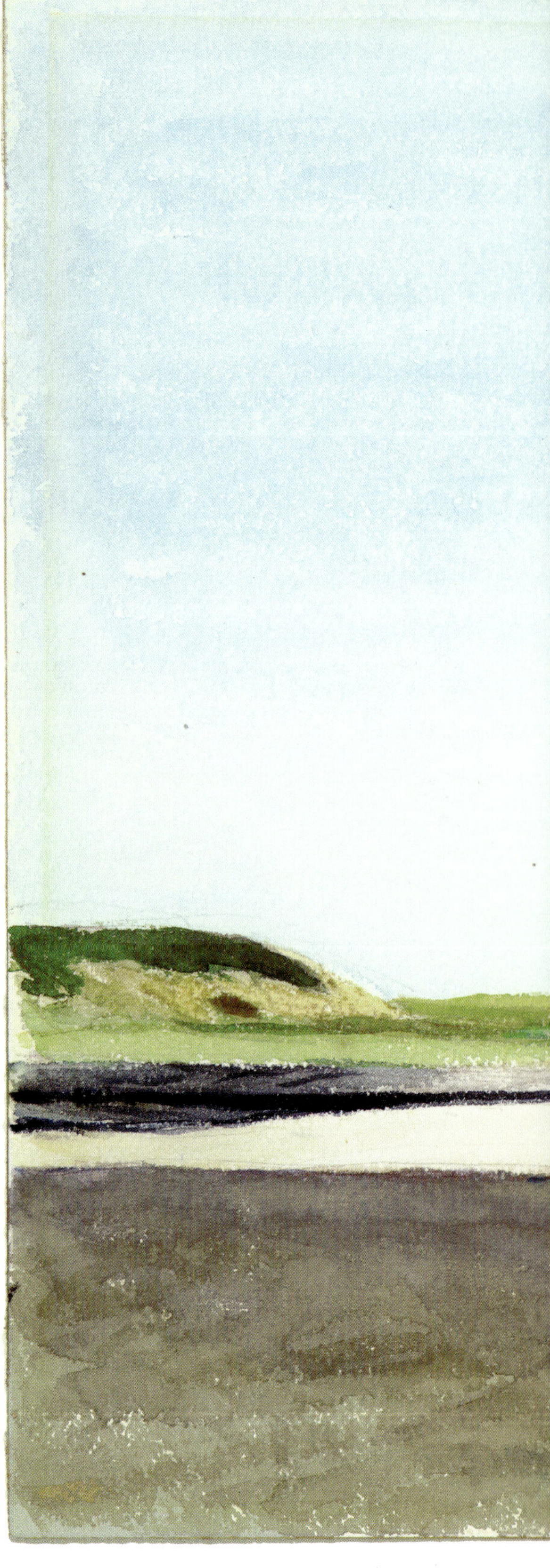

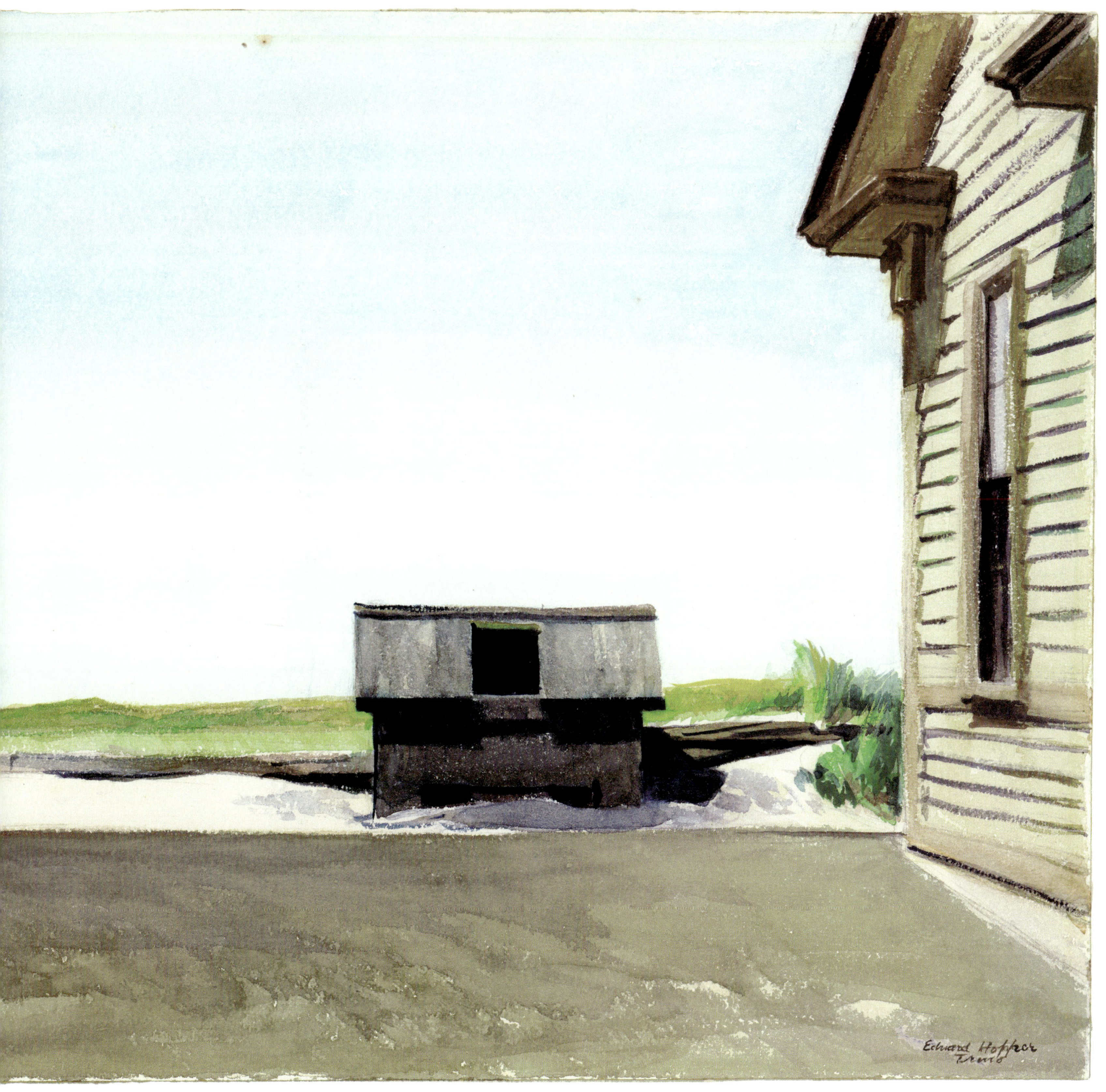

Cat. 36

37

Edward Hopper
Marshall's House, 1932
Opaque and transparent watercolor, over graphite, on thick wove paper [from watercolor paper block]
14 × 20 in. (35.6 × 50.8 cm)
Signed lower right: Edward Hopper
Ex coll.: with Frank K. M. Rehn Gallery, New York, 1932
Purchased through the gift of Henry and Walter Keney, 1933.93

In 1932, Hopper turned fifty. He had never been so confident, both artistically and financially. He participated in more than twenty exhibitions across the country that year, and was profiled in a feature article in *Vanity Fair*.[1] He declined membership in the National Academy of Design, feeling sufficiently assured of his professional stature to remain independent of the artistic establishment. Despite the Depression, he had faith that his work would continue to sell well, and so he took over the large front apartment on the top floor of 3 Washington Square North, where he had lived since 1913. And—while he sometimes had difficulty finding subjects he wanted to paint—this year he was highly productive: in the few months he spent in Truro, he painted two oils and eight watercolors, among them *Marshall's House*.

The house itself still stands on Old County Road in South Truro and is owned by descendants of the family who lived there in Hopper's day. Marshall's house appears in the lower left corner of a map Jo Hopper drew of their neighborhood in South Truro (fig. 1).[2] The house is not far from the cottage the Hoppers rented from local postmaster A. B. Burleigh Cobb their first several summers in Truro, and not much more than a mile (via "car tracks—home made short cut," as Jo labeled it) from the house they would build in 1934 near Camel's Hump overlooking Cape Cod Bay. Hopper, an inveterate walker, traveled the "short cut" regularly; it led past houses occupied over various summers by friends and acquaintances, including such well-known figures as John Dos Passos and Ben Shahn (q.v.), and others, such as the Lewises, Jennesses, and Marshalls, whose names have come down to us because of his watercolors.

Now surrounded by foliage and modernized somewhat, from the outside the house nonetheless appears basically the same, a typical Cape Cod "house and a half." Hopper painted a view of the house that featured the screened-in porch off the ell, rather than focusing on what was presumably the more formal entrance around the other side. He thus emphasized the house's unassuming qualities, what Jo Hopper, describing the watercolor in Hopper's record book, called a "Most matter of fact statement, perfectly conventional little house & arrangement."[3]

The house's "matter of fact" quality was the foil for a deeply satisfying rendering of late summer light, as Jo then described: "but—sunlight on red roof over house & porch so simply just *there* & light on most uneventful field of timothy so serene."[4] Hopper's watercolor technique, never self-advertising or virtuosic, is at its most evocative here: by means of careful scraping out in the foreground, thin curved lines of revealed paper suggest the bristly, bleached stalks of grass waving in the breeze. Dense, nearly opaque color describes the red tiled roof baking in the sun, while streaky layers of brown and gray wash indicate the dusty translucency of the porch screens. In the sky, pale blue washes against the bright white of reserved paper suggest high clouds; the patterns in the sky seem so fugitive that by contrast the little house appears all the more solid and steadfast.

Critics responded enthusiastically to the humble majesty Hopper revealed in old vernacular buildings like Marshall's house, finding in them, in an era of intense nationalism, an expression of a genuine American spirit. E. C. Sherburne, reviewing Hopper's 1933 exhibition at the Museum of Modern Art for the *Christian Science Monitor*, began his article with a tribute to images such as *Marshall's House* (which the Atheneum lent to the show): "Wherever Edward Hopper sets up his easel, America sits for its portrait. On the walls of the Museum of Modern Art . . . are to be seen his pictures of dwellings that are without style but that have enormous character. . . . He makes art, then, out of the familiar scene; and, often, the scene is so homely that we have had to wait for him to discover its connotations of beauty for us."[5]

1. Frank Crowninshield, "A Series of American Artists, No. 3—Edward Hopper," *Vanity Fair* 38 (June 1932): 11, 30–31.
2. Edward Root Papers, Archives, Munson-Williams-Proctor Arts Institute, Utica, New York.
3. Hopper Record Book 2:37, Whitney Museum of American Art, quoted in *Edward Hopper: A Catalogue Raisonné*, by Gail Levin (New York: Whitney Museum of American Art in association with W. W. Norton, 1995), 2:W-286, 255.
4. Ibid.
5. E. C. Sherburne, "The Hopper Exhibition," *Christian Science Monitor*, 6 November 1933.

Fig. 1. Josephine Hopper, *Hand Drawn Map of South Truro, Cape Cod*, c. 1955. Munson-Williams-Proctor Institute Archives, Edward Root Papers

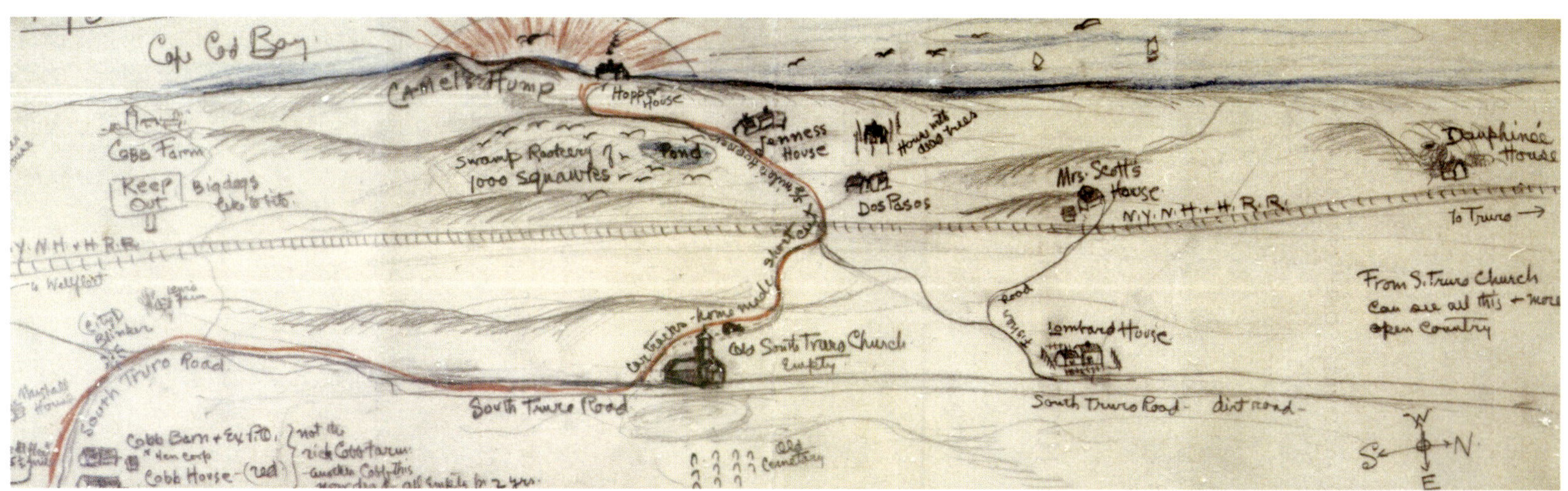

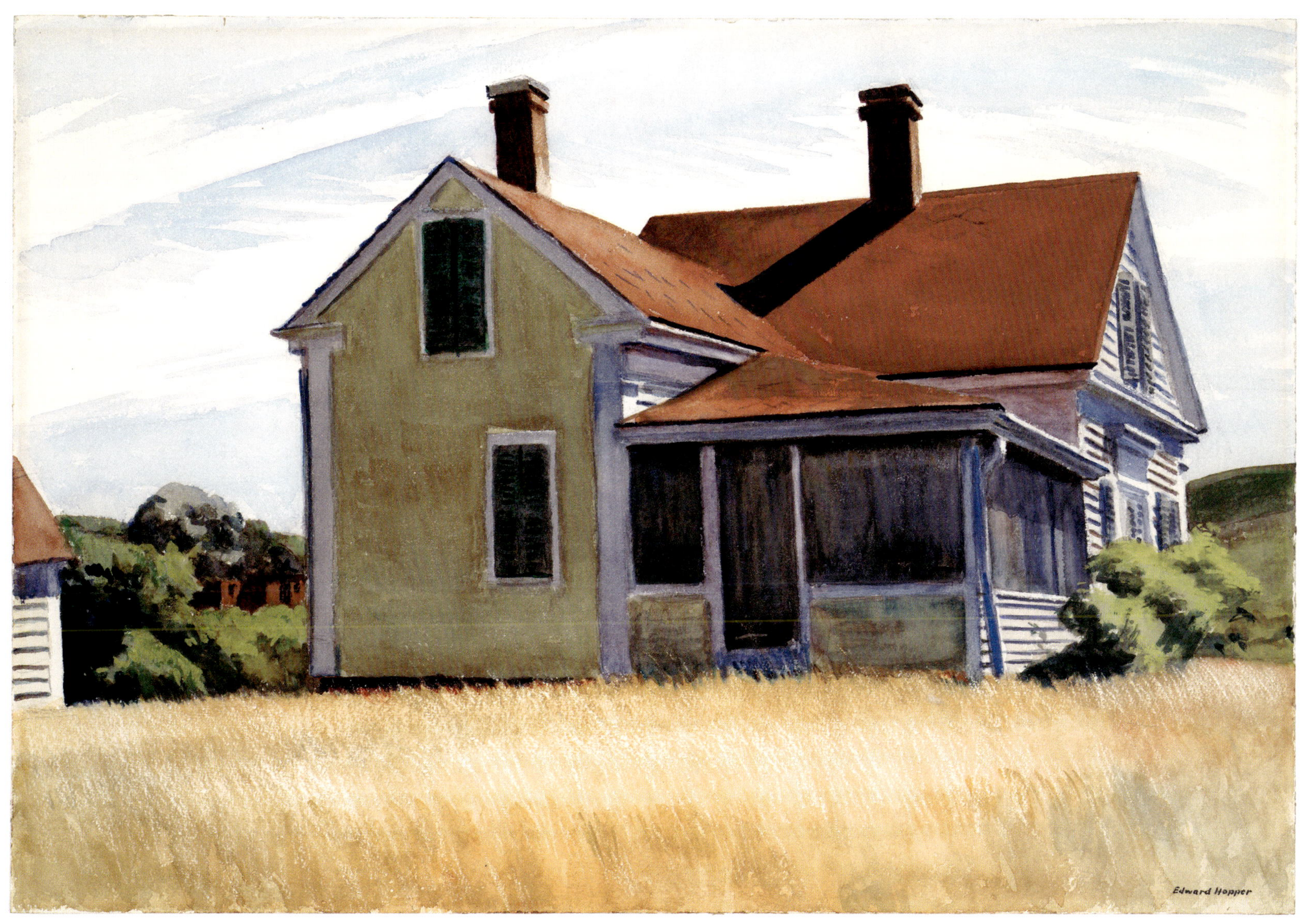

Cat. 37

Charles Sheeler

Born in Philadelphia, 1883;
died in Dobbs Ferry, New York, 1965

Charles Sheeler was an American modernist who explored the relationships between photography, film, and more traditional media such as painting and drawing. He studied art from 1900 to 1906, first at the School of Industrial Art, Philadelphia, and then under William Merritt Chase at the Pennsylvania Academy of the Fine Arts. Sheeler traveled to Europe with Chase and his class in 1904 and 1905 and returned on his own in 1909.

Sheeler took up photography to support himself in 1910. He moved to Bucks County, Pennsylvania, where he photographed the simple, unadorned architecture of the rural setting in a sharp-focus style. Sheeler's austere photographs attracted the attention of Alfred Stieglitz, who later proclaimed Sheeler, along with Morton Schamberg and Paul Strand, the "Trinity of Photography." His reputation as a painter developed more slowly; however, six of his paintings were included in the famous Armory Show, held in New York in 1913. In about 1916–17 Sheeler created a series of photographs based on a house in Doylestown, Pennsylvania, which he later translated into paintings.

Sheeler was already closely allied with a number of leading modernist artists and collectors—Stieglitz, Marius de Zayas, Walter Arensberg—when he moved to New York in 1919. The following year, he collaborated with Paul Strand on a short film called *Manhatta*, which depicted a day in the life of New York. The film is considered a landmark in the history of avant-garde cinema. Sheeler married in 1921, and in 1926 he and his wife moved to South Salem, New York. The next year, Sheeler spent six weeks photographing the Ford Motor Company's River Rouge Plant in Michigan. These photographs provided industrial themes for future paintings.

In 1931 Sheeler joined the Downtown Gallery, where he had the first of nine one-man shows. He was honored with a large-scale retrospective that included paintings, drawings, and photographs, at the Museum of Modern Art, New York, in 1939. Sheeler served as an artist-in-residence at the Phillips Academy, Andover, Massachusetts, in 1946, and the Currier Gallery of Art, Manchester, New Hampshire, in 1948. A stroke in 1959 left him unable to paint or take photographs. In 1963, two years before his death, Sheeler was elected to the National Institute of Arts and Letters.

Select Bibliography

Martin L. Friedman. *Charles Sheeler*. New York: Watson/Guptill, 1975.

Carol Troyen and Erica E. Hirshler. *Charles Sheeler: Paintings and Drawings*. Boston: Museum of Fine Arts, 1987.

Theodore E. Stebbins Jr., Gilles Mora, and Karen Haas. *The Photography of Charles Sheeler: American Modernist*. Boston: Bulfinch Press, 2002.

Charles Brock. Charles Sheeler: *Across Media*. Washington, D.C.: National Gallery of Art, 2006.

38

Charles Sheeler
The Stove, 1931
Black Conté crayon on wove paper laid down to paperboard with heat-set tissue
6 7/8 × 9 3/8 in. (17.5 × 23.9 cm)
Signed and dated at lower right: Sheeler 1931
Ex coll.: The Downtown Gallery, New York; Philip L. Goodwin, New York, 1931
The Collection of Philip L. Goodwin through James L. Goodwin and Henry Sage Goodwin, 1958.232

Sheeler's goal for his art, he once explained, was "to combine the memory and the present."[1] Among the "memories" he drew upon throughout his career were those preserved in his photographs of an eighteenth-century fieldstone house he rented in Doylestown, Pennsylvania (near Philadelphia), beginning in 1910. The exhibition of the Doylestown house pictures to significant acclaim in 1917 marked the beginning of Sheeler's successful career as a photographer. However, over the next fifteen years his reputation as a painter and draftsman languished, and Edith Halpert, the enterprising proprietor of the Downtown Gallery in New York, suggested that the public might be confused by his displaying paintings and drawings of subjects depicted in his photographs. If he wanted to succeed as a painter, she advised, he should stop exhibiting the photographs. This was in 1931, the year he made *The Stove*.

The Stove was one of a group of sixteen drawings in Conté crayon that Sheeler produced in the 1930s. Conté crayon, made of clay and carbon black and available in a variety of densities, can be used to create anything from fine lines (the outline of the chopping block, here) to dense shading (the body of the stove). With a stump (a pointed roll of leather or paper), it can be blended to create even gradations of tone, as in the shadow on the windowsill. Its ability to yield both crisp contours and soft, velvety areas of shadow must have had special appeal for Sheeler at a time when he was rethinking the relationship of his photography to his work in other media; he noted that his Conté drawings were the works that "most closely approach photography."[2]

The Stove was based on the photograph *Doylestown House, Stove, Horizontal* (fig. 1). Sheeler derived Conté drawings from other photographs of the house; from stills from his 1920 film *Manhatta*; from photographs he made in 1929 of the Ford Motor Company plant at River Rouge, Michigan; and even from a snapshot-sized image of his cat.[3] Of these drawing-photograph pairs, *The Stove* is perhaps closest to its source. It is almost exactly the same size (the photograph is 6 1/2 × 9 1/4 inches, the drawing is 6 7/8 × 9 3/8 inches) and nearly matches the photograph detail for detail. In fact, Sheeler acknowledged that the Conté drawings "were made to see how much exactitude I could attain."[4] Yet—what Halpert feared the public would not understand—the expressive character of the two works is profoundly different.

The eerie quality of the photograph derives from the radical cropping of the stove, which is seen so close up that there is little sense of the surrounding space. Sheeler lit the stove from behind, so it appears as a hulking black form that is spookily present. The drawing, with its surfaces more abstracted and

Fig. 1. Charles Sheeler, *Doylestown House, Stove, Horizontal*, c. 1917. Gelatin silver print, 6 1/2 × 9 1/4 in. (16.5 × 23.5 cm). Museum of Fine Arts, Boston. The Lane Collection, L95.3.73. © 2009, Museum of Fine Arts, Boston

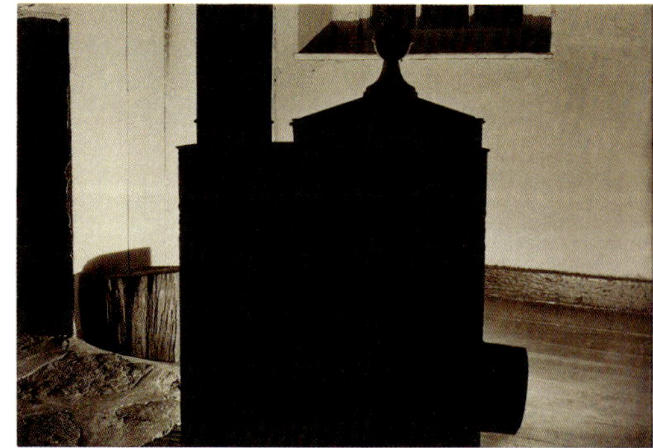

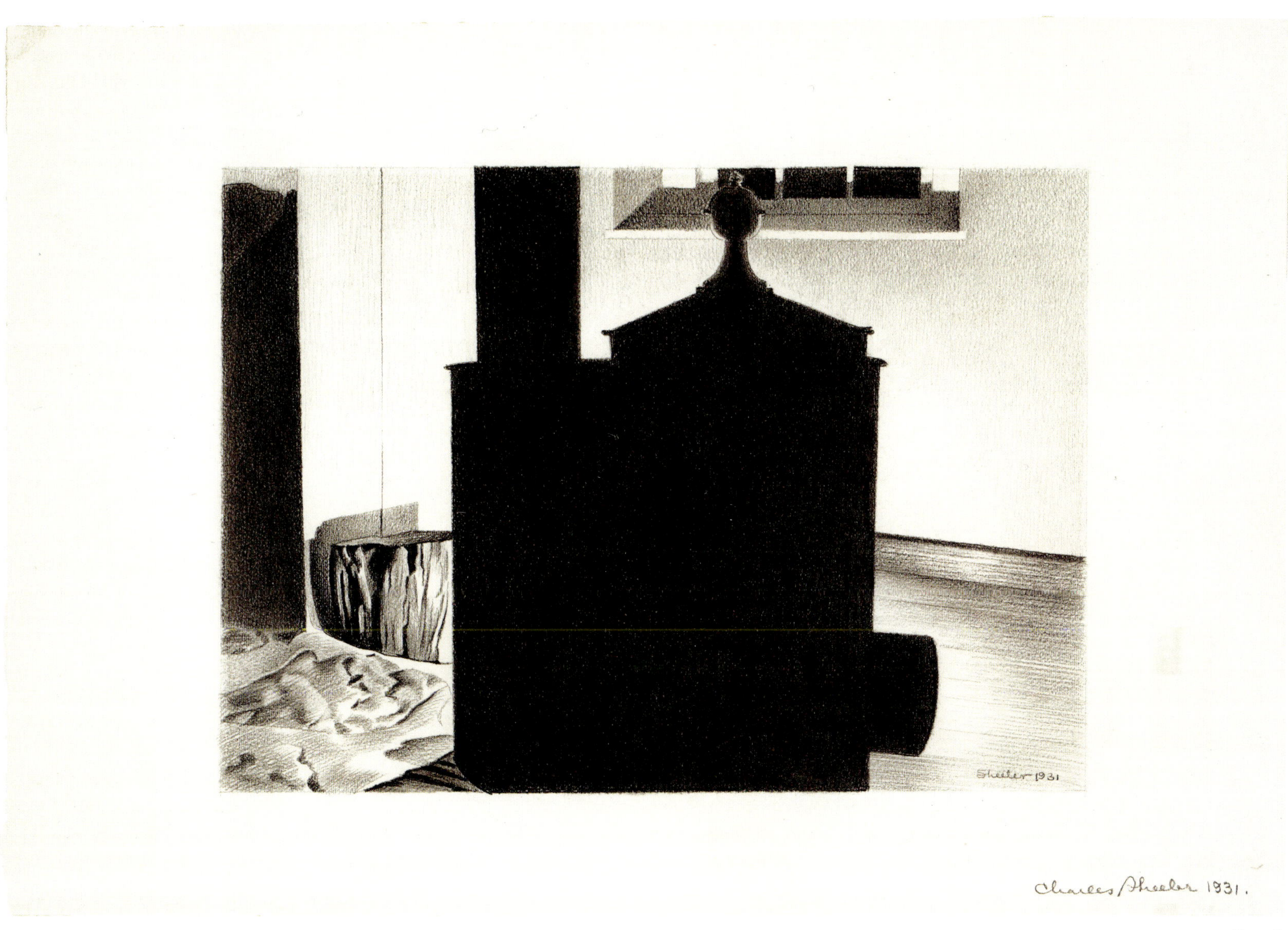

Cat. 38

shapes flatter, presents an idealized view of the interior. Textures are simplified: while in the photograph the splintery surface of the chopping block contrasts with the roughness of the fieldstone hearth, in the drawing they become complimentary fluidities. Yet despite its experimental composition and its mysterious transformation of mundane objects, the photograph has a nostalgic quality, suggesting the quiet deterioration of eloquent things. In contrast, in the drawing the interior appears pristine. Signs of wear on the plaster walls and doorjambs are eliminated, and the scuffs and dents visible along the old baseboard are smoothed over. As they do in memories, imperfections and signs of aging disappear. The past, brought into the present, takes on a kind of timeless perfection. The Doylestown house, which Sheeler gave up in 1926, had been both a muse and a refuge. *The Stove* was the first of many works Sheeler created to honor its memory.

The Stove was probably one of the five drawings that were shown, along with a group of recent oils, in Sheeler's inaugural exhibition at the Downtown Gallery in November 1931. The show was widely praised in the press. A laudatory *New York Times* review concluded, "The drawings reveal both the painter and photographer and emphasize his ability to simplify—when he wishes—almost to the point of abstraction."[5] This association of the two media must have especially pleased Sheeler. Equally gratifying were the sales. The works sold quickly, and for strong prices, to some of the most esteemed collectors of American and avant-garde art: Abby Aldrich Rockefeller, Walter Arensberg, and Edsel Ford. *The Stove* was bought by New York architect and patron of the arts Philip L. Goodwin, whose family—longtime supporters of the Atheneum—gave it to the museum in 1958.
CT

1. Charles Sheeler, undated manuscript, Sheeler Papers, Archives of American Art, Smithsonian Institution, as quoted in Theodore E. Stebbins Jr., "The Memory and the Present: Romantic American Painting in the Lane Collection," in *The Lane Collection: 20th-Century Paintings in the American Tradition*, by Stebbins and Carol Troyen (Boston: Museum of Fine Arts, 1983), 32.
2. Charles Sheeler, quoted in "Charles Sheeler—1946," *Art News* 45 (March 1946): 30.
3. For example, *The Open Door* (1932; Metropolitan Museum of Art, New York) and *Interior with Stove* (1932; National Gallery of Art, Washington, D.C.), both related to the Doylestown House photographs; *Totems in Steel* (1935; Harvard University Art Museums), from *Manhatta*; *Ballet Méchanique* (1931; Memorial Art Gallery, University of Rochester) from the River Rouge photographs; and *Feline Felicity* (1934; Harvard University Art Museums), from a personal photograph now in the Lane Collection.
4. "Charles Sheeler—1946," 30.
5. H. V. D., "Art: Charles Sheeler's Exhibition," *New York Times*, 19 November 1931. The exhibition—Sheeler's first paintings show in more than five years—featured a half dozen oils that would become his most famous works: *Upper Deck*, *Home Sweet Home*, *Americana*, *Cactus*, *American Landscape*, and *Classic Landscape*.

Rockwell Kent

Born in Tarrytown, New York, 1882;
died in Au Sable, New York, 1971

Rockwell Kent was one of the best-known American artists during the course of his sixty-five year career, gaining a reputation through his talents as a painter, illustrator, writer, book designer, artist-explorer, and political activist. As a young man he enrolled in the Horace Mann School, New York, where he studied mechanical drawing, woodworking, and casting. The experience fostered a lifelong respect for craftsmanship that is seen in his precise work as a draftsman, designer, and printmaker. Kent studied architecture at Columbia University, New York, and received a scholarship at William Merritt Chase's summer school in Shinnecock Hills, Long Island. In 1904 Kent enrolled at the New York School of Art (formally the Chase School of Art and now Parsons the New School for Design), where he attended Robert Henri's art classes and met George Bellows and Edward Hopper (q.v.).

As an avid traveler, Kent sought adventure in remote locations for his rugged landscape and marine paintings. At the suggestion of Henri, Kent first visited Monhegan Island, off the coast of Maine, where he worked as a carpenter and lobster fisherman. Inspired by Winslow Homer, Kent painted winter seascapes, and fishing scenes of the island and its coast. His time on Monhegan set a lifetime pattern for travel to unspoiled northern regions. Kent set off every few years, leaving his growing family behind, to travel to regions that became the subject of his art and writing. He spent extended periods in Newfoundland, Greenland, and Alaska, and then traveled south to Tierra del Fuego, and to France and Ireland.

By 1908 Kent had joined the Socialist Party. While Kent was an outspoken and committed political activist, advocating for social justice and civil liberties, his views were not openly expressed in his art. In 1920 Kent settled in Vermont, where he published his first book, *Wilderness*, and was encouraged by the print connoisseur and dealer Carl Zigrosser to create wood engravings. He moved to the Adirondacks, in New York State, where he purchased Asgaard Farm, his principal residence for the remainder of his life. His mature paintings, prints, and illustrations demonstrate the artist's awareness of modernism, seen in their reductive detail. Kent's illustrations for the 1930 edition of Herman Melville's novel *Moby-Dick* are considered to be among his greatest artistic achievements.

Select Bibliography

Rockwell Kent. *It's Me O Lord: The Autobiography of Rockwell Kent.* New York: Dodd and Mead, 1955. Reprint, New York: Da Capo Press, 1977.

David Traxel. *An American Saga: The Life and Times of Rockwell Kent.* New York: Harper and Row, 1980.

Fridolf Johnson, ed. *Rockwell Kent: An Anthology of His Works.* New York: Alfred A. Knopf, 1982.

Jake Milgram Wien. *Rockwell Kent: The Mythic and the Modern.* Manchester, Vt.: Hudson Hills Press in association with the Portland Museum of Art, 2005.

39 a and b

Rockwell Kent
Illustration for Moby-Dick, Chapter CXXXV (Whaleboat and Crew Tossed into the Sea), c. 1929
Black ink applied using pen and brush over traces of graphite on wove paper laid down on paperboard
10 3/8 × 7 3/8 in. (26.4 × 19.7 cm)
Signed at bottom: Rockwell Kent
Ex coll.: likely acquired from the artist after 1930 by Erhard Weyhe, Weyhe Gallery, New York, until 1955
Gift of E. Weyhe, 1955.398

Illustration for Moby-Dick, Chapter LXXXII (Man on Dolphin Attacking Whale), c. 1929
Black ink applied using pen and brush over traces of graphite on wove paper laid down on paperboard
6 7/8 × 7 1/2 in. (17.5 × 19.1 cm)
Signed at lower right: Rockwell Kent
Ex coll.: likely acquired from the artist after 1930 by Erhard Weyhe, Weyhe Gallery, New York, until 1955
Gift of E. Weyhe, 1955.399

Kent's drawings for *Moby-Dick; or, The Whale*, which he completed for the 1930 edition of Herman Melville's famous novel, remain among his most famous works. His background as a draftsman and his love of maritime travel and adventure made him particularly well suited to take on the illustration of Melville's great epic. In 1926, the Lakeside Press of R. R. Donnelley & Sons in Chicago made plans to produce a series of first-class limited-edition books with illustrations by noted artists that would "contribute something to the improvement of standards in the making of books in America."[1]

They turned to Rockwell Kent, then the best-known artist working in the field of book illustration, asking him to choose an American classic for their series. He selected *Moby-Dick*, the tale of Ahab's quest for the great white whale, which inspired Kent's own obsessive northern journeys. Kent was commissioned to make the drawings for a three-volume set, and he executed approximately 300 ink drawings in the end.[2] In addition, he was allowed to oversee all aspects of the book's production.

Determined to capture his subject with authenticity, Kent spent time researching whaling lore and visiting whaling museums and New York's American Museum of Natural History. After he had completed about half of the drawings, his project was interrupted when he decided to travel to Greenland. On the voyage, Kent nearly lost his life in a shipwreck on the island's west coast. Following in the footsteps of other artist-explorers, he spent the summer on the island, enchanted by the isolation. There he met two Arctic ethnographers and returned with them to their native Denmark, where Kent completed the illustrations for *Moby-Dick*.[3] His firsthand exposure to the polar seas and his great admiration for and sensitivity to Melville's novel inspired these powerful illustrations.

Working on good-quality paper, Kent first drew with pencil and then used pen and ink for his illustrations. Both *Whaleboat* and *Man on Dolphin* are energetic, closely cropped drawings. They display strong and deliberate lines that produce a flat and clear image. In *Whaleboat*, the vessel plunges forward into the sea, throwing the three bare-chested sailors toward the ocean below, while two other sailors have already met their fate, and only their thrusting legs are visible in the water. Sets of wooden oars fly in all directions. In the tightly cropped drawing *Man on Dolphin*, a nude mythic figure riding on the back of a dolphin holds a spear and shield in hand to attack the midsection of the enormous whale's body. The whale's lower jaw and teeth are seen at the lower right, and its massive tail swings up and out of the picture plane.

In each case, the drawings address man's struggle against nature. As Bruce Robertson has remarked, "The poles of Kent's art were his passionate identifications with the North and with the working class. He ennobled hard labor and suffering in his art, identifying class struggle not with the urban proletariat but with the honest peasant."[4]

Working with the publishing firm's designer William Kittridge, Kent oversaw all aspects of the publication's design, including the selection of a paper that could take a heavy black ink, and an appropriate typeface for the book. He spoke poetically about the book: "The *color*, so far as I can see, *is* determined;

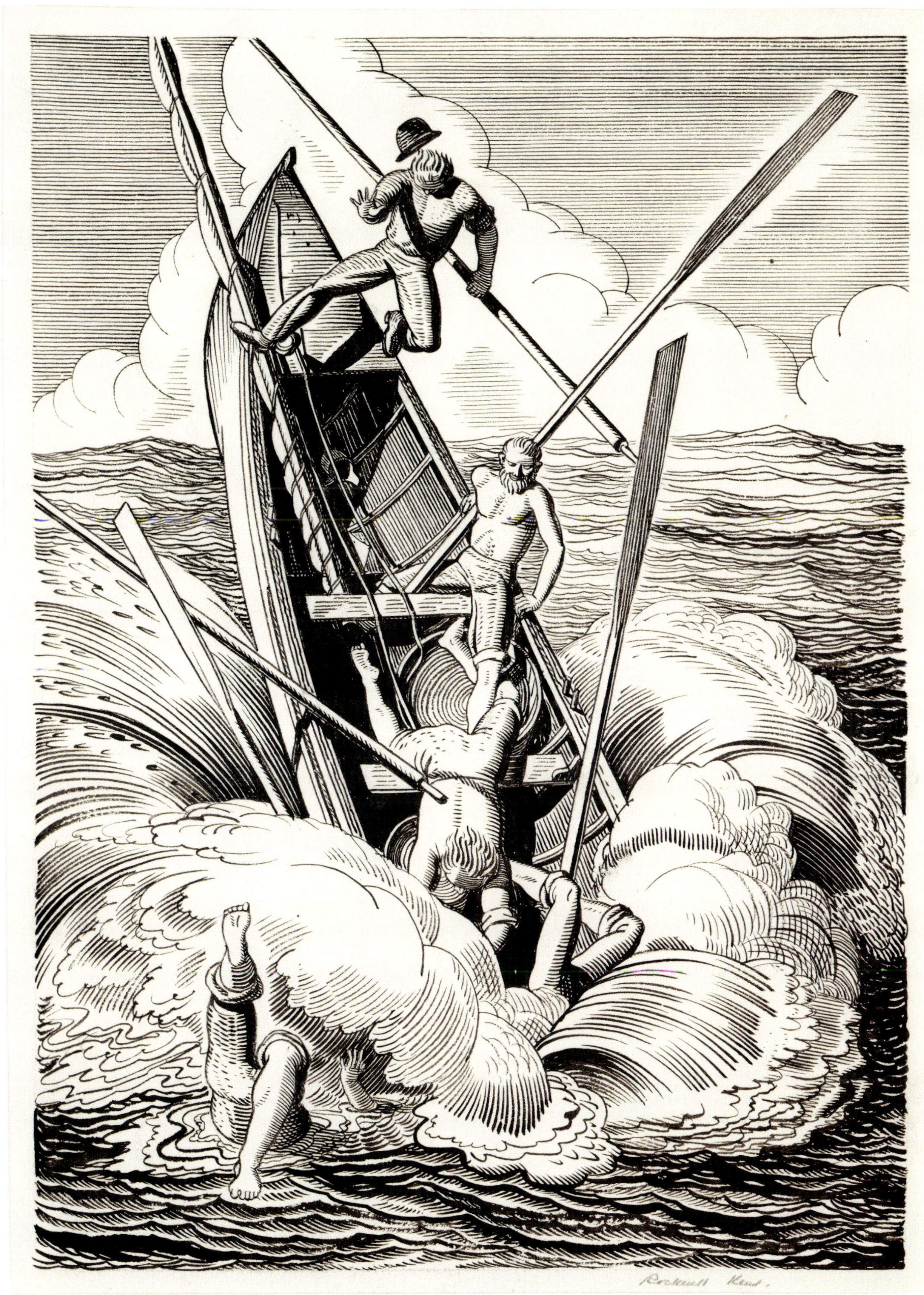

Cat. 39a

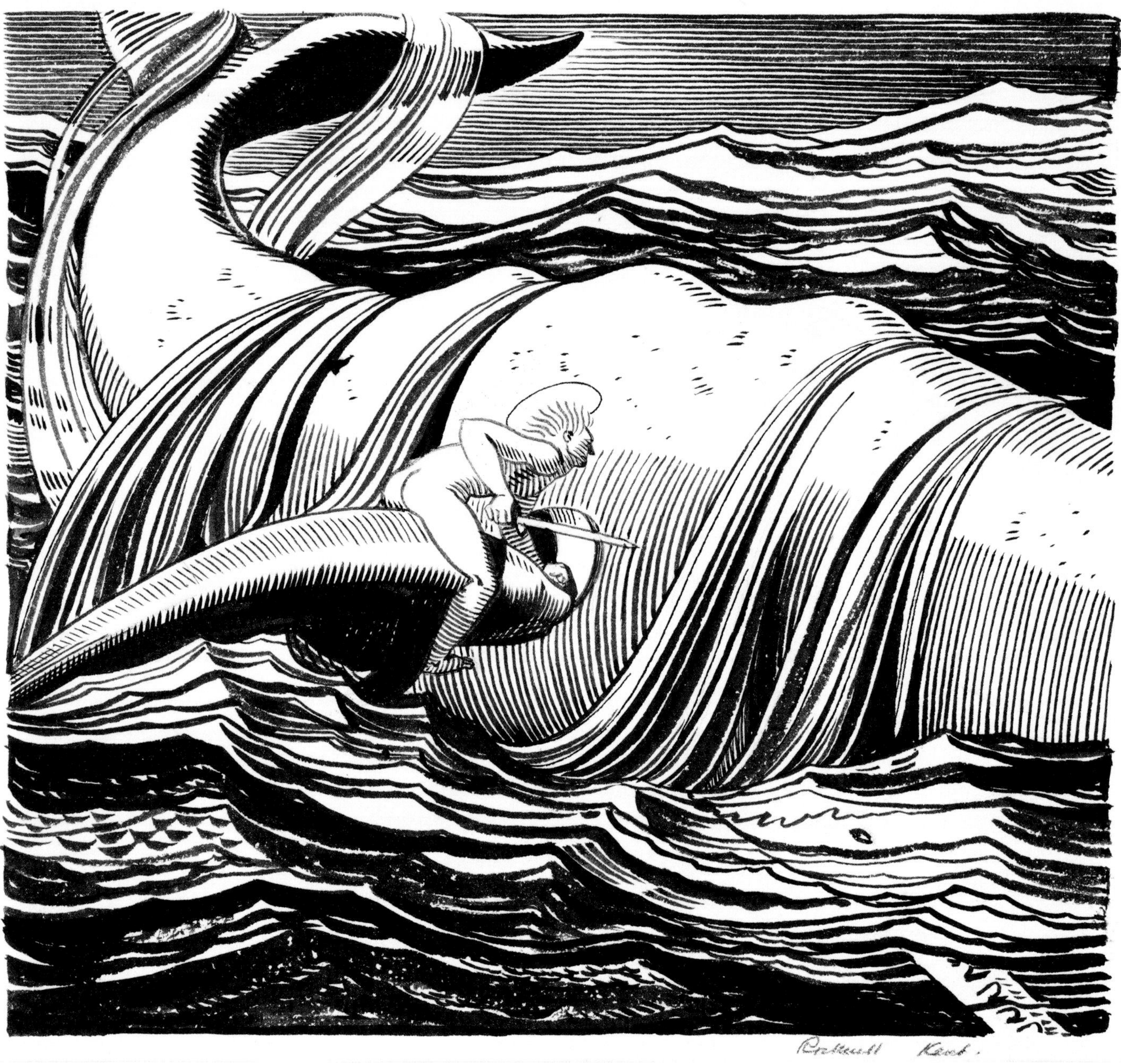

Cat. 39b

night, the midnight darkness enveloping human existence, the darkness of the human soul, the abyss—such is the mood of Moby Dick."[5] The original three-volume set, in an aluminum slipcase, sold out quickly, despite its substantial $75 price. The popularity of the series led to many successive editions of the books.[6]

The dealer Erhard Weyhe acquired these two drawings from Rockwell Kent, who had exhibited his watercolors and drawings at the Weyhe Gallery in the 1920s. Weyhe established his fine art print gallery in New York in 1919. In 1955 Weyhe gave to the Atheneum the two drawings published here, as well as two additional drawings by Kent: *Illustration for Moby-Dick, Chapter LXXXI, Three Whale Boats Attacking Whale* and *Illustration for Moby-Dick, Chapter XL, Five Men around a Capstan.* At the same time, he gave the Atheneum 143 prints by a number of twentieth-century artists, including 15 by Rockwell Kent.
EMK

1. David Traxel, *An American Saga: The Life and Times of Rockwell Kent* (New York: Harper and Row, 1980), 159.
2. Jake Milgram Wein, *Rockwell Kent: The Mythic and the Modern* (Manchester, Vt.: Hudson Hills Press in association with the Portland Museum of Art, 2005), 134, provides a history of the limited edition and successive editions of *Moby-Dick*.
3. Traxel, *An American Saga*, 159.
4. Bruce Robertson, *Reckoning with Winslow Homer: His Late Paintings and Their Influence* (Cleveland: Cleveland Museum of Art, 1990), 105.
5. Quoted in ibid., 134; Rockwell Kent to William Kittredge, 11 November 1926.
6. Traxel, *An American Saga*, 166.

Stuart Davis

Born in Philadelphia, 1892;
died in New York, 1964

Stuart Davis was born into a family that was very involved with the arts: his parents studied with Thomas Anshutz at the Pennsylvania Academy of the Fine Arts and his father was the art editor at the *Philadelphia Press*. Davis studied with Robert Henri at the Art School of New York from 1909 to 1912. Early on, he was influenced by the aesthetic of the Ashcan school and, like his teacher, he took as his subject matter the everyday urban environment. Davis exhibited five watercolors at the legendary Armory Show in 1913. These works showed the influence of the paintings of the European avant-garde, such as Vincent van Gogh, Paul Gauguin, and Henri Matisse. During the 1910s Davis experimented with a variety of styles of European modernism, including Postimpressionism and Cubism.

After Davis's first encounter with radical European art, the American scene remained his favored subject matter. For Davis, jazz, radio, movies, and consumer products epitomized contemporary American life. In the 1920s, he began experimenting with Synthetic Cubism and developed the elements of his mature style: a flat, linear style in which geometric forms are combined with bold, high-key color. In 1927 his abstract style reached its culmination in his Egg Beater series; that same year, Edith Halpert from the Downtown Gallery, New York, became his dealer.

Davis spent one year in Paris (1928–29), where, as he painted cafés and street scenes, he forged important friendships with leading American modernists such as John Graham, Arshile Gorky (q.v.), and Willem de Kooning. This experience strengthened his knowledge of contemporary abstract movements and made him one of America's strongest advocates of abstract art in the first half of the twentieth century.

Upon his return to the United States, in 1929, Davis moved to Greenwich Village and spent most of his summers in the seaside town of Gloucester, Massachusetts. In the 1930s he was active in organizations such as the American Artists' Congress and Artists' Union. From 1931 to 1932 he taught at New York's Art Students League, and he worked for the mural division of the Public Works Project from 1933 to 1939.

During the last two decades of his life, Davis's art became bolder, and he increased his clarity of conception. He reworked earlier ideas into large-scale paintings defined by planes of bright color and simplified, recognizable images. The Museum of Modern Art gave him his first major retrospective in 1945. Other important exhibitions included traveling retrospectives in 1957 (organized by the Walker Art Center, Minneapolis); 1965 (National Gallery of Art, Washington, D.C.); and 1978 (the Brooklyn Museum).

Select Bibliography

H. Harvard Arnason. *Stuart Davis Memorial Exhibition.* Washington, D.C.: National Collection of Fine Arts, Smithsonian Institution, 1965.

John R. Lane. *Stuart Davis: Art and Art Theory.* Brooklyn: Brooklyn Museum, 1978.

Karen Wilkin. *Stuart Davis.* New York: Abbeville Press, 1987.

Ani Boyajian and Mark Rutkoski, eds. *Stuart Davis: A Catalogue Raisonné.* 3 vols. New Haven, Conn.: Yale University Press, 2007.

40

Stuart Davis
Gas Pumps, 1935
Opaque watercolor with pen and black ink on illustration board
(board ink-stamped: Joseph Torch Pen-Art)
16 5/6 × 15 in. (42.8 × 38.1 cm)
Signed and dated at lower right:
STUART DAVIS 1925–35
Ex coll.: the artist; Henry E. Schnakenberg, Newtown, Connecticut, as of 1941
Gift of Henry E. Schnakenberg, 1952.388

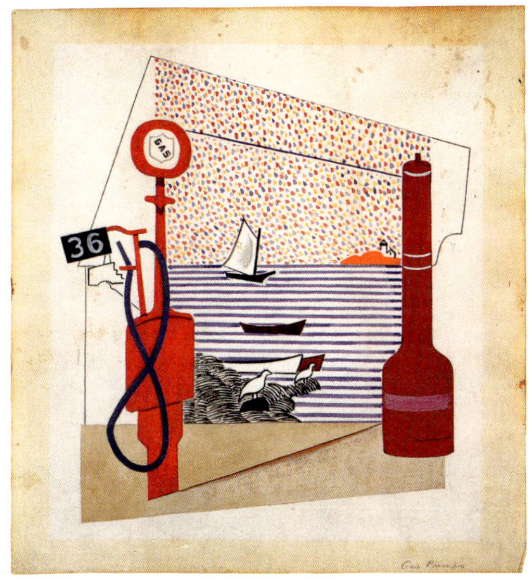

Fig. 1. Stuart Davis, *Gas Pumps*, 1925. Watercolor and traces of pencil on paper, 14 1/2 × 12 1/2 in. (36.8 × 31.8 cm). Rose Art Museum, Brandeis University, Waltham, Mass. Gift of Mrs. Teresa Jackson Weill, New York, 1975.67W

In 1913 Stuart Davis visited Provincetown, Massachusetts, for the first time, and from that moment onward he was "a continuing addict of the New England coast."[1] Two years later, he spent the first of many summers in the seafaring town of Gloucester, Massachusetts, which had a thriving artist colony dating to the nineteenth century. Gloucester played an important role in Davis's art; its working harbor and artifacts of the fishing community inspired the shapes and patterns of his work of the 1920s and '30s.[2] The composition, as the title indicates, is based on the ordinary but essential fixture of modern times, the gas pump. Davis contrasts the bright new red gas pump, a symbol of modernity, against the picturesque Gloucester harbor. As Davis explained, "I [juxtaposed] the gas pumps against a familiar waterfront scenery. It is difficult to realize today the stimulus of this sense of the new when the gas pump is omnipresent in all environments."[3]

Davis executed three variations of *Gas Pumps*: the original composition (fig. 1), followed by the Atheneum version, completed in 1935, and a final version in 1938 (private collection). In each case, he retained the essentials of the original design—a waterfront view with two vertical forms in the foreground (a gas pump and a marker or buoy) and a picturesque background (complete with sailboat, seagulls, rocky coastline, and quaint lighthouse)—but also made each work distinct. The Atheneum version reflects Davis's stylistic development in the mid-1930s. Whereas the earliest watercolor appears decorative and controlled, ten years later the composition is energetic and full of motion. Using opaque rather than transparent watercolor, Davis redefines the background with three horizontal bands of solid color. The addition of descriptive details—the passing clouds, the coil of rope—and decorative elements, such as the ribbonlike motif to unify the two vertical forms, gives the design greater visual impact.

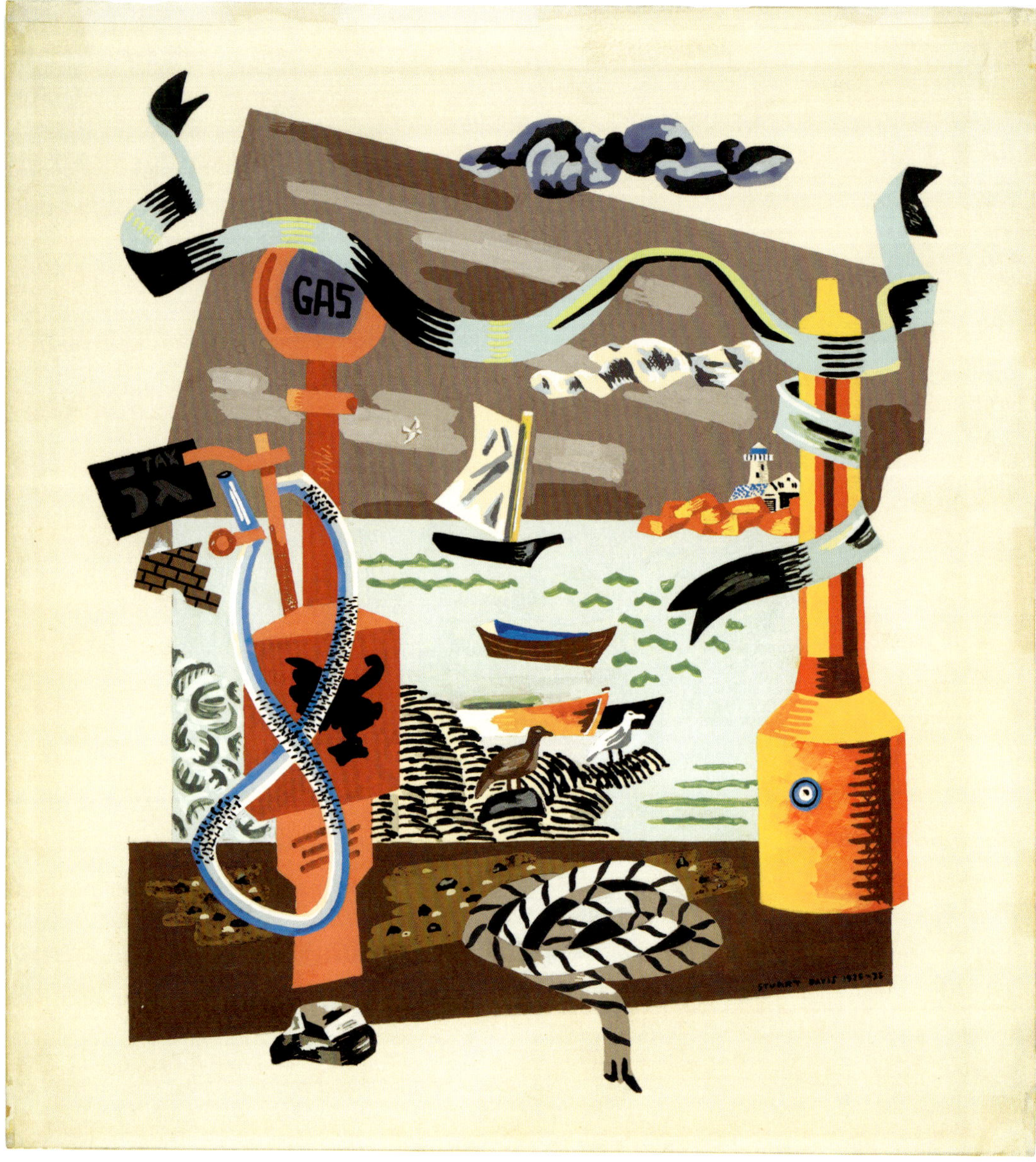

Cat. 40

Davis's imagery, like his painting style, fused opposing tendencies: tradition and modernity, realism and abstraction. Dubbed an "American Cubist," Davis delighted in the fragmented designs and vivid colors of European modernism and used these aesthetics to reinterpret the local flavor of American subject matter. In *Gas Pumps* the overlapping shapes and patterns set against a background of solid colors recalls the flat, decorative appearance of Cubist collage. As in Pablo Picasso's early Cubist collages, Davis parodies the limits of realism using trompe l'oeil to mimic the coiled rope hanging over a virtual edge.

The proliferation of advertising became an important inspiration for twentieth-century American artists. In *Gas Pumps*, for example, Davis introduced contemporary, commercial objects into his work and cleverly blurred the boundary between high and low art.
ECM

41

Stuart Davis
Yellow Truck (or *Yellow Hand Truck*), 1939
Opaque watercolor and black ink with traces of pencil on wove paper
$11\frac{15}{16} \times 15\frac{7}{8}$ in. (30.3 × 40.3 cm)
Signed at lower right: Stuart Davis
Ex coll.: with the artist; Mrs. Seymour Resor as of 1949; Mr. Resor (son of Mrs. Seymour Resor), as of 1950; Mrs. James Laughlin, Norfolk, Connecticut
Gift of Mrs. James Laughlin, 1981.61

On the occasion of Stuart Davis's 1965 memorial exhibition, the art historian H. Harvard Arnason observed: "[With Davis,] the establishment of an exact chronology of stylistic development is even more difficult than it is in the case of many artists and—I am sure Davis himself would insist—perhaps even more pointless. We continually find him returning to earlier ideas, suddenly creating paintings out of drawings that he had laid aside for years."[1] In many ways, the Atheneum's two works on paper by Davis, *Yellow Truck* and *Gas Pumps* (cat. 40), uphold Arnason's comments. Both compositions were reconfigured and reworked, at least twice, years after the original idea was conceived. Davis often recorded the evolution of his ideas and composition in his sketchbooks.

In the case of *Yellow Truck*, for example, the original sketch appeared as a pen and ink drawing in a notebook in 1938. Then Davis made two colorful, more finished, compositions—*Yellow Truck*, seen here, and *Night Dock* (1953; collection of James and Barbara Palmer). Motifs from these earlier versions reappeared in the right half of the painting *Deuce*, completed in 1954 (fig. 1).[2]

Fig. 1. Stuart Davis, *Deuce*, 1954. Oil on canvas, $26 \times 42\frac{1}{4}$ in. (66 × 107.3 cm). San Francisco Museum of Modern Art. Gift of Mrs. E. S. Heller, 55.4734

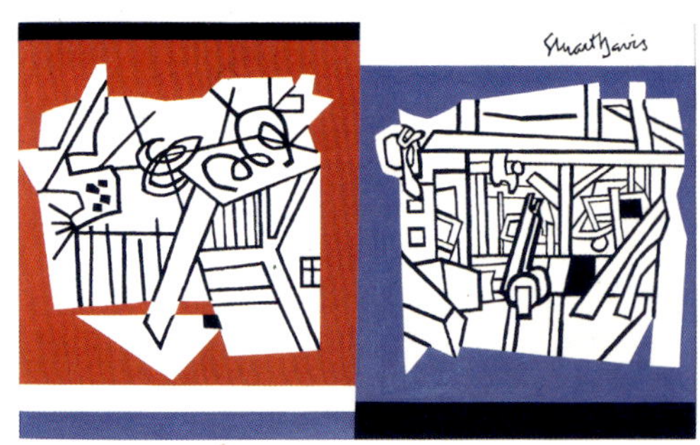

1. Diane Kelder, *Stuart Davis* (Fort Worth, Tex.: Amon Carter Museum, 1986), 24.
2. Karen Wilkin, *Stuart Davis in Gloucester* (West Stockbridge, Mass.: Hard Press, 1999), 56.
3. Stuart Davis to Charles C. Cunningham, 2 May 1954, curatorial files, Wadsworth Atheneum.

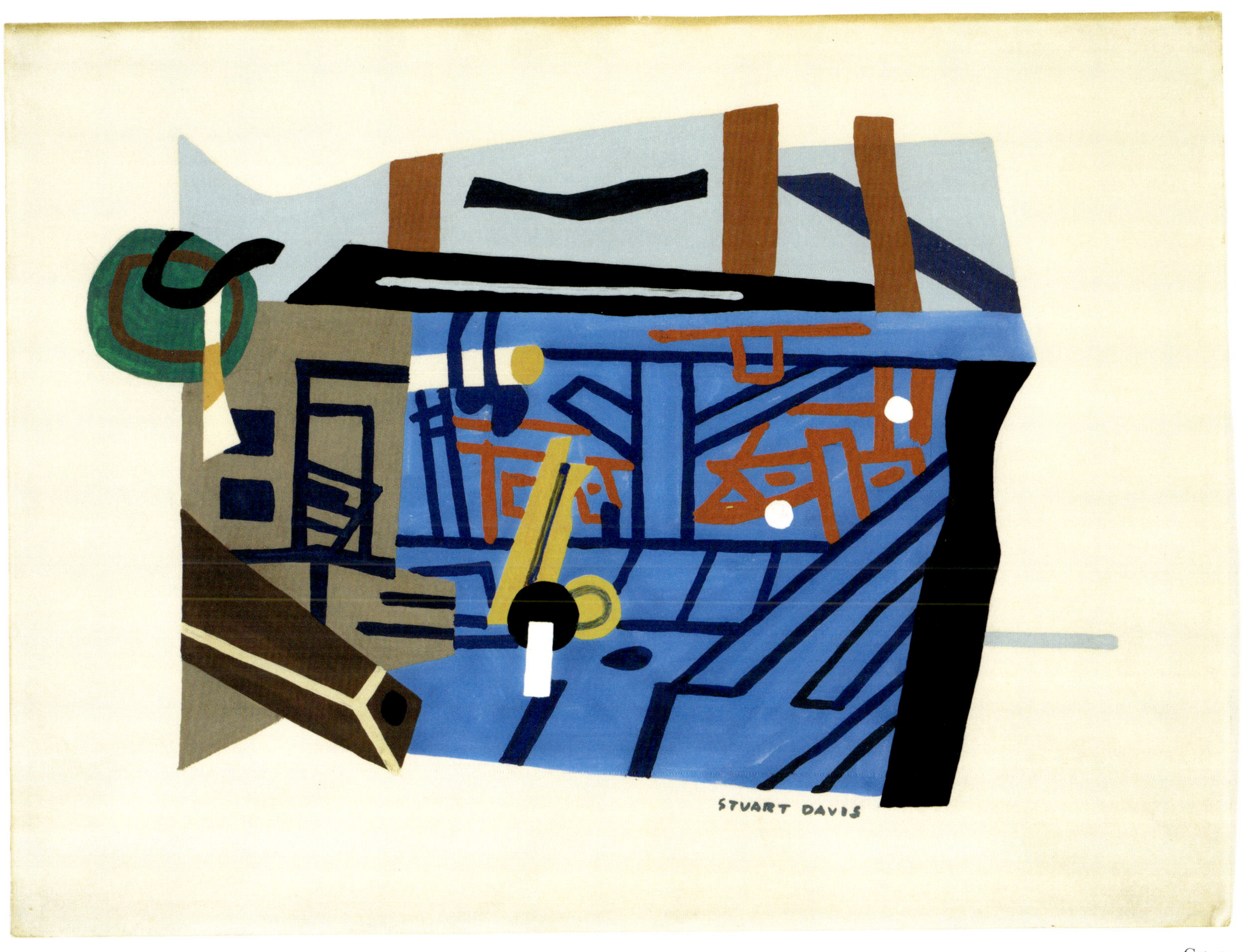

Cat. 41

As the title of the Atheneum's work indicates, the central image is a yellow hand truck used to transport heavy objects. The scene in which it is set is a visual hodgepodge of abstract circles and lines suggestive of a schematic diagram rather than a real location. According to Davis's notes, however, it is a dock scene.[3] In his sketchbooks, Davis made numerous drawings of the docks and sailboats in Gloucester, Massachusetts, where he summered. In *Yellow Truck*, the sailboat masts and nautical lines are translated into a patterned landscape of color and line. The environment represented is almost illegible; shapes appear to overlap and intersect at random, and even Davis's use of color seems arbitrary. At the same time, however, the composition is visually engaging and cheery–the yellow truck draws the viewer into the scene.

1. H. H. Arnason, *Stuart Davis Memorial Exhibition* (Washington, D.C.: National Collection of Fine Arts, Smithsonian Institution, 1965), 22.
2. Ani Boyajian and Mark Rutkoski, eds., *Stuart Davis: A Catalogue Raisonné*, 3 vols. (New Haven, Conn.: Yale University Press, 2007), cat. 1243 for *Yellow Truck* and cat. 1677 for *Deuce*. According to loan activities noted in Stuart Davis's Account Book I, this work was noted by the title "Yellow Hand Truck" in September 1940, but two months later was titled "Yellow Truck." See the Estate of Stuart Davis Archives, Harvard University.
3. In the remarks in the catalogue raisonné entry for *Deuce*, Davis wrote of this two-sectioned composition, "Made necessary change in the extreme right area of 26 × 42 drawing on canvas, yet unnamed, consisting of 2 major elements-a Dock Scene and a Table. Canvas divided in half vertically." Boyajian and Rutkoski, *Stuart Davis*, 3:388.

Milton Avery

Born in Altmar, New York, 1893;
died in New York, 1965

Milton Avery was born in upstate New York, the son of a tanner. The Avery family moved to the Hartford, Connecticut, area when Avery was thirteen. After working in local factories to help support his family, he enrolled in the night school at the Connecticut League of Art Students under the direction of Charles Noel Flagg in order to pursue a career as an artist. By 1918, he had transferred to the School of the Art Society in Hartford.

In 1925 Avery went to Gloucester, Massachusetts, to join the art colony there, and in the fall of that year he moved to New York to be closer to Sally Michel, a student at the Art Students League, whom he would marry that year. During the 1920s, Avery painted traditional figurative and genre subjects in a Postimpressionist style. He attended evening classes at the Art Students League, where, influenced by Kenneth Hayes Miller and Yasuo Kuniyoshi (q.v.), he began to simplify his forms and use broader expanses of color in his work. While his paintings became increasingly abstract, he never fully abandoned representational forms in his figural works, landscapes, seascapes, and still lifes. He developed close friendships with Adolph Gottlieb, Marsden Hartley, Barnett Newman, and Mark Rothko. The Phillips Collection in Washington, D.C., purchased a work by Avery in 1929 and gave him his first solo museum exhibition in 1944. In 1960, the Whitney Museum of American Art held a retrospective of his work. During his lifetime, he exhibited his work with that of his wife Sally Avery and their daughter, March Avery Cavanaugh, also artists. Avery's work in color abstraction is credited with paving the way for the Abstract Expressionists.

Select Bibliography

Hilton Kramer. *Milton Avery: Paintings, 1930–1960.* New York: A. S. Barnes, 1962.

Adelyn D. Breeskin. *Milton Avery.* Washington, D.C.: National Collection of Fine Arts, 1970.

Cheryl A. Brutvan. *Milton Avery: Works on Paper.* Williamstown, Mass.: Sterling and Francine Clark Art Institute, 1980.

Barbara Haskell. *Milton Avery.* New York: Harper & Row in association with the Whitney Museum of American Art, 1982.

Robert Hobbs. *Milton Avery.* New York: Hudson Hills Press, 1990.

42

Milton Avery
Church by the Sea, 1939
Opaque and transparent watercolor on thick wove paper
(Whatman watermark at bottom edge)
22 9/16 × 30 13/16 in. (58.1 × 78.4 cm)
Signed at lower left, on side of boat: Milton Avery
Ex coll.: with the Grace Borgenicht Gallery, New York, by 1981; purchased by CIGNA for the CIGNA Museum and Art Collection, Philadelphia, Pennsylvania, in 1981 to 2005
Gift of CIGNA, 2005.3.1

In the summer of 1938, Milton Avery and his family traveled to the Gaspé Peninsula, in the French-speaking province of Quebec in southeastern Canada. Fascinated by the isolated landscape and the distinctive white light of this region, Avery produced a series of watercolors that capture this light and the vibrant color harmonies that he observed there. The result, as Barbara Haskell notes, "was a unique luminosity of color."[1] Avery would spend the next two years translating these works on paper into oils. *Church by the Sea*, dated 1939, is based on the previous summer's work on the Gaspé Peninsula, and depicts the peninsula's rugged terrain and coastline.

Avery used a series of shorthand notations, alternating between translucent and opaque watercolor, to delineate the boats on the water, the waves, beach, coastline, and the land. He transformed nature into a series of squiggly lines, broad wavy brushstrokes, and variations in color. The small white church in the distance is portrayed as a spare, abstract form in white and black. This work and the approximately two hundred watercolors Avery produced at Gaspé Peninsula are considered a breakthrough for the artist in their freedom of execution and simplicity of form.[2] The works benefited from the artist's use of expensive watercolor paper, which adds to their luminosity of color.

The inspiration for the Gaspé Peninsula series may have been, in part, Avery's admiration for Marsden Hartley's work, as well as their shared interest in American vernacular and folk arts.[3] Following his return to America in 1934, Hartley developed a spare, consciously primitivist modern style for his New England subjects. In 1935 he traveled to Nova Scotia, where he lived in a remote island setting with a French-Canadian fishing family, whom he came to revere. Paintings such as *Northern Seascape, Off the Banks* (1936; Milwaukee Art Museum), painted shortly after Hartley left Nova Scotia, with its pared-down, abbreviated, and roughly applied brushstrokes, may have served as inspiration for the shift in style found in Avery's own scenes of the Canadian shoreline.[4]

EMK

1. Barbara Haskell, *Milton Avery* (New York: Harper & Row in association with the Whitney Museum of American Art, 1982), 72.
2. Robert Hobbs, *Milton Avery* (New York: Hudson Hills Press, 1990), 96.
3. Ibid., 108–9; and Elizabeth Mankin Kornhauser, "Marsden Hartley and Folk Art," *Antiques* (January 2003): 150–58.
4. For a discussion of the relationship between Avery and Hartley see Hobbs, *Milton Avery*, 108–10. Hobbs suggests that the two artists shared both a friendship and a rivalry, and that Avery may in fact have influenced Hartley. Also see Elizabeth Mankin Kornhauser, ed., *Marsden Hartley* (New Haven, Conn.: Yale University Press, 2003), 196, 244, 245, 311.

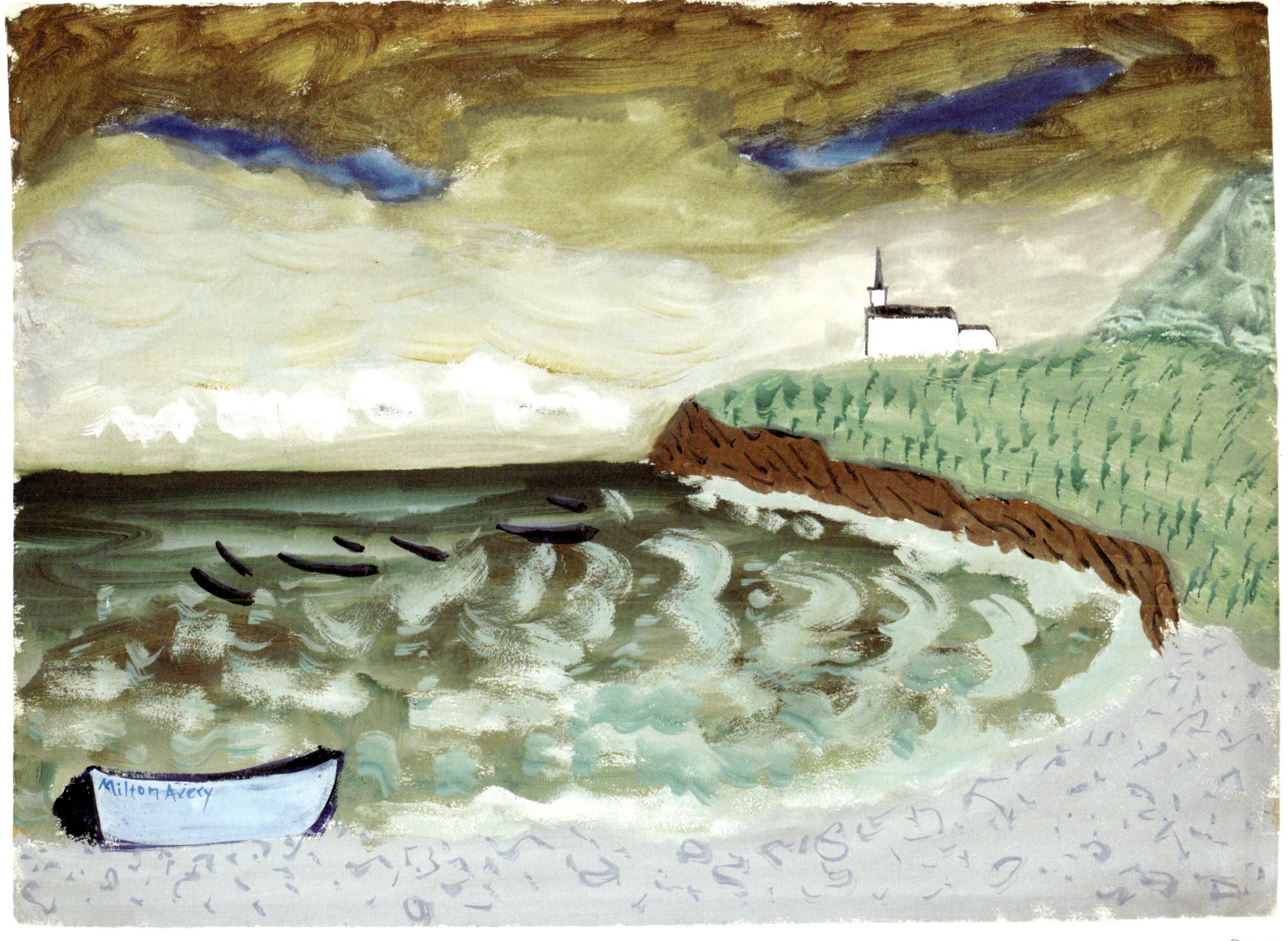

Cat. 42

Jacob Lawrence

Born in Atlantic City, New Jersey, 1917;
died in Seattle, 2000

Jacob Lawrence was a leading figurative painter of the twentieth century who documented the African-American experience through his artwork. Lawrence and his family moved to Harlem in 1924, where he engaged in the vibrant black intellectual, cultural, and artistic life. He first took art classes at the Utopia Children's Center, where he studied with the artist Charles H. Alston. Alston mentored Lawrence, introducing him to the leading intellectuals of the era, such as the painter Aaron Douglas and the writers Langston Hughes and Alain Locke. Their progressive ideas and beliefs inspired Lawrence to commit to depicting the history of black Americans, a commitment he maintained for the rest of his career.

Lawrence enrolled in classes with the Works Progress Administration (WPA) in New York from 1934 to 1937 and studied at the Harlem Art Workshop in 1935. His first significant body of paintings from 1936 includes genre scenes of Harlem street life painted in a social realist style. In 1941, his landmark series The Migration of the American Negro was exhibited at the Downtown Gallery in New York, bringing Lawrence international recognition. That year Lawrence became the first African-American artist to be represented in the collection of the Museum of Modern Art, New York. Many of his best-known series from the 1940s chronicle important moments in African-American history through individuals such as Toussaint L'Ouverture, Harriet Tubman, and Frederick Douglass.

After World War II, Lawrence taught briefly at Black Mountain College, North Carolina, where he was influenced by Josef Albers's interest in form and design. In the 1950s his realism became more stylized, and his subject matter shifted to the political atmosphere surrounding racism in America. In 1970 Lawrence and his wife, painter Gwendolyn Knight, moved to Seattle, where he accepted a teaching position at the University of Washington. He retired with emeritus status in 1986. His numerous accolades include honorary degrees from eighteen schools and the Spingarn Medal, the highest honor awarded by the NAACP. From the 1970s to the 1990s Lawrence completed numerous public commissions, including a seventy-two-foot-long mosaic titled *New York in Transit*, installed in the Times Square subway complex in 2001. In 1999 Lawrence and his wife established the Jacob and Gwendolyn Lawrence Foundation for the creation, presentation, and study of American art, with a special emphasis on work by African-American artists. Jacob Lawrence was still painting until a few weeks before his death at age eighty-two.

Select Bibliography

Milton W. Brown. *Jacob Lawrence*. New York: Whitney Museum of American Art, 1974.

Ellen Harkins Wheat. *Jacob Lawrence: American Painter*. Seattle: University of Washington Press, 1986.

P. T. Nesbett and M. Dubois, eds. *Jacob Lawrence: Paintings, Drawings and Murals, 1935–1999: A Catalogue Raisonné*. Seattle: University of Washington Press, 2001.

43

Jacob Lawrence
Rain, 1937
Opaque watercolor heightened with graphite on thick wove paper
28 × 20³/₄ in. (71.1 × 52.7 cm)
Signed and dated at lower right: J. Lawrence 37
Ex coll.: Jacob and Gwendolyn Knight Lawrence, New York and Seattle; with the Francine Seders Gallery, Seattle
The Ella Gallup Sumner and Mary Catlin Sumner Collection Fund, 1990.30

Inspired by the Harlem community where Jacob Lawrence and his family were living at the time, *Rain* is part of a series depicting scenes from the neighborhood. Jacob Lawrence began the series when he was just twenty years old and on the verge of an important career as a social realist artist. His art and philosophical outlook were influenced largely by the culture of this close-knit neighborhood, which impressed upon him the importance of his African-American identity.[1]

In this early Harlem series, Lawrence developed reductive, cartoonlike figures using flat areas of color. As Lawrence recalled, his ideas for brightly colored patterns were inspired by decorative, inexpensive furnishings at home: "[They] must have had some influence [on my work], all the color and everything. Because we were so poor, [color was] a means of brightening their life."[2] In *Rain*, three figures tend to a leaking tenement roof. The two at left direct their gazes toward the black cracks in the wall while the third, seated figure sponges water into a bucket. At this time, Lawrence's palette was dominated by somber blacks and grays, symbolizing the harsh realities of poverty, but it was also punctuated with bright colors. The dismal setting is enlivened by accents of burnt orange and yellow in the clothing and the towels.

Over time, Lawrence's subject matter became more provocative, as did his use of color. He tackled more serious subjects with an ambitious, narrative format. Lawrence's John Brown series (1955), for example, chronicled in twenty-two individual frames the story of the nineteenth-century abolitionist who fought to his death to overthrow slavery in America.[3] In no. 2 in the series, *For 40 years, John Brown reflected on the hopeless and miserable conditions of the slaves*, the composition centers around the pious John Brown, at the head of the table, praying for strength and guidance (fig. 1). The emotive power of Lawrence's bold colors and reductive style is further heightened by the historical significance of the stories he retold.
ECM

Fig. 1. Jacob Lawrence, no. 2 in the John Brown series, *For 40 years, John Brown reflected on the hopeless and miserable conditions of the slaves*, 1977. Screenprint on paper, 26 × 20 in. (66 × 50.8 cm). Wadsworth Atheneum Museum of Art. Purchased through the Bequest of Hanna Newburger and Gift of Howard Fromson, 1991.4.2

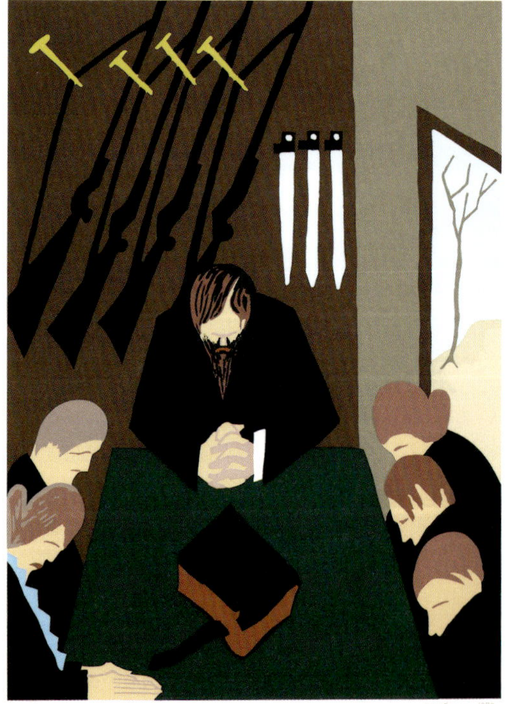

1. Ellen Harkins Wheat, *Jacob Lawrence: American Painter* (Seattle: University of Washington Press, 1986), 30. At Charles Alston's studio, Lawrence encountered seminal figures such as Alain Locke, Langston Hughes, Aaron Douglas, Richard Wright, and Ralph Ellison.
2. Jacob Lawrence, conversation with Ellen Harkins Wheat, 15 February 1983. Reprinted in ibid., 29.
3. *The Legend of John Brown* (Detroit: Founders Society, Detroit Institute of Arts, 1978). The series was completed in 1941, first as gouache on paper and then later reproduced as silkscreens in 1977. As Ellen Harkins Wheat explained, it is considered to be the apogee of Lawrence's dramatic narrative abilities. To preserve the important series, the Detroit Institute of Arts, which received the originals as a gift in 1955, collaborated with the artist to produce the series as a limited edition of screen prints. The end result was not simply a replication of the originals but rather a reinterpretation–with input from the artist to the printer–in a new medium.

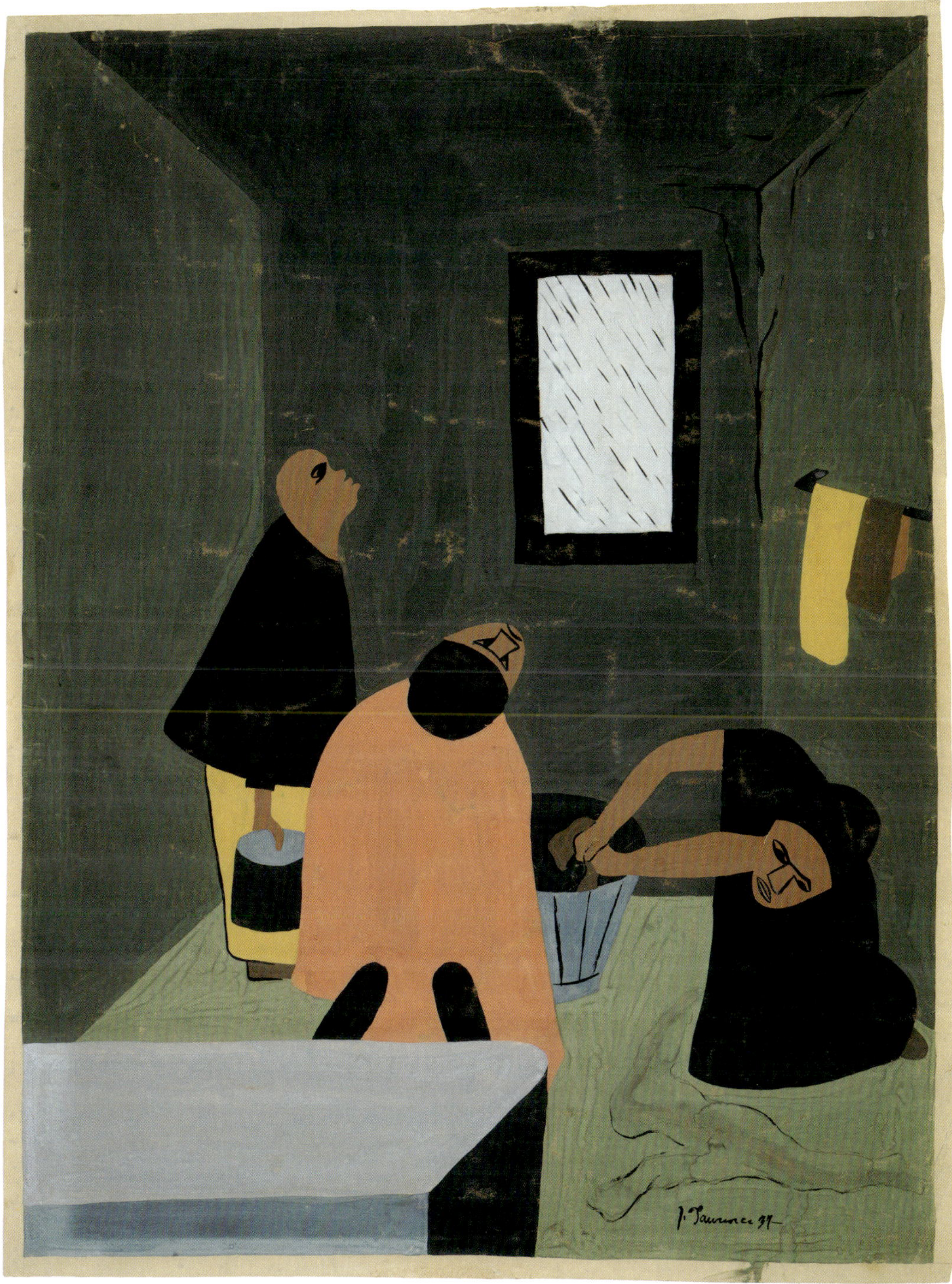

Cat. 43

Ben Shahn

Born in Kovno, Lithuania, 1898;
died in New York, 1969

Ben Shahn was an American painter, photographer, and lithographer. He was born into a family of Jewish craftsmen who emigrated in 1906, settling in Brooklyn, New York. From 1913 to 1917, he served as an apprentice in Hessenberg's Lithography Shop in Manhattan, and attended high school in the evenings in Brooklyn. He studied academic subjects at New York University and then City College of New York before enrolling in the National Academy of Design in 1922 to pursue a career as an artist. He became famous for his social realist paintings that championed liberal political ideals, among them the landmark series of 1932, Passion of Sacco and Vanzetti, which explored the theme of the trials and execution of immigrant anarchists Nicola Sacco and Bartolomeo Vanzetti.

After he married in 1922, Shahn and his wife traveled to North Africa, Spain, and France. Upon their return, they moved to Brooklyn Heights in 1925. There he met Walker Evans, with whom he shared a studio, and became interested in photography. Also at this time, he spent summers in the artist colony of Truro, near Provincetown, Massachusetts, painting seascapes and landscapes. Shahn traveled abroad again from 1927 to 1929, and in 1930 was given his first one-man exhibition at the Downtown Gallery, New York. In the 1920s, Shahn developed his hallmark style, and by 1932 he had become known as a social realist. To his social realist subject matter, he applied a unique painting style characterized by strong linearity and distortion used to convey emotion.

During the 1930s and '40s, Shahn painted murals for the Works Progress Administration's Federal Art Project and was also employed by the Farm Security Administration. He assisted Diego Rivera with the contentious, politically charged Rockefeller Center murals and completed a mural for the Federal Social Security Building, Washington, D.C., in 1942.

Throughout the 1950s and '60s, Shahn completed numerous mural commissions throughout the country that celebrate his Jewish heritage. Among them was a mosaic mural for the Congregation Mishkan, Israel, in Hamden, Connecticut. His major retrospective at the Museum of Modern Art in 1961 toured internationally. His last solo exhibition was at the Kennedy Galleries, in 1968, one year before he died.

Select Bibliography

James T. Soby. *Ben Shahn: His Graphic Art.* New York: George Braziller, 1963.

Howard Greenfeld. *Ben Shahn: Artist's Artist, People's Painter.* New York: Random House, 1998.

Deborah Martin Kao, Laura Katzman, and Jenna Webster. *Ben Shahn's New York: The Photographs of Modern Times.* Cambridge, Mass.: Fogg Art Museum, Harvard University Art Museums, 2000.

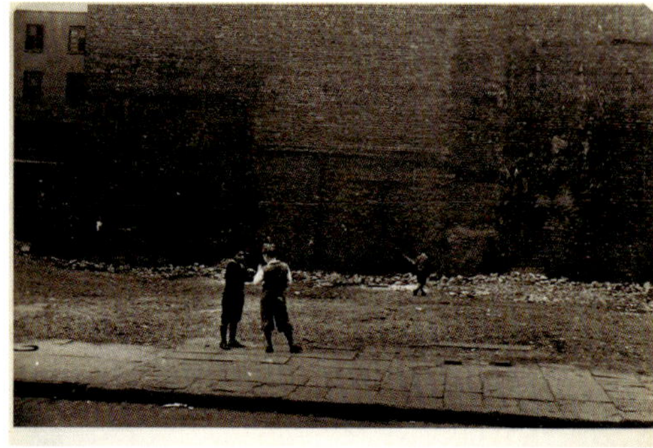

Fig. 1. Ben Shahn, *Untitled (New York City)*, 1932–34. Gelatin silver print, 6 7/16 × 9 3/4 in. (16.4 × 24.8 cm). Harvard Art Museum, Fogg Art Museum. Gift of Bernarda Bryson Shahn, P1970.722

44

Ben Shahn
Vacant Lot, 1939
Watercolor and gouache on paper laid down on Masonite with rabbit skin glue (materials identified by artist)
19 × 23 in. (48.3 × 58.4 cm)
Signed at lower right: Ben Shahn
Ex coll.: with Julien Levy Gallery, New York
The Ella Gallup Sumner and Mary Catlin Sumner Collection Fund, 1941.390

In 1930, during a summer of work and soul-searching on Cape Cod, Ben Shahn came to a decision about the path he wanted to follow as an artist. "I had seen all the right pictures and read all the right books," he recalled, "but it still didn't add up to anything . . . I [realized] I liked stories and people."[1] This impulse directed Shahn to create art with social and political meaning. He began to observe ordinary people in everyday settings, first documenting his surroundings with a handheld camera, creating photographs that he later translated into paintings. In 1932 Shahn, his first wife, and their young daughter moved from Brooklyn Heights to the Lower East Side, then the cultural center of the New York art scene.

In the 1930s Shahn developed his hallmark style when he joined the vanguard of the social documentary movement, making street photographs that captured New York life through the prosaic activities and expressive gestures of ordinary people.[2] Shahn often adapted certain aspects–placement of figures, configuration of buildings, leisure activities, and so forth–for his painted compositions. He often altered the painted compositions by eliminating representational details and cropping them to create a symbolic feeling or mood.

This painting was based on a photograph of three boys playing in an empty gravel lot (fig. 1). The lot was located on the corner of Bethune and Greenwich streets, near Shahn's studio at the time.[3] To the right, one boy plays a game of stickball against a brick wall while the other two look on from behind. With their backs to the camera, all three seem unaware of its presence and, perhaps more poignantly, impervious to the desolation of their urban playground. A comparison of the photograph with *Vacant Lot* shows significant alterations and deviations from photograph to painting. Shahn heightened the mood of the painting; as he explained, "[I presented] it in the most dramatic way I [could] by exploring the big and little relationships of color and tone, like the big red brick wall dwarfing the boy playing ball all alone."[4]

Two noteworthy changes to *Vacant Lot* emphasize a particular mood: the boys in the foreground have been removed, and the entire scene is cropped, eliminating the view of nearby buildings in the background. As a result, the little boy who remains appears dwarfed by his dark, empty surroundings and isolated from the rest of the world. According to the artist, the vacant area "drew the usual contingent of youngsters, but that [painting] is no actual happening, nor real boy. It's simply a sort of response to the attraction and the sense of lonliness [*sic*] that such a place has. It's an emptiness full of something that was there before."[5] Like Edward Hopper's empty diners or Walker Evans's street scenes, Shahn's *Vacant Lot* engages the viewer with a haunting absence; all these artists highlighted the mysterious qualities that haunt the most familiar places.
ECM

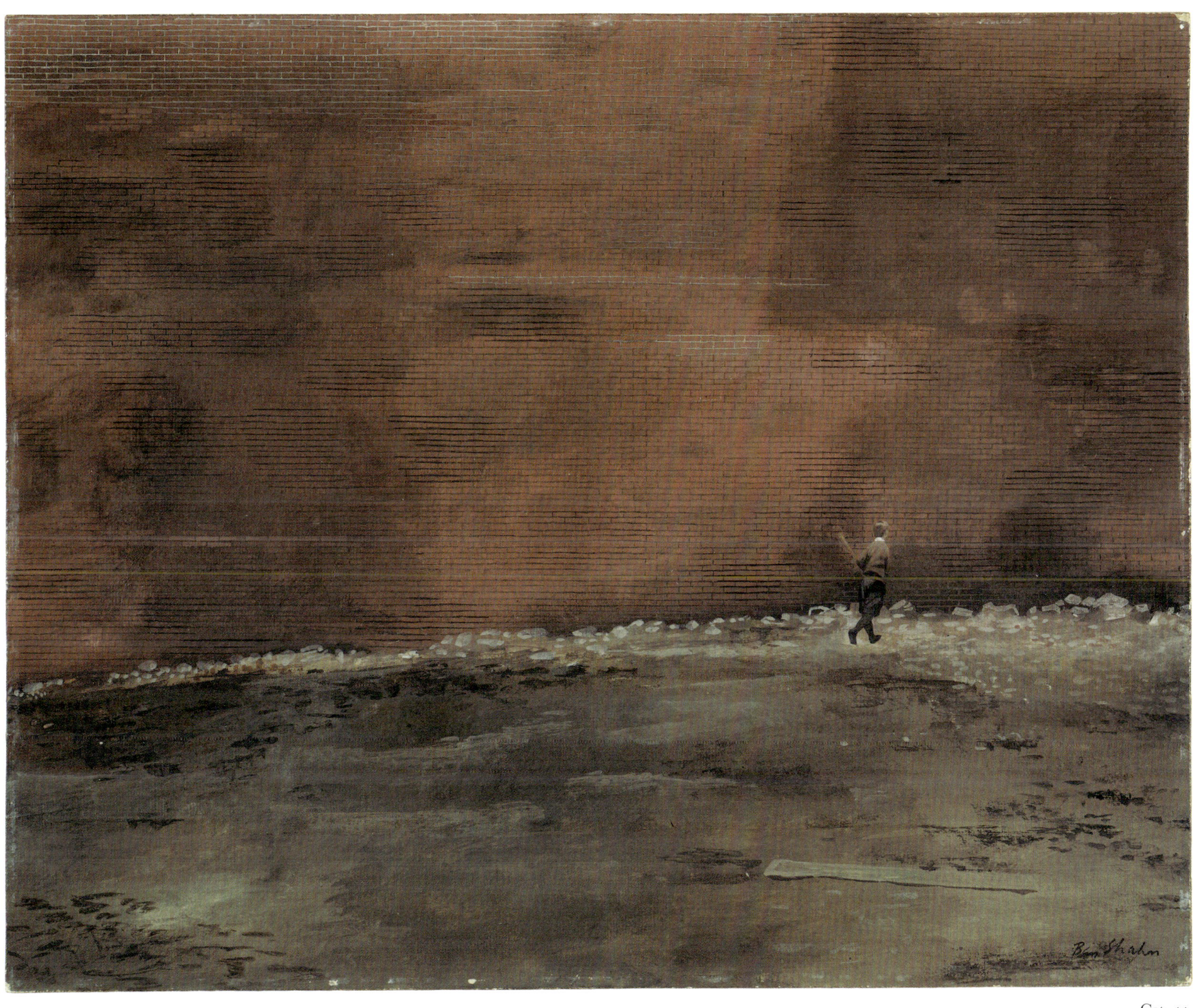

Cat. 44

1. "Ben Shahn, Painter of Social Themes, Is Dead at 70," *New York Times*, 16 March 1969.
2. Deborah Martin Kao, Laura Katzman, and Jenna Webster, *Ben Shahn's New York: The Photographs of Modern Times* (Cambridge, Mass.: Fogg Art Museum, Harvard University Art Museums, 2000). Walker Evans and Ben Shahn shared a studio for several years in the early 1930s.
3. Ben Shahn to Charles C. Cunningham, 26 January 1953. Wadsworth Atheneum Archives.
4. *Vacant Lot* was completed the same year as his well-known painting *Handball* (1939; Museum of Modern Art, New York). Details from both compositions appear in Shahn's mural *The Meaning of Social Security* (1942–44; now in the headquarters of the Voice of America, Washington, D.C.).
5. John D. Morse, "Ben Shahn: An Interview," *Magazine of Art* 37 (April 1944): 61.

George Overbury "Pop" Hart

Born in Cairo, Illinois, 1868;
died in New York, 1933

Early in life, George Overbury Hart acquired, and later preferred, the nickname "Pop" to his given name, George. Hart left home as a teenager and thus began an itinerant life at a young age. Primarily a self-taught artist—although he attended classes intermittently at the Art Institute of Chicago from 1894 to 1897—he began working as a sign painter in Chicago in 1892. In 1897 he embarked on a period of travel that included trips within the United States and abroad to Cuba, Central America, Iceland, and Europe.

Upon his return to the United States in 1907, Hart settled in Coytesville, New Jersey, where he opened a sign-painting business. Among his regular commissions were signs at the Palisades Amusement Park and stage sets for the World Pictures film studio based in Fort Lee, New Jersey. Hart became active in Fort Lee artistic circles, and among the more significant artists he met and became close friends with was Walt Kuhn (1877–1949). Several years later Hart lived for a brief period in New Orleans, where he shared an apartment with the French painter Jules Pascin (1885–1930). The influence of Pascin's expressionistic style can be seen in Hart's mature works. Also at this time, beginning in 1914, Hart made annual trips to the West Indies, where he sketched and made watercolors. His personal response to the life of the natives of tropical countries has been compared to Paul Gauguin's love of Tahiti.

In 1921, like other American artists before him such as Edward Hopper (q.v.), John Sloan (q.v.), and Max Weber (q.v.), Hart began to experiment with printmaking, exploring a variety of techniques such as drypoint, aquatint, and lithography. He continued printmaking and painting in watercolor for the rest of his life.

Although he traveled abroad regularly, Hart was active in the New York art scene in the late 1920s and early 1930s. He was a member of the American Watercolor and New York Watercolor societies and was twice president of the Brooklyn Society of Etchers. In 1927 the Downtown Gallery began representing him, and two years later his work was included in the Museum of Modern Art's important exhibition *Paintings by Nineteen Living Americans.* In December 1932, just nine months before his death, Hart's artistic achievements were honored in a solo exhibition at the New Jersey State Museum in Trenton. A large-scale memorial retrospective was held at the Newark Museum in 1935.

Select Bibliography

"'Pop' Hart, Artist, Philosopher, Dies." *New York Times*, September 19, 1933.

George Overbury "Pop" Hart, 1868–1933. Newark, N.J.: Newark Museum, 1935.

Irving H. Sandler. "Arthur B. Davies, 'Pop' Hart and Yasuo Kuniyoshi." *Art News* 61 (March 1962): 50.

Gregory Gilbert. *George Overbury "Pop" Hart: His Life and Art.* New Brunswick, N.J.: Rutgers University Press, 1986.

45

George Overbury "Pop" Hart
Street Fair: Fort Lee Special, 1930
Transparent watercolor over charcoal on wove paper
18 × 35½ in. (45.7 × 90.2 cm)
Signed at lower right: Hart 30
Ex coll.: The Downtown Gallery, New York
The Ella Gallup Sumner and Mary Catlin Sumner Collection Fund, 1947.401

Pop Hart sketched the people and the landscape of distant places such as Egypt, Tahiti, and Mexico, but he was equally attracted to the local scene of New York and its environs.[1] This included Coytesville, a neighborhood in Fort Lee, New Jersey, where the artist resided intermittently from 1907 until his death in 1933. Fort Lee bordered an area known as Cliffside Park, home of the thirty-eight-acre Palisades Amusement Park. As an experienced sign painter, Hart completed numerous signs and placards for restaurants and sideshows at Palisades Park.[2]

Hart's familiarity with the ambience of amusement parks likely informed his lively interpretation of a small, local street fair in Fort Lee, seen here. (The sign for the circus tent in the background harkens back to his earlier commissions.) His carnival-like setting includes a selection of familiar rides and attractions. The merry-go-round, Ferris wheel, and barker promoting games of chance and skill are painted with a spirited, impressionistic brushstroke. Hart conveyed the hot, brightly lit night by alternating yellow and blue-black, and rendered the crowds of people in shorthand as squiggly patches of color.[3]

Pop Hart excelled as printmaker and painter, but watercolor constituted a major part of his creative effort. His late watercolors were characterized by a freer, simplified and abstract style.[4] In *Street Fair*, for instance, the motion of the merry-go-round in the lower right corner is represented in quick, abbreviated brushstrokes that borders on nonobjective painting. Also at this time, Hart's work began to attract increasing critical attention in the art world. In 1927, Edith Gregor Halpert at the Downtown Gallery became his dealer. Halpert represented other American modernists such as Stuart Davis (q.v.), Yasuo Kuniyoshi (q.v.), and John Marin (q.v.) at this time.[5] This watercolor was purchased directly from the gallery in 1947.
ECM

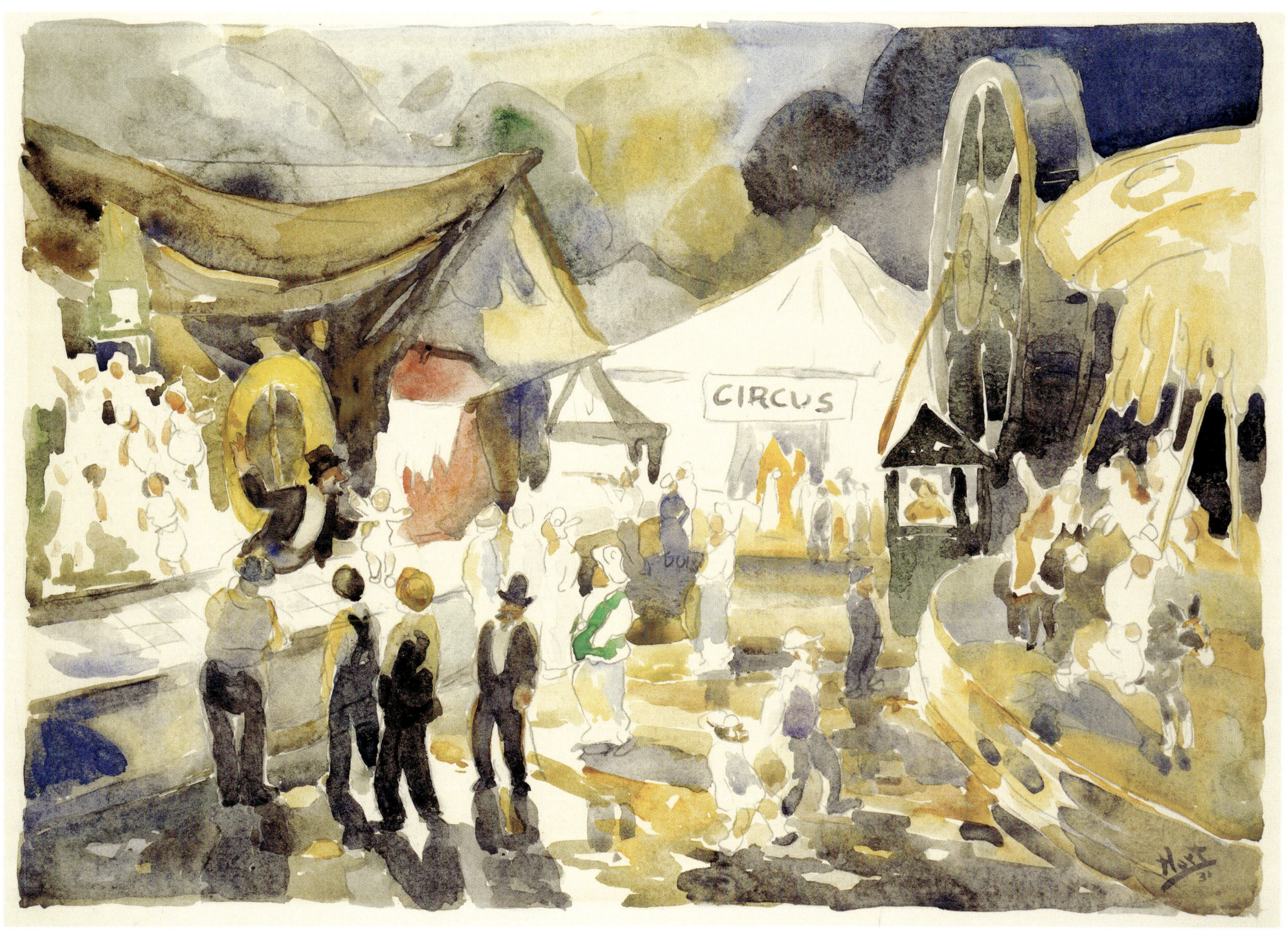

Cat. 45

1. Charles T. Butler, ed., *Lines of Discovery: 225 Years of American Drawings* (Columbus, Ga.: Columbus Museum, 2006), 143.
2. Gregory Gilbert, *George Overbury "Pop" Hart: His Life and Art* (New Brunswick, N.J.: Rutgers University Press, 1986), 30. For a more detailed and visual history of the park, see http://www.palisadespark.com/history.htm and http://www.fortleeonline.com/palpark/.
3. "Picture of the Month," August 4, 1958, Wadsworth Atheneum Archives.
4. Gilbert, *George Overbury "Pop" Hart*, 75.
5. In addition to promoting American modernism, Edith Halpert also collected American folk art. In its combination of regional subject matter and a progressive style, Hart's work would have appealed to Halpert's modernist and folk art tastes.

Guy Pène du Bois

Born in Brooklyn, New York, 1884;
died in Boston, 1958

Guy Pène du Bois was a painter, teacher, and art critic. In his paintings and watercolors, he presented satirical views of New York society. As early as high school, he showed a talent for drawing and enrolled in the New York School of Art, where he studied with William Merritt Chase. He later trained with the realist artists Kenneth Hayes Miller and Robert Henri. In 1905 he traveled to Paris, where one of his paintings was shown at the Salon. He returned to New York the following year, after his father's unexpected death. To support the family, he worked as an illustrator and a music and art critic for the *New York American*, his father's former employer. In 1913, he became editor of *Arts and Decoration* magazine.

After he left *Arts and Decoration* in 1921, Pène du Bois devoted more time to painting and to teaching at the Art Students League. In the 1920s his style matured, and he abandoned the dark palette and quick, gestural brushstrokes of his teachers for a style dominated by simplified and stylized figures. Between 1922 and 1946, he had regular solo exhibitions at the Kraushaar Galleries in New York. Pène du Bois depicted the nouveaux riches of New York and Parisian society and became best known for portraits of fashionable women, in groups or at parties. He and his family moved to France in 1924, but returned to New York after the Wall Street crash of 1929.

Between 1932 and 1950 he ran a school in Stonington, Connecticut, where he spent his summers. Throughout his career he wrote about art and was regarded as an astute critic. He produced several monographs on artists such as Edward Hopper (q.v.) and John Sloan (q.v.), and wrote a book, *Artists Say the Silliest Things* (1940).

Select Bibliography

Guy Pène du Bois. *Artists Say the Silliest Things.* New York: American Artists Group and Duell, Sloan and Pearce, 1940.

Betsy Fahlman. *Guy Pène du Bois: Artist about Town.* Washington, D.C.: Corcoran Gallery of Art, 1980.

Betsy Fahlman. *Guy Pène du Bois, Painter of Modern Life.* New York: Quantuck Lane Press, 2004.

46

Guy Pène du Bois
Roosevelt!, 1938
Transparent watercolor with pen and black ink on thick wove paper
14 11/16 × 11 15/16 in. (37.3 × 30.3 cm)
Signed and dated at lower left:
Guy Pène du Bois '38
Ex coll.: with Kraushaar Galleries, New York; George J. Dyer, Norfolk, Connecticut
Gift of George J. Dyer, 1963.500

Guy Pène du Bois made the world of money, fashion, and social status of New York, with which he was well acquainted, the subject of his satires.[1] His work from the late 1930s and '40s often referred to contemporary politics and political figures, as in the case of *Roosevelt!* Following a successful first term as president, from 1933 to 1937, Franklin D. Roosevelt lost favor with the public at the beginning of his second term. His proposed reforms to the Supreme Court were perceived as an attempt to rig the judiciary system; this seeming impropriety made the year 1938 the low point of his presidency.[2]

The anti-Roosevelt sentiment provided the context for Pène du Bois's watercolor, as the title indicates. The artist portrays two well-dressed gentlemen engaged in a lively discussion from a perspective likened to that of "an amused spectator of the passing show."[3] The passing show, in this instance, is the conversation between the two men. These patrons lean against the bar in poses that suggest an extended discourse over cocktails and cigarettes. Pène du Bois's style is characterized by somewhat distorted, almost cartoonlike figures. There is an overall washy texture to which sporadic details have been added in black ink. Behind the two men, the bartender appears somewhat indistinct. (Except for a silhouette of the server's head and torso, neither he nor the bottles behind him are easy to discern.) That the working man is barely visible in this composition suggests Pène du Bois's attraction to "the smart foibles of the Gotham world style."[4]

This watercolor may also relate to change in Pène du Bois's financial well-being. In 1924, having sold his home in Westport, Connecticut, he moved to France with his family. When the U.S. stock market crashed in 1929, the economic downturn had far-reaching effects, and Pène du Bois was forced to return home.[5] Upon his return, he, like many artists, anxiously sought patronage and financial stability. He participated in the Works Progress Administration (WPA), under Roosevelt's relief programs collectively known as the New Deal, and completed two commissions for murals in federal buildings, in 1936 and 1937. The $1,200 stipend for these projects was paid in three installments, and for an artist in need of money, this proved frustrating.[6] It is perhaps this frustration with the government that led Pène du Bois to mock the men at the bar, who presumably didn't need its support and, furthermore, were out of touch with those who did.
ECM

1. Hilton Kramer, "A Lover of Beauty, Guy Pène du Bois Painted His Ideal," *New York Observer*, 30 May 2004. Kramer's piece was a review of the exhibition *Guy Pène du Bois: Painter of Modern Life*, at John Graham & Sons Gallery, New York.
2. Franklin D. Roosevelt Presidential Library and Museum, Hyde Park, N.Y., www.fdrlibrary.marist.edu/fdrbio.html.
3. Betsy Fahlman, *Guy Pène du Bois, Painter of Modern Life* (New York: Quantuck Lane Press, 2004), 9.
4. Ibid.
5. John Kraushaar to Guy Pène du Bois, 9 January 1930: "I am very sorry to have to write to you that the first of April [1930] will be the last payment I will be able to make to you, owing to the conditions in business on this side." Reprinted in ibid., 42.
6. Guy Pène du Bois to Edward G. Rowan, superintendent of the Treasury's Section of Painting and Sculpture, 9 March 1938, National Archives and Records Administration (NARA), College Park, Maryland, reprinted in Fahlman, *Guy Pène du Bois*, 54. Pène du Bois wrote, "I haven't been paid yet. Could anything at all be done to hurry the check? I need it terribly."

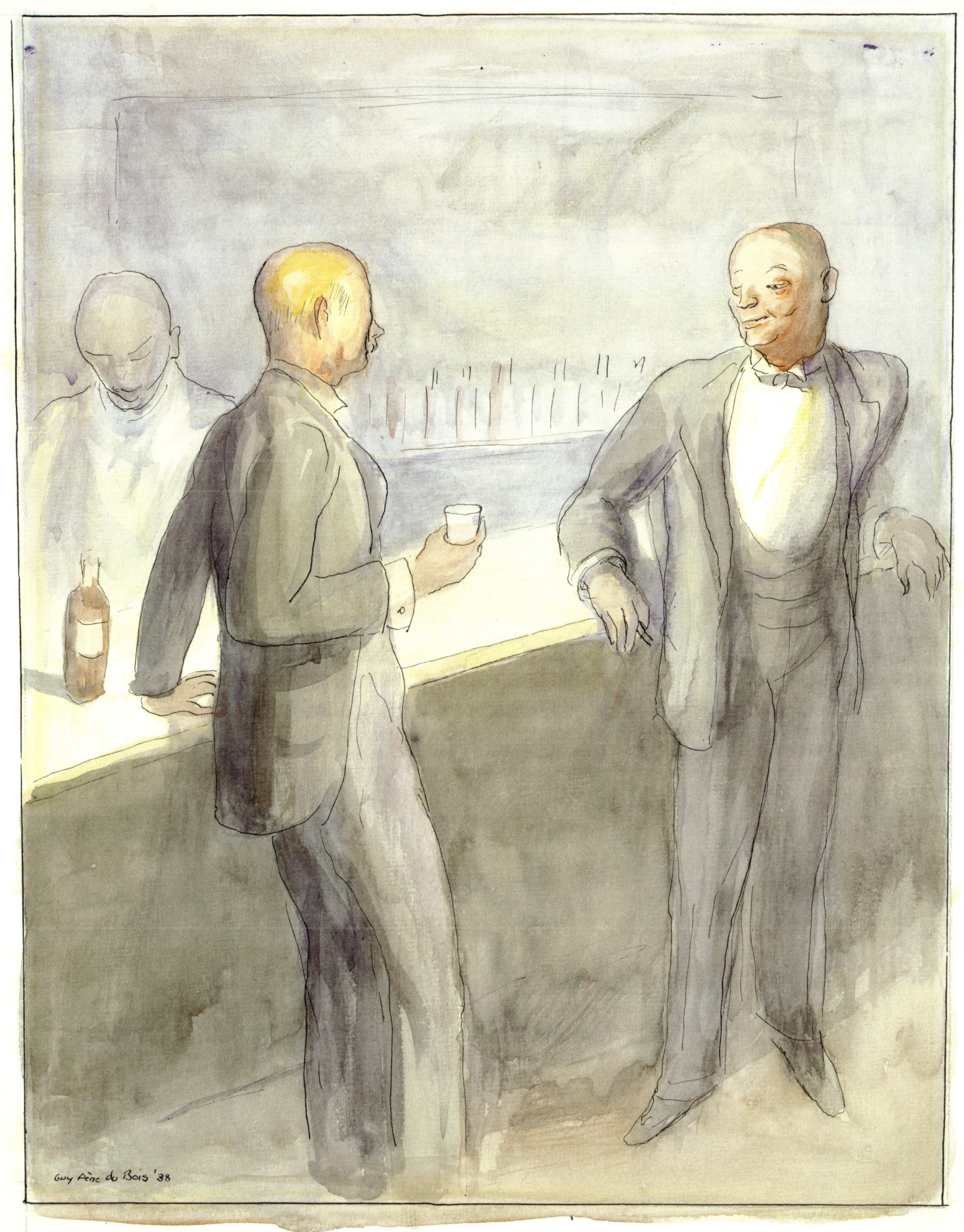

Cat. 46

Reginald Marsh

Born in Paris, 1898;
died in Dorset, Vermont, 1954

Marsh was born to American parents who were living and studying art in Paris. As an undergraduate at Yale University, New Haven, he served as art editor and cartoonist for the *Yale Record*. After graduating in 1920, he moved to New York City, where he studied at the Art Students League under John Sloan (q.v.), George Luks, and Kenneth Hayes Miller. When he finished his studies, he went on to work as an illustrator for the *Daily News* and the *New Yorker*.

Marsh worked in a variety of media, from printmaking to oil painting to drawing with pen and ink, but he excelled in watercolor. In 1929 Thomas Hart Benton (q.v.) introduced him to the medium of egg tempera, and from 1929 to 1940 tempera became his preferred medium for major works. Marsh became successful in the early 1930s: he secured Frank Rehn as his dealer in 1930 and was given solo exhibitions almost every year at the gallery for the rest of the artist's life. His work was distinct from his social realist colleagues in that he rarely focused on the injustices and social evils of American society; rather, he portrayed tawdry urban subjects in New York City, from the seedy burlesque theaters to the crowds at Coney Island.

Marsh's rhythmic compositions, full of movement, were influenced by Renaissance and Baroque masters, especially Peter Paul Rubens. They are nonetheless deeply rooted in the harsh realities of 1930s America. From 1935 until his death, Marsh taught at the Art Students League. He also completed two murals for the United States Treasury Department, in 1935 and 1937. In 1943 Marsh began to explore yet another new medium: Chinese ink drawing. He created hundreds of large-scale Chinese ink drawings before his death in 1954.

Select Bibliography

Lloyd Goodrich. *Reginald Marsh*. New York: Abrams, 1972.

Edward Laning. *The Sketchbooks of Reginald Marsh*. New York: New York Graphic Society, 1973.

Marilyn Cohen. *Reginald Marsh's New York: Paintings, Drawings, Prints and Photographs*. New York: Dover, in association with the Whitney Museum of American Art, 1983.

Avis Berman and William Benton. *Reginald Marsh's New York*. New York: DC Moore Gallery, 1996.

47

Reginald Marsh
New York, 1938
Opaque and transparent watercolor over graphite on wove paper [from watercolor paper block]
13¾ × 20 in. (34.9 × 50.8 cm)
Signed and dated at lower right: Reginald Marsh 1938
Ex coll.: with Frank K. M. Rehn Gallery, New York
The Ella Gallup Sumner and Mary Catlin Sumner Collection Fund, 1939.209

Beginning in the late 1920s, Marsh produced many paintings and prints of the Manhattan skyline. Most of these were done on the spot, showing the city from across the river. Marsh explored the city constantly, and so there are views of the Hudson as well as of the East River; often, as here, a tugboat steaming through the middle distance creates a sense of connection between the viewer and the skyline. Marsh's interest in these watercolors appears to have been more impressionistic than topographical. In *New York*, for example, although the bridge in the middle distance can be identified as the Manhattan Bridge, and the paired skyscrapers are most likely the Chrysler and the Empire State Buildings, their forms are generalized and appear as soft silhouettes.

While the Manhattan Bridge, connecting lower Manhattan and Brooklyn, was not as popular an artistic subject as the Brooklyn Bridge, it did attract the interest of a number of Marsh's contemporaries. In the 1920s Edward Hopper (q.v.) painted watercolors from and of the majestic span and also produced a monumental oil, *Manhattan Bridge Loop* (1928; Addison Gallery of American Art, Andover, Mass.), that depicts the trolley turnaround at the end of the bridge. Berenice Abbott made a number of photographs in 1936 and 1937 that focus on the panoramas visible from the bridge, and on dramatic views of the structure's girders, piers, and walkways. But Marsh was not interested in revealing the modernism inherent in the bridge's architecture, as Abbott was, or its metaphoric embrace of the breadth of the city, which captivated Hopper. Rather, he used it to form a transparent screen that separates Manhattan in the distance from the dock on the near side of the river, where a conversational group forms the chief subject of the picture.

What distinguishes this watercolor from Marsh's other skyline views is the activity in the foreground, as the artist himself commented. "The picture is rare in that figures have been introduced, sketched rapidly from life,"[1] he wrote to Atheneum director Charles C. Cunningham in 1946. In fact, its novelty stems not only from the presence of these figures, but also from their ordinariness—they are not the Bowery bums, floozies, and carnival freaks that comprise Marsh's usual cast of characters, but a group of quietly dressed, unexceptional people: three adults gathered around a baby carriage, and a single woman behind them on the dock.

In another letter to Cunningham, Marsh noted that he made this picture in "an hour or hour & a half."[2] His uncomplicated technique reflects the spontaneity of the sketch. The grainy softness of the pigments indicates that Marsh wet the paper first and put down several layers of pale wash to suggest a hazy sky and, in the foreground, the worn wooden boards of the dock. The figures are drawn with denser strokes of pigment over light pencil outlines, and the color is subdued, almost monochrome. In this, as in most of Marsh's watercolors, the style is essentially graphic, reflecting the artist's background in illustration and his habit of sketching constantly.
CT

1. Reginald Marsh to Charles C. Cunningham, New York, 1 October 1946, curatorial files, Wadsworth Atheneum.
2. Marsh to Cunningham, New York, 22 April 1951, curatorial files, Wadsworth Atheneum.

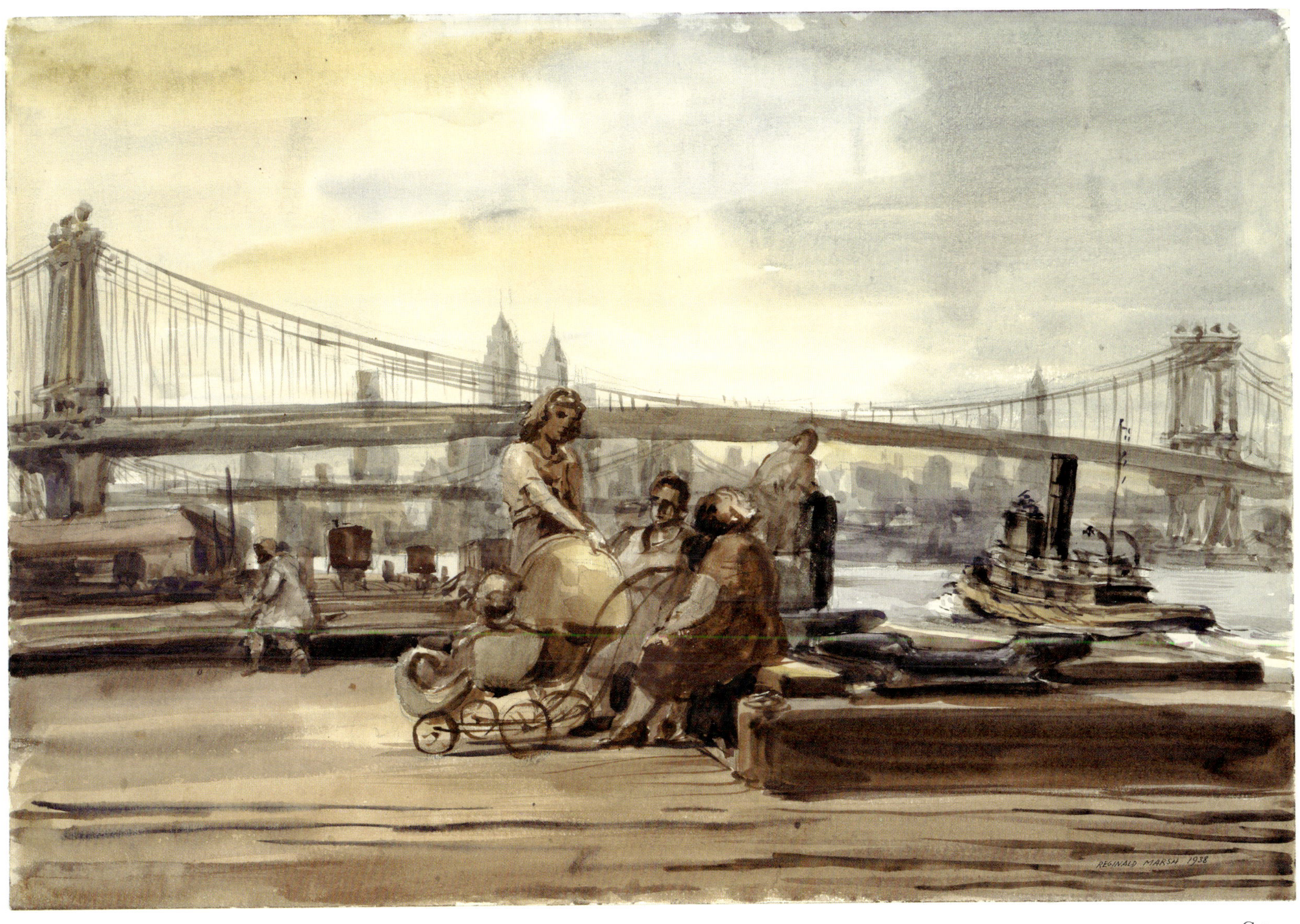

Cat. 47

48

Reginald Marsh
Woman Walking (formerly *Walking Girl*), 1945
Opaque and transparent watercolor over traces of black chalk on wove paper [from watercolor paper block]
19 1/2 × 13 1/4 in. (49.5 × 33.7 cm)
Signed and dated at lower right: REGINALD MARSH / 1945
Inscription on purse: FM
Ex coll.: the artist; William Benton, Southport, Connecticut, to 1961
Gift of Mr. and Mrs. William Benton, 1961.158

Marsh drew and painted "walking women" many times during his career. In addition to striding through some of New York's seamier neighborhoods (*Eyes Tested*, 1944; private collection) or toward the ticket window of a movie theater (*Twenty Cent Movie*, 1939; Whitney Museum of American Art, New York), they also appear in simpler compositions, in which the focus is on them alone. Sometimes Marsh locates these women on the El, sometimes on Fourteenth Street, and sometimes before an unidentified New York building, as here. They are young, attractive, and confident.

Marsh has been described as "an urban diarist, but [also] a documenter of his own personal fantasy."[1] His women tend to be quite voluptuous, and in these compositions Marsh frequently emphasizes their brazen sexuality by including a man, often down-and-out, who watches the women from the background but makes no attempt to interact (fig. 1).[2] While his images of self-assured women may have alluded to a social reality in Depression-era and wartime America—the insecurity of men in straitened economic times and in the face of increasing numbers of women in the workforce—they were also reflections of Marsh's own desires. As his friend Edward Laning noted, "Marsh's omnipresent girl strides through his work . . . , *dea ex machina* in a world of men without women. She is not real, but merely a projection of Marsh's fantasy. If Marsh is Ishmael, she is the Great White Whale."[3]

In contrast to the many highly sexualized versions of the walking woman, the Atheneum's watercolor is surprisingly subdued. This woman is pretty, rather than provocative, and Marsh's handling emphasizes her refinement. Rather than using the exaggerated contours and bold tones of his other images, here he has rendered the figure with graceful lines and soft washes, restricting his palette to warm grays with touches of yellow and salmon pink. His interpretation of the figure is more sympathetic, as well: though her dress clings to her body, her curves are not pneumatic. Her features are attractive, not hardened or masked by excessive makeup. The dejected male whose presence suggests frustrated desire in many of Marsh's walking women images is replaced here by a young woman—another shopper, perhaps—who is quietly dressed. The unusually restrained tone of this watercolor may have roots in Marsh's biography, as is signaled by the initials "FM" on the woman's handbag. In 1934 Marsh married the artist Felicia Meyer, and began making portraits of her. Although the woman in this watercolor bears only a general resemblance to Felicia Meyer Marsh, the monogram on the handbag suggests that Marsh may have made this watercolor in tribute to his wife.
CT

1. Avis Berman, "Reginald Marsh: Eros and the City," in *Reginald Marsh's New York*, by Berman and William Benton (New York: DC Moore Gallery, 1996), 1.
2. Among the many examples are *Girl on 14th Street*, transparent and opaque watercolor over graphite (1939; Brooklyn Museum), *Seated Man and Walking Woman*, watercolor and Chinese ink on paper (1943; Whitney Museum of American Art), and, perhaps the most salacious of these images, the engraving *Girl Walking–Pillar–Soldier* (1942).
3. Edward Laning, introduction to *The Sketchbooks of Reginald Marsh* (New York: New York Graphic Society, 1973), 28.

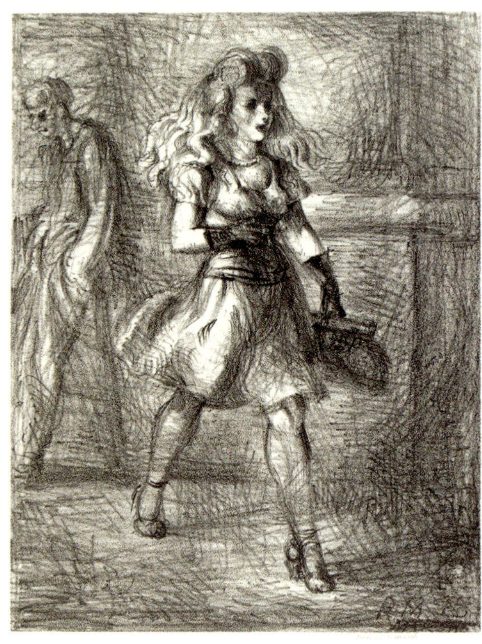

Fig. 1. Reginald Marsh, *Girl Walking*, 1945. Lithograph on paper, 10 3/4 × 8 in. (27.3 × 20.3 cm). Smithsonian American Art Museum. Museum Purchase, 1966.64.32

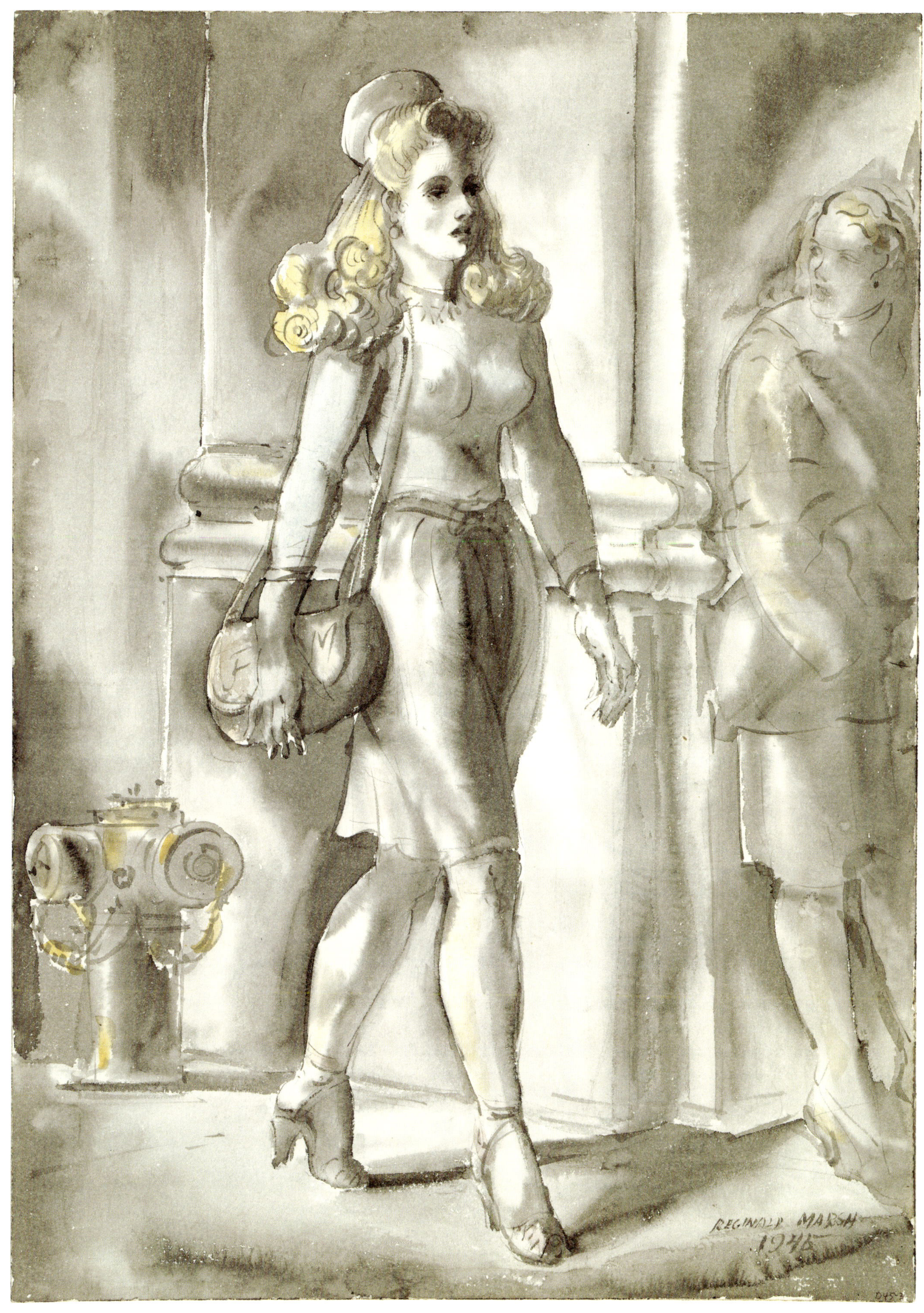

Cat. 48

Thomas Hart Benton

Born in Neosho, Missouri, 1889;
died in Kansas City, Missouri, 1975

Thomas Hart Benton attended the Art Institute of Chicago (1906–7) before making the traditional art pilgrimage to Paris, where he lived between 1908 and 1911 and studied briefly at the Académie Julian. There he spent time in cafés and at the studios of important personalities such as Leo Stein, brother of the famous Gertrude, John Marin (q.v.), Diego Rivera, and Stanton MacDonald-Wright. He experimented with various modernist styles, including Impressionism, Postimpressionism, Cubism, and Synchromism.

Benton returned to the United States in 1912 and moved to New York, setting up a studio in nearby Fort Lee, New Jersey, home to a burgeoning movie industry. There he met emerging American artists such as "Pop" Hart (q.v.) and Arthur B. Davies. Around 1916, Benton's early interest in abstraction began to wane, and he began painting American subjects. He eventually became known, along with John Steuart Curry and Grant Wood, as one of the foremost Regionalist or American Scene painters. Throughout his career, murals were the major vehicle for this effort.

As one of the central figures of the Regionalist art movement, Benton traveled widely throughout the United States, gathering material for his murals and other paintings. In the 1930s he completed numerous mural commissions for American colleges, government buildings, and libraries. His famous series The Arts of Life in America (1932), originally made for the library of the Whitney Museum of American Art, was relocated to the New Britain Museum of American Art, Connecticut, in 1953.

Benton was a prolific teacher, and among his most famous students from his time at the Art Students League (1926 to 1935) was Jackson Pollock. He moved to Kansas City permanently in 1935 and began teaching at the Kansas City Art Institute and School of Design, where he remained until 1940. Throughout the 1940s and '50s, Benton completed nearly a dozen mural commissions in between several trips abroad to France, Italy, and Spain. Important exhibitions of his work were organized by the New Britain Museum of American Art (1954), and the Rutgers University Art Gallery, New Brunswick, New Jersey (1972).

Select Bibliography

Thomas Hart Benton. *An Artist in America.* New York: Robert M. McBride, 1937.

Matthew Baigell. *Thomas Hart Benton.* New York: Harry N. Abrams, 1973.

Henry Adams. *Thomas Hart Benton: An American Original.* New York: Alfred A Knopf, 1989.

49

Thomas Hart Benton
Oil Barge (formerly *Loading Racks on the Mississippi*), c. 1943–44
Pen and black ink and sepia ink heightened with opaque white watercolor on wove paper
13 3/4 × 16 1/2 in. (34.9 × 41.9 cm)
Inscription at lower right: Oil Barge / Benton
Ex coll.: The Standard Oil Company, New Jersey, 1949 to 1951
Gift of Esso Standard Oil Company, The Standard Oil Company Collection, 1951.231

Thomas Hart Benton's art was rooted in the fabric of American life, particularly its rural and agricultural scenery. In the 1940s he sketched the construction of a troop ship in Pittsburgh, which he then followed down the Mississippi River to New Orleans. This was the first of several river trips that Benton took—he was fascinated with the river as a hotbed of activity and a test of his powers of observation. As he recalled, "While the banks of the lower river as seen from a boat deck are interminably monotonous, the river itself is not so, at least for those who can read its face."[1] Benton, like other American artists, began to document the mobilization of the oil industry for war.[2] While in Louisiana, he made a number of sketches of oil rigs and refineries, as seen here, that resulted in his painting of a Baton Rouge oil refinery, *Fluid Catalytic Crackers* (1945; Massachusetts Institute of Technology, List Visual Arts Center, Cambridge).[3]

This drawing records two significant components of oil production: the Esso Standard Oil Company's Baton Rouge refinery, in the far distance, and the *Sprague*, the famous sternwheeler towboat, seen here moving up the river.[4] These towboats were used for pushing barges carrying oil up and down inland rivers. Benton outlines each structure using a fine ink line. The absence of color is remedied by meticulous drawing with touches of sepia wash and crosshatched lines for shading. In the foreground, our attention is directed to the oil barge and the pilothouse of another sternwheeler (cropped on the right by the edge of the sheet). The barge, at least momentarily, is docked and inactive. In a style more typical of his completed paintings and narrative murals, Benton uses a horizontal format to enhance the rhythmic interplay of shapes. The pipes and tubes running the length of the barge at the center are echoed in the tall vertical piles on the right. Similarly, the triangular cargo boom at the edge of the barge is repeated in the steps on the right near the pilothouse, where a deckhand stands idle. The perspective suggests that Benton completed the drawing while standing on a bank, where he was known to have waited for days to observe a riverbank loading in process.[5]
ECM

1. Thomas Hart Benton, *An Artist in America* (New York: Robert M. McBride, 1937), 131. Benton devoted an entire chapter to rivers; see chapter 5, "The Rivers."
2. The Standard Oil Company of New Jersey sponsored artists in the 1940s to document their oil refineries. This drawing clearly relates to this series, but it is uncertain if it was a commissioned work. Many of these sketches were in preparation for the painting *Fluid Catalytic Crackers* (1945; oil over egg tempera on Masonite, 48 × 58 in. [121.9 × 147.3 cm]; Gift of The Standard Oil Company of New Jersey, MIT, List Visual Arts Center). See http://listart.mit.edu:8080/Obj2$15 (accessed 18 February 2009).
3. Henry Adams, *Thomas Hart Benton: An American Original* (New York: Alfred A. Knopf, 1989), 316.
4. Curatorial files, Wadsworth Atheneum. According to the National Mississippi River Museum and Aquarium, Port of Dubuque, Iowa, the *Sprague* was the largest steam towboat ever, and its maker, Peter Sprague (1828–1900), is in their National Rivers Hall of Fame.
5. Benton, *An Artist in America*, 137. Benton describes a similar journey to Red River, Louisiana, when he camped for an entire week waiting for a boat to sketch.

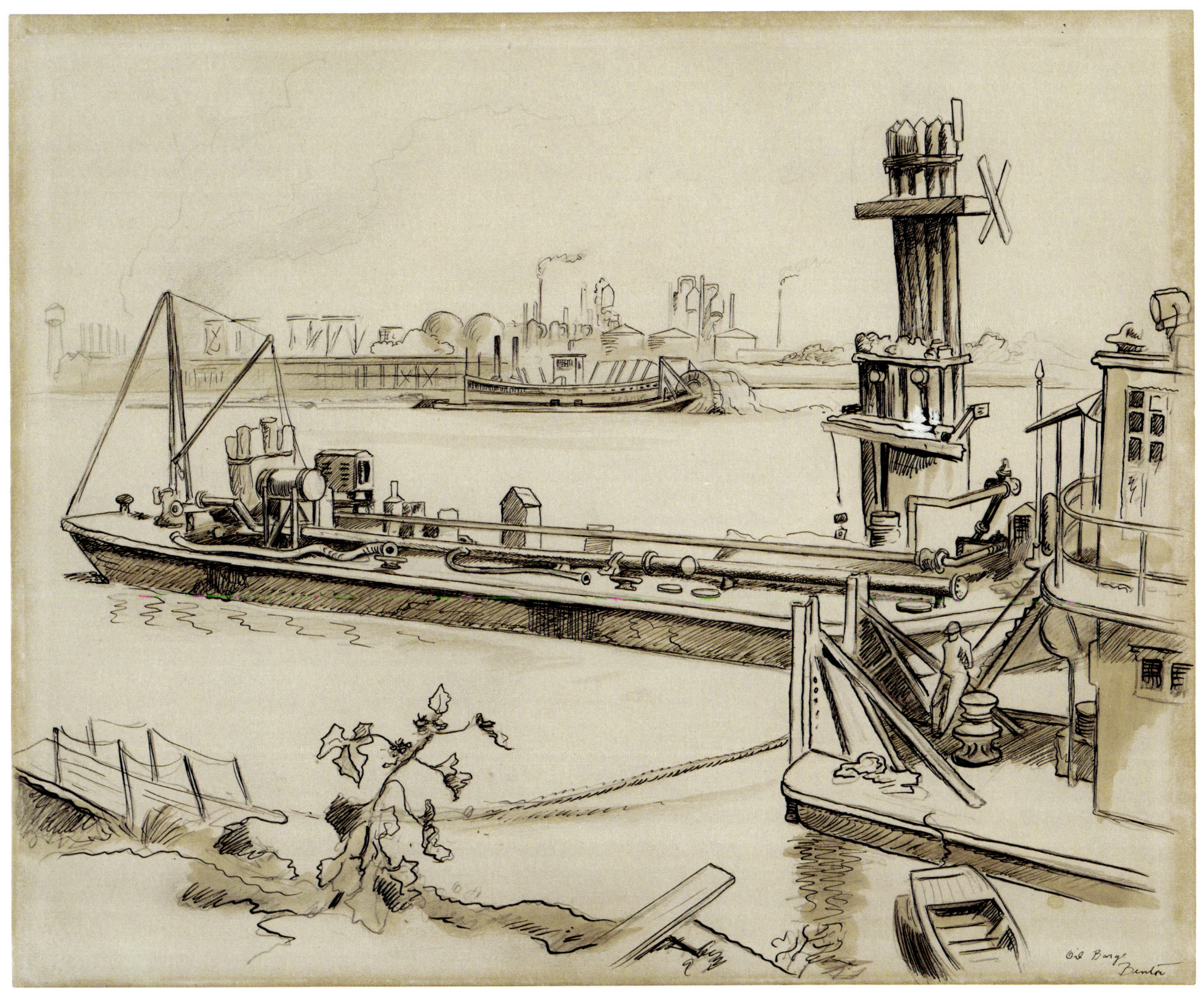

Cat. 49

George Grosz

Born in Berlin, 1893;
died in Berlin, 1959

Grosz was a German painter, draftsman, and illustrator particularly recognized for his caustic caricatures of the ruling classes in Germany. Born Georg Ehenfried Groß, in 1916 he anglicized his name to George Grosz (the double-s or ß sign in German is technically "sz"). He graduated from the Royal Saxon Academy of Fine Arts, Dresden, in 1911 and continued his studies briefly at the Berlin Arts and Crafts School. He served as a combat soldier in World War I and was discharged in 1917. The horrors of the war inspired in him an antiwar political stance; his earliest images depicted victims of war, and criticized those who benefited from it.

Grosz chronicled the Weimar Republic, which came into power in 1919, with great insight and savagery, condemning bourgeois corruption and denouncing Nazi leaders. Eventually, the political climate made it dangerous for Grosz to remain in Germany, and he moved to New York City in 1933, just days before Hitler came into power. He taught at the Art Students League from 1933 to 1936, and intermittently from 1940 to 1950. He was also active in Provincetown, Massachusetts, from 1937 to 1945. In 1954, he had a retrospective exhibition at the Whitney Museum of American Art. After several visits to Germany, he returned in May 1959 to West Berlin, where he died two months later.

Grosz's presence in the New York art scene had an impact on American social realists, and even on a later generation of Pop artists such as James Rosenquist.

Select Bibliography

John I. H. Baur. *George Grosz*. New York: Macmillan, 1954.

The Autobiography of George Grosz: A Small Yes and a Big No. Translated by Arnold J. Pomerans. 1955; reprint, New York: Allison & Busby, 1982.

Uwe M. Schneede. *George Grosz: His Life and Work*. Translated by Susanne Flatauer. New York: Universe Books, 1979.

M. Kay Flavell. *George Grosz: A Biography*. New Haven, Conn.: Yale University Press, 1988.

50

George Grosz
The Fire, 1933
Opaque and transparent watercolor on wove paper (watermark: PM Fabriano)
17 3/4 × 22 in. (45.1 × 55.9 cm)
Signed and dated at lower right:
Grosz 5 33 NY
Ex coll.: with C. Philip Boyer, Washington, D.C., as of 1948
The Ella Gallup Sumner and Mary Catlin Sumner Collection Fund, 1948.481

George Grosz immigrated from Berlin to New York in 1933, just as Adolf Hitler became chancellor of Germany. Up to that moment, Grosz's art had been politically motivated, and his reputation was based on biting satirical drawings and illustrations that indicted the German bourgeoisie. His arrival in New York thus marked a major shift in the tone and images he considered personally relevant.[1] As a teacher at the Art Students League, he had little time for his own art and as a result turned to drawing and watercolor, which were portable and less laborious than oil painting. Coinciding with Grosz's technical transition was a personal struggle to reconcile his strong German heritage with a desire to assimilate to American life and culture. As he explained, "The second phase of my life began in America, but with it came an inner conflict over the break with my past."[2]

This struggle was revealed in his watercolors from the early 1930s, which often depicted dueling or disconnected worlds. As John I. H. Baur observed, Grosz frequently synthesized the city rather than recorded it and many of his compositions were composite images.[3] For example, *The Fire* depicts two parallel but disjointed worlds. The house fire on the left is juxtaposed with a ghostlike forest on the right. Each area is distinguished by expressive colors—rich browns and bright reds on the left; cool blues on the right—that symbolize, respectively, life and death. The morbid overtones are suggested by the Grim Reaper–like skeleton emerging from the forest, ready to claim the life of the woman screaming from the inferno. From the top window a crucifix-like shape emerges from the fire that perhaps signifies the sacrifice of human life. The ominous mood is enhanced by Grosz's use of transparent washes and the wet-blended technique, in which colors have soft, fuzzy edges.[4] In *The Fire*, the billowing smoke and ethereal clouds are accentuated by the vague, misty qualities of this style.

The Fire illustrates themes of death and destruction. Other watercolors dating to his first years in New York, such as *This Burning World* (1933; Cleveland Museum of Art) and *Punishment* (1934; Museum of Modern Art, New York), contain similar apocalyptic images of physical destruction, particularly by fire. Though Grosz was settled safely in America by this time, these images suggest he was still processing the horrors of World War I, which he had witnessed firsthand. As Grosz explained, "The new visions and dreams [in America] were no longer distortions or caricatures. They were not created or designed to improve or educate man. They were now composed of apocalyptic fire and intimated the duality of the world."[5]
ECM

1. John I. H. Baur, *George Grosz* (New York: Macmillan, 1954), 24. Baur explains, "From the moment he stepped foot in the city, he began to draw, avidly collecting faces, bits of architecture, ash cans, street signs, and every sort of humanity from dowagers to burlesque queens."
2. *The Autobiography of George Grosz: A Small Yes and a Big No*, trans. Arnold J. Pomerans (1955; repr., New York: Allison & Busby, 1982), 276.
3. Baur, *George Grosz*, 27.
4. Eliot O'Hara, *Watercolor at Large* (New York: Minton, Balch, 1946), 64. O'Hara cites Grosz specifically as having excelled in the wet-blended technique.
5. *Autobiography of George Grosz*, 276.

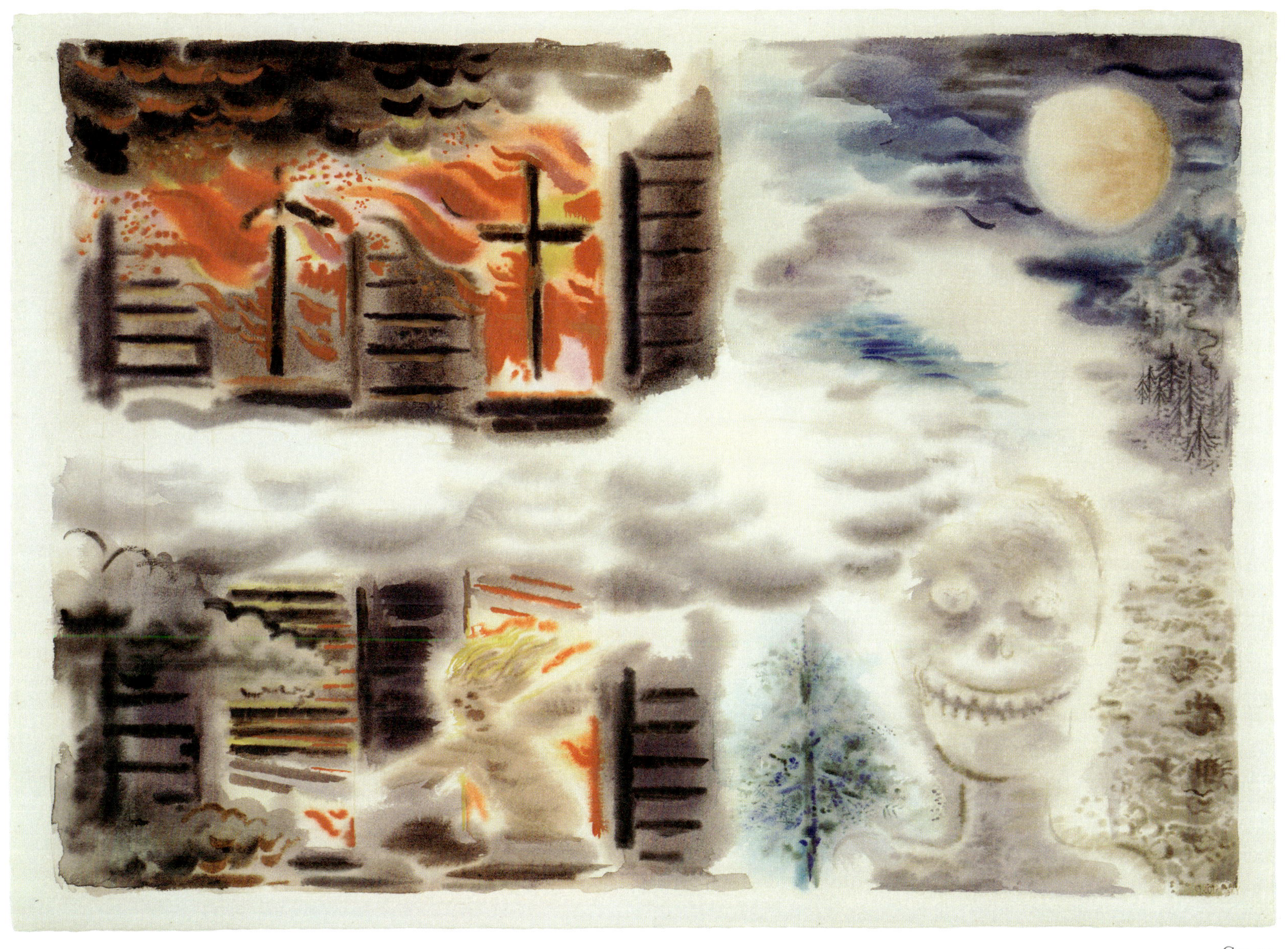

Cat. 50

Peggy Bacon

Born in Ridgefield, Connecticut, 1895;
died in Kennebunk, Maine, 1987

Peggy Bacon was a satirist, author, and illustrator who integrated marriage, family, and a career at a time when few women did. Born to artistic parents—her father, Charles Roswell Bacon, studied at the Art Students League under Robert Henri and her mother, Elizabeth Chase, was a talented miniature painter—Bacon's talents emerged at an early age. After high school, she enrolled in the Art Students League in New York City, where she studied under John Sloan (q.v.), Kenneth Hayes Miller, and George Bellows. At the Art Students League, Bacon soon discovered her affinity for printmaking, specifically drypoint and lithography.

Bacon summered in the artist colonies of Woodstock, New York, and Provincetown, Massachusetts, respectively. In Woodstock she met the American painter Alexander Brook, whom she married in 1920. Brook worked with Juliana Force at the Whitney Studio Club (later the Whitney Museum of American Art) and introduced Bacon to the New York gallery scene. The dealers and collectors she encountered at social gatherings included notable figures such as Georgia O'Keeffe (q.v.), Alfred Stieglitz, and Edith Gregor Halpert, owner of the Downtown Gallery. These gatherings and contacts provided source material for Bacon's printed caricatures of the 1920s and '30s. One critic commented on the occasion of her solo show at the Downtown Gallery, in 1931, "No one has brought a greater wit and penetration to caricature than she." Two years later, Bacon received a Guggenheim Fellowship and published a portfolio of caricatures of art world figures called *Off with Their Heads.*

After 1940, the year of her divorce from Brook, Bacon began summering in Martha's Vineyard and Ogunquit, Maine. In the 1950s she took up painting and began producing scenes of small-town life that, while quiet in mood, often contained subtle oddities and witty detail. Bacon eventually moved to Maine permanently and remained a prolific illustrator and author until the 1970s, when failing eyesight prohibited her from continuing working.

Select Bibliography

Peggy Bacon Papers, 1893–1973. Archives of American Art, Smithsonian Institution, Washington, D.C.

Paul Rosenfeld. "Art: Caricature and Peggy Bacon." *Nation* 132 (3 June 1931): 617.

Peggy Bacon. *Off with Their Heads.* New York: Robert M. McBride, 1934.

Peggy Bacon: Personalities and Places. Washington, D.C.: Smithsonian Institution Press, 1975.

Roberta K. Tarbell. "Peggy Bacon's Pastel and Charcoal Caricature Portraits." *Women's Art Journal* 9, no. 2 (Autumn 1988–Winter 1989): 32–37.

51

Peggy Bacon
Afternoon Off, or The House of the Dead Witch, 1953
Opaque and transparent watercolor with pen and black ink on wove paper
17 7/8 × 12 in. (45.4 × 30.5 cm)
Inscription at lower left:
Afternoon Off, or The House of the Dead Witch / Peggy Bacon 1953
Ex coll.: with Kraushaar Galleries, New York; Henry E. Schnakenberg, Newtown, Connecticut
Gift of Henry E. Schnakenberg, 1954.117

Following a successful period as a printmaker, Peggy Bacon returned to painting and drawing in the 1950s. This technical change was accompanied by a shift from the satirical tone of her illustrations and portraits toward a more narrative content. This change is clearly illustrated by two of Bacon's drawings, separated by twenty years, in the Atheneum's collection.[1] The first example, *Heywood Broun at the Typewriter,* exemplifies Bacon's prowess as a caricaturist (fig. 1). The portrait, drawn from life, shows the liberal columnist at his desk, in a chaotic mess of letters and litter.[2] The loose lines accentuate the anxiety of the writer at work, who, as Bacon put it, wears the "must-get-the-article-in look."[3]

In contrast, her later work demonstrates her renewed interest in the medium of watercolor and the narrative subject. In *Afternoon Off, or The House of the Dead Witch,* the satire is not as intense; rather, strains of lyricism and fantasy are more prominent.[4] Bacon sets this scene in an enchanted, dreamlike setting using a mixture of memory and imagination to enhance the tale. As the artist explained, the idea was inspired by a small cottage in Oak Bluffs, Martha's Vineyard, where she had vacationed numerous times: "It is the cook's and housemaid's day off, they have gone into the forest to pick mushrooms, have come

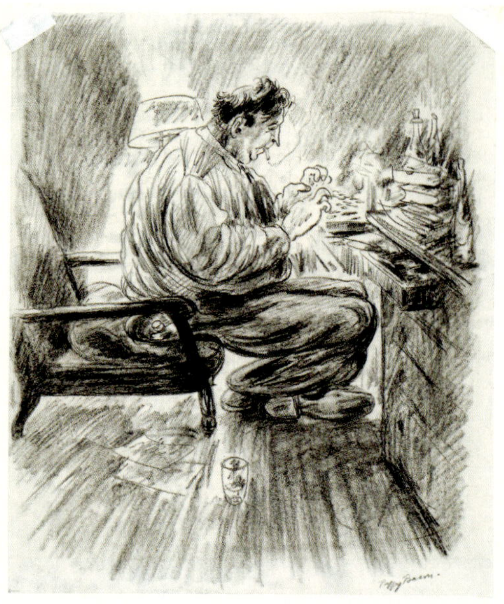

Fig. 1. Peggy Bacon, *Heywood Broun at the Typewriter,* 1953. Charcoal on paper, 16 3/4 × 13 3/4 in. (42.6 × 34.9 cm). Wadsworth Atheneum Museum of Art. Gift of Henry E. Schnakenberg, 1954.115

by accident upon the haunted hut, and being superstitious and nervous, are suddenly startled and alarmed by the woodpecker up in the pine tree."[5] Set in a densely wooded area, the two women appear anxious, their eyes alert and poses hesitant. Behind them is a tiny, uninhabited house with a mossy roof and darkened windows. Discarded objects in the yard indicate a dormant, neglected existence. In the foreground is a lively array of plant life and wildflowers primarily native to woodland settings. The large foxglove prominently placed in the center, however, is unusual, as this variety was not native to the environment.[6] The flower is medicinally and highly toxic; its inclusion suggests a symbolic warning to the wandering women.

In this work, Bacon combined her printmaker's eye for detail with her experience as an illustrator. She used a large-scale composition and filled it with rich detail and color. While the figures are drawn using loose, gestural lines, recalling the expressiveness of her caricatures, the details of the foliage and scenery are meticulous. The texture of the bark and the weathered shingles, for example, is carefully articulated with black ink. Similarly, detailed areas of bright orange and light purple emerge from within the woodland setting. (Only the careful observer will locate the woodpecker in one of the trees.) Though the techniques used here recall Bacon's earlier genres, this pictorial demonstrates the intertwinement of fantasy and reality in her later work.[7]

ECM

1. The Atheneum also owns a related pen and ink drawing of Heywood Broun, c. 1934 ($11^{1}/_{4} \times 9^{3}/_{8}$ in.; Gift of Henry E. Schnakenberg, 1954.116).
2. Peggy Bacon to Charles C. Cunningham, 3 January 1955, Wadsworth Atheneum Archives. The finished version of this drawing was published in Bacon's books of caricatures, *Off with Their Heads* (New York: Robert M. McBride, 1934).
3. In Bacon, *Off with Their Heads*; cited in "The Radical Impulse" in *Life of the People: Realist Prints and Drawings from the Ben and Beatrice Goldstein Collection, 1912–1948*, ed. Harry L. Katz (Washington, D.C.: Library of Congress, 2000), http://www.loc.gov/exhibits/goldstein/goldrad.html (accessed February 18, 2009).
4. *Peggy Bacon: Personalities and Places* (Washington, D.C.: Smithsonian Institution Press, 1975), 50. Bacon's fondness for storytelling, as made apparent in this work, also extended into her literary projects. The same year she completed this watercolor, her mystery novel *The Inward Eye* won the Edgar Allan Poe Mystery Award.
5. Bacon to Cunningham, 3 January 1955, Wadsworth Atheneum Archives.
6. My thanks to Anne Mankin Masury, horticulturist, for identifying the flowers (from left to right): yellow lady's slipper, white trillium, Dutchman's-breeches, jack-in-the-pulpit, and Indian pipe.
7. *Peggy Bacon*, 54.

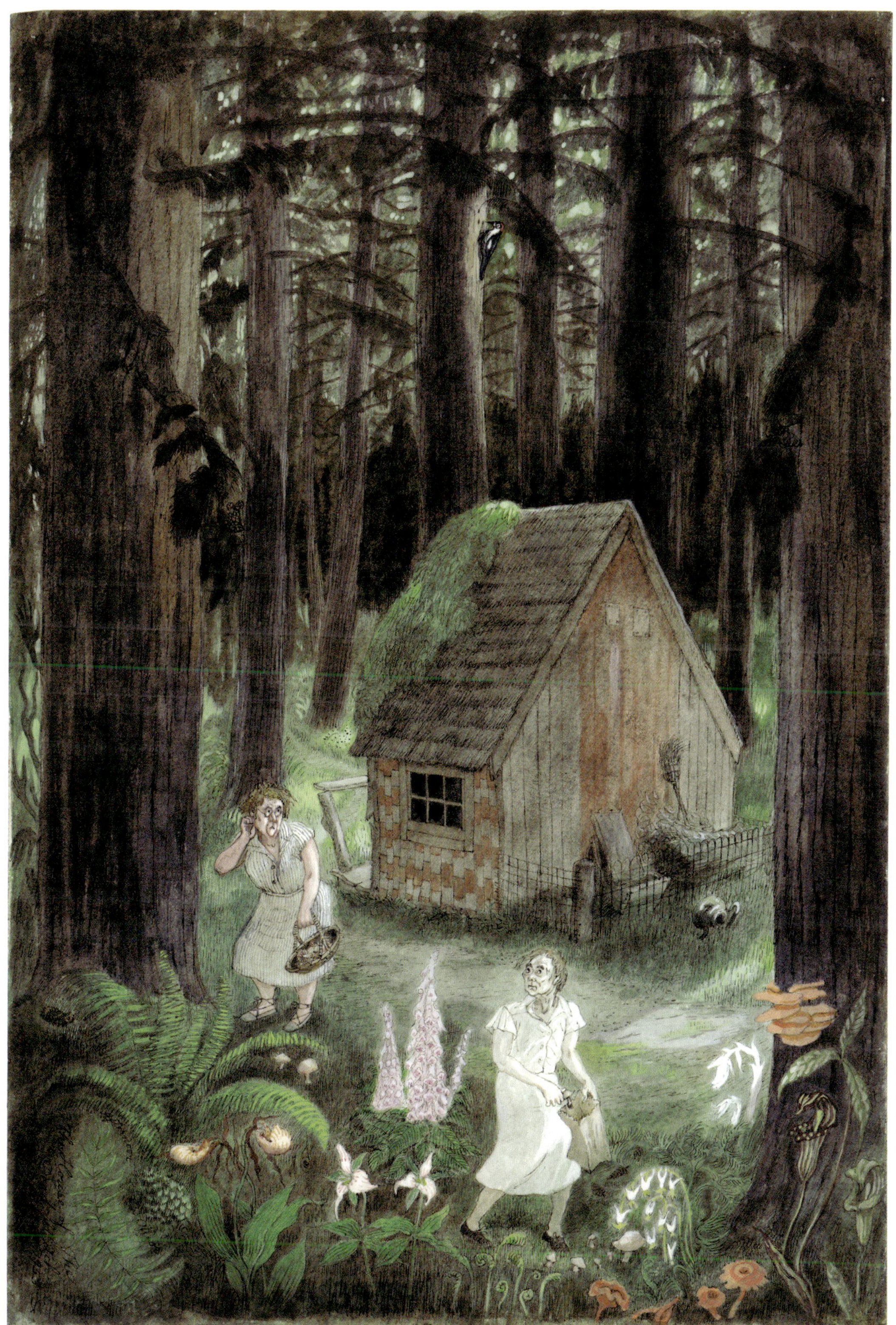

Cat. 51

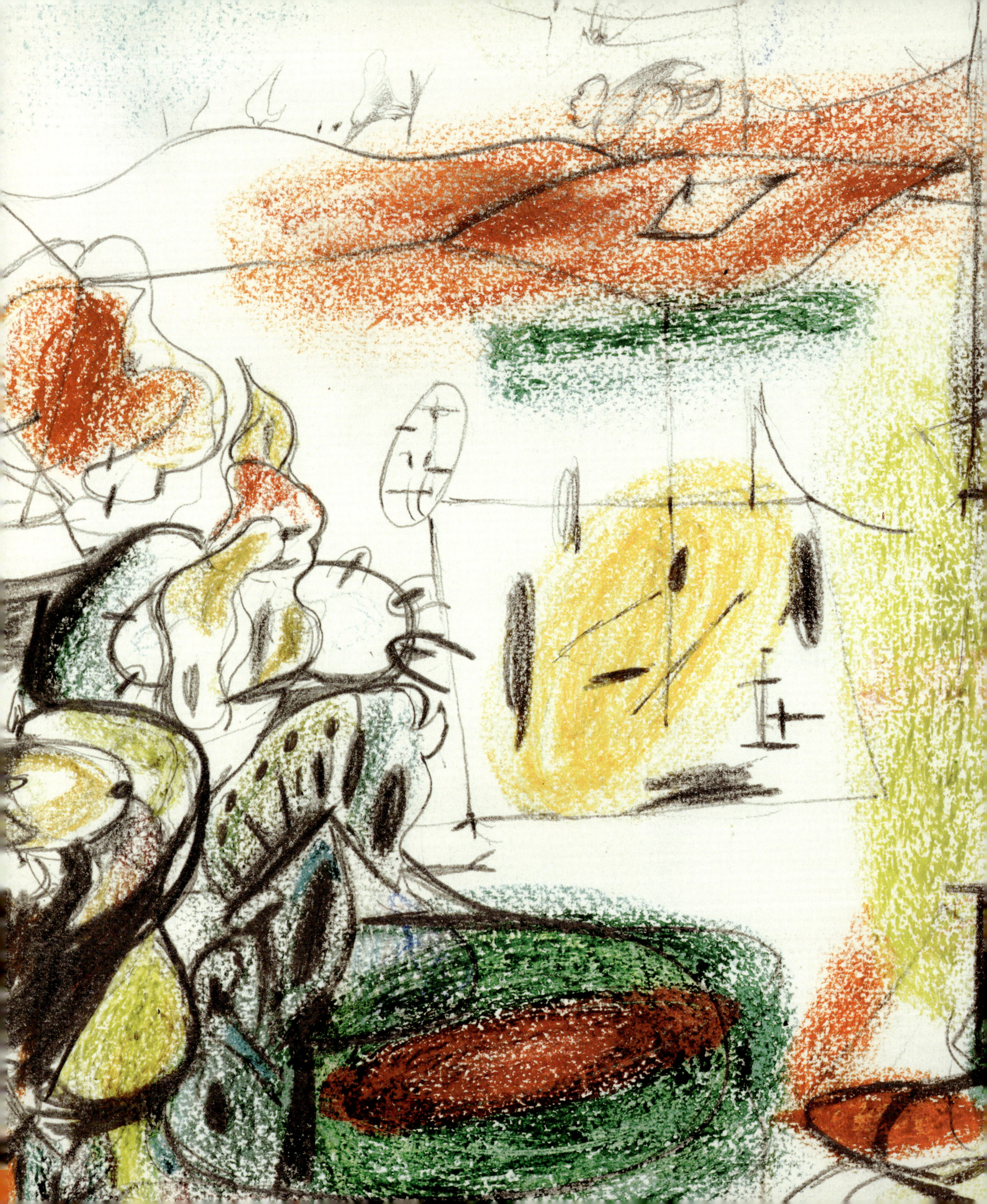

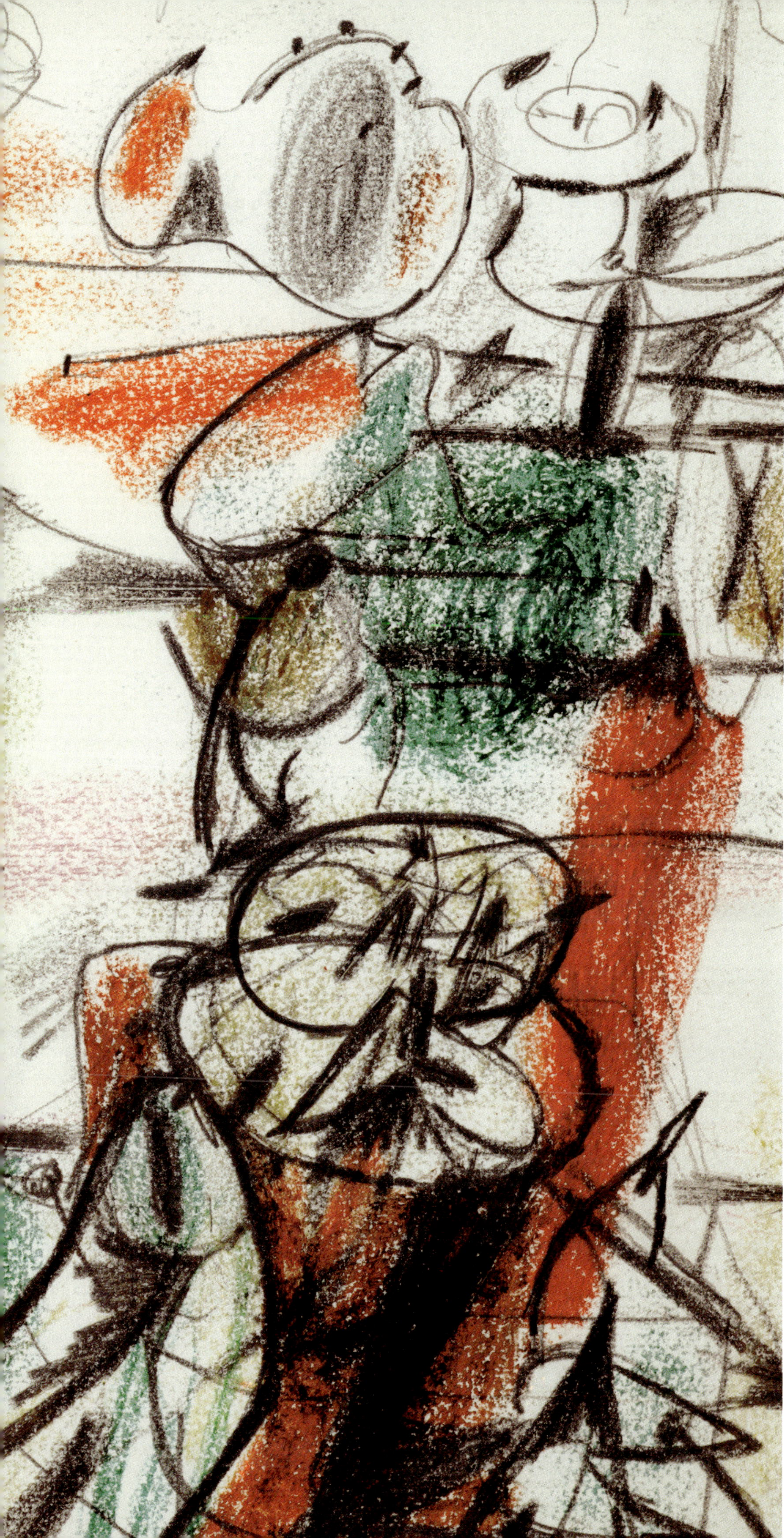

3.
Surrealism and Neo-Romanticism

Pavel Tchelitchew

Born in Moscow, 1898; died in Rome, 1957

Pavel Tchelitchew was born into an aristocratic family and was educated by private tutors. Following the Bolshevik Revolution of 1918, the family was forced to flee Moscow and relocated to Kiev. In Kiev, Tchelitchew attended drawing classes at the academy and was encouraged by Alexandra Exter, who was an accomplished Constructionist stage designer, and by the Cubist painter and set designer Isaac Rabinovitch.

In 1926 Tchelitchew was included in a significant exhibition at the Galerie Druet, in Paris, with the Dutch artist Kristians Tonny (q.v.) and others. Although they did not consider themselves a group or movement and painted very differently from one another, these artists were allied in their reaction against the dominant trends in painting and inserted a nostalgic, human sentiment into their art. In 1931 the group was presented as the "Neo-Romantics" in a show at the Wadsworth Atheneum Museum of Art. During this period, Tchelitchew explored a range of subjects using metamorphic or anthropomorphic imagery that was inspired by Surrealism. He had a number of solo shows in Paris and London. Tchelitchew moved to New York in 1934 and was given his first solo show in America at the Julien Levy Gallery in the same year.

Tchelitchew was a prolific set and costume designer for the ballet and theater. He was well acquainted with the Russian choreographer George Balanchine and Ballets Russes founder Sergey Diaghilev. This circle of friends also included the renowned Wadsworth Atheneum director Everett A. "Chick" Austin. At least in part through his friendship with Austin, Tchelitchew was commissioned to design the invitation, costumes, and decorations for the Paper Ball, part of the Hartford Festival, a celebration of the performing arts held at the Wadsworth Atheneum in 1936.

From 1933 to 1940, Tchelitchew established a studio in Weston, Connecticut, and during the following two years he painted in Vermont, where he was inspired by the New England landscape. During this period he renewed his interest in metamorphosis and anthropomorphic landscapes. In 1939 he began his large canvas *Hide-and-Seek* (Museum of Modern Art, New York), perhaps his best known work. He traveled to Europe in 1949, spending most of his time in Italy. He intended to return to the United States, but bad health kept him in Italy until his death.

Select Bibliography

James Thrall Soby. *Tchelitchew: Paintings, Drawings.* New York: Museum of Modern Art, 1942.

Lincoln Kirstein. *Pavel Tchelitchew.* New York: Gallery of Modern Art, 1964.

Parker Tyler. *The Divine Comedy of Pavel Tchelitchew.* New York: Fleet, 1967.

Lincoln Kirstein. *Tchelitchev.* Santa Fe, N.Mex.: Twelvetrees Press, 1994.

52 a and b

Pavel Tchelitchew
Design for the Paper Ball Invitation, Hartford Festival, 1936
Pen and ink and graphite on paper
10 1/2 × 7 1/4 in. (26.7 × 18.4 cm)
Signed and dated lower left:
P. Tchelitchew/N.Y 36
Ex coll.: the artist
The Ella Gallup Sumner and Mary Catlin Sumner Collection Fund, 1936.20

Sketch for the Paper Ball, 1936
Black and brown ink applied using pen and brush and opaque and transparent watercolor on paperboard
10 × 7 in. (25.4 × 17.8 cm)
Signed and dated lower right:
P. Tchelitchew/N.Y 1936
Ex coll.: the artist; George Platt Lynes, New York, to 1955; Mr. and Mrs. Russell Lynes, New York
Gift of Mr. and Mrs. Russell Lynes, 1989.67

The Paper Ball took place in the Avery Court of the Wadsworth Atheneum on February 15, 1936. The court was decorated by Tchelitchew, who sought to create a dazzling "Ragpicker's Ball" (or, as he called it, a "Cirque de Chiffoniers"), with all costumes and settings made of worthless materials.[1] Hartford's fete had its historic origins in actual balls held in the nineteenth century in disreputable neighborhoods of Paris for rag pickers, street sweepers, slaughterhouse workers, and other members of the underclass; it was modeled after the shabby-chic imitations of those balls staged by the French aristocracy.[2]

The ball's *style pauvre* theme was introduced in the sketches Tchelitchew made for the invitation to the party. The sketches show a group of charming ragamuffins in heroic, if tattered, attire putting up a poster announcing the festivities to come. In one drawing, which was not used, the poster is enigmatically inscribed "Calendar." In the other, which became the invitation, the "Paper Ball" is advertised beneath a stylized musical score. The children's poses are theatrical, with a cartoonish, mock-classical flavor (in "Calendar," the figure with a sheathed sword caricatures the declamatory stance of the *Apollo Belvedere*). Their clothes, even in these pen-and-ink sketches, seem to be made of stiff paper, cardboard, and rags.

The idea of a costume party was clearly appealing. The Paper Ball was attended by hundreds of luminaries from New York and Hartford, the last of whom staggered out of Avery Court at 6:30 a.m.[3] And although the event lost money and the behavior of some guests irritated the museum's staid trustees, it became a landmark in the institution's history. On October 22, 1966, the Atheneum reprised the ball. Avery Court was decorated by James Rosenquist, and paper costumes were created by Rudi Gernreich, Bill Blass, and other celebrated designers of the era.[4]
CT

1. "Ragpickers' Ball Held in Hartford," *New York Times*, 16 February 1936.
2. For a contemporary description of such a ball, see Wirt Sikes, "The Blousard in his Hours of Ease," *Lippincott's Magazine of Popular Literature and Science* 15 (June 1875): 684–92.
3. The Paper Ball is discussed in detail in Eugene R. Gaddis, *Magician of the Modern: Chick Austin and the Transformation of the Arts in America* (New York: Alfred A. Knopf, 2000), 290–308.
4. See Judy Klemesrud, "But Will Paper Dresses Pass the Test of Time?" *New York Times*, 24 October 1966. The most sensational costume was Rudi Gernreich's clear plastic dress with strategically placed circular paper decals.

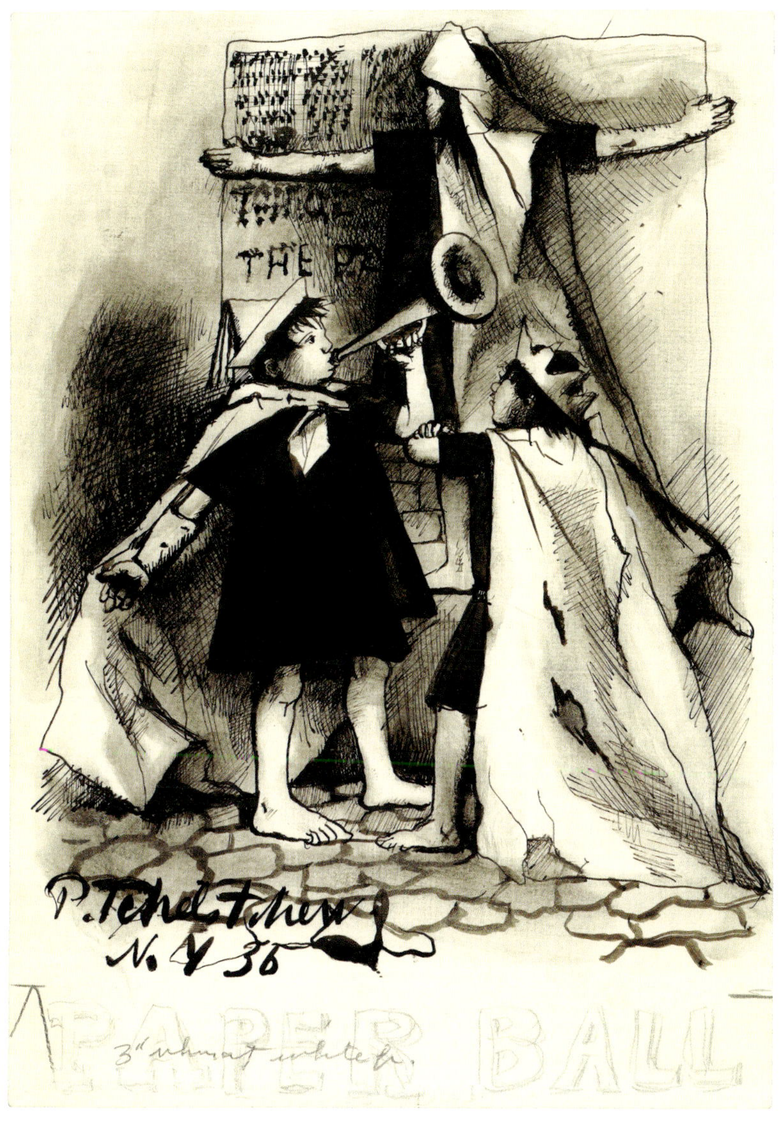

Cat. 52a

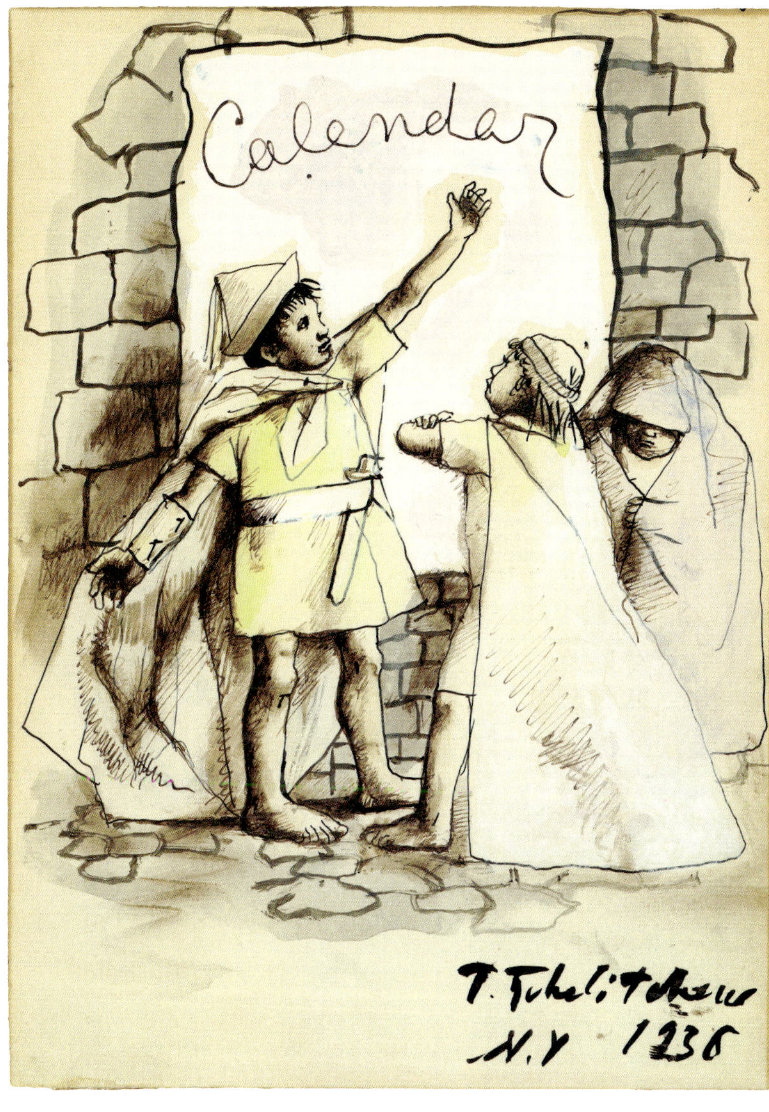

Cat. 52b

53

Pavel Tchelitchew
Cover for Program for Hartford Festival, 1936
Pen and black ink, transparent watercolor, and white opaque watercolor on cut and printed paper laid down on blue wove paper
11 5/8 × 8 3/4 in. (29.5 × 22.2 cm)
Signed at lower right: P. Tchelitchew
Ex coll.: the artist
The Ella Gallup Sumner and Mary Catlin Sumner Collection Fund, 1936.21

Describing the decorations he was planning for the Paper Ball, which would be the culminating social event of the Wadsworth Atheneum's Hartford Festival, the Russian émigré artist Pavel Tchelitchew told a reporter, "There were [*sic*] be draperies and garlands and vases of paper between the boxes, some of them with flowers, and some with feathers. . . . Oh, it will be very gay. Like a valentine."[1] In fact, the festival was held during the week of Valentine's Day, 1936 (9–16 February); fittingly, Tchelitchew's program cover resembles an old-fashioned cut-paper valentine: delicate, sentimental, and ephemeral.

The festival was a week-long celebration of the arts, during which the Atheneum hosted concerts, films, vocal performances, and ballets. It was an ambitious and exuberant demonstration of director Chick Austin's conviction that the Atheneum should be an arena for all art forms and "a museum of living things."[2] To that end, in late 1935 he solicited participation and commissioned works from many of his favorite painters, composers, and choreographers. Among them was Tchelitchew, who was invited to be the principal designer for the festival. Tchelitchew was already known in Hartford: his paintings and drawings had been shown in several exhibitions at the Atheneum beginning in the early 1930s; he also had designed backdrops for performances staged there. In a few frantic months, working first in New York and then in Hartford, Tchelitchew created decorations and costumes for the Paper Ball, sets and costumes for George Balanchine's new ballet *Serenata*, which premiered on Valentine's Day, and the cover for the festival's program booklet.

The cover, a sweet, fanciful collage of gouache and ink and newspaper cut and pasted onto dark blue paper (now faded), features two young dancers, their transparent bodies

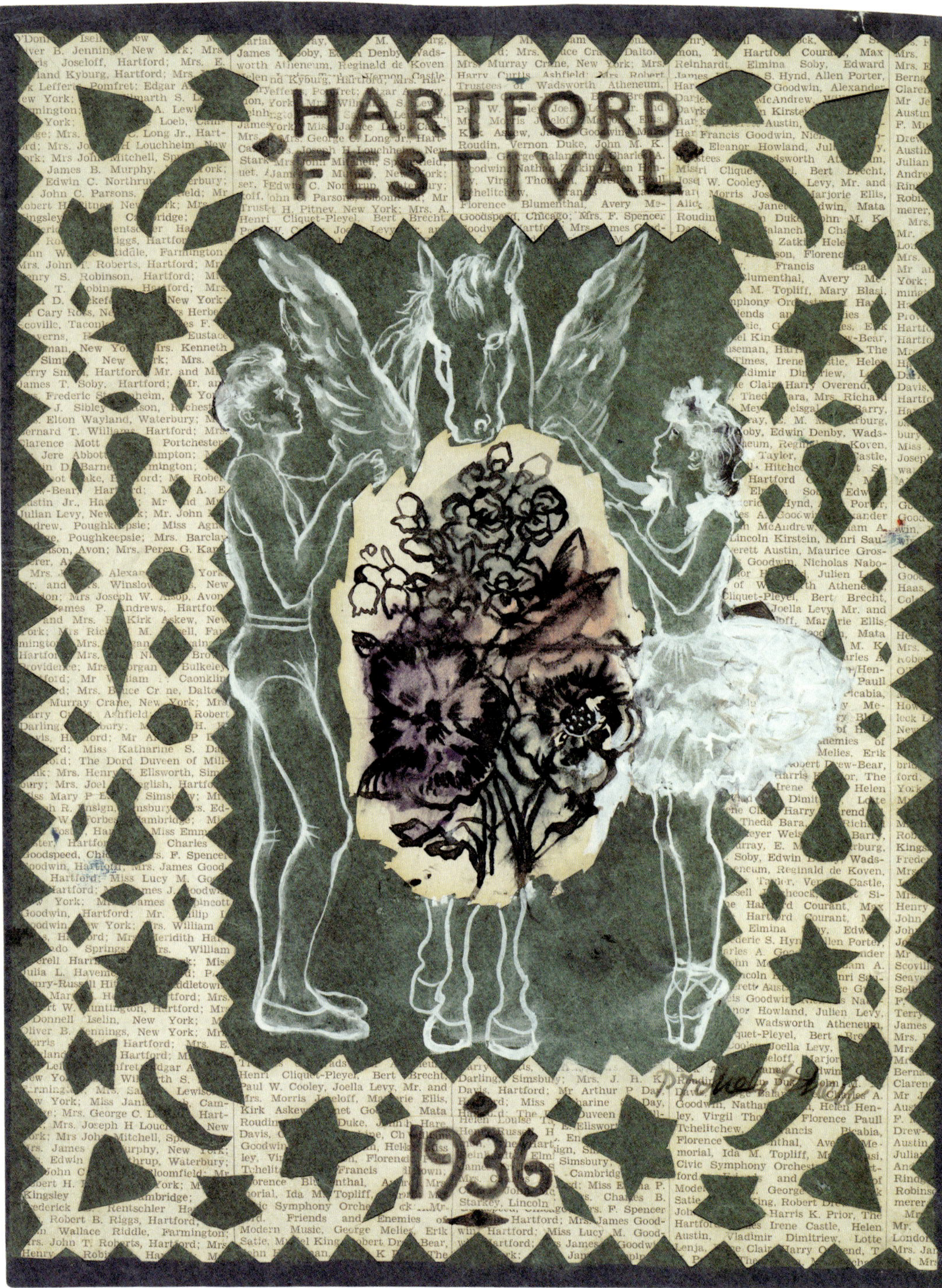

Cat. 53

outlined in white opaque watercolor. The female dancer is shown *en pointe*, in a frothy tutu; the male dancer wears rehearsal attire. They flank a bouquet of oversize flowers, drawn in ink and toned loosely with purplish red, teal, and violet. The flowers are painted onto an oval placard with jagged edges that was cut out of blank newsprint and pasted on the blue paper. The placard appears to be held by the transparent figures; like them, it is a play on substance versus illusion, reality versus fantasy. Behind the placard stands a winged horse, also transparent and outlined in white; it gazes down benignly at the flowers. The horse (with all its associations of fantasy and flight) was a motif favored by Tchelitchew and his fellow Neo-Romantics. Tchelitchew in fact spoke of his own "horsey behavior" and his tendency to go "galloping off in all directions"[3] – an apt image for the multifaceted festival itself. Framing the figures is an ersatz newspaper article (set by the *Hartford Times*) with stars, moons, diamonds, and hearts cut out of the newsprint. The "article" lists the names of contemporary painters, composers, performers, curators, critics, art dealers, impresarios, and supporters of the arts.[4] Conspicuous among the last were trustees of the Wadsworth Atheneum and other local patrons, whose support Austin needed for the success of the festival.

Tchelitchew's design was reproduced on the cover of the program. Austin himself contributed $200 toward the cost of production to ensure the quality of the color.[5] The collage was subsequently bought by the Atheneum. It was one of twelve works for which Tchelitchew was paid $750 as partial compensation for his contributions to the festival and Paper Ball, and is one of the few tangible souvenirs of those magical events.

CT

1. "'Ragpickers' Circus' for the Paper Ball," *Hartford Times*, 21 December 1935, Scrapbooks December 1934–December 1935, box 19, Wadsworth Atheneum Archives.
2. Austin, fragment of typescript, Austin Papers, Wadsworth Atheneum Archives, cited in Eugene R. Gaddis, *Magician of the Modern: Chick Austin and the Transformation of the Arts in America*, 309.
3. Lincoln Kirstein, *Tchelitchev* (Santa Fe, N.Mex.: Twelvetrees Press, 1994), 68.
4. Among those mentioned are Tchelitchew, Erik Satie, Irene Castle, Virgil Thomson, Edward Denby, Julien Levy, Lincoln Kirstein, Philip L. Goodwin, The Friends and Enemies of Modern Music, and trustees of the Wadsworth Atheneum.
5. Gaddis, *Magician of the Modern*, 308.

54a–c

Pavel Tchelitchew
Ring Master (Mr. Austin).
Paper Ball, Hartford Festival, 1936
Opaque and transparent watercolor over graphite on thick gray cardboard
16 3/4 × 7 5/8 in. (42.6 × 19.4 cm)
Ex coll.: the artist
The Ella Gallup Sumner and Mary Catlin Sumner Collection Fund, 1936.22

Ring Mistress (Mrs. R. M. Bissell).
Paper Ball, Hartford Festival, 1936
Opaque and transparent watercolor on thick gray cardboard
16 3/4 × 7 5/8 in. (42.6 × 19.4 cm)
Ex coll.: the artist
The Ella Gallup Sumner and Mary Catlin Sumner Collection Fund, 1936.23

Summer (Mrs. Austin).
Paper Ball, Hartford Festival, 1936
Opaque and transparent watercolor over graphite on thick gray cardboard
16 7/8 × 7 5/8 in. (42.9 × 19.4 cm)
Ex coll.: the artist
The Ella Gallup Sumner and Mary Catlin Sumner Collection Fund, 1936.26

In his biography of Chick Austin, Eugene Gaddis begins his chapter devoted to the Hartford Festival with the observation, "No costume was more appropriate for Chick to wear at the Paper Ball of 1936 than the one Tchelitchew designed for him. He was to be the Ringmaster. With a top hat and a red coat, he would lead a procession of fantastically bedecked merrymakers through his museum, cracking a whip."[1] Other principals attending the ball were equally suitably clad: Marie Bissell, chairman of the Paper Ball Committee and a longtime Austin friend and supporter who found most of the Hartford elite tediously staid, was dressed as the Ring Mistress in a tight, wasp-waisted black gown, leather boots, and a silvery-gray whip. For pretty Helen Austin, who had a sweet and forgiving temperament, Tchelitchew designed a lacy, tutu-like costume, with bows at the shoulders and a floral headdress (fig. 1). She personified Summer, and as indicated by his sketch, Tchelitchew envisioned her in a basket made of flowers and pulled through the air by a fleet of white doves. Choreographer George Balanchine, ballet impresario Lincoln Kirstein, and financier and patron Edward Warburg (the last two quite wealthy) were attired in magnificent beggars' costumes. In all, there would be twelve major groups of costumed figures (some of them outfitted by Eugene Berman [q.v.] and Alexander Calder [q.v.]). Led by the Ringmaster, these revelers, representing "Poets," "A Calendar of Trees," "The Ruins of Hartford 3095," "Modern Art," and so on, strolled in procession from the Morgan Memorial wing of the Atheneum through the Tapestry Hall and into Avery Court.[2] As Kirstein would later recall, the elegantly austere International style Avery Court had been transformed into a "lobby of a continental opera house whose loges were filled with flowers, chairs, and spectators," all fashioned out of newspaper.[3]

The drawings Tchelitchew created for the Paper Ball costumes have the finely detailed, brightly colored, and strongly silhouetted quality of paper dolls. Although he worked on cheap cardboard (which has since discolored), Tchelitchew's drawings are not rough, rapid sketches but precisely rendered designs in opaque watercolor. The color schemes are highly decorative: Tchelitchew used posterlike red, black, and white for the Ringmaster; black, white, and silvery gray for the Ring Mistress; and sugary pastels for Summer.

When discussing his plans for the Paper Ball, Tchelitchew predicted, "Each lady will want . . . to have a costume design for her own personality."[4] Those costumes, and the implied commentary on the wearer, were meant in fun. But the notion of imparting fantastic identities to friends and associates would resurface in Tchelitchew's enormous canvas *Phenomena* (State Tretyakov Gallery, Moscow), completed in 1938 but probably already under way when he was working on the Hartford Festival. That painting, full of grotesque, visceral, shocking figures, featured "libelous identifiable portraits of living personages."[5] A number of those personages (among them poet and critic Parker Tyler and composer Virgil Thomson) Tchelitchew had already dressed, but far more kindly, for the Paper Ball. CT

1. Eugene Gaddis, *Magician of the Modern: Chick Austin and the Transformation of the Arts in America* (New York: Alfred A. Knopf, 2000), 290.
2. Ibid., 305.
3. Lincoln Kirstein, *Pavel Tchelitchew: An Exhibition in the Gallery of Modern Art* (New York: Foundation for Modern Art, 1964), 37.
4. Pavel Tchelitchew, *Hartford Times*, 21 December 1935.
5. Lincoln Kirstein, *Tchelitchev* (Santa Fe, N.Mex.: Twelvetrees Press, 1994), 72.

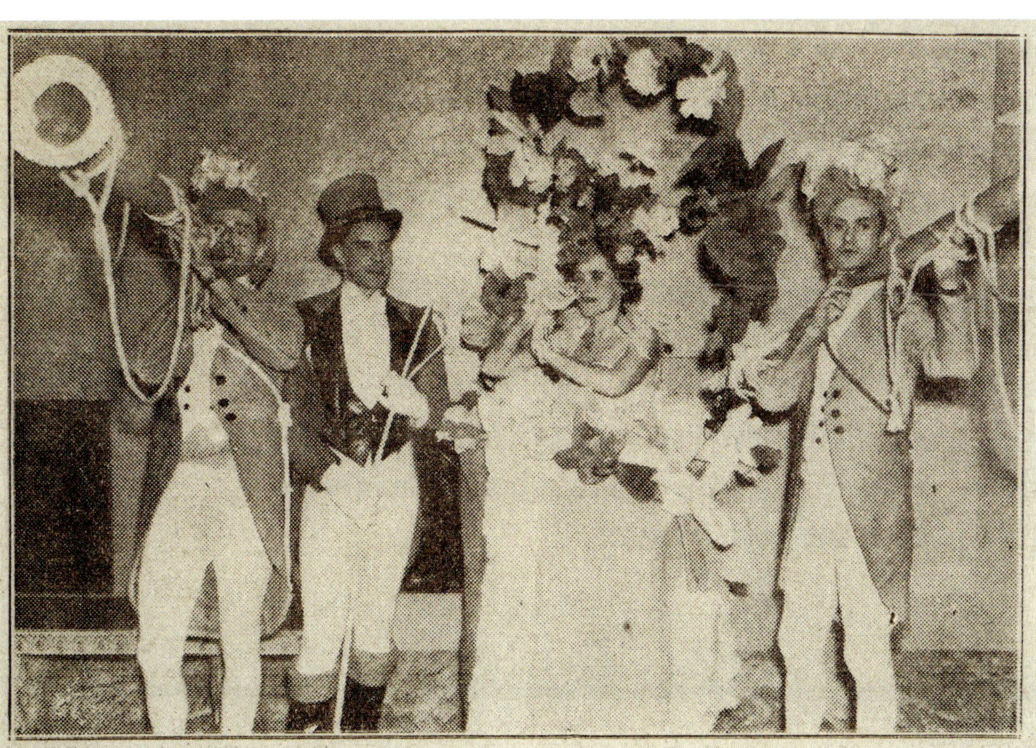

Fig. 1. Chick and Helen Austin in their Paper Ball costumes, *Hartford Courant*, 17 February 1936. Archives, Wadsworth Atheneum Museum of Art

Cat. 54a

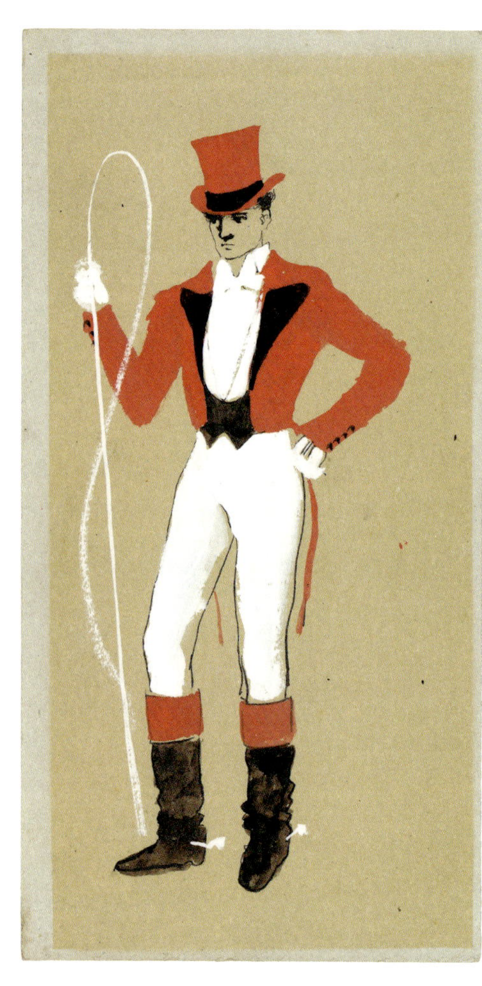

Cat. 54b

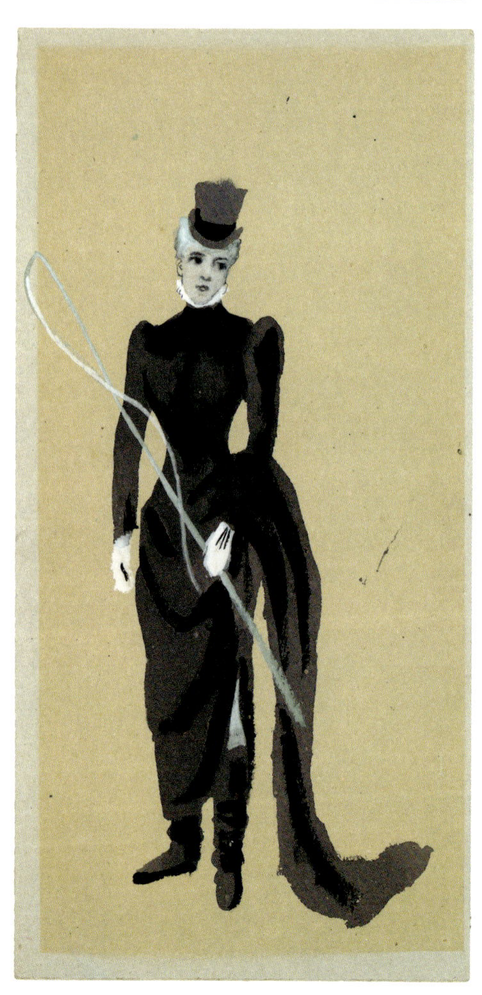

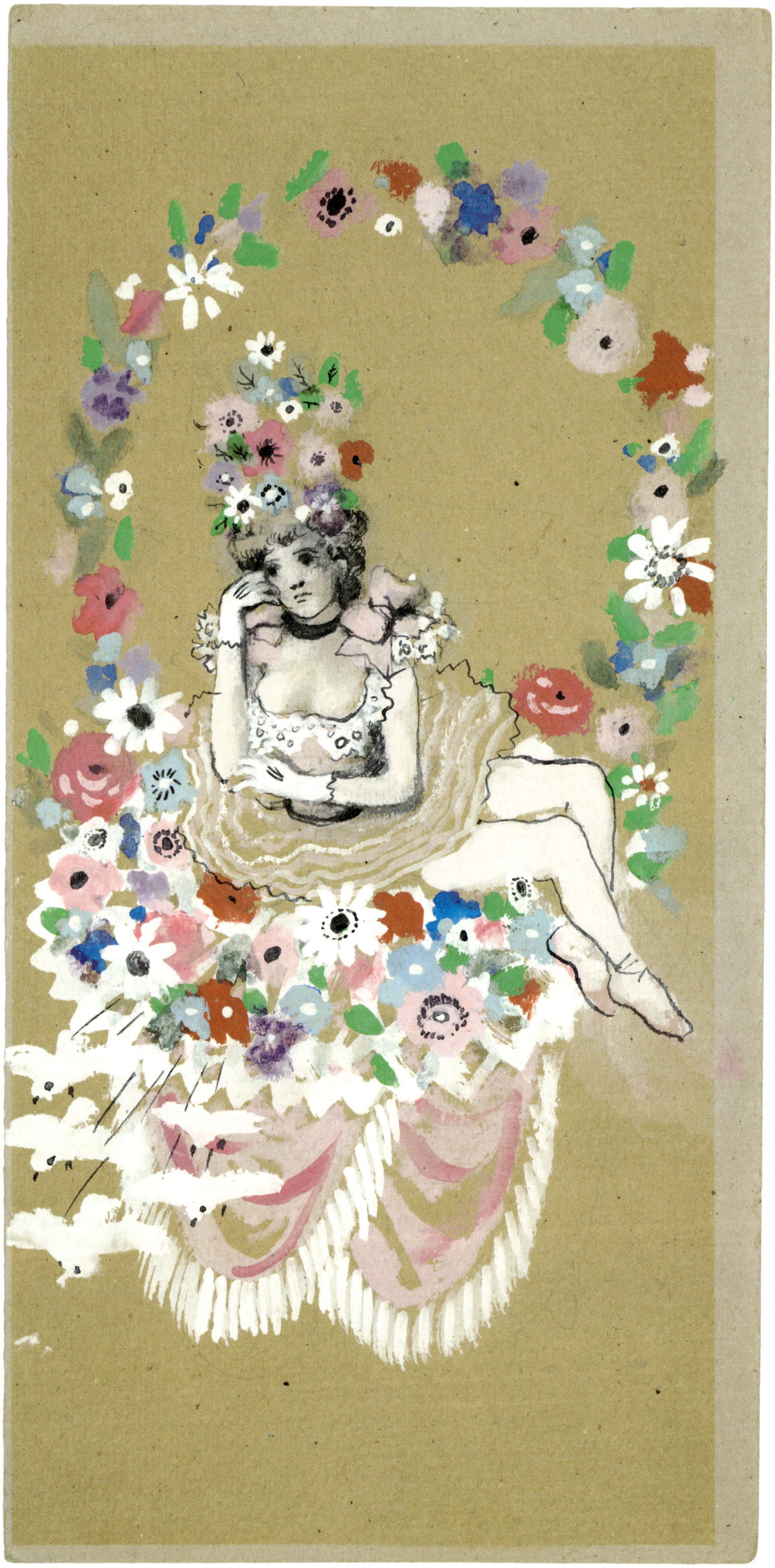

Cat. 54c

55

Pavel Tchelitchew
Constance Askew, 1938
Black ink applied using pen and brush on thin wove paper
16 7/8 × 13 7/8 in. (42.9 × 35.2 cm)
Signed and dated at lower right:
P. Tchelitchew 1938
Ex coll.: Constance Askew, New York; to her daughter Pamela Askew
Gift of Pamela Askew, 1996.35.1

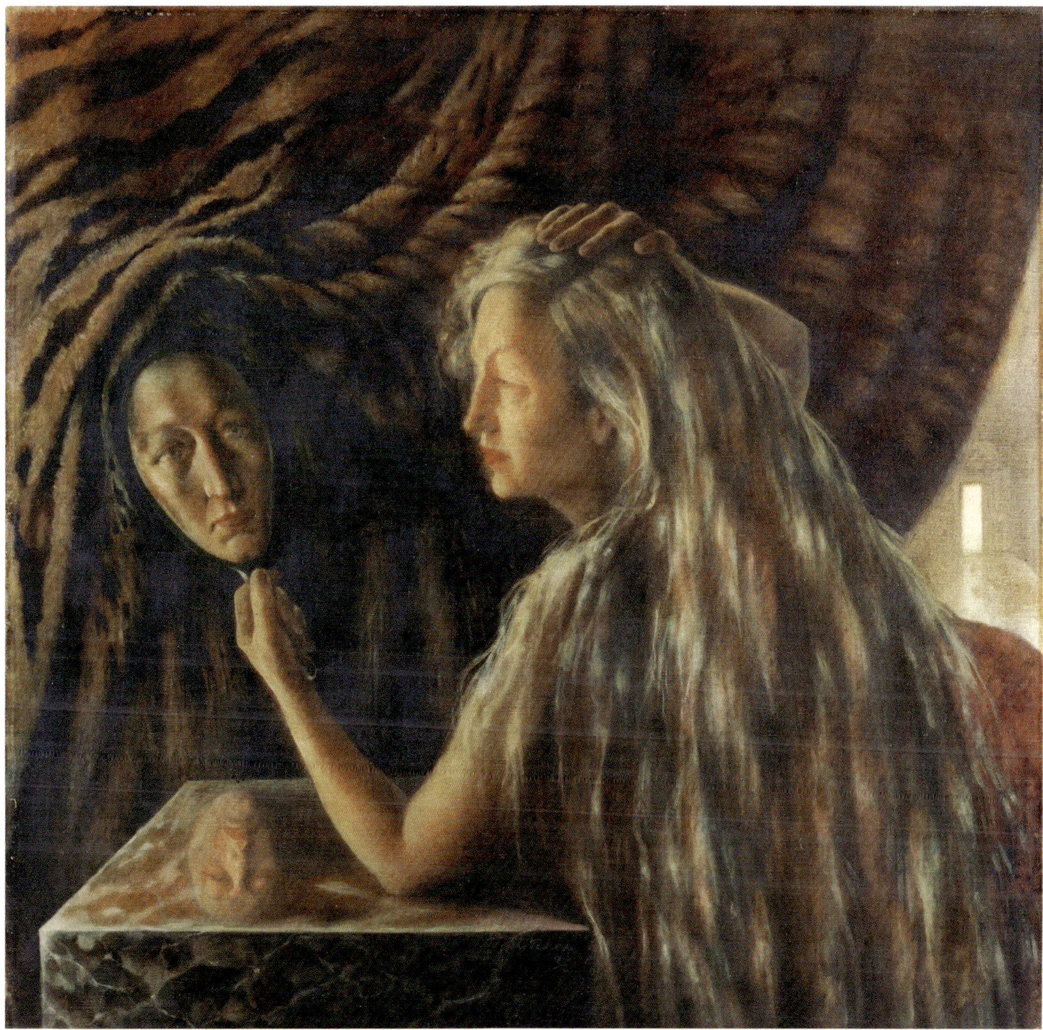

Fig. 1. Pavel Tchelitchew, *Constance Askew*, 1938. Oil on canvas, 39 × 39 in. (99.1 × 99.1 cm). Wadsworth Atheneum Museum of Art. Gift of Mrs. Kirk Askew, 1976.78

In a letter of about 1940 to his English patron Edith Sitwell, Tchelitchew described Kirk and Constance Askew as "the only people I see regularly . . . absolutely wonderful and real people."[1] The artist had started attending the Askews' Sunday soirees shortly after he came to the United States in the fall of 1934 for a solo show at the Julien Levy Gallery in New York City. The Levys were close friends of the Askews. They were regulars at their weekly parties, which served as a lively meeting place for the avant-garde in New York in the 1930s—not just for painters, dealers, and patrons, but also for writers, composers, dancers, and balletomanes.[2]

Kirk Askew was a dealer at Durlacher Brothers, an established art gallery on Fifty-seventh Street that specialized in old master, particularly Baroque, paintings. The Askews had a taste for modern art as well; their personal collection contained examples of both. Askew became Tchelitchew's dealer in 1942, taking over from Levy, who was in the army. He and Constance were great supporters of Tchelitchew's, and eventually owned more than twenty works by the artist in all media, ranging in date from about 1927 to 1951.[3]

In the late 1930s, Tchelitchew was engaged in a series of portraits of his friends (many of whom attended the Sunday soirees). This drawing is from that period, and presumably was made at the same time as Tchelitchew's celebrated—and highly inventive—oil portrait of Constance. In that painting, she is dressed in a mink coat and has waist-length hair (in fact, she wore her hair short); she admires herself in a hand mirror while her face is reflected in the polished top of the table at which she sits (fig. 1). In the drawing, on the other hand, Tchelitchew recorded what Constance actually looked like, and the likeness on the whole is more sympathetic. Yet, while not a preparatory study in any conventional sense, the drawing may well have functioned as a rehearsal for Tchelitchew's rendering of her features in oil, where two of the three faces show her as she might have looked as she aged (the image on the table suggests a death mask).[4]

Since about 1930 Tchelitchew had been producing double images, working in ink and silverpoint as well as in oil. His drawing of Constance Askew is not as surreal as some—his silverpoint portrait of Frederick Ashton, made the same year as the Askew drawing, shows the choreographer's head twice, once upside down, the fringe of his hair continuing from his scalp across the picture surface (fig. 2). In contrast, *Constance Askew* is one of Tchelitchew's most affecting double images. Askew is shown full face; a second head, turned away slightly, floats behind. Tchelitchew's ink line is sharp and precise; gray wash, applied economically at her cheeks and temples and in her hair, softens the face in the foreground. The second head, rendered with loose ink lines and pale, silky wash, appears somewhat ghostly, as though it were the memory of a face.

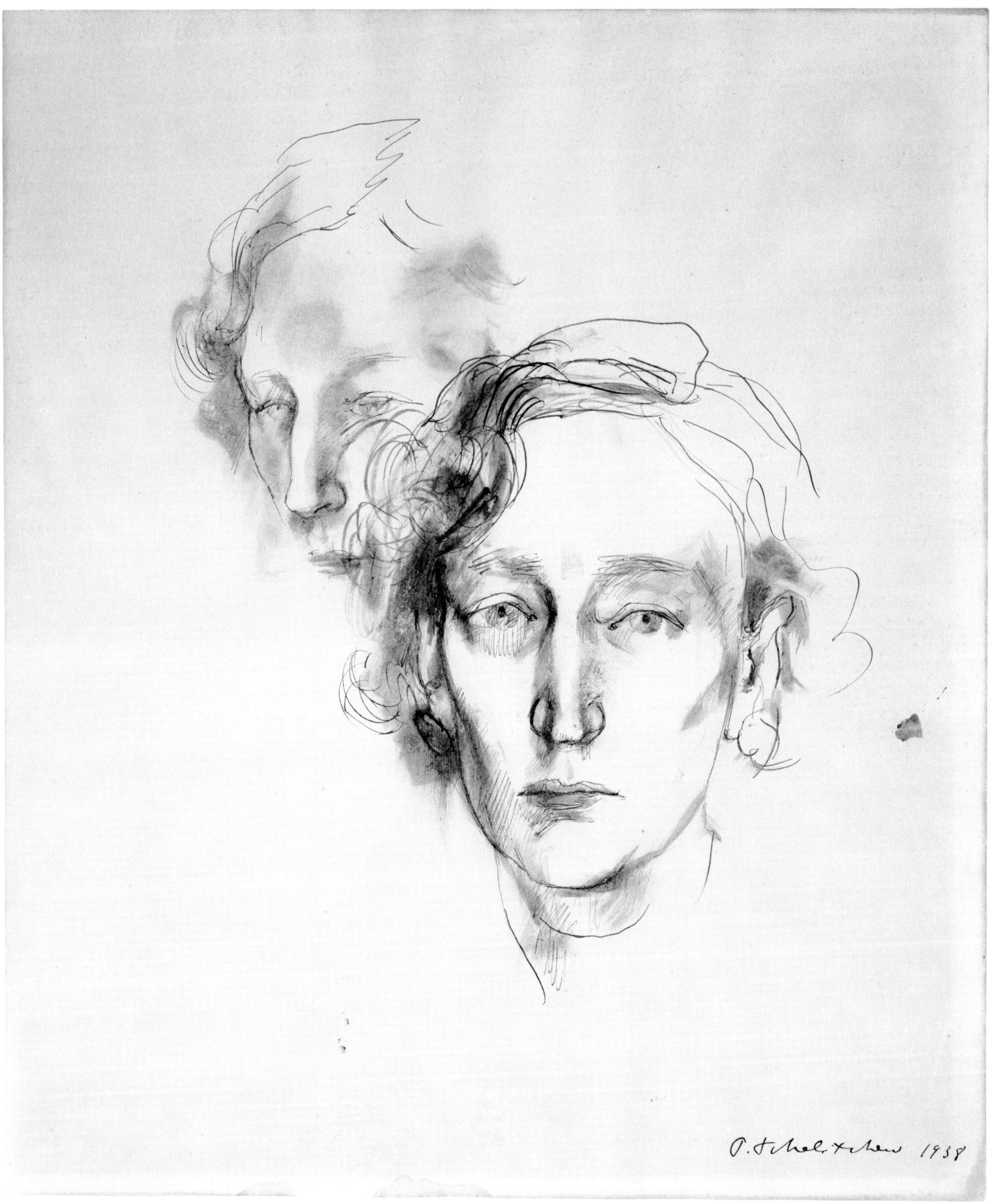

Cat. 55

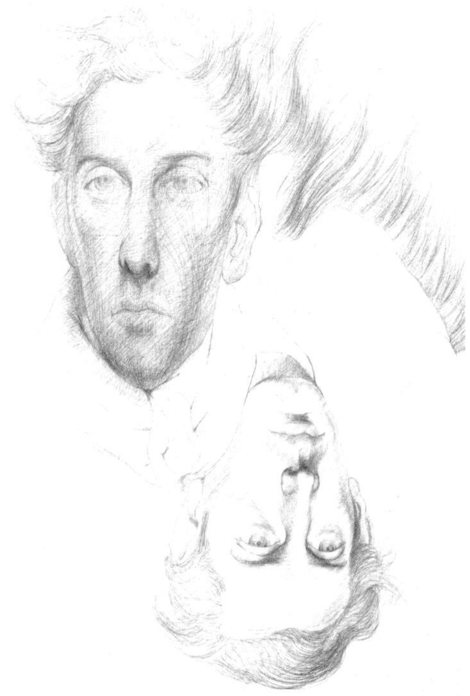

Fig. 2. Pavel Tchelitchew, *Frederick Ashton* (1904–1988), 1938. Silverpoint on white prepared paper, 20 × 12 1/2 in. (50.8 × 31.8 cm). Harvard Art Museum, Fogg Art Museum. Gift of Meta and Paul J. Sachs, 1959.165

Despite Tchelitchew's predilection for ambiguity in his double images, this portrait seems to be a clear presentation of both Askew's appearance and her character: she is shown as a handsome, sensitive, and somewhat reserved woman. Virgil Thomson (who a few years earlier had created a series of musical portraits of his friends, including the Askews) described her as "a New England woman of means, of broad cultural experience, and of striking beauty," and also wrote of her "related visage, as calm as that of Garbo." His words could serve as the caption for this portrait.[5]
CT

1. Parker Tyler, *The Divine Comedy of Pavel Tchelitchew* (New York: Fleet, 1967), 446.
2. For a description of the Askews' Sunday parties, see Virgil Thomson, *Virgil Thomson* (1966; repr., New York: E. P. Dutton, 1985), 215–17.
3. For a sense of the extent of the Askews' collection of Tchelitchews, see their loans to the 1964 exhibition *Pavel Tchelitchew* at the Gallery of Modern Art (New York: Foundation for Modern Art, 1964).
4. "Constance Askew," in *American Paintings before 1945 in the Wadsworth Atheneum*, by Elizabeth Mankin Kornhauser with contributions from Elizabeth R. McClintock and Amy Ellis (New Haven, Conn.: Yale University Press, 1996), 2: cat. no. 435, 711.
5. Thomson's "Portraits for Piano Solo" depicting the Askews were composed in 1935. His description of Constance Askew is found in Thomson, *Virgil Thomson*, 215.

56a–c

Pavel Tchelitchew
Sketch #4 for Niobe
(Derby Hill Theme, Winter), 1940
Black ink applied using pen and brush and graphite with traces of green wash on thin wove paper
8 1/2 × 11 in. (21.6 × 27.9 cm)
Signed and dated at lower right:
P. Tchelitchew 40
Ex coll.: James Thrall Soby, New York
Gift of James Thrall Soby, 1942.623

Sketch #5 for Niobe
(Derby Hill Theme, Winter), 1942
Black ink applied using pen and brush and graphite with traces of green wash on thin wove paper
8 1/2 × 11 in. (21.6 × 27.9 cm)
Signed and dated at lower right:
P. Tchelitchew 42
Ex coll.: James Thrall Soby,
West Hartford, Connecticut
Gift of James Thrall Soby, 1942.624

Sketch #6 for Niobe
(Derby Hill Theme, Winter), 1942
Black ink applied using pen and brush and graphite on thin wove paper
8 1/2 × 11 in. (21.6 × 27.9 cm)
Signed and dated at lower right:
P. Tchelitchew 42
Ex coll.: James Thrall Soby,
West Hartford, Connecticut
Gift of James Thrall Soby, 1942.625

In the summer of 1940, Tchelitchew moved to Derby Hill, a pre-Revolutionary house on Rupert Mountain, near the village of Pawlet, Vermont. Inspired by his view of pastureland and the Green Mountains beyond, he created a group of landscapes known as Theme and Variations: Derby Hill that combine his characteristic meticulous realism and his equally characteristic interest in fantasy. During this period Tchelitchew was deeply involved with the notion of metamorphosis; that is, with unrelated and unexpected images emerging from the basic forms of a composition. Highly suggestive and intriguing, such paintings offer a kind of visual rebus; or, as Tchelitchew's first biographer James Thrall Soby explained it, metamorphosis presents an "interior magic, creating its own mystery but never becoming a dominant illusion."[1]

The four paintings forming Tchelitchew's Theme and Variations represent the seasons of the year, and are metamorphic at the same time.[2] *Fata Morgana (Derby Hill Theme, Summer)*, 1940 (collection Ruth Ford, New York) shows the figure of a nude woman defined by the landscape's green, rolling hills. The last three–*David and Goliath (Derby Hill Theme, Autumn)*, 1942 (Harvard University Art Museums, Fogg Art Museum), *Hiawatha (Derby Hill Theme)*, 1940 (Wadsworth Atheneum Museum of Art), and *Niobe (Derby Hill Theme, Winter)*, 1942 (fig. 1)–all show a mountain in the middle distance with a large face seeming to emerge from the foliage. The drawings in this exhibition, which illustrate the genesis of that face and other hidden forms, are for *Niobe*, the bleakest and most theatrical painting of the group.[3]

The story of Niobe, queen of Thebes, is one of the most tragic in Greek mythology. She had fourteen children and foolishly boasted of them to the Titan Leto, whose own children, Apollo and Artemis, were fathered by Zeus. In revenge, Leto had all Niobe's children killed. Niobe fled to Mount Sipylus (in present-day Turkey) and was turned to stone, from which a stream emerged, fed by her endless tears. The story is particularly suited to Tchelitchew's interest in metamorphosis, for the mountain has a natural rock formation resembling a woman's face that appears to "weep" whenever rainwater seeps through it.

The hallucinatory image that Tchelitchew derived from the myth was the product of careful preparation. The Wadsworth Atheneum owns six sketches for the painting; in them, the tree form that is *Niobe*'s central motif evolves from a naturalistic, if emotionally overwrought, image to a grotesque and unsettling one. In the first three drawings, Tchelitchew outlined the twisted branches in pencil, using a minimum of crosshatched shading (see fig. 2). He initially rendered the branches stretching from right to left; by the third drawing, he arrived at the orientation he would use in the final composition.

For the last three drawings, Tchelitchew used ink and wash.[4] The drawings are increasingly complex, combining smooth applications of wash with nervous, hatched pen lines. In the fifth drawing, certain passages, including the apex of the tree and the dark area in the center, are so heavily worked that the paper is almost torn through, creating a sense of violence that carries over to the finished work. The background also takes shape in the three ink drawings. The face in the hills begins to appear, as does the figure of Niobe. In the last drawing, her face looms out from under the bending branch while her nude body huddles next to the trunk of the tree. In the final version, these two forms are combined into a single floating, ghostly profile.

CT

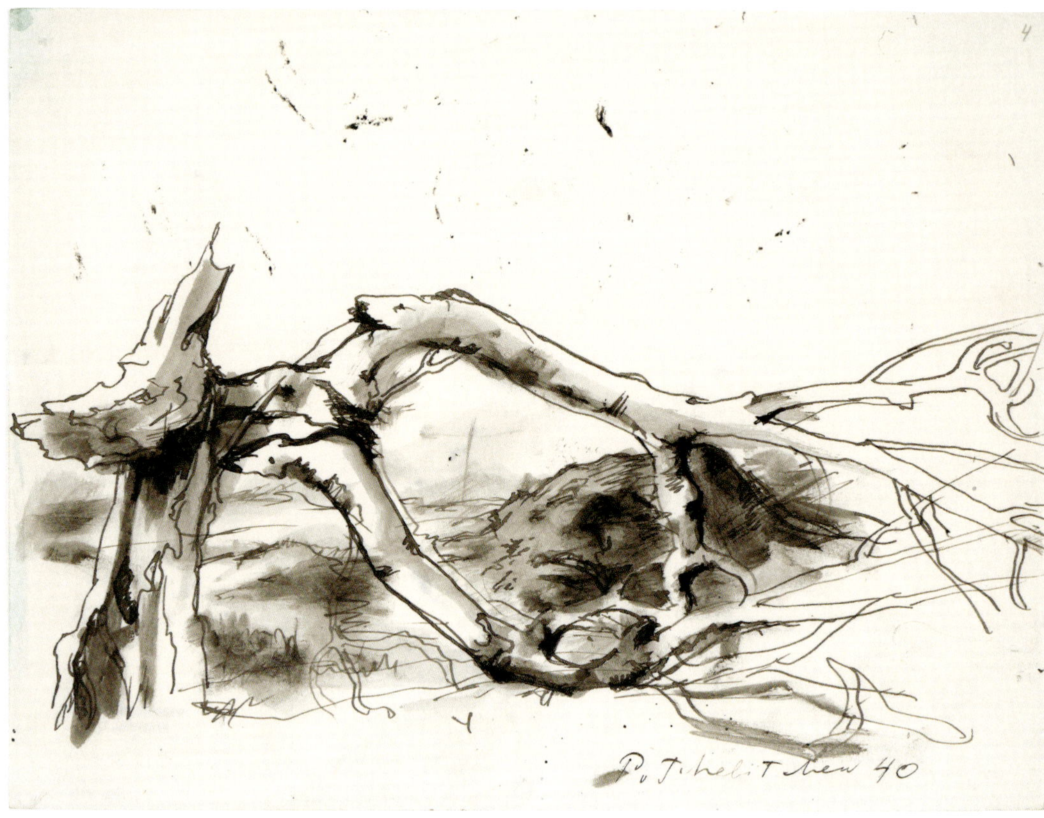

Cat. 56a

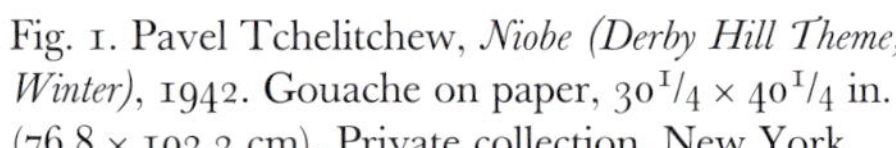

Fig. 1. Pavel Tchelitchew, *Niobe (Derby Hill Theme, Winter)*, 1942. Gouache on paper, 30 1/4 × 40 1/4 in. (76.8 × 102.2 cm). Private collection, New York

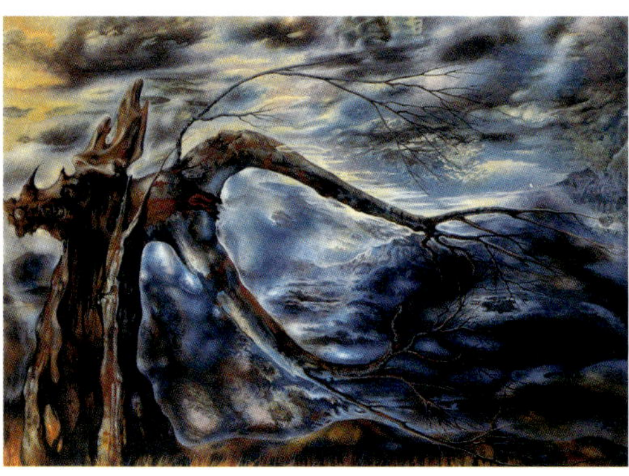

Fig. 2. Pavel Tchelitchew, *Sketch for Niobe (Derby Hill Theme, Winter)*, 1942. Pencil on paper, 8 1/2 × 11 in. (21.6 × 27.9 cm). Wadsworth Atheneum Museum of Art. Gift of James Thrall Soby, 1942.622

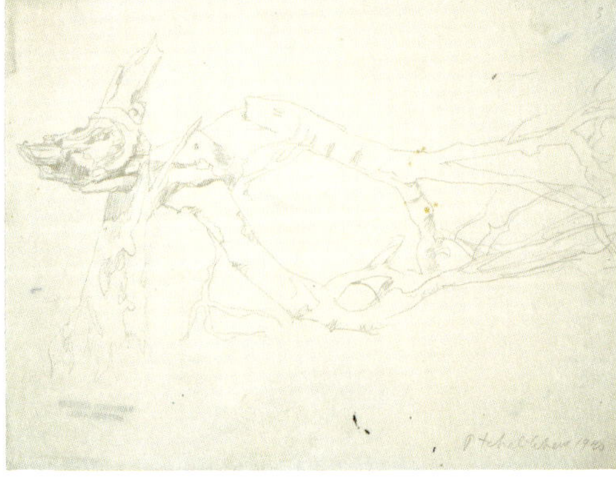

1. James Thrall Soby, *Pavel Tchelitchew* (New York: Museum of Modern Art, 1942), 19.
2. The finished works form a perplexing group. The sizes of the works are not consistent, and some are oil and some are gouache. Those that are dated bear the date 1940 (except for the picture at Harvard, which is dated both 1940 and 1942). Some of the *Niobe* drawings are dated 1940 and some 1942 (and so after the finished work); it is possible that Tchelitchew inscribed them at the time James Thrall Soby acquired them.
3. As described by Lincoln Kirstein, another of Tchelitchew's supporters, *Niobe* is "a winterscape in silver, lead, steel and crimson, suggest[ing] brooding cruelty and loss . . . at once mysterious and powerful." Kirstein, *Tchelitchev* (Santa Fe, N.Mex.: Twelvetrees Press, 1994), 84.
4. This was the medium he used for preparatory drawings for other oils in the series. See, for example, *Study for David, for "Derby Hill Theme: David and Goliath,"* 1942, black ink and gray wash on buff paper, 11 × 8 7/6 in. (27.9 × 21.5 cm), Harvard University Art Museums, Fogg Art Museum.

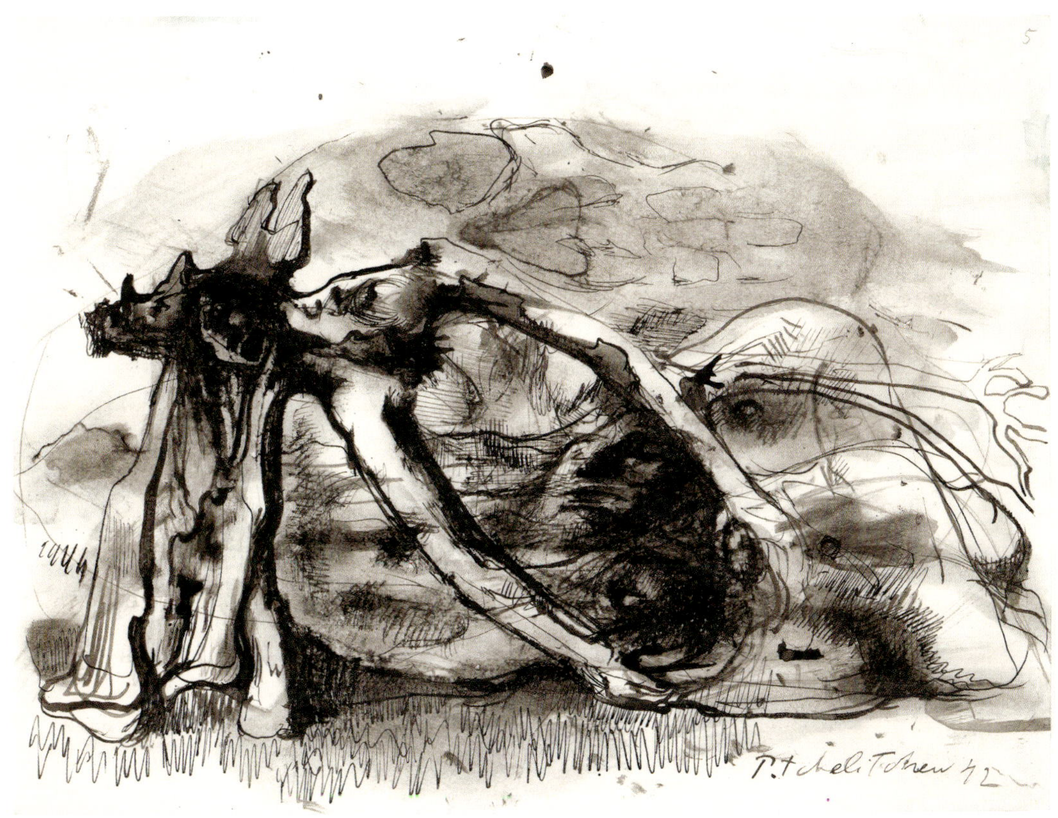

Cat. 56b

Cat. 56c

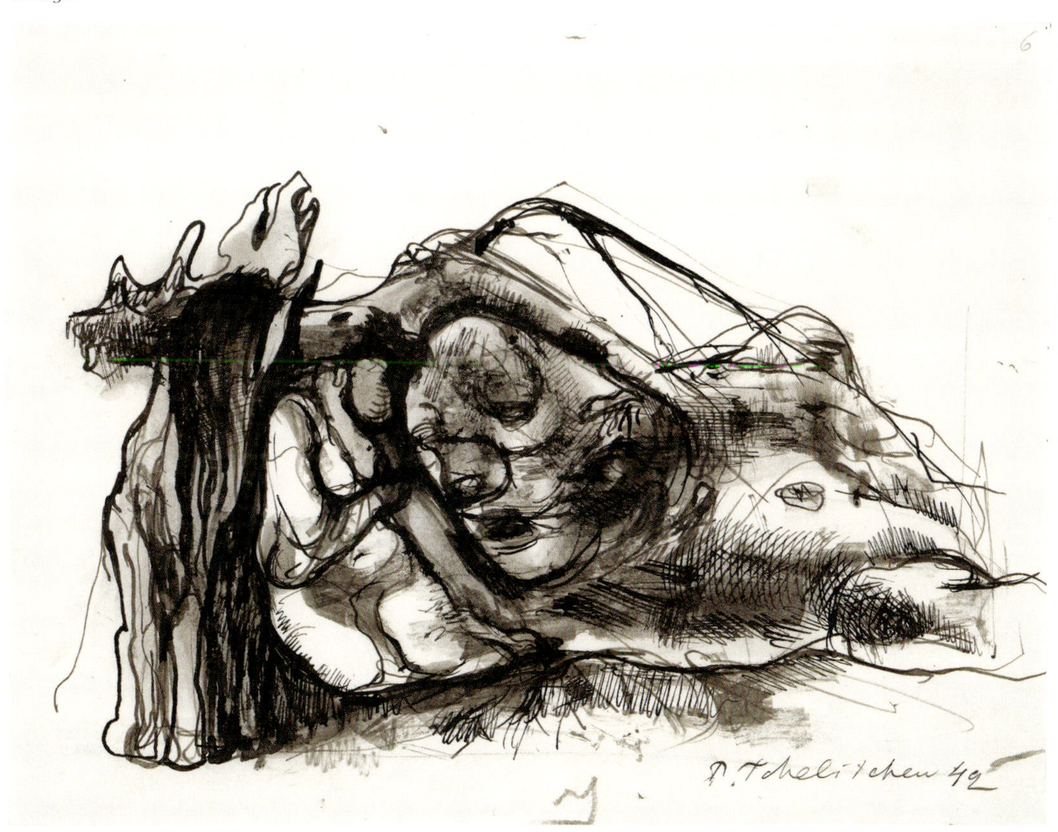

Eugene Berman

Born in St. Petersburg, Russia, 1899;
died in Rome, 1972

Having studied in Germany, Switzerland, and France for much of his youth, Berman returned to St. Petersburg, his birthplace, in 1914 to train under the Russian painter Pavel Naumov and the architect Sergey Gruzenberg. Berman's early attraction to architecture was fostered by the buildings of his native Russia, as well as his exposure to the architectural traditions of western Europe, Italy in particular. His early predilection for architecture would remain one of the recognizable influences in his painting style for the rest of his career. Returning to France in 1918, Berman enrolled at the Académie Ranson in Paris, studying under Édouard Vuillard and Maurice Denis. Among his fellow pupils were his elder brother Leonid, as well as Christian Bérard.

Berman first exhibited in Paris in 1924 at the Galerie Druet, and only two years later he began exhibiting with the Neo-Romantic painters, a group whose members included his brother as well as Bérard, Kristians Tonny (q.v.), and Pavel Tchelitchew (q.v.). Neo-Romanticism developed in response to the growing influence of Cubism. These artists admired the poetic melancholy of Picasso's Rose and Blue periods, and sought to reintroduce the humanistic and the emotional into an art world they saw as increasingly analytical. Berman was introduced to De Chirico and Surrealism in 1926; Surrealism would be a significant influence on the Russian artist's style.

The influential dealer Julien Levy introduced Berman's work to American audiences in 1930. The following year, Berman was included in an exhibition at the Wadsworth Atheneum, *Tonny Tchelitchew Berard Berman Leonide* [*sic*], celebrating the Neo-Romantic movement. Berman did not travel to the United States until four years later, on the occasion of his solo exhibition at the Atheneum. On that trip, he visited A. Everett "Chick" Austin, the Atheneum's director, in Hartford. Austin later commissioned Berman to design musical sets and costumes for various events during the Hartford Festival in 1936. Berman's relationship with Austin was long-lived, and in 1958 the artist contributed an essay, "Legendary Chick," to an anthology dedicated to the museum director's influential presence in the art world.

In addition to his design work for the Hartford Festival, after moving to America, Berman was commissioned to create costumes for ballet and other theatrical performances, and to paint mural decorations for private residences, including James Thrall Soby's in Farmington, Connecticut. Beginning in 1940, Berman made his permanent home in America, first in New York and then in Los Angeles. In 1944 he became an American citizen and was awarded two Guggenheim fellowships, in 1947 and 1949, to travel to Mexico. Berman returned to Europe in 1950, and after a 1955 residency at the American Academy in Rome, he settled there permanently. He worked there until his death in 1972.

Select Bibliography

George Amberg. *The Theater of Eugene Berman.* New York: Museum of Modern Art, 1947.

Julien Levy. *Eugene Berman.* New York: American Studio Books, [1947].

Eugene Berman. *The Graphic Work of Eugene Berman.* New York: Clarkson N. Potter, 1971.

Michael Duncan. *High Drama: Eugene Berman and the Legacy of the Melancholic Sublime.* New York: Hudson Hills Press, 2004.

57

Eugene Berman
Brooklyn Bridge, 1935
Pen and black ink and ink wash on wove paper
10½ × 15 in. (26.7 × 38.1 cm)
Signed lower right: E B 1935
Ex coll.: with Julien Levy, New York, 1935
Purchased through the gift of Henry and Walter Keney, 1935.64

As a young man, the Neo-Romantic artist Eugene Berman studied architecture in his native Russia. Later, as he pursued a career as a painter and set designer, he continued to find buildings, bridges, and urban plazas fascinating subjects for his art. He was not, however, especially attracted to contemporary architecture. In the early 1930s, for example, he painted Paris's celebrated bridges, all dating from the nineteenth century and before. When he came to the United States in the spring of 1935, one of the first subjects to engage his interest was the Brooklyn Bridge. Characteristically, he did not approach it as an icon of modernism, as American artists had done for the previous twenty years, but as part of a tradition of historical structures, as a monument of the past.

In this melancholy drawing, Berman concentrated his pictorial energies in the foreground, painting with deep black strokes a number of figures in a rather bleak landscape. The bridge, in the middle distance, is a flat, uniform medium gray. Its span is described by a long, low arc; its famous towers with Gothic arches (Berman shows only one) are vaguely anthropomorphized. The tall buildings of the Manhattan skyline are shadowy shapes in pale gray. None of the skyscrapers is particularly identifiable; rather, some have spires and domed tops more suggestive of European (and even Russian) cathedrals than of the ambitious new structures of New York.

The bridge is a time-honored symbol of transition;[1] the perspective Berman chose—looking across the East River from Brooklyn toward Manhattan's soaring towers—was often used to signal aspiration. But in Berman's vision, the mood is quiet, even resigned; there is little sense that the city holds promise. Of the many figures who populate his foreground, only one gazes at the skyline.[2] The others, who are clothed in long, shapeless robes (markedly different from the fitted styles and sharp silhouettes of the 1930s), sit or stand quietly, their heads down. They seem indifferent to the promise of the bridge and the allure of the city. Rather, in the words of critic Russell Lynes, they inhabit "a world that had no noise in it, a frozen world in which nothing was happening but in which a great deal seemed to have happened, a world of pervasive loneliness."[3]

CT

1. The classic study of this motif is Adele Holbomb, "The Bridge in the Middle Distance: Symbolic Elements in Romantic Landscape," *Art Quarterly* 36 (Spring 1974): 49–53.
2. Berman continued to find this view appealing. In a series of pencil drawings dated 1936, for example, Berman again recorded the Manhattan skyline from a vantage point in Brooklyn. Buildings, though still appearing somewhat fanciful, are rendered with much greater precision and attention to architectural detail. In some of the drawings, Berman included a number of spectators gazing across the river. In at least one, their view is framed by the span of the bridge, with its arched openings and crenellated towers silhouetted against the sky. The drawings are illustrated in *The Graphic Work of Eugene Berman* (New York: Clarkson N. Potter, 1971), n.p.
3. Russell Lynes, foreword, ibid.

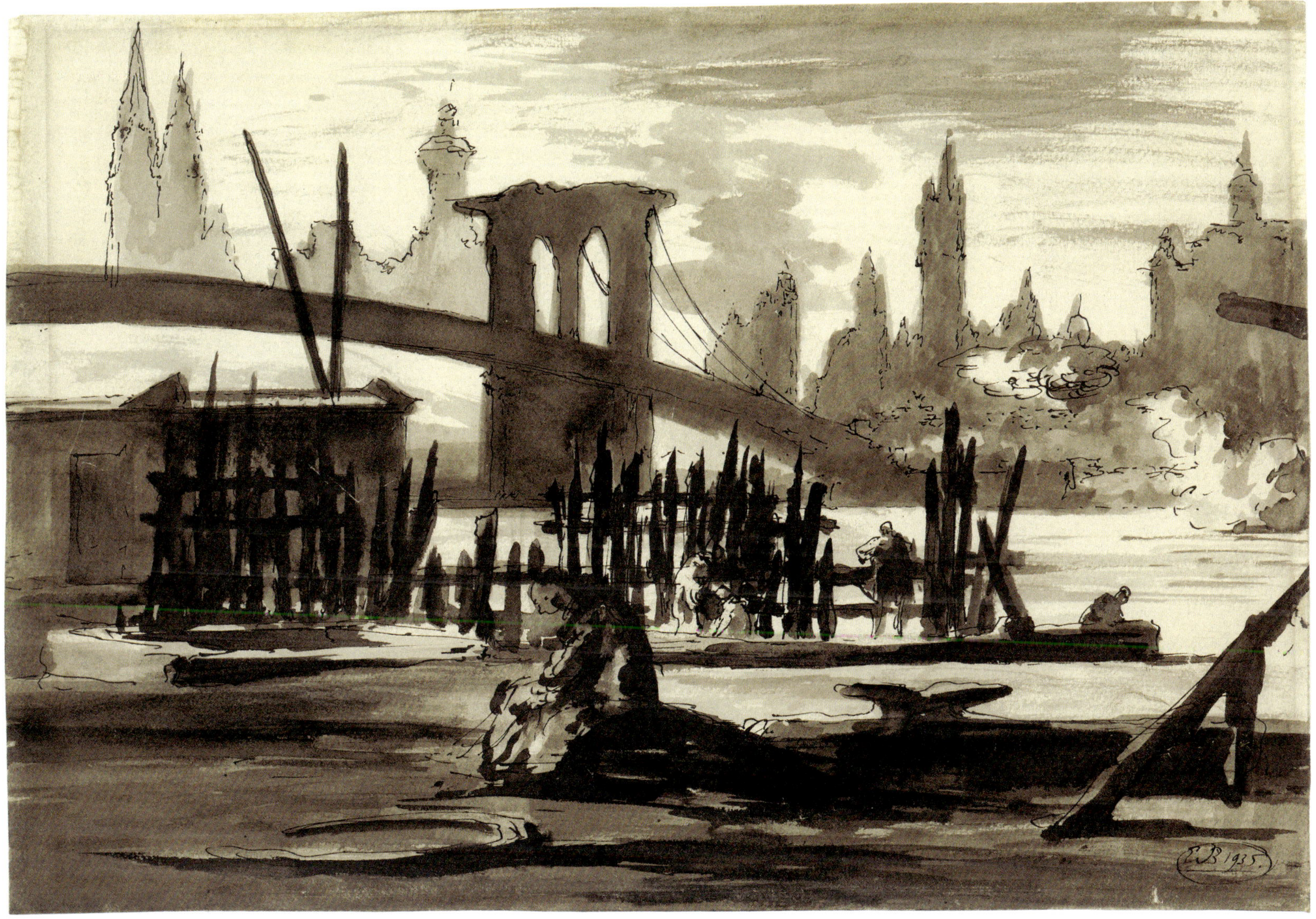

Cat. 57

58 a and b

Eugene Berman
Sketch for Stage Set Used in Hartford Festival, February 16, 1936
Opaque and transparent watercolor with pen and black ink on gray laid paper
9 3/4 × 12 5/8 in. (24.8 × 32.1 cm)
Inscribed: The Wadsworth Atheneum Theater, Hartford, Connecticut
The Ella Gallup Sumner and Mary Catlin Sumner Collection Fund, 1936.2

Sketch for Stage Set Used in Hartford Festival, February 16, 1936
Opaque and transparent watercolor with pen and black ink on gray cardboard
10 1/2 × 16 in. (26.7 × 40.6 cm)
Inscribed upper left: The Wadsworth Atheneum / Theater / Hartford, Connecticut
The Ella Gallup Sumner and Mary Catlin Sumner Collection Fund, 1936.6

The Hartford Festival, a multimedia extravaganza organized by museum director Chick Austin, took place at the Wadsworth Atheneum in February 1936. Like the hugely successful Venetian Fete held there eight years earlier, its purpose was to raise money for the Atheneum. Austin also undoubtedly hoped to persuade conservative Hartford of the excitement of the avant-garde by involving some of the liveliest artists of the day in his week-long social and cultural pageant. The culmination of the Festival was the Paper Ball, a glorious costume party in which the guests and the museum itself were decked out in fantastic creations, all made of paper. Closing the week was a "Matinée Musicale" in the Avery Theater, a concert of rarely heard music from the eighteenth century to the present. Virgil Thomson conducted; the scenic backdrop was designed by Eugene Berman.[1]

Although Berman had clearly been thinking about stage design and had painted several "experimental stage models" before he got to Hartford,[2] this was his first experience with creating an actual set, and he embraced the task with gusto. As Thomson recalled, "Berman had dreamed of theatrical settings all his grown life. When Chick suggested his actually designing one, almost overnight he made thirty-four water-color sketches, all evocative of seventeenth-century Italian ruins and all showing mud puddles in the foreground."[3]

Of these watercolor sketches, some, such as 1936.2 (cat. 58a), contain elements reminiscent of the eerie empty spaces and oddly scaled figures of Giorgio de Chirico, whom Berman admired. In other images, he used similar classical motifs, but drew on the symmetry and grace of the architecture of Alberti and other Renaissance masters. The structures of these theatrical designs resonated with Berman's easel paintings, many of which were themselves like stage sets. Throughout his career, Berman frequently would use architectural forms to demarcate the space and create evocative vistas; many of his figures occupy a proscenium-like area in the foreground. In 1936.6 (cat. 58b), the use of classical busts, placed high off the stage and arranged at measured intervals, echoed the decorations he provided for the Avery Theater's lobby: there, too, he created a Neo-Romantic dream world, with pseudo-Roman busts on tall pedestals surrounded by swags of fabric (fig. 1).[4] And the truncated architectural forms, which suggest both structures not yet finished and buildings in ruins, recurred in the costumes Berman created for the Paper Ball: they formed a procession of broken columns and other architectural fragments that Austin dubbed "Les Ruines de Hartford, 3095."[5]

For the actual backdrop (see fig. 2) Berman combined elements from several of the watercolor sketches. He was praised in the *Hartford Courant* for integrating the traditional and the contemporary in his design, and thereby creating a fitting complement to the festival's concluding program of "ancient and modern chamber music": "The setting is Neo-Romantic in temper, combining the melancholic penchant for ruins and fragments of classical architecture of the true Romantic movement, with a new smartness and recherche elegance of design."[6]

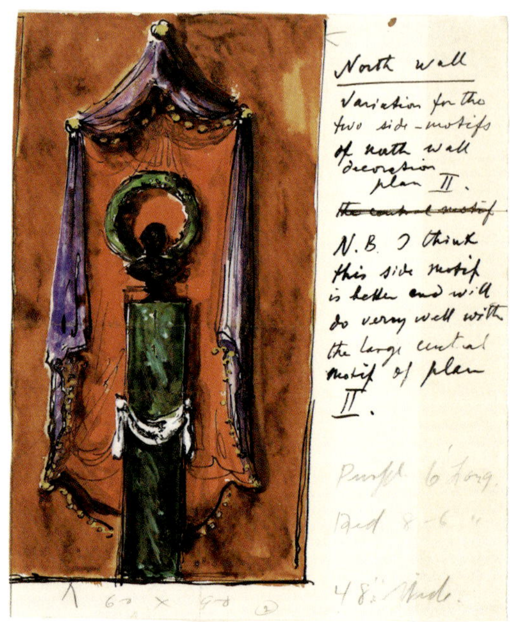

Fig. 1. Eugene Berman, *Design for Hartford Festival, Avery Lobby*, 1936. Watercolor on paper, 8 1/4 × 4 1/4 in. (21 × 10.8 cm). Wadsworth Atheneum Museum of Art. Gift of an anonymous donor, 1936.65

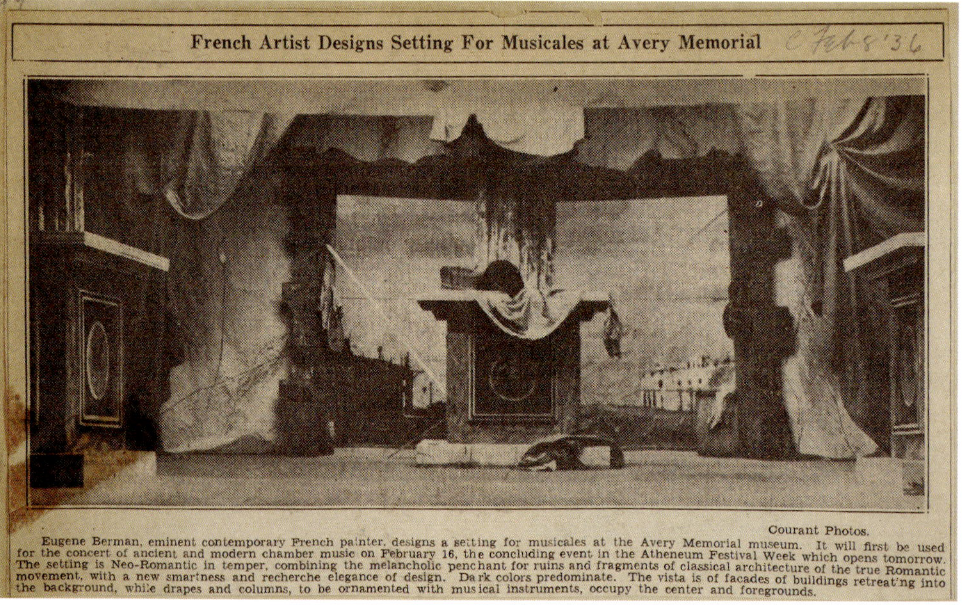

French Artist Designs Setting For Musicales at Avery Memorial

Courant Photos.

Eugene Berman, eminent contemporary French painter, designs a setting for musicales at the Avery Memorial museum. It will first be used for the concert of ancient and modern chamber music on February 16, the concluding event in the Atheneum Festival Week which opens tomorrow. The setting is Neo-Romantic in temper, combining the melancholic penchant for ruins and fragments of classical architecture of the true Romantic movement, with a new smartness and recherche elegance of design. Dark colors predominate. The vista is of facades of buildings retreating into the background, while drapes and columns, to be ornamented with musical instruments, occupy the center and foregrounds.

Fig. 2. "French Artist Designs Sets for Musicales at Avery Memorial." *Hartford Courant*, 8 February 1936. Archives, Wadsworth Atheneum Museum of Art

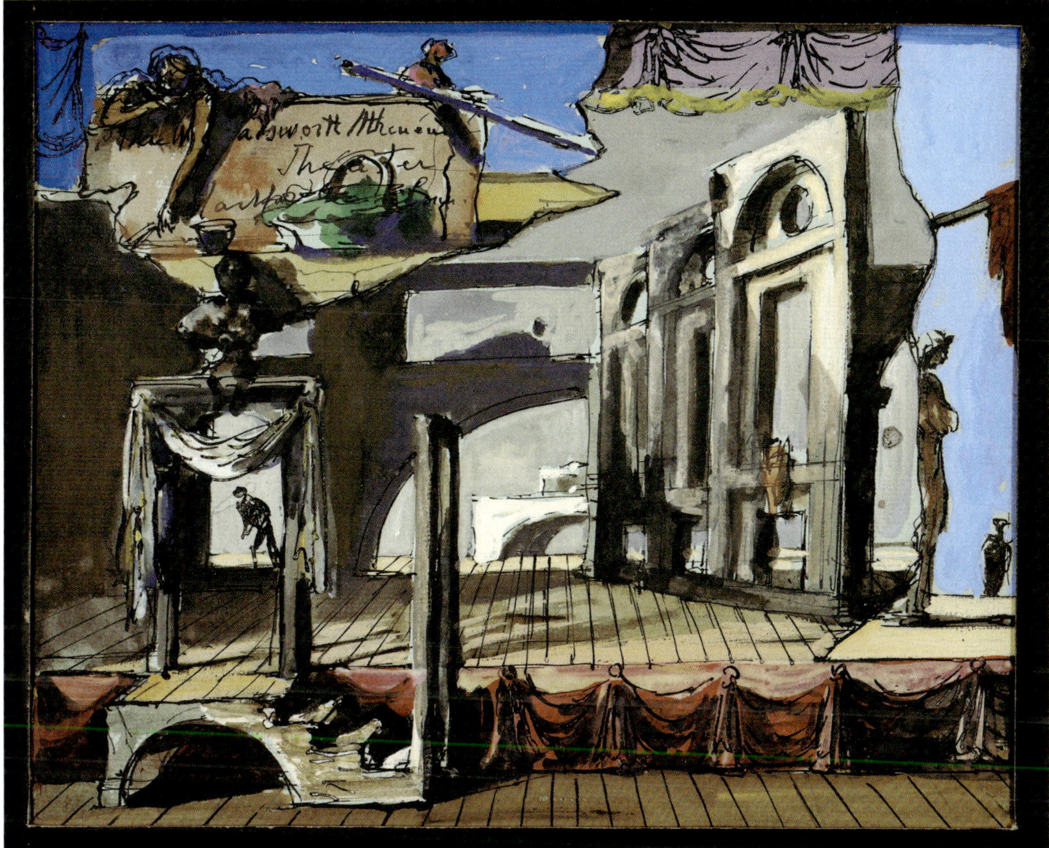

Cat. 58a

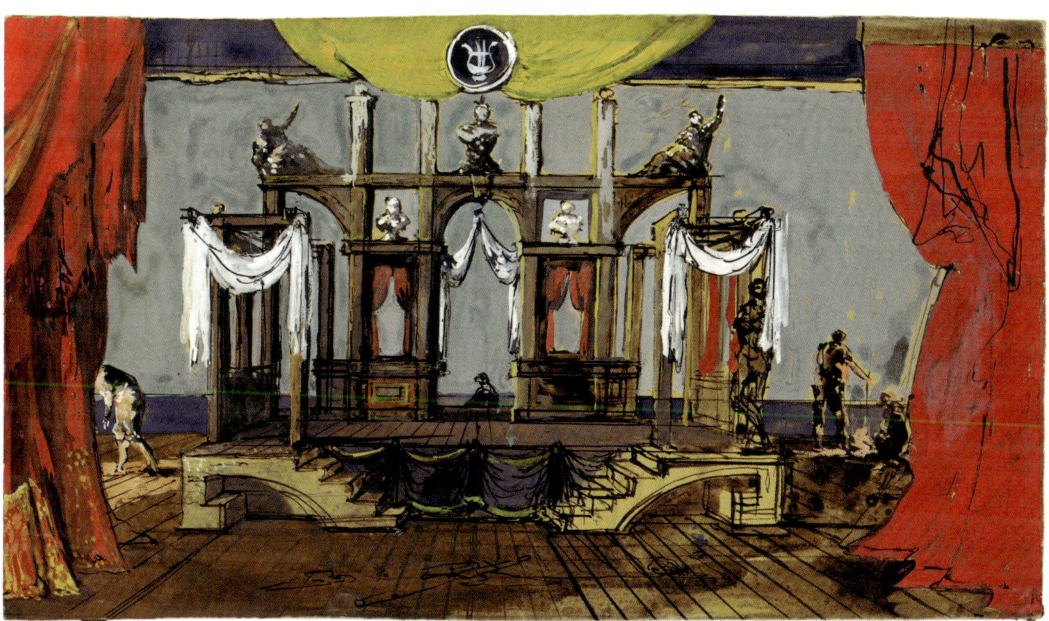

Cat. 58b

After the Hartford Festival, several of Berman's stage set sketches were exhibited at his solo exhibition at Julien Levy's New York gallery, where they elicited restrained praise from *New Yorker* critic Lewis Mumford: "Perhaps the most interesting examples in the present show are the water-color drawings for stage designs; these often have a fine architectural sense, and they are far less subdued than the oils."[7] Mumford, once relatively enthusiastic about the Neo-Romantics, had recently lost interest; his reaction may also reflect the difficulty of exhibiting set designs as independent works of art. On the other hand, in Avery Theater, the combination of the rich, opulent, mysterious sets; the exotic music (some of it played on period instruments); and the excitement of being present at such a rarefied event must have been dazzling. As *New York Sun* critic Henry McBride said of the Matinée Musicale, it "was so beautiful that all agreed it was perfection."[8]
CT

1. For a full and lively discussion of the Hartford Festival, see Eugene Gaddis, *Magician of the Modern: Chick Austin and the Transformation of the Arts in America* (New York: Alfred A. Knopf, 2000), 289–310.
2. Julien Levy suggested that the murals Berman had painted for his New York apartment and for the Farmington, Connecticut, home of James Thrall Soby prepared Berman for the leap in scale required by stage designs. Julien Levy, "Eugene Berman," in *Eugene Berman* (New York: American Studio Books, 1947), ix.
3. Virgil Thomson, *Virgil Thomson* (New York: E. P. Dutton, 1966), 255.
4. In a cavalier disregard for historic American art, Berman defaced the busts with paint and smashed their noses. As he described it: "I improvised a last-minute decoration for the lobby of the Auditorium in which all the spectacles and concerts took place, a decoration with contrasting vivid draperies and fake marbleized busts on pedestals for which I used whatever plaster heads of American statesmen I could lay my hands on in the cellars of the museum. By smashing in a few noses and by freely dousing them with running colors to achieve astonishing effects of real marble and painting in some cracks and characteristic features, I was able to transform them into Roman Emperors, Matrons or Baroque heroes." Eugene Berman, "Legendary Chick," in *A. Everett Austin, Jr.: A Director's Taste and Achievement* (Hartford, Conn.: Wadsworth Atheneum, 1958), 49.
5. Gaddis, *Magician of the Modern*, 300, 305.
6. "French Artist Designs Setting for Musicales at Avery Memorial," *Hartford Courant*, 8 February 1936, Wadsworth Atheneum Archives.
7. Lewis Mumford, "Drawings and Illustrations–Pictures for the Public," *New Yorker* 12 (16 May 1936), in *Mumford on Modern Art in the 1930s*, ed. Robert Wojtowicz (Berkeley and Los Angeles: University of California Press, 2007), 198.
8. Henry McBride, *New York Sun*, 22 February 1936, 26.

59

Eugene Berman
Costume for Hat Vendor from the prelude to *Devil's Holiday*, Ballet Russe de Monte Carlo, 1939
Opaque and transparent watercolor with pen and black ink over traces of pencil on laid paper
12 1/2 × 9 3/4 in. (31.8 × 24.8 cm)
Inscribed upper left:
Prologue. / Vendeur de Chapeaux
Signed and dated at center left: E B 1939
Ex coll.: James Thrall Soby, New York
Gift of Mr. and Mrs. James Thrall Soby, 1939.697

"Berman . . . has given us five more [back-drops] . . . which are as brilliant as any Baroque Burnacini, but full of a contemporary intimate and personal sentiment . . . and his costumes are the most wonderful imaginable . . . like a fashion show in heaven."[1] So wrote dance critic Edwin Denby in his review of the Ballet Russe de Monte Carlo's comic ballet *Devil's Holiday (Le Diable s'amuse)*, with choreography by the young Frederick Ashton and music by Vincenzo Tommasini based on themes of Paganini. *Devil's Holiday* was intended for the fall 1939 season in London; however, the outbreak of the war necessitated moving the premiere to New York, where the ballet was performed at the Metropolitan Opera on October 26 of that year. It was Berman's first set design for an American production since the Hartford Festival three years earlier, and it allowed him to indulge both in his fondness for Italy—the opera is set in Venice during Carnival—and his penchant for the surreal and phantasmagoric—the story centers on a puckish devil who meddles in human affairs.

The hat seller is one of a number of picturesque characters participating in the pageantry of Carnival, in which costumes and disguises are required for all; he appears in the ballet's prologue. He carries a dozen hats, which are decorated with plumes and feathers, or sport outlandishly large brims; they are rendered in opaque watercolor in lush hues of lavender, magenta, and green to underscore their playful aspect. The figure himself, arms held gracefully aloft to hold the hats and feet in third position, seems poised for movement, as though the ballet were about to begin.
CT

1. Edwin Denby, "Ashton's 'Devil's Holiday,'" *Modern Music* 17 (October 1939): 56.

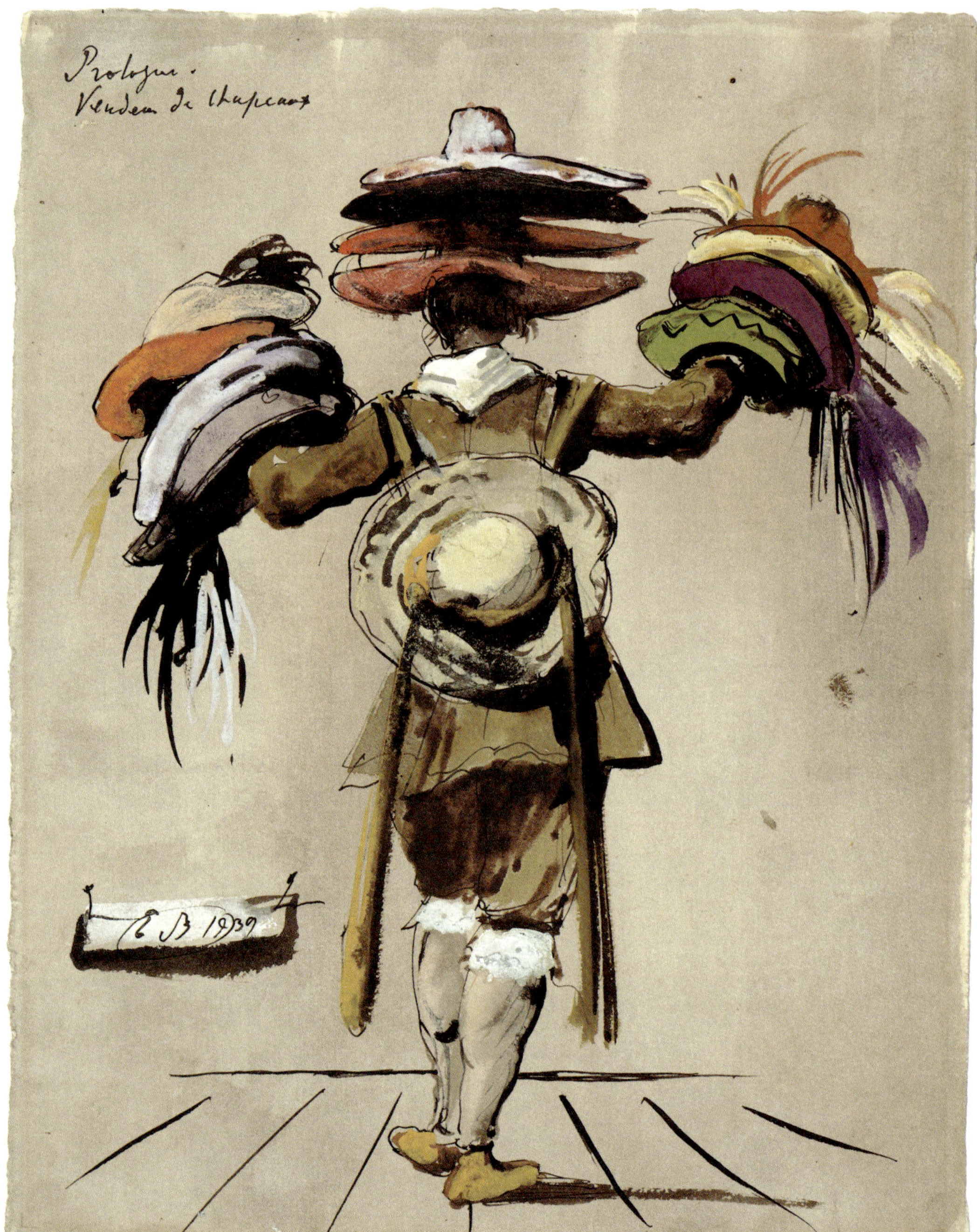

Cat. 59

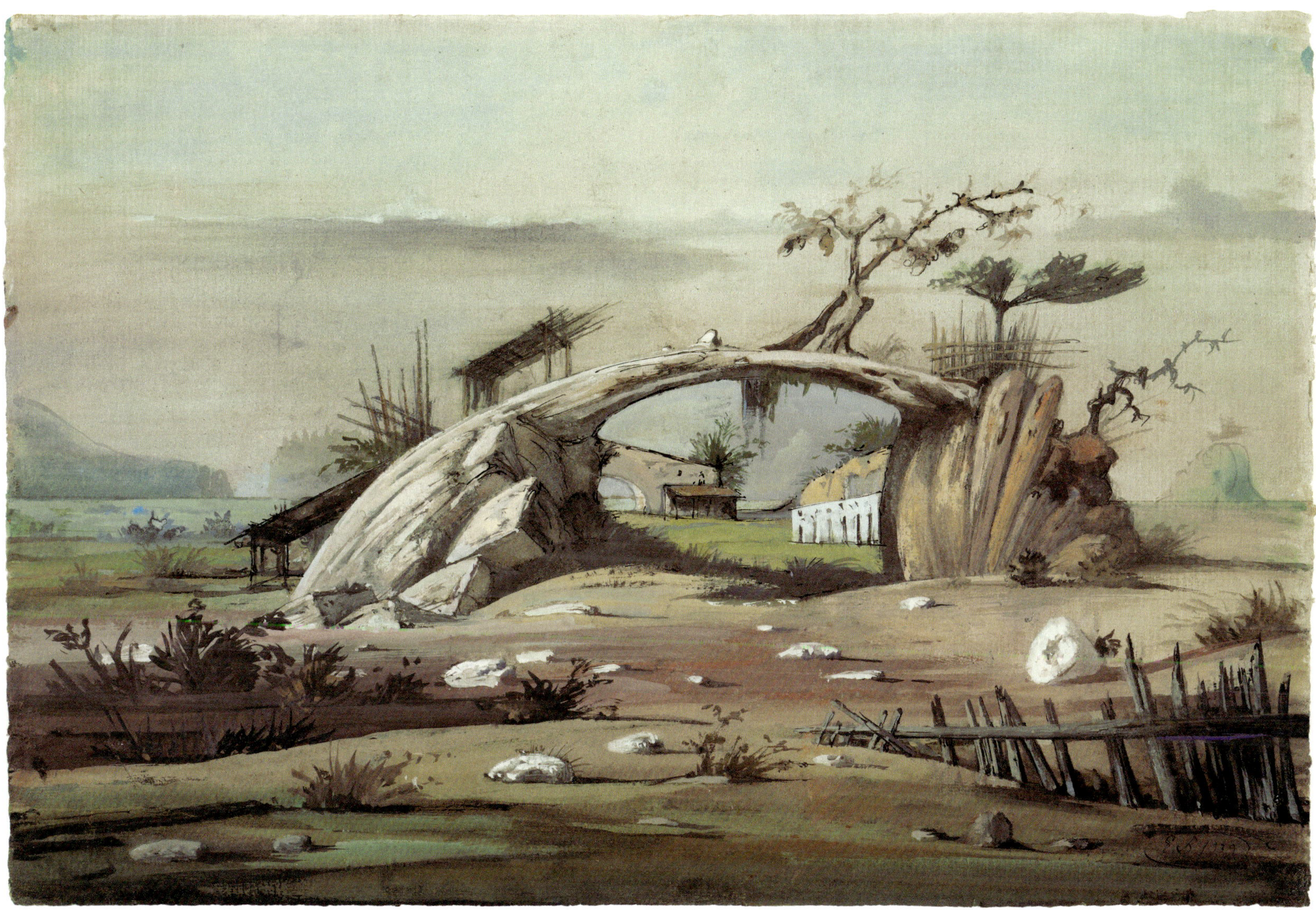

Cat. 60

60

Eugene Berman
"Natural Bridge," sketch for *Devil's Holiday*, 1939
Opaque and transparent watercolor with pen and black ink over traces of pencil on gray laid paper
13 × 19 in. (33 × 48.3 cm)
Signed and dated lower right: E. B. 1939
Ex coll.: with Julien Levy Gallery, New York, 1941
The Ella Gallup Sumner and Mary Catlin Sumner Collection Fund, 1941.388

Devil's Holiday describes the actions of the devil, who–just to amuse himself–causes the daughter of an impoverished Venetian nobleman to abandon her wealthy fiancé on the eve of their wedding for the love of a young beggar disguised as a prince.[1] This ballet required a variety of sets, and so Berman created a nobleman's palace, a ballroom scene garishly lit to complement the devil's machinations, and an eerily empty piazza that is lined with outsize arcades on top of which living statues posture and turn and swirl long turquoise banners. In addition to architectural settings, the story called for landscapes. Berman envisioned the third scene as taking place in a rock-strewn field with a natural bridge in the center[2]–an evocative backdrop for the wanderings of the lonely beggar-prince, seeking his love.

Despite the comic nature of *Devil's Holiday*, distinguished critic John Bowlt called Berman's sets for the ballet "one of his most disturbing designs," and noted that the vision of "unending wastelands" introduced there recurs in the artist's later sets.[3] Berman reprised the natural bridge motif almost immediately, in a 1940 backdrop for the ballet *Giselle*, where the writhing natural forms echo the turbulence of the ballet's action.[4] Here, the color–the watercolor is softly painted in silvery tones of grayish green and lavender–mitigates somewhat the desolation of the landscape, and creates a wistful, dreamlike setting.
CT

1. Horst Koegler, *Concise Oxford Dictionary of Ballet*, 2nd ed. (London: Oxford University Press, 1982), 124.
2. Allison Delarue, "The Stage and Ballet Designs of Eugene Berman," *Dance Index* 5 (January 1946): 10–11.
3. John E. Bowlt, "Eugene Berman," in *International Encyclopedia of Dance*, ed. Selma Jeanne Cohen (New York: Oxford University Press, 2004), 1:437.
4. See Berman's sketches for *Giselle* reproduced in *The Theater of Eugene Berman*, by George Amberg (New York: Museum of Modern Art, 1947), 25.

Kristians Tonny

Born in Amsterdam, 1907;
died in Amsterdam, 1977

Kristians Tonny, son of the Dutch artist A. Kristians, moved with his parents to Paris in 1913. Tonny studied art with his father in his Paris studio and developed an interest in cinema at an early age. He had his first exhibition in the gallery Mouninou, Paris, in 1920 when he was only thirteen years old. By the 1920s Tonny was part of the Paris circle of artists promoted (if only briefly) by American poet, writer, and collector Gertrude Stein. Stein purchased several works by Tonny; he also painted her portrait (cat. 61). He exhibited his works with four other artists who were working in Paris at this time and who came to be called the Neo-Romantics: the French artist Christian Bérard, Pavel Tchelitchew (q.v.), and the brothers Eugene Berman (q.v.) and Leonid [Berman]. Tonny married Marie Claire Ivanoff and traveled to the United States in 1937, also making trips to Mexico and Guatemala.

In 1931 Tonny exhibited with the Neo-Romantics in a show referred to as *Five Young Painters* that was organized by A. Everett "Chick" Austin Jr., director of the Wadsworth Atheneum (see Carol Troyen, "Modernism and Antimodernism," in this volume). Austin supported this group of artists, acquiring a number of works by Tonny and his colleagues. In 1937, he commissioned Tonny to produce murals for the new Avery Theater (see cats. 62a and b). The artist spent the early 1940s in southern France, and took up residence in Paris by 1944. By 1949, he returned to the Netherlands, settling in Amsterdam, where he died in 1977.

Select Bibliography

A. Everett Austin Jr. *Tonny Tchelitchew Berard Berman Leonide.* Hartford, Conn.: Wadsworth Atheneum, 1931.

Frida de Jong and Laurens Vancrevel. *Kristians Tonny.* Amsterdam: Meulenhoff Nederland, 1979.

61

Kristians Tonny
After van Eyck [Gertrude Stein], c. 1930–36
Black ink over tempera on primed Masonite adhered to cardboard
24 × 17 7/8 in. (61 × 45.4 cm)
Inscription on verso:
No. 3 Homage a Van Eyck
Ex coll.: with Julien Levy Gallery, New York, 1937
The Ella Gallup Sumner and Mary Catlin Sumner Collection Fund, 1937.38

Kristians Tonny first visited Gertrude Stein in her celebrated house at 27, rue de Fleurus in 1927, when he was twenty years old. He had had an exhibition in Paris, which Stein had seen, and was one of a group of painters known as the Neo-Romantics, who had recently captured her attention: "The group then consisted of the Russian [Tchelitchew], a Frenchman [Bérard], a very young dutchman [Tonny] and two Russian brothers [the Bermans]. All of them except the dutchman about twenty-six years old."[1]

For about four years, Tonny was a member of Stein's inner circle. They collaborated on projects for which Stein and Georges Hugnet, a young French poet and another of Stein's favorites at the time, wrote the text and Tonny and others provided illustrations. She bought one of his paintings (*Bateau d'ivre*, 1927; location unknown) and arranged for her friends Carl Van Vechten and Paul Bowles to take some of his drawings to the United States to sell; the Cone sisters of Baltimore were among the buyers. Some time before the summer of 1930, Tonny produced a pen and ink portrait of Stein with her dog Basket.[2] Then—as happened to so many of Stein's favorites—there was a falling-out.[3] His painting was exiled to her "salon des refuses," and there was no more talk about helping Tonny sell drawings. This image of her, which she may never have seen, came to New York for Tonny's first American solo exhibition, held at Julien Levy's gallery in February 1937. The Wadsworth Atheneum bought the portrait from that show for $200.

Exhibited with the title "After van Eyck," the work attracted attention and inventive commentary. The critic for *Parnassus* named it "the best of the paintings" in the show and described it as a "cardinal-like figure seated before a tall Gothic campanile (. . . a steal from a van der Weyden)."[4] In fact, it was a Jan van Eyck, the exquisite *St. Barbara*, that Tonny appropriated for this picture (fig. 1).

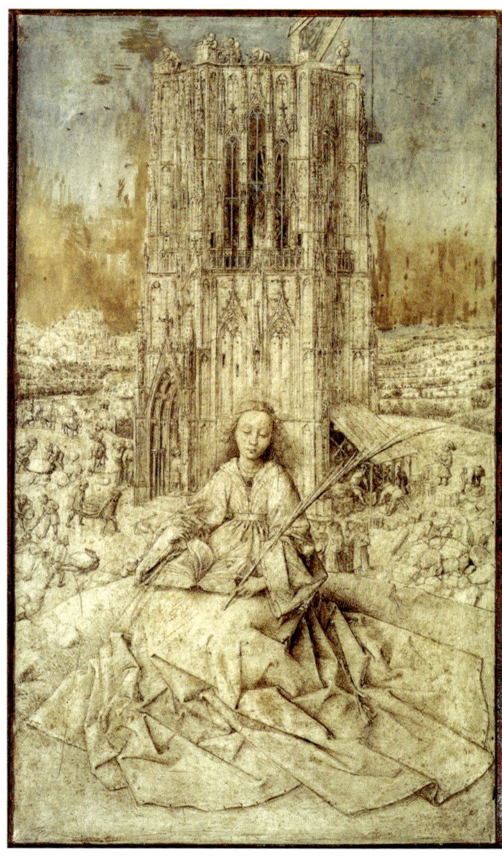

Fig. 1. Jan van Eyck, *St. Barbara*, 1437. Brush and chalk on paper, 12 11/16 × 7 1/3 in. (32.2 × 18.5 cm). Koninklijk Museum voor Schone Kunsten, Antwerp

Although Tonny's picture is about twice the size of van Eyck's, and wider in proportion, he carried over the principal features of his model: a woman seated before a Gothic tower, with incidental figures behind. Tonny's landscape, with warm yellow light suffusing the middle distance, is essentially *en grisaille*, in imitation of the Netherlandish master. (Van Eyck's painting is an outline drawing made with a pointed brush on a chalk ground, with the only color being a brownish gray pigment used for shading and modeling.) However, van Eyck's panel is both a devotional image (the tower is Saint Barbara's symbol) and a representation of everyday life (all the incidental figures are workmen—carpenters, masons—who labor busily on the cathedral[5]). Tonny's image, on the other hand, is pure fantasy. It is dominated by a "gutted gothic building . . . seemingly made out of witch's materials, broomsticks and livers, dried herbs and dead birds."[6] There are a number of gargoyles spaced at regular intervals along the tower, as well as spikes, orbs, and, near the top, a six-pointed yellow star.

The auxiliary figures have no clear identity, though they are far from the busy little workers who populate van Eyck's scene. Confined to a band of space in the middle distance, with a flat Netherlandish landscape stretching to a low horizon behind them, they are quite generalized. The figures at left could be pilgrims of some sort; in any case, they seem to be moving in a rhythmic line toward the tower. The figures at right are more troubling. They gather around a reclining or fallen figure; the raised staff held by one makes them seem like tormentors. Yet the figures at far right (one of which is so summarily painted as to seem transparent) look like a pair of docile peasant women derived from Jean-François Millet.

Gertrude Stein is rendered with somewhat greater precision, but with no clearer meaning. Much smaller and more self-contained than her saintly predecessor, she does not wear her habitual brown corduroy suit and sandals[7] but a long dress in a startling saffron color. Her facial features are summarily rendered, and are made more indistinct by the shadow cast by her broad-brimmed straw hat. We know her chiefly by her bulk: she sits, foursquare, arms folded at her waist, knees apart with drapery clinging to them, like some archaic Madonna. Other portraits of Stein—by Lipschitz, Man Ray, and especially Picasso—captured with some affection her imposing presence, her fierce intellect, and her dramatic mass. Tonny presents her as a stern creature from a disconcerting fairy tale or (in the words of the critic for *Parnassus*), a "fairly polite nightmare."[8]
CT

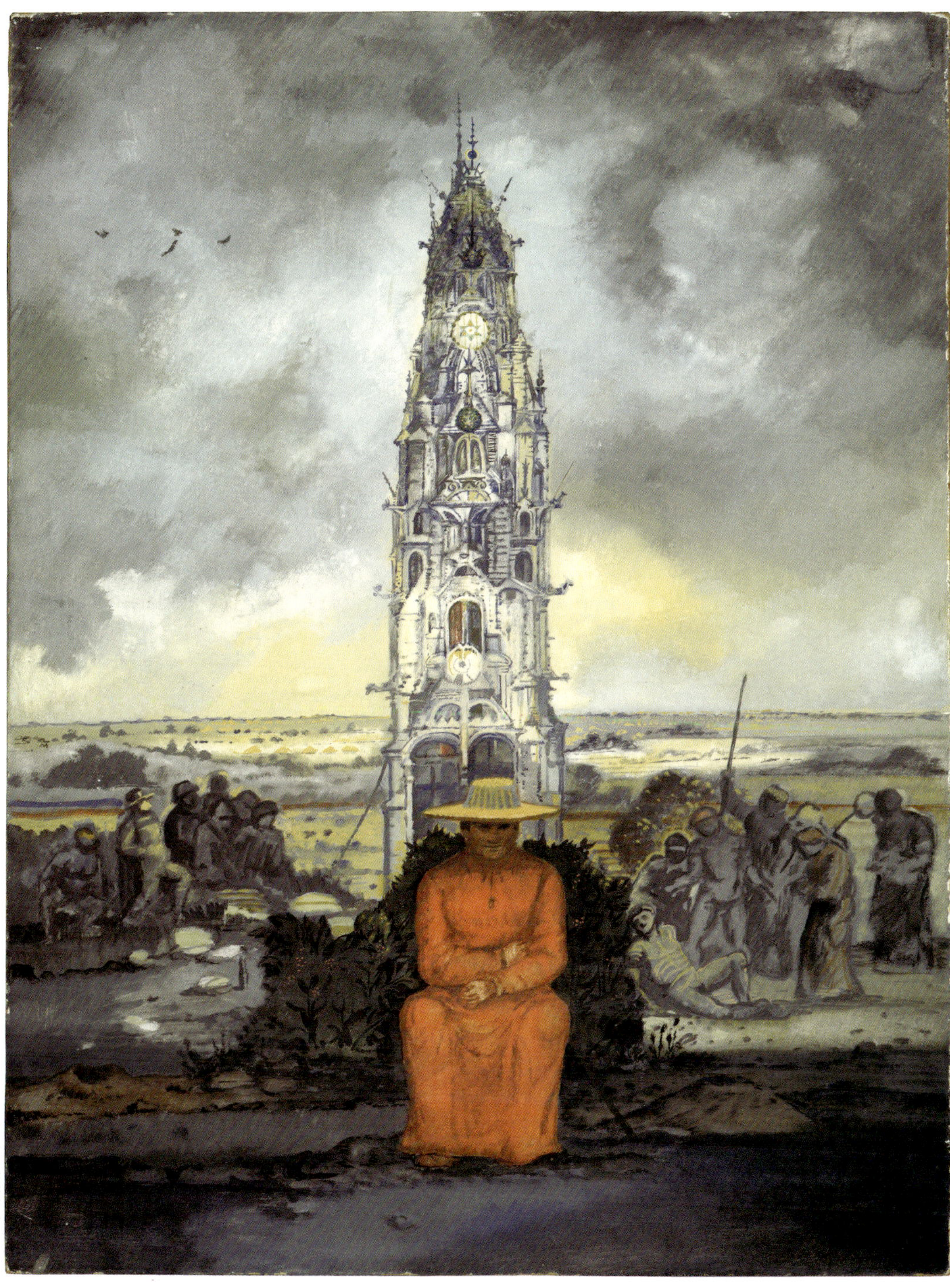

Cat. 61

1. Gertrude Stein, *The Autobiography of Alice B. Toklas* (1933; New York: Vintage Books, 1990), 226. For Stein, there was something talismanic about the age of these young artists: "I remember very well the impression I had of Hemingway that first afternoon. He was an extraordinarily good-looking young man, twenty-three years old. It was not long after that that everybody was twenty-six. It became the period of being twenty-six. During the next two or three years all the young men were twenty-six years old. It was the right age apparently for that time and place. There were one or two under twenty . . . but they did not count as Gertrude Stein carefully explained to them. If they were young men they were twenty-six." Ibid., 212.
2. Paul Bowles, *Without Stopping: An Autobiography* (New York: G. P. Putnam's Sons, 1972), 197; Stein to Van Vechten, Bilignin par Belley, 15 October 1930: "as to my portrait you bet your life I posed and so did Basket," in *The Letters of Gertrude Stein and Carl Van Vechten 1913–1946*, ed. Edward Burns, 2 vols. (New York: Columbia University Press, 1986), 1:229.
3. Gertrude Stein to Carl Van Vechten, Paris, 17 January 1932: "we have quarreled beginning with Bravig Imbs going on through Tonny and Georges Hugnet and ending with Virgil Thomson and now we don't see any of them any more," in Burns, *Letters of Stein and Van Vechten*, 233. See also Paul Bowles to Aaron Copland, Paris, 28 November 1931: "Gertrude is fachée [angry] because I stayed with Tonny, whom she detests at the moment. I daresay he doesn't know it," in *In Touch: The Letters of Paul Bowles*, ed. Jeffrey Miller (New York: Farrar, Straus & Giroux, 1994), 92.
4. "H.W.," "Notes," *Parnassus* 9 (March 1937): 39.
5. Saint Barbara's tower is said to have been modeled on an actual structure, possibly Cologne Cathedral, which is not far from van Eyck's native Bruges and was under construction in the 1430s when he was working on this painting. Elisabeth Dhanens, *Hubert and Jan van Eyck* (New York: Alpine Fine Arts, 1980), 264.
6. H. W., "Notes," 39.
7. Stein, *Toklas*, 116.
8. H. W., "Notes," 39.

62 a and b
Kristians Tonny
Sketch for a Mural in Avery Auditorium (Left Wall with White City), 1937
Opaque and transparent watercolor on wove paper
21 3/4 × 37 1/4 in. (55.3 × 94.6 cm)
Ex coll.: the artist
Museum purchase, 1938.24A

Sketch for a Mural in Avery Auditorium (Right Wall with Volcano), 1937
Opaque and transparent watercolor on wove paper
21 3/4 × 32 in. (55.3 × 94.6 cm)
Ex coll.: the artist
Museum purchase, 1938.23A

In the spring of 1937 Atheneum director Chick Austin approached the young Dutch painter Kristians Tonny about painting murals to decorate the walls of the newly built Avery Theater at the Wadsworth Atheneum. Tonny was not known as a muralist; in fact, his most highly regarded works were his drawings, small, delicate sketches in pencil or pen and ink. However, Austin was enthusiastic about Tonny's Neo-Romantic style – images that were wistful, dreamy, melancholic, and painted in a traditional manner. Austin also had a penchant for facilitating the unexpected. And Tonny was happy to take on this unconventional assignment, which would raise his profile in the United States.

The correspondence between Tonny and Austin finalizing the arrangement for the murals consists largely of Tonny requesting an advance on his fee ($1,500 plus the cost of materials) and Austin pleading for some sketches with which he could persuade the Atheneum trustees to approve the commission. There is no discussion of what the murals should look like: neither Tonny's conception for the images, nor Austin's wishes for the design, are mentioned.[1] In fact, Austin's only requirement was that they not have too specific a subject, so they could complement the many and varied productions he envisioned taking place on the Avery stage. Tonny finally produced four sketches in gouache (these two, for the left and right walls of the front half of the auditorium, and two others for the rear portions of those walls [see fig. 1]), which the trustees approved. The artist completed the murals in time for the January 6, 1938, performance of the Ballet Caravan, a troupe directed by Lincoln Kirstein. Both murals and ballet were cheered by the press.[2]

Tonny met Austin's requirements for the content of the auditorium decorations. In an era when most murals designed for civic buildings in the United States were either geometric abstractions or, more often, patriotic reenactments of episodes in America's past done in a realistic, illustrative manner, Tonny's murals have no clear subject, no narrative content. The sketches, and the murals based on them, are populated by galloping horses and their spear-wielding nude riders pursuing wild cattle. High above the hunt, in one of the sketches for the mural at the left, is a fantastic medieval town, the skeletal spires of its buildings piercing a bank of clouds. In the sketch for the wall opposite, a group of monkeys sets fire to a cart loaded with hay.[3]

These bizarre images, rendered in gray and white, with yellow and orange providing bright accents against an atmospheric gray ground, are both violent and whimsical. Their tiny figures scattered almost randomly across an amorphous space bring to mind prehistoric cave paintings. At the same time the murals evoke the most sophisticated rococo decorations, for they are filled with exotic creatures arranged, in the artist's words, in "a series of rhythmic arabesques, without a formal composition."[4] And in their capricious, sensational, and dreamlike content they are linked to contemporary Surrealism, of which Austin was an early champion. As Tonny explained, "I think the best kind of composition comes without consciousness."[5]
CT

1. A. Everett Austin Papers, Wadsworth Atheneum Archives.
2. Three ballets were performed by Ballet Caravan on the evenings of 6 and 7 January 1938: *Filling Station*, in its world premiere, with music by Virgil Thomson, choreography by Lew Christensen, and costumes by Paul Cadmus; Eugene Loring's *Yankee Clipper*; and Erick Hawkins's *Show Piece*. For a discussion of these ballets and their reception in the press, see Eric M. Zafran, Eugene R. Gaddis, and Susan Hood, *Ballets Russes to Balanchine: Dance at the Wadsworth Atheneum* (Hartford, Conn.: Wadsworth Atheneum Museum of Art, 2004), 35–37; and Eugene R. Gaddis, *Magician of the Modern: Chick Austin and the Transformation of the Arts in America* (New York: Alfred A. Knopf, 2000), 323–25. The art critics for both local papers were enthusiastic about Tonny's designs. Marian Murray, writing for the *Hartford Times*, called them "satisfying but unconventional composition[s]" ("Avery Ready to Unveil Kristians Tonny Murals," 6 January 1938); T. H. Parker, in the *Hartford Courant*, praised their "exceptionally fine drawing, . . . lively sense of decoration, . . . rhythmic, lyric approach" ("Veil Drawn on Tonny's Work Here," 7 January 1938, 95). Clippings in Scrapbooks, vol. 18 (1937), Wadsworth Atheneum Archives.
3. Adjacent to the burning hay wagon in the sketch but not in the final mural is a tree with a volcano-shaped trunk whose branches host groups of monkeys and of men.
4. Tonny, quoted in Murray, "Kristians Tonny Murals."
5. Tonny, in ibid.

Fig. 1. *Avery Theater after the installation of the murals by Kristians Tonny*, 1938. Archives, Wadsworth Atheneum Museum of Art

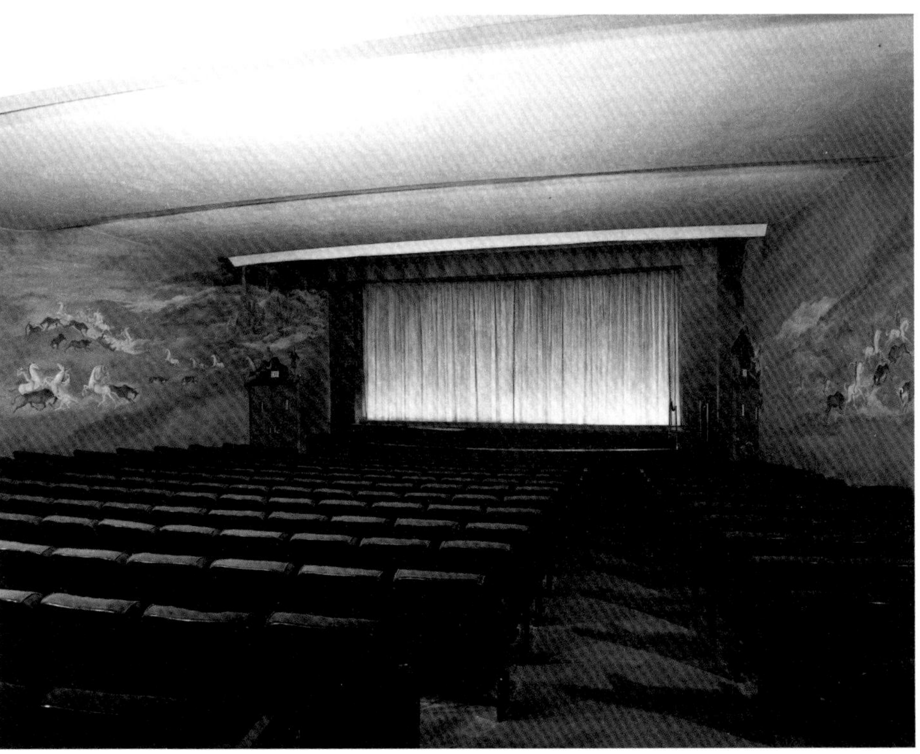

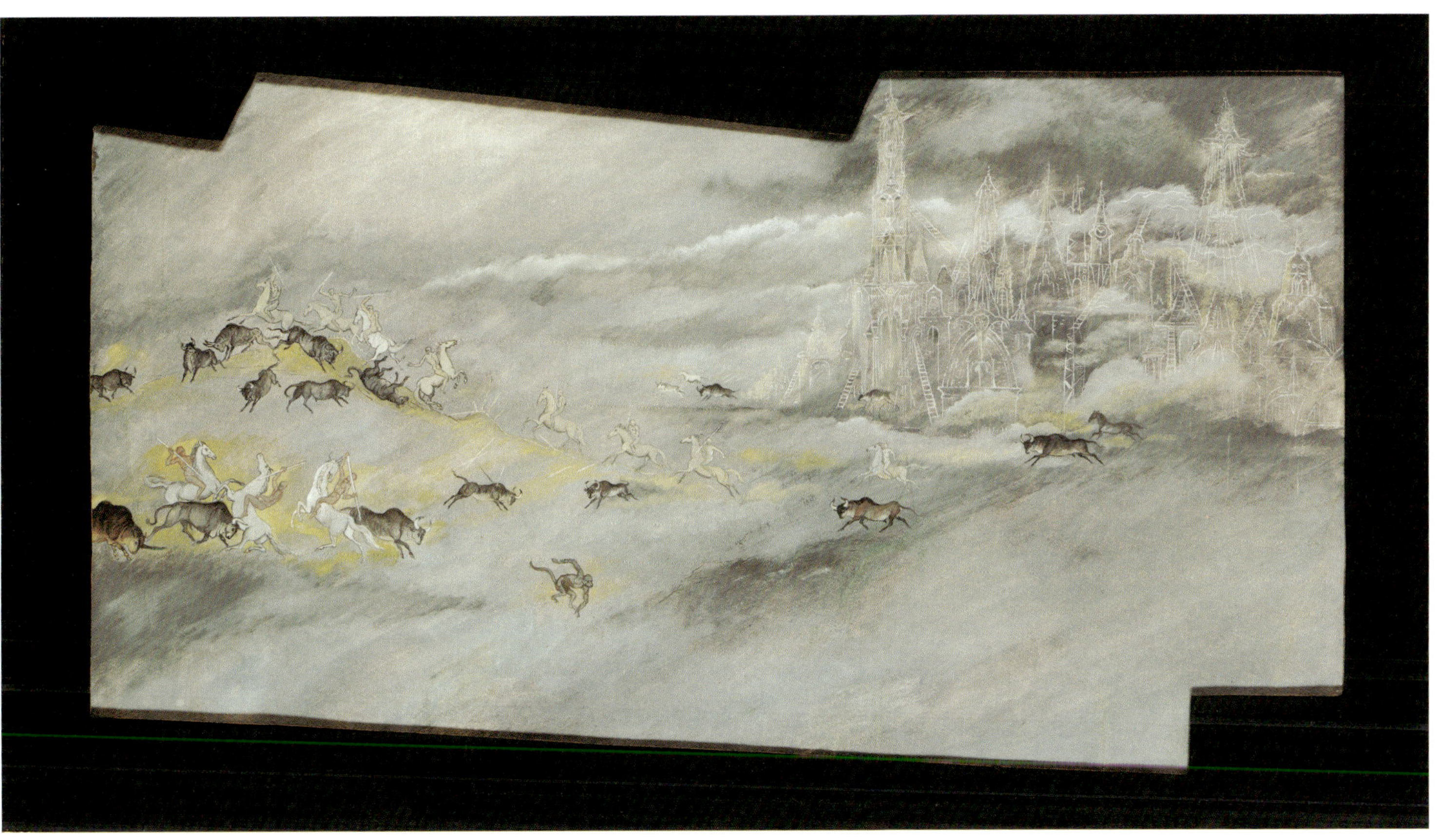
Cat. 62a

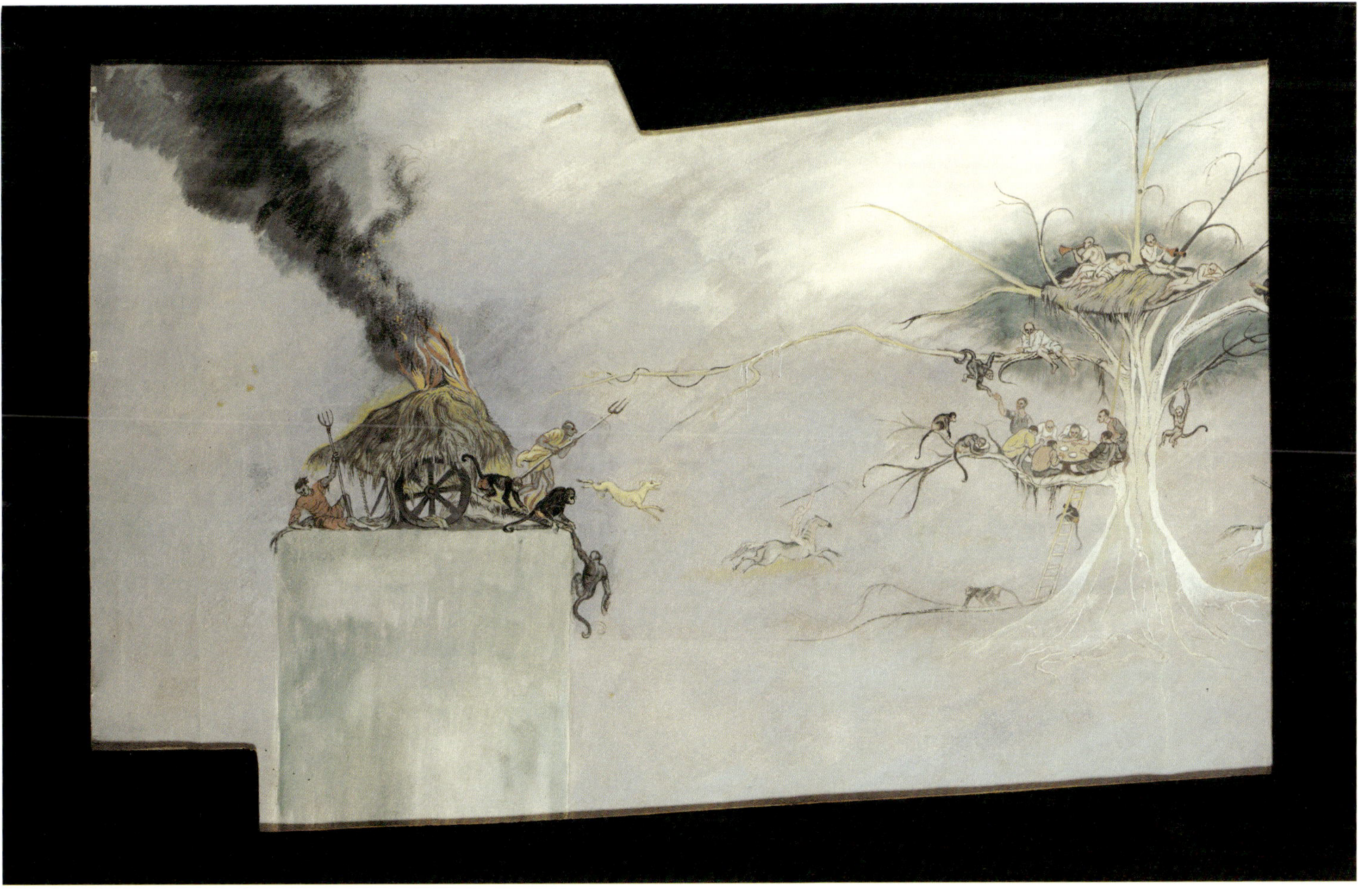
Cat. 62b

Salvador Dalí

Born in Figueras, Spain, 1904;
died in Figueras, Spain, 1989

Salvador Dalí was a leading member of the Surrealist movement and a master of illusion. His childhood was divided between Figueras and nearby Cadaqués, Spain, where his family owned a second house. His first work, dated 1910, depicted a landscape near Figueras. Dalí studied drawing, painting, and sculpture at the San Fernando School of Fine Arts in Madrid in 1921. There he was exposed to European modernist styles including Futurism, Cubism, and Pointillism, which would influence his art. While there, he befriended Luís Buñuel, Eugenio Montes, and Federico García Lorca. Later, Dalí was expelled after being accused of encouraging students to challenge authority.

In the year 1929, on a trip to Paris to work with Buñuel on the film *Un Chien Andalou*, Dalí met Joan Miró, who introduced him to the Parisian Surrealists. He joined the group at this time. On this same trip, Dalí met Paul Éluard, who was a fellow member of the Surrealist group in later years. That summer Éluard and his wife, Gala, visited Dalí in Cadaqués. Gala eventually left her husband for Dalí, and the two were married.

In 1931, Everett A. "Chick" Austin, then director of the Wadsworth Atheneum, arranged for the first exhibition of Surrealist work in America, which was held at the Atheneum. Ten paintings by Dalí were included in the show, *Newer Super-Realism*, along with works by Max Ernst, Giorgio de Chirico, and Pablo Picasso. Dalí's now iconic painting, *Persistence of Memory*, was included in the show and offered to the museum for $350. Another painting, *La Solitude*, was acquired instead, making it the first of Dalí's works to enter a museum's collection.

Dalí and Gala returned to Hartford in 1934 to attend the first public performance by the School of American Ballet. At the event, Austin invited Dalí to lecture at the Wadsworth Atheneum, and Dalí accepted. On December 18, 1934, the artist gave a slide lecture in French at the museum on the subject of his Surrealist works. An exhibition of Dalí's paintings from the early 1930s accompanied the lecture, and from these, the museum acquired two more of the artist's works for its collection: *Paranoiac–Astral Image* (1934) and a figure study (cat. 64). His prominence in Hartford notwithstanding, at this point Dalí had been expelled from the Surrealist group for adopting a more classical style.

Dalí fled France after the German invasion in 1940, taking refuge in the United States. In 1948 he returned to Europe, dividing his time between Paris and Port Lligat, Spain. A retrospective of his work was held at the Museum of Modern Art in 1941. In the 1970s, a museum devoted to his work opened in his native city of Figueras, Spain.

Select Bibliography

James Thrall Soby. *Salvador Dali: Paintings, Drawings, Prints*. New York: Museum of Modern Art, 1941.

Robert Descharmes. *The World of Salvador Dalí*. New York: Harper and Row, 1962.

S. Wilson. *Salvador Dalí*. London: Tate Gallery, 1980.

Dawn Ades. *Dalí's Optical Illusions*. New Haven, Conn.: Yale University Press in association with the Wadsworth Atheneum, 2000.

Dawn Ades and Michael R. Taylor. *Dalí*. Philadelphia: Philadelphia Museum of Art, 2004.

63

Salvador Dalí
Study of the Nurse for Weaning of Furniture–Nutrition, 1934
Graphite and pen and ink on card
5 3/8 × 5 3/4 in. (13.7 × 14.6 cm)
Ex coll.: Eleanor Howland Bunce, Bloomfield, Connecticut
Bequest of Eleanor H. Bunce, 1999.29.20

This drawing is one of several studies related to the painting *Weaning of Furniture–Nutrition* (fig. 1). In one of these studies (1932–33; Salvador Dalí Museum, St. Petersburg, Florida), a small pencil drawing containing motifs used in several different oils, Dalí sketched a preliminary version of the seated figure. Tiny, rudimentary drawings of the nightstand are also scattered across the sheet. Another drawing (1932–33; Salvador Dalí Museum, St. Petersburg, Florida) is a compositional study, and includes the boats along the shore and the terraced hills in the distance. The Atheneum's drawing, of just the nurse and the nightstand, is the smallest of the three. It is not a reduction: the forms are approximately the same size as the forms in the oil. The quick, sure pencil lines are reinforced with ink, suggesting that Dalí may have made the drawing after the fact. The beach has been replaced with some sort of flooring, and the lines defining the edges of the boards suggest an exercise in linear perspective, converging at a point visible through the nightstand-shaped hole in the woman's body. All three drawings show the figure in reverse.

As interpreted by several Dalí scholars, in *Weaning of Furniture–Nutrition* Dalí represents his beloved childhood nurse posed like the women mending fishing nets that he saw on the beach near his home at Port Lligat, Spain. It expresses his "nostalgic desire to return to the maternal body."[1] During the mid-1930s, Dalí, like many Surrealists, was deeply interested in Freudian psychology, and used meticulously rendered dream images to reveal subconscious desires. The principal motifs in *Weaning of Furniture–Nutrition* appear in many of Dalí's paintings of the period: the crutch, often indicating death or impotence but also conveying a sense of solemnity, and the night table (which Dalí as a child associated with his nurse), standing for the female body.[2] The latter association is made literal here: the night table is carved out of the woman's torso, which then requires a crutch for support.

The oil *Weaning of Furniture–Nutrition* was first seen in an exhibition at the Julien Levy Gallery in New York in November 1934. A reduced version of Levy's show—nine oils and two drawings—was then presented at the Wadsworth Atheneum. Presumably because the pictures were so small, they were hung in director Chick Austin's office rather than in

Fig. 1. Salvador Dalí, *The Weaning of Furniture–Nutrition*, 1934. Oil on panel, 7 × 9 1/2 in. (17.8 × 24.1 cm). Salvador Dalí Museum, St. Petersburg, Florida

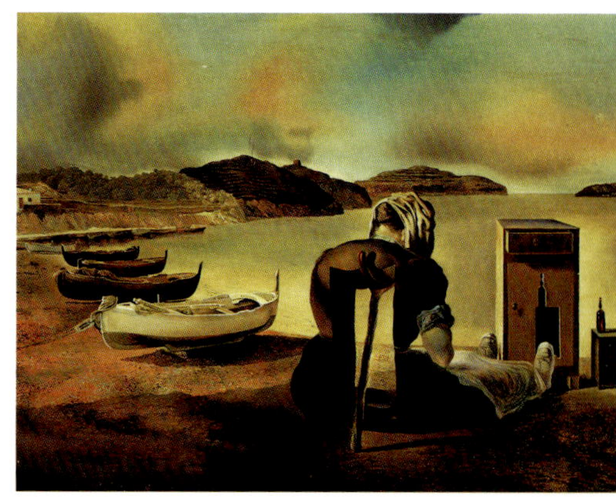

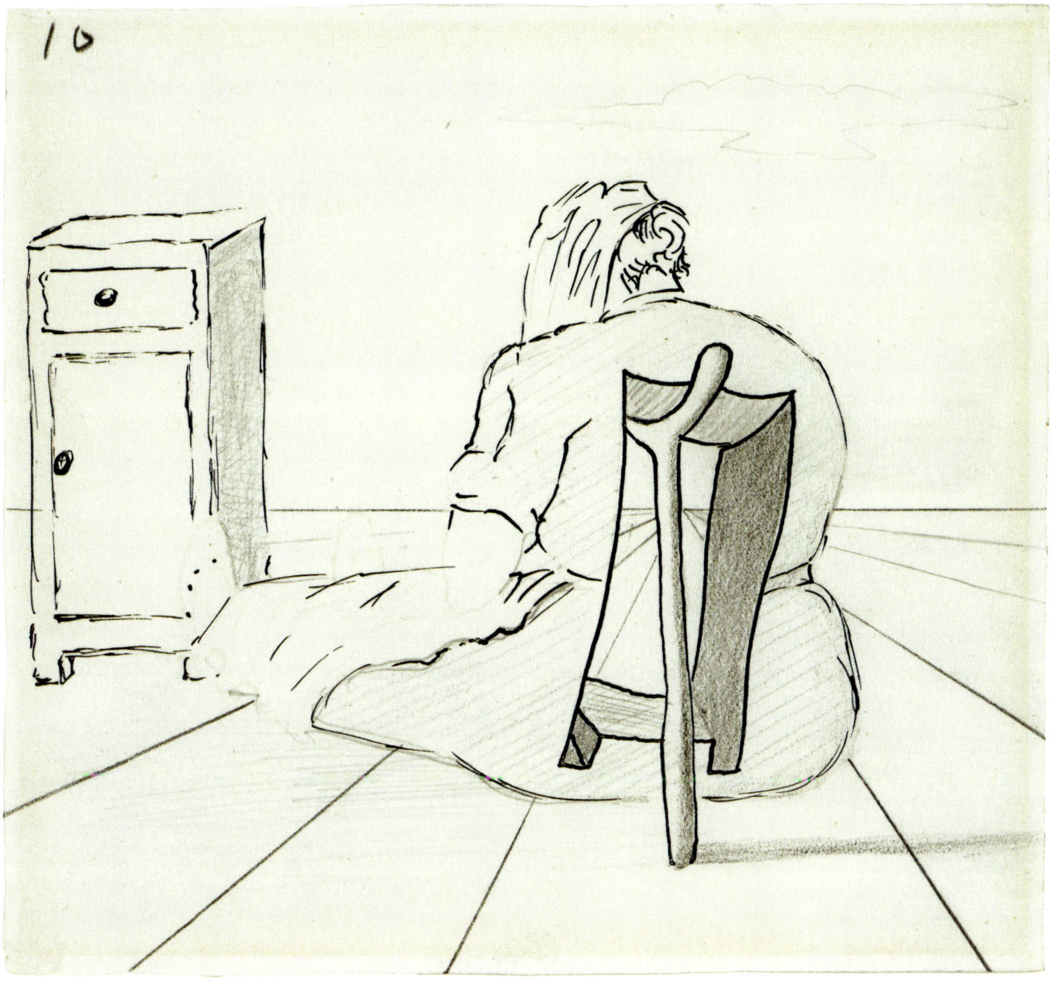

Cat. 63

one of the galleries. This was Dalí's first solo show at an American museum (although his work had been included in three earlier Atheneum shows[3]), and the artist came to Hartford for the opening, at which time he gave a lecture at the museum and attended a screening of his film *Un Chien Andalou.* Dalí had been to Hartford a few weeks earlier to attend a premier performance by the School of American Ballet. At the party afterward, the artist apparently spent quite some time chatting with (and ogling) Austin's assistant, Eleanor Howland, later Eleanor H. Bunce.[4] Afterward he gave (or perhaps sold) her this drawing as a memento of the evening. It was one of a number of works Howland received from artists—among them Eugene Berman (q.v.), Pavel Tchelitchew (q.v.), Yves Tanguy (q.v.), and Alexander Calder (q.v.)—she befriended during their visits to Hartford. Many of these objects were bequeathed to the Atheneum at her death in 1999.
CT

1. Richard S. Lubar, *Dalí: The Salvador Dalí Museum Collection* (Boston: Bulfinch Press, 2000), 97.
2. The crutch appears in *The Specter of Sex Appeal* (1934; Fundació Gala–Salvador Dalí, Figueres, Spain) and *The Ghost of Vermeer of Delft Which Can Be Used as a Table* (1934; Salvador Dalí Museum, St. Petersburg, Florida) among other paintings; the nightstand can be seen in *Cardinal, Cardinal* (1934; Munson-Williams-Proctor Arts Institute, Utica, New York) and *Skull with Its Lyric Appendage Leaning on a Bedside Table Which Should Have the Exact Temperature of a Cardinal's Nest* (1934; Salvador Dalí Museum). The meaning of these forms is discussed in Lubar, *Dalí*, and in Dawn Ades and Michael R. Taylor, *Dalí* (Philadelphia: Philadelphia Museum of Art, 2004), 232.
3. Dalí was well represented in the 1931 exhibition *Newer Super-Realism.* Austin also included his work in *Trends in Twentieth Century Painting* (1932) and *Literature and Poetry in Painting since 1850* (1933). In addition, in 1934 Austin hung two paintings by Dalí that he borrowed from Julien Levy. See Eric M. Zafran, "'I Am Not a Madman': Salvador Dalí in Hartford," in *Dalí's Optical Illusions*, by Dawn Ades (Hartford, Conn.: Wadsworth Atheneum in association with Yale University Press, 2000), 38–49.
4. Zafran, "I Am Not a Madman," 44–46; and Eugene Gaddis, *Magician of the Modern: Chick Austin and the Transformation of the Arts in America* (New York: Alfred A. Knopf, 2000), 26.

64

Salvador Dalí
Figure Studies, 1934
Graphite on wove paper
10 3/4 × 7 in. (27.3 × 17.8 cm)
Signed and dated at lower right:
Salvador Dalí 1934
Ex coll.: with Julien Levy Gallery, New York, 1934
The Ella Gallup Sumner and Mary Catlin Sumner Collection Fund, 1935.11

This delicate pencil drawing shows the right arm, chest, and back of a man seen in profile, a shoulder-to-knee view of a frontal female nude, and a young boy, shown nude and from the back. Only the boy has a head. This sheet of figure studies may have been among the drawings included in Dalí's November 1934 exhibition at Julien Levy's gallery in New York. The presentation at Levy's was the artist's second solo show in the United States; after it closed, the core of the exhibition was sent to the Wadsworth Atheneum, where it was on view for three weeks over the Christmas holidays. The Atheneum then acquired two of the works: *Paranoiac–Astral Image* (1934; oil on panel) for $620, and this drawing for $100.[1]

Such a traditional life drawing seems anomalous in the oeuvre of an artist known for populating his paintings with disturbingly deformed figures and body parts. In fact, although Dalí did not create this sketch in anticipation of a painting, a number of his preparatory studies are similarly precise—as though such faithful studies from the nude model enabled him to render anatomical distortions with greater conviction.[2] Dalí made at least one other drawing in this manner in the mid-1930s (fig. 1).

This sheet illustrates Dalí's continued dedication to traditional craftsmanship. It is also—especially in contrast to the anguished, absurd imagery and frantic accumulation of detail of the paintings of this period—remarkably calm. The contours of the figures are assured and elegant; the shading is pale and velvety. Yet Dalí's demographic (a man, a woman, and a young boy, each shown in a different view and each drawn from a model), the disparity in scale among the figures, and the combination of the fully modeled and the two-dimensional, the sculptural and the ephemeral, give the drawing a vaguely unsettling quality.
CT

1. *Paintings by Salvador Dalí* was presented at the Julien Levy Gallery November 21–December 10, 1934. The exhibition at the Wadsworth Atheneum was installed in the director's office December 18, 1934–January 7, 1935. See Eric M. Zafran, "'I Am Not a Madman': Salvador Dalí in Hartford," in *Dalí's Optical Illusions*, by Dawn Ades (Hartford, Conn.: Wadsworth Atheneum in association with Yale University Press, 2000), 48–50.

2. See, for example, *The City of Drawers*, pencil on paper (1936; Art Institute of Chicago), a study for *The Anthropological Cabinet*, oil on panel (1936; Kunstsammlung Nordrhein-Westfalen, Düsseldorf).

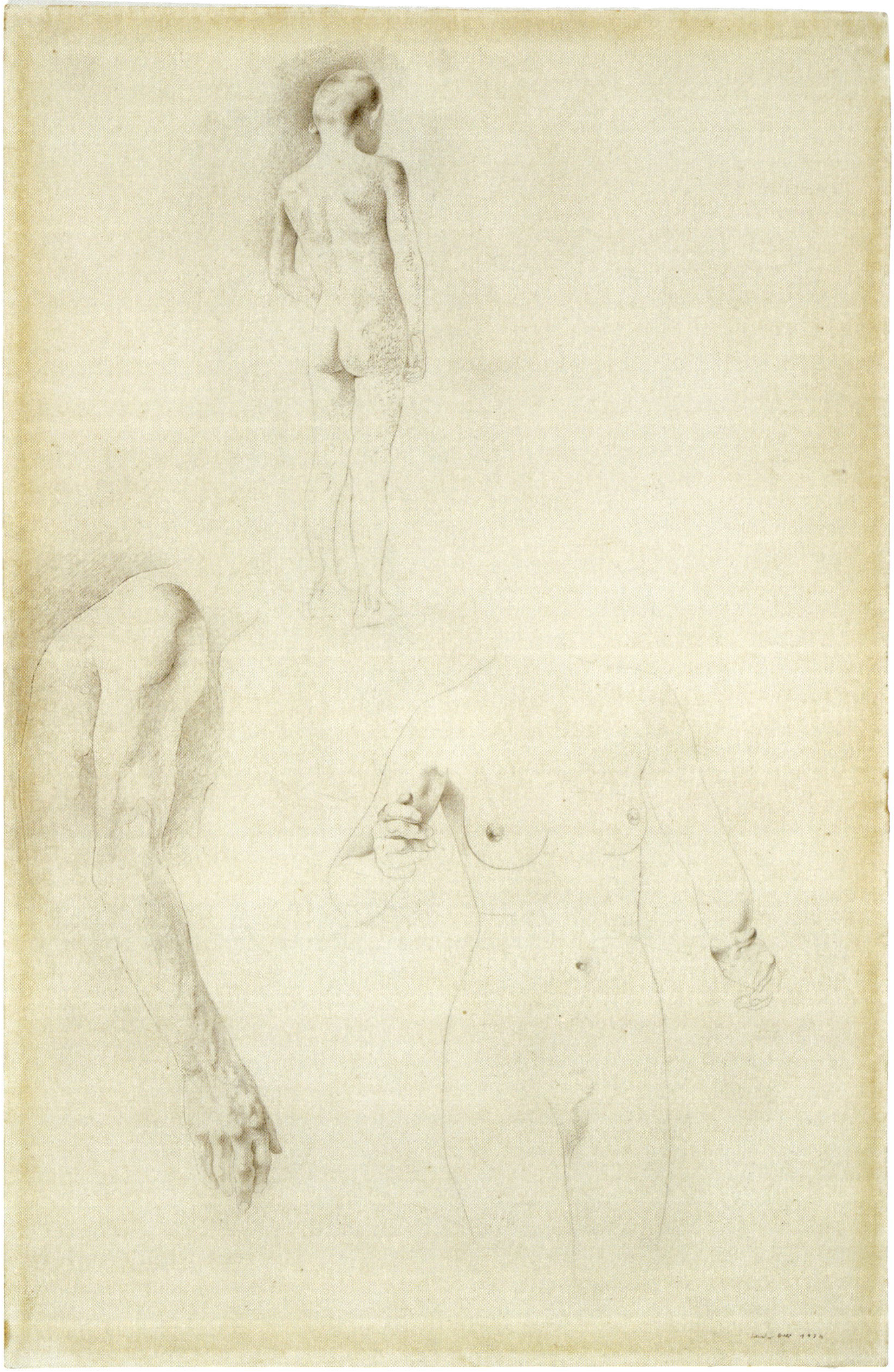

Fig. 1. Salvador Dalí, *Studies of a Nude*, 1935. Pencil on paper, 6 7/8 × 5 1/2 in. (17.5 × 14 cm). Museum of Modern Art, New York. James Thrall Soby Bequest, 908.1979

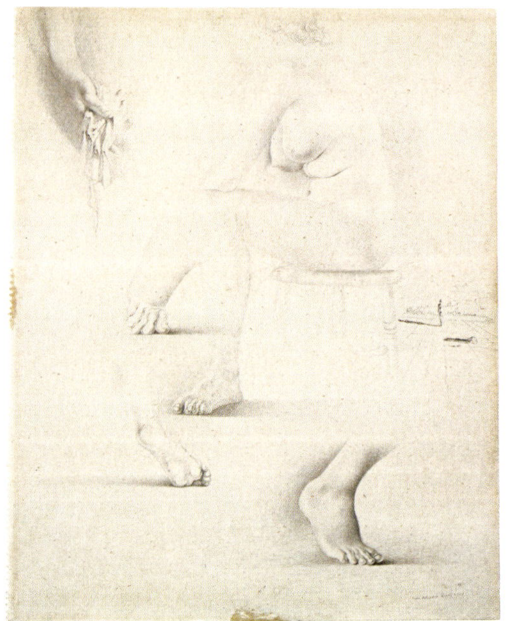

Cat. 64

Gaston Lachaise

Born in Paris, 1882;
died in New York, 1935

Gaston Lachaise studied sculpture at the École Bernard Palissy and the Académie Nationale des Beaux-Arts, and he exhibited his early works in the Paris Salons of 1899, 1901, 1902, and 1904. Shortly thereafter, in 1906, Lachaise traveled to Boston, at least in part to follow Isabel Nagle, a married woman whom he had met as a student. Lachaise moved to New York City in 1912 and became a U.S. citizen in 1916. He married Ms. Nagle, who had been recently divorced, the next year.

Lachaise exhibited the plaster sculpture *Statuette* in the Armory Show of 1913, and he gained widespread recognition by 1918, the year of his first one-man exhibition at Stephan Bourgeois Galleries in New York. Throughout his career, Lachaise's figurative sculptures were often exercises in portraiture. Besides his wife, who served as his primary muse and model, Lachaise depicted numerous friends and cultural beacons in the New York art world, including Alfred Stieglitz, Georgia O'Keeffe (q.v.), Henry McBride, Lincoln Kirstein, E. E. Cummings, and John Marin (q.v.). In drawing, the artist found a medium by which he could produce works quickly, expressing the figure through the lyricism of line. The artist produced drawings in concentrated periods and treated these works as separate from and independent of his sculptures.

In 1930, Lachaise's work was featured in a show at the Harvard Society for Contemporary Art, the famous gallery that counted Lincoln Kirstein as one of its founders. Kirstein, founder of the New York City Ballet, was Lachaise's greatest patron. Lachaise's standing sculptures—among them *Man Walking* (1933; Whitney Museum of American Art, New York), a portrait of Kirstein—were some of his most celebrated works. Kirstein organized Lachaise's retrospective exhibition at the Museum of Modern Art, New York, in 1935.

Select Bibliography

Gaston Lachaise. *The Sculpture of Gaston Lachaise.* With an essay by Hilton Kramer and appreciations by Hart Crane, E. E. Cummings, Marsden Hartley, Lincoln Kirstein, A. Hyatt Mayor, and Henry McBride. New York: Eakins Press, 1967.

Gerland Nordland. *Gaston Lachaise: The Man and His Work.* New York: G. Braziller, 1974.

Carolyn Kinder Carr and Margaret C. S. Christman. *Gaston Lachaise: Portrait Sculpture.* Washington, D.C.: National Portrait Gallery, Smithsonian Institution Press, 1985.

65

Gaston Lachaise
Male Nude, c. 1932
Graphite on wove paper
23 11/16 × 18 3/4 in. (60.2 × 47.6 cm)
Inscribed at lower left:
To My Friend Lincoln Kirstein
Signed at lower left: G Lachaise
Ex coll.: Lincoln Kirstein, New York
Gift of Lincoln Kirstein, 1934.21

In 1934 Lincoln Kirstein, cofounder of the New York City Ballet and its affiliate the School of American Ballet, gave the Atheneum two figure drawings by Gaston Lachaise (cat. 65 and fig. 1). The drawings were given in honor of Kirstein's friend and then museum director, A. Everett ("Chick") Austin. As Kirstein explained in a letter to Austin, the drawings were a conciliatory gesture as he would be unable to attend the premiere of Virgil Thomson's opera *Four Saints in Three Acts* at the museum on February 7, 1934.[1] The gift honored the rich history of ballet and dance that Austin brought to the Atheneum during his tenure. As a Harvard alumnus, Austin was well acquainted with prominent figures and tastemakers of both the visual arts and performance of the late 1920s and '30s: Kirstein, also a Harvard graduate, was among the most notable and significant of these.

Kirstein was among Lachaise's earliest supporters; the two met at a party in New York in 1931, where the former was living after graduation from Harvard. According to contemporary accounts, Lachaise was immediately taken by the young man's handsome features. Thus began for Kirstein, as Carolyn Kinder Carr put it, "a role as protector and promoter of the sculptor—a role that would continue long after the artist's death."[2] During his lifetime, Lachaise portrayed Kirstein numerous times and dedicated work to him as well, including the drawings given to the Atheneum, both of which were inscribed, one in English and the other in French, "To my friend Kirstein."[3]

This pair of drawings possesses the robust energy and expressive force for which Lachaise was celebrated. In his sculptures and drawings of the 1930s, Lachaise reached the heights of his expressive power. He replaced the refined, classical aesthetic of his earlier nudes, such as the marble *Statue of a Youth* (1927; Wadsworth Atheneum), with exaggerated proportions and distorted features, bordering on the grotesque, as in the drawing here

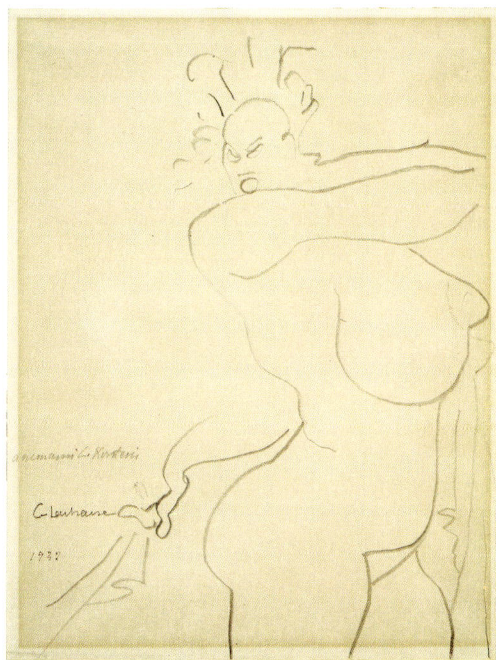

Fig. 1. Gaston Lachaise, *Female Nude*, 1932. Graphite on wove paper, 11 7/8 × 8 7/8 in. (30.2 × 22.5 cm). Wadsworth Atheneum Museum of Art. Gift of Lincoln Kirstein, 1934.22

and its companion, *Female Nude*. In *Male Nude*, the musculature of the upper body of the figure is overstated by large pectoral muscles. This is contrasted to the feminine qualities of the lower half, such as the narrow waist, rounded hips, and diminutive phallus. *Female Nude* is equally bizarre, with its atypical anatomy, angry face, and unruly hair. Her silhouette is determined by a large, bulbous breast and a strange appendage above her buttocks, perhaps an arm reaching around from the front. These drawings reveal the variety of stylistic influences that informed Lachaise's style, from the classicism of Auguste Rodin to Asian and African influences such as Indian and Egyptian art. Lachaise borrowed elements from these disparate sources to create original and unorthodox nudes.

The articulation of an expressive physical form rather than an anatomically accurate one distinguished Lachaise from the sculptors of his time. As Hilton Kramer has noted, "In Lachaise the mold of classical tradition is broken—broken, one may say, by a sense of life too forceful and too confident, too unbounded, to contain it."[4] Kramer astutely observed that the combination of the sacred and profane was more pronounced in the late work, when "the pressure of Lachaise's erotic fantasy yielded a truly amazing variety of sculptural ideas and realizations."
ECM

1. Lincoln Kirstein to Chick Austin, 20 January 1934, reprinted in Eugene R. Gaddis, *Magician of the Modern: Chick Austin and the Transformation of the Arts in America* (New York: Alfred A. Knopf, 2000), 238.
2. Carolyn Kinder Carr and Margaret C. S. Christman, *Gaston Lachaise: Portrait Sculpture* (Washington, D.C.: National Portrait Gallery, 1985), 140.
3. Lachaise completed two portraits of Kirstein in bronze, *Head of Lincoln Kirstein* (1932; private collection) and *Man Walking* (1933; Whitney Museum of American Art).
4. *The Sculpture of Gaston Lachaise*, with an essay by Hilton Kramer (New York: Eakins Press, 1967), 13–14.

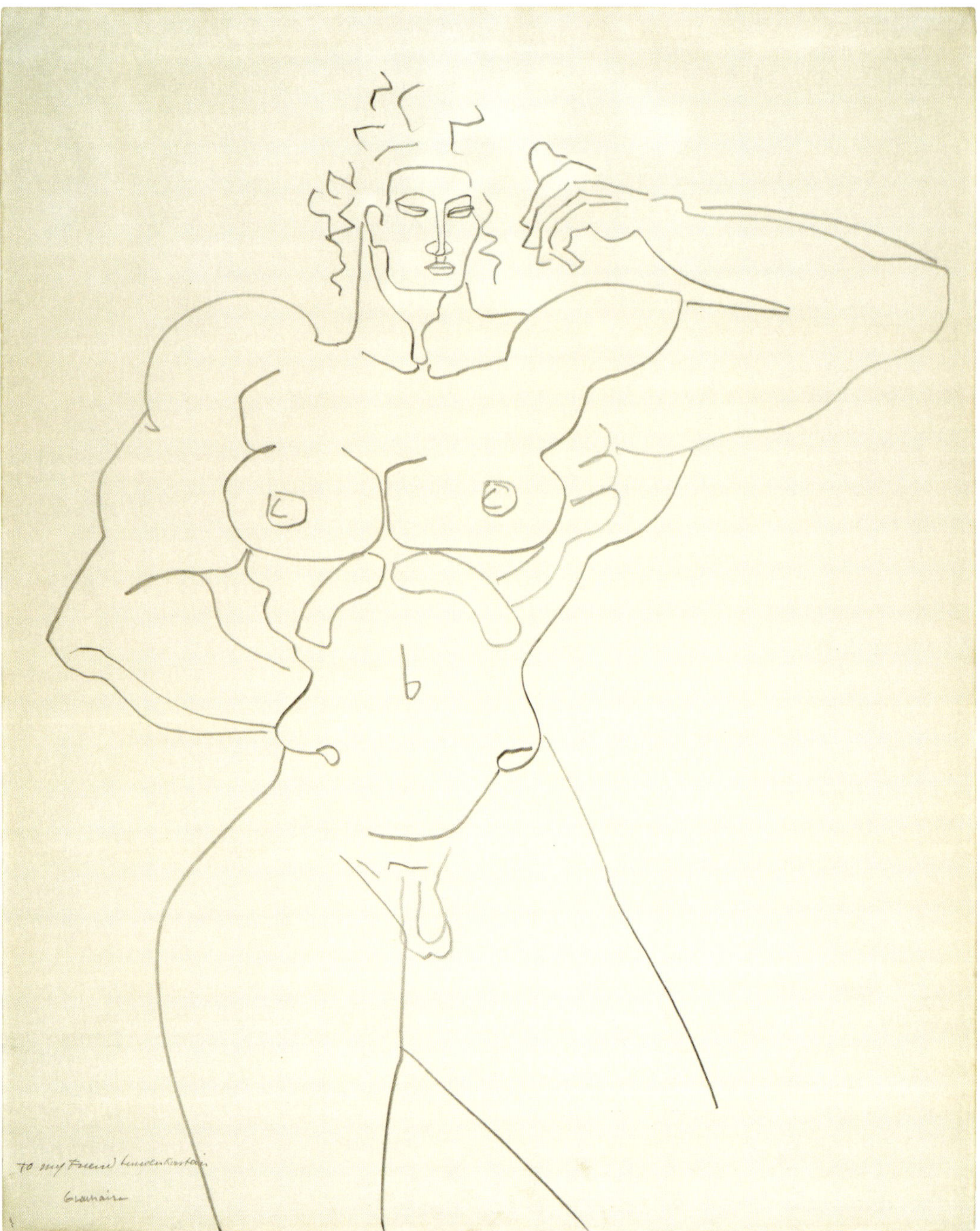

Cat. 65

Alexander Calder

Born in Lawnton, Pennsylvania, 1898;
died in New York, 1976

Alexander Calder was born into a family of artists: his father was a sculptor, and his mother a painter. Although Calder experimented artistically in his youth, he did not immediately pursue formal artistic training. Instead, he studied mechanical engineering, graduating from the Stevens Institute of Technology in Hoboken, New Jersey, in 1919. This engineering background probably played a large part in Calder's development of kinetic abstract sculpture. From 1923 to 1926, he studied drawing and painting at the Art Students League in New York City.

In 1925 Calder was employed by the *National Police Gazette* in New York to sketch the Barnum and Bailey Circus in performance. After moving to Paris in 1926, Calder turned this subject matter into sculptural creations of wire and cloth that became *Calder's Circus*, which was received with amusement and enthusiasm. While in Paris, he became well acquainted with leading members of the modernist art movement such as Joan Miró and Piet Mondrian. Calder himself regarded a 1930 visit to Mondrian's studio as a pivotal moment in his development. Calder's three-dimensional translation of Mondrian's work was recognized by A. Everett Austin Jr., who exhibited Calder's sculptures alongside Mondrian's work in a 1935 group exhibition at the Wadsworth Atheneum. Calder's sculpture in the 1930s, pieces of metal and wood connected by wires and rods, began as "stabiles" and eventually became works in motion, "mobiles," as named by Marcel Duchamp. His abstract works were first exhibited in 1931, the year he married Louisa James. The couple returned to America in 1933 and settled in Roxbury, Connecticut.

Calder's early prominence in modernist circles in Paris prefigured an international reputation. He was highly regarded on both sides of the Atlantic, and exhibited widely in Europe and America. In 1943, Calder was given a retrospective exhibition at the Museum of Modern Art in New York. Beginning in 1953, Calder established residences in both France and America, and would travel frequently between them for the rest of his life.

Following the success of his retrospective at MoMA, Calder was chosen to represent the United States at the 1952 Venice Biennale, where the sculptor took home first prize. Toward the end of the 1950s, he began creating monumental stabiles, and exhibited these new works in Paris in 1959. Beginning in the 1960s Calder received a large number of international commissions for these stabiles, among them the 1972 commission by the Connecticut State Capital Commission of Sculpture for the towering crimson *Stegosaurus*. This type of large-scale public sculpture dominated Calder's work in the last decade of his life. Calder's art was shown at two major retrospective exhibitions: one at the Solomon R. Guggenheim Museum in New York in 1964, and another in 1976 at the Whitney Museum of American Art, the year of the artist's death. There would be many retrospectives in the following decades. An exhibition at the Wadsworth Atheneum in 2000, *Calder in Connecticut*, explored the influence of the Connecticut countryside on the sculptor's work.

Select Bibliography

Jean Lipman. *Calder's Universe*. New York: Whitney Museum of American Art, 1999.

Eric M. Zafran. *Calder in Connecticut*. With Elizabeth Mankin Kornhauser and Cynthia Roman; introductory essay by Alexander S. C. Rower; afterword by Arthur Miller. Hartford, Conn.: Wadsworth Atheneum in association with Rizzoli, 2000.

Joan Simon and Brigitte Léal, eds. *Alexander Calder: The Paris Years, 1926–1933*. New York: Whitney Museum of American Art, 2008.

66

Alexander Calder
A Strip-tease (with Guide), 1936
Pen and black ink, ink wash, blue pencil, white opaque watercolor, and collage on wove paper laid down on card stock
22 7/8 × 30 in. (58.1 × 76.2 cm)
Inscribed at lower center:
A strip-tease (with guide) / in the jungle / a rather obvious mucilage, / to Nellie, with high esteem / 5/2/36 Sandy
Ex coll.: Eleanor Howland [Bunce], Hartford, Connecticut, 1936
Bequest of Eleanor H. Bunce, 1999.29.16

The "Nellie" to whom Calder dedicated this collage was Eleanor Howland (later Eleanor H. Bunce), Chick Austin's assistant in the mid-1930s, when the artist first became involved with the Atheneum. It is one of a number of collages Calder presented to friends. Shortly after giving this one to Howland, he sent a collage to Austin that contains a humorous plea for inclusion in the director's next "impresariol adventure." Calder later made amusing collages for James Thrall Soby, a longtime patron and close friend, and for Alex Matter, his godson and namesake.

While some of the imagery in *A Strip-tease* clearly relates to the events that linked Calder and Howland, the significance of other motifs – for example, the improbably green "Matador" rose at the center–no longer seems, as the inscription on the work claims, "rather obvious." The scrap of paper bearing the logo "Transition" is from the literary magazine that published Dada and Surrealist manifestos and imagery in the 1920s and '30s, including works by a number of artists supported by the Atheneum. The various sexual references–the label for "Klymax" Clothes Line, the mostly nude strip-tease artist and her vaudevillian "guide"–may allude to a joke between Calder and Howland whose meaning has been lost over time. However, the delightfully fantastic animals–lion, giraffe, elephant with a horse's body, monkey with the face of a wildebeest–recall the costumes Calder designed for the Paper Ball held at the Atheneum a few months earlier (for the ball, see cat. 58), the culminating event of the week-long Hartford Festival. Calder, one of several artists creating costumes for the ball, designed "A Nightmare Side Show"– a collection of jungle creatures more charming than nightmarish–for Soby's group of revelers, which included Howland.[1]

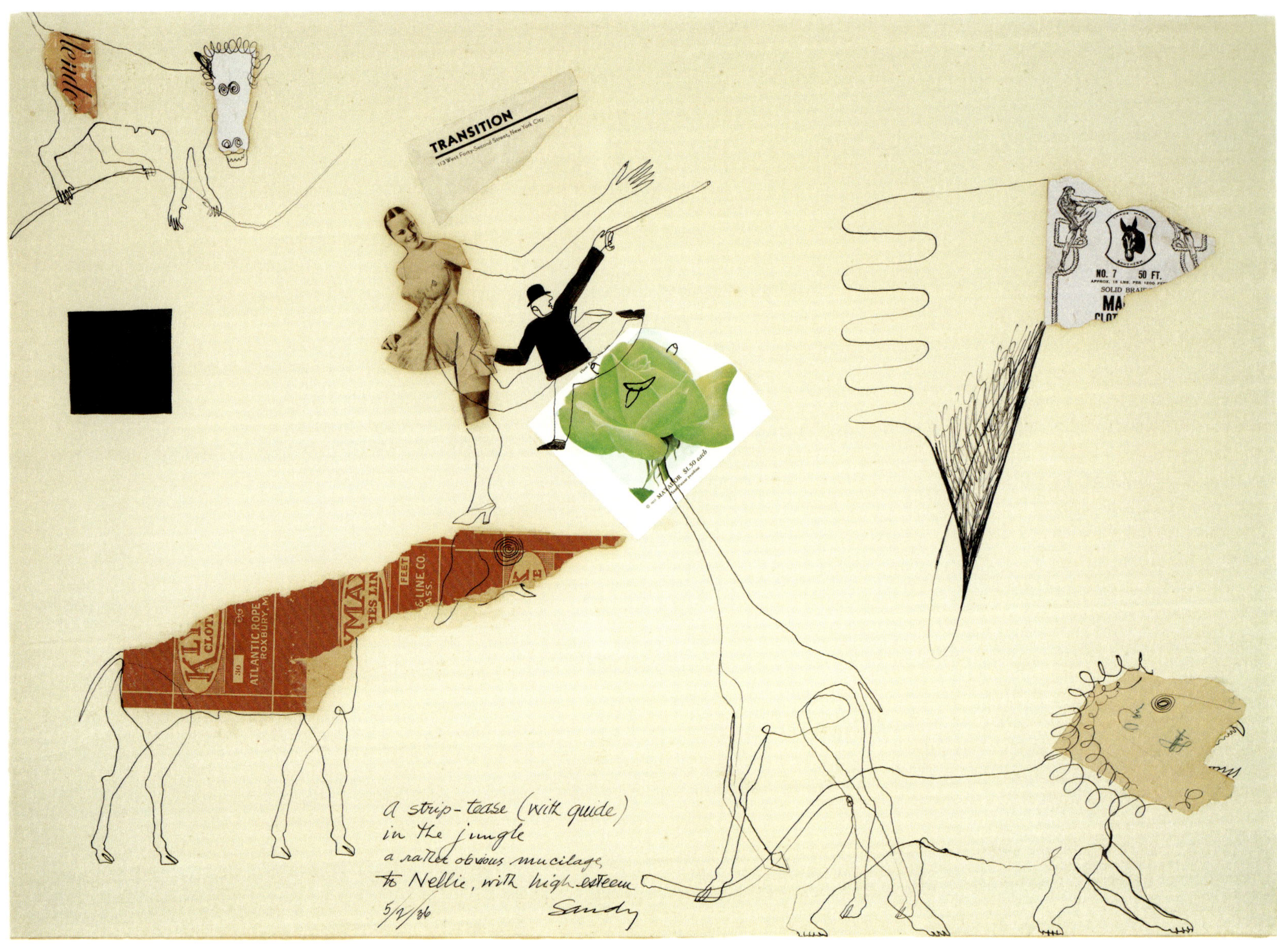

Cat. 66

The animals animating this collage had long been part of Calder's vocabulary. In the late 1920s he began making wire sculptures of animals; these evolved alongside *Calder's Circus*, first presented to an American public in 1931.[2] In 1931, Calder made a group of circus drawings. He referred to the wire sculptures as "three-dimensional line drawings";[3] conversely, the drawings look like the wire sculptures pressed onto the page. They seem spontaneous, improvisational; most of them were made essentially from a single, continuous line. These features link *A Strip-tease* with the automatic writing of the Surrealists, who also employed the collage technique. (Calder here used the term *mucilage* – an adhesive – as synonymous with *collage*.) Collage allowed the provocative juxtaposition of unrelated images.[4] But in his collages for Howland and other friends, Calder tempered the unsettling randomness characteristic of many Surrealist collages with an elegant compositional sense and, above all, with a spirit of playful exuberance and affection.

CT

1. Eric M. Zafran, *Calder in Connecticut* (Hartford, Conn.: Wadsworth Atheneum in association with Rizzoli, 2000), 38; Eugene Gaddis, *Magician of the Modern: Chick Austin and the Transformation of the Arts in America* (New York: Alfred A. Knopf, 2000), 302–03.
2. Calder began making his wire sculptures of animals about 1928, and showed them at Weyhe Gallery, New York, that year. He gave a number of private performances of *Calder's Circus* in Paris and the United States beginning about 1926; they were first shown widely to an American public in 1929. See Alexander S. C. Rower, "The Surrealist Years: 1926–1947," in *The Surreal Calder*, by Mark Rosenthal (Houston: Menil Collection, 2006), 111–18.
3. Calder, quoted in Marla Prather, *Alexander Calder: 1898–1976* (Washington, D.C.: National Gallery of Art, 1998), 21.
4. See Martica Sawin, *Surrealism in Exile and the Beginning of the New York School* (Cambridge, Mass.: MIT Press, 1995), 334.

Yves Tanguy

Born in Paris, 1900;
died in Woodbury, Connecticut, 1955

Raymond Georges Yves Tanguy was born in Paris in 1900. He showed no predilection for art in his youth, stumbling upon his future vocation rather abruptly upon his return to Paris following military service. After seeing work by the Surrealist Giorgio de Chirico in a Parisian gallery in 1923, Tanguy took up painting. In 1925, he met André Breton and joined the burgeoning Surrealist art movement. From the outset Tanguy was an active member of the Surrealist circle in Paris, and in 1928 he participated in the Surrealist group exhibition at the Galerie Sacre du Printemps.

Tanguy's work is largely characterized by strange, imaginary landscapes, which merge the recognizable with the fantastical. Following a brief dry spell in the early 1930s, Tanguy entered a prolific period in which his work was exhibited simultaneously in several shows internationally, including a number of group exhibitions of Surrealism. In 1935, his reputation in America was reinforced by the purchase of two works by the Museum of Modern Art. The following year, MoMA director Alfred H. Barr Jr. included thirteen works by the artist in the exhibition *Fantastic Art, Dada, Surrealism.*

In 1937, Tanguy met the influential art dealer Peggy Guggenheim and opened a solo exhibition at the new Guggenheim Jeune Gallery in London in 1938. The following year, while vacationing with Breton and others in the Surrealist circle in the Rhone Valley in France, Tanguy met the American painter Kay Sage, whom he followed to America in November 1939. Immediately following, he had a solo show at the Pierre Matisse Gallery in New York. Sage and Tanguy were married in 1940 in Nevada (both had prior marriages that ended in divorce) and the two settled in New York. The couple moved in 1946 to Woodbury, Connecticut, to a farmhouse that included a double barn where the two artists set up separate studios. Two years after moving to Woodbury, Tanguy became an American citizen. The artist's move to America in 1938 is discernible in his work: his paintings display a brighter palette, a more expansive treatment of space, and an increasingly bizarre and diverse formal vocabulary.

The European Surrealists received early attention from the Wadsworth Atheneum under the tenure of A. Everett Austin Jr., who organized the first large-scale Surrealist exhibition in America in 1931. The Atheneum purchased Tanguy's painting *Time and Again* from a Matisse Gallery group show in 1942 at the urging of trustee James Thrall Soby, who would maintain a friendship with Tanguy for the remainder of his life. The Atheneum held a solo exhibition for Tanguy in 1940, and in 1954 held a joint exhibition for Tanguy and Sage. While he did not go back to Europe often after his original emigration in 1939—he returned for the first time with Sage in 1953—Tanguy continued to retain a presence in museums and gallery exhibitions there through the 1940s and '50s. Plagued by health problems in his later years, Tanguy died of a cerebral hemorrhage on January 15, 1955, in a Woodbury hospital. That same year Soby organized a memorial retrospective of Tanguy's work at the Museum of Modern Art, and Sage began work on a catalogue raisonné of her husband's work, which was published in 1963.

Select Bibliography

Yves Tanguy, quoted in "Symposium: The Creative Process," *Art Digest* 28 (15 January 1954): 14.

James Thrall Soby. *Yves Tanguy*. New York: Museum of Modern Art, 1955.

Karin von Maur, ed. *Yves Tanguy and Surrealism*. With contributions by Susan Davidson, Gordon Onslow Ford, Konrad Klapheck, Karin von Maur, and Beate Wolf. Ostfildern-Ruit: Hatje Cantz, 2001.

67

Yves Tanguy
Dream Landscape, c. 1935
Opaque watercolor on thin paper laid down on mat board
3 7/16 × 11 1/4 in. (8.7 × 28.6 cm)
Signed and dated at lower right:
YVES TANGUY 3[5]
Ex coll.: with Julien Levy Gallery, New York
The Ella Gallup Sumner and Mary Catlin Sumner Collection Fund, 1936.59

The unusual panoramic format of *Dream Landscape* occurs in a number of miniature gouaches Tanguy painted beginning about 1931. The earliest of these, like Tanguy's contemporary work in other media, have a clearly articulated horizon line. But by mid-decade, his images are characterized by an "ambiguous melting of land into sky."[1] In *Dream Landscape*, the result is a space that is both friezelike and infinite.

Land and sky are rendered in chalky colors with soft yet imperceptible brushstrokes. They provide an atmospheric backdrop for Tanguy's solid, carefully delineated forms, painted with a miniaturist's patience and precision. The setting is dreamy and evocative, suggesting perhaps a beach at twilight or a lunar surface, while the carefully articulated forms seem, in the words of poet John Ashbery, "real if non-existent."[2] Tanguy's bony creatures have been compared to biomorphic sculpture by Swiss artist Hans Arp;[3] several of the vertical shapes are reminiscent of Picasso, but without the emotional intensity.

Unlike some of Tanguy's earlier works, in which his peculiar objects seem to multiply on the picture surface, *Dream Landscape* is rather spare. There is a measured distribution of forms and careful attention to the intervals between them. This regular procession of ossified but peculiarly mobile objects across the bleached landscape establishes a "pristine order"[4] of almost hallucinatory clarity, yet the elegance of execution mitigates any disquieting quality.

Dream Landscape was included in Tanguy's second solo exhibition in America, which was held at Julien Levy's gallery in New York in March 1936.[5] That show elicited a strong response from Hartford's promoters of the avant-garde. Prominent collector James Thrall Soby, who had already profiled Tanguy in his landmark study *After Picasso* (1935), contributed a statement to Levy's catalogue. Chick Austin bought *Dream Landscape* for the

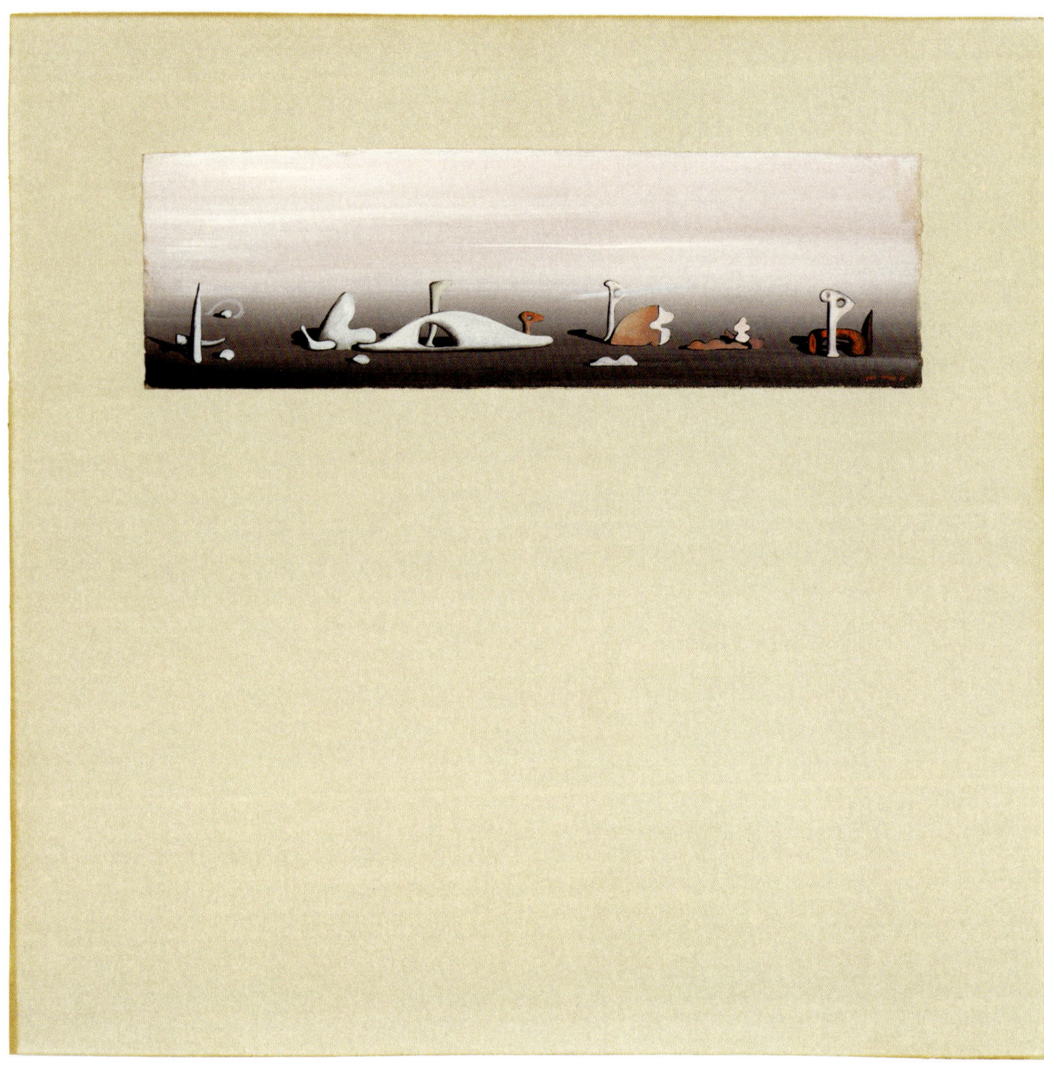

Cat. 67

Atheneum for $35; his assistant Paul Cooley bought a closely related gouache (untitled, 1930s; collection Timothy Baum, New York) for his own collection. Those gouaches and an oil owned by Soby would be featured in the Atheneum's 1940 presentation of Tanguy's works, the artist's first solo museum exhibition in the United States.
CT

1. James Thrall Soby, *Yves Tanguy* (New York: Museum of Modern Art, 1955), 18.
2. John Ashbery, "Tanguy–The Geometer of Dreams," in *Yves Tanguy* (New York: Acquavella Galleries, 1974), n.p.
3. Alfred H. Barr Jr., *Cubism and Abstract Art* (New York: Museum of Modern Art, 1936), 186.
4. Soby, *Yves Tanguy*, 22.
5. The first was held at the Stanley Rose Gallery, Hollywood, California, in November 1935.

68

Yves Tanguy
Untitled, 1949
Pen and black ink on card stock
22 1/8 × 28 1/4 in. (56.2 × 71.8 cm)
Signed and dated at lower right:
YVES TANGUY 49
Ex coll.: the artist and his wife,
Kay Sage Tanguy; to Kay Sage Tanguy,
Woodbury, Connecticut, in 1955
Bequest of Kay Sage Tanguy, 1963.51

In the late 1940s Tanguy produced a group of large pen and ink drawings. He rarely titled them, although most would be well described by the title he gave to the drawing now at the Metropolitan Museum of Art, New York: *Fantastic Construction* (fig. 1). In most of these drawings, the linear patterns are intricate and the sheet is densely decorated with a profusion of diminutive, interconnected forms. The Atheneum's drawing, in contrast, is calm and austere. In it, the "construction" itself is large, occupying much of the sheet, but because it is created in pure outline, with no modeling, shading, or touches of color and only a few busy areas of tiny details, it seems massive and, at the same time, serenely insubstantial.

Tanguy described his method as governed by "the element of surprise."[1] He clearly worked additively here, with one quasi-mechanistic

Fig. 1. Yves Tanguy, *Fantastic Construction*, 1949. Pen and ink, pencil, and cut and pasted paper on paper, 19 7/8 × 14 3/4 in. (50.5 × 37.5 cm). The Metropolitan Museum of Art, New York. Bequest of Kay Sage Tanguy

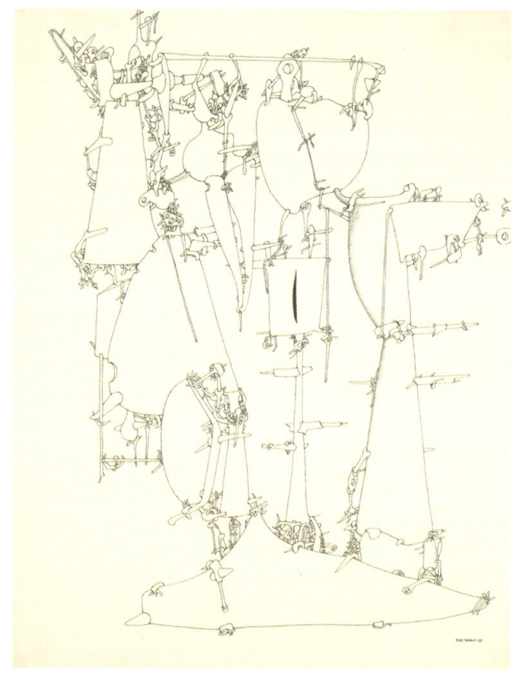

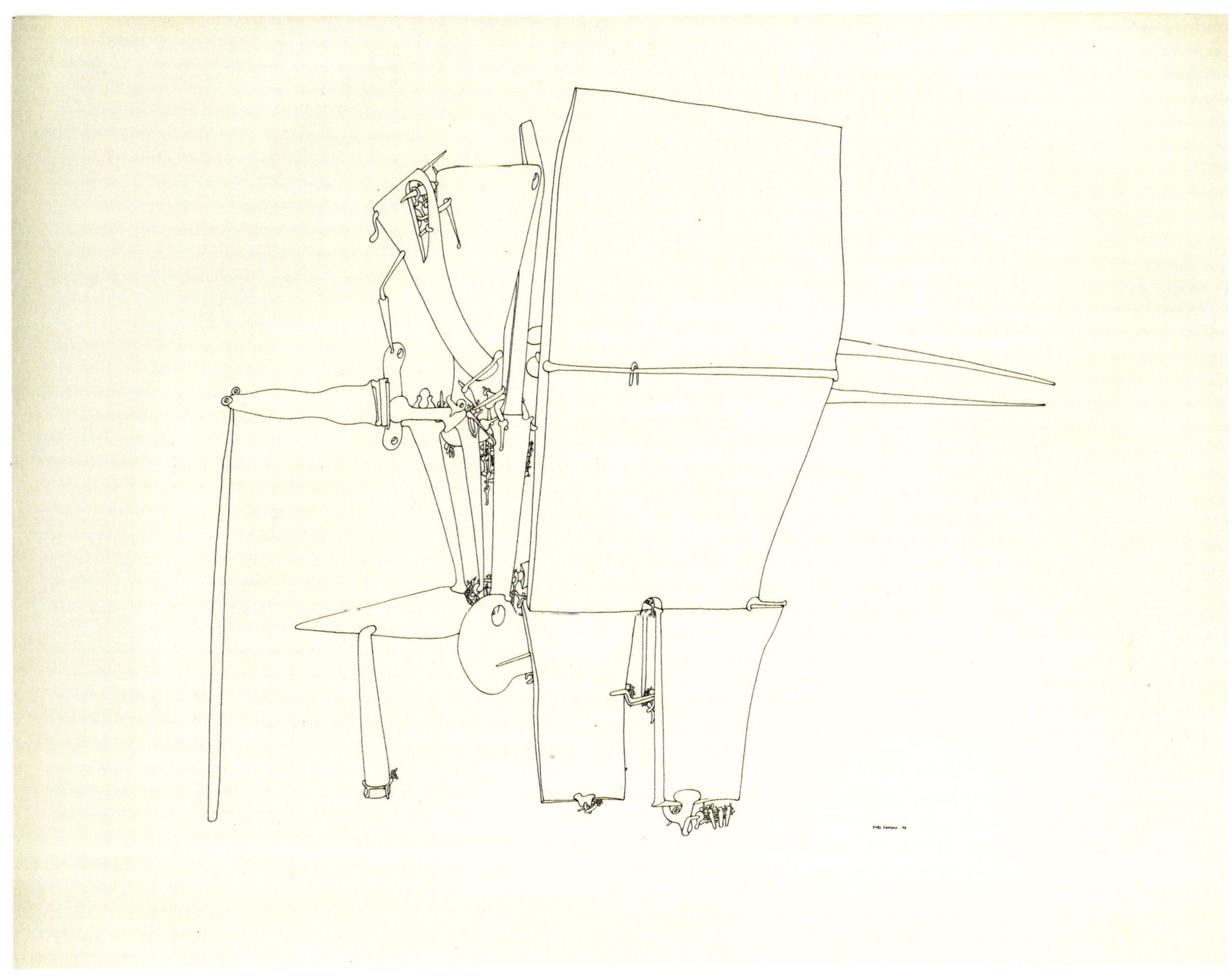

Cat. 68

form growing out of another. As explained by collector and curator James Thrall Soby, Tanguy believed in the "spontaneous generation of forms." He was interested in unpredictability, in the way one shape or motif suggested another: "a chain reaction, as of bundled firecrackers."[2] This method links Tanguy with his fellow Surrealists, and yet distinguishes him from them. The image in the Atheneum's drawing is "automatic" in that it was not conscious or planned. Yet unlike the roughly worked, seemingly scribbled fantasies of contemporaries like Matta (q.v.) or Arshile Gorky (q.v.), Tanguy's visions are meticulous, neat, and "communicated with the utmost finesse."[3]
CT

1. Yves Tanguy, quoted in "Symposium: The Creative Process," *Art Digest* 28 (15 January 1954): 14.
2. James Thrall Soby, *Yves Tanguy* (New York: Museum of Modern Art, 1955), 17.
3. Ibid., 19.

Matta (Roberto Antonio Sebastián Matta Echaurren)

Born in Santiago, Chile, 1911 or 1912; died in Tarquinia, Italy, 2002

Roberto Matta Echaurren, known as Matta, was influenced by Parisian modernism while he was a student at the Academia de Bellas Artes in Santiago, Chile. Matta's drawing teacher at the Academia had worked for the French painter Fernand Léger. In 1934, Matta moved to Paris and began working in the atelier of the architect Le Corbusier.

Matta traveled extensively throughout Europe in the late 1930s. Still, his primary influences were the Spanish and South American poets Federico García Lorca and Pablo Neruda, whom he met in Spain between 1936 and 1937. Around the same time, Matta met Salvador Dalí (q.v.) and André Breton, and was later asked to join their Surrealist group. His early work was almost entirely on paper, and a selection of these drawings was included in an important show, the Exposition Internationale du Surréalisme in Paris in 1937.

Like other émigré artists, Matta left France and moved to New York as World War II erupted. At this time, he began painting in oil. While in New York, Matta became acquainted with a number of American artists. For a brief period he ran workshops instructing his colleagues (among them William Baziotes [q.v.], Robert Motherwell, and Jackson Pollock) in the use of automatist methods. During World War II, Matta's art became increasingly agitated. He used a vocabulary of irregular shapes coupled with smudgy shading and precise lines of color in works that seem frenzied and violent.

Matta later split from the Surrealist group. It has been suggested that his affairs with women, among them Arshile Gorky's wife, may have precipitated the split from the Surrealists. Following this schism, he left the United States permanently and later divided his time between Paris and Tarquinia, Italy. Retrospectives of Matta's work were held at the Museum of Modern Art in New York (1957) and at the Pompidou Center in Paris (1985).

Select Bibliography

William Rubin. *Matta.* New York: Museum of Modern Art, 1957.

Matta: Centre Georges Pompidou. Paris: Editions du Centre Pompidou, 1985.

Elizabeth A. T. Smith and Colette Dartnall. *Matta in America: Paintings and Drawings of the 1940s.* Chicago: Museum of Contemporary Art, 2001.

69

Matta

Untitled (Personnages Transparence), c. 1941–42

Graphite and colored crayon on wove paper

19 11/16 × 25 1/2 in. (50 × 64.8 cm)

Ex coll.: with Pierre Matisse Gallery, New York

The Ella Gallup Sumner and Mary Catlin Sumner Collection Fund, 1942.280

In his memoirs, the art dealer Julien Levy observed that Matta had "a powerful obsession with space and could make it vast and inhuman. . . . Translating his perspective into limitless voids past the horizon and beyond the vanishing point, Matta seems to have arrived at his own strange outer world."[1] By the early 1940s, when he made this drawing, Matta had abandoned any sense of conventional perspective and instead created an irregular, irrational space. Here his forms seem utterly free of gravity, coupling and colliding in random patterns through overlapping spheres of space. At once organic and mechanistic, they bring to mind jellyfish with their stinging tentacles streaming behind them, or fragments of fuselage dropping through the sky.

Matta's drawings of this period, rooted in Surrealist automatism, became increasingly disturbing as World War II intensified. His shapes here seem vaguely sinister, knotted, and tense, their impending collisions more aggressive than playful. The precision of execution—Matta used sharp pencil lines, a reflection of his early training as an architect, and coupled them with smudgy shading and color embellishments—makes the drawing all the more unnerving.

Matta gave his drawings Spanish, French, or English titles; many he did not name at all. This drawing, made shortly before the artist's first solo show at the Pierre Matisse Gallery in late March 1942 (but probably not included in it),[2] was acquired for the Wadsworth Atheneum for $125 at the time of the show. It was identified simply as "Drawing" in the exhibition *Painters in Attendance*, held at the Atheneum that May, and as "Composition" in the Museum of Modern Art's *Modern Drawings* exhibition in 1944. At some later point, the drawing became known as *Personnages Transparence*—transparent beings.[3]

The title connects the drawing with a theory of transparency developed by Matta and his mentor, the Surrealist leader André Breton, in about 1942. The theory was first spelled out in Breton's "Prolegomena to a Third Manifesto of Surrealism or Else," published in the periodical *VVV* in June 1942. That essay was illustrated with a reproduction of Matta's large drawing *The Great Transparent Ones* (1942; private collection, Paris),[4] which contains forms similar to those in the present drawing. These "transparent ones"—expressed by Matta's hallucinatory shapes—defined a universe that was not rational and of which "man is perhaps not the center, the focus," in Breton's words. These beings "exist above him;" their behavior is "alien to him . . . completely escaping his frame of reference," and thus out of his control. Derived from Surrealism's denial of the rationality of civilization, and its dedication to the new worlds accessible through the subconscious, "transparency" was proposed as a new mythology, one that relieved humankind of responsibility for the horrors of contemporary events. Rather, it was the transparent ones, the "hypothetical beings, which obscurely manifest themselves to us in fear and the feeling of chance," who governed "perturbations like the cyclone, in the face of which man is powerless to be anything but victim or witness, or like war."[5]

CT

1. Levy, *Memoirs of an Art Gallery* (1977; Boston: MFA Publications, 2003), 247. Levy was Matta's first dealer in the United States, giving the artist a solo show in April 1940. When Levy joined the army in 1942, Pierre Matisse became Matta's representative.
2. The show featured ten oil paintings as well as seven drawings in the unusual medium of "oil pencil." None of those drawings, bearing Surrealist titles such as *Vampire and Centaur* and *Gods and Dogs*, can be definitively identified with this one. One of the paintings, *Rain*, was already owned by Atheneum trustee James Thrall Soby, who had also bought three drawings for himself the previous fall, and may have seen this one at the time.

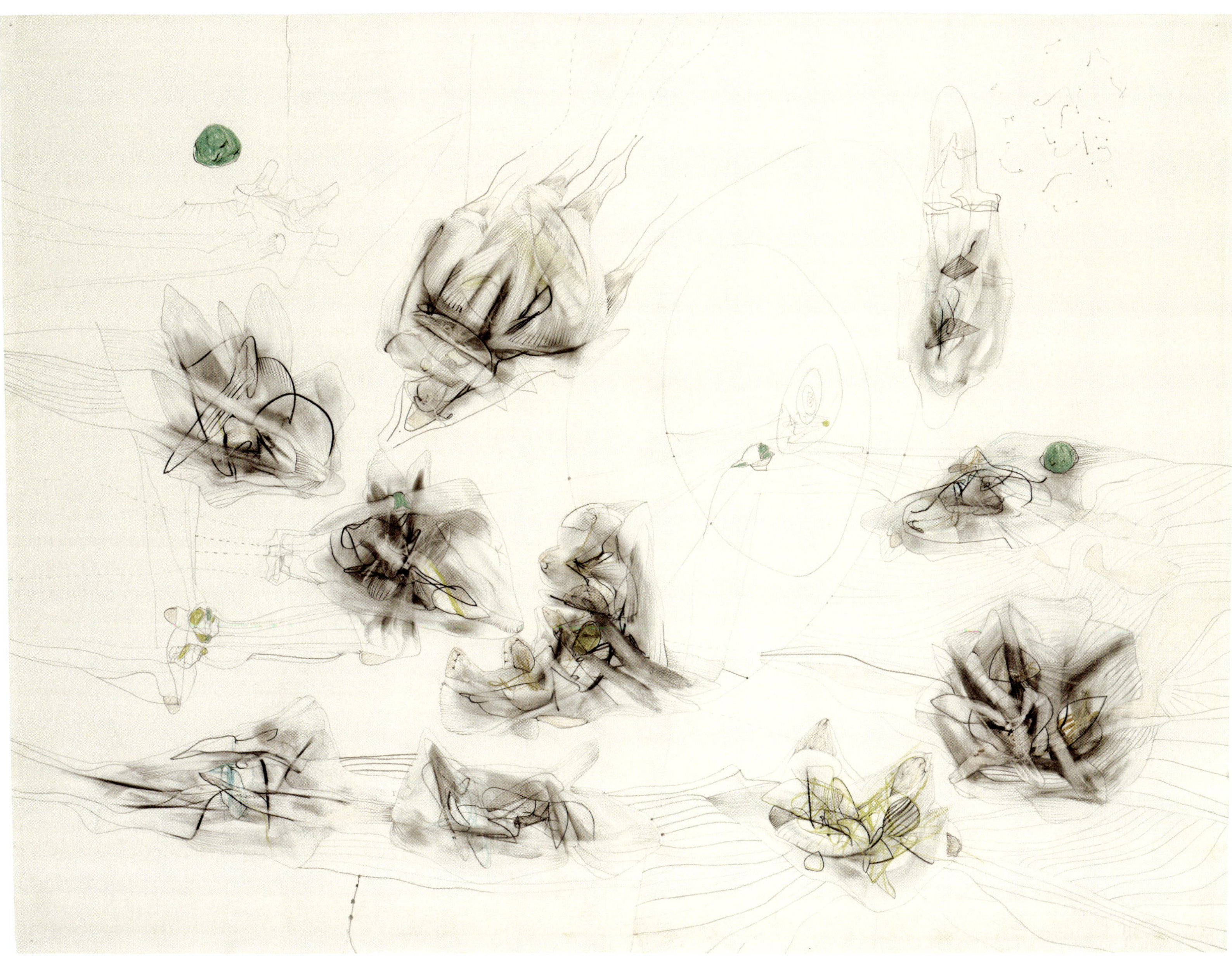

Cat. 69

3. In a letter of 30 March 1948 to Charles C. Cunningham, Samuel Green, curator of prints at Wesleyan University, Middletown, Connecticut, referred to the drawing as "Personage Transparents." By 1968, it was identified as "Composition Drawing (Personnages Transparence)" in an exhibition at the Museum of Natural History, Washington, D.C.; see Philip C. Ritterbush, *The Art of Organic Forms* (Washington, D.C.: Smithsonian Institution, 1968), 103.
4. The drawing is reproduced in *Matta* (Paris: Centre Georges Pompidou, 1985), 131.
5. André Breton, quoted in William Rubin, "Matta," *Bulletin of the Museum of Modern Art* 25, no. 1 (1957): 7.

Arshile Gorky

Born in Khorkom, Armenia, 1904;
died in Sherman, Connecticut, 1948

Experiencing great tragedy throughout his short life, Arshile Gorky became one of the most important abstract artists in America. He was born "Vosdanik Adoian" in the village of Khorkum in the Van province of Armenia in 1904; escalating violence with Turkey forced the family to flee the Van province in 1914. After witnessing the death of his mother in 1919, Gorky immigrated to the United States with his sister, arriving at Ellis Island in February 1920 before settling in Watertown, Massachusetts, with relatives. Gorky began attending classes at the Boston New School of Design, studying there until 1924, when he relocated to New York City. It was at this point in his career that he shed his birth name in favor of "Arshile Gorky," a name with Russian and Armenian roots. In New York in 1925, Gorky began study at the Grand Central Art School, and a year later he was offered a faculty position. He taught there until 1931.

Gorky's work from the 1920s reflects an aesthetic derived from close study of the Postimpressionist work of Paul Cézanne. The still lifes, landscapes, and portraits Gorky produced during this period are explicitly modeled on works of the French artist, whose treatment of form and space appealed to the Armenian's artistic sensibilities as he explored the movement toward abstraction. In the late 1920s and early '30s, Gorky's focus shifted from Postimpressionism to Cubism, specifically to the work of Pablo Picasso. Gorky immersed himself in the progressive art movement and befriended the artists Stuart Davis (q.v.) and John Graham. While Davis and Graham would remain focused on Cubism, Gorky was drawn to the Surrealist movement, which made an entrance on the American art scene in the years leading up to and during World War II.

Beginning around 1930, Gorky was also exposed to Surrealist art through a variety of exhibitions in New York. Gorky began participating in group shows around this time; in 1934 he had his first solo show anywhere at the Mellon Galleries in Philadelphia. The next year, the Guild Art Gallery gave him his first solo show in New York, *Abstract Drawings by Arshile Gorky*, which the *New York Times* hailed as "brilliantly effective." However, during the Depression, critical success did not necessarily lead to financial success. Like many fellow artists who were also struggling, Gorky joined the government-organized Works Progress Administration's Federal Art Project, and worked on designs for several murals.

The increasing presence of Surrealism as well as the influence of Wassily Kandinsky can be seen in Gorky's work as it matured in the late 1930s into the 1940s. Kandinsky's brightly hued, expressionistic watercolors provided a source of inspiration for Gorky as he continued to explore abstraction. Another major source of influence for the artist was the work of Spaniard Joan Miró. Gorky was attracted to the psychological space explored by Miró, as well as to the biomorphic shapes and the method of automatism espoused by the European Surrealists of André Breton's circle, such as Max Ernst and Matta (q.v.).

The artist's personal circumstances changed significantly upon meeting Agnes Magruder in 1941; he would marry her later that year. In the summer of 1943, Gorky and his young family made their first visit to Crooked Run Farm, his in-laws' home, in Hamilton, Virginia. This rural setting had a lasting effect on the artist, inspiring a style that synthesized the abstraction and palette of Kandinsky with the Surrealist approach to organic forms and psychological exploration. Gorky would eventually settle in Sherman, Connecticut, in 1945, sharing the home of the architect Henry Hebbeln. That same year was the beginning of Gorky's contract with dealer Julien Levy, and the first show at his gallery.

In January 1946, a fire destroyed much of his Sherman studio. Shortly after the tragic fire, the artist underwent treatment for cancer. This series of traumatic events continued into 1948 when a car accident left the artist with a broken neck and severe arm injuries. The artist committed suicide in his Sherman studio a month following the accident. In November of the same year Levy held a memorial show for the artist, which was followed in 1951 by a memorial retrospective at the Whitney Museum of American Art.

Select Bibliography

Ethel Schwabacher. *Arshile Gorky Memorial Exhibition.* New York: Whitney Museum of American Art, 1951.

Jim M. Jordon and Robert Goldwater. *The Paintings of Arshile Gorky: A Critical Catalogue.* New York: New York University Press, 1980.

Diane Waldman. *Arshile Gorky, 1904–1948: A Retrospective.* New York: Harry N. Abrams in collaboration with the Solomon R. Guggenheim Museum, 1981.

Harry Rand. *Arshile Gorky: The Implication of Symbols.* Berkeley and Los Angeles: University of California Press, 1991.

Matossian Nouritza. *Black Angel: The Life of Arshile Gorky.* New York: Overlook Press, 2000.

70

Arshile Gorky
Untitled, 1943
Colored crayon heightened with graphite on thick wove paper (partial watermark: . . . Linen 2)
19 3/4 × 27 3/4 in. (50.2 × 70.5 cm)
Signed and dated at left margin: A. Gorky / 1943
Ex coll.: Estate of the artist; with Sidney Janis Gallery, New York, until 1955
The Ella Gallup Sumner and Mary Catlin Sumner Collection Fund, 1955.275

In early June 1943, Gorky, his wife, and their infant daughter traveled from New York City to rural Hamilton, Virginia, to stay on his in-laws' farm. They remained five months, and the visit marked a turning point in Gorky's art. He was remarkably prolific during that period, going out into the fields to draw practically every day, and producing well over a hundred drawings, including this one. As though to explain this outpouring of creativity, Gorky wrote to his sister, "It is as if some ancient Armenian spirit within me moves my hand to create so far from our homeland the shapes of nature we loved in the gardens, wheatfields, and orchards of our Adoian family in Khorkom."[1] In fact, the low, lush, rolling hills of Virginia bore little resemblance to the arid, mountainous landscape of his homeland,[2] but the security and contentment Gorky found among family in Virginia seems to have been as sustaining and stimulating as his earliest childhood memories were. Beginning that summer in Virginia, his imagery began to come from his surroundings, supplanting the people and places remembered from Armenia that had dominated his previous work. The stimulation of new subjects to draw and paint enabled him to shed his earlier dependence on other artists—Picasso, Cézanne, the Surrealists—and forge an original style.[3]

Even though Gorky was clearly working from nature, the forms in *Untitled* are not readily identified. Perhaps the most conventionally legible image is the spider web hovering just above the horizon at upper right. Yet its position in space—it seems to be floating in the sky above the landscape—and its scale defy easy understanding. The pileup of organic shapes to left and right of center can variously be read as human or vegetal. The shapes on the right might be seen as describing a rather genial figure, with splayed orange legs, a greenish torso, rounded shoulders and arms rendered with pencil, and then a neck and incomplete oval for a head. The identity of shapes at left is even less certain, except for Gorky's familiar spotted pupa/butterfly form at the edge of the foliage at lower center. But whatever their meaning, these accumulations of shapes at left and right and the penciled horizon line two-thirds of the way up the sheet establish a space that is classical, almost Claudean, in its structure. In this landscape, natural elements on either side of the composition part to reveal a view into the far distance. Or, as Gorky reportedly told his mother-in law, who wondered how he could make drawings

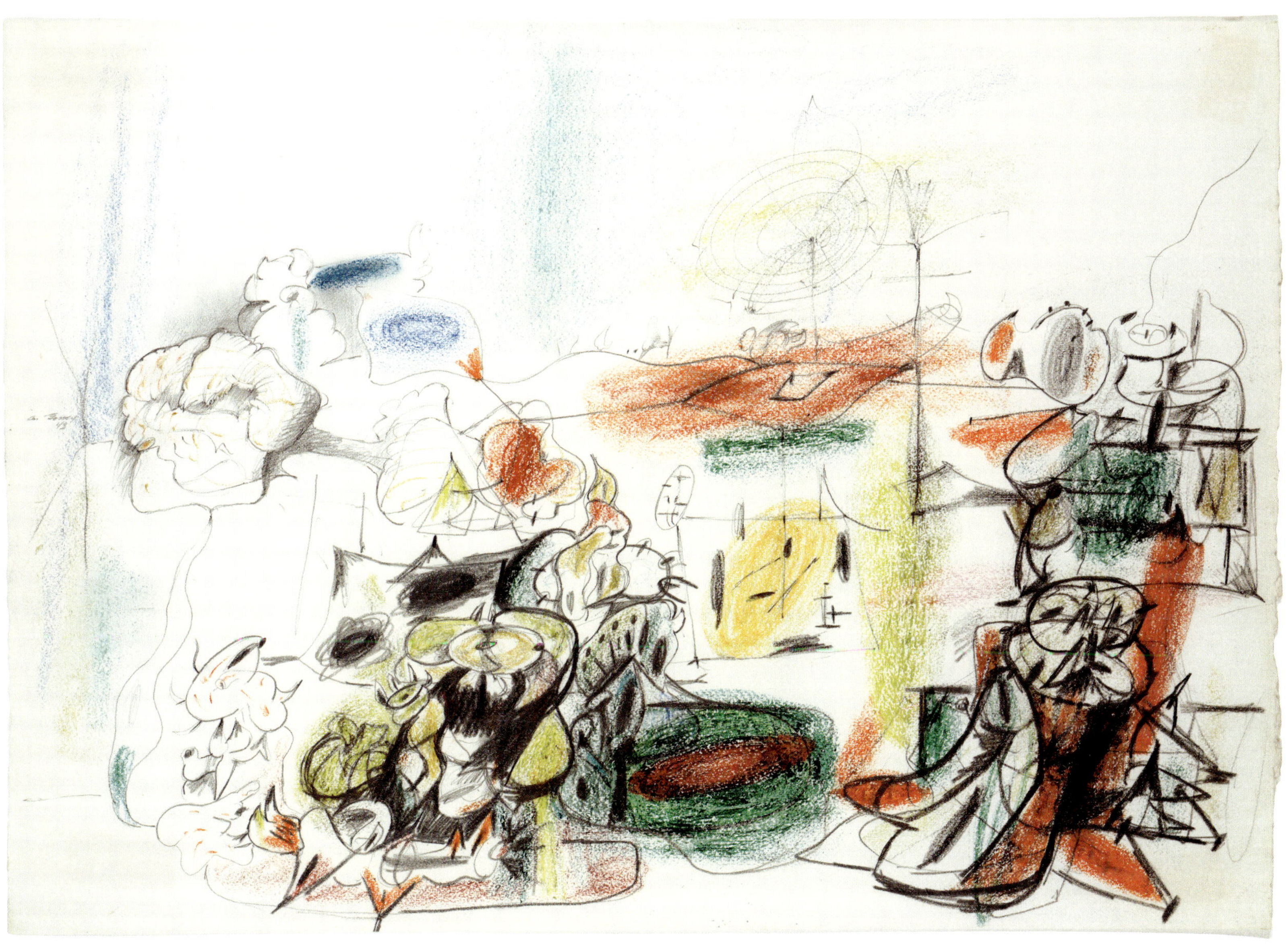

Cat. 70

like this one from such beautiful trees and plants and hills on their property, "I'm not drawing the trees. I'm drawing the space between the trees."[4]

In this drawing, like many others produced during his months in Virginia, Gorky kept areas of color – crayon, sometimes gently stroked across the paper surface but more often rubbed in hard – separated from rather lacy pencil underpinnings that locate his forms in space. After applying the crayon, he came back again with pencil to work the surface very heavily in places, so that the shininess of those penciled areas plays off against the waxiness of the crayon. This counterpoint of line and color contributes to the drawing's spatial complexity, setting up a telescoping of near and far distance. At the same time, Gorky's densely interwoven shapes pulsate with energy on the drawing's surface; his color is riotous, and the whole image reflects an intense, even exuberant, physicality. When Gorky returned from Virginia, he used many of the drawings to create paintings that are now seen as masterpieces, among them *The Liver Is the Cock's Comb* (1944; Albright-Knox Art Gallery, Buffalo) and *One Year the Milkweed* (1944; National Gallery of Art, Washington, D.C.). Whereas the Atheneum's drawing apparently was not used later as a sketch for a painting, its dynamism testifies to Gorky's joy at having found his own voice that summer. It is part of an astonishing body of work that inaugurated Gorky's period of greatest achievement.
CT

1. Gorky to Vartoosh Adoian Mooradian, April 1944, quoted in Karlen Mooradian, "The Letters of Arshile Gorky to Vartoosh, Moorad, and Karlen Mooradian," *Ararat* 12 (Fall 1971): 29–30, as quoted in Jim M. Jordan, "Arshile Gorky at Crooked Run Farm," *Arts Magazine* 50 (March 1976): 99.
2. Hayden Herrera, *Arshile Gorky, His Life and Work* (New York: Farrar, Straus and Giroux, 2003), 413.
3. See Harry Rand, *Arshile Gorky: The Implication of Symbols* (1981; repr., Berkeley and Los Angeles: University of California Press, 1991), 112; and Melvin P. Lader, "What the Drawings Reveal: Some Observations on Gorky's Working Method," in *Arshile Gorky: A Retrospective of Drawings*, by Janie C. Lee and Lader (New York: Whitney Museum of American Art, 2003), 42. As noted at the time by critic James Johnson Sweeny, "Then last summer Gorky decided to put art out of his mind, the galleries of Fifty-seventh Street and the reproductions of Picasso, Léger, and Miró, and 'look into the grass,' as he put it." "Five American Painters," *Harper's Bazaar* (April 1944): 123.
4. Herrera, *Gorky*, 421.

Sonja Sekula

Born in Lucerne, Switzerland, 1918; died in Zurich, 1963

Sonja Sekula and her family immigrated to New York in 1936 when Sekula's father moved his business there. Sekula studied art as well as philosophy and poetry at Sarah Lawrence College. In 1941 she began studying at the Art Students League, where she worked under George Grosz (q.v.) and Morris Kantor. Due in large part to her family's position in New York's European cultural circles, in the 1940s Sekula became well acquainted with New York's growing community of Surrealists, among them Matta (q.v.), Robert Motherwell, and Max Ernst.

Sekula's first solo exhibition was held in 1946 at Peggy Guggenheim's Art of This Century Gallery, then the hub for European Surrealists in America. Two years later Sekula was given a second solo show, this time at the Betty Parsons Gallery, where she would continue to exhibit until 1957. Sekula's most prolific years were the 1940s in New York. During this time she forged friendships with key members of the New York artistic avant-garde, not only painters but also such influential figures as the choreographer Merce Cunningham and composer John Cage. In 1949 Sekula embarked on a year-and-a-half-long trip throughout Europe and North Africa. Throughout her life Sekula documented her travels in sketchbooks with written entries as well as small-scale watercolors and drawings.

Returning to New York in the spring of 1951, Sekula was shown alongside Mark Rothko at the Betty Parsons Gallery. That same year, she participated in the Brooklyn Museum's biennial watercolor exhibition. At this point her work was beginning to reflect Abstract Expressionist tendencies as well as demonstrating the influence of Surrealist artists, Joan Miró in particular. Although she chose to work on a smaller scale than many of the male Abstract Expressionists (such as Jackson Pollock or Barnett Newman), critics and colleagues appreciated the vibrant intensity of her abstract forms, strong lines, and use of color.

Sekula's fragile mental state is a well-documented aspect of her artistic persona. Several mental breakdowns interrupted her work and caused her to withdraw from New York art circles. Suffering from a severe breakdown in 1952, she returned with her mother to Switzerland, where she was admitted to a clinic for treatment. While Sekula continued to appear in exhibitions in New York, she would not return to the city until her final solo show at the Betty Parsons Gallery in May 1957. The artist did not remain in New York long, returning to Switzerland that same year. Although she continued to work once she returned to Switzerland, the increasing severity of her mental instability is evident in her decline in productivity. Despite this decline, Sekula continued to work in oil as well as on paper, and began experimenting with collage in the early 1960s. She remained in Switzerland until her long battle with mental illness ended in her 1963 suicide in Zurich.

Select Bibliography

Nancy Foote. "Who Was Sonia Sekula?" *Art in America* 54 (September/October 1971): 73–79.

Walter Robinson. "Sonja Sekula Abstract Expressionist, Lesbian and Mad." *Artnet Magazine*, 21 September 1996. http://www.artnet.sk/magazine_pre2000/features/robinson/robinson9-21-96.asp.

Dieter Schwartz. *Sonja Sekula, 1918–1963*. New York: Swiss Institute, 1996.

71

Sonja Sekula
Spring . . . (Hurtings), 1950
Opaque and transparent watercolor and black ink applied with pen and brush on wove paper
14 15/16 × 22 1/2 in. (38 × 57.2 cm)
Signed and dated at lower right: Spring . . . (Hurtings) / Sekula 50
Inscribed on verso: Paris.1950
Ex coll.: Mr. and Mrs. Burton Tremaine, New York City, by 1951
Gift of Mr. and Mrs. Burton Tremaine, 1975.158

The Swiss-born Sonja Sekula was part of a generation of artists in transition from Surrealism to Abstract Expressionism. During the early 1940s she associated with other émigrés, among them André Breton, who befriended her, and Matta (q.v.), who introduced her to the practice of automatism.[1] By 1946 she was exhibiting at Peggy Guggenheim's Art of This Century Gallery, where Jackson Pollock and Mark Rothko also showed; like them, she subsequently moved to the Betty Parsons Gallery, where she exhibited frequently, beginning in 1948.

Although *Spring . . . (Hurtings)* probably was not included in Sekula's April 1951 exhibition at the Parsons Gallery (noted collector Emily Tremaine bought it in January of that year),[2] the show featured a number of similar, small-scale, lively watercolors. Those works caught the attention of *Art News* critic Thomas Hess, who praised their "free calligraphic abstractions" as "handsomely decorative and vigorous. Squirls, squiggles, dabs, dots and dashes, all related by their bright, chalky colors, build fancy skyscrapers."[3]

In the late 1940s Sekula produced a number of city-inspired watercolors containing fanciful architectural motifs. The earliest of these (*When the People Had Left the Town*, 1948; Munson-Williams-Proctor Arts Institute, Utica) was created while she was working in a loft on the Lower East Side of Manhattan. *Spring . . . (Hurtings)* was made in Paris during a period of travel to Europe and Morocco between the spring of 1949 and the winter of 1950–51.[4] But none of these watercolors refers to a particular place; rather, Sekula presents in them a fantastic environment, a dreamscape. Here, arched forms and square shapes capped with lunettes suggest windows and doorways; slim verticals crisscrossed by swaying linear girders evoke buildings under construction; cascading trapezoids conjure up a majestic staircase.

Sekula began by laying down an allover pattern of ink lines. Her wandering pen created a succession of elegant geometric details that are at once flat and three-dimensional, resting on the surface while gliding into space. Her seemingly random, free-associative method has roots in the Surrealist technique of automatic writing (or, in Sekula's pretension-deflating term, "telefonedoodling"[5]). At the same time, her use of tiny linear shapes to create a vast city is reminiscent of the work of her countryman Paul Klee, as are her penchant for pale soft tones and her enthusiasm for the medium of watercolor. Her palette here is limited, consisting of smoky grays and chalky blue washes with some touches of opaque white. The orange orb in the center—the only brightly colored shape in the picture and the only one unbounded by line—demands to be read as the sun. Like Klee's work, *Spring . . . (Hurtings)* is playful, decorative—yet not unserious.

The title Sekula gave to this watercolor is enigmatic and somewhat dispiriting. It may reflect her personal struggle with mental illness and her difficulty in making her way in the aggressively masculine culture of Abstract Expressionism.[6] Yet the painting itself is vibrant, even exuberant. A letter Sekula wrote to her mother some years before, speaking of her aspirations for her city pictures, provides an explanation for the optimistic vision presented here: "[I want] to speak of the New, the new

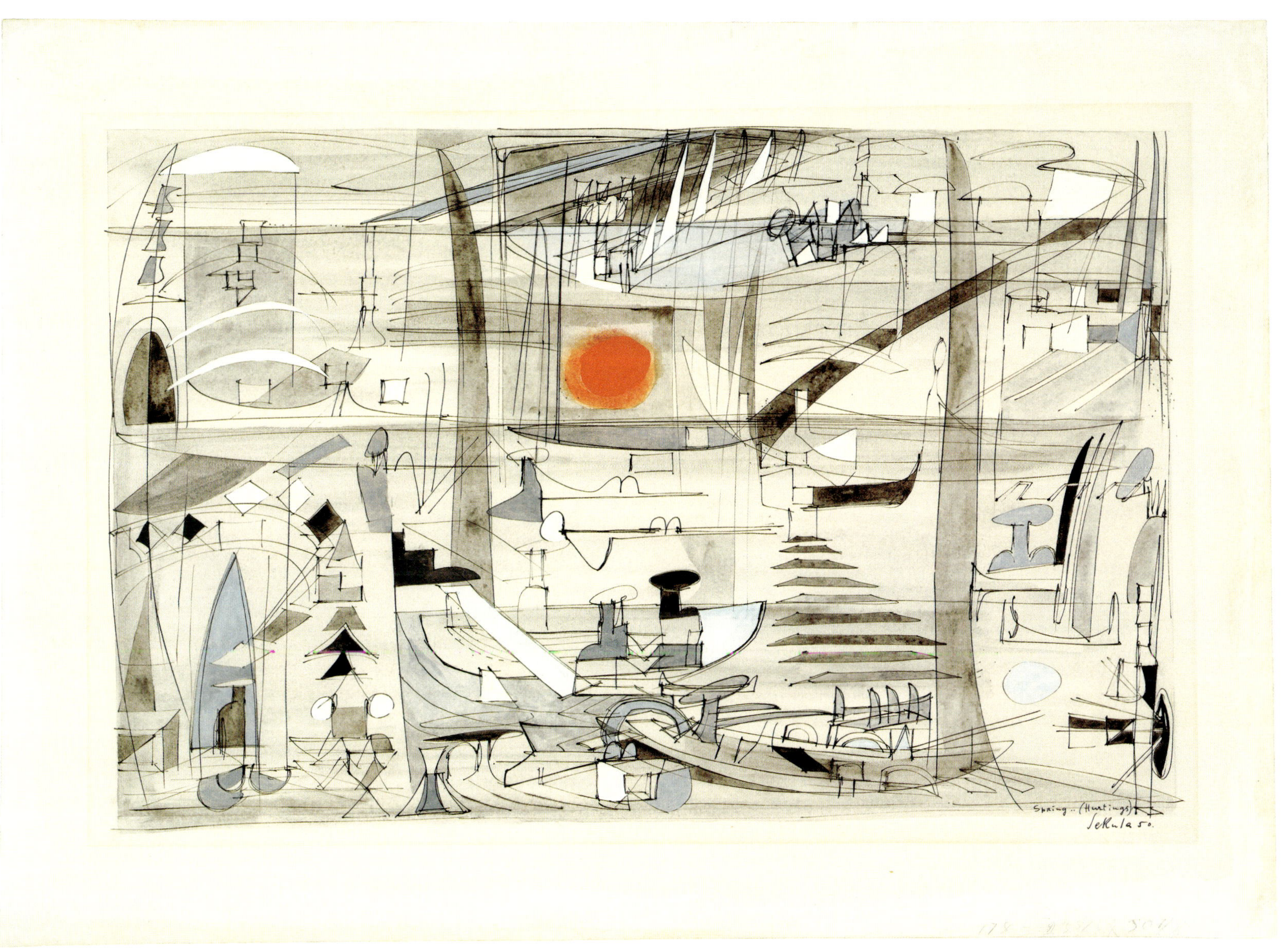

Cat. 71

cities that are shooting up along the river, the new settlements in which humanity shall dwell, the new space in which children shall throw up and spread their arms . . . a future we begin to feel underneath the current of war and strife and uncertainty."[7]
CT

1. That she was an integral part of this émigré community is indicated by her collaboration with Breton, Ernst, Matta, and others on a piece published in the Surrealist journal *VVV* in 1943.
2. Letter from Emily Hall Tremaine to Betty Parsons, 3 January 1951, requesting shipment of the work to Connecticut. Betty Parsons Papers, Archives of American Art, Smithsonian Institution, Washington, D.C.
3. T[homas] B. H[ess], "Sonia Sekula," *Art News* 20 (April 1951): 48.
4. Biographical sources disagree on the exact date of Sekula's return to the United States. The Internet site www.sonja-sekula.org/timeline.htm (accessed October 2008) cites her return in November 1950 from Hamburg; other publications describe her coming back in time for her April 1951 exhibition at the Parsons Gallery.
5. Walter Robinson, "Sonja Sekula Abstract Expressionist, Lesbian and Mad," *Artnet Magazine*, 21 September 1996, http://www.artnet.sk/magazine_pre2000/features/robinson/robinson9-21-96.asp.
6. For a thoughtful discussion of how Sekula–schizophrenic and openly lesbian–was marginalized by the New York School, see Ann Eden Gibson, *Abstract Expressionism: Other Politics* (New Haven, Conn.: Yale University Press, 1997), 127–30. However, Sekula's work may have kept these experiences at a distance, as is suggested by Brian O'Doherty in Nancy Foote, "Who Was Sonia Sekula?" *Art in America* 54 (September/October 1971): 74. O'Doherty observes, "While suffering her pain, she did not seem able to experience it. It eluded her as a subject."
7. Sekula, quoted in Foote, "Who Was Sonia Sekula?" 76.

Theodore Roszak

Born in Pozna, Poland, 1907;
died in New York, 1981

The Polish-born Roszak was raised in Chicago from the age of two. He studied at the Art Institute of Chicago from 1925 to 1926 and then briefly attended the National Academy of Design, New York, in 1926. Dissatisfied with the program, he returned to Chicago in 1927 and was soon appointed a full-time faculty member at the Art Institute. Roszak began as a painter and throughout his career continued to explore ways of expressing his ideas in a variety of media, including drawing and lithography.

The decade of the 1930s marked a turning point in Roszak's development. A visit to Europe in 1929–30 provided crucial exposure to modernist trends. His encounters with Surrealism, Constructivism, and Bauhaus styles through art as well as avant-garde magazines and books helped him find his mature voice. Roszak built his first sculptures using clay and plaster, but from 1932 to 1945, he made constructions using painted wood, metal, and plastic, which reflected utopian Constructivist ideals.

During World War II, Roszak taught aircraft mechanics and built airplanes. After the war, however, Roszak's art underwent a major shift. He explored the darker side of the technological progress that had caused tremendous death and destruction. His faith in the natural world was renewed, and he used a more expressive style for his welded, brazed metal sculptures. His later work included large drawings, many with cosmological themes, and large-scale sculptures, including a spire and bell tower for Eero Saarinen's chapel at the Massachusetts Institute of Technology (1960).

Select Bibliography

H. H. Arnason. *Theodore Roszak*. Minneapolis: Walker Art Center, 1956.

Douglas Dreishpoon. *Theodore Roszak: Constructivist Works, 1931–1947; Paintings, Constructions, Drawings, Photograms*. New York: Hirschl & Adler Galleries, 1992.

Joan M. Marter. *Theodore Roszak: The Drawings*. New York: Drawing Society, 1992.

72

Theodore Roszak
Four Studies for "Firebird," 1949
Black ink, applied using pen and brush, on wove paper
14 3/4 × 20 in. (37.5 × 50.8 cm)
Signed and dated at lower center: Fury–T.J. Roszak '49 / Firebird
Verso: Study for Firebird
Ex coll.: the artist; Belle K. Ribicoff, West Hartford, Connecticut, by 1961
Gift of Belle K. Ribicoff, 1991.156

A brilliant and prolific draftsman, Roszak made drawings for many purposes. Sometimes, as here, he made several sketches on a single sheet, in energetic anticipation of a sculpture. Other drawings are refined presentations of forms and ideas also expressed in metal. In addition, he created highly imaginative, sprawling compositions that exist independent of work in any other medium. Frequently, motifs introduced in one forum reappear in another–for example, the long, slender, spiderlike legs and crescent-shaped, hornlike form in the present drawing from 1949 recur in the iron, bronze, and brass sculpture *Firebird* (Metropolitan Museum of Art, New York), and in the larger, more formal preparatory drawing (also Metropolitan Museum of Art), both made the next year (fig. 1).[1] Related images also occur in the explosive, large-scale ink drawing *Study for "The Furies"* (1950; Whitney Museum of American Art, New York). Roszak may have used the present sketch as a jumping-off point for both the sculpture and the Whitney's drawing, for he inscribed it "Fury" as well as "Firebird."

Like a number of artists of his generation, Roszak was profoundly disturbed by the events of World War II. About 1945, he renounced his earlier utopian Constructivist style and began searching for imagery that expressed both his rage at the violence and destruction and his faith in human endurance.[2] The firebird proved to be an ideal image through which Roszak could express these feelings. In 1949 he attended a New York City Ballet performance of Stravinsky's *Firebird*, and was captivated by the magical creature.[3] He was further inspired by conversations with Joseph Campbell, his friend and fellow faculty member at Sarah Lawrence College, about universal myths. The firebird (which appears in Russian, Chinese, and Native American folktales) glowed with a supernatural light that transformed its surroundings while generating a heat so intense that it destroyed itself. But (like its cognate, the phoenix) the firebird then rose again from its own ashes–a metaphor for destruction and regeneration, vulnerability and power.

Although Roszak's drawings were rooted in the gestural abstraction of much postwar art, they are also in some manner baroque, in their theatrical dynamism and in their classical structure and balance. The variant sketches on this sheet reveal Roszak's search for a configuration that was flamboyant but also harmonious. He used a thin ink outline to give shape to a creature that, especially in the largest sketch, is spectacularly balletic, elegant yet grotesque. His system of cross-hatching, shaggy strokes, and dots of ink creates evocative surface textures. Roszak used wash (or its absence, as in the reserved paper on the crescent shape) to model his form and locate it in space, generating a sense of looming three-dimensionality. Layers of gray wash form a backdrop for the whirling firebird, while a pool of more densely colored wash at the base forms a ground plane from which the graceful, formidable bird rises, as if *en pointe*.
CT

Fig. 1. Theodore J. Roszak, *Study for "Firebird,"* 1950. Pen and ink, watercolor, and pencil on paper, 28 7/8 × 34 7/8 in. (73.3 × 88.6 cm). The Metropolitan Museum of Art, New York. The Muriel Kallis Steinberg Newman Collection, Gift of Muriel Kallis Newman, in memory of the artist, 1982, 1982.16.2

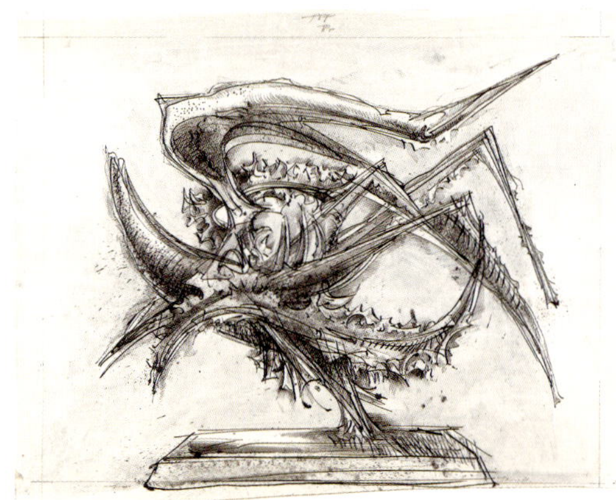

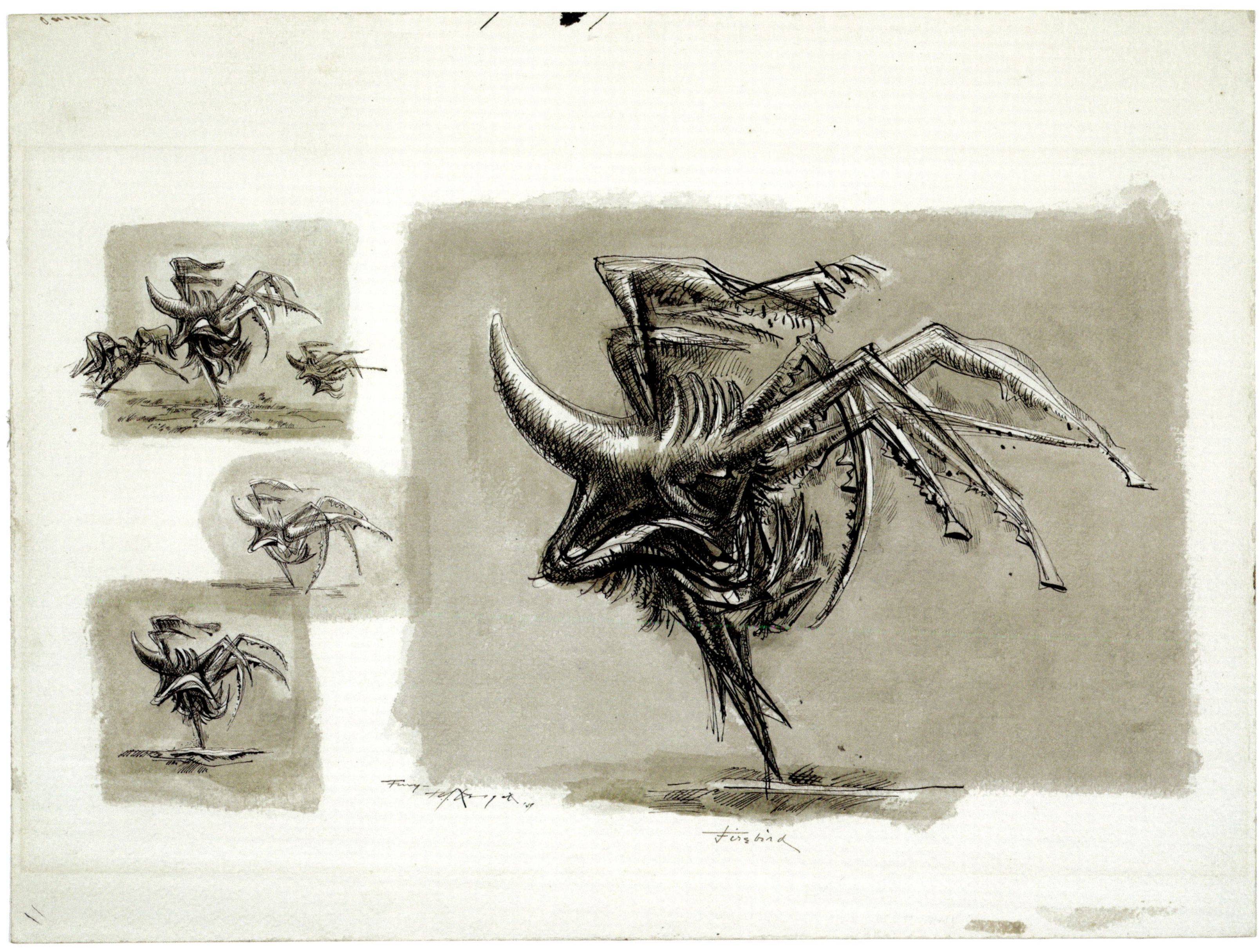

Cat. 72

1. There were undoubtedly a number of preparatory studies for the sculpture. See, for an additional example, the pen and ink and wash *Firebird* (c. 1949; estate of Theodore Roszak [in 1992]), reproduced in Joan M. Marter, *Theodore Roszak: The Drawings* (New York: Drawing Society, 1992), 23.

2. As he explained in 1955, "The forms that I find necessary to assert, are meant to be blunt reminders of primordial strife and struggle, reminiscent of those brute forces that not only produce life, but in turn threatened to destroy it. I feel that if necessary, one must be ready to summon one's total being with an all-consuming rage against those forces that are blind to the primacy of life-giving values. Perhaps by this sheer dedication, one may yet merge force and grace." Theodore Roszak, "In Pursuit of an Image," lecture delivered at the School of the Art Institute of Chicago, March 1955, *Quadrum* 2 (November 1956): 54.

3. Roszak recalled, "[Stravinsky] has these slow smoldering chords that accelerate and then whip up into a terrific frenzy of sound . . . [the firebird] embodied a kind of ritualistic experience that found its habitat in practically any part of the world that has . . . [gone] through this smoldering and phoenix-like emergence out of a complete desolation and affirming its position all over again in terms of affirming life." James H. Elliott, "Interview with Theodore Roszak," 13 February 1956, Roszak Papers, Archives of American Art, Smithsonian Institution, Washington, D.C.

Seymour Lipton

Born in New York, 1903;
died in New York, 1986

Seymour Lipton began his professional career as a dental surgeon, graduating from Columbia University in 1927. He began pursuing a career as an artist in 1932, and five years later had his first solo exhibition, at the ACA Gallery in New York.

While he described himself as a sculptor, Lipton was dedicated to drawing, and this commitment runs throughout his artistic career, functioning as an integral step in his artistic process. For Lipton, drawing provided a means of working through preliminary ideas for his finished sculptures. Working mainly in black oil crayon, he often produced multiple sketches before turning to three-dimensional work.

During the 1940s Lipton's art underwent several transitions–most notably he began to explore different metals for his sculpture, working first in lead and then bronze. Inspired by Constructivism, Lipton built his sculptures by assembling sheets of metal and manipulated them through brazing: bendable materials easily lent themselves to abstract forms. In the 1940s, he investigated the natural forces of the universe, the cycles of life and death, and the human condition. His work reflects a fascination with and concern for the emotional effects of war and suffering on the human condition, an interest that he shared with his artistic contemporaries in the postwar period.

Lipton was part of a group of sculptors working in New York that brought their medium to the elevated status previously achieved only by painting. In 1951 the Museum of Modern Art in New York recognized this new status by giving postwar Constructivist sculptors a significant presence in its monumental *Abstract Painting and Sculpture in America* show. In addition to Lipton, David Smith (q.v.), Alexander Calder (q.v.), Isamu Noguchi (q.v.), and Richard Lippold were featured in the exhibition.

Lipton showed regularly at the Betty Parsons Gallery in New York City between 1948 and 1961. In 1958 he represented the United States at the Brussels World Fair as well as the Venice Biennale, where he was featured in a solo exhibition. Throughout his career, Lipton explored the relationship between man and nature, which he echoed in the dynamic movement of his sculpture.

Select Bibliography

Harry Rand. *Seymour Lipton, Aspects of Sculpture.* Washington, D.C.: Smithsonian Institution Press, 1979.

Lori Verderame. *An American Sculptor: Seymour Lipton.* University Park: Pennsylvania State University, 1999.

Martica Sawin. *Seymour Lipton: A Sculptor's Odyssey.* New York: Michael Rosenfeld Gallery, 2005.

73

Seymour Lipton
Untitled [Study for Earth Forge #1], 1954
Black crayon on thin wove paper
(Watermark: Riverside Bond)
8 1/2 × 11 in. (21.6 × 27.9 cm)
Signed and dated at lower right: Lipton '54
Ex coll.: Terese and Alvin S. Lane Foundation, New York
Gift from the Terese and Alvin S. Lane Foundation, 1962.156

"I usually begin with a rough crayon drawing,"[1] Lipton wrote to Atheneum director Charles C. Cunningham in 1956. He was describing the process leading to the metal sculpture *Earth Forge #1*, which the Atheneum had acquired the previous year (fig. 1). In fact, Lipton generally made scores of drawings (most of them in Conté crayon on an 8 1/2 × 11–inch sheet of bond paper, as here) in anticipation of his sculptures, which themselves were often produced in series. The Atheneum owns a second drawing for *Earth Forge #1* (fig. 2); the sculpture *Earth Forge #2* (nickel silver over steel; Brooklyn Museum) was completed in 1955.

Lipton's imagery from the mid-1950s combined the organic and the mechanical, as his title, *Earth Forge*, suggests. It also reflected his perception—one shared with other abstract sculptors of his day—that tension and conflict were required for progress and growth.[2] Drawings were key to expressing this conflict: "I was concerned at the time with a mood of violent struggle conveyed through a formal feeling of monumental simplicity. Specifically, from nature it grew out of such things as twisted giant cacti and gnarled roots. Yet in a sense it was purely a formal search for newness . . . in the course of several sketches, the sense of growth, intertwining and a somewhat hidden interior emerged."[3]

Lipton designed *Earth Forge* to be seen in the round; in the Atheneum's drawings, he represented it rotated ninety degrees.[4] As he moved from those sketches to the final sculpture, he made significant changes. In this drawing, he laid out the knotted shape that

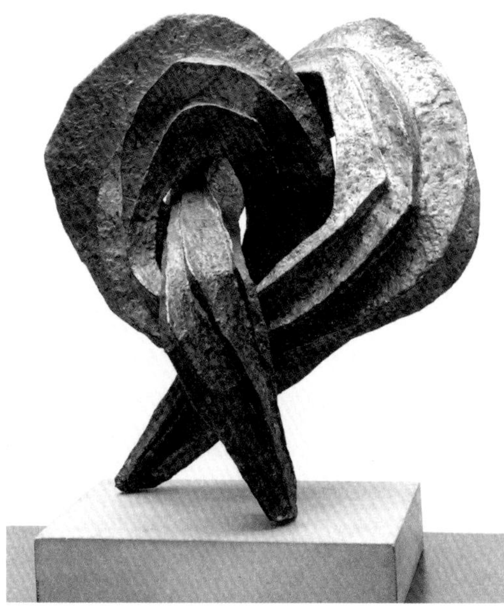

Fig. 1. Seymour Lipton, *Earth Forge #1*, 1954. Nickel silver over steel, 29 in. (73.7 cm). Wadsworth Atheneum Museum of Art. Gift of Susan Morse Hilles, 1955.282

Fig. 2. Seymour Lipton, *Untitled [Study for Earth Forge #1]*, 1954. Black crayon on paper, 8 1/2 × 11 in. (21.6 × 27.9 cm). Wadsworth Atheneum Museum of Art. Gift from The Terese and Alvin S. Lane Foundation, 1962.10

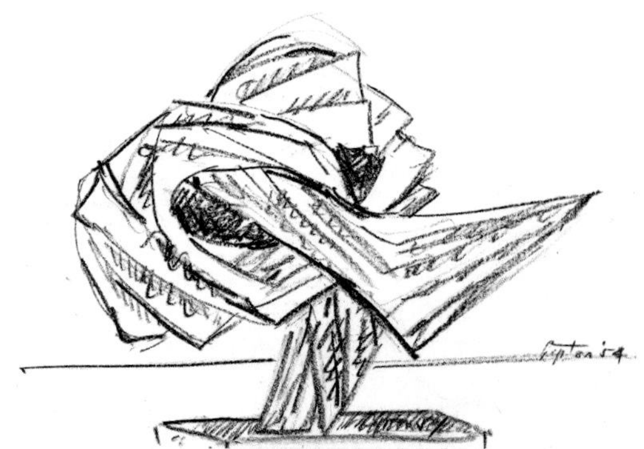

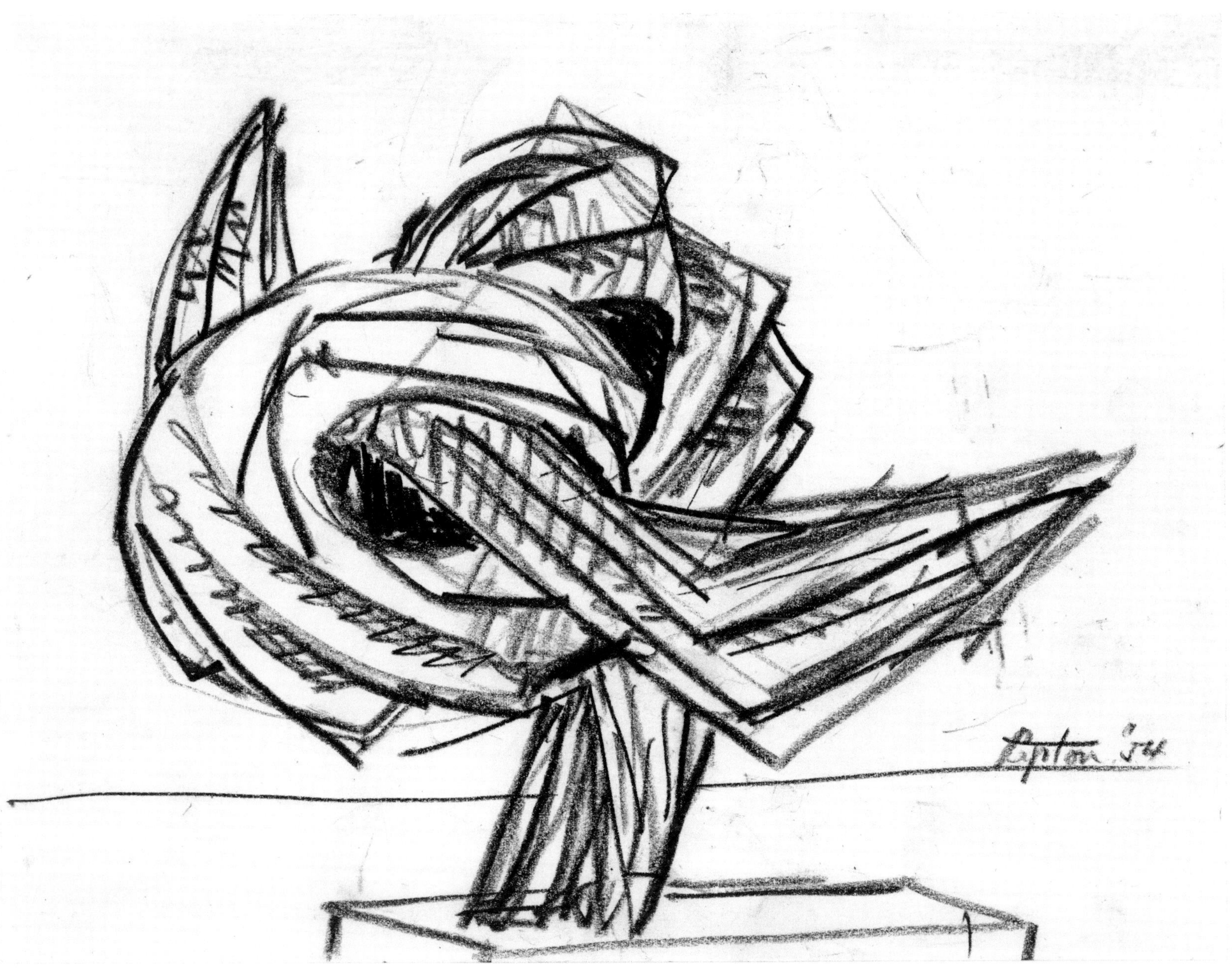

Cat. 73

would define the finished piece, and worked to give form to the tension between centrifugal and centripetal energy that was a recurring theme in his work. That energy seems more dynamic, tougher, less controlled than in the sculpture. By eliminating the second triangular "arm" that reaches out from the body of the form, Lipton arrived at a sculpture that is more contained, dense, self-involved. (The other drawing also has only one "arm" and as a result is more compact, but less gestural and anthropomorphic.) In addition, as the piece was reoriented for mounting, the massive trunk of the drawings became two legs, and the metal form assumed a dancelike posture that is at once casual and taut.

To envision his sketch in three dimensions (or, as Lipton explained, "so [the drawing] is a schema for a sculpture, never just a graphic conception"[5]), Lipton drew a base beneath his form. Here the form rises from one end of the base. By locating it off center, Lipton accentuated its dynamism. He also drew a horizon line, which provided a resting place for his signature and created "the illusion of an object standing on the ground."[6]
CT

1. Seymour Lipton to Charles C. Cunningham, 6 January 1956, Wadsworth Atheneum Archives.
2. Lori Verderame, *An American Sculptor: Seymour Lipton* (University Park: Pennsylvania State University, 1999), 27, citing Albert Elsen, "Seymour Lipton: Odyssey of the Unquiet Metaphor," *Art International* 5 (1 February 1961): 38–44.
3. Lipton to Cunningham, 6 January 1956.
4. That Lipton regarded a different view of the piece as the primary one is indicated in a letter to Cunningham of 8 December 1955, in which he provided a sketch of the sculpture resting on a wooden base. Wadsworth Atheneum Archives.
5. Tal Streeter, "The Sculptor's Role: An Interview with Seymour Lipton," *Register of the Museum of Art of the University of Kansas* 2 (April 1962): 29, quoted in Verderame, *American Sculptor*, 52.
6. Seymour Lipton Papers, "Notes," 1 March 1967, Archives of American Art, Smithsonian Institution, quoted in Verderame, *American Sculptor*, 53.

Paul Cadmus

Born in New York, 1904;
died in Weston, Connecticut, 1999

Paul Cadmus was born to artistic parents and enjoyed drawing and painting from an early age. His first preoccupation was with drawing, and he remained devoted to the medium throughout his career. At fifteen, Cadmus entered the National Academy of Design, where he studied until 1925. He continued his formal training at the Art Students League, where he enrolled in a lithography class with Joseph Pennell (q.v.). He continued taking classes there from 1928 to 1931 while he was employed as a commercial illustrator.

Cadmus's artistic career truly began when he quit commercial work in order to travel to Europe with his friend and fellow artist Jared French. Cadmus and French remained abroad for two years, eventually setting up a studio in Mallorca, a town off the coast of Spain. Cadmus's Mallorcan paintings and drawings included portraits, harbor scenes, and landscapes.

In 1933, after having read about the American Scene movement, Cadmus returned home to New York City to become one of the first participants in the Public Works of Art Project (PWAP), established in December of that year by the U.S. Treasury Department. His focus on the figurative and his background as an illustrator was well suited to the sociopolitical subject matter of government commissions. What Cadmus became known for, however, was the provocative and satirical undertones in his paintings, which often stirred up controversy. The first instance was when his painting *The Fleet's In!* (1934)–a depiction of uniformed sailors on leave soliciting prostitutes and engaging in homosexual activity–was removed from the initial PWAP exhibition in Washington, D.C. He continued to receive important painting and mural commissions but often with mixed reactions. For example, a 1940 commission by *Life* magazine to paint the labor struggle in the United States was rejected on political grounds.

Throughout the 1940s, Cadmus gained recognition as a major American artist, exhibiting regularly at the Midtown Galleries in New York City. During this time, his painting style was associated with magic realism, a term first associated with certain European artists but brought into wider use in the 1940s. Cadmus was included in the landmark exhibition *American Realists and Magic Realists* at the Museum of Modern Art in 1943. The term *magic realism* was used to describe painting in which strange or "unreal" elements were pictured in a realistic, often meticulous style. Cadmus was among several notable magic realists who used egg tempera, a technique borrowed from the Italian Renaissance.

Cadmus was part of a circle of writers, artists, musicians, and choreographers whom he considered colleagues and friends. These included W. H. Auden, George Balanchine, Christopher Isherwood, Lincoln Kirstein (his brother-in-law), and George Platt Lynes. Cadmus moved to Weston, Connecticut, in 1975, and continued to paint until his death at the age of ninety-four.

Select Bibliography

Guy Davenport. *The Drawings of Paul Cadmus.* New York: Rizzoli, 1989.

Jonathan Weinberg. *Paul Cadmus: Visionary Realist.* New Haven, Conn.: Yale University Art Gallery, 1997.

Philip Eliasoph. "A Tribute to Paul Cadmus." *American Art* 14, no. 3 (Fall 2000): 94.

74

Paul Cadmus
Ignis Fatuus, 1950
Colored crayon on black wove charcoal paper
18 3/4 × 24 1/4 in. (47.6 × 61.6 cm)
Signed at lower left: Cadmus
Ex coll.: with Midtown Galleries, New York; Henry E. Schnakenberg, Newtown, Connecticut
Gift of Henry E. Schnakenberg, 1953.218

The phrase *ignis fatuus*, the title of Cadmus's drawing, translates from Latin as "foolish fire" and is more poetically defined as "a deceptive goal or hope." This is a preparatory drawing for the background of the painting in the Atheneum's collection, *Architect* (fig. 1). The completed painting is an imaginative portrait of an architect and his tools. Upon closer inspection the composition presents a deeper, symbolic criticism of modernity.[1] At center, a man stares intently toward the viewer. His chiseled features and cold stare make him appear robotic, emotionless. The tools of the trade surround him: a T-square, two cubes on the desk, and a third mysterious glass box sitting atop a blueprint. The starkness and rigidity of the central figure–the architect–contrasts with the softness and sensuality of the male nude reflected in the window.

Cadmus's study focuses entirely on the architectural background, visible through the windowpanes in the finished product. Using black paper to create the evening setting, he meticulously defines the framework of the buildings with touches of white and yellow crayon. The lattice pattern represents hundreds of office spaces, identical in size and generic in their appearance. The view of clustered buildings was adapted from the view seen from the artist's apartment in New York City's West Village.[2] Despite the familiar setting, Cadmus infuses the scene with a feeling of detachment. The glow of incandescent interior lights from the office buildings feigns a "real" human presence. The *ignis fatuus* is thus the rub of the modern era; the false hope that the increased physical proximity of people will create real, tangible connections.

Cadmus's interest in different professions inspired two earlier paintings: *Aviator* (1941; private collection, New York), and *Inventor* (1946; collection James and Barbara Palmer). *Architect* can be seen as a companion piece to this group. As a figurative painter, Cadmus's paintings highlight male figures, all of which

Fig. 1. Paul Cadmus, *Architect*, 1950. Egg tempera on Masonite panel, 25 1/2 × 25 1/2 in. (64.8 × 64.8 cm). Wadsworth Atheneum Museum of Art. Gift of an anonymous donor, 1992.79

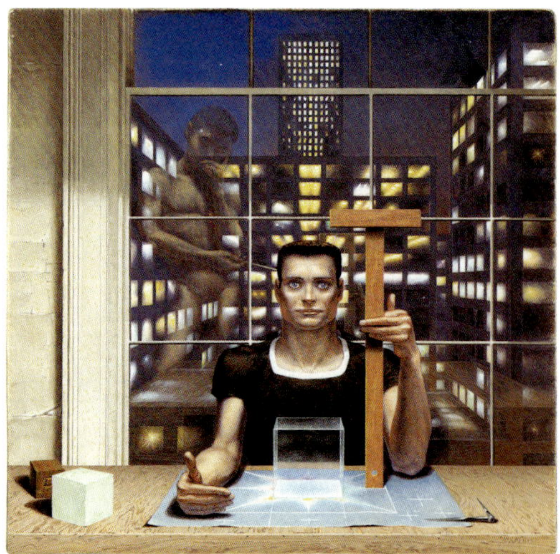

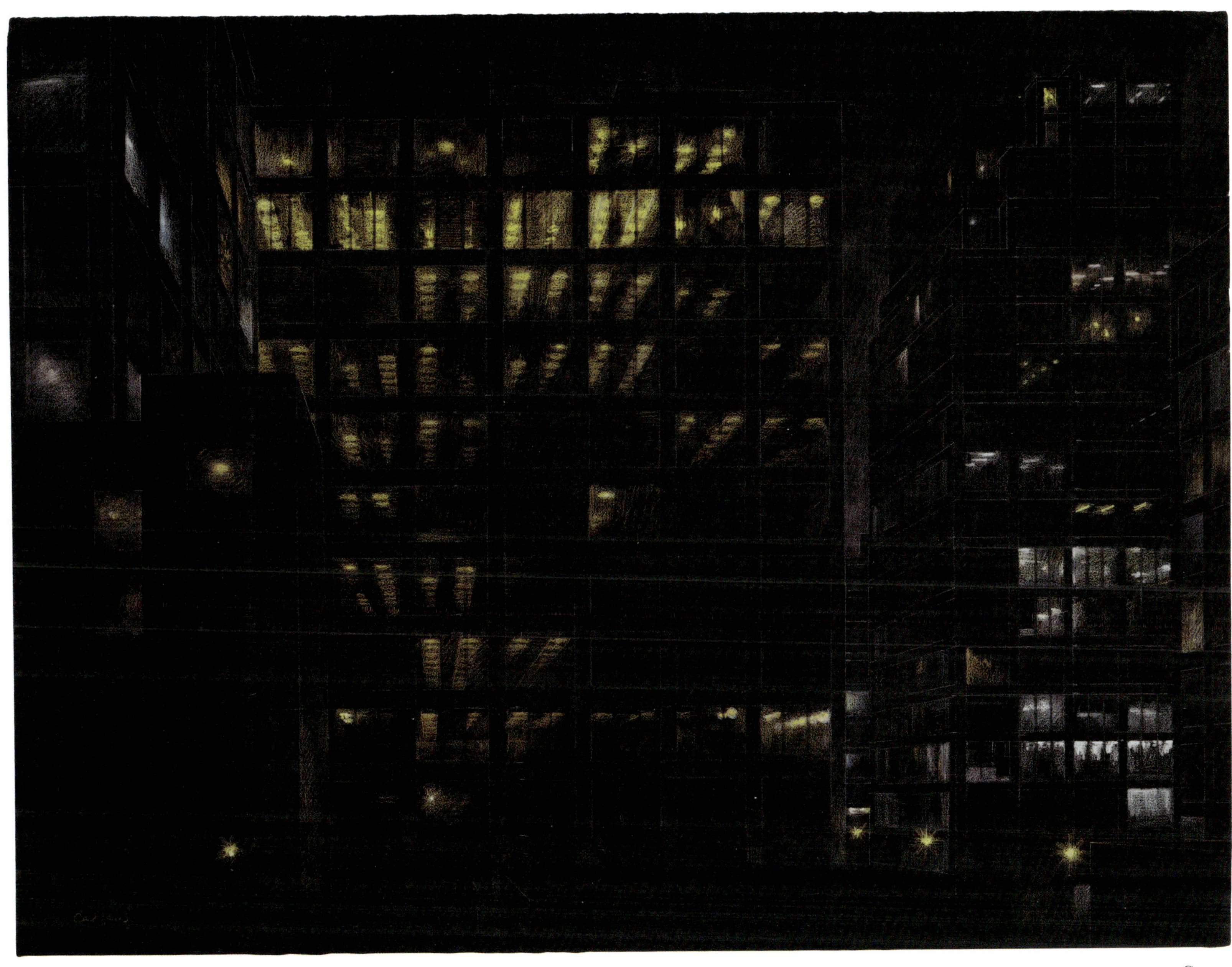

Cat. 74

were based on people he knew. Although homosexuality was not Cadmus's raison d'être for his art, the male figure played an important and often autobiographical role in his paintings: in *Architect*, the central model is Charles "Chuck" Howard, and the nude figure is the artist George Tooker, Cadmus's partner at that time.[3] *Architect* symbolizes the rift between the rigidity and starkness of modernism and the sensuality and beauty of the human form. The inclusion of a male nude "suggests that for Cadmus, the measure of all things is not some abstract system, but the human body itself."[4]
ECM

1. Guy Davenport, *The Drawings of Paul Cadmus* (New York: Rizzoli, 1989), 15: "In Cadmus we have a rare balance that few artists achieve in any medium: compassion and contempt."
2. Paul Cadmus to Charles C. Cunningham, 29 June 1954, Wadsworth Atheneum Archives. Writing from 5 St. Luke's Place, New York City, Cadmus explained that the drawing was "very much based on the view from my windows here overlooking a playground towards a school and various office buildings."
3. Philip Eliasoph, "A Tribute to Paul Cadmus," *American Art* 14, no. 3 (Fall 2000): 94. Eliasoph quotes Cadmus as saying, "Gayness is not the raison d'être of my work."
4. Jonathan Weinberg, *Paul Cadmus: Visionary Realist* (New Haven, Conn.: Yale University Art Gallery, 1997), 2.

Peter Blume

Born in Smorgon, Russia, 1906;
died in New Milford, Connecticut, 1992

Peter Blume painted dreamlike, painstakingly detailed works that made him one of the best known artists in the United States in the 1930s and '40s. Born in Russia, after the revolution he immigrated with his family to Brooklyn, New York, in 1911, when he was five years old. From 1921 to 1924 he studied art at the Educational Alliance, the Beaux-Arts Institute of Design, and the Art Students League in New York. He began showing his work at the Charles Daniel Gallery, New York, in 1925, and had his first solo show there in 1930. In the 1920s Blume painted precisely rendered architectural motifs that related to Precisionism; several of the Precisionists, including Charles Demuth (q.v.), Charles Sheeler (q.v.), and Niles Spencer, were also represented by the Charles Daniel Gallery. At this time, he began to introduce Surrealist juxtapositions of recognizable objects that did not relate to one another. Displaying a curious hybrid of American and European artistic traditions and disparate styles, Blume's work became famous for its meticulous rendering of forms and humanistic themes in a style perhaps best defined as magic realism. In his most famous works, he explored the dangers of technology, the horrors of fascism, and the isolation of urban existence through disturbing dreamlike imagery. His labor-intensive method resulted in a small body of work.

Blume won a Guggenheim Fellowship in 1932 and traveled to Italy, where he made preliminary drawings for his most famous painting, *The Eternal City* (1934–37; Museum of Modern Art, New York). This politically charged work depicted a green-headed Il Duce as a jack-in-the-box and was exhibited in 1937 at the Julien Levy Gallery, New York. He gained international acclaim in 1934 when his Surrealist-inspired painting *South of Scranton* (1931; Carnegie Museum of Art, Pittsburgh) won first prize at the Carnegie International Exhibition of Paintings in Pittsburgh.

Blume spent much of his career in Sherman, Connecticut, and was a member of the group of modern artists, writers, and critics who were drawn to the northwestern corner of the state.

Select Bibliography

Robert Ulric Godsoe. "Peter Blume–A New Vision." *Creative Art* 10 (September 1932): 11–15.

Charles E. Buckley. *Peter Blume: Paintings & Drawings in Retrospect, 1925 to 1964*. Manchester, N.H.: Currier Gallery of Art, 1964.

Dennis Adrian and Peter Blume. *Peter Blume*. Chicago: Museum of Contemporary Art, 1976.

75

Peter Blume
Sketch for "The Italian Straw Hat," c. 1952
Oil paint and black ink over graphite on wove paper, mounted on a sheet of black wove paper
$4^{1}/_{2}$ × 6 in. (11.4 × 15.2 cm)
Ex coll.: with Peter Blume, Sherman, Connecticut, until 1956
Gift of Peter Blume, 1956.482

Peter Blume made a gift of three preliminary drawings for his painting *The Italian Straw Hat* (fig. 1) to the Wadsworth Atheneum in 1956 because, as he expressed in a letter to Atheneum director Charles C. Cunningham, "they belong with the painting."[1] Cunningham had purchased the painting a year earlier using the Henry Schnakenberg Fund (see Elizabeth Mankin Kornhauser, "Galvanizing Hartford," in this volume), and had written to the artist inquiring about this seemingly enigmatic work. A second-floor room is filled with an odd assortment of objects that appear to take on a life of their own. Blume explained:

> *I was trying to clarify my approach to picture composition by, as it were, nailing down the relationships of extremely familiar objects and their peculiarities. There is no better place to study this problem than in one's own bedroom. It's at once the world within and the world without, and I tried to convey a sense of being inside of a house with the world around it.*[2]

Blume moved to Sherman, Connecticut, in 1930, following in the footsteps of his Greenwich Village left-wing colleagues, the writers Malcolm Cowley, Matthew Josephson, and Robert Coates. There he bought a farmhouse directly across from Cowley on Church Road, surrounded by farmland, with an eighteenth-century cemetery nearby, just out of sight. Alexander Calder (q.v.) joined the group, settling in nearby Roxbury, Connecticut.

In observing his second-story bedroom (this room had earlier served as his studio), Blume chose to emphasize a number of disparate objects for his finished oil painting and included views of local scenery through the windows – cows grazing in the fields and the cemetery just down the road from his house.

The oil and watercolor study for the painting focuses on the room interior and its objects, and does not address the exterior views. Blume includes a straw hat hanging on the back wall, and that serves as the title for the painting.[3] The artist had returned from Italy in 1952, around when *The Italian Straw Hat* was made. Near the hat, Blume painted a rendition of a mobile that his friend and neighbor Alexander Calder had made for him, *Untitled Mobile* (c. 1942; private collection).[4] Other elements in the room include a blue painted dresser at right with a pitcher (filled with flowers in the finished oil) placed on top, a country chair holding a knitting basket at the center of the room, a striped rug on the floor that seems to spring to life, and a bright yellow curtain at the window. The study is executed in roughly applied brushstrokes using both thin oil paint and areas of watercolor, and it lacks the precision of the finished painting, which is executed with Blume's characteristic meticulous, hyperreal detail. In addition to this study, Blume also gave the Atheneum a pencil sketch and a crayon study done in the same year, both also entitled *Sketch for "The Italian Straw Hat."*

EMK

Fig. 1. Peter Blume, *The Italian Straw Hat*, 1952. Oil on paper on board, $22^{1}/_{4}$ × $30^{3}/_{8}$ in. (56.5 × 77.2 cm). Wadsworth Atheneum Museum of Art. The Schnakenberg Fund, 1955.32

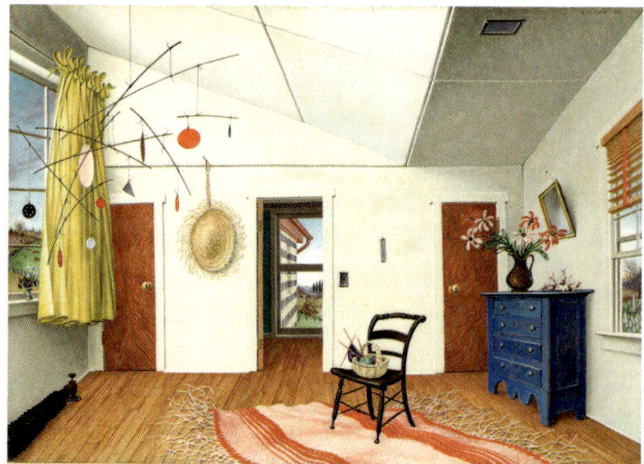

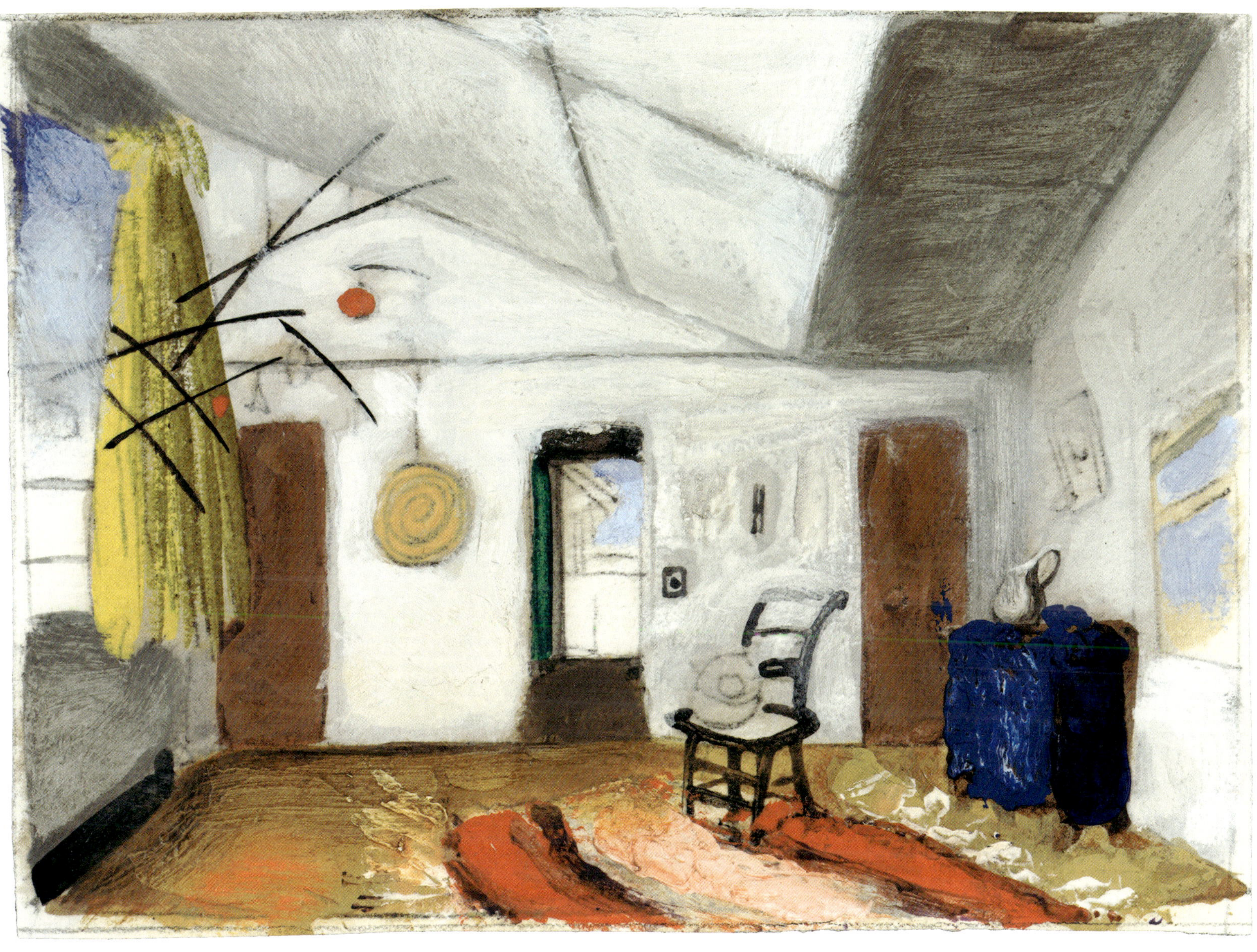

Cat. 75

1. Peter Blume to Charles C. Cunningham, 23 August 1956, Wadsworth Atheneum Archives.
2. Blume to Cunningham, 1 February 1955, Wadsworth Atheneum Archives.
3. It is not clear whether the artist was making a reference in the title for his painting to the popular comedy by Eugène Labiche and Marc Michel published in 1851, *An Italian Straw Hat*, and which was later made into René Clair's 1927 film *The Italian Straw Hat*.
4. Eric M. Zafran, with contributions by Elizabeth Mankin Kornhauser and Cynthia Roman, *Calder in Connecticut* (Hartford, Conn.: Wadsworth Atheneum in association with Rizzoli, 2000), 68–69.

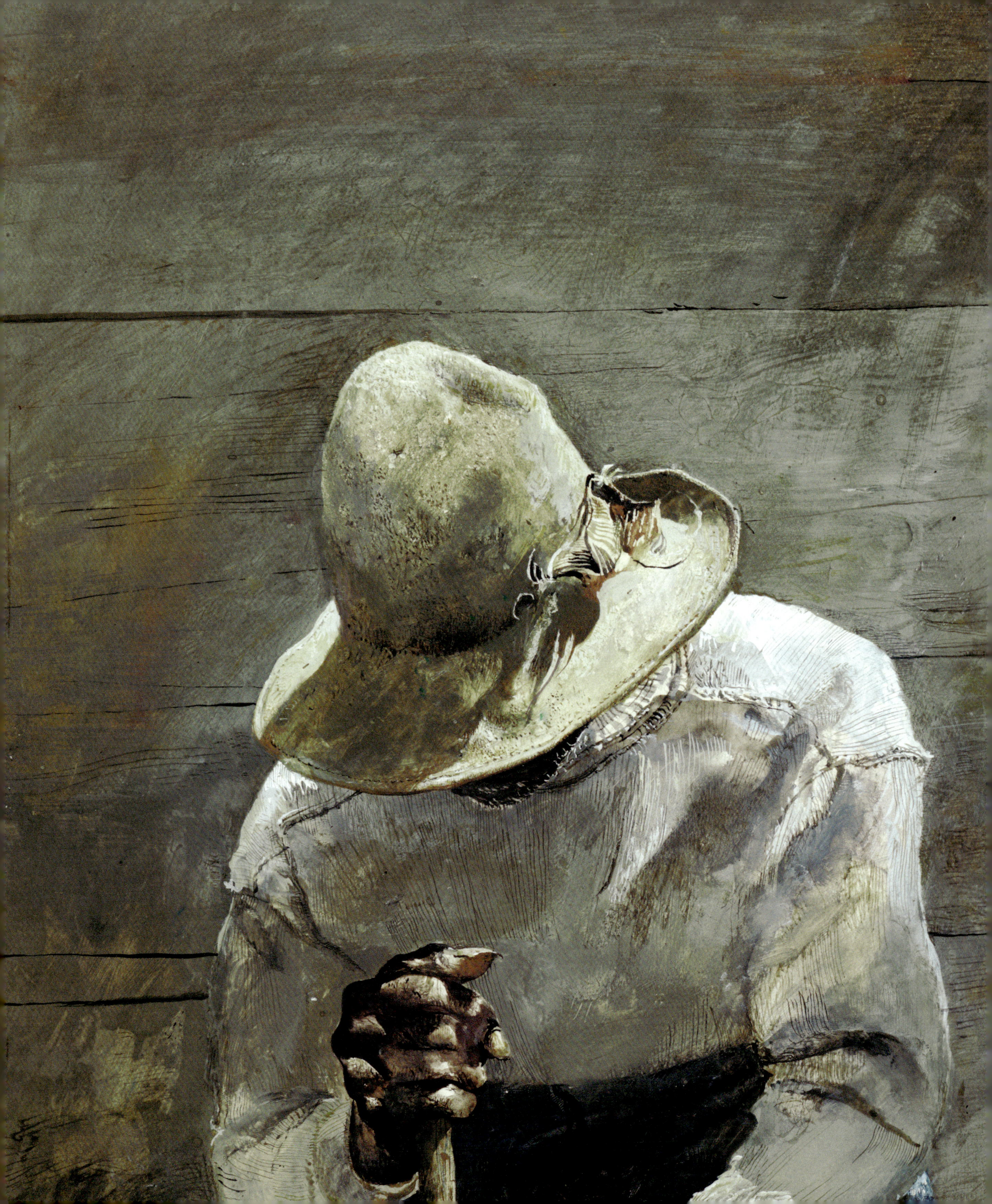

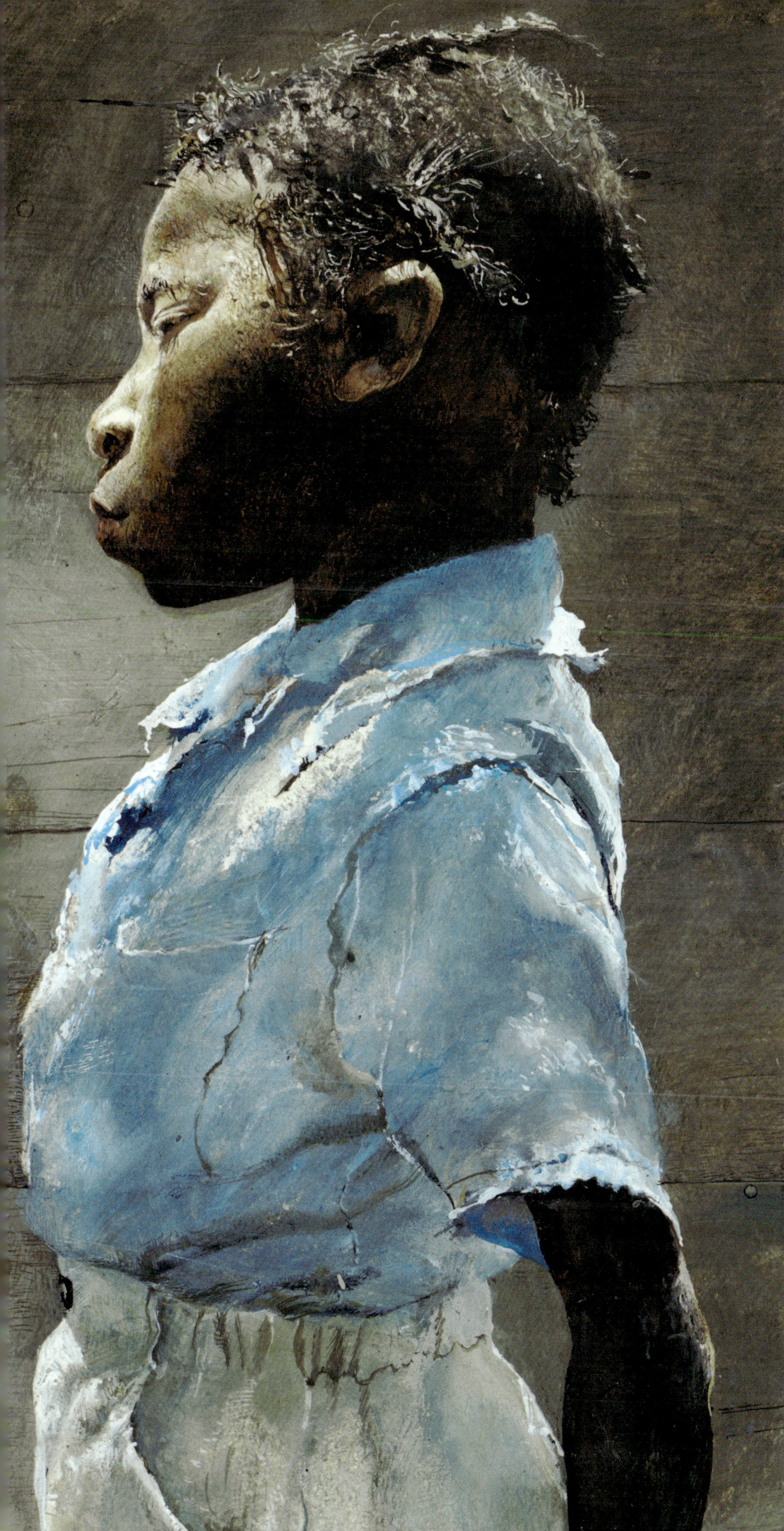

4.

Postwar Abstraction and the Resurgence of Realism

Morris Cole Graves

Born in Fox Valley, Oregon, 1910;
died in Loleta, California, 2001

Morris Graves was born and raised in the Puget Sound region and always maintained a strong spiritual connection to the culture and terrain of the Pacific Northwest. Mostly self-taught, Graves combined two principal influences in his art: the spirit of American transcendentalism and Eastern philosophy. He was associated with the Northwest school of painting, known for its combination of Eastern philosophies and an appreciation for the natural world. Graves developed a visual vocabulary of bird and flower imagery that symbolized his love of nature. He began as an oil painter, but by the late 1930s his preferred media had become tempera, watercolor, gouache, and ink.

As a teenager, Graves joined the merchant marines and made three trips to the Far East. There he encountered Eastern religions such as Taoism and Buddhism. In the United States, he pursued his interest in Asian art while working at the Seattle Art Museum, which had an extensive Asian collection. In the mid-1930s, Graves was supported by the Works Progress Administration's Federal Art Project. Through the project he met the painter Mark Tobey (q.v.), whose interest in Zen Buddhism was an important influence on his art and spirituality. Zen, which offers a path to enlightenment through meditation, was of great importance to many artists in the Pacific Northwest and became a central theme in Graves's art. In 1938 Graves also met the composer John Cage, with whom he shared his interest in Zen.

Graves's professional breakthrough was in 1942, when nineteen of his paintings of emblematic birds, known as the Inner Eye series, were included in the Museum of Modern Art's *Americans 1942* exhibition. The exposure brought him immediate recognition. In 1946 he was awarded a Guggenheim Fellowship for study in Japan, but the Allied occupation of the country prevented this, and he traveled to Hawaii instead. Graves's career peaked in the late 1950s; he was given a major retrospective in 1956 at the Whitney Museum of American Art. He became an honorary member of the American Watercolor Society in 1968.

Graves traveled extensively in the 1950s, '60s, and '70s. In his late career, he moved away from images of animals and turned to spare, richly colored floral paintings. In 1964 he bought twenty-five acres of redwood forest and established a studio on the northern California coast. His idyllic home, known as "The Lake," became an artist's retreat and is presently the site of the Morris Graves Foundation.

Select Bibliography

George Michael Cohen. "The Bird Paintings of Morris Graves." *College Art Journal* 18, no. 1 (Autumn 1958): 3–5.

Ida E. Rubin, ed. *The Drawings of Morris Graves.* New York: New York Graphic Society for the Drawing Society, 1974.

Ray Kass. *Morris Graves: Vision of the Inner Eye.* New York: George Braziller, 1983.

Sheryl Cokelton and Laura Landau. *Northwest Mythologies: The Interactions of Mark Tobey, Morris Graves, Kenneth Callahan, and Guy Anderson.* Seattle: University of Washington Press in association with the Tacoma Art Museum, 2003.

76

Morris Graves
The Myth of Division and Separation, 1940
Opaque and transparent watercolor on thin laid paper (red ink stamped in right margin: Made in China)
23 × 20 3/4 in. (58.4 × 52.7 cm)
Signed and dated at lower right:
M Graves 1940
Ex coll.: The artist; Henry Schnakenberg, New York City, as of 1942
Gift of Henry Schnakenberg, 1952.298

Born and raised near Seattle, Washington, Morris Graves appreciated at an early age the natural beauty of the Pacific Northwest. Graves was influenced by Zen Buddhism, which nurtured his existing love for the natural world. Zen religion emphasizes a meditative existence, in which practitioners seek knowledge of the self in relation to the universe and aim to create a oneness between the two.[1] For Graves, the act of painting was meditative, and his imagery was highly symbolic. He was best known for his paintings of birds, a creature he chose to symbolize the quiet inner life of the artist.

In the spring of 1940, Graves relocated from mainland Washington to Fidalgo, one of the San Juan Islands in the Puget Sound, living alone in a small shack built with his own hands. This remote setting provided the solace he needed for contemplation and meditation.[2] Among the works he completed that year was *The Myth of Division and Separation*, a painting that represents a critical moment in Graves's early career when he began experimenting with "white-writing," a technique inspired by oriental calligraphy that he learned from fellow painter Mark Tobey (q.v.). Not long after seeing Tobey's work, Graves began the Inner Eye series, which launched his breakout exhibition at the Museum of Modern Art in 1942.[3] Simultaneously, Graves experimented with watercolor, using Asian media and techniques such as *sumi-e* ink and rice paper.[4]

This combination of techniques can be seen in this work. Graves used a simple palette of white and black ink and an extremely thin Chinese paper that enhanced the delicacy of the work. He applied the pigment with varying degrees of opacity so the natural texture of the paper support is visible. Two basic forms—a bird and a radiating circular form—are placed in a shallow space against a divided background. Graves painted numerous "birds of solitude," as one critic described them, birds that, marked by large, vacant eyes, appear against a blank background. Some scholars believe the solitary bird in Graves's paintings symbolized man's inner loneliness and reticence.[5] In the case of *The Myth of Division and Separation*, however, the title suggests a metaphor more closely related to Graves's interest in Zen Buddhism: that the division of man from nature, symbolized by light and dark, bird and background, is a "myth." The artist's belief in the unity of man and the natural world is reinforced by the prominent white circle at the right, reminiscent of the *enso* in Zen art, the ultimate symbol for oneness (fig. 1).[6]

ECM

Fig. 1. Mishima Ryojun, *"What Is This?" Enso* (detail), 20th century. Ink on paper, 13 × 17 1/4 in. (33 × 43.8 cm). Courtesy of Robyn Buntin Gallery, Honolulu, Hawaii

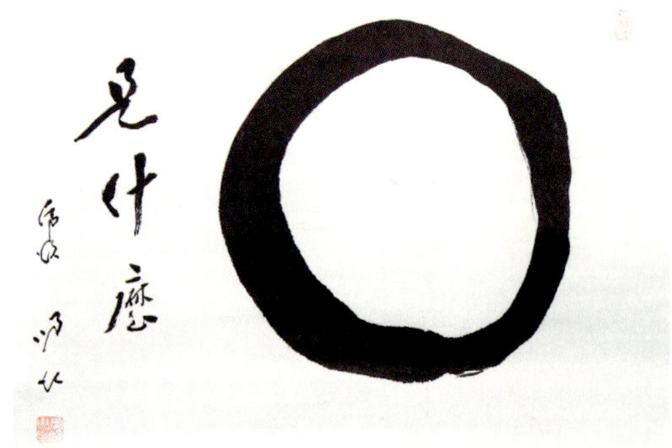

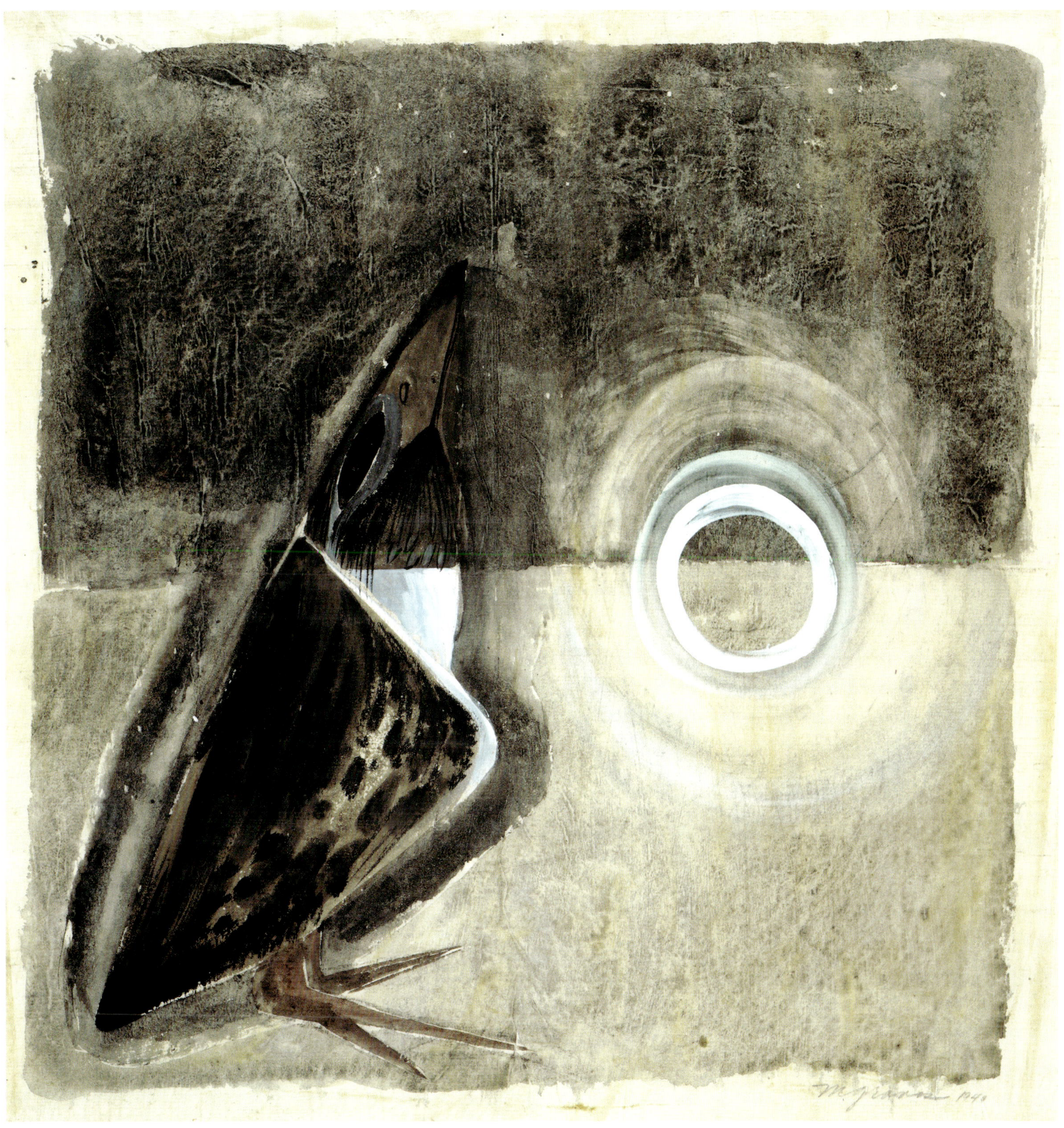

Cat. 76

1. George Michael Cohen, "The Bird Paintings of Morris Graves," *College Art Journal* 18, no. 1 (Autumn 1958): 3–5. Cohen directs the reader to detailed accounts of Zen Buddhism, including Alan Watts, *Spirit of Zen* (London: John Murray, 1948), 104–30. Zen religion "seeks the meditative, stills the surface of the mind, and lets the inner surface bloom."
2. Daniel du Bois, *Morris Graves: Reconciling Inner and Outer Realities, 1932–1983* (New York: Schmidt Bingham Gallery, 1992), 10.
3. Ray Kass, *Morris Graves: Vision of the Inner Eye* (New York: George Braziller, 1983), 30.
4. Ibid. It is speculated that Tobey inspired this transition.
5. Cohen, "Bird Paintings," 8.
6. Http://zenart.shambhala.com/browse-gallery.htm?selectedBrowseKey=2488 (accessed February 27, 2009).

Hans Hofmann

Born Johann Georg Hofmann
in Weissenburg, Germany, 1880;
died in New York, 1966

A teacher and prolific artist, Hans Hofmann was one of the most important figures of postwar American art. He was raised and educated in Munich and, after taking classes in science and mathematics, he began studying art in 1898. With the support of Berlin art patron Phillip Freudenberg, Hofmann was able to move to Paris in 1904, taking classes at both the Académie de la Grande Chaumière (with fellow student Henri Matisse) and the Académie Colarossi.

In Paris, Hofmann observed and absorbed the innovations of the most adventurous artists of the day, including Pablo Picasso, Georges Braque, Robert and Sonia Delaunay, Fernand Léger, and Henri Matisse, many with whom he met and became friendly. He remained in Paris until 1914, when the advent of World War I required him to return to Germany. Unable to enroll in the military due to a respiratory ailment, he opened an innovative school for art in Munich. The school's reputation spread internationally, especially after the war, attracting students from Europe and the United States.

In 1933 Hofmann immigrated to the United States and established the Hans Hofmann School of Fine Arts in New York and another school in Provincetown, Massachusetts, then a thriving artists' colony. As a teacher he brought to America direct knowledge of the work of a celebrated group of European modernists and developed his own philosophy of art. In the late 1950s, Hofmann focused on his own career as an artist and turned to painting full-time. Although Hofmann did not come to the United States until he was over fifty, he is embraced as an American painter and regarded as a key member of the Abstract Expressionists.

Hofmann was close to seventy years old when, in a burst of energy, he painted most of the large, highly recognizable canvases of the late 1950s and '60s that secured his reputation. He is best known for his paintings of solid color blocks on fragmented backgrounds. His legacy as a teacher is evident in the careers of students that included American artists such as Helen Frankenthaler, Red Grooms, Lee Krasner, Louise Nevelson, and Frank Stella. By 1960, noted art historian Clement Greenberg called Hofmann "in all probability the most important art teacher of our time."

Select Bibliography

Sara T. Weeks and Bartlett H. Hayes Jr., eds. *The Search for the Real and Other Essays.* Andover, Mass.: Addison Gallery of American Art, Phillips Academy, 1948.

Cynthia Goodman. *Hans Hofmann.* New York: Abbeville Press, 1986.

Karen Wilkin. *Hans Hofmann: A Retrospective.* Naples, Fla.: Naples Museum of Art, 2003.

77

Hans Hofmann
Provincetown, 1942
Colored crayon on wove paper
14 × 17 in. (35.6 × 43.2 cm)
Signed and dated at lower right:
VII.14.42 HH
Ex coll.: the artist; with the Samuel Kootz Gallery, New York; Hazel McKinley, West Cornwall, Connecticut, as of 1959
Gift of the Hazel McKinley Gallery in memory of A. Everett Austin Jr., 1959.37

Provincetown belongs to a series of still lifes and landscapes from 1935 to 1943 inspired by the picturesque Cape Cod town. Hofmann ran an art school there during the summers and thus painted daily, often *en plein air*, with his students. Most drawings were based on actual views that, when filtered through Hofmann's eyes, became focused studies of line and color. For example, in this drawing Hofmann depicts the town hall building, which still stands today, crowned with a distinctive clock tower and cupola.[1] These prominent architectural elements are reduced to intersecting geometric shapes such as the triangles for the pointed roof and the circle for the clock. Surrounding this central grouping are energetic hatch marks that represent the neighboring houses and buildings.

The Provincetown drawings are highly diversified in their appearance, ranging from fairly traditional representation to experiments with spontaneous abstraction.[2] These stylistic differences are easily traced because, with little exception, Hofmann dated each composition. Whereas Hofmann's earlier drawings were typically unsigned and undated, the Provincetown drawings are inscribed with the month (often using roman numerals) and the day.[3] This meticulous dating creates a visual diary of Hofmann's summer months. Present-day viewers can trace changes in his palette and his designs on a weekly, even daily, basis. For example, in the span of a few days, Hofmann worked with red crayon in a fractured, Cubist style (*Untitled*, 7 July 1942; private collection); then transitioned to complementary colors—oranges and blues, reds paired with greens—using a greater degree of abstraction as in the Atheneum's drawing; and, finally, two days later, combined black ink and colored crayons (fig. 1).

The importance of these drawings was noted by the artist himself, who remarked in 1941, "[I feel] a very deep need to draw and I have already made quite a number . . . I think I am on the way to a new orientation with amazing results . . . so I hope."[4] These daily experiments with color and line undoubtedly aided Hofmann's stylistic development and his artistic theories. Years later, he published his famous "push and pull" theory that addressed the visual effects achieved by colors of varied intensity: some recede, others project.[5] Though Hofmann didn't officially publish this theory and its methodology until 1948, the drawings from the earlier part of the decade show the refinement of these ideas.

ECM

Fig. 1. Hans Hofmann, *Untitled VII.16.42*, 1942. Pen, ink, and crayon on paper, 14 × 16 15/16 in. (35.6 × 43 cm). Hirshhorn Museum and Sculpture Garden, Smithsonian Institution, Washington, D.C. Museum purchase, 1977

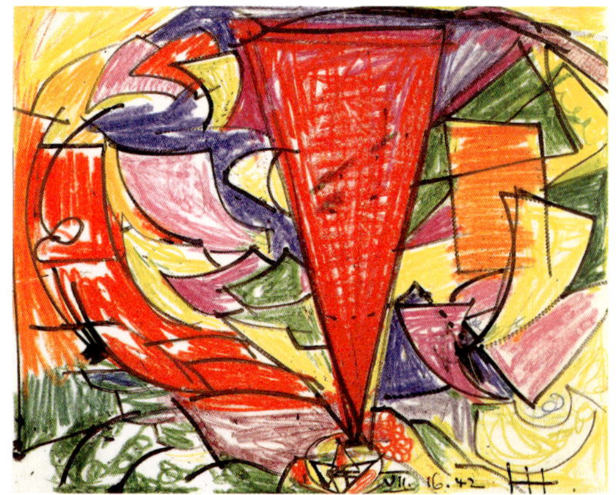

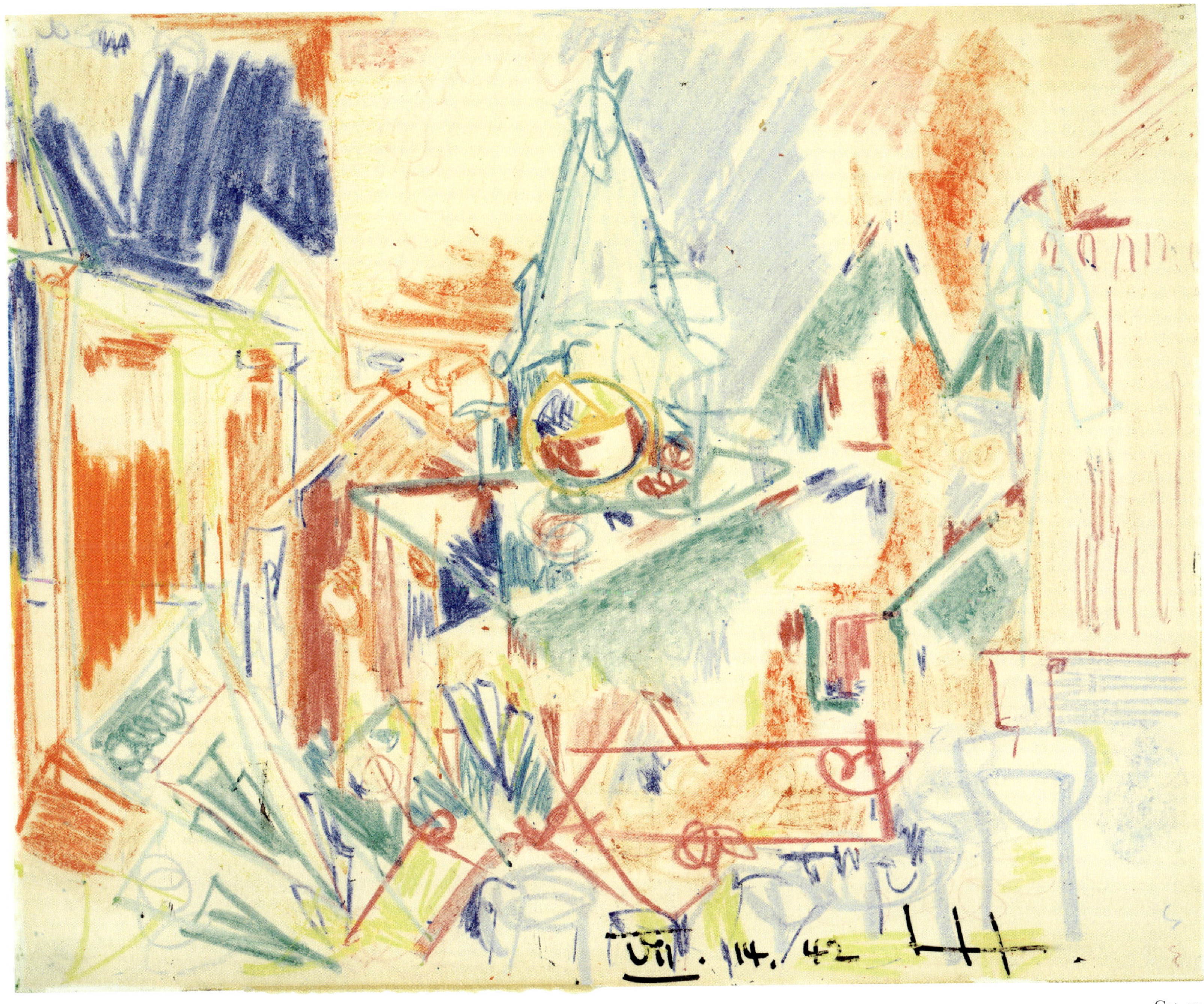

Cat. 77

1. My thanks to Christine M. McCarthy, Provincetown Art Association and Museum, and Stephen Borkowski, Provincetown Art Commission, for their help identifying this building.
2. *Flying Tigers: Painting and Sculpture in New York, 1939–1946* (Providence, R.I.: Bell Gallery, 1985), 56.
3. For more information on the drawings from 1941 to 1943, see *Hans Hofmann: Pictures of Summer; Provincetown, 1941–1942* (New York: André Emmerich Gallery, 1986), and *Hans Hofmann: Provincetown Landscapes, 1941–1943* (New York: André Emmerich Gallery, 1979). For more information on Hofmann in Provincetown, see *Hans Hofmann: Four Decades in Provincetown* (Provincetown, Mass.: Provincetown Art Association and Museum, 2000). In a 1977 exhibition of Hofmann's work at André Emmerich Gallery, Barbara Rose noted in her essay that, for the most part, Hofmann's drawings were neither signed nor dated. Barbara Rose, *Hans Hofmann: Drawings, 1930–1944* (New York: André Emmerich Gallery, 1977), 5.
4. Hans Hofmann to Alice Hodges and Lillian Kiesler, 14 July 1941, reprinted in Cynthia Goodman, *Hans Hofmann* (Munich: Prestel, 1990), 53.
5. Irving Sandler, "Hans Hofmann: The Dialectical Master," in Goodman, *Hans Hofmann*, 77–98. Sandler described Hofmann's push and pull idea: "The problem was to adjust high-keyed color shapes, pushing and pulling them, as it were, so as to achieve an equilibrium and overall intensity."

78

Hans Hofmann
Untitled, 1948
Black ink, applied using pen and brush, and colored crayon on wove paper
16 15/16 × 14 in. (43 × 35.6 cm)
Signed and dated at lower right:
Hans Hofmann 48
Ex coll.: Samuel Kootz Gallery, New York; Mr. Herrick Jackson, Orleans, Massachusetts, bought in the 1940s
Gift of Mr. Herrick Jackson, 1976.109

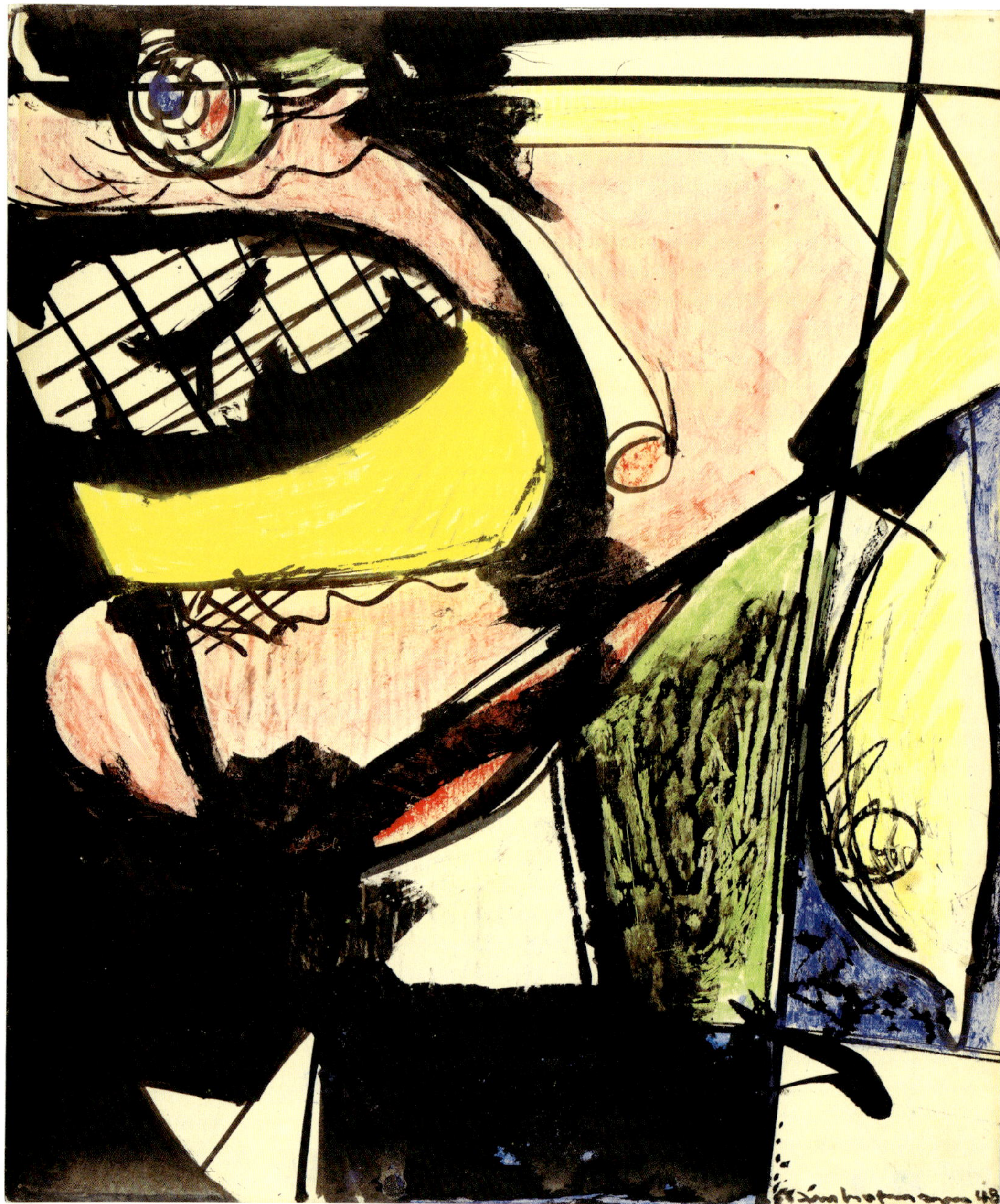

Cat. 78

The 1940s marked a decisive period in Hans Hofmann's career, one of rapid stylistic transition largely fostered by drawing, both in black and white and in color. During this time, Hofmann moved toward an increasingly free and automatic drawing style. He often simplified and reduced natural forms to a degree of abstractness that departed significantly from his earlier, academic drawings.[1] This abstraction was also reflected in his paintings, but the drawings specifically helped Hofmann work through certain stylistic tendencies.[2] Not only was drawing a practical tool (Hofmann used the practice to limber his wrist), but it also allowed focused studies of line and color on a more intimate scale.

Untitled is a still life that has been abstracted to its most elemental form. The combined influences of Cubism and linear abstraction on Hofmann's aesthetic are evident: the bowls and pieces of fruit are reduced to curvilinear outlines, silhouetted in black, and tilted askew.[3] At the center is a banana, painted as an irregular yellow half moon juxtaposed by a lattice design. Circles and silhouettes suggesting other fruits are interspersed among the patches of black ink. Throughout the composition, black ink, with varying thicknesses, is layered over blocks of color. The picture plane is tilted toward the viewer, so the blocks of color and blocks of black appear simultaneously in the foreground and the background. The emphasis on flatness reveals the lasting impact of Cézanne and Mondrian, respectively, on Hofmann's stylistic development.[4]

Hofmann completed this drawing the same year he published his seminal treatise *The Search for the Real in the Visual Arts*, which explained the limitations of translating the three-dimensional world into two dimensions.[5] According to Hofmann, an important part of a successful work of art is to find tension between space, form, color, and planes, or "the push and pull effect." This tension became apparent in the paintings of the 1950s, which are characterized by overlapping blocks of vivid color. Thus, in retrospect, *Untitled* belongs to an important period of experimentation from which "emerged the visual symbols [which] are now recognized as Hofmann's characteristic signature forms."[6]
ECM

1. Barbara Rose, *Hans Hofmann: Drawings, 1930–1944* (New York: André Emmerich Gallery, 1977), n.p.
2. Ibid.
3. Cynthia Goodman, *Hans Hofmann* (Munich: Prestel, 1990), 61.
4. Ibid., 58.
5. Hans Hofmann, "Search for the Real," reprinted in *The Search for the Real and Other Essays*, ed. Sara T. Weeks and Bartlett H. Hayes Jr. (Andover, Mass.: Phillips Academy, 1948).
6. Sam Hunter, *Hans Hofmann* (New York: Harry N. Abrams, 1964), 23.

Mark Tobey

Born in Centerville, Wisconsin, 1890;
died in Basel, Switzerland, 1976

Mark Tobey was a painter and printmaker whose wide-ranging influences included the teachings of the Bahá'í World Faith, East Asian painting, and calligraphy. He first took art classes in high school and later studied watercolor and oil painting at the Art Institute of Chicago. Tobey began his career in Chicago as an illustrator. From 1913 to 1917, he divided his time between New York and Chicago, working as a fashion illustrator and doing portrait drawings on the side.

Tobey had his first one-man exhibition at the Knoedler Gallery in New York in 1917. The following year he converted to the Bahá'í faith; this spiritual redirection was an important aspect of his artistic development. As a follower of Bahá'í, Tobey espoused humanistic, mystical beliefs. In 1922, he moved to Seattle to teach and met the Chinese painter Teng Kuei, who taught him Chinese calligraphy techniques. Thus began a period of great experimentation when Tobey reacted against traditional ideas of compositional space and order and worked to "smash the image in space." At this time, he became associated with the school of painting developing in the Pacific Northwest.

In 1930 Tobey accepted a position to teach and paint in England, where he remained for eight years. He traveled regularly, including several trips to China, where he studied calligraphy, and to Japan, where he spent time in a Zen monastery. Upon his return, Tobey began experimenting with a new technique he later described as "white writing"–using swift, calligraphic brushstrokes, often in white, over a colored background. The white writing paintings debuted in a solo exhibition at the Willard Gallery in New York in 1944. At the time, Tobey's gestural abstractions paralleled the work of the Abstract Expressionists, such as Jackson Pollock's drip paintings, but he remained independent from this group. Instead, Tobey was part of the Northwest school, a group of artists from the Pacific Northwest whose paintings had mystical or visionary qualities.

From the late 1940s to the early 1950s, Tobey's white writing style evolved to include darker colors on a lighter background. In 1958, he became the second American awarded first prize at the Venice Biennale, confirming his international reputation. Whereas his earlier compositions were smaller in scale, he began producing monumental canvases in the 1960s, often in a somber palette. In 1960 he moved to Basel, Switzerland, where he lived and worked until his death.

Select Bibliography

Edward B. Thomas. *Mark Tobey: A Retrospective Exhibition from Northwest Collections.* Seattle: Seattle Art Museum, 1959.

William C. Seitz. *Mark Tobey.* New York: Museum of Modern Art, 1962.

Eliza E. Rathbone. *Mark Tobey: City Paintings.* Washington, D.C.: National Gallery of Art, 1984.

Mark Tobey: Works on Paper from Northern California and Seattle Collections, Celebrating the Centenary of the Artist's Birth. Stanford, Calif.: Stanford University Museum of Art, 1990.

79

Mark Tobey
Broadway Afternoon, 1950
Opaque and transparent watercolor on laid paper
19 × 24 1/2 in. (48.3 × 62.2 cm)
Signed and dated at lower right: Tobey '50
Ex coll.: the artist; Willard Gallery, New York, as of 1955
The Ella Gallup Sumner and Mary Catlin Sumner Collection Fund, 1955.263

In 1935, Mark Tobey began using a new technique described as "white writing," in both his paintings and his works on paper. This technique of meandering, abstract lines painted over an initial composition was largely influenced by the Oriental brushwork and calligraphy Tobey learned from the Chinese painter Teng Kuei, whom he had met in Seattle several years earlier. Tobey completed his first paintings in the white writing style in the 1940s. He painted a series inspired by the urban streetscape of New York City, where he had lived intermittently from 1911 to 1922. Unlike the representational genre scenes painted by Ashcan school artists or the realists of the 1930s, Tobey relied upon abstraction to express his fascination with the city as a living organism.[1] He translated its vitality and energy into a visual frenzy of overlapping calligraphic lines. In *Broadway Afternoon*, for example, a dense web of lines and colors represents the people and architecture of the busy neighborhood.

Tobey's initial depictions of New York were night scenes, characterized by white writing over a dark background, as in *Electric Night* (fig. 1). In comparison, *Broadway Afternoon* is characterized by dark lines over a

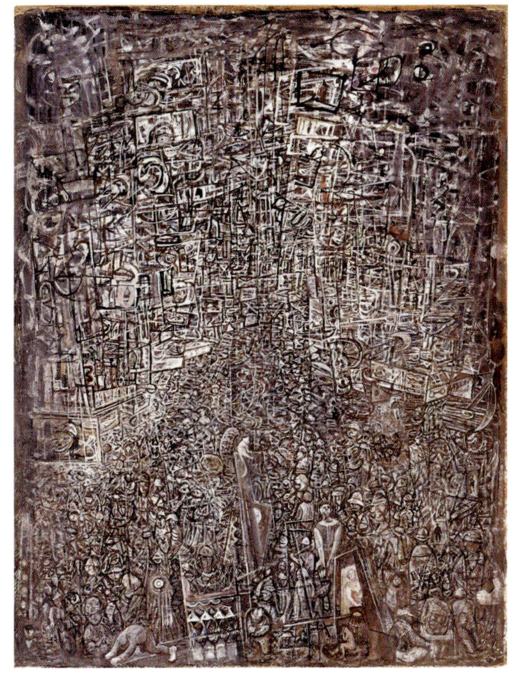

Fig. 1. Mark Tobey, *Electric Night*, 1944. Tempera on board, 17 1/2 × 13 in. (44.5 × 33 cm). Seattle Art Museum. Eugene Fuller Memorial Collection, 44.78

light background and evidences the evolution of Tobey's style in the 1950s. In his later works, discernable details such as street signs, for instance, are de-emphasized and hidden by the allover abstraction. In addition, his use of color became more intricate, requiring careful study of each composition.[2] *Broadway Afternoon* reveals subtle tonalities of blue, green, and red, emerging from dense blacks. Fragments of faces, such as the pair of almond-shaped eyes in the lower right quadrant, emerge from within this composition.

Tobey's meditative, gestural style had certain affinities to Abstract Expressionism, specifically Jackson Pollock's drip paintings, which Pollock began to paint around the same time. In Pollock's *Number 9* (fig. 2), for example, the allover compositional style recalls *Broadway Afternoon*. Both compositions consist of layered colors, lines of varying thicknesses, and an obvious lack of depth. Unlike Pollock's pure abstraction, however, Tobey's composition is oriented as a landscape, with a distinct top and bottom. The lower section has a greater concentration of color and line, emulating the congestion of pedestrians and traffic at street level. The lines in the upper layer are looser and more dispersed, suggesting the skyline. ECM

1. Eliza E. Rathbone, *Mark Tobey: City Paintings* (Washington, D.C.: National Gallery of Art, 1984), 23.
2. Ibid., 35.

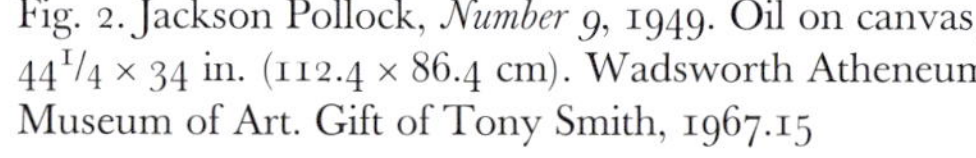

Fig. 2. Jackson Pollock, *Number 9*, 1949. Oil on canvas, $44\frac{1}{4} \times 34$ in. (112.4 × 86.4 cm). Wadsworth Atheneum Museum of Art. Gift of Tony Smith, 1967.15

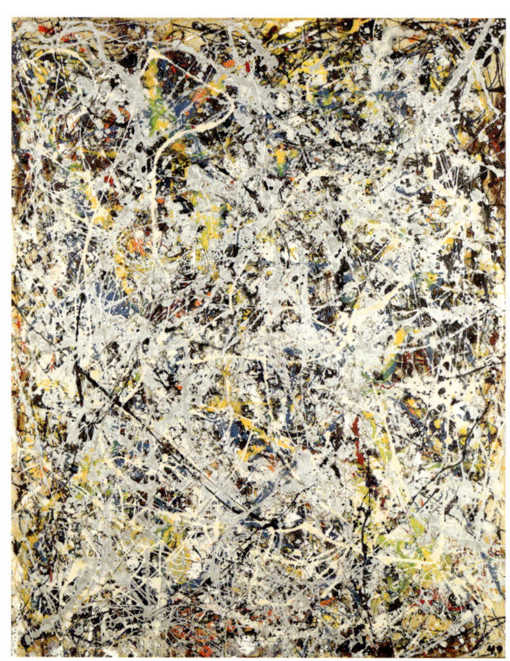

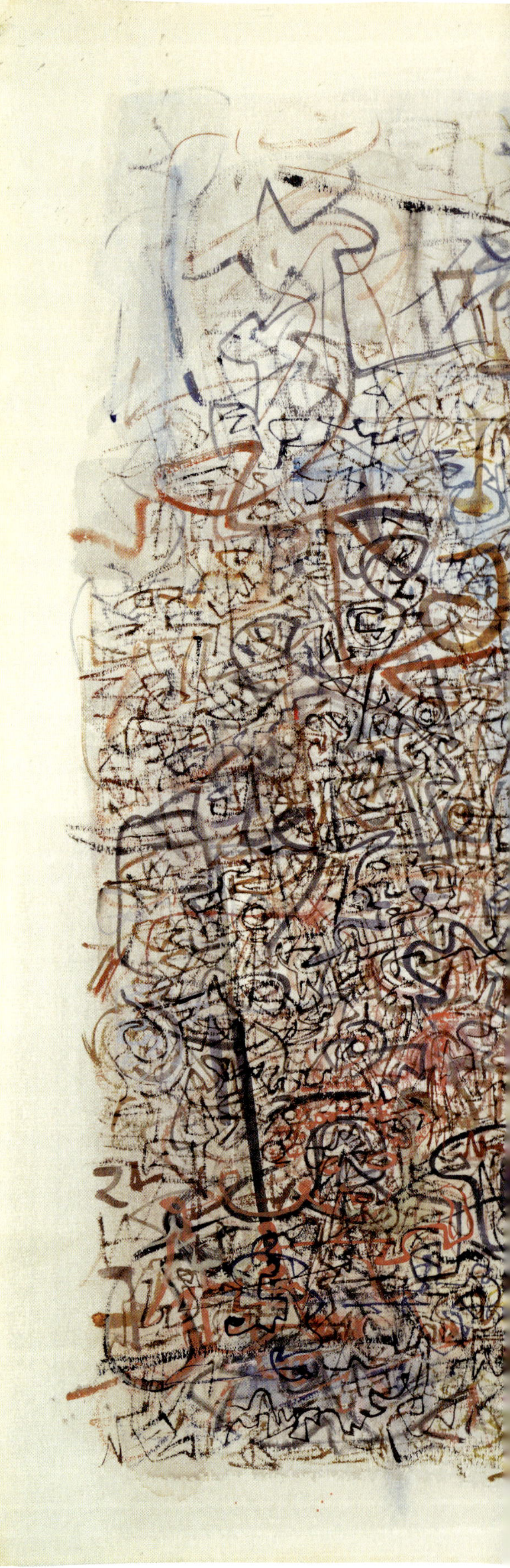

Cat. 79

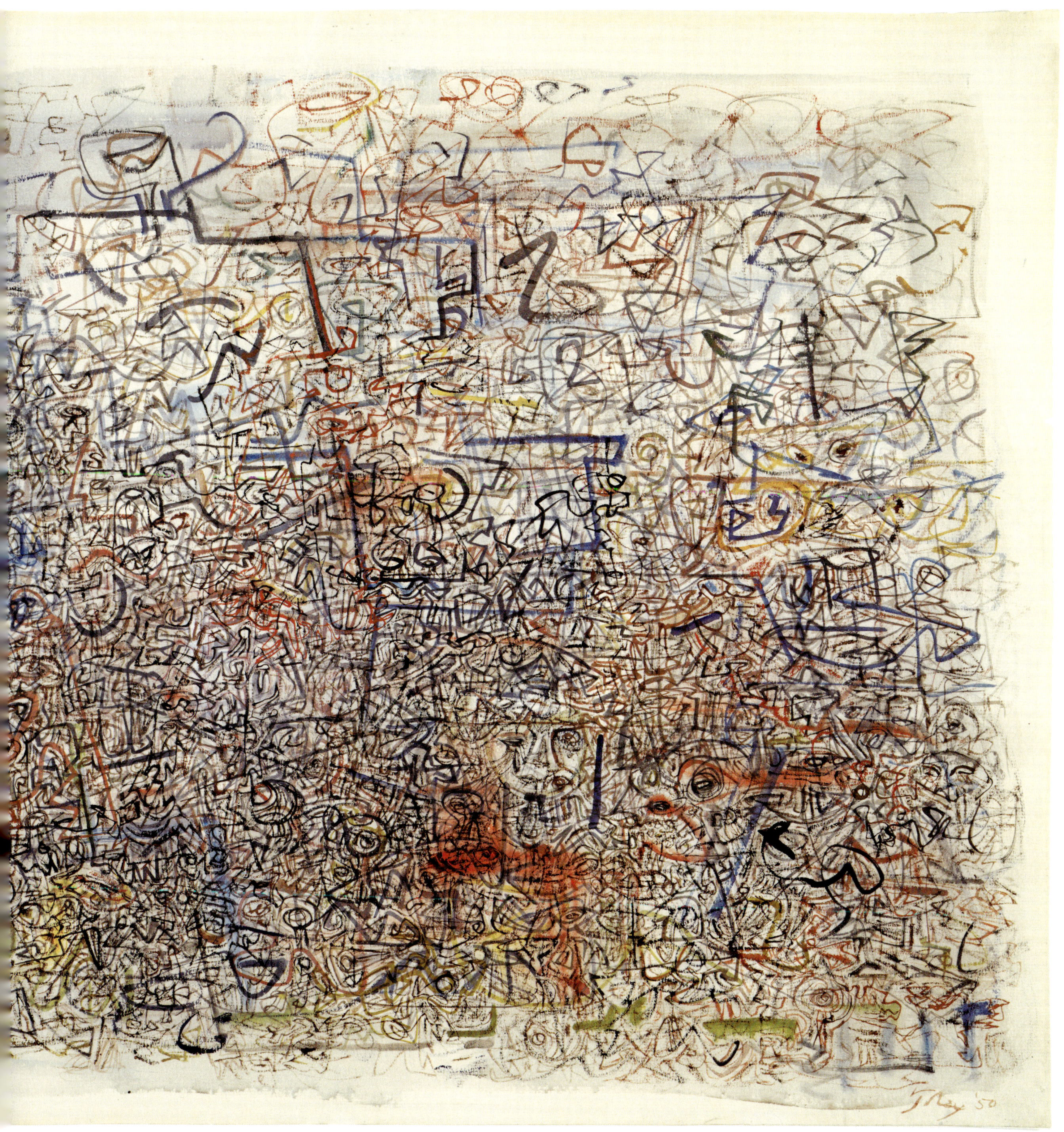

William Baziotes

Born in Pittsburgh, 1912;
died in New York, 1963

The son of Greek parents, William Baziotes grew up in Reading, Pennsylvania. From 1931 to 1933, while working at the Case Glass Company antiquing glass and running errands, he attended evening sketch classes. There he met the Reading poet Byron Vazakas, who became a lifelong friend. Vazakas introduced him to the work of Charles Baudelaire and Symbolist poetry, which provided continued inspiration for his art.

In 1933, Baziotes moved to New York and enrolled in the National Academy of Design. In 1936 he was hired by the Works Progress Administration to teach art at the Queens Children's Museum. Influenced by the Surrealist émigrés he met in New York, he began to experiment with automatism. Baziotes was one of the few Americans invited by André Masson to participate in an important Surrealist exhibition at the Whitelaw Reid Mansion in 1942. Two years later, he was given his first solo exhibition at Peggy Guggenheim's Art of This Century Gallery, New York.

Like the Surrealists and Abstract Expressionists, Baziotes was fascinated by the power of myth. His titles and imagery often made references to mythology and/or prehistoric past. From 1941 to 1942, Baziotes abandoned painting in order to focus entirely on automatic drawing. Through automatic drawing he developed a personal vocabulary of abstract symbols, which he would use for the remainder of his life. In his art, these symbols took the form of biomorphic imagery, shapes that suggested living organisms but had no specific identity.

Baziotes's major breakthrough period is considered to be from 1946 to 1950, when he changed his compositions significantly, and his work became more closely associated with Abstract Expressionism. Also during this time he founded the short-lived Subjects of the Artist School on Eighth Street in New York, with David Hare, Robert Motherwell, and Mark Rothko. (Influenced by Motherwell in particular, Baziotes's late work consisted of simpler compositions in which several large, biomorphic shapes appear to float in fields of soft, glowing color.) Throughout his career he taught in New York: at the Brooklyn Museum Art School from 1949 to 1952, and at Hunter College from 1952 until his death.

Two years after his death, the Solomon R. Guggenheim Museum in New York presented a memorial exhibition of Baziotes's work. In 1978 the Newport Harbor Art Museum, Newport Beach, California, organized a traveling retrospective.

Select Bibliography

Lawrence Alloway. *William Baziotes: A Memorial Exhibition.* New York: Solomon R. Guggenheim Museum, 1965.

Irving Sandler. "Baziotes: Modern Mythologist." *Art News* 63, no. 10 (February 1965): 28–30.

Michael Preble, Barbara Cavaliere, and Mona Baziotes Hadler. *William Baziotes: A Retrospective Exhibition.* Newport Beach, Calif.: Newport Harbor Art Museum, 1978.

Michael Preble. *William Baziotes: Paintings and Drawings, 1934–1962.* Milan: Skira, in association with the Peggy Guggenheim Collection, Venice, 2005.

80 a and b

William Baziotes
Pompeii, 1953
Pastel over charcoal on gray wove paper (watermark: Ingres/Canson & Montgolfier France)
19 × 24 7/8 in. (48.3 × 63.2 cm)
Signed at lower left: Baziotes / III
Ex coll.: with the Samuel Kootz Gallery, New York; Philip L. Goodwin, New York, as of 1954
Gift of Philip L. Goodwin, 1957.603

Figure in Foliage, 1954
Pastel over charcoal on gray laid paper (blind stamp: Strathmore)
19 × 24 7/8 in. (48.3 × 63.2 cm)
Signed at lower right: Baziotes
Inscribed on verso: Figure [in] Foliage / 1954
Ex coll.: with the Samuel Kootz Gallery, New York
The Ella Gallup Sumner and Mary Catlin Sumner Collection Fund, 1955.266

In his review of William Baziotes's 1965 retrospective, Irving Sandler described the artist as "a modern mythologist," whose style of painting linked ancient myth to contemporary art.[1] Like the Surrealists and Abstract Expressionists, Baziotes was fascinated by the power of myth and experimented with automatism, a technique that gave free rein to unconscious imagery. He created a repertoire of swollen, biomorphic shapes, rendered in solid color and belonging to a distant allegorical or fantasy world, as the title of many of these images suggests.

The Atheneum's two pastels, *Pompeii* and *Figure in Foliage*, date to late in Baziotes's career, when his compositions became tighter and his use of color more controlled.[2] In these examples, the distinct shapes and forms are neatly outlined with delicate black lines. By using such outlines, Baziotes accentuates the subtle tones and coloration–intermingling cool and warm colors. The works contain the amorphous, abstract forms that populated Baziotes's visionary fantasy world. In both compositions, a single anthropomorphic form is set against a background of solid color. These shapes are simply and roughly drawn but nonetheless suggestive; the standing form in *Figure in Foliage* could be a curvaceous nude, and in *Pompeii* a one-eyed cat hovers above the horizon. The use of softly textured pastels enhances the mesmerizing, dreamlike quality of these strange distant worlds. Baziotes further emphasized his forms by setting them in extremely shallow spaces with minimal detail; only fragmented shapes help identify or codify the different environments. With its green, leafy cluster hanging from above, presumably the "foliage," *Figure in Foliage*

Fig. 1. William Baziotes, *Pompeii*, 1955. Oil on canvas, 60 × 48 in. (152.4 × 121.9 cm). Museum of Modern Art, New York. Louise Reinhardt Smith Fund, 189.1955

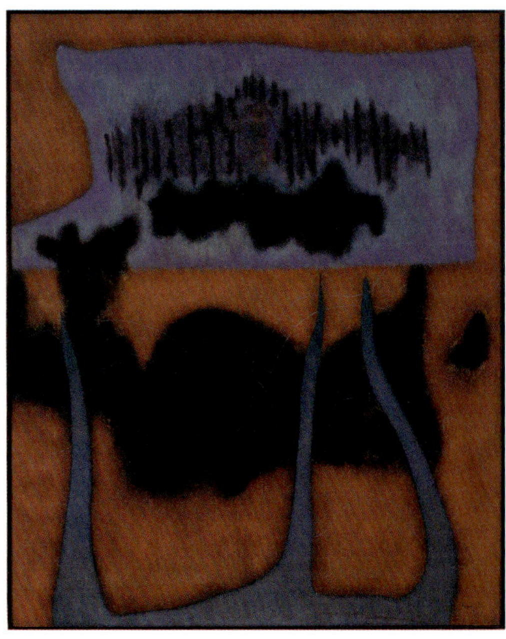

becomes an earthly Eden. The setting of *Pompeii*, on the other hand, appears architectural because of the black columnar form at right and the jagged structure at the bottom.

In the late 1940s and early 1950s, Baziotes spent countless hours in the Metropolitan Museum of Art and the Museum of Natural History, immersing himself in prehistoric and primeval subjects.[3] Since he was of Greek ancestry, he found personal significance in these early objects, and accordingly his paintings from this time were given titles such as *Cyclops*, *Dwarf*, and *Pompeii*, the latter named after the Roman city tragically destroyed by Mount Vesuvius in 79 AD.[4] This subject appears to have been of particular interest to Baziotes, who completed two works with the same title, the Atheneum's pastel and an oil painting two years later (fig. 1). There does not appear to be any visual connection between the two, but both can be seen as meditations on the theme of a lost city and civilization.
ECM

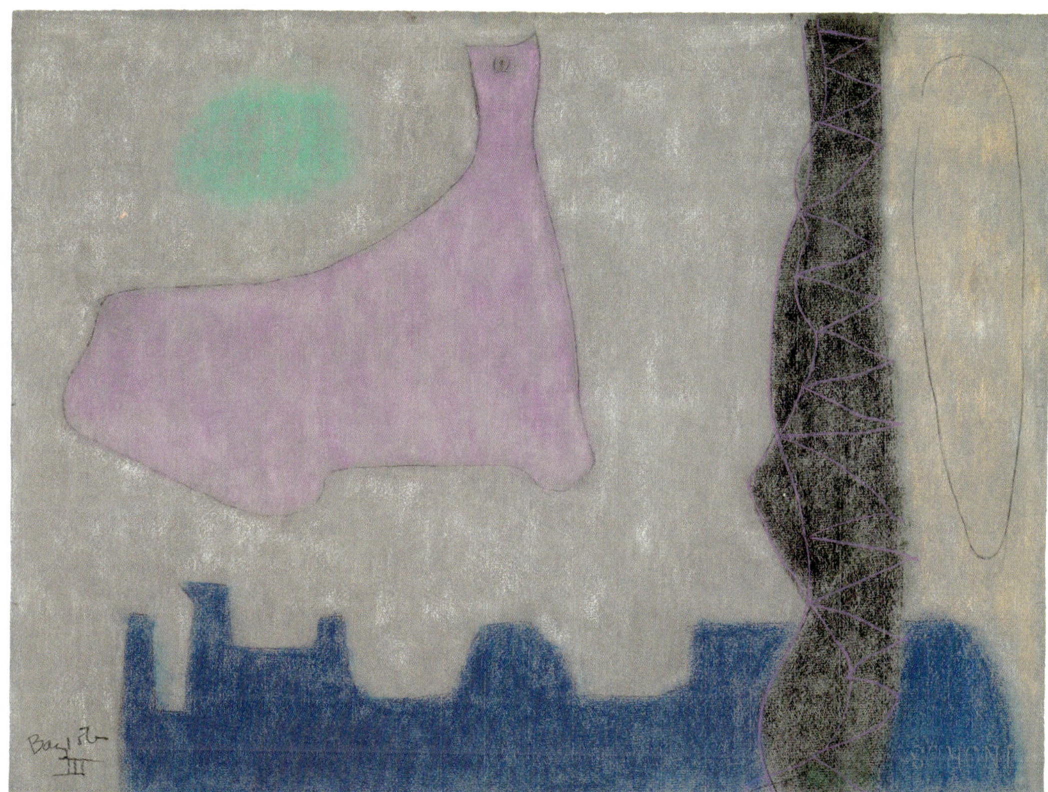

Cat. 80a

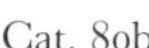

Cat. 80b

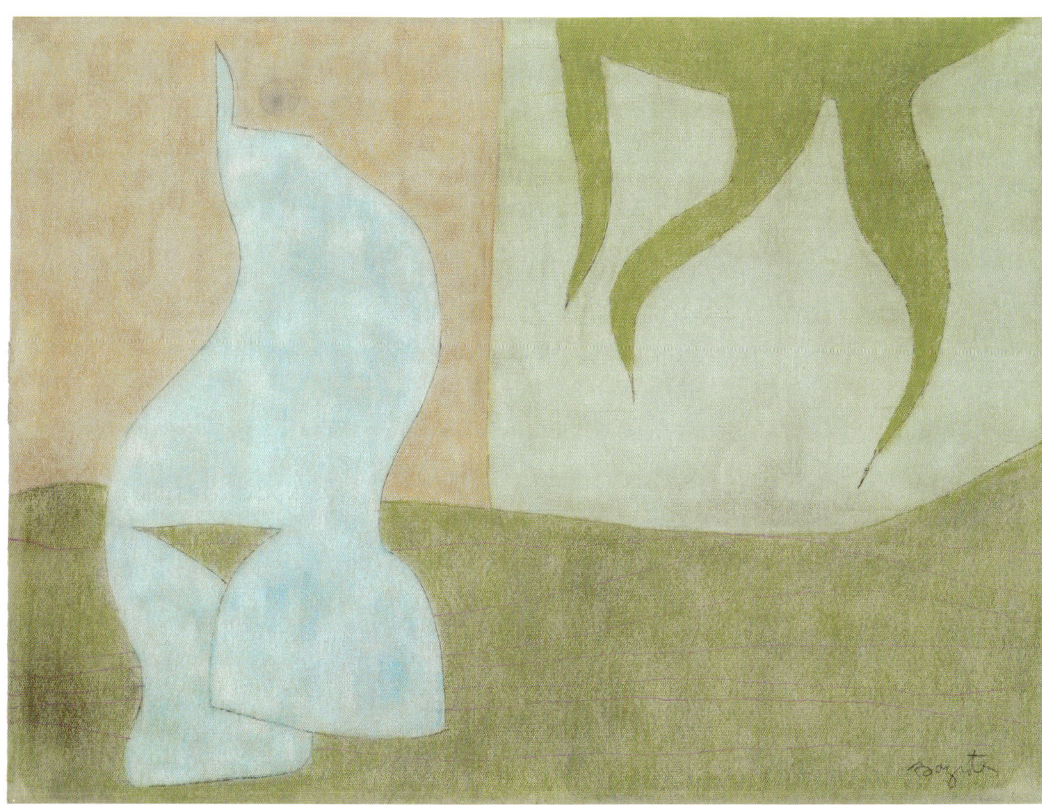

1. Irving Sandler, "Baziotes: Modern Mythologist," *Art News* 63, no. 10 (February 1965): 66.
2. Ibid. "There was a growing concern with the definition of form rather than the spread of color."
3. Mona Hadler, "William Baziotes: Four Sources of Inspiration," in *William Baziotes: A Retrospective Exhibition* (Newport Beach, Calif.: Newport Harbor Museum, 1978), 79.
4. Ibid., 79. There is correspondence between Dorothy Miller and William Baziotes discussing the painting *Pompeii*, but he does not mention the pastel. Museum collection files, Department of Painting and Sculpture, Museum of Modern Art, New York. For a thorough description of the painting *Pompeii*, see ibid., 92–95.

David Smith

Born in Decatur, Indiana, 1906;
died in Bennington, Vermont, 1965

David Smith was the preeminent American sculptor of the postwar era and a prolific draftsman. Born and raised in the Midwest, he moved to New York City at age twenty, intending to pursue a career as a painter. He enrolled at the Art Students League, where his teacher, the Czech-born Cubist painter Jan Matulka (1890–1972), introduced him to the welded sculptures of Julio González and Pablo Picasso. Smith then realized that the skills he had obtained while working at a Studebaker automobile plant years earlier could be used to make art. While in New York, Smith also met fellow American artists John Graham, Stuart Davis (q.v.), and Arshile Gorky (q.v.), who introduced him to European modernism.

By the 1930s, Smith was devoting himself increasingly to sculpture. Smith worked at the Terminal Iron Works in Brooklyn, alongside commercial welders, and his early constructions explored a wide range of stylistic influences, including Surrealism and Cubism. In January 1938 Smith had his first one-man show of welded iron sculptures and drawings at Marian Willard's East River Gallery in New York. In the spring of 1940, Smith and his wife, the artist Dorothy Dehner, moved to Bolton Landing, an eighty-six-acre property near Lake George. He later named this studio-workshop Terminal Iron Works after the Brooklyn shop.

In 1950, a fellowship from the John Simon Guggenheim Memorial Foundation provided Smith with financial security and allowed the purchase of materials in quantity. His sculpture became larger and more ambitious, as seen in important series such as Tanktotems (1953–60), made from boiler parts, and Sentinels (1956), made from industrial I-beams. Smith became famous for his imaginative use of industrial materials and scrap metal parts.

In his late works, Smith's constructions became more geometricized, more purely abstract, and larger. In the last phase of his career, from 1960 to 1965, some of his sculptures were as high as fifteen feet, such as the stainless steel Cubi series. Smith died tragically in a car accident in 1965. A major memorial retrospective was organized by the Museum of Modern Art, New York, the following year.

Select Bibliography

David Smith, 1906–1965: A Retrospective Exhibition. Cambridge, Mass.: Fogg Art Museum, Harvard University, 1966.

Cleve Gray, ed. *David Smith by David Smith.* New York: Holt, Rinehart and Winston, 1968.

Paul Cummings. *David Smith: The Drawings.* New York: Whitney Museum of American Art, 1979.

Karen Wilkin. *David Smith.* New York: Abbeville Press, 1984.

David Smith: A Centennial. New York: Guggenheim Museum, 2006.

81 a and b

David Smith
Untitled, 1951
Opaque and transparent watercolor on wove paper
25 3/4 × 19 7/8 in. (65.4 × 50.5 cm)
Signed and dated at lower left: ΔΣ 51
Ex coll.: the artist; private collection
Promised gift

Untitled (formerly *Three Vertical Forms*), 1953
India ink, egg yolk, and watercolor on laid paper
19 3/4 × 15 11/16 in. (50.2 × 39.8 cm)
Signed and dated at lower left: Δ Σ 15/5/4/53
Ex coll.: the artist; private collection
Promised gift

In 1950, David Smith received a John Simon Guggenheim Memorial Foundation Fellowship that ushered in an intensely fertile period of his career. The award not only boosted the artist's confidence but also provided financial stability that inspired larger and more ambitious welded series sculptures. This creative burst was mirrored in his drawings, too. Beginning in the 1950s, Smith made 300 to 400 drawings per year, and these works became an independent part of his oeuvre. As Karen Wilkin observed, "Smith's drawings [of the 1950s] seem quite different. . . . [They become] self-sufficient pictures, not simply visualizations of objects planned to exist in other materials."[1]

In his drawings and in his sculptures, Smith explored semi-abstract forms that were amorphous yet suggestive of forms in nature. For example, in *Untitled*, 1951, an allover composition of black and purple lines zigzags across the page. The lines angle sharply and create a skeletal, sinewy form. As evidenced by *Chicken Bones* Δ Σ *1951* (1951; estate of David Smith), Smith based his composition on "real" objects. In these two examples, the bony protrusions were likely inspired by the animal skeletons he studied during visits to the American Museum of Natural History in New York.[2]

In the 1953 drawing *Untitled*, Smith demonstrates his fascination with the human form. Using a monochromatic palette, he depicts the three linear pairs.[3] The semi-abstract shapes resemble three couples whose bulging and curving bodies intertwine in a sexually suggestive manner. Smith used similar linear forms in his Tanktotems series of sculptures, begun the same year. In these he combined tall, freestanding metal shapes with convex and concave attachments. Smith's interest in the human body and his attraction to ambiguous sexually charged appendages is apparent in his welded works and drawings from this period.[4]

Shortly after it was made, *Untitled* was selected for the cover of the October 1, 1953, issue of *Art Digest* (fig. 1). At the time, the journal offered artists the opportunity to submit art for the cover of each issue. The project was overseen by art critic Belle Krasne, who was then editor of the journal.[5] Krasne and Smith first became friends in the early 1950s and she received these two drawings directly from the artist.

ECM

Fig. 1. David Smith, *Art Digest* cover. October 1, 1953

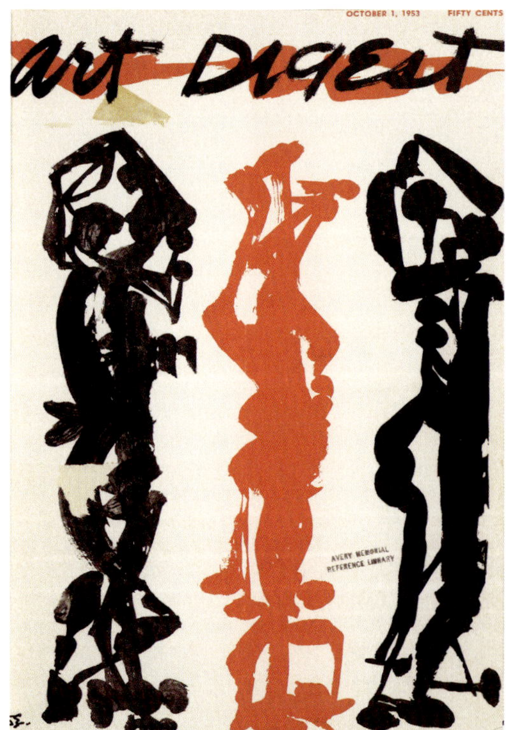

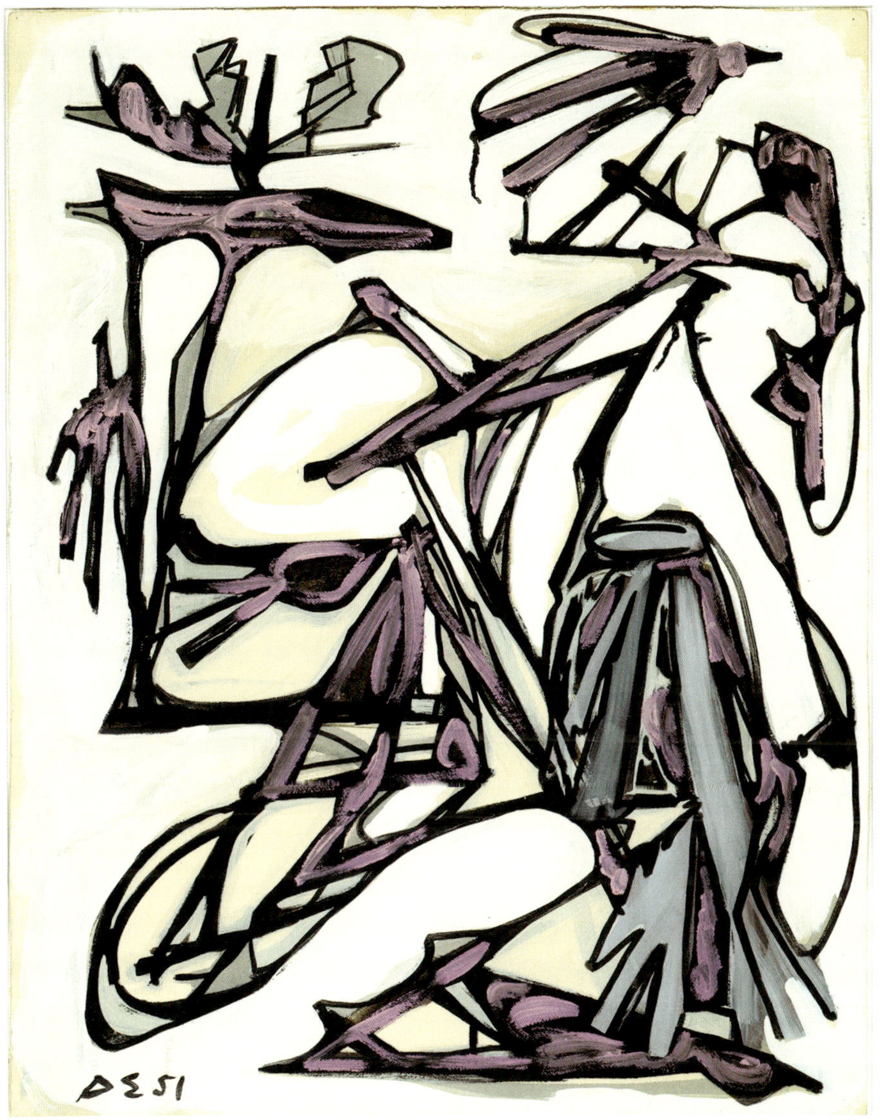

Cat. 81a

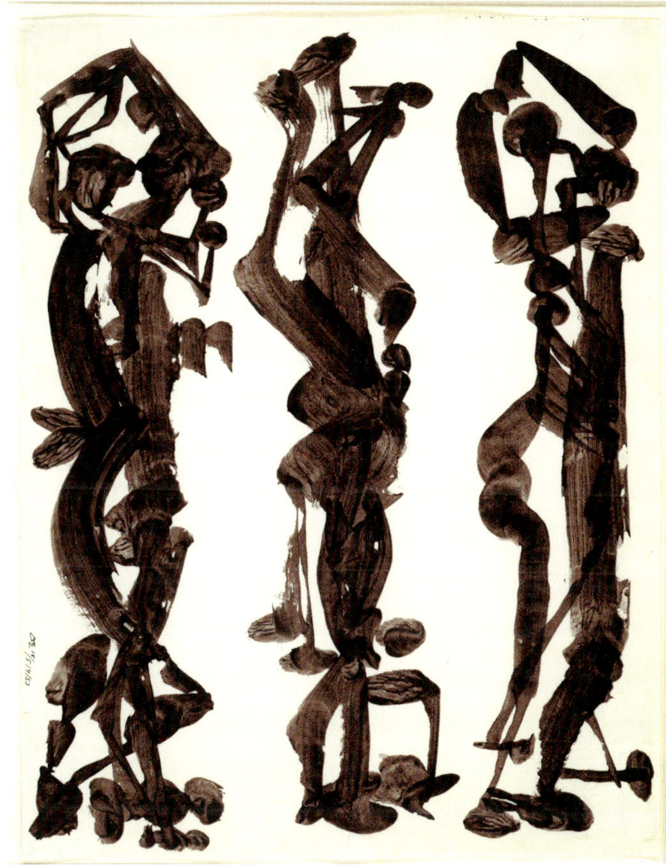

Cat. 81b

1. Karen Wilkin, "David Smith: A Sculptor Draws," *Master Drawings* 40, no. 1 (Spring 2002): 43–56.
2. *David Smith: A Centennial* (New York: Guggenheim Museum, 2006), 404.
3. Special thanks to Susan Cooke, associate director, Estate of David Smith, for her insight into the orientation of *Untitled* as either a vertical or horizontal composition. The location of the signature suggests the composition may have been conceived as horizontal but, as Cooke explained, Smith was known to change the orientation of his works. Erin Monroe, conversation with Susan Cooke, July and August 2009.
4. *David Smith*, 410.
5. Krasne was editor in chief of *Art Digest*, 1949–54.

Andrew Wyeth

Born in Chadds Ford, Pennsylvania, 1917; died in Chadds Ford, Pennsylvania, 2009

Andrew Wyeth was born and raised in a small Pennsylvania town, the youngest of five children in a family of artists; his father, Newell Convers (N. C.) Wyeth, a celebrated painter and illustrator, would become his teacher and mentor. Owing to frail health, he was taught at home by tutors and received artistic training from his father. When Andrew was only twenty, his father arranged for an exhibition of his watercolors at the Macbeth Gallery, New York, that was an immediate success. In the early 1930s, Wyeth saw an exhibition of Winslow Homer's watercolors that prompted him to paint the fleeting effects of light and movement. Whereas his early works are marked by a freedom of handling, his mature style is more refined and detailed.

In the early 1940s, Wyeth was introduced by his brother-in-law, the artist Peter Hurd, to the medium of egg tempera. He also used a dry brush technique for his watercolors that involved squeezing moisture from the brush until only fairly dry pigment was left at the tip. Wyeth's working method was slow and deliberate, and the tempera limited his palette to subdued earth colors. He often worked in a combination of media for both his work on paper and his large paintings. His works on paper include pencil-and-ink preparatory sketches for his paintings as well as highly finished compositions, such as *Granddaughter* (cat. 82).

A turning point in Wyeth's work was the tragic death of his father—his mentor and teacher—in 1945. After that, his imagery is more solemn, more introspective, and has a strain of melancholy. This is apparent in paintings such as *Christina's World* (1948; Museum of Modern Art, New York), one of Wyeth's most celebrated works and among the most recognized images in the history of art. Wyeth is often categorized as a postwar realist for his representational images, which became immensely popular in the 1950s.

From the 1950s to the 1970s, Wyeth regularly painted the world around him—the people and places he observed on a daily basis in Pennsylvania and Maine, the two regions of the United States where he spent his life. His style and subject matter changed little throughout his career, yet his work remains enormously popular both in the United States and abroad; it has been shown several times in Japan. He was honored by a retrospective at the Museum of Modern Art, New York (1976). Wyeth remained in his hometown of Chadds Ford, Pennsylvania, until his death. In his later years, he was a familiar sight around Chadds Ford, driving his beat-up GMC Suburban through the fields and riverbeds with a sketch pad on the seat.

Select Bibliography

Wanda M. Corn. *The Art of Andrew Wyeth.* Greenwich, Conn.: New York Graphic Society, 1973.

Andrew Wyeth and Betsy James Wyeth. *Andrew Wyeth: Close Friends.* Seattle: University of Washington Press, 2001.

Anne Knutson, Kathleen Foster, Michael Taylor, and Christopher Crosman. *Andrew Wyeth: Memory and Magic.* New York: Rizzoli in association with the High Museum, Atlanta, 2005.

Michael Kimmelman. "Andrew Wyeth, Famed and Infamous Artist Dies at 91." *New York Times,* 16 January 2009.

82

Andrew Wyeth
Granddaughter, 1956
Drybrush and opaque watercolor on thick wove paper; edges laid down on brown paper, mounted to wood strainer
16 5/8 × 23 1/4 in. (42 × 59 cm)
Signed at lower right: Andrew Wyeth
Ex coll.: Mr. and Mrs. Robert Montgomery, Canaan, Connecticut, as of 1970; to Mrs. Robert Montgomery, Canaan, Connecticut
Gift of Mrs. Robert Montgomery, 1991.79

Fig. 1. Andrew Wyeth, *Day of the Fair*, 1963. Drybrush and watercolor on paper, 14 7/8 × 19 7/8 in. (37.8 × 50.5 cm). Saint Louis Art Museum. Museum purchase, 56:1963

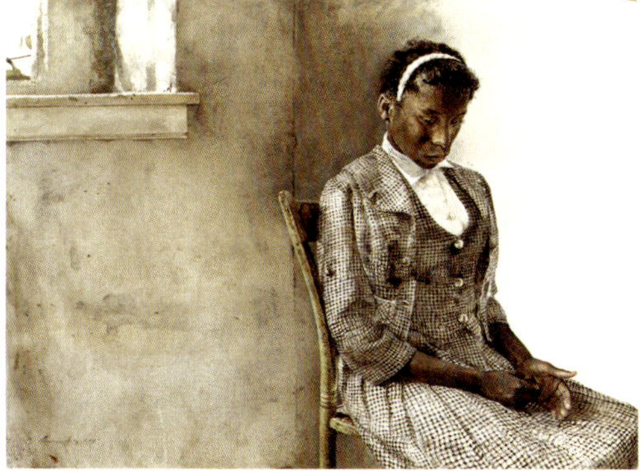

Andrew Wyeth was regarded as "America's Painter," even though his images are rooted—both emotionally and physically—in the two remote towns he divided his time between: Chadds Ford, Pennsylvania, and Cushing, Maine. His most compelling and poignant images were portraits of neighbors and friends, many of whom never ventured outside their small-town existence, but nevertheless had a lasting impact on the artist. Much of Wyeth's work explores the relationships and bonds forged in small towns. As Wanda Corn observes, "Without the knowledge that comes from books or wider acquaintances, [Wyeth's people] continually impressed him with their innocence, their individuality and their pragmatic wisdom."[1]

Granddaughter depicts two of Wyeth's acquaintances from Dilworthtown, a small community just outside of Chadds Ford. Seated is the elderly grandfather Alexander Chandler, dozing in the sun, and standing at center is his granddaughter, Cathy Hunt. As Wyeth recalled, Chandler, though blind, was an unofficial figure of authority who kept watch over the children as they played. He would often throw pennies for them to scamper after and pick up.[2] Cathy waits to get her grandfather's attention, perhaps to collect a few pennies of her own. With hands crossed and downcast eyes, she waits impatiently, not knowing if her grandfather has dozed off or is simply reluctant to meet her request.

From the 1950s onward, Wyeth often painted his African-American acquaintances. These friends often served as models for his paintings, both in and out of the studio. These "real" glimpses into the community touched upon themes of life and death and the aging process. In this respect, the two figures in *Granddaughter* can be seen as symbols of youth and old age. Their poses contrast with one another, like character foils in a play. The elder is seated and slumped over, seemingly tired or asleep, whereas the girl is upright, full of life. Seven years later, Wyeth painted Cathy again, as a young woman dressed up for the annual May Fair dance in *Day of the Fair* (fig. 1). In place of the childish arrogance in *Granddaughter*, the adolescent Cathy appears self-conscious and insecure. She is positioned off-center, in the corner of the room, as if to say the viewer should only give her a passing glance. This pair of paintings gives rise to nostalgia as they capture the passing of time and highlight the fragility of youth and innocence.
ECM

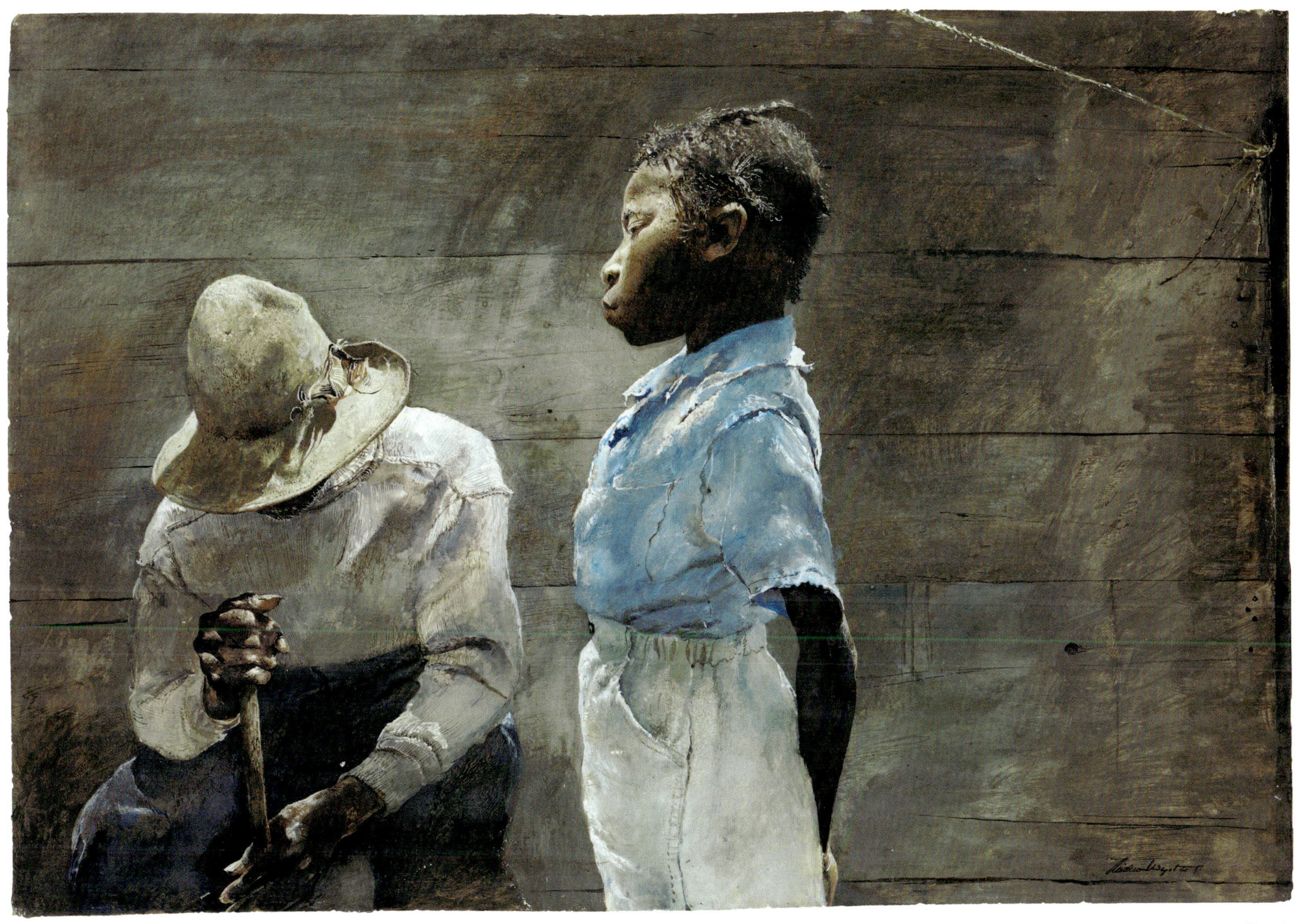

Cat. 82

1. Wanda M. Corn, "The Art of Andrew Wyeth," in *The Art of Andrew Wyeth* (Greenwich, Conn.: New York Graphic Society, 1973), 146.
2. For more information on Alexander Chandler, see *Andrew Wyeth: Close Friends* (Seattle: University of Washington Press, 2001), 18; and *Andrew Wyeth* (Boston: Museum of Fine Arts, 1970), 83, cat. no. 34. The entry suggests the granddaughter is waiting for her grandfather to "give her a nickel to spend at the store."

Philip Pearlstein

Born in Pittsburgh, 1924

Philip Pearlstein is a contemporary American realist painter whose talents were recognized at an early age. When he was seventeen, he received top prize for painting in a national high school art exhibition, for which Reginald Marsh (q.v.) was a juror. The prizewinning paintings were reproduced in *Life* magazine.

Pearlstein graduated from the Carnegie Institute of Technology in 1949 and moved to New York City. That summer, he lived with Andy Warhol, his former classmate, in a run-down apartment in Greenwich Village. In 1950 Pearlstein pursued his master's in art history at the Institute of Fine Arts, New York. At that time he became involved with the Club, the celebrated meeting place of the Abstract Expressionists. The 1950s were of crucial importance to Pearlstein's early paintings, which owe a debt to Abstract Expressionism. In 1954, Clement Greenberg included Pearlstein in the Kootz Gallery's *Emerging Talent* exhibition. The following year, Pearlstein had his first solo exhibition at the Tanager Gallery.

A turning point in Pearlstein's stylistic development took place in 1959, when he joined a weekly drawing group that aroused his interest in studying the human form. These sessions inspired Pearlstein to paint from life models, and in 1962 he exhibited his first figure painting and figurative wash drawings. Pearlstein, like other American artists such as Alex Katz and Chuck Close, was part of an important group of figurative painters that emerged in the 1960s in response to the abstract tendencies of the previous decade.

Pearlstein has garnered numerous awards and recognitions throughout his life. Most notable are a Fulbright Grant, the John Simon Guggenheim Memorial Foundation Fellowship, and the National Endowment for the Arts Fellowship. In 2008, Pearlstein received the National Academy's Lifetime Achievement Award. In addition, he has taught at the Pratt Institute, Yale University, Brooklyn College, and the Skowhegan School of Painting and Sculpture, Maine. He remains active in the New York City art world.

Select Bibliography

Philip Pearlstein. "Figure Paintings Today Are Not Made in Heaven." *Art News* 61 (Summer 1962): 51–52.

Linda Nochlin. *Philip Pearlstein*. Athens: Georgia Museum of Art, University of Georgia, 1970.

Russell Bowman. *Philip Pearlstein: The Complete Paintings*. New York: Alpine Fine Arts Collection, 1983.

John Perreault, *Philip Pearlstein: Drawings and Watercolors*. New York: Harry N. Abrams, 1988.

John L. Ward. *American Realist Painting*. Ann Arbor: UMI Research Press, 1989.

83

Philip Pearlstein
Standing Figure (Back View), 1962
Sepia wash on wove paper
14 × 11 in. (35.6 × 27.9 cm)
Signed and dated at lower left: Pearlstein / 62
Ex coll.: Alex Katz, New York
Gift of Alex Katz, 1971.96

In 1959, Pearlstein joined a weekly drawing group led by the artist and teacher Mercedes Matter. The group included emerging New York painters such as Philip Guston, Alex Katz, Lois Dodd, George McNeil, Sidney Tillim, and Jack Tworkov. These sessions sparked Pearlstein's interest in depicting the human figure, and he quickly developed a distinctive drawing style of running-dash lines, often in transparent watercolor wash, to illustrate the contours of the body.[1] Pearlstein also credits Matter with encouraging him to work from live models, a practice he began in 1962, the same year he completed *Standing Figure*.[2]

Since the early 1960s, Pearlstein has depicted the nude with great single-mindedness, in both small-scale works on paper and large oil paintings. His drawings functioned as preparatory studies for specific paintings or, as in *Standing Figure*, exercises in depicting the body in a variety of poses and positions. Given its early date, this drawing presages the compositional format of Pearlstein's mature paintings, which explore spatial tension between the figure and its surroundings.

As with most of his paintings, the face is hidden from view (either by the nature of the pose or the cropping of the composition). The model is also illuminated by harsh, artificial light to create shadow.[3] The composition emphasizes shadows on the contours of the body using broad brushstrokes.

Unlike the paintings, however, this drawing is an isolated study of the figure. Whereas the finished paintings included objects observed in the room, ranging from the obvious (furniture and rugs) to the obscure (fake flamingos and hobby horses), this composition focuses exclusively on the human form.

The year 1962 was a crucial one for Pearlstein and for the image of the figure in American art. That year, he exhibited a figure painting and figurative brushwork drawings in two different gallery shows.[4] In conjunction with his drawings exhibition, his essay "Figure Paintings Today Are Not Made in Heaven" was published in *Art News*.[5] The broader significance of Pearlstein's discussion of a new figurative realism was made clear when the Museum of Modern Art opened an exhibition, *Recent Painting USA: The Figure*, on a similar theme later that year.

ECM

1. Charles T. Butler, ed., *Lines of Discovery: 225 Years of American Drawings* (Columbus, Ga.: Columbus Museum, 2006), 202.
2. John L. Ward, *American Realist Painting* (Ann Arbor: UMI Research Press, 1989), 139.
3. Ibid.
4. Russell Bowman, *Philip Pearlstein: The Complete Paintings* (New York: Alpine Fine Arts Collection, 1983), 254. Pearlstein exhibited one painting at the Tanager Gallery, New York, January–February. His drawings were shown at the Allan Frumkin Gallery, New York, in June 1962.
5. Philip Pearlstein, "Figure Paintings Today Are Not Made in Heaven," *Art News* 61 (Summer 1962): 51–52.

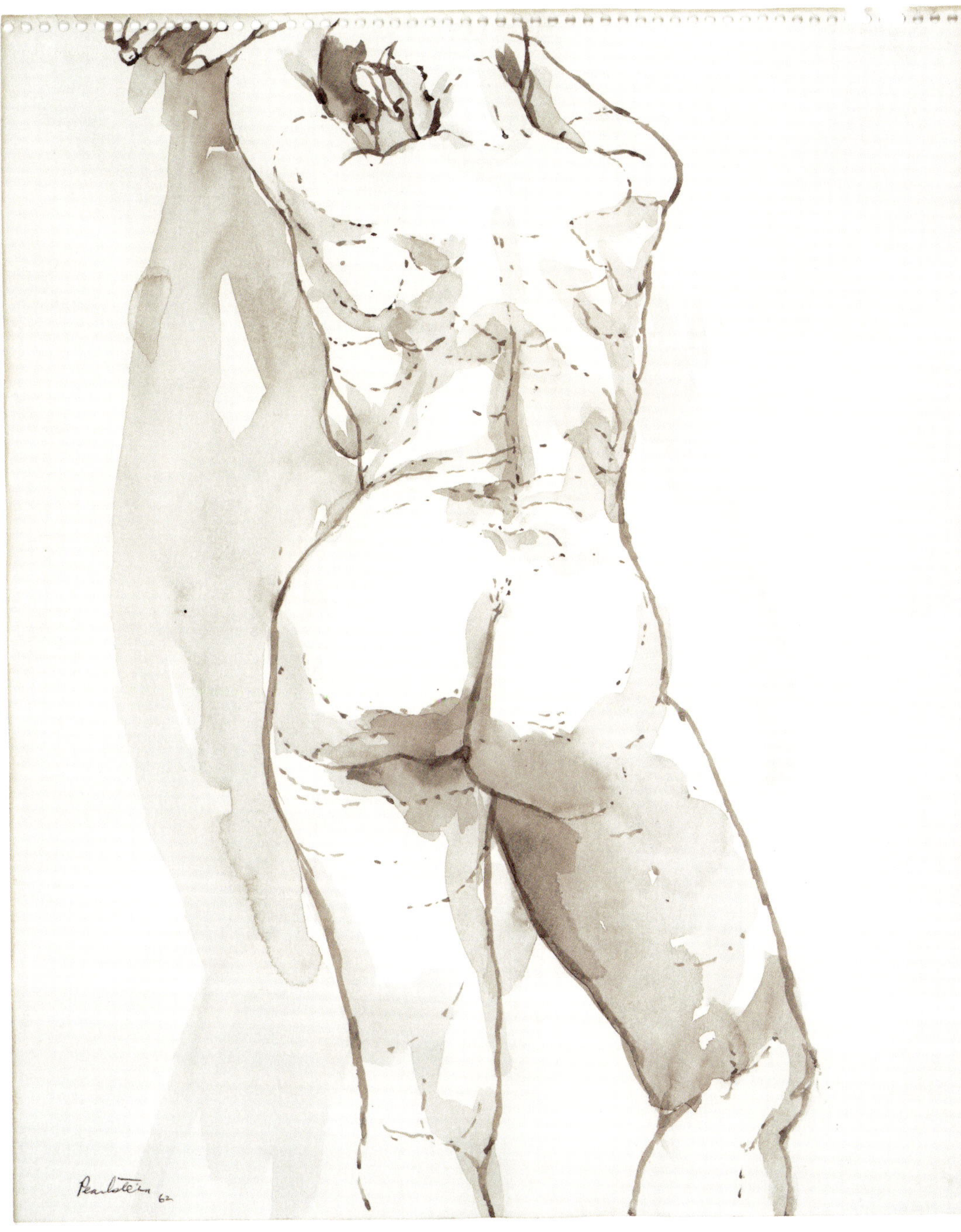

Cat. 83

Ellsworth Kelly

Born in Newburgh, New York, 1923

Ellsworth Kelly is a painter and sculptor whose work emphasizes the simplicity of form. He studied at the Pratt Institute, Brooklyn, from 1941 to 1943. After military service from 1943 to 1945, he attended the School of the Museum of Fine Arts, Boston, 1946–47. The following year, he moved to Paris and enrolled at the École des Beaux-Arts under the GI Bill; he remained there until 1954.

In France, Kelly met and was influenced by the artists of the School of Paris, such as Jean Arp, Constantin Brancusi, and Alexander Calder (q.v.). Calder had the most significant impact on Kelly's career, and they maintained a close friendship when they returned to the United States. Through these artists, Kelly was introduced to geometric and biomorphic abstraction and Surrealism, and began to experiment with these styles in his own work. In 1950 Kelly began making shaped wood reliefs, collages, and shaped paintings in which the canvas is painted a single color. His first solo exhibition was held at the Galerie Arnaud, Paris, in 1951.

Kelly returned to the United States in 1954 and eventually settled in a studio apartment in Coenties Slip, an area of Lower Manhattan facing the East River. (This neighborhood was home to fellow artists who wanted to distance themselves from the Abstract Expressionists, such as Robert Indiana, Agnes Martin, and James Rosenquist.) Kelly's work began to attract critical attention at this time. His first solo exhibition in the United States was at the Betty Parsons Gallery, New York, in 1956, and that same year the Whitney Museum of American Art purchased one of his works—the first museum to do so.

Using a variety of media, Kelly continues to explore the connection between abstraction and nature, from which he extrapolates his forms and colors. He is known for his vocabulary of geometric forms in painting, drawings, prints, photography, and freestanding sculptures. Kelly's first retrospective was held at the Museum of Modern Art, New York, in 1973. In 1996 the Solomon R. Guggenheim Museum, New York, presented a career retrospective that traveled internationally. Since 1970, Kelly has lived in a small town in the Hudson River Valley, with his studio in nearby Chatham, New York, in an old theater.

Select Bibliography

Diane Upright. *Ellsworth Kelly: Works on Paper.* New York: Harry N. Abrams, 1987.

Diane Waldman, ed. *Ellsworth Kelly: A Retrospective.* New York: Guggenheim Museum, 1996.

Ellsworth Kelly. *Line, Form, Color.* Cambridge, Mass.: Harvard University Art Museums, 1999.

84

Ellsworth Kelly
Corn (11), 1959
Transparent watercolor on wove paper
22 1/2 × 28 1/2 in. (57.2 × 72.4 cm)
Signed and dated on verso:
CORN 11 / 12 JULY 1959 / Kelly 3589
Ex coll.: the artist
The Ella Gallup Sumner and Mary Catlin Sumner Collection Fund, 1975.57

In 1975, Ellsworth Kelly was the first artist featured in the Wadsworth Atheneum's now legendary MATRIX, a program that presented exhibitions, performances, and lectures by emerging artists (see Elizabeth Mankin Kornhauser, "Galvanizing Hartford," in this volume). Kelly's solo exhibition included twelve works: ten drawings from 1959, and two steel sculptures from 1974. The drawings were part of a series based on cornstalks Kelly was growing on the roof of his New York City apartment, and it was the first time they had been exhibited publicly. The compositions included both preparatory drawings in pencil, such as *Corn (10)* (fig. 1), and finished watercolors. In honor of the occasion, the museum purchased *Corn (11)*. Presently it is the only work from the series in a public collection; all others are owned by the artist or are in private hands.[1]

The 1975 exhibition was accompanied by a simple typewritten checklist and brief narrative by Andrea Miller-Keller, then curator of contemporary art, in which she praised the drawings for their elegance. She also noted how the drawings were reminiscent of the artist's large-scale minimalist paintings and metal sculptures of solid color. As she explained, "Careful observation will show that they share the same interest in shape and perimeters seen in his paintings and sculpture."[2]

In the postmodern era, Kelly's use of a traditional medium such as watercolor was significant. The immediacy and intimacy of working on paper allowed the artist to reconnect with his interest in shape and the space in and around forms. By silhouetting the cornstalks against a blank background, Kelly's still life becomes modern and abstract. In *Corn (11)*, as in his paintings on shaped canvases, form and color were no longer independent from one another but rather became one. ECM

Fig. 1. Ellsworth Kelly, *Corn (10)*, 1959. Pencil on paper, 22 1/2 × 28 1/2 in. (57.2 × 72.4 cm). Collection of Ellsworth Kelly, Spencertown, New York

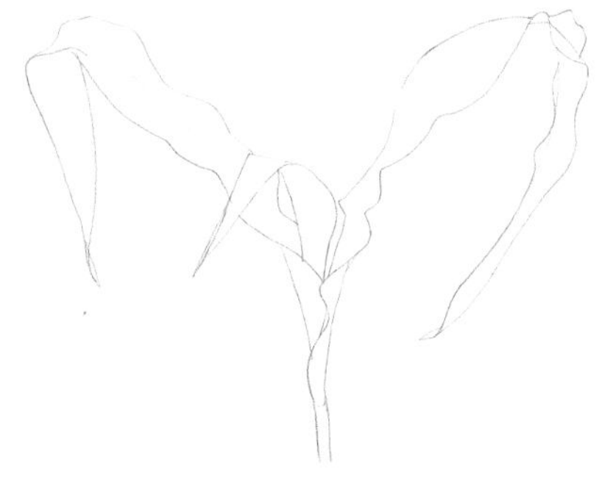

1. My thanks to Eva H. Walters, archivist for Ellsworth Kelly, for information regarding the other drawings in the series.
2. Andrea Miller-Keller, typewritten checklist for *Ellsworth Kelly: MATRIX 1*, Wadsworth Atheneum Museum of Art, January–February 1975.

85

Ellsworth Kelly
Briar, 1961
Pen and black ink on wove paper
22 1/2 × 28 1/2 in. (57.2 × 72.4 cm)
Signed and dated on verso:
Briar 2 31, July 1961 (pencil) / EK (ink)
Ex coll.: the artist; Samuel Wagstaff, New York, as of 1973
Gift of Mr. Samuel Wagstaff in memory of Elva McCormick, 1980.7

Briar belongs to a series of plant drawings Ellsworth Kelly started producing in 1949 and continues to make to this day.[1] These line drawings in black ink are characterized by exceptional simplicity and beauty, important principles Kelly admired in the works of Jean Arp and Constantin Brancusi, which he encountered in Paris, where he lived from 1948 to 1954. The influence of these artists is seen in the changes that took place in Kelly's work during this period: figurative paintings from 1948 were replaced by abstract forms and focused studies of plants and fruit. Belonging to the latter group, *Briar* is representative of these large-scale studies of a single natural form or cluster centered on the page.[2]

At first sight, *Briar* and similar drawings such as *Apples* (1949; Museum of Modern Art, New York) appear antithetical to Kelly's other abstract works: they are representational, usually totally linear, and black and white.[3] As Theodore Stebbins noted, "[they are] as austere as if . . . shaped in piano wire."[4] The drawings, however, reflected Kelly's continuing interest in minimalism and also revealed his obsession with the purity of essential forms. The plant drawings were his earliest ventures into the relationship between straight and curved lines and the interaction of positive and negative spaces. In *Briar*, each leaf, thorn, and stem is rendered by a single, unbroken sweep of line, just as Kelly's shaped canvases were defined by their silhouettes. The branch spreads across the page, almost touching the edges of the sheet and thereby creating visual tension. The contours and flattened forms in the plant drawings were reminiscent of his shaped canvases.

Briar is one of two works on paper by Ellsworth Kelly given to the museum by Samuel J. Wagstaff Jr., who joined the curatorial staff in 1961 (see Elizabeth Mankin Kornhauser, "Galvanizing Hartford," in this volume).[5] These gifts demonstrate both Wagstaff's admiration for the Atheneum and his personal friendship with Ellsworth Kelly. In addition to *Briar*, Wagstaff gave the museum Kelly's screenprint, *Untitled* (c. 1977). The print, a large solid green ovoid in the center of the sheet, was affectionately inscribed: "For Sam / Artist's Proof."[6] The screenprint highlights the graphic qualities of Kelly's hard-edged designs. In fact, many of Kelly's sparse ink drawings, such as *Briar*, were later translated into lithographs. ECM

1. Diane Waldman, ed., *Ellsworth Kelly: A Retrospective* (New York: Guggenheim Museum, 1996), 32. Many of the plant drawings were later printed as lithographic suites; the plant lithographs were first published by Maeght Editeur, Paris, 1964–66.
2. Diane Waldman, *Ellsworth Kelly: Drawings, Collages, Prints* (Greenwich: New York Graphic Society, 1971), 15.
3. Barbara Knowles Debs, "Ellsworth Kelly's Drawings," *Print Collector's Newsletter* 3, 4 (September–October 1972): 73.
4. Theodore E. Stebbins Jr., *American Master Drawings and Watercolors* (New York: Harper and Row, 1976), 404. Stebbins quotes from E. C. Goossen, "Ellsworth Kelly," *Derrière le Miroir* 110 (Paris, 1958): 8–9.

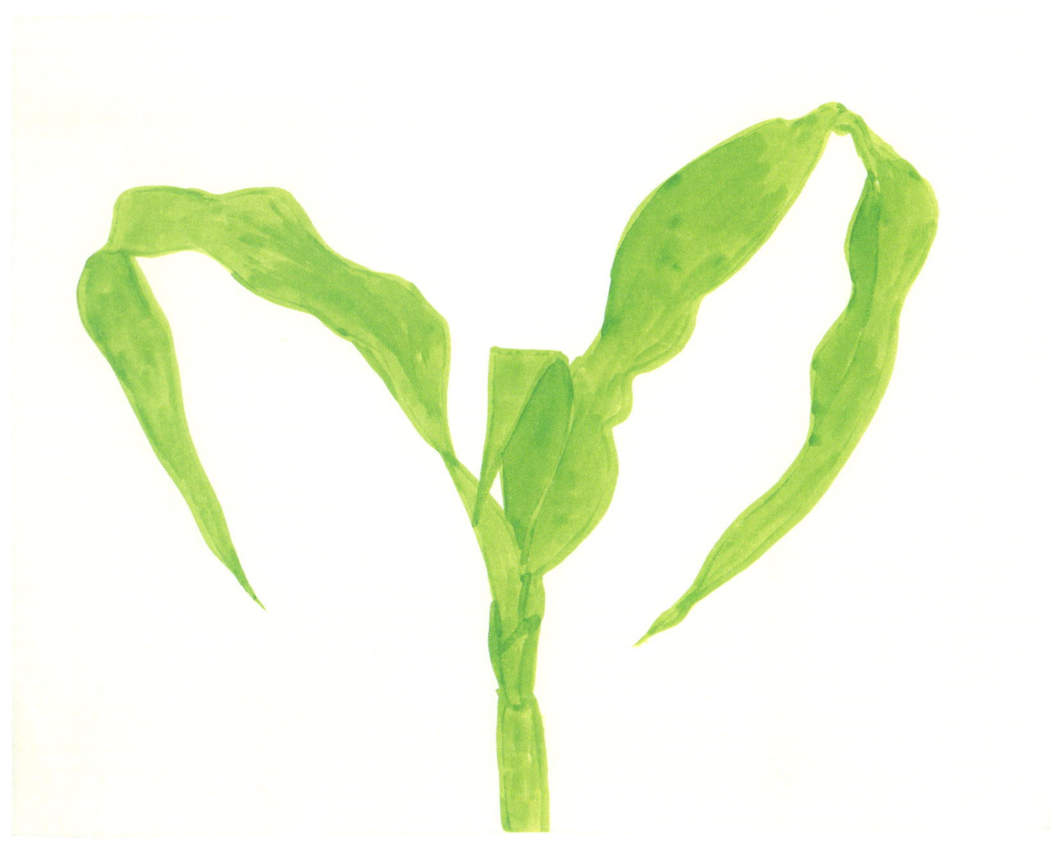

Cat. 84

Cat. 85

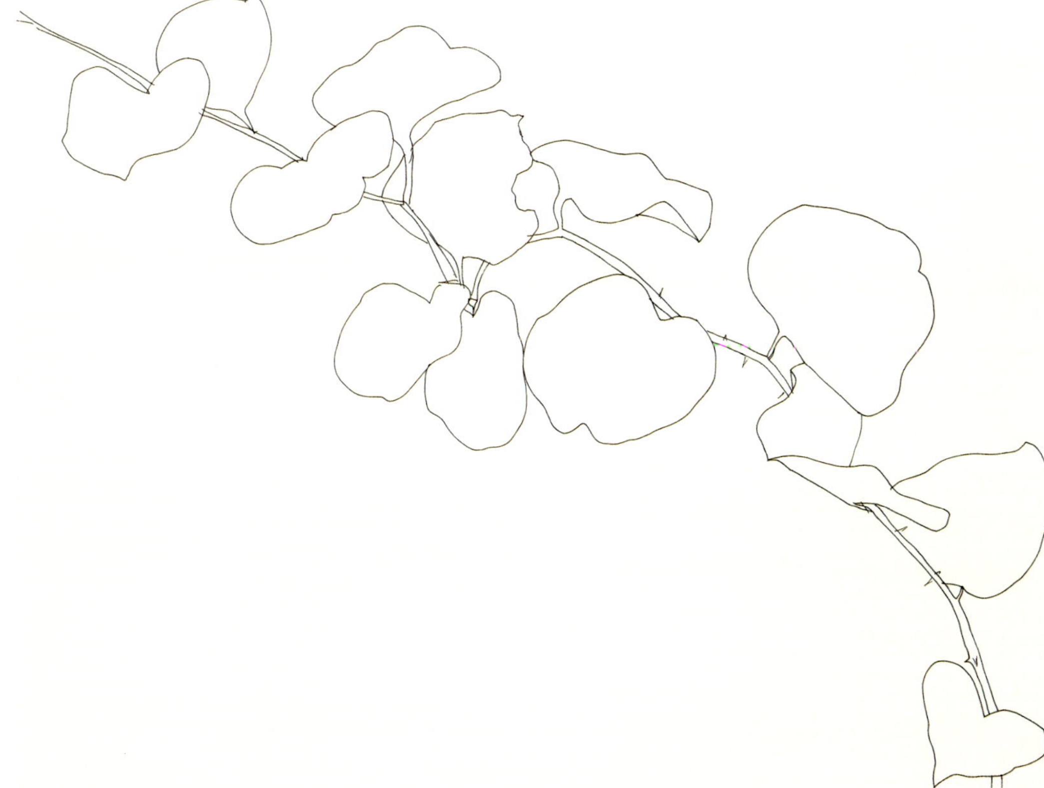

5. During his seven-year tenure in Hartford, Wagstaff began voluminous correspondence with a number of contemporary artists, including Kelly. As early as 1962, they were corresponding about the artist's recent work and the anticipated production of a portfolio of lithographs (based on his plant drawings). See Samuel J. Wagstaff to Ellsworth Kelly, 19 June 1963, Wadsworth Atheneum Archives.
6. *Briar* was given by Wagstaff in memory of Elva B. McCormick (1902–1980), who was manager of the gift shop at the Wadsworth Atheneum at the time, and before that managed Brentano's bookstore in Hartford.

Selected Bibliography

Books on individual artists can be found at the end of the artist biographies.

Adams, Henry. *American Drawings and Watercolors in the Museum of Art, Carnegie Institute.* Pittsburgh: University of Pittsburgh Press, 1985.

Agee, William C., and Susan C. Faxon. *Coming of Age: American Art, 1850s to 1950s.* New Haven, Conn.: Yale University Press, 2006.

Alvin, Martin. *American Realism: Twentieth-Century Drawings and Watercolors.* New York: Harry N. Abrams in association with the San Francisco Museum of Modern Art, 1986.

American Moderns, 1900–1950. Giverny, France: Musée d'Art Américain, 2000.

Avery, Kevin J. *American Drawings and Watercolors in the Metropolitan Museum of Art.* Vol. 1, *A Catalogue of Works by Artists Born before 1835.* New York: Metropolitan Museum of Art in association with Yale University Press, 2002.

Balken, Debra Bricker. *Debating American Modernism: Stieglitz, Duchamp, and the New York Avant-Garde.* New York: American Federation of Arts in association with Distributed Art Publishers, 2003.

Berman, Greta. *Realism and Realities: The Other Side of American Painting, 1940–1960.* New Brunswick, N.J.: Rutgers University Art Gallery, 1981.

Braun, Emily. *New York Collects: Drawings and Watercolors, 1900–1950.* New York: Pierpont Morgan Library, 1999.

Burroughs, Alan. *A History of American Watercolor Painting.* New York: L. F. White, 1942.

Cohn, Marjorie B. *Wash and Gouache: A Study of the Development of the Materials of Watercolor.* Cambridge, Mass.: Center for Conservation and Technical Studies, Fogg Art Museum, 1977.

De Grazia, Diane, and Carter E. Foster, eds. *Master Drawings from the Cleveland Museum of Art.* Cleveland: Cleveland Museum of Art in association with Rizzoli, 2000.

Ferber, Linda S., and Barbara Dayer Gallati. *Masters of Color and Light: Homer, Sargent and the American Watercolor Movement.* Washington, D.C.: Smithsonian Institution Press, 1998.

Finch, Christopher. *American Watercolors.* New York: Abbeville Press, 1986.

——. *Twentieth-Century American Watercolors.* New York: Abbeville Press, 1988.

Gaddis, Eugene. *Avery Memorial: The First Modern Museum.* Hartford, Conn.: Wadsworth Atheneum, 1984.

——. *Magician of the Modern: Chick Austin and the Transformation of the Arts in America.* New York: Alfred A. Knopf, 2000.

Goodrich, Lloyd. *American Watercolor and Winslow Homer.* Minneapolis: Walker Art Center, 1945.

Greenough, Sarah, ed. *Modern Art in America: Alfred Stieglitz and His New York Galleries.* Washington, D.C.: National Gallery of Art, 2000.

Hall, Lee. *Betty Parsons: Artist, Dealer, Collector.* New York: H. N. Abrams, 1991.

Haskell, Barbara. *The American Century: Art and Culture, 1900–1950.* New York: Whitney Museum of American Art in association with W. W. Norton, 1999.

Howat, John K., Victor Koshkin-Youritzin, and Stephen Rubin. *American Watercolors from the Metropolitan Museum of Art.* New York: American Federation of the Arts in association with Harry N. Abrams, 1991.

Kantor, Sybil Gordon. *Alfred H. Barr, Jr. and the Intellectual Origins of the Museum of Modern Art.* Cambridge, Mass.: MIT Press, 2002.

Kornhauser, Elizabeth Mankin. *American Paintings before 1945 in the Wadsworth Atheneum.* With contributions by Elizabeth R. McClintock and Amy Ellis. 2 vols. New Haven, Conn.: Yale University Press, 1996.

Kornhauser, Elizabeth Mankin, Amy Ellis, and Maura Lyons. *Stieglitz, O'Keeffe and American Modernism.* Hartford, Conn.: Wadsworth Atheneum, 1999.

Kramer, Hilton. *The Age of the Avant-Garde: An Art Chronicle of 1956–1972.* New York: Farrar, Straus and Giroux, 1973.

Levy, Julien. *Memoir of an Art Gallery.* Boston: Museum of Fine Arts, 2003.

Lines of Discovery: 225 Years of American Drawings. Columbus, Ga.: Columbus Museum of Art in association with GILES, 2006.

Messinger, Lisa Mintz. *Abstract Expressionism: Works on Paper; Selections from the Metropolitan Museum of Art.* New York: Metropolitan Museum of Art, 1992.

Murray, Mary E., and Gail Levin. *American Twentieth-Century Watercolors at the Munson-Williams-Proctor Arts Institute.* Utica, N.Y.: Brodock Press, 2000.

O'Hara, Eliot. *Watercolor at Large.* New York: Minton, Balch & Company, 1946.

Phillips, Lisa. *The American Century: Art and Culture, 1950–2000.* New York: Whitney Museum of American Art in association with W. W. Norton, 1999.

Pollock, Lindsay. *The Girl with the Gallery: Edith Halpert and the Making of the Modern Art Market.* New York: Public Affairs, 2006.

Reed, Sue Welsh, and Carol Troyen. *Awash in Color: Homer, Sargent, and the Great American Watercolor.* Boston: Museum of Fine Arts in association with Bulfinch Press, Little, Brown, 1993.

Rose, Barbara. *Readings in American Art since 1900: A Documentary Study.* New York: F. A. Praeger, 1968.

Sadik, Marvin. *Edith Halpert and the Downtown Gallery.* Storrs: Benton Museum, University of Connecticut, 1968.

Soby, James Thrall. *After Picasso.* Hartford, Conn.: Edwin Valentine Mitchell, 1935.

Stebbins, Theodore E., Jr. *American Master Drawings and Watercolors.* New York: Harper & Row, 1976.

Stebbins, Theodore E., Jr., and Carol Troyen. *The Lane Collection: 20th-Century Paintings in the American Tradition.* Boston: Museum of Fine Arts, 1983.

Stebbins, Theodore E., Jr., Kimberly Orcutt, and Virginia Anderson, eds. *American Paintings at Harvard.* Vol. 2, *Paintings, Watercolors, Pastels, and Stained Glass by Artists Born 1826–1856.* Cambridge, Mass.: Harvard Art Museum in association with Yale University Press, 2008.

Stieglitz, Alfred. *Stieglitz: Memorial Portfolio, 1864–1946.* New York: Twice a Year Press, 1946.

Strickler, Susan E., ed. *American Traditions in Watercolor: The Worcester Art Museum Collection.* New York: Abbeville Press, 1987.

Tsujimoto, Karen. *Images of America: Precisionist Painting and Modern Photography.* Seattle: University of Washington Press, 1982.

Turner, Elizabeth Hutton. *In the American Grain: Arthur Dove, Marsden Hartley, John Marin, Georgia O'Keeffe, and Alfred Stieglitz; The Stieglitz Circle at the Phillips Collection.* Washington, D.C.: Counterpoint, 1995.

Ward, John L. *American Realist Painting, 1945–1980.* Ann Arbor, Mich.: UMI Research Press, 1989.

Weber, Nicholas Fox. *Patron Saints: Five Rebels Who Opened America to a New Art, 1928–1943.* New York: Alfred A. Knopf, 1992.

Wilmerding, John. *Drawings and Watercolors.* Vol. 1 of *American Art in the Princeton University Art Museum.* Princeton, N.J.: Princeton University Art Museum in association with Yale University Press, 2004.

Zafran, Eric M. *Ballets Russes to Balanchine: Dance at the Wadsworth Atheneum.* Hartford, Conn.: Wadsworth Atheneum, 2004.

——, ed. *Renaissance to Rococo: Masterpieces from the Wadsworth Atheneum Museum of Art.* New Haven, Conn.: Yale University Press in association with the Wadsworth Atheneum, 2004.

Zafran, Eric M., and Paul Paret. *Surrealism and Modernism from the Collection of the Wadsworth Atheneum Museum of Art.* New Haven, Conn.: Yale University Press in association with the Wadsworth Atheneum, 2003.

Index

Note: Pages with illustrations are indicated in italics.

Photo Credits

Photo credits and copyright notices other than those indicated in the captions are as follows:

Betty Cunningham Gallery, cat. 83; Burchfield-Penney Art Center, cat. 26 fig. 1; Godel & Company Fine Art, New York, cat. 31 fig. 1; © Edward Gorey Charitable Trust, cat. 31 fig. 2; Harvard Art Museum. Photo: Imaging Department © President and Fellows of Harvard College, cat. 44 fig. 1; Koninklijk Museum voor Schone Kunsten, Antwerp. Photo: Scala/Art Resource, NY, cat. 61 fig. 1; Kraushaar Galleries, Inc., NY, cats. 2 and 51, cat. 51 fig. 1; The Metropolitan Museum of Art. Image © Art Resource, NY, cat. 11 fig. 1, cat. 35 fig. 1, cat. 68 fig. 1, cat. 72 fig. 1; The Museum of Modern Art. Licensed by SCALA/Art Resource, NY, cat. 64 fig. 1, and Digital Images © Licensed by SCALA/Art Resource, NY, Troyen essay, figs. 3 and 6; Princeton University Art Museum. Photo: Bruce M. White, Troyen essay, fig. 7; Robyn Buntin Gallery, cat. 76 fig. 1; Seattle Art Museum. Photo: Paul Macapia, cat. 79 fig. 1; Wadsworth Atheneum Museum of Art: © Milton Avery Trust/Artists Rights Society (ARS), New York, cat. 82; © Estate of William Baziotes (Ethel Baziotes), cat. 80; © T.H. Benton and R.P. Benton Testamentary Trust/UMB Trustee/Licensed by VAGA, NY, cat. 49; © The Education Alliance, Inc./Estate of Peter Blume/Licensed by VAGA, NY, cat. 75, cat. 75 fig. 1; Reproduced with permission from the Charles E. Burchfield Foundation, cats. 26–31; © Calder Foundation/Artists Rights Society (ARS), NY, cat. 66; © Estate of Paul Cadmus, cat. 74; © Gala-Salvador Dalí Foundation/Artists Rights Society (ARS), NY, cats. 63–64; © Estate of Stuart Davis/Licensed by VAGA, New York, NY, cats. 40–41, cat. 40 fig. 1, cat. 41 fig. 1; © Delaware Art Museum/Artists Rights Society (ARS), NY, cats. 3–4, cat. 3 fig. 1; Courtesy of Demuth Museum, Lancaster, Pa., cat. 18a–b, cat. 18a–b figs. 1–2, cats. 19–20, cat. 21 fig. 1, cat. 35 fig. 1; © Estate of Arthur G. Dove, cats. 23–24, cat. 23 fig. 1, cat. 24 fig. 2, cat. 25a–f, cat. 25a–f fig. 1; © Estate of William Glackens, cat. 2, cat. 2 fig. 1; Gorky/Artists Rights Society (ARS), NY, cat. 70; © Morris Graves Foundation, cat. 76; © Estate of George Grosz/Licensed by VAGA, NY, cat. 50; © Renate, Hans & Maria Hofmann Trust/Artists Rights Society (ARS), NY, cats. 77–78, cat. 77 fig. 1; © Ellsworth Kelly, cats. 84–85, cat. 84 fig. 1; Kent: Copyright © 1930 R.R. Donnelley & Sons, Inc., and The Plattsburgh State College Foundation, Inc. All rights reserved, cat. 39a–b; © Estate of Yasuo Kuniyoshi/Licensed by VAGA, NY, cat. 16a–b; The Lachaise Foundation, cat. 65, cat. 65 fig. 1; © The Jacob and Gwendolyn Lawrence Foundation, Seattle/Artists Rights Society (ARS), New York, cat. 43, cat. 43 fig. 1; © The LeWitt Estate/Artists Rights Society (ARS), NY, Kornhauser essay, figs. 22–23; © Estate of Seymour Lipton, Michael Rosenfeld Gallery, LLC, NY, cat. 73, cat. 73 figs. 1–2; Courtesy of MaineMemory.net item #16548, cat. 33 fig. 1; © Estate of John Marin/Artists Rights Society (ARS), NY, Kornhauser essay, fig. 20, cats. 9–13, cat. 11 figs. 1–2; © Estate of Reginald Marsh/Art Students League/Artists Rights Society (ARS), NY, cats. 47–48, cat. 48 fig. 1; Matta: © ADAGP, Paris/Artists Rights Society (ARS), NY, cat. 69; © The Isamu Noguchi Foundation and Garden Museum, New York/Artists Rights Society (ARS), NY, cat. 17; © Georgia O'Keeffe Museum/Artists Rights Society (ARS), New York, cat. 15; James Graham & Sons, New York and the Estate of Yvonne Pène du Bois, cat. 46; © The Pollock-Krasner Foundation/Artists Rights Society (ARS), NY, cat. 79 fig. 2; © Estate of Theodore Roszak/Licensed by VAGA, NY, cat. 72, cat. 72 fig. 1; © Estate of Ben Shahn/Licensed by VAGA, NY, cat. 44, cat. 44 fig. 1; © Estate of David Smith/Licensed by VAGA, NY, cat. 81a–b; © Estate of Yves Tanguy/Artists Rights Society (ARS), NY, cats. 67–68, cat. 68 fig. 1; © Estate of Mark Tobey/Artists Rights Society (ARS), NY, cat. 79; © Andrew Wyeth, cat. 82, cat. 82 fig. 1; Zabriskie Gallery, cats. 5–6.